OXFORD ENGLISH DRAMA

General Editor: Michael Cordner

Associate General Editors: Peter Holland · Martin Wiggins

THE DEVIL IS AN ASS

AND OTHER PLAYS

BEN JONSON, the greatest dramatic satirist of the English Renaissance, was born in London in 1572. As a young man he worked as a bricklayer and served as a soldier in the Netherlands, and in 1594 embarked on a new career as an actor. Three years later he began to write plays, and with the accession of James I in 1603, he also began to compose court masques, often in collaboration with Inigo Jones. He wrote prolifically for both the court and the public theatres, and also established himself as one of the finest poets of the period. His tumultuous private life included several spells in prison, a commuted death sentence for murder, and possible involvement in the Gunpowder Plot. In 1618 he walked to Scotland, where his wittily opinionated views of his contemporaries were recorded by William Drummond. In 1628 Jonson's public life was suddenly terminated by a stroke, and he lay paralysed in bed for the last nine years of his life. He died in 1637, and was buried in Westminster Abbey.

MARGARET JANE KIDNIE is Senior Lecturer at South Bank University, London. She has previously edited Philip Stubbes's *Anatomie of Abuses*, and published articles on bibliography, early modern drama and Shakespeare on film.

MICHAEL CORDNER is Reader in the Department of English and Related Literature at the University of York. He has edited George Farquhar's *The Beaux' Stratagem*, the *Complete Plays* of Sir George Etherege, *Four Comedies* of Sir John Vanbrugh, and, for Oxford English Drama, *Four Restoration Marriage Plays* and Sheridan's *The School for Scandal and Other Plays*. He is writing books on *The Comedy of Marriage* and *Shakespeare and the Actor*.

PETER HOLLAND is Professor of Shakespeare Studies and Director of the Shakespeare Institute, University of Birmingham.

MARTIN WIGGINS is a Fellow of the Shakespeare Institute and Lecturer in English at the University of Birmingham.

OXFORD ENGLISH DRAMA

J. M. Barrie
Peter Pan and Other Plays

Aphra Behn
The Rover and Other Plays

George Farquhar
The Recruiting Officer and Other Plays

John Ford
*'Tis Pity She's a Whore and
Other Plays*

Ben Jonson
The Alchemist and Other Plays

Ben Jonson
The Devil is an Ass and Other Plays

Christopher Marlowe
Doctor Faustus and Other Plays

John Marston
The Malcontent and Other Plays

Thomas Middleton
*A Mad World, My Masters and Other
Plays*

Richard Brinsley Sheridan
*The School for Scandal and
Other Plays*

J. M. Synge
*The Playboy of the Western World and
Other Plays*

John Webster
The Duchess of Malfi and Other Plays

Oscar Wilde
*The Importance of Being Earnest and
Other Plays*

William Wycherley
The Country Wife and Other Plays

Court Masques
ed. David Lindley

Five Romantic Plays
ed. Paul Baines & Edward Burns

Four Jacobean Sex Tragedies
ed. Martin Wiggins

Four Restoration Marriage Plays
ed. Michael Cordner

Four Revenge Tragedies
ed. Katharine Maus

*The New Woman and Other
Emancipated Woman Plays*
ed. Jean Chothia

OXFORD WORLD'S CLASSICS

———

BEN JONSON

Poetaster, or, The Arraignment
Sejanus his Fall
The Devil is an Ass
The New Inn, or, The Light Heart

———

Edited with an Introduction and Notes by
MARGARET JANE KIDNIE
General Editor
MICHAEL CORDNER
Associate General Editors
PETER HOLLAND   MARTIN WIGGINS

OXFORD
UNIVERSITY PRESS

OXFORD
UNIVERSITY PRESS

Great Clarendon Street, Oxford OX2 6DP

Oxford University Press is a department of the University of Oxford.
It furthers the University's objective of excellence in research, scholarship,
and education by publishing worldwide in

Oxford New York

Athens Auckland Bangkok Bogotá Buenos Aires Calcutta
Cape Town Chennai Dar es Salaam Delhi Florence Hong Kong Istanbul
Karachi Kuala Lumpur Madrid Melbourne Mexico City Mumbai
Nairobi Paris São Paulo Shanghai Singapore Taipei Tokyo Toronto Warsaw

with associated companies in Berlin Ibadan

Oxford is a registered trade mark of Oxford University Press
in the UK and in certain other countries

Published in the United States
by Oxford University Press Inc., New York

Editorial matter © Margaret Jane Kidnie 2000

British Library Cataloguing in Publication Data

Data available

Library of Congress Cataloging in Publication Data

Data available

ISBN 0–19–813229–8

1 3 5 7 9 10 8 6 4 2

Typeset in Ehrhardt
by RefineCatch Limited, Bungay, Suffolk
Printed in Great Britain by
Cox & Wyman Ltd.
Reading, Berkshire

CONTENTS

ACKNOWLEDGEMENTS

I am grateful to Roberta Barker for checking the modernized play texts against the original editions and to John Jowett for chats about editorial practice. Gene Giddens and James Purkis kindly read early drafts of the Introduction, providing a range of useful comments and suggestions. I should also like to thank Martin Wiggins, the series' Associate General Editor, for his support and enthusiasm from beginning to end, and for the rigour with which he commented on and queried early drafts of the edition; the volume has benefited immensely from his scrupulous attention to detail. Michael Cordner, the series' General Editor, gave of his time and experience at a busy point in the academic year to oversee with care the transition from typescript to proof. Judith Luna, Jeff New, and Elizabeth Stratford at Oxford University Press were consistently helpful and responsive to my concerns throughout the production process, and I am especially pleased to acknowledge their contribution to the volume. Special thanks are owed to Ian Butler for generously providing a quiet workplace and a floor to sleep on when they were needed most.

This edition is dedicated to James Purkis, whose perceptive critique and supportive encouragement throughout its preparation have proved invaluable.

INTRODUCTION

Controversy and scandal dogged Ben Jonson throughout the course of a professional career lasting more than thirty years and extending over the reigns of three monarchs. He was thrown into Marshalsea Prison in 1597 for 'seditious and slanderous matter' found in his collaborative play, *The Isle of Dogs*, and was saved from hanging after killing his fellow actor Gabriel Spencer in a duel the following year only by pleading benefit of clergy, a legal loophole which allowed any person who was able to read a verse from the Latin Bible to escape capital punishment once. He was interrogated by Lord Chief Justice Popham in 1601 for libellous material in *Poetaster*, summoned before the Privy Council a few years later to defend *Sejanus*, and in 1605 found himself in danger of having his nose slit and ears cut for satirical passages in *Eastward Ho*. In 1606 Jonson was required to appear before the London Consistory Court for recusancy, having converted to Catholicism while in prison eight years earlier, and he remained a practising Catholic until 1610. While visiting the Scottish poet William Drummond during the Christmas season of 1618–19, he mentioned that he had been asked by the king to 'conceal' the satirical content of *The Devil is an Ass*, and in 1628 he was questioned by the Privy Council, perhaps once again with regard to *Sejanus*, in connection with the assassination of the Duke of Buckingham. Both in his life and his writings, Jonson constantly pushed against the limits imposed by early modern state authorities. Similarly, in his construction of an authorial identity for himself in the commercial theatres he pushed against the limits imposed by fee-paying audiences, regularly—and at times vociferously—disagreeing with popular estimations of theatre and art.

Jonson was born on 11 June 1572, and his mother, widowed during the pregnancy, took as her second husband a London bricklayer. Before eventually being apprenticed to his stepfather's trade, Jonson studied under the scholar William Camden at the College of St Peter at Westminster, and this education, over the course of which he was introduced to Latin and Greek classical literature, proved to have a formative influence on his subsequent career as a poet and dramatist. Sometime probably before the autumn of 1594, when it is thought he married Anne Lewis, he enlisted with the English army and saw military service in the Low Countries where, as he later proudly recounted to Drummond, 'he had in the face of both the camps, killed an enemy and taken *opima spolia* [rich spoils] from him'. Returning to London, Jonson embarked on an uncertain career of acting and writing for the stage, and during these early years was forced for financial reasons periodically to maintain his membership in the guild of tilers and bricklayers. When the theatre company with which he was associated, the Lord Pembroke's Men, effectively dissolved with the closing of the theatres after the scandal of *The Isle of Dogs*, he wrote plays for the Lord Admiral's Men and the Lord Chamberlain's Men.

With the death of Elizabeth I and the accession to the throne of James I in 1603, Jonson began to establish himself in court circles. His first masque produced at court was *The Masque of Blackness* in 1605, and he thereafter wrote a masque nearly every year for performance during the Christmas season. The years from 1606 to 1614 in which he wrote the comedies *Volpone*, *Epicene*, *The Alchemist*, and *Bartholomew Fair* are usually regarded as Jonson's most successful creative period, and culminated in his recognition by the king in 1616 as 'the royal poet', a prestigious and lucrative appointment which coincided with the publication of *The Works of Benjamin Jonson* in folio the same year. Jonson had no plays performed on the professional stage for ten years after 1616, and the destruction of all his books and papers by fire in 1623 prevents subsequent readers from gaining a clear sense of the direction in which his writing was developing during that time. When he returned to the stage in 1626 with *The Staple of News* the theatrical climate had significantly changed, at least partly in response to the death of James I and the accession of his son, Charles I, in 1625, and Jonson never fully regained the royal favour and popular esteem he had enjoyed during the previous reign. He was rendered bedridden after a paralytic stroke in 1628, and although he continued to write plays, masques, and poetry until his death in 1637, his last years were marked by illness and financial insecurity.

Jonson was regarded at his death as one of the pre-eminent playwrights of his age, but his reputation since then has been overshadowed by the critical estimation which has grown up around the name of Shakespeare. As Shakespeare increasingly became associated with the articulation of a notion of universal human experience, Jonson became identified with widely respected, but nonetheless off-putting, scholasticism. His plays are commonly awarded classic status, but resisted as difficult—they are often regarded as long and wordy, and if not filled with obscure topical references to the events and customs of early modern London, then steeped in increasingly obscure allusions to the literature of the classical world. T. S. Eliot identified in the 1920s the paradox surrounding the critical reception of Jonson's plays: 'To be universally accepted; to be damned by the praise that quenches all desire to read the book; to be afflicted by the imputation of the virtues which excite the least pleasure; and to be read only by historians and antiquaries—this is the most perfect conspiracy of approval.' This critical heritage has encouraged few modern readers or theatrical companies to explore the Jonsonian canon beyond his four mature comedies.

But there has been a renewal of interest in Jonson in recent years, and scholars have begun to challenge that received estimation by highlighting in his writings previously unexplored critical territory, such as a developing understanding of the concept of the author, the tension surrounding the relationship which should ideally pertain between the poet and the monarch, and an engagement with and critique of state politics. This critical re-evaluation has been given added impetus with the successful mounting of major modern productions of lesser-known plays such as *The New Inn* and *The Devil is an Ass* which have given audiences the opportunity to consider their theatrical merits afresh. The four plays in this volume are indicative of the broad range of Jonson's career as a writer for the professional stage, not only extending from the closing years of the reign of Elizabeth through to the reign of Charles, but also presenting a variety of genres in which he worked, including satirical comedy, tragedy, city comedy, and romance.

Jonson began to establish a reputation for himself as a dramatist in the years 1599–1602, when he engaged in an acrimonious exchange of plays with the competing playwright John Marston. The conflict between the men focused on their relative merits as writers for the stage but quickly deteriorated into personal attack, each playwright lampooning his rival by means of satirical stage portraits. The controversy escalated when a third playwright, Thomas Dekker, entered the fray on the side of Marston. One of the later contributions to the 'Poetomachia' or 'War of the Theatres'—as this set of plays subsequently became known—is Marston's *What You Will*, in which Jonson's propensity for asserting his own creative excellence as a poet is comically ridiculed in the character of Lampatho Doria. The likelihood that it was Marston who triggered the controversy is supported by Jonson's claim that 'he had many quarrels with Marston, beat him and took his pistol from him, wrote his Poetaster on him; the beginning of them were that Marston represented him in the stage'. Jonson, learning that Dekker was working on *Satiromastix, or The Untrussing of the Humorous Poet*, pre-empted his efforts by writing *Poetaster* in what was for him the unusually short period of fifteen weeks.

Poetaster, as the title suggests, takes as its subject fraudulent or trivial rhymesters who merely pretend to the status of poet, and Jonson presents his rivals Marston and Dekker as the sartorially and intellectually threadbare characters Crispinus and Demetrius. Horace, by contrast, the play's moral and artistic touchstone, is usually regarded as the mouthpiece for Jonson's own views. Audiences' ability to identify these characters with their Elizabethan originals would have been encouraged in the earliest performances through visual caricature. The dialogue indicates, for example, that the boy actor playing Crispinus parodied Marston's typical appearance by sporting a red beard and wearing a distinctive 'ash-coloured feather' in his hat, and it is probably safe to assume that such costuming choices would have been supplemented further by unscripted stage business which we are not able to discern in the printed text. Reproduction in the characters' dialogue of Marston's and Dekker's distinctive vocabulary and speech patterns provides further identifying clues to an audience or readership attuned to the likelihood of parody. An awareness that at least part of the function of these characters is contemporary satire contributes a comic edge to the scene in which Horace, bewildered, finds himself plagued by the 'land-remora' Crispinus, who obstinately attaches himself to the renowned writer as he walks along the street. Likewise, Horace's triumph over the poetasters in the final scene when, with the allowance of Caesar, they are convicted of libel amongst an eminent group of true poets and punished according to Horace's wishes, can be read as Jonson staging a moral victory over his fellow dramatists. Horace's resolution to make Crispinus a better writer through the administration of a purgative which leads him violently to vomit his words into a basin can be seen, from a literal and literary perspective, as Jonson's own form of poetic justice.

An understanding of the specific manner in which *Poetaster* intervened in the London theatrical world at the time of its first production not only influences our perception of the play's satire, but also provides a clearer sense of the play's reception amongst its earliest audiences. Moreover, it allows us to maintain a sceptical distance from Livor's conviction, as asserted in the prologue, that Jonson's decision to set the drama in Rome necessarily forestalls critical attempts to interpret it in terms of London personalities and politics. The long opening speech by Livor (a name which translates from the Latin as

Envy) is to this extent disingenuous in its insistence that the play can have no topical application. Jonson used the play not only to burlesque two of his fellow dramatists but also to satirize actors, lawyers, and military captains, a creative decision which led to trouble with the authorities and resulted in the censorship from the first published quarto of some of the more offensive passages, including an 'Apologetical Dialogue' which features a character called 'the Author' discussing his right as a satirist to 'spare the persons, and to speak the vices'.

It is important to resist, however, the idea that *Poetaster* is interesting *solely* in terms of the role it played in the so-called War of the Theatres. This was a problem in the Victorian era, when the flurry of debate around the play was misguidedly rooted entirely in tenuous arguments which attempted to determine which real-life dramatists were 'really' behind Jonson's portrayal of classical poets such as Ovid and Virgil. A key strand of criticism which stands apart from a discussion of Elizabethan personalities centres on the function of the poet within the commonwealth.

Poetaster is set in Augustan Rome at the height of classical art and literature, and Jonson dramatizes his satirical portraits of Marston and Dekker alongside Roman literary figures such as Ovid, Tibullus, Virgil, and Horace. The dramatic action opens with a soliloquy by Ovid, who is in the midst of composing the fifteenth elegy of the first book of the *Amores*. The relevance of this passage and of Ovid's subsequent encounter with his father to the arraignment of trivial rhymesters is not immediately apparent, and the scene has been criticized as potentially misleading, in that some audience members and readers might assume that Ovid is the titular poetaster. However, delaying the entrance of Crispinus, the true poetaster, to the beginning of the second act allows Jonson the opportunity to broaden the scope of inquiry beyond mere denunciation of artistic incompetence to include an exploration of the cultural and political significance of poetry within the state. The character of Ovid is central to this larger issue. Unlike Crispinus, who uses poetry as a means to seduce the jeweller's wife Chloë, and whose attacks on Horace in verse, written in conjunction with Demetrius, are motivated by nothing more than professional jealousy, Ovid demonstrates an avowed commitment to his art by pursuing it in face of his father's disapproval and anger. But the opposition between these two characters is not a simple one, since our view of Ovid is qualified by intratextual comments which suggest that he misuses his talents.

The complexity of our response to the character of Ovid is most apparent during the masquerade banquet held at court in Act 4. The conceit is that each guest dresses up as and impersonates a different Roman god or goddess throughout the banquet, and the centrality of Ovid to the plan is implicit in the fact that he and his mistress, the emperor's daughter Julia, enact the roles of the quarrelling couple Jupiter and Juno. However, a certain unease about the intended revelry is registered early on in the act when Cytheris quizzes Ovid's friends, Gallus and Tibullus, about their presumption in transforming mortals into divine beings. The pride and arrogance underpinning the poets' blithe confidence in their creative prerogative is exposed when Caesar, informed of the proceedings by spies, bursts in on the banquet, threatens to kill his daughter, and banishes Ovid from the court. The violence of Caesar's attack derives explicitly from the belief that, in counterfeiting the gods, the poets have profaned true divinity, and this moral distinction between performed identity and inner truth is one to which the emperor returns throughout his enraged outburst. In abusing his imagination by using it to trivialize the divine, and thus upsetting the hierarchy of order in which gods are necessarily elevated above humans, Ovid threatens similarly to undermine the social order on which Caesar's political power depends.

The issue at the heart of one's understanding of this character is the extent to which we are to interpret his banishment from court as justified. In the banquet scene of Act 4 Ovid demonstrates poor judgement. Transported by his blinding love for Julia, he indulges his poetic imagination without due respect for the responsibilities attendant on his chosen vocation to improve human moral agency in a manner compatible with the needs of state authority. And for this reason he must be abandoned by a judicious state. By contrast, the favour Caesar shows to Virgil in the fifth act when the poet reads to him from the *Aeneid* suggests the prestige and honour which will fall to a poet better able within this political system to balance these competing pressures. What is less certain, however, is the extent to which Jonson presents these limitations on the poetic imagination as proper, or even unexceptional. Directorial decisions concerning Act 4, Scene 4, in which Ovid surreptitiously visits his lover's balcony to bid her farewell before leaving the court, will have an important influence on an audience's perception of the banishment. This scene, reminiscent of the lovers' parting balcony scene in *Romeo and Juliet*, can be played either sympathetically or with irony. If the latter interpretation is put forward, then the poignancy of the scene could seem artificial and self-conscious—yet another excess of imagination on the part of a talented, but immature, poet—and the audience's distance from his plight would thus be reinforced. But if the potential for irony is resisted, then our views are less clearly aligned with those of Caesar, and space is opened to reflect critically on his judgements as pronounced during the banquet scene.

It is difficult to make sense of Horace's objection that the banquet is a minor instance of high spirits maliciously misrepresented as treason by the politically ambitious tribune Lupus, if one entirely accepts the interpretation of the event as voiced by Caesar. Caesar is the ultimate authority within the social world of the play, but Horace tends to function for the audience as its reliable commentator. The audience is thus presented with a conflict of opinion which potentially opens up an alternative understanding of the relationship of the poet to the state in which Ovid is the victim of 'application', the determination to (mis)interpret an essentially harmless event or text through reference to unrelated contemporary circumstances and personalities. By this alternative reading, Ovid is brought down by Caesar's decision to allow himself to be influenced by spiteful attention-seekers, and the play is not so much concerned to pass moral judgement on Ovid's indiscretions as a poet and contrast his failures with the wisdom of Virgil as the ideal counsellor of state, as it is interested in interrogating the function and power of spies such as Lupus within a tyranny. Horace thus emerges as occupying a crucial position within Caesar's court as a poet who is prepared to comment, sometimes critically, on policy and events, but whose beneficial guiding impact on the mechanisms of state is limited by the perils of pursuing the ideal of free speech within a tyranny. The vulnerability of even a character as highly regarded by Caesar as Horace is demonstrated in Act 5, when he is forced to defend the meaning of one of his own emblems from the treasonous interpretation imposed on it by Lupus.

These broader political issues not only begin to explain why the Elizabethan authorities might have felt concerned enough about this play to censor it before allowing its printed publication, but also offer some insight into Jonson's developing ideas about the appropriate function of the poet within a monarchical order. Livor's despair when confronted by a Roman setting is not enough to distance the action from the War of the Theatres, but the armed Prologue who subsequently enters takes care to lay out the more general, and more significant, principle that the worthy poet, the fitting counsellor to state, must seek to protect his reputation and writings from the petty ambitions of less able minds. The related issues of informers and free speech as either fostered or undermined within a repressive political climate is a subject Jonson developed in a more thematically controlled manner in his next work, *Sejanus*, this time in the tragic mode.

Sejanus was written by Jonson in collaboration with an unidentified dramatist (who may have been George Chapman) in 1603, but it was almost certainly not performed in the public theatres until 1604 since the theatres were closed in the spring after the death of Queen Elizabeth, and remained closed on account of the plague throughout the rest of the year. The first performance, therefore, may have been in the court of James I in December 1603, or during the early winter of 1604. No evidence survives to indicate what this original performance text might have looked like, however, since when Jonson came to revise the play for publication in quarto in 1605 he systematically rewrote the contributions of his fellow dramatist. The extant quarto text is remarkable on account of its visual presentation: each page of dialogue is accompanied by a tightly packed column of marginal annotation. These sidenotes, referring the reader to specific passages in the Greek and Latin source texts, are intended, as Jonson explains in his prefatory letter to the reader, to demonstrate his 'integrity in the story'; that is, the sidenotes are evidence of the accuracy with which he claims to reproduce the events as narrated by classical historians. In effect, Jonson uses these marginal annotations to limit the potential scope of a reader's interpretation by insisting that he is merely presenting historically documented events in a dramatic form. He may have considered this a necessary precaution in light of the play's politically sensitive subject-matter, and indeed, we know that at some point he was summoned before the Privy Council to defend himself and his play from accusations of 'popery and treason' alleged by the Earl of Northampton. It is impossible to be certain whether it was the earliest performances or the revised printed playtext which offended Northampton, but if it was the latter, then we have a situation in which Jonson anticipated trouble before publication and took steps—to no avail—to protect himself.

Discussion of the controversy surrounding the play is hampered by the fact that we no longer know the precise nature of the charges brought against Jonson. Although Jonson protests throughout the prefatory material that his play should not be read in terms of current affairs, most critics have assumed that this is exactly what Northampton did, interpreting *Sejanus* as a thinly veiled allusion to the events surrounding the downfall of Elizabeth I's favourite the Earl of Essex, who was executed in 1601, or to the circumstances surrounding the trial of Sir Walter Ralegh in 1603, or even possibly as a generalized, but none the less potentially seditious, exploration of contemporary *Realpolitik*. The manipulation and exercise of state power was a dangerous choice of subject-matter in the early seventeenth century, and the volatility of this period of Roman history is suggested by the speech made by Sir John Eliot during the parliamentary impeachment hearings of 1626 in which George Villiers, Duke of Buckingham, was attacked as a Sejanus.

Jonson defends his choice of subject-matter by asserting that he has dramatized accurately the events of history, a defence which implies that it is possible to write historical drama from an ideologically impartial perspective. However, the play's lengthy prefatory material and copious sidenotes perhaps signal an anxiety which belies that confidence. An awareness that the retelling of history is necessarily an act of interpretation, and therefore always political and ideological, is tellingly demonstrated through the trial of the historian Cordus in the third act. Cordus has written the chronicles of Rome from the time of Pompey to the present reign, times which, as Natta notes in the play's opening scene, 'are somewhat queasy to be touched', and he is accused of treason on the grounds that his praise of men such as Brutus and Cassius casts aspersion on Rome's current rulers. Cordus' spirited and lengthy defence of his work is an extraordinary dramatic achievement, in that Jonson has inserted into his drama a direct translation of the historian's speech as recorded in Tacitus' *Annals*. What is particularly interesting, however, is that, in sharp contrast to the manner in which Jonson chose to defend *Sejanus*, Cordus justifies his work through an articulate advocacy of freedom of speech as essential to the healthy functioning of a well-governed state. Far from arguing that his *Annals* are irrelevant to contemporary politics, he cites with approval examples of historians writing in previous ages who were permitted by the authorities to comment critically on government policy; although their opposition may have been ignored or rebutted, it was not suppressed. The suggestion implicit in Cordus' speech is that a ruler's inability to tolerate criticism is symptomatic of institutional corruption at the highest levels. The extremity of that intolerance is emphasized at the end of the trial, when Cordus' work is censored and condemned to the flames. This scene is in many ways reminiscent of the relationship tentatively explored in *Poetaster* in which the worthy poet interacts with the ruler as an adviser of state, but significantly, the political climate dramatized in *Sejanus* is very different.

The court of Tiberius, as portrayed by Jonson, is an oppressively claustrophic environment dominated by spies and informers, in which courtiers jockey for power and promotion by currying favour with the emperor's minion Sejanus. A sense of the degrading sycophancy which characterizes the court is conveyed in the opening moments by Sabinus' repulsive description of Tiberius' hangers-on in terms of their soft and glutinous bodies; like snails, not men, they creep up the wall to success. Despite his claims to the contrary, Jonson massages the historical record in order to present the action of the play in terms of a distinct split between two opposed camps. On the one side are Sejanus and Tiberius and the morally corrupt parasites in attendance on them, while on the other side is the virtuous, but powerless, Germanican faction, including amongst its numbers such characters as Agrippina, Silius, and Arruntius. The political alliances of individual characters, as well as some sense of the ideological divide which separates the factions, is visually represented in the opening scene through the dramatic technique of ranging ever-growing clusters of gossiping courtiers on either side of the stage.

This conflict between the Germanicans and the imperial forces, however, is finally revealed as being of only secondary importance to the balance of power. The Germanicans, especially characters such as Arruntius and Lepidus, serve an important function in that they provide the audience with a moral perspective from which to assess the events of the play, and to some extent the effect of Arruntius' commentary, often delivered as a series of asides punctuating the dialogue, is that of a chorus mediating between the action and the audience. In political terms, however, the Germanicans are entirely ineffectual. Incapable of mounting a coherent resistance to Sejanus and Tiberius, they retreat into passive stoic forbearance; as Agrippina counsels her son at the beginning of Act 4, 'though you do not act, yet suffer nobly'. Scholars have tended to put forward widely varying estimations of this group of characters: they are morally just but politically weak and, as such, present themselves as helpless sacrifices to Sejanus' ambition. Arruntius operates as a moral touchstone, but the only reason his life is spared is because his relentless carping is for the moment useful to Sejanus' machinations. While we might respect the values of the Germanicans, it is difficult to support as viable their strategies for survival within the political realities of Tiberius' Rome.

As the plot unfolds, our real interest becomes increasingly focused on the power-struggle between the emperor and his favourite. The play's dramatic energy is generated by the tension between these two

central characters, each of whom is determined to wield ultimate political control. Sejanus is the villain on whom our attention is focused
from the beginning. It is Sejanus who seduces Livia, plots the murder
of Tiberius' son Drusus, and brings about the downfall of the powerful military general and stalwart of the Germanican faction Silius. The
heinousness of such plotting, according to his enemies, is exacerbated
by his low birth. To the Germanican aristocrats, acutely aware of
social rank, Sejanus is an upstart whose origins can be traced back to a
time when he was a cup-bearer who obscenely prostituted his body to
noblemen's lust. Characters such as Arruntius and Drusus register
genuine bewilderment as to why such a person should be permitted to
consolidate personal power within the court without significant opposition from Tiberius, and apparently without the emperor even being
aware of his designs.

However, the dynamics of the relationship between the emperor
and Sejanus are more complicated than Arruntius assumes. Arruntius
presents Tiberius as a canny politician who is nonetheless unaware of
the extent to which the balance of power is shifting against him. But
this is probably one instance in which we should maintain a critical
distance from this character's perspective and commentary. During
the private meeting between Tiberius and Sejanus in the second act,
Tiberius gives the impression of seeking Sejanus' advice about how
best to handle the threat to his authority posed by Agrippina's faction.
It at first appears that Sejanus is fully in control, firmly setting out the
manner in which Tiberius must destroy their enemies. This perception is exposed as false, however, when Tiberius finally lets fall the
mask of irresolution which he had adopted to test his adviser, demon-
strating that the interview had been stage-managed from beginning to
end. When Sejanus inadvertently reveals in the third act the height of
his ambitions by asking for permission to marry into the emperor's
family, Tiberius immediately recognizes the threat and sets in place a
counter-attack. Believing that Tiberius has become politically com-
placent, more concerned to indulge his sexual appetites in Capri than
to safeguard his authority in Rome, Sejanus remains oblivious to his
intentions; he badly underestimates the emperor's political astuteness,
a mistake which gives Tiberius the opportunity to outmanoeuvre him
in the final act.

Tiberius does not appear again on stage after the third act. Remark-
ably, Sejanus' precipitous fall from power and ultimate destruction is
orchestrated by the physically absent emperor through his instrument
Macro, and by means of a letter read out loud in open Senate. Far from

being a weakness of construction, this decision to present the emperor as pure word, pure authority, establishes him beyond question as the play's consummate Machiavel. It is difficult to read *Sejanus* in terms of a traditional Aristotelian analysis of tragedy, because although the hero's fall can be explained as a punishment for upstart pride, his destruction in no way brings to an end the political corruption in Rome which is perpetuated in the person of Tiberius. The gods in Jonson's construction of Rome are presented as having no effective agency; Dame Fortune, to whom Sejanus appeals in the fifth act, merely has power to confirm the outcome already set in place by the emperor. Rather than attempting to make sense of the fall of Sejanus in terms of social disorder, moral justice, or divine agency, it is perhaps most useful to approach this play as a study in the vicissitudes of power as played out in a tyrannical state in which free speech has been silenced through surveillance and censorship.

The Roman settings of *Sejanus* and *Poetaster* are important for different reasons to a critical understanding of the dramatic action. In the former Jonson relies on the well-documented accuracy of his geographically and historically remote setting to forestall accusations of political topicality, while in the latter the distant location discourages an Elizabethan audience from reading the drama exclusively in terms of contemporary theatrical disputes and alerts them to the playwright's more general analysis of the function of art within the state. However, while Jonson's portrayal of the ancient world in *Sejanus* is not only devoid of anachronism but carefully researched in order to create and maintain the effect of Roman verisimilitude, *Poetaster*, by occasionally evoking early modern London through casual references to such recognizably Elizabethan details as doublets and rapiers, coaches and fans, shows more blurring of dramatic location. Therefore, even though during the prologue Livor specifies the play's Roman setting by reading the place-name on display on signboards at the back of the stage, the setting of *Poetaster* remains to a large extent unlocalized, and an audience needs to hold both ancient Rome and early modern London in their minds while engaging with the action.

Most of the action of *The Devil is an Ass*, by contrast, takes place exclusively in London, as the opening scene in Hell makes explicit. Pug, a junior devil and keen to show off a supposed talent for leading human souls to damnation, begs permission of Satan to insinuate himself into London society, where he promises to accomplish great wonders in the service of Hell. This claim is supported by the sudden entrance of the Vice character, Iniquity, whose account of infernal activities on earth leads the imaginations both of Pug and the audience along a circuitous and detailed route through the streets and alleys of London from St Paul's Cathedral south to the docks and along the Strand to Westminster. His monologue is abruptly cut short by Satan, however, who flatly states that traditional vices like Iniquity are now considered out of fashion, reminding both them and us of the date: 1616. Such specificity of location in terms of time and place is crucial to note since it would have made the earliest audiences, watching a performance of *The Devil is an Ass* in the autumn of 1616, aware that the London dramatized on the stage before them is supposed to be a replica of their own social world. This effect is further heightened by the meta-theatrical device of portraying Fitzdottrel's eager, but ultimately frustrated, attempts to see the first performance of *The Devil is an Ass* at the Blackfriars Theatre. His intention is to advertise himself a fashionable gentleman by sitting on the stage in his finery and disrupting the action by getting up to leave the play early, a plan which implicitly draws attention to the behaviour of those audience members with whom the actor playing Fitzdottrel already shares the Blackfriars stage.

The attention given in the opening scene to details of urban, particularly London, life prepares the audience for a comedy in keeping with some of Jonson's earlier drama in which the manners and behaviour peculiar to the residents of the city of London provide the focus of the playwright's satiric gaze. This genre of play—city comedy—is primarily populated by outspoken, domineering women, effeminate courtiers, smooth-talking gallants, grasping, dishonest merchants, and gullible dupes, and the dramatic action centres on the variety of stratagems by which men are cheated of their money and cuckolded by their wives. *The Devil is an Ass*, based on a complex set of interlocking scams, is no exception. Merecraft, assisted by his agent Engine, preys on wealthy English men and women by persuading them to finance any of a range of proposed ideas for commercial monopolies, and Fitzdottrel, sucked in by Merecraft's sales-patter and the prospect of huge profits, agrees to enter into a partnership to drain the Norfolk fens, a tract of potentially arable land of which he expects eventually to be made duke. While Merecraft and his accomplices try to hook Fitzdottrel's money, Wittipol, a city gallant, attempts to seduce his wife, having already gained a meeting with her by bribing her husband with an expensive cloak. These separate plot-lines come together at the end of Act 4 when Wittipol is suborned by Merecraft to pose as the 'Spanish lady', an English widow capable of educating

Mistress Fitzdottrel in the subtle ways of city women, and in the course of this scene Fitzdottrel is persuaded to sign over the management of his entire estate to a third party, Wittipol's friend Manly. In the final act Fitzdottrel attempts to regain his estate through law by feigning demonic possession, an elaborate performance which is only abandoned when the revelation arrives from Newgate prison that one of the recently admitted thieves (Pug) was really the devil in disguise.

The Devil is an Ass is a slightly unusual city comedy, however, in that the satiric content and characterization are not relentlessly sharp or bitter. Instead of cuckolding Fitzdottrel by taking advantage of Frances Fitzdottrel's desperate marital situation, Wittipol takes pity on his virtuous mistress's plight and agrees to assist her as a friend to achieve financial independence from her foolish husband. Moreover, through his intervention in the disguise of the Spanish lady, Wittipol ensures that the projector's designs on the Fitzdottrel estate are foiled, but not exposed, with his friend Manly making an unlikely appeal in his closing speech to the con-artists' better consciences. The action is thus to some extent only provisionally resolved, since after the final scene Fitzdottrel is still a fool, Mistress Fitzdottrel remains trapped in an empty marriage with no hope of relief, and Merecraft is free to re-establish himself as an entrepreneur within London society.

Jonson further adapts the city comedy format through the introduction of elements of the traditional devil play, or interlude, a genre which was especially popular in the mid-sixteenth century. The opening scene in Hell sets in place expectations of a type of drama in which the devil, in the company of his chosen Vice figure, comes to earth to disrupt the community; the playwright comically subverts the conventions of this genre by presenting his audience with a devil who has trouble competing with, or even keeping abreast of, the vices practised daily in the capital. Most of the time Pug is simply a shocked witness to human duplicity, but occasionally he finds himself reluctantly drawn into the action, as during the scenes in which he is conned out of a jewel or unwittingly used as the means by which to arrange a clandestine lovers' meeting. The extent to which Jonson turns the interlude form on its head is emblematized in Pug's final scene in Newgate: usually in devil plays the fiend leaves the stage bearing the Vice character on his back, but here, as Iniquity points out, the fiend is carried out by the Vice. The presence on stage throughout the play of an astounded devil pleading to return to Hell before the conclusion of his assigned time in London comically reinforces the outrageous conduct of the con-artists and ladies of fashion amongst whom he finds himself, and confirms the satirist's view that 'Hell is | A grammar school to this!'

Jonson told Drummond, however, that 'he was accused' for this play, which suggests that its satire extends beyond a critique of London fashions and morals to engage in a very specific manner with the political circumstances of this period in the reign of James I. Merecraft's far-fetched 'projects' are in effect proposals for royal monopolies, and monopolies had become the object of intense scrutiny just prior to the writing of *The Devil is an Ass*. The licence granted to Alderman Cockayne in 1613 to dye and dress English cloth for export to foreign markets was seen as particularly controversial, because it posed competition to the exclusive rights held by another company, the Merchant Adventurers, to export undressed cloth. Cockayne's project initially enjoyed the support of influential courtiers and even of the king himself, but as it became increasingly associated with corruption and financial failure, the monopolist found himself abandoned by his backers. Just months after the earliest performances of Jonson's play the company was dissolved. Jonson's satirical treatment of projectors thus offers a timely and politically relevant analysis of a practice already in some disfavour.

A second important context underlying the play's dramatic action is the practice of witchcraft, a subject which became increasingly politicized in the aftermath of the Overbury scandal. Frances Howard had secretly conspired with the sorceress, Anne Turner, to escape from an unwanted marriage to the Earl of Essex in order to marry her lover, the Earl of Somerset. After the annulment was granted, Howard further conspired with Turner to poison Sir Thomas Overbury, a noble who forcefully opposed the proposed marriage between Howard and Somerset. In November 1615 Anne Turner was hanged as a witch, and Howard and Somerset were convicted of murder the following spring. Jonson's comedy clearly recollects the circumstances of the Overbury trial by flirting with such topical issues as unhappy marriages and devil-worshipping. However, its preoccupation with sorcery, real and bogus, can also be seen to cut in another direction. To the embarrassment of two circuit judges who had been unable to perceive the deception, James I had recently intervened in a celebrated court case in Leicestershire to expose a fraudulent case of possession by the devil which had led to the execution of nine local women as witches. Jonson's portrayal of Fitzdottrel's failed ruse to regain his estate in Act 5 can thus be seen as an implicit compliment to the king and a castigation of justices of the peace such as Sir Paul Eitherside who are incapable of seeing justice done, either through neglect or stupidity. The possibility that Eitherside might have allowed himself to have been misled by self-interest is not only suggested by the mention of his close business relationship with Merecraft, but also by his name, which signals an ability and willingness to argue either side of a case regardless of justice.

But it was his discourse of the Duke of Drowned-land that James I specifically asked Jonson to conceal. The need to curb, or at least disguise, the play's portrayal of Fitzdottrel's gullible belief that Mere-craft has solved the engineering problems associated with draining the fens suggests that a recognizable contemporary figure underpins the fictional character. Various critics have speculated on who the original of the Duke of Drowned-land might have been, the most convincing suggestion being Sir Robert Carr, a nobleman and Gentleman of the Prince's Bedchamber who was granted sole rights in a very similar enterprise in 1614. Crucially, the faction with which Carr was associated was in decline in 1616, and this combination of circumstances again suggests that Jonson's satire is politically motivated, contributing to the complex and fluctuating court politics centred around the person of the king. Jonson is sometimes discussed, and even dismissed, as a royalist playwright who carefully formulated his views in keeping with a perceived monarchical agenda, but the questioning, satirical manner in which the narrative threads of *The Devil is an Ass* intersect with current Jacobean events suggests a more distanced perspective, which acts less as a congratulatory affirmation of government policy than as a salutary prompt to decision-making. It is important, however, not only to register the potential distance between the views of Jonson and those of the state authorities, but to recognize also the extent to which the playwright is carving out for himself a distinctive authorial identity as a cautious and impartial advisor to the throne. This politically engaged and sometimes even critical relationship of the poet to his king is reminiscent of the function of art as tentatively explored in much-earlier dramas such as *Poetaster* and *Sejanus*.

The difficulties attendant on interpreting the politics of the drama written by Jonson up to 1616 are magnified when one considers the plays written after his return to the stage in 1626. Critical estimation of Jonson's late plays tends to vary widely, and *The New Inn*, in particular, has been subject over the years to radically different readings. The alterations in Jonson's personal circumstances after the death of James I in 1625—his increasingly poor health, straitened financial means, and lack of favour in the court of Charles I—seem to some scholars to have provided the catalyst for a new departure in Jonson's stagecraft. Others, interpreting the canon in terms of artistic continuity, locate in Jonson's dramatic style after 1626 the same satiric and didactic impulses which underpin much of his earlier work.

The New Inn is an exceptional piece, in that it is the only extant play in which Jonson experiments with the genre of romantic comedy. In the manner of Shakespearian drama such as *As You Like It* and *A Midsummer Night's Dream*, Jonson allows his lovers the freedom to interact with each other outside of the usual constraints imposed by society through the device of setting the action entirely in a wayside inn, The Light Heart, in the market town of Barnet, a resort area on the outskirts of London. The holiday atmosphere prompted by the lovers' temporary relocation outside the city walls is further developed not only by their Host's passionate commitment to good fellowship and revelry, but also by the establishment of a mock Court of Love presided over by Queen Prudence, Lady Frampul's chambermaid. As a result of formative encounters over the course of the day's activities at The Light Heart, the lovers arrive at a maturity and understanding both of themselves and each other which ultimately enable them to embrace true love at the close of the action. Superimposed on this romantic comedy framework is a fifth act which partakes of the romance tradition. Jonson scoffed at his audience's supposed preference for some 'mouldy tale' such as *Pericles* in the 'Ode to Himself' printed at the end of the drama, but the sense of strangeness and wonder which results from a comic resolution effected through a sudden flurry of inexplicable and unexpected revelations indicates the extent to which, in this play at least, he was influenced by the very dramatic conventions he derides. In light of the surprising twists in Act 5, readers unfamiliar with the plot of *The New Inn* are advised not to continue reading this introduction, but to read the play first.

At the end of Act 4, there seems little likelihood that the Host will achieve his ambition to see his guests merry: the Court of Love has been dissolved, Lady Frampul and her maid have quarrelled, and Lovel has retired to bed to 'dream away the vapour of love'. It is only with Fly's announcement that Lord Beaufort has married Laetitia in the stables that the Host's original failed plot can be reworked to a comic resolution. The entry of the newlyweds at the beginning of Act 5 seems a guaranteed source of mirth at the expense of the gullible Beaufort, since it provides Pru and her mistress with the opportunity to reveal that Laetitia is really the Host's son, Frank, in disguise. But this disclosure is hastily followed by the Nurse's revelation that the deception is even more complex, and that Frank is not a boy after all, but her daughter who was dressed up as a boy before their arrival at the inn. Beaufort's subsequent dismay and anger at the prospect of having married a beggar prompts a series of further developments in the plot that no audience could either know in advance or predict: Laetitia is Lord Frampul's daughter and the missing sister to Frances, the Nurse is Frampul's long-lost wife, and the Host is the absent Lord Frampul himself. The young lord's impetuous elopement thus rescues the plot from disarray by inadvertently providing the means by which the long-separated family achieves reconciliation.

The manner in which the action of *The New Inn* is brought to a conclusion is dramatically unusual, however, in that Frank's true identity prior to the closing moments is known only to her mother and kept a secret from everyone else both on stage and in the audience. The members of Jonson's earliest audience, in particular, accustomed to the dramatic convention that a boy actor dressed as a woman should be interpreted as a woman unless informed otherwise, are given no clue which might prepare them for the sudden reversals in the fifth act. It seems especially important to avoid reading in advance of the play the extensive preliminary material published by the irate dramatist to ensure that his reading audience, unlike his theatrical audience, would be able to make sense of the action: we do not know—and are not supposed to know—that there is any mystery surrounding the Host's son until the Nurse announces his/her true origins. Moreover, one should resist examining too closely the implications of the characters' hidden identities on the early scenes since it otherwise quickly appears ludicrous that a wife and husband, living together for years under the same roof, could fail to see through an eyepatch and a false beard, and that neither parent would reveal himself or herself to their daughter upon her arrival at the inn. The magic summoned up by the final scene, if inscrutable, is entirely typical of the romance genre in which an audience is often left without a credible explanation for the events as they unfold.

The play's dominant motif is the world as a stage, and this motif is established early in the opening scene through the Host's description of himself as a spectator comfortably seated to watch the drama of life unfold before him. Jonson develops this initial presentation of life as performance in two distinct ways. First, many of the characters, including both guests and serving-staff, agree to enact the roles assigned to them in the play within a play, or Court of Love, conducted in the third and fourth acts. Such self-conscious role-play is crucial to the drama's successful outcome, since it is only by means of this theatrical game that Lovel is persuaded to abandon his ineffectual melancholy and Lady Frampul learns to know herself better, thereby appreciating fully the merits of her suitor. Secondly, in a related vein, the day's activities at The Light Heart demonstrate the transform-ational power of costume itself, as the audience unexpectedly finds that the characters are suited to the clothing they seemingly assumed in jest. Frank, for example, dresses up as one of Lady Frampul's close female relations, only for it to be revealed at the close of the action that the Host's adopted son is, indeed, of the gender and social rank he/she feigns. Similarly, Pru takes on with some misgivings the finery and trappings of those of gentry status, only to be reinvented as a noble-woman in the final moments through Lord Latimer's proposal of mar-riage. The power of costume is emphasized most clearly, however, when the Host transforms himself from an innkeeper to Lord Fram-pul by assuming the robes of his former life.

Clothing is portrayed not simply as an indicator of gender or social status, but as a potent means by which personal identity may be formed and transformed. This is not to say, however, that the oper-ation of its magic is available to all; on the contrary, the point that its efficacy must remain restricted to a select elite is forcefully demon-strated when the tailor's wife, Pinnacia Stuff, is stripped of her count-ess's dress and, as punishment for her presumption, is subjected to the public ridicule and humiliation of a whore. Nonetheless, the theatrical-ity of costume as presented in *The New Inn* marks a thematic sea-change for Jonson. In his earlier drama he articulated a deep mistrust of shape-shifting: Sejanus, for instance, despite assuming a position of power and privilege, remains a base upstart, while the costume ban-quet in *Poetaster* leads directly to the banishment of Ovid. In these plays Jonson sets forward the reactionary view that clothing should be an unproblematic sign of one's true personal identity, a politics which is itself the source of tension in the illusory world of early modern theatre in which commoners play kings, and boy actors play women. But the comic resolution of *The New Inn*, premissed on the successful transformation of personal identity, sets forward the possibility that the power of costume, at least in this play, can be a positive and rejuvenating force.

By this reading, the romance elements of the drama should be taken at face value, and the scenes involving the Stuffs and the below-stairs regiment led by Fly and Tipto can be seen as designed to highlight the gap between the ideal world achieved by the lovers and the mundane, even tedious, reality experienced by the lowlife characters. Another strand of criticism, however, is sceptical of readings which posit that over a ten-year absence from the stage Jonson revised not only his views on the potential of human relationships, but also his well-known distaste for dramatic forms such as romance and romantic comedy. Scholars who take a more cynical view of what Jonson was attempting to accomplish with *The New Inn* argue that his tale of reconciliation and forgiveness is an elaborate, but perhaps overly subtle, parody of the Caroline court. The Court of Love scenes, far from advocating Platonic love and Senecan valour, burlesque attitudes made popular in courtly circles by the Queen of England, Henrietta Maria.

Suspicions about the royal court are raised early in Act I during a dispute between Lovel and the Host about the merits of the education gained there by young courtiers; according to the Host, the modern English gentry have so lost sight of ancestral nobility that he would rather kill his son himself, 'mak[ing] a clean riddance' of him, than allow him to be raised as a page. The sports which follow the arrival of Lady Frampul and her entourage at the inn may be read as evidence of the truth of courtly decadence, and the participants in the mock court, either swayed by Lovel's eloquence, or themselves thoroughly steeped in the same culture, praise his discourses as utterly convincing. In a tradition which can be traced back to the medieval Courts of Love, Lovel is assigned two separate hours in which formally to address his mistress on a subject determined by the assembled court. Lovel uses his first hour to define love, arguing, in a series of set speeches heavily dependent on Ficino's commentary on Plato's *Symposium*, that the more exalted form of love is that in which lovers are able to set aside carnal lust—the banquet of sense—to find full satisfaction in an intellectual apprehension of the object of desire. Significantly, this session reworks attitudes made fashionable by the foreign queen of Charles I, whose advocacy of Platonic love, although undoubtedly sincere for her own part, led to a widespread popular understanding of true love as being apart from and unrestricted by the codes of conventional morality as regulated through the institution of marriage. In his second hour Lovel advocates the view that valour is defined not by anger generated by a perceived slight to one's personal pride or honour, but by a Stoic fortitude which enables the truly valorous man to identify and defend worthy causes in a spirit of calm self-possession.

Although Jonson provides no on-stage voice capable of challenging the authority of Lovel's discourse, there is reason to believe that the playwright may have expected his audience to maintain a critical distance from the proceedings. First, Lovel's disquisition on Platonic love is comically counterpointed by the behaviour of Lord Beaufort who, plainly lusting after Laetitia and snatching kisses from his beloved at all opportunities, provides a clear and constant reminder throughout the scene of the sexual intimacy Lovel so carefully attempts to dismiss as a meaningless distraction. Secondly, Lovel himself fails to live up to the high ideals he advances in the Court of Love. Not only does he angrily stalk off-stage at the end of Act 4, claiming that he has allowed himself to be baffled by a chambermaid, behaviour which stands in sharp ironic contrast to his preceding discussion of true valour, he then eagerly exits at the end of Act 5 to enjoy a night of what one presumes will be something other than Platonic love in the arms of his mistress. Finally, the below-stairs action which portrays Fly holding court over his mock militia parodies and deflates the action above-stairs in which courtiers participate in a mock court ruled by a chambermaid. In these scenes, Lovel's vision of love is replaced by Peck's visions of fraud and roguery, while the open brawl sparked by Hodge Huffle's comic vapouring provides an earthy reminder of the realities of human interaction which Lovel's discourse on valour threatens to overlook. In a similar manner, the tailor's wife, Pinnacia Stuff, who enacts and then willingly imparts to the other characters her husband's elaborate sexual fantasies, provides a larger-than-life testimony to the very real power of sex and sensuality which implicitly makes less compelling the dry intellectualism embraced by those who punish her.

In these ways an audience remains emotionally distanced from the play's comic resolution through an ironic awareness that the reconciliations dramatized in the closing moments are premissed on self-deception. However, unlike *Poetaster* or *Sejanus*, in which the characters of Horace and Arruntius provide the audience with a guiding perspective through which to appraise the action, and unlike *The Devil is an Ass*, in which fraudsters such as Merecraft and Engine keep us informed of their deceits as they unfold, the audience is left to interpret and judge the satiric implications of the action of *The New Inn* for themselves. This technique could represent a further development in the stagecraft of Jonson the satirist, but if so, then it is probably a failed experiment since the play's irony is too subtle for an audience to acknowledge with any certainty. Conversely, *The New Inn* could suggest a development in the playwright's dramatic style away from satire altogether; and indeed, as Anne Barton has argued, if

Jonson's purpose was satire, then it seems odd that he gives no indication of it in his lengthy explanatory notes included as part of the printed version of the play. The appeal of an interpretation of this late play as parody is that the image of Jonson which it implies—the playwright as satirical poet, taking upon himself an almost moral obligation to admonish the perceived failings of the court—is an authorial identity with which we are familiar from his early drama. The familiarity of such a construction, however, should not blind us to the possibility that this was an identity which Jonson had, indeed, himself already abandoned.

None of the four plays included in this volume was a box-office hit for Jonson. His claim that *Poetaster*'s 'Apologetical Dialogue' was spoken just once on the stage may allude to censorship, but equally, may indicate that the play was not long in the repertory of the Children of the Chapel at the Blackfriars (see *Poetaster*, Additional Passage E). The critical reception afforded *Sejanus*, almost certainly performed first at court by the King's Men and then subsequently at the Globe, seems to have been a major and unexpected disappointment for Jonson, an assumption implied by his careful revision and preparation of the text for print publication, and made explicit by the commendatory poem signed 'Ev. B.' which describes the audience's 'beastly rage, | Bent to confound thy grave and learned toil'. There is no clear evidence to confirm whether or not the earliest production of *The Devil is an Ass* by the King's Men at Blackfriars was a success, but the fact that there is no record of a revival during Jonson's lifetime perhaps suggests that the response was indifferent. And *The New Inn*, attacked by Dryden as one of Jonson's 'dotages' and vilified by its earliest audience when acted by the King's Men at Blackfriars, probably saw only one performance in 1629; the fact that a second epilogue written for a projected performance at court was never spoken suggests that it was removed from the company's repertory altogether. Blaming an ignorant audience for the play's failure, Jonson penned the vitriolic 'Ode to Himself', and attempted to make the action more accessible to his reading audience by prefacing the printed text with character and plot descriptions.

The predominantly negative assessments of these four plays by Jonson's contemporaries have not, by and large, been challenged by their subsequent stage history, which is characterized by neglect. No records after their earliest productions survive of any of these plays in performance prior to the twentieth century. Within the last hundred years *Poetaster* and *Sejanus* have each been given only a single, limited run, by William Poel in London on 26–7 April 1916 and 12 February 1928 respectively, while *The New Inn* has been revived only twice, and *The Devil is an Ass* three times. The disinclination of theatre companies to present these plays perpetuates the unwarranted assumption that they somehow lack theatrical merit. Significantly, however, such revivals as have been attempted have proved successful, and the recent productions, in particular, of *The Devil is an Ass* and *The New Inn* by the Royal Shakespeare Company at the Swan Theatre were mounted to widespread critical acclaim. To some extent, Jonson's deliberate efforts to ossify in print the theatrical potential of his dramatic works must be blamed for a modern reluctance to tackle his lesser-known plays on stage more frequently. But these plays—and none more so than *Poetaster* and *Sejanus*—richly deserve major new productions.

NOTE ON THE TEXT

The four plays in this volume have been edited afresh from the earliest printed texts. No systematic collation of the extant copies of the original texts has been prepared, but I have silently incorporated into the plays the collation work carried out by previous editors. Spelling and punctuation are modernized in accordance with the guidelines set out by Stanley Wells in *Re-editing Shakespeare for the Modern Reader*, and so, for example, 'and' (where it means 'if'), 'sodaine', 'Gods a me', 'powring', 'porpentine', and 'publique' are standardized to their modern equivalents ('an', 'sudden', 'God sa' me', 'pouring', 'porcupine', and 'public'). Words which are historically distinct from more recognizable modern words with similar meanings have been preserved, however, such as 'rand' (not 'rant') and 'gripe' (not 'grip'). An exception to these general principles is that archaic or obsolete forms are preserved where required by either metre or rhyme. Jonson's use of a now obsolete form of punctuation involving an apostrophe between words ('She' is') to indicate elision, rather than contraction, is omitted.

Emendation has been introduced cautiously, where the early printed text is clearly in error, and is recorded and discussed in the Explanatory Notes only if unique to this edition. Jonson's act and scene breaks are preserved in *Poetaster*, *The Devil is an Ass*, and *The New Inn*, where new scenes tend to occur with the entrance of a character or group of characters signalling a significant development in the action. Only act breaks are marked in the original editions of *Sejanus*, however, and scene breaks are introduced in this edition in square brackets according to the customary principle that a new scene begins when the stage is cleared of actors. All of the original texts, in accordance with the conventions for learned drama, provide massed entries at the beginning of new scenes indicating all of the characters who will appear in the scene, regardless of whether they are on-stage from the beginning or enter midway through; this practice is adapted here by cueing the entrance of a character only at the point at which he or she appears on-stage. The cast lists of *Poetaster* and *Sejanus* are reorganized and brief explanations of some of the characters are added in square brackets to make these plays more accessible to the general reader. Names of characters are silently standardized in the speech headings and stage directions, and some of the Latin speech prefixes printed in *Sejanus* are standardized to their English equivalent. Latin stage directions are translated. Added speech prefixes, along with stage directions inserted to help the reader visualize stage business clearly implied in the dialogue, are signalled with square brackets; stage directions not provided in square brackets are original to the early printed texts. The Explanatory Notes are used freely to explore the manner in which particular moments or scenes might potentially be staged in performance.

The edition of Jonson's plays to which every subsequent editor is indebted is the eleven-volume complete works prepared by C. H. Herford and Percy and Evelyn Simpson (1925–52); recommended single-volume editions are cited below after the textual discussion of individual plays.

Poetaster

Poetaster was printed twice in Jonson's lifetime, once in 1602 in quarto format (four leaves or eight pages printed to a sheet), and again in 1616 as part of the *Works of Benjamin Jonson* printed in folio format (two leaves or four pages printed to a sheet). The play is significantly different in each printed version. Beyond the revision of individual words and short phrases ('traduce' becomes 'bewitch', '*Numa in Decimo nono*' becomes 'Nay, I will see it', 'Acoutrements' becomes 'habillaments'), the folio text omits all references to knights found in the quarto and renames Livor, a character appearing in the prologue, Envy. The folio also departs from the quarto in printing a short dedicatory letter to Richard Martin and including four lengthy passages of dialogue not previously printed. The likely provenance of the four passages of dialogue varies. Jonson notes in the Apologetical Dialogue that his satirical attack on such professions as actors, lawyers, and military captains was considered hugely controversial when the play was first performed. It seems probable that two of the excerpts not printed in the quarto edition, but included in the folio—the ones satirizing actors and lawyers—were deliberately omitted from the earliest printed text as the result either of official or self-censorship (see Introduction, p. xiii, and Additional Passages B and C). Jonson's justification of his work, the Apologetical Dialogue, was performed at least once on stage, but not printed until well after the controversy had passed, again, probably as the consequence of some form of censorship. The highly literary scene between the characters of Horace and Trebatius, on the other hand, presented in the folio as Act 3, Scene 5, was probably newly written by Jonson for the 1616 printing as a retrospective response to criticisms made of the play at the time of its first performance. This scene, a lengthy discussion and justification of the poet's satirical art, is a loose translation of a passage in Horace's *Satires* (ii. 1).

This edition takes as its control text the earliest printed version of the play, the quarto of 1602, on the grounds that this version, rather than the folio version revised for print publication more than a decade later, will more closely approximate to the play as performed on stage in 1601. Passages found only in the folio version are printed at the end of the play as Additional Passages. Readers interested to reconstruct the text of *Poetaster* as it may have looked in its original production should consider the likelihood that Additional Passages B, C, and E were acted at Blackfriars. An excellent single-volume edition of the play which takes the folio as its copy-text has recently been prepared by Tom Cain as part of the Revels Plays series (Manchester: MUP, 1995).

Sejanus

There are two extant versions of *Sejanus*, the quarto published in 1605 and the version as printed in the folio *Works* of 1616. Jonson's peculiar relationship with the theatre is nowhere more evident than in the quarto text of *Sejanus*, which was presented to the reader less as a blueprint for dramatic performance than as a finished literary masterpiece, with the classical sources for the drama carefully and copiously documented in the margins of the play. The text's literary quality is further highlighted through the use of a page layout intended to create for the reader a Roman 'feel'—the opening lines of Tiberius' letter in the Senate of Act 5, for example, is printed in capital letters and punctuated with full-stops between each word in the manner of a Roman inscription. Although there are a few verbal differences between the quarto and folio versions, the major difference between the two texts is that stage directions were incorporated into the latter, and its presentation adapted to bring it more into conformity with the layout of the other plays included in the *Works*.

Sejanus was not a theatrical success, and Jonson explains in his Letter to the Readers that he revised the play heavily for print publication, rewriting entirely the contributions of his collaborator. This edition takes as its control text the quarto of 1605, and passages included in the folio but not in the quarto are printed at the end of the play as Additional Passages. While issues of presentation (marginal notes, layout of the text on the page) are indicative of the manner in which Jonson engaged with the play when reworking it for print publication, these features disappear from performance, and consequently have not been preserved in this edition. The play text of *Sejanus* is one instance, however, in which an early performance text is certainly irretrievable. No records exist to indicate what *Sejanus* as it was first performed may have looked like, and all that is available to modern readers is the text as revised for print. The play's historical circumstances, along with the quarto's bookish layout, the entire lack of scene breaks and stage directions, the large number of missing cues for characters' entrances and exits, the unusual practice of indicating location for the readers' benefit by means of a headnote in Acts 3 and 5 ('The Senate'), and non-specific massed entrances (the end of a list of characters required on stage often ends with the vague catch-all '&c.') indicate that the printer's copy underlying the quarto came not from the playhouse but from Jonson's study. The best and most easily available single-volume edition of *Sejanus* is the Revels Plays edition prepared by Philip J. Ayres (Manchester: MUP, 1990, repr. 1999), which is based on the 1605 quarto. Other useful editions have been prepared by W. D. Briggs for the Heath Belles Lettres series (Boston: Heath, 1911), Jonas A. Barish for the Yale Ben Jonson (New Haven: Yale UP, 1965), and W. F. Bolton for the New Mermaids series (London: Ernest Benn, 1966).

The Devil is an Ass

The Devil is an Ass was first printed in 1631, when Jonson undertook to publish a second volume to the folio *Works* of 1616. In addition to *The Devil is an Ass*, this second collection was to include *Bartholomew Fair* and *The Staple of News*. Jonson was dissatisfied with his printer's standard of work, however, and abandoned the project after all three plays were printed. The second volume to the *Works* eventually appeared in 1640 after Jonson's death, but the text of *The Devil is an Ass* included in most of the copies of that book is comprised of the pages printed nine years earlier, in 1631. A shortage of copies of *The Devil is an Ass* for the 1640 folio prompted a second printing of the play in 1641 by T. Harper.

This edition of *The Devil is an Ass* takes as its control text the 1631 printed edition which was published as part of the second volume of *The Works of Benjamin Jonson* in 1640. It is impossible to know how similar the 1631 text is to the play as first performed at Blackfriars in 1616, since Jonson may well have revised the play for print publication after complaints were voiced about his use of satire (see Introduction, pp. xxiii–xxiv). The original play text is in places unclear about exits and stage business (see, for example, the discussion in the explanatory notes at 4.6.41 about the exit of Mistress Fitzdottrel, and the discussion at 1.6.148 about the manner in which the interview between Wittipol and Mistress Fitzdottrel is staged in performance). In addition, the 1631 text includes a number of marginal directions which are fictional rather than theatrical. Rather than illuminate the staging, they interrupt the flow of the action and are therefore relocated to the Explanatory Notes. These novelistic sidenotes, alongside the ambiguities about staging, indicate that the printer's copy underlying the 1631 edition was an authorial or scribal manuscript deriving from Jonson's study, rather than a playhouse manuscript marked up by the bookkeeper. A solid and reliable edition of *The Devil is an Ass* has recently been prepared by Peter Happé for the Revels Plays series (Manchester: MUP, 1994).

The New Inn

The New Inn was printed in 1631 in octavo format (eight leaves or sixteen pages printed to a sheet). This is the only original printed text of the play available, and it has been used as the control text for this edition. The first performance of *The New Inn* in 1629 was disastrously received by its audience, an event which on the play's title-page Jonson blames on the actors and spectators: 'THE | NEW INNE | OR, | *The light Heart.* | A COMOEDY. | As it was neuer acted, but most | negligently play'd, by some, | the Kings Seruants. | And more squeamishly beheld, and censu- | red by others, the Kings Subiects. | 1629. | Now, at last, set at liberty to the Readers, his Maties | Seruants, and Subiects, to be iudg'd. | 1631. | By the Author, *B. Ionson.* | Hor. . . . . *me lectori credere mallem:* | *Quàm spectatoris fastidia ferre superbi* [Horace: I prefer to entrust myself to a reader rather than to bear the disdain of a scornful spectator].' Disappointed by the play's reception in the theatre, Jonson included in the printed text's preliminary material explanatory character outlines and lengthy descriptions of the plot to help his readers interpret the action. He also explains in a second Epilogue appended to the printed text, apparently never performed on stage, that there was some controversy about the original name of Lady Frampul's chambermaid, Cis. This character

name is revised in the printed text to Pru. These revisions and additions, along with missing entrances and exits, suggest that the copy
from which the printer set the play came from Jonson's study, not the
playhouse. Michael Hattaway's edition of *The New Inn*, prepared for
the Revels Plays series (Manchester: MUP, 1984), is highly
recommended.

SELECT BIBLIOGRAPHY

The best biographical studies are *Ben Jonson: A Life* by David Riggs (Cambridge, Mass: Harvard UP, 1989), and *Ben Jonson: His Life and Work* by Rosalind Miles (London: Routledge & Kegan Paul, 1986); W. David Kay's *Ben Jonson: A Literary Life* (Basingstoke: Macmillan, 1995) offers insightful readings of the literary work alongside an account of the author's life. There are a number of excellent book-length literary studies of Jonson available, including Anne Barton's *Ben Jonson, Dramatist* (Cambridge: CUP, 1984), Ian Donaldson's *Jonson's Magic Houses: Essays in Interpretation* (Oxford: Clarendon, 1997), and Peter Womack's *Ben Jonson* (Oxford: Basil Blackwell, 1986). John Creaser's 'Enigmatic Ben Jonson', in Michael Cordner, Peter Holland, and John Kerrigan (eds.), *English Comedy* (Cambridge: CUP, 1994), 100–18, is a good article-length piece on the author and his work. Julie Sanders explores the plays from a previously overlooked political perspective in *Ben Jonson's Theatrical Republics* (Basingstoke: Macmillan, 1998), while Richard Dutton's *Ben Jonson: To the First Folio* (Cambridge: CUP, 1983) offers a well-written and insightful analysis of the folio edition of 1616. Richard Cave's theatrical study in *Ben Jonson* (Basingstoke: Macmillan, 1991) is the best of its kind available, and the discussion of the plays in performance is developed further in *Ben Jonson and Theatre: Performance, Practice and Theory* (London: Routledge, 1999) by Richard Cave, Elizabeth Schafer, and Brian Woolland. Lois Potter's 'The Swan Song of the Stage Historian', in Martin Butler (ed.), *Re-Presenting Ben Jonson: Text, History, Performance* (Basingstoke: Macmillan, 1999), 193–209, offers an excellent discussion of Jonson in performance in the Swan Theatre, Stratford-upon-Avon. Two recent collections of essays, *New Perspectives on Ben Jonson* (London: Associated UP, 1997) edited by James Hirsh, and *Refashioning Ben Jonson: Gender, Politics, and the Jonsonian Canon* (Basingstoke: Macmillan, 1998) edited by Julie Sanders, with Kate Chedgzoy and Susan Wiseman, embrace a variety of critical approaches to Jonson, and offer some excellent readings of his lesser-known plays. *Ben Jonson: The Critical Heritage, 1599–1798* (London: Routledge, 1990), edited by D. H. Craig, gathers together the early secondary material on Jonson. George E. Rowe Jr. examines Jonson's fashioning of an authorial identity in 'Ben Jonson's Quarrel with Audience and its Renaissance Context', *Studies in Philology*, 81: 4 (1984), 438–60.

The most convincing analysis of *Poetaster* as a study in a poet's moral responsibilities is offered by Anne Barton in *Ben Jonson, Dramatist*. David Bevington's *Tudor Drama and Politics: A Critical Approach to Topical Meaning* (Cambridge, Mass: Harvard UP, 1968) is one of the earliest and best books to interpret the play in terms of state politics, but issues of state politics and sexuality are pursued in a slightly different vein in an excellent article by Alan Sinfield called '*Poetaster*, the Author, and the Perils of Cultural Production', *Renaissance Drama*, NS 27 (1996), 3–18. Topical allusions to the controversy surrounding the Earl of Essex are explored by Tom Cain in '"Satyres, That Girde and Fart at the Time": *Poetaster* and the Essex Rebellion', in *Refashioning Ben Jonson*, 48–70. Annabel Patterson's *Censorship and Interpretation: The Conditions of Writing and Reading in Early Modern England* (Madison: U. of Wisconsin Press, 1984), Richard Dutton's *Mastering the Revels: The Regulation and Censorship of English Renaissance Drama* (London: Macmillan, 1991), and Janet Clare's '*Art made tongue-tied by authority': Elizabethan and Jacobean Dramatic Censorship* (Manchester: MUP, 1990) provide interesting discussions of the censorship issues surrounding both *Poetaster* and *Sejanus*.

Issues of authority, primarily in relation to *Sejanus*, but also with reference to *Poetaster* are analysed by John G. Sweeney III in '*Sejanus* and the People's Beastly Rage,' *ELH* 48: 1 (1981), 61–82. Jonathan Goldberg provides a thought-provoking discussion of *Sejanus* in terms of Jonson's presentation of power politics in *James I and the Politics of Literature: Jonson, Shakespeare, Donne, and Their Contemporaries* (Baltimore: Johns Hopkins UP, 1983), while excellent explorations of body politics and sexuality are found in Gail Kern Paster's *The Idea of the City in the Age of Shakespeare* (Athens: U. of Georgia Press, 1985), and Mario DiGangi's *The Homoerotics of Early Modern Drama* (Cambridge: CUP, 1997). Those interested in Jonson's use of history should read Richard Dutton's 'The Sources, Text, and Readers of *Sejanus*: Jonson's "integrity in the Story"', *Studies in Philology*, 75: 2 (1978), 181–98, and Philip Ayres's 'The Nature of Jonson's Roman History', *ELR* 16 (1986), 166–81. Also good is Blair Worden's 'Ben Jonson among the Historians', in Kevin Sharpe and Peter Lake (eds.), *Culture and Politics in Early Stuart England* (Basingstoke: Macmillan, 1994), 67–89. An excellent discussion of the interpretive implications of Jonson's sidenotes is offered by John Jowett in '"Fall before this Booke": The 1605 Quarto of *Sejanus*', *TEXT*, 4 (1988), 279–95.

Less has been written on *The Devil is an Ass* than on the other three plays in this volume, and much of the recent critical attention focuses on the play's topicality. The earliest discussion of this nature is Leah Marcus's *The Politics of Mirth: Jonson, Herrick, Milton, Marvell, and the Defense of Old Holiday Pastimes* (Chicago: U. of Chicago Press, 1986), which is developed significantly by Robert C. Evans in 'Political Contexts of *The Devil is an Ass*', in *Jonson and the Contexts of His Time* (London: Associated UP, 1994). The play's love plot has been analysed by Helen Ostovich in relation to contemporary paradigms of female behaviour in 'Hell for Lovers: Shades of Adultery in *The Devil is an Ass*', in *Refashioning Ben Jonson*, 155–82.

The best discussions of Jonson's treatment of the romance genre in *The New Inn* are provided by L. A. Beaurline in *Jonson and Elizabethan Comedy: Essays in Dramatic Rhetoric* (San Marino: Huntington Library, 1978) and Anne Barton, '*The New Inn* and the Problem of Jonson's Late Style', *ELR* 9 (1979), 395–418, while the case for a satirical reading is forcefully argued by E. B. Partridge in *The Broken Compass: A Study of the Major Comedies of Ben Jonson* (London: Chatto and Windus, 1958) and Larry S. Champion in *Ben Jonson's 'Dotages': A Reconsideration of the Late Plays* (Lexington: U. of Kentucky Press, 1967). Martin Butler discusses the possibility that Jonson may have been positing an ideal, not actual, world in 'Late Jonson', in Gordon McMullan and Jonathan Hope (eds.), *The Politics of Tragicomedy: Shakespeare and After* (London: Routledge, 1992), 166–88. Harriett Hawkins offers an engaging reading of the theatricality of the play in 'The Idea of a Theater in Jonson's *The New Inn*', *Renaissance Drama*, 9 (1966), 205–26, while in an article of relevance both to *The New Inn* and *Poetaster*, Frank Kermode analyses the origins of 'The Banquet of Sense' in *Shakespeare, Spenser, Donne: Renaissance Essays* (London: Routledge & Kegan Paul, 1971).

A CHRONOLOGY OF BEN JONSON

1572   (11 June) Ben Jonson born, posthumous son of a minister.

1573(?)   Remarriage of Jonson's mother to a bricklayer.

1579–89(?)   Attends Westminster School.

1589–91(?)   Works as a bricklayer.

1591–2   Military service in the Low Countries.

1594   (14 November) marriage to Anne Lewis.

1597   Employed as an actor; imprisoned for his contribution to *The Isle of Dogs*, a (lost) play regarded as seditious.

1598(?)   *Every Man in His Humour* performed by the Lord Chamberlain's Men at the Curtain Theatre in Shoreditch; *The Case is Altered* performed; (22 September) kills Gabriel Spencer, a fellow actor, in a duel; avoids death sentence by pleading benefit of clergy; converted to Roman Catholicism while in prison.

1599   (January) imprisoned for debt.

1599–1602   'War of the Theatres'.

1599   Marston satirizes Jonson in *Histriomastix*; *Every Man out of His Humour* performed by the Lord Chamberlain's Men at the Globe and at court.

1600   Marston satirizes Jonson in *Jack Drum's Entertainment*.

1601   Jonson satirizes Marston and Dekker in *Cynthia's Revels* (acted by the Children of Queen Elizabeth's Chapel); Marston satirizes Jonson in *What You Will*; Jonson satirizes Marston and Dekker in *Poetaster* (performed by the Children of the Chapel at the Blackfriars); Dekker (possibly assisted by Marston) satirizes Jonson in *Satiromastix*; (25 September) Jonson writes additions to Kyd's *Spanish Tragedy*.

1602   (22 June) Jonson commissioned to write a play called *Richard Crookback* (i.e. Richard III); the play, which may not have been completed, is lost.

1603   *Sejanus* performed by the King's Men; (25 June) *King's Entertainment at Althorpe* performed.

1604(?)   Jonson examined by Privy Council.

1604   (15 March) *King's Coronation Entertainment*; (19 March) *A Panegyre*; and (1 May) *Entertainment at Highgate* performed.

1605   (6 January) *Masque of Blackness* performed; imprisoned for his contribution to *Eastward Ho*; (9 October) present at a dinner party attended by several Catholics who were later exposed as Gunpowder Plot conspirators.

1606   (5 and 6 January) *Hymenaei* performed; (April) indicted (with his wife) as a recusant; *Volpone* performed by the King's Men in Oxford, Cambridge, and London.

1608   (10 January) *The Masque of Beauty* performed; (9 February) *The Haddington Masque* performed.

1609   (2 February) *The Masque of Queens* performed.

1609   (or early 1610) *Epicene* performed by the Children of the Queen's Revels at the Whitefriars.

1610   (January) *Prince Henry's Barriers* performed; *The Alchemist* performed by the King's Men at the Globe; granted a pension by the king; reconverted to Anglicanism.

1611   (1 January) *Oberon, The Fairy Prince* performed; (3 February) *Love Freed from Ignorance and Folly* performed; *Catiline* performed by the King's Men.

1612   (6 January) *Love Restored* performed.

1612–13   Travels in France as tutor to Walter Ralegh (son of Sir Walter).

1613   (27 December, and 1 January 1614) *A Challenge at Tilt* performed; (29 December, and 3 January 1614) *The Irish Masque* performed.

1614   *Bartholomew Fair* performed by the Lady Elizabeth's Men at the Hope Theatre (31 October) and at court (1 November).

1615   *Mercury Vindicated* performed.

1616   (1 and 6 January) *The Golden Age Restored* performed; granted royal pension; publication of Folio *Works*; *The Devil is an Ass* performed by the King's Men at the Blackfriars; (December) *Christmas His Masque* performed.

1617   (6 and 19 January) *Vision of Delight* and (22 February) *Lovers Made Men* performed.

1618   (6 January) *Pleasure Reconciled to Virtue* and (27 February) *For the Honour of Wales* performed.

1618–19   Visit to Scotland.

1619   (17 July) awarded honorary MA by Oxford University.

1620   (17 January and 29 February) *News from the New World* and (May) *Entertainment at the Blackfriars* performed; (19 June) *Pan's Anniversary* scheduled for performance (and possibly performed) at Greenwich.

1621   *The Gypsies Metamorphosed* performed at Burley-on-the-Hill (3 August), Belvoir Castle (5 August), and Windsor (September).

1622	(6 January) *The Masque of Augurs* performed.
1623	(January) *Time Vindicated* performed.
1623	(or 1624) *Pan's Anniversary* performed.
1624	(6 January) *Neptune's Triumph* scheduled for performance but cancelled and (19 August) *The Masque of Owls* performed.
1625	(9 January) *The Fortunate Isles* performed.
1626	*The Staple of News* performed by the King's Men at the Blackfriars.
1628	Paralysed by a stroke.
1629	(19 January) *The New Inn* performed by the King's Men.
1630	(26 March) royal pension increased by King Charles and supplemented with an annual cask of canary wine.
1631	(9 January) *Love's Triumph through Callipolis* and (22 February) *Chloridia* performed; *Bartholomew Fair*, *The Devil is an Ass*, and *The Staple of News* printed together in folio, but Jonson was unsatisfied with the quality of work and the collection was not offered for sale.
1632	*The Magnetic Lady* performed by the King's Men at the Blackfriars.
1633	*A Tale of a Tub* performed by Queen Henrietta's Men at Cockpit and (January 1634) at Whitehall; (31 May) *King's Entertainment at Welbeck* performed.
1634	(30 July) *Love's Welcome at Bolsover* performed.
1637	(16 August) death of Jonson.

POETASTER,

or,

The Arraignment

THE PERSONS THAT ACT°

Augustus Caesar [first emperor of Rome]°

Julia [only daughter of Augustus and Ovid's lover]°

Maecenas [patron of the arts]°

Virgil [poet]°

Horace [poet and satirist]°

Fu[scus] Aristius [friend of Horace]

[Tibullus, poet]°

Plautia [mistress of Tibullus]

Cor[nelius] Gallus [poet]°

Cytheris [mistress of Gallus]

Pub[lius] Ovid [poet]°

Propertius [poet]°

Hermogenes [musician]°

Mar[cus] Ovid [Ovid Sr, father of Publius Ovid]°

Tucca [disbanded soldier]°

[Rufus Laberius] Crispinus [writer of mimes]°

De[metrius] Fannius [hack writer]°

Lupus [tribune]°

Histrio [actor]°

Albius [jeweller]

Chloë [wife of Albius]

Minos [apothecary]

[Luscus, servant of Ovid and Ovid Sr]

Pyrgi [servants of Tucca]°

Lictors [attendants to magistrates]

Maids

[Equites Romani, attendants to the emperor]°

[Livor]°

AD LECTOREM.°

Ludimus innocuis verbis, hoc iuro potentis
Per genium Famae Castalidumque gregem
Perque tuas aures, magni mihi numinis instar,
Lector inhumana liber ab Inuidia.

Mart[ial]

[Prologue]

[Enter] Livor [after the second sounding, arising in the midst of the stage]°

[LIVOR] Light, I salute thee, but with wounded nerves,
Wishing thy golden splendour pitchy darkness.
What's here? *Th'Arraignment?* Ay, this, this is it,°
That our sunk eyes have waked for all this while:
Here will be subject for my snakes and me.   5
Cling to my neck and wrists, my loving worms,
And cast you round in soft and amorous folds
Till I do bid uncurl; then break your knots,
Shoot out yourselves at length, as your forced stings
Would hide themselves within his maliced sides°   10
To whom I shall apply you. Stay! The shine
Of this assembly here offends my sight;
I'll darken that first, and outface their grace.°
Wonder not if I stare. These fifteen weeks°
(So long as since the plot was but an embryon)   15
Have I, with burning lights, mixed vigilant thoughts
In expectation of this hated play,
To which, at last, I am arrived as Prologue.
Nor would I you should look for other looks,
Gesture, or compliment from me than what   20
Th' infected bulk of envy can afford,
For I am ris here with a covetous hope°
To blast your pleasures and destroy your sports
With wrestings, comments, applications,
Spy-like suggestions, privy whisperings,   25
And thousand such promoting sleights as these.°
Mark how I will begin. The scene is—ha?
Rome? Rome? And Rome? Crack eyestrings, and your balls°
Drop into earth—let me be ever blind!
I am prevented. All my hopes are crossed,   30
Checked, and abated; fie, a freezing sweat
Flows forth at all my pores, my entrails burn!
What should I do? Rome! Rome! Oh, my vexed soul,
How might I force this to the present state?°
Are there no players here? No poet-apes,°   35

5

That come with basilisks' eyes, whose forkèd tongues
Are steeped in venom, as their hearts in gall?
Either of these would help me; they could wrest,
Pervert, and poison all they hear or see
With senseless glosses and allusions.   40
Now if you be good devils, fly me not.
You know what dear and ample faculties
I have endowed you with; I'll lend you more.
Here, take my snakes among you; come and eat,
And while the squeezed juice flows in your black jaws,   45
Help me to damn the author. Spit it forth
Upon his lines, and show your rusty teeth°
At every word or accent; or else choose
Out of my longest vipers to stick down
In your deep throats, and let the heads come forth   50
At your rank mouths, that he may see you armed
With triple malice, to hiss, sting, and tear
His work and him, to forge and then declaim,
Traduce, corrupt, apply, inform, suggest:
Oh, these are gifts wherein your souls are blest.   55
What? Do you hide yourselves? Will none appear?
None answer? What, doth this calm troop affright you?°
Nay, then I do despair. Down, sink again.
      [*Livor begins to descend*]
This travail is all lost with my dead hopes.
If in such bosoms spite have left to dwell,   60
Envy is not on earth, nor scarce in hell.
    [*The third sounding. Enter*] Prologus [*in armour*]
[PROLOGUS] Stay, monster! Ere thou sink, thus on thy head
  Set we our bolder foot, with which we tread
  Thy malice into earth.
      [*Exit Livor*]
               So spite should die,
Despised and scorned by noble industry.   65
If any muse why I salute the stage,
An armèd Prologue, know 'tis a dangerous age,
Wherein, who writes, had need present his scenes
Forty-fold proof against the conjuring means
Of base detractors and illiterate apes   70
That fill up rooms in fair and formal shapes.
'Gainst these have we put on this forced defence,

6

Whereof the allegory and hid sense
Is that a well-erected confidence
Can fright their pride, and laugh their folly hence.   75
Here now, put case our author should once more
Swear that his play were good; he doth implore
You would not argue him of arrogance,°
Howe'er that common spawn of ignorance,
Our fry of writers, may beslime his fame   80
And give his action that adulterate name.
Such full-blown vanity he more doth loathe
Than base dejection: there's a mean 'twixt both,
Which with a constant firmness he pursues,
As one that knows the strength of his owne Muse.   85
And this he hopes all free souls will allow;
Others that take it with a rugged brow,
Their moods he rather pities, than envies:
His mind it is above their injuries.
    [*Exit*]

1.1

    [*Enter*] *Ovid*
OVID   Then, when this body falls in funeral fire,
            My name shall live, and my best part aspire.°
    It shall go so. [*Writes*]
    [*Enter Luscus*]
LUSCUS Young master, Master Ovid, do you hear? God sa' me!° Away
    with your songs and sonnets, and on with your gown and cap   5
    quickly—here, here, your father will be a man of this room pres-
    ently.° Come, nay, nay, nay, nay, be brief. These verses, too, a poi-
    son on 'em, I cannot abide 'em; they make me ready to cast,° by the
    banks of Helicon. Nay look, what a rascally untoward thing this
    poetry is; I could tear 'em now.   10
OVID Give me. How near's my father?
LUSCUS Heart a' man! Get a law book in your hand, I will not answer
    you else. Why, so; now there's some formality in you. By Jove, and
    three or four of the gods more, I am right of mine old master's
    humour for that; this villainous poetry will undo you, by the   15
    welkin.

7

OVID What, hast thou buskins° on, Luscus, that thou swear'st so
    tragically and high?

LUSCUS No, but I have boots on, sir, and so has your father, too, by
    this time, for he called for 'em, ere I came from the lodging.   20

OVID Why, was he no readier?

LUSCUS Oh no, and there was the mad skeldering° captain with the
    velvet arms° ready to lay hold on him as he comes down—he that
    presses every man he meets, with an oath, to lend him money, and
    cries, 'Thou must do 't, old boy, as thou art a man, a man of   25
    worship.'

OVID Who? Pantilius Tucca?

LUSCUS Ay, he, and I met little master Lupus, the tribune, going
    thither, too.

OVID Nay, an he be under their arrest, I may (with safety enough)   30
    read over my elegy before he come.

LUSCUS God sa' me! What'll you do? Why, young master, you are not
    Castalian mad,° lunatic, frantic, desperate? Ha?

OVID What ailest thou, Luscus?

LUSCUS God be with you, sir, I'll leave you to your poetical fancies   35
    and furies. I'll not be guilty, I.

    Exit Luscus

OVID Be not, good ignorance; I'm glad th' art gone,
    For thus alone, our ear shall better judge
    The hasty errors of our morning Muse.
        [*Reads*]
        Envy, why twit'st thou me my time's spent ill?   40
        And call'st my verse fruits of an idle quill?
        Or that (unlike the line from whence I sprung)
        War's dusty honours I pursue not young?
        Or that I study not the tedious laws,
        And prostitute my voice in every cause?   45
        Thy scope is mortal; mine, eternal fame,
        Which through the world shall ever chant my name.°
        Homer will live whilst Tenedos stands, and Ide,
        Or to the sea fleet Simois doth slide;°
        And so shall Hesiod, too, while vines do bear,   50
        Or crooked sickles crop the ripened ear.°
        Callimachus, though in invention low,
        Shall still be sung, since he in art doth flow.°
        No loss shall come to Sophocles' proud vein,°
        With sun and moon Aratus shall remain.°   55

8

Whilst slaves be false, fathers hard, and bawds be whorish,
Whilst harlots flatter, shall Menander flourish.°
Ennius, though rude, and Accius' high-reared strain,°
A fresh applause in every age shall gain.
Of Varro's name, what ear shall not be told?°   60
Of Jason's Argo, and the fleece of gold?
Then shall Lucretius' lofty numbers die,°
When earth and seas in fire and flames shall fry.
Tityrus, Tillage, Aenee shall be read°
Whilst Rome of all the conquered world is head.   65
Till Cupid's fires be out, and his bow broken,
Thy verses, neat Tibullus, shall be spoken.
Our Gallus shall be known from east to west;
So shall Lycoris, whom he now loves best.°
The suff'ring ploughshare or the flint may wear,   70
But heavenly poesy no death can fear.
Kings shall give place to it, and kingly shows,
The banks o'er which gold-bearing Tagus flows.°
Kneel hinds to trash; me let bright Phoebus swell,°
With cups full-flowing from the Muses' well.   75
The frost-dread myrtle shall impale my head,°
And of sad lovers I'll be often read.
Envy, the living, not the dead, doth bite:
For after death all men receive their right.°
Then, when this body falls in funeral fire,   80
My name shall live, and my best part aspire.

1.2

[Enter] Ovid Senior, Luscus, Tucca, [and] Lupus

OVID SENIOR Your name shall live, indeed, sir, you say true, but how
infamously, how scorned and contemned in the eyes and ears of the
best and gravest Romans, that you think not on; you never so much
as dream of that! Are these the fruits of all my travail and expenses?
Is this the scope and aim of thy studies? Are these the hopeful   5
courses wherewith I have so long flattered my expectation from
thee? Verses? Poetry? Ovid, whom I thought to see the pleader,
become Ovid the playmaker?
OVID No, sir.

OVID SENIOR Yes, sir! I hear of a tragedy of yours coming forth for   10
the common players there, called *Medea*.° By my household gods,
if I come to the acting of it, I'll add one tragic part more than is yet
expected to it—believe me when I promise it. What, shall I have my
son a stager now? An ingle for players? A gull? A rook? A shot-clog
to make suppers, and be laughed at? Publius, I will set thee on the   15
funeral pile first.°

OVID Sir, I beseech you to have patience.

LUSCUS Nay, this 'tis to have your ears dammed up to good counsel. I
did augur all this to him aforehand, without poring into an ox's   20
paunch for the matter, and yet he would not be scrupulous.

TUCCA [*to Luscus*] How now, goodman slave? What, roll poll?° All
rivals, rascal? [*To Ovid Senior*] Why, my knight of worship,°
dost hear? Are these thy best projects? Is this thy designs and thy   25
discipline, to suffer knaves to be competitors with commanders
and gent'men? [*To Luscus*] Are we parallels, rascal? Are we
parallels?

OVID SENIOR [*to Luscus*] Sirrah, go get my horses ready. You'll still be
prating.   30

TUCCA Do, you perpetual stinkard, do; go talk to tapsters and ostlers,
you slave, they are i' your element, go. Here be the emperor's
captains, you ragamuffin rascal, and not your comrades.
      [*Exit Luscus*]

LUPUS Indeed, Sir Marcus Ovid, these players are an idle generation,   35
and do much harm in a state, corrupt young gentry very much, I
know it; I have not been a tribune thus long and observed nothing.
Besides, they will rob us, us that are magistrates, of our respect,
bring us upon their stages, and make us ridiculous to the plebeians;
they will play you, or me, the wisest men they can come by still—   40
me! Only to bring us in contempt with the vulgar, and make us
cheap.

TUCCA Th'art in the right, my venerable cropshin, they will, indeed;
the tongue of the oracle never twanged truer. Your courtier cannot
kiss his mistress' slippers in quiet for 'em, nor your white innocent   45
gallant pawn his revelling suit to make his punk a supper. An honest decayed commander cannot skelder, cheat, nor be seen in a
bawdy house, but he shall be straight in one of their wormwood°
comedies. They are grown licentious, the rogues; libertines, flat
libertines. They forget they are i' the statute, the rascals, they are   50
blazoned there, there they are tricked,° they and their pedigrees:
they need no other heralds, iwis.

OVID SENIOR Methinks if nothing else, yet this alone, the very
reading of the public edicts should fright thee from commerce with
them, and give thee distaste enough of their actions. But this   55
betrays what a student you are; this argues your proficiency in the
law.

OVID They wrong me, sir, and do abuse you more,
That blow your ears with these untrue reports.°
I am not known unto the open stage,   60
Nor do I traffic in their theatres.
Indeed, I do acknowledge, at request
Of some near friends, and honourable Romans,
I have begun a poem of that nature.

OVID SENIOR You have, sir? A poem? And where is 't? That's the law   65
you study!

OVID Cornelius Gallus borrowed it to read.

OVID SENIOR Cornelius Gallus? There's another gallant, too, hath
drunk of the same poison: and Tibullus, and Propertius. But these
are gentlemen of means and revenues now. Thou art a younger   70
brother, and hast nothing but thy bare exhibition;° which I protest
shall be bare indeed, if thou forsake not these unprofitable by-
courses, and that timely, too. Name me a professed poet, that his
poetry did ever afford him so much as a competency. Ay, your god
of poets there (whom all of you admire and reverence so much),   75
Homer, he whose worm-eaten statue must not be spewed against
but with hallowed lips and grovelling adoration, what was he? What
was he?

TUCCA Marry, I'll tell thee, old swagg'rer: he was a poor, blind, rhyming rascal, that lived obscurely up and down in booths° and tap-   80
houses, and scarce ever made a good meal in his sleep, the whoreson
hungry beggar.

OVID SENIOR He says well. Nay, I know this nettles you now, but
answer me: is 't not true? Is't not true? You'll tell me his name shall
live, and that now (being dead) his works have eternized him and   85
made him divine; but could this divinity feed him while he lived,
could his name feast him?

TUCCA Thou speak'st sentences, old Bias.°

OVID SENIOR Well, the day grows old, gentlemen, and I must leave
you. Publius, if thou wilt hold my favour, abandon these idle, fruit- 90
less studies that so traduce thee. Send Janus home his backface
again,° and look only forward to the law: intend that. I will allow
thee what shall suit thee in the rank of gentlemen, and maintain thy

society with the best; and under these conditions, I leave thee. My blessings light upon thee, if thou respect them; if not, mine eyes may drop° for thee, but thine own heart will ache for itself; and so farewell.   95

[*Enter Luscus*]

What, are my horses come?

LUSCUS Yes, sir, they are at the gate without.

OVID SENIOR That's well. Asinius Lupus, a word. Captain, I shall take my leave of you?   100

TUCCA No, my little knight errant, dispatch with cavalier Cothurnus° there; I'll attend thee, I.

LUSCUS [*aside*] To borrow some ten drachmas, I know his project.   105

OVID SENIOR [*to Lupus*] Sir, you shall make me beholding to you. Now, Captain Tucca, what say you?

TUCCA Why, what should I say? Or what can I say, my most magnanimous mirror of knighthood? Should I say thou art rich? Or that thou art honourable? Or wise? Or valiant? Or learned? Or liberal? Why, thou art all these, and thou knowest it, my noble Lucullus,° thou knowest it; come, be not ashamed of thy virtues, old stump. Honour's a good brooch to wear in a man's hat at all times. Thou art the man of war's Maecenas,° knight. Why shouldst not thou be graced then by them, as well as he is by his poets?   110   115

[*Enter 1 Pyrgus and whispers to Tucca*]

How now, my carrier, what news?

LUSCUS [*aside*] The boy has stayed within for his cue this half hour.

TUCCA Come, do not whisper to me, but speak it out. What, it is no treason against the state, I hope, is 't?   120

LUSCUS [*aside*] Yes, against the state of my master's purse.

1 PYRGUS Sir, Agrippa desires you to forbear him till the next week—his mules are not yet come up.

TUCCA His mules? Now the bots, the spavin, and the glanders, and some dozen diseases more, light on him and his mules. What, ha' they the yellows,° his mules, that they come no faster? Or are they foundered?° ha? His mules ha' the staggers belike, ha' they?   125

1 PYRGUS Oh no, sir. [*Aside*] Then your tongue might be suspected for one of his mules.°

TUCCA He owes me almost a talent,° and he thinks to bear it away with his mules, does he? Sirrah, you, nut-cracker: go your ways to him again, and tell him I must ha' money, I. I cannot eat stones and turfs, say. What, will he clem me and my followers? Ask him and he   130 will clem me—do, go. He would have me fry my jerkin, would he? Away, setter, away! Yet stay, my little tumbler;° the knight shall supply now. I will not trouble him, I cannot be importunate, I; I cannot be impudent.   135

I PYRGUS [*aside*] Alas, sir, no: you are the most maidenly blushing creature upon the earth.

TUCCA Dost thou hear, my little six and fifty, or thereabouts? Thou 140
art not to learn the humours and tricks of that old bald cheater, Time; thou hadst not this chain° for nothing. Men of worth have their chimeras as well as other creatures, and they do see monsters sometimes; they do, they do.

I PYRGUS [*aside*] Better cheap than he shall see you, I warrant him. 145

TUCCA Thou must let me have six, six drachmas, I mean, old boy; thou shalt do it—I tell thee, old boy, thou shalt, and in private, too, dost thou see? [*To 1 Pyrgus*] Go, walk off: there, there. [*To Ovid Senior*] Six is the sum. Thy son's a gallant spark, and must not be put out of a sudden. [*To Ovid*] Come hither, Callimachus. Thy 150
father tells me thou art too poetical, slave; thou must not be so; thou must leave them, young novice, thou must. They are a sort of poor starved rascals that are ever wrapped up in foul linen, and can boast of nothing but a lean visage, peering out of a seam-rent suit; the very emblems of beggary. No, dost hear? Turn lawyer. Thou 155
shalt be my solicitor.
    [*Ovid Senior gives Tucca money*]
'Tis right, old boy, is't?

OVID SENIOR You were best tell° it, captain.

TUCCA No—fare thou well, mine honest knight, and thou, old beaver. Pray thee, knight, when thou comest to town, see me at my lodging, 160
visit me sometimes. Thou shalt be welcome, old boy; do not balk° me, good swagg'rer. Jove keep thy chain from pawning, go thy ways; if thou lack money, I'll lend thee some. I'll leave thee to thy horse now. Adieu.

OVID SENIOR Farewell, good captain.   165

TUCCA [*aside to 1 Pyrgus*] Boy, you can have but half a share now, boy.
    Exit [*Tucca, followed by 1 Pyrgus*]

OVID SENIOR 'Tis a strange boldness that accompanies this fellow. Come.

OVID I'll give attendance on you to your horse, sir, please you —

OVID SENIOR No, keep your chamber and fall to your studies; do so. 170
The gods of Rome bless thee.
    Exit [*Ovid Senior, with Lupus and Luscus*]

13

OVID And give me stomach to digest this law;
    That should have followed sure, had I been he.
    O sacred poesy, thou spirit of arts,
    The soul of science, and the queen of souls,   175
    What profane violence, almost sacrilege,
    Hath here been offered thy divinities!
    Hmh! That thine own guiltless poverty should arm
    Prodigious ignorance to wound thee thus!
    For thence is all their force of argument   180
    Drawn forth against thee; or from the abuse
    Of thy great powers in adult'rate brains.
    When, would men learn but to distinguish spirits,
    And set true difference 'twixt those jaded wits
    That run a broken pace for common hire,   185
    And the high raptures of a happy soul,
    Borne on the wings of her immortal thought,
    That kicks at earth with a disdainful heel
    And beats at heaven gates with her bright hooves,
    They would not then with such distorted faces,   190
    And dudgeon censures, stab at poesy.°
    They would admire bright knowledge, and their minds
    Should ne'er descend on so unworthy objects
    As gold or titles; they would dread far more
    To be thought ignorant, than be known poor.   195
    The time was once when wit drowned wealth; but now,
    Your only barbarism's to have wit, and want.
    No matter now in virtue who excels,
    He that hath coin, hath all perfection else.

1.3

    [*Enter*] *Tibullus*
TIBULLUS Ovid?
OVID   Who's there? Come in.
TIBULLUS   Good morrow, lawyer.
OVID Good morrow, dear Tibullus, welcome. Sit down.
TIBULLUS Not I. What, so hard at it? Let's see, What's here?
    Numa in decimo nono?
OVID   Pray thee away.°

TIBULLUS [*reads*] If thrice in field a man vanquish his foe,   5
          'Tis after in his choice to serve, or no.
    How now, Ovid! Law cases in verse?
OVID In troth, I know not—they run from my pen
    Unwittingly, if they be verse. What's the news abroad?°
TIBULLUS Off with this gown, I come to have thee walk.   10
OVID No, good Tibullus; I'm not now in case.°
    Pray thee, let me alone.
TIBULLUS   How? Not in case!
    'Slight, thou 'rt in too much case, by all this law.°
OVID Troth, if I live, I will new dress the law
    In sprightly poesy's accoutrements.   15
TIBULLUS The hell thou wilt. What, turn law into verse?
    Thy father has schooled thee, I see. Here, read that same.
    There's subject for you; and if I mistake not,
    A supersedeas to your melancholy.
OVID How! Subscribed 'Julia'! Oh, my life, my heaven!   20
TIBULLUS Is the mood changed?
OVID Music of wit! Note for th' harmonious spheres!
    Celestial accents, how you ravish me!
TIBULLUS What is it, Ovid?
OVID That I must meet my Julia, the Princess Julia.   25
TIBULLUS Where?
OVID Why at—heart, I have forgot; my passion so transports me.
TIBULLUS I'll save your pains: it is at Albius' house,
    The jeweller's, where the fair Lycoris lies.
OVID Who? Cytheris, Cornelius Gallus' love?   30
TIBULLUS Ay, he'll be there, too, and my Plautia.
OVID And why not your Delia?
TIBULLUS   Yes, and your Corinna.°
OVID True—but my sweet Tibullus, keep that secret:
    I would not, for all Rome, it should be thought
    I veil bright Julia underneath that name.   35
    Julia, the gem and jewel of my soul,
    That takes her honours from the golden sky,
    As beauty doth all lustre from her eye.
    The air respires the pure elysian sweets
    In which she breathes; and from her looks descend   40
    The glories of the summer. Heaven she is,
    Praised in herself above all praise; and he
    Which hears her speak would swear the tuneful orbs

Turned in his zenith only.
TIBULLUS   Publius, thou'lt lose thyself.°
OVID Oh, in no labyrinth can I safelier err,   45
  Than when I lose myself in praising her.
  Hence law, and welcome, Muses; though not rich,
  Yet are you pleasing: let's be reconciled,
  And new made one. Henceforth, I promise faith,
  And all my serious hours to spend with you;   50
  With you, whose music striketh on my heart,
  And with bewitching tones steals forth my spirit
  In Julia's name. Fair Julia! Julia's love
  Shall be a law, and that sweet law I'll study;
  The law and art of sacred Julia's love: 55
  All other objects will but abjects prove.
TIBULLUS Come, we shall have thee as passionate as Propertius anon.
OVID Oh, how does my Sextus?
TIBULLUS Faith, full of sorrow for his Cynthia's death.
OVID What, still?   60
TIBULLUS Still, and still more; his griefs do grow upon him,
  As do his hours. Never did I know
  An understanding spirit so take to heart
  The common work of fate.
OVID   Oh, my Tibullus,
  Let us not blame him, for against such chances   65
  The heartiest strife of virtue is not proof.
  We may read constancy and fortitude
  To other souls, but had ourselves been struck
  With the like planet, had our loves (like his)
  Been ravished from us by injurious death,   70
  And in the height and heat of our best days,
  It would have cracked our sinews, shrunk our veins,
  And made our very heart strings jar like his.°
  Come, let's go take him forth, and prove° if mirth
  Or company will but abate his passion.   75
TIBULLUS Content, and I implore the gods it may.
       Exeunt

2.1

[*Enter*] *Albius* [*and*] *Crispinus*

ALBIUS Master Crispinus, you are welcome; pray, use a stool, sir. Your cousin, Cytheris, will come down presently. We are so busy for the receiving of these courtiers here, that I can scarce be a minute with myself for thinking of them. Pray you sit, sir, pray you sit, sir.   5

CRISPINUS I am very well, sir. Ne'er trust me, but you are most delicately seated here, full of sweet delight and blandishment; an excellent air, an excellent air.

ALBIUS Ay, sir, 'tis a pretty air. These courtiers run in my mind still, I must look out. For Jupiter's sake, sit, sir, or please you walk into the   10
garden. There's a garden on the backside.

CRISPINUS I am most strenuously well, I thank you, sir.

ALBIUS Much good do you, sir.

Exit [*Albius. Enter Chloë with two maids*]

CHLOË Come, bring those perfumes forward a little, and strew some roses and violets here.   15

[*Enter Albius*]

Fie, here be rooms savour the most pitifully rank that ever I felt°—
I cry the gods mercy, my husband's in the wind of us.

ALBIUS Why, this is good, excellent, excellent—well said,° my sweet Chloë. Trim up your house most obsequiously.

CHLOË For Vulcan's° sake, breathe somewhere else; in troth, you   20
overcome our perfumes exceedingly, you are too predominant.

ALBIUS Hear but my opinion, sweet wife.

CHLOË A pin for your 'pinion. In sincerity, if you be thus fulsome° to me in everything, I'll be divorced. Gods my body!° You know what you were before I married you; I was a gentlewoman born, I. I lost   25
all my friends to be a citizen's wife because I heard, indeed, they kept their wives as fine as ladies, and that we might rule our husbands like ladies, and do what we listed—do you think I would have married you else?

ALBIUS I acknowledge, sweet wife. [*To Crispinus*] She speaks the best   30
of any woman in Italy, and moves as mightily; which makes me I had rather she should make bumps on my head, as big as my two fingers, than I would offend her.° [*To Chloë*] But, sweet wife—

17

CHLOË Yet again? Is't not grace enough for you that I call you husband, and you call me wife, but you must still be poking me against   35
my will to things?

ALBIUS But you know, wife, here are the greatest ladies and gallant'st
gentlemen of Rome to be entertained in our house now; and I
would fain advise thee to entertain them in the best sort, i'faith,
wife.   40

CHLOË In sincerity, did you ever hear a man talk so idly? You would
seem to be master? You would have your spoke in my cart? You
would advise me to entertain ladies and gentlemen? Because you
can marshal your pack-needles, horse-combs, hobby-horses, and
wall candlesticks° in your warehouse better than I, therefore you   45
can tell how to entertain ladies and gentlefolks better than I?

ALBIUS O my sweet wife, upbraid me not with that: 'gain savours
sweetly from anything.' He that respects to get, must relish all
commodities alike, and admit no difference betwixt woad and
frankincense, or the most precious balsamum and a tar barrel.°   50

CHLOË Marry faugh! You sell snuffers, too, if you be remembered,
but I pray you, let me buy them out of your hand; for I tell you true,
I take it highly in snuff to learn how to entertain gentlefolks of you,
at these years, i'faith. Alas, man, there was not a gentleman came to
your house i' your tother wife's time, I hope? Nor a lady? Nor   55
music? Nor masques? Nor you, nor your house, were so much as
spoken of before I disbased myself from my hood and my farthingale to these bumrolls and your whalebone bodies.°

ALBIUS Look here, my sweet wife, I am mum,° my dear mummia, my
balsamum, my spermaceti, and my very city of—° [*To Crispinus*]   60
She has the most best, true, feminine wit in Rome.

CRISPINUS I have heard so, sir, and do most vehemently desire to
participate° the knowledge of her fair features.

ALBIUS Ah, peace, you shall hear more anon. Be not seen yet, I pray
you, not yet; observe.   65
        Exit Albius

CHLOË 'Sbody,° give husbands the head a little more, and they'll be
nothing but head shortly. What's he there?

1 MAID I know not, forsooth.

2 MAID Who would you speak with, sir?

CRISPINUS I would speak with my cousin Cytheris.   70

[2] MAID He is one, forsooth, would speak with his cousin Cytheris.

CHLOË Is she your cousin, sir?

CRISPINUS Yes, in truth, forsooth, for fault of a better.°

CHLOË She is a gentlewoman?

CRISPINUS Or else she should not be my cousin, I assure you.   75

CHLOË Are you a gentleman born?

CRISPINUS That I am, lady; you shall see mine arms,° if 't please
you.

CHLOË No, your legs do sufficiently show you are a gentleman born,
sir, for a man borne upon little legs is always a gentleman born.°   80

CRISPINUS Yet, I pray you, vouchsafe the sight of my arms, mistress,
for I bear them about me, to have 'em seen. My name is Crispinus,
or Cri-spinas, indeed, which is well expressed in my arms: a face
crying in chief,° and beneath it a bloody toe, between three thorns
pungent.°   85

CHLOË Then you are welcome, sir; now you are a gentleman born, I
can find in my heart to welcome you, for I am a gentlewoman born,
too, and will bear my head high enough, though 'twere my fortune
to marry a flat-cap.°

[*Enter Albius. He is still going in and out*]

ALBIUS Dear wife, be not angry.   90

CHLOË God's my passion!

ALBIUS Hear me but one thing: let not your maids set cushions in the
parlour windows, nor in the dining-chamber windows, nor upon
stools in either of them in any case, for 'tis tavern-like, but lay them
one upon another in some out-room, or corner of the dining-
chamber.   95

CHLOË Go, go, meddle with your bed-chamber only, or rather with
your bed in your chamber only, or rather with your wife in your bed
only, or on my faith, I'll not be pleased with you only.

ALBIUS Look here, my dear wife, entertain that gentleman kindly, I   100
prithee—mum.

Exit Albius

CHLOË Go, I need your instructions, indeed. Anger me no more, I
advise you. City-sin,° quoth'a! She's a wise gentlewoman, i'faith,
will marry herself to the sin of the city.

[*Enter Albius*]

ALBIUS But this time, and no more, by heaven, wife: hang no pictures   105
in the hall, nor in the dining-chamber, in any case, but in the gallery
only, for 'tis not courtly else, on my word, wife.

CHLOË 'Sprecious, never have done!

[*She makes a threatening gesture*]

ALBIUS Wife—

Exit Albius

CHLOË Do I not bear a reasonable corrigible° hand over him,   110
Crispinus?

CRISPINUS By this hand, lady, you hold a most sweet hand over him.
    [*Enter Albius*]

ALBIUS And then for the great gilt andirons?

CHLOË Again! Would the andirons were in your great guts, for me.

ALBIUS I do vanish, wife.   115
    Exit Albius

CHLOË How shall I do, Master Crispinus? Here will be all the bravest
ladies in court presently to see your cousin Cytheris—O the gods!
How might I behave myself now, as to entertain them most courtly?

CRISPINUS Marry, lady, if you will entertain them most courtly, you
must do thus: as soon as ever your maid or your man brings you   120
word they are come, you must say, 'A pox on 'em, what do they
here?' And yet when they come, speak them as fair, and give them
the kindest welcome in words that can be.

CHLOË Is that the fashion of courtiers, Crispinus?

CRISPINUS I assure you it is, lady, I have observed it.   125

CHLOË For your pox, sir, it is easily hit upon; but 'tis not so easy to
speak fair after, methinks?
    [*Enter Albius*]

ALBIUS O wife, the coaches are come, on my word, a number of
coaches and courtiers.

CHLOË A pox on them, what do they here?   130

ALBIUS How now, wife! Would'st thou not have them come?

CHLOË Come? Come, you are a fool, you. [*To Crispinus*] He knows not
the trick on 't. [*To Albius*] Call Cytheris, I pray you.
    [*Exit Albius*]
And good Master Crispinus, you can observe, you say; let me
entreat you for all the ladies' behaviours, jewels, jests, and attires,   135
that you marking as well as I, we may put both our marks together
when they are gone, and confer of them.

CRISPINUS I warrant you, sweet lady; let me alone to observe, till I
turn myself to nothing but observation.
    [*Enter Albius with Cytheris*]
Good morrow, cousin Cytheris.   140

CYTHERIS Welcome, kind cousin. What, are they come?

ALBIUS Ay, your friend Cornelius Gallus, Ovid, Tibullus, Propertius,
with Julia, the emperor's daughter, and the lady Plautia are lighted
at the door; and with them Hermogenes Tigellius, the excellent
musician.   145

CYTHERIS Come, let us go meet them, Chloë.
CHLOË Observe, Crispinus.
CRISPINUS At a hair's breadth, lady, I warrant you.

2.2

[*Enter*] *Gallus, Ovid, Tibullus, Propertius, Hermogenes,*
Julia, [and] Plautia

GALLUS Health to the lovely Chloë! [*To Cytheris*] You must pardon
me, mistress, that I prefer° this fair gentlewoman.

CYTHERIS I pardon, and praise you for it, sir; [*to Julia*] and I beseech
your excellence, receive her beauties into your knowledge and
favour.   5

JULIA Cytheris, she hath favour and behaviour that commands as
much of me; and sweet Chloë, know I do exceedingly love you, and
that I will approve° in any grace my father the emperor may show
you. Is this your husband?

ALBIUS For fault of a better, if it please your highness.   10

CHLOË [*aside to Cytheris*] Gods my life! How he shames me!

CYTHERIS Not a whit, Chloë, they all think you politic and witty;
wise women choose not husbands for the eye, merit, or birth, but
wealth and sovereignty.

OVID Sir, we all come to gratulate for the good report of you.   15

TIBULLUS And would be glad to deserve your love, sir.

ALBIUS My wife will answer you all, gentlemen; I'll come to you again
presently.
          Exit Albius

PLAUTIA You have chosen you a most fair companion here, Cytheris,
and a very fair house.   20

CYTHERIS To both which, you and all my friends are very welcome,
Plautia.

CHLOË With all my heart, I assure your ladyship.

PLAUTIA Thanks, sweet Mistress Chloë.

JULIA You must needs come to court, lady, i'faith, and there be sure   25
your welcome shall be as great to us.

OVID She will well deserve it, madam. I see, even in her looks, gentry,
and general worthiness.

TIBULLUS I have not seen a more certain character° of an excellent
disposition.   30

[*Enter Albius*]

ALBIUS Wife.

CHLOË Oh, they do so commend me here, the courtiers! What's the
matter now?

ALBIUS For the banquet, sweet wife.

CHLOË Yes—and I must needs come to court, and be welcome, the   35
princess says.

        Exit [*Chloë, with Albius*]

GALLUS Ovid and Tibullus, you may be bold to welcome your mis-
tresses here.

OVID We find it so, sir.

TIBULLUS And thank Cornelius Gallus.   40

OVID Nay, my sweet Sextus, in faith thou art not sociable.

PROPERTIUS In faith, I am not, Publius, nor I cannot.
   Sick minds are like sick men that burn with fevers,
   Who, when they drink, please but a ling'ring taste,
   And after bear a more impatient fit.   45
   Pray, let me leave you; I offend you all,
   And myself most.

GALLUS   Stay, sweet Propertius.

TIBULLUS You yield too much unto your griefs and fate,
   Which never hurts, but when we say it hurts us.

PROPERTIUS Oh, peace, Tibullus; your philosophy   50
   Lends you too rough a hand to search my wounds.
   Speak they of griefs that know to sigh and grieve;
   The free and unconstrainèd spirit feels
   No weight of my oppression.

        Exit Propertius

OVID   Worthy Roman!
   Methinks I taste his misery, and could   55
   Sit down and chide at his malignant stars.

JULIA Methinks I love him, that he loves so truly.

CYTHERIS This is the perfect'st love, lives after death.

GALLUS Such is the constant ground of virtue still.

PLAUTIA It puts on an inseparable face.°   60

        [*Enter Chloë*]

CHLOË Have you marked everything, Crispinus?

CRISPINUS Everything, I warrant you.

CHLOË What gentlemen are these? Do you know them?

CRISPINUS Ay, they are poets, lady.

CHLOË Poets? They did not talk of me since I went, did they?   65

CRISPINUS Oh yes, and extolled your perfections to the heavens.

CHLOË Now, in sincerity, they be the finest kind of men that ever I knew. Poets? Could not one get the emperor to make my husband a poet, think you?

CRISPINUS No, lady, 'tis love and beauty make poets; and since you like poets so well, your love and beauties shall make me a poet.   70

CHLOË What, shall they? And such a one as these?

CRISPINUS Ay, and a better than these; I would be sorry else.

CHLOË And shall your looks change? And your hair change? And all, like these?   75

CRISPINUS Why, a man may be a poet, and yet not change his hair, lady.

CHLOË Well, we shall see your cunning; yet if you can change your hair, I pray, do.°

    [*Enter Albius*]

ALBIUS Ladies and lordings, there's a slight banquet stays within for   80
you, please you draw near and accost it.

JULIA We thank you, good Albius, but when shall we see those excellent jewels you are commended to have?

ALBIUS At your ladyship's service. [*Aside*] I got that speech by seeing a play last day, and it did me some grace now; I see 'tis good to   85
collect sometimes. I'll frequent these plays more than I have done, now I come to be familiar with courtiers.

GALLUS Why, how now, Hermogenes? What ailest thou, trow?

HERMOGENES A little melancholy, let me alone, pray thee.

GALLUS Melancholy! How so?   90

HERMOGENES With riding—a plague on all coaches for me.

CHLOË Is that hard-favoured gentleman a poet, too, Cytheris?

CYTHERIS No, this is Hermogenes; as humorous as a poet, though. He is a musician.

CHLOË A musician? Then he can sing.   95

CYTHERIS That he can excellently; did you never hear him?

CHLOË Oh, no—will he be entreated, think you?

CYTHERIS I know not. [*To Gallus*] Friend, Mistress Chloë would fain hear Hermogenes sing; are you interested in him?°

GALLUS No doubt his own humanity will command him so far, to the   100
satisfaction of so fair a beauty; but rather than fail, we'll all be suitors to him.

HERMOGENES 'Cannot sing.

GALLUS Pray thee, Hermogenes.

HERMOGENES 'Cannot sing.   105

GALLUS For honour of this gentlewoman, to whose house I know thou mayst be ever welcome.

CHLOË That he shall in truth, sir, if he can sing.

OVID What's that?

GALLUS This gentlewoman is wooing Hermogenes for a song.   110

OVID A song? Come, he shall not deny her. Hermogenes?

HERMOGENES 'Cannot sing.

GALLUS No, the ladies must do it,° he stays but to have their thanks acknowledged as a debt to his cunning.°

JULIA That shall not want; ourself will be the first shall promise to   115
pay him more than thanks, upon a favour so worthily vouchsafed.

HERMOGENES Thank you, madam; but 'will not sing.

TIBULLUS Tut, the only way to win him is to abstain from entreating him.

CRISPINUS Do you love singing, lady?   120

CHLOË Oh, passingly.°

CRISPINUS Entreat the ladies to entreat me to sing then, I beseech you.

CHLOË I beseech your grace, entreat this gentleman to sing.

JULIA That we will, Chloë; can he sing excellently?   125

CHLOË I think so, madam, for he entreated me to entreat you to entreat him to sing.

CRISPINUS Heaven and earth! Would you tell that?

JULIA Good sir, let's entreat you to use your voice.

CRISPINUS Alas, madam, I cannot in truth.   130

PLAUTIA The gentleman is modest; I warrant you he sings excellently.

OVID Hermogenes, clear your throat; I see by him, here's a gentleman will worthily challenge you.

CRISPINUS Not I, sir, I'll challenge no man.   135

TIBULLUS That's your modesty, sir; but we, out of an assurance of your excellency, challenge him in your behalf.

CRISPINUS I thank you, gentlemen, I'll do my best.

HERMOGENES Let that best be good, sir, you were best.

GALLUS Oh, this contention is excellent. What is 't you sing, sir?   140

CRISPINUS 'If I freely may discover,' etc. Sir, I'll sing that.

OVID One of your own compositions, Hermogenes. He offers you vantage enough.

CRISPINUS Nay, truly, gentlemen, I'll challenge no man—I can sing but one staff of the ditty neither.   145

GALLUS The better—Hermogenes himself will be entreated to sing the other.

[CRISPINUS (*sings*)]

> *If I freely may discover*
> *What would please me in my lover,*
>   *I would have her fair and witty,*   150
>   *Savouring more of court than city;*
>   *A little proud, but full of pity;*
>   *Light, and humorous in her toying;*
>   *Oft building hopes, and soon destroying;*
>   *Long, but sweet in the enjoying;*   155
> *Neither too easy, nor too hard:*
> *All extremes I would have barred.*°

GALLUS Believe me, sir, you sing most excellently.

OVID If there were a praise above excellence, the gentleman highly
deserves it.   160

HERMOGENES Sir, all this doth not yet make me envy you, for I know
I sing better than you.

TIBULLUS Attend Hermogenes now.

[HERMOGENES (*sings*)]

>   *She should be allowed her passions,*
>   *So they were but used as fashions;*   165
>   *Sometimes froward, and then frowning,*
>   *Sometimes sickish, and then swooning,*
>   *Every fit with change still crowning.*
>   *Purely jealous I would have her,*
>   *Then only constant when I crave her;*   170
>   *'Tis a virtue should not save her.*
>   *Thus, nor her delicates would cloy me,*°
>   *Neither her peevishness annoy me.*

JULIA Nay, Hermogenes, your merit hath long since been both known
and admired of us.   175

HERMOGENES You shall hear me sing another; now will I begin.

GALLUS We shall do this gentleman's banquet too much wrong that
stays for us, ladies.

JULIA 'Tis true, and well thought on, Cornelius Gallus.   180

HERMOGENES Why, 'tis but a short air, 'twill be done presently; pray,
stay—strike music.

OVID No, good Hermogenes; we'll end this difference within.

JULIA 'Tis the common disease of all your musicians, that they know
no mean to be entreated, either to begin or end.   185

ALBIUS Please you lead the way, gentles?

ALL Thanks, good Albius.

Exeunt [all but Albius]

ALBIUS   Oh, what a charm of thanks was here put upon me! O, Jove, what a setting forth it is to a man to have many courtiers come to his house! Sweetly was it said of a good old housekeeper, 'I had   190
rather want meat, than want guests'—specially if they be courtly guests. For never trust me, if one of their good legs° made in a house be not worth all the good cheer a man can make them. He that would have fine guests, let him have a fine wife; he that would have a fine wife, let him come to me.   195

[Enter Crispinus]

CRISPINUS   By your kind leave, Master Albius.

ALBIUS   What, you are not gone, Master Crispine?

CRISPINUS   Yes, faith, I have a design° draws me hence; pray, sir, fashion me an excuse to the ladies.

ALBIUS   Will you not stay and see the jewels, sir? I pray you stay.   200

CRISPINUS   Not for a million, sir, now. Let it suffice, I must relinquish;° and so in a word, please you to expiate this compliment.

ALBIUS   Mum.   205

Exit [Albius]

CRISPINUS   I'll presently go and ingle some broker° for a poet's gown, and bespeak a garland—and then, jeweller, look to your best jewel, i'faith.

Exit

3.1

[*Enter*] *Horace, Crispinus* [*following*]

HORACE Hmh? Yes, I will begin an ode so; and it shall be to Maecenas.

CRISPINUS 'Slid, yonder's Horace! They say he's an excellent poet, Maecenas loves him. I'll fall into his acquaintance if I can; I think he be composing as he goes i' the street. Ha! 'Tis a good humour, an he be—I'll compose too.   5

HORACE   Swell me a bowl with lusty wine,
                  Till I may see the plump Lyaeus swim°
                       Above the brim.
                  I drink as I would write:
                  In flowing measure, filled with flame and sprite.°   10

CRISPINUS Sweet Horace! Minerva and the Muses° stand auspicious to thy designs. How farest thou, sweet man? Frolic? Rich? Gallant? ha?

HORACE Not greatly gallant, sir; like my fortunes, well. I'm bold to take my leave, sir; you'd naught else, sir, would you?

CRISPINUS Troth, no; but I could wish thou didst know us, Horace.   15
We are a scholar, I assure thee.

HORACE A scholar, sir? I shall be covetous of your fair knowledge.

CRISPINUS Gramercy, good Horace. Nay, we are new turned poet, too, which is more; and a satirist,° too, which is more than that—I write just in thy vein, I. I am for your odes or your sermons,° or   20
anything, indeed. We are a gentleman besides: our name is Rufus Laberius Crispinus; we are a pretty stoic, too.

HORACE To the proportion of your beard,° I think it, sir.

CRISPINUS By Phoebus, here's a most neat fine street, is 't not? I protest to thee, I am enamoured of this street now, more than of   25
half the streets of Rome again, 'tis so polite and terse. There's the front of a building now. I study architecture, too; if ever I should build, I'd have a house just of that prospective.°

HORACE [*aside*] Doubtless this gallant's tongue has a good turn when he sleeps.   30

CRISPINUS I do make verses when I come in such a street as this. Oh, your city ladies, you shall ha' 'em sit in every shop like the Muses—°
[*pauses*] off'ring you the Castalian dews, and the Thespian liquors,° to as many as have but the sweet grace and audacity to—[*pauses*] sip of their lips. Did you never hear any of my verses?   35

HORACE No, sir. [*Aside*] But I am in some fear I must now.

27

CRISPINUS I'll tell thee some (if I can but recover 'em) I composed
    e'en now of a velvet cap I saw a jeweller's wife wear, who, indeed,
    was a jewel herself—I prefer that kind of tire° now. What's thy
    opinion, Horace?   40

HORACE With your silver bodkin° it does well, sir.

CRISPINUS I cannot tell, but it stirs me more than all your court curls,
    or your spangles, or your tricks; I affect not these high gable-ends,
    these Tuscan tops, nor your coronets, nor your arches, nor your
    pyramids.° Give me a fine sweet—[pauses] little velvet cap, with a   45
    bodkin, as you say, and a mushroom for all your other ornatures.

HORACE [aside] Is't not possible to make an escape from him?

CRISPINUS I have remitted° my verses all this while, I think I ha'
    forgot 'em.

HORACE [aside] Here's he could wish you had else.   50

CRISPINUS Pray Jove I can entreat 'em of my memory.

HORACE You put your memory to too much trouble, sir.

CRISPINUS No, sweet Horace, we must not ha' thee think so.

HORACE I cry you mercy. [Aside] Then they are my ears
    That must be tortured; well, you must have patience, ears.   55

CRISPINUS Pray thee, Horace, observe.

HORACE Yes, sir: your satin sleeve begins to fret at the rug that is
    underneath it,° I do observe. And your ample velvet hose are not
    without evident stains of a hot disposition naturally.°

CRISPINUS Oh—[pauses] I'll dye them into another colour at pleasure.   60
    How many yards of velvet dost thou think they contain?

HORACE Heart! I have put him now in a fresh way
    To vex me more. Faith, sir, your mercer's book
    Will tell you with more patience than I can,
    For I am crossed, and so's not that, I think.°   65

CRISPINUS 'Slight, these verses have lost me again; I shall not invite
    'em to mind now.

HORACE Rack not your thoughts, good sir, rather defer it
    To a new time. I'll meet you at your lodging,
    Or where you please. Till then, Jove keep you, sir.   70

CRISPINUS Nay, gentle Horace, stay—I have it now.

HORACE Yes, sir. [Aside] Apollo, Hermes, Jupiter,
    Look down upon me.

CRISPINUS Rich was thy hap, sweet velvet cap,°
                    There to be placed,   75
                Where thy smooth black, sleek white may smack,°
                    And both be graced.

'White' is there usurped for her brow, her forehead; and then 'sleek'
as the parallel to 'smooth' that went before. A kind of paronomasy,
or agnomination; do you conceive, sir?   80

HORACE Excellent. Troth, sir, I must be abrupt and leave you.

CRISPINUS Why, what haste hast thou? Pray thee, stay a little; thou
shalt not go yet, by Phoebus.

HORACE [aside] I shall not? What remedy? Fie, how I sweat with
suffering.   85

CRISPINUS And then—

HORACE Pray, sir, give me leave to wipe my face a little.

CRISPINUS Yes, do, good Horace.

HORACE Thank you, sir.
    [Aside] 'Death! Must crave his leave to piss anon,   90
    Or that I may go hence with half my teeth,°
    I am in some such fear. This tyranny
    Is strange, to take mine ears up by commission
    (Whether I will or no) and make them stalls°
    To his lewd solecisms and worded trash.°   95
    Happy the bold Bolanus now, I say,°
    Rome's common buffoon. His free impudence
    Would, long ere this, have called this fellow fool,
    And rank and tedious fool, and have slung jests
    As hard as stones till he had pelted him   100
    Out of the place; whilst my tame modesty
    Suffers my wit be made a solemn ass
    To bear his fopperies—

CRISPINUS Horace, thou art miserably affected to be gone, I see.
But—[pauses] pray thee, let's prove° to enjoy thee awhile. Thou   105
hast no business, I assure me. Whither is thy journey directed?
ha?

HORACE Sir, I am going to visit a friend that's sick.

CRISPINUS A friend? What's he? Do not I know him?

HORACE No, sir, you do not know him. [Aside] And 'tis not the worse   110
for him.

CRISPINUS What's his name? Where's he lodged?

HORACE Where I shall be fearful to draw you out of your way, sir; a
great way hence. Pray, sir, let's part.

CRISPINUS Nay, but where is't? I pray thee say.   115

HORACE On the far side of all Tiber yonder, by Caesar's gardens.

CRISPINUS Oh, that's my course directly; I am for you. Come, go—
why stand'st thou?

HORACE Yes, sir. Marry, the plague is in that part of the city; I had
    almost forgot to tell you, sir.   120

CRISPINUS Faugh! It's no matter, I fear no pestilence, I ha' not
    offended Phoebus.

HORACE [aside] I have, it seems, or else this heavy scourge
    Could ne'er have lighted on me—

CRISPINUS Come along.   125

HORACE I am to go down some half mile this way, sir, first, to speak
    with his physician. And from thence to his apothecary, where I shall
    stay the mixing of divers° drugs—

CRISPINUS Why, it's all one. I have nothing to do, and I love not to be
    idle; I'll bear thee company. How call'st thou the 'pothecary?   130

HORACE [aside] Oh, that I knew a name would fright him now.
    [To him] Rhadamanthys,° sir.
    There's one so called is a just judge in hell,
    And doth inflict strange vengeance on all those
    That, here on earth, torment poor patient spirits.   135

CRISPINUS He dwells at the Three Furies, by Janus' temple?

HORACE Your apothecary does, sir.

CRISPINUS Heart, I owe him money for sweetmeats, and he has laid to
    arrest me, I hear, but—

HORACE Sir, I have made a most solemn vow: I will never bail any   140
    man.

CRISPINUS Well then, I'll swear and speak him fair, if the worst come.
    But his name is Minos, not Rhadamanthys, Horace.

HORACE That may be, sir; I but guessed at his name by his sign. But
    your Minos is a judge, too, sir!   145

CRISPINUS I protest to thee, Horace, do but taste me once, if I do
    know myself and mine own virtues truly, thou wilt not make that
    esteem of Varius,° or Virgil, or Tibullus, or any of 'em, indeed, as
    now in thy ignorance thou dost, which I am content to forgive. I
    would fain see which of these could pen more verses in a day, or   150
    with more facility than I, or that could court his mistress, kiss her
    hand, make better sport with her fan, or her dog!

HORACE I cannot bail you yet, sir.

CRISPINUS Or that could move his body more gracefully, or dance
    better. You should see me, were it not i' the street.   155

HORACE Nor yet.

CRISPINUS Why, I have been a reveller, and at my cloth of silver suit
    and my long stocking° in my time, and will be again—

HORACE If you may be trusted, sir.

CRISPINUS And then for my singing, Hermogenes himself envies me, 160
that is your only master of music you have in Rome.

HORACE Is your mother living, sir?

CRISPINUS Agh! Convert thy thoughts to somewhat else, I pray thee.

HORACE You have much of the mother in you,° sir. Your father is
dead? 165

CRISPINUS Ay, I thank Jove, and my grandfather, too, and all my
kinsfolks, and well composed in their graves.

HORACE [aside] The more their happiness that rest in peace,
Free from th' abundant torture of thy tongue;
Would I were with them, too. 170

CRISPINUS What's that, Horace?

HORACE I now remember me, sir, of a sad fate
A cunning woman, one Sabella, sung,°
When in her urn she cast my destiny,
I being but a child. 175

CRISPINUS What was 't, I pray thee?

HORACE She told me I should surely never perish
By famine, poison, or the enemy's sword;
The hectic fever, cough, or pleurisy°
Should never hurt me; nor the tardy gout; 180
But in my time, I should be once surprised°
By a strong tedious talker, that should vex
And almost bring me to consumption.
Therefore (if I were wise) she warned me shun
All such long-winded monsters as my bane. 185
For if I could but 'scape that one discourser,
I might, no doubt, prove an old aged man.
By your leave, sir?

CRISPINUS Tut, tut—abandon this idle humour, 'tis nothing but
melancholy. 'Fore Jove, now I think on't, I am to appear in court 190
here to answer to one that has me in suit. Sweet Horace, go with
me, this is my hour; if I neglect it, the law proceeds against me.
Thou art familiar with these things; pray thee, if thou lovest
me, go.

HORACE Now let me die, sir, if I know your laws, 195
Or have the power to stand half so long
In their loud courts, as while a case is argued.°
Besides, you know, sir, where I am to go,
And the necessity—

CRISPINUS 'Tis true— 200

HORACE [*aside*] I hope the hour of my release be come.
He will, upon this consideration, discharge me, sure.

CRISPINUS Troth, I am doubtful what I may best do; whether to leave
thee, or my affairs, Horace?

HORACE O Jupiter, me, sir, me, by any means! I beseech you, me, sir.   205

CRISPINUS No, faith, I'll venture those now. Thou shalt see I love
thee. Come, Horace.

HORACE Nay then, I am desperate. I follow you, sir. 'Tis hard contending with a man that overcomes thus.

CRISPINUS And how deals Maecenas with thee? Liberally, ha? Is he   210
open-handed? Bountiful?

HORACE He's still himself, sir.

CRISPINUS Troth, Horace, thou art exceeding happy in thy friends
and acquaintance; they are all most choice spirits, and of the first
rank of Romans. I do not know that poet, I protest, has used his   215
fortune more prosperously than thou hast. If thou wouldst bring
me known to Maecenas, I should second thy desert well. Thou
shouldst find a good sure assistance of me: one that would speak all
good of thee in thy absence, and be content with the next place, not
envying thy reputation with thy patron. Let me not live, but I think   220
thou and I (in a small time) should lift them all out of favour, both
Virgil, Varius, and the best of them, and enjoy him wholly to
ourselves.

HORACE [*aside*] Gods, you do know it, I can hold no longer;
This breeze hath pricked my patience. [*To him*] Sir, your silkness   225
Clearly mistakes Maecenas, and his house,
To think there breathes a spirit beneath his roof
Subject unto those poor affections
Of undermining envy and detraction,
Moods only proper to base, grovelling minds.   230
That place is not in Rome, I dare affirm,
More pure or free from such low, common evils.
There's no man grieved that this is thought more rich,°
Or this more learned; each man hath his place,
And to his merit, his reward of grace,   235
Which with a mutual love they all embrace.

CRISPINUS You report a wonder! 'Tis scarce credible, this.

HORACE I am no torturer to enforce you to believe it, but 'tis so.

CRISPINUS Why, this inflames me with a more ardent desire to be his
than before; but I doubt I shall find the entrance to his familiarity   240
somewhat more than difficult, Horace.

HORACE Tut, you'll conquer him as you have done me. There's no
    standing out against you, sir, I see that. Either your importunacy, or
    the intimation of your good parts, or—
CRISPINUS Nay, I'll bribe his porter and the grooms of his chamber;   245
    make his doors open to me that way first, and then I'll observe my
    times. Say he should extrude° me his house today; shall I therefore
    desist, or let fall my suit tomorrow? No, I'll attend him, follow him,
    meet him i' the street, the highways, run by his coach, never leave
    him. What! 'Man hath nothing given him in this life without much   250
    labour.'°
HORACE [aside] And impudence.
    Archer of heaven, Phoebus, take thy bow,
    And with a full-drawn shaft, nail to the earth
    This python, that I may yet run hence and live;°   255
    Or brawny Hercules, do thou come down,
    And (though thou mak'st it up thy thirteenth labour)
    Rescue me from this Hydra of discourse here.

3.2

    [Enter] Aristius
ARISTIUS Horace! Well met.
HORACE   Oh welcome, my redeemer!
    [Horace takes Aristius to one side]
    Aristius, as thou lovest me, ransom me.
ARISTIUS What ailst thou, man?
HORACE   'Death! I am seized on here
    By a land-remora—I cannot stir,°
    Not move, but as he please.
CRISPINUS   Wilt thou go, Horace?   5
HORACE 'Heart! He cleaves to me like Alcides' shirt,°
    Tearing my flesh and sinews. Oh, I ha' been vexed
    And tortured with him worse than forty fevers.
    For Jove's sake, find some means to take me from him.
ARISTIUS Yes, I will. But I'll go first, and tell Maecenas.   10
CRISPINUS Come, shall we go?
ARISTIUS The jest will make his eyes run, i'faith.
HORACE Nay, Aristius!
ARISTIUS Farewell, Horace.

HORACE 'Death! Will a leave me? Fuscus Aristius, do you hear? Gods   15
    of Rome! You said you had somewhat to say to me in private.

ARISTIUS Ay, but I see you are now employed with that gentleman;
    'twere sin to trouble you. I'll take some fitter opportunity.
    Adieu.   20

      Exit [Aristius]

HORACE Mischief and torment! O my soul and heart,
    How are you cramped with anguish! Death itself
    Brings not the like convulsion. Oh this day,
    That ever I should view thy tedious face!

CRISPINUS Horace, what passion, what humour's this?   25

HORACE Away, good prodigy, afflict me not.
    A friend, and mock me thus! Never was man
    So left under the axe—how now?

3.3

      [Enter] Minos [and two] Lictors

MINOS That's he, in the embroidered hat there, with the ash coloured
    feather. His name is Laberius Crispinus.

1 LICTOR Laberius Crispinus, I arrest you in the emperor's name.

CRISPINUS Me, sir? Do you arrest me?

1 LICTOR Ay, sir, at the suit of Master Minos, the apothecary.   5

HORACE Thanks, great Apollo! I will not slip° thy favour offered me
    in my escape, for my fortunes.

      Exit [Horace]

CRISPINUS Master Minos? I know no Master Minos. Where's
    Horace? Horace? Horace?

MINOS Sir, do not you know me?   10

CRISPINUS Oh, yes, I know you, Master Minos, 'cry you mercy. But
    Horace? God's 'lid, is he gone?

MINOS Ay, and so would you, too, if you knew how. Officer, look to
    him.

CRISPINUS Do you hear, Master Minos? Pray, let's be used like a man   15
    of our own fashion. By Janus and Jupiter, I meant to have paid you
    next week, every drachma. Seek not to eclipse my reputation thus
    vulgarly.°

MINOS Sir, your oaths cannot serve you; you know I have forborne
    you long.   20

CRISPINUS I am conscious of it, sir. Nay, I beseech you, gentlemen, do not exhale me° thus; remember 'tis but for sweetmeats—

1 LICTOR Sweet meat must have sour sauce, sir. Come along.

CRISPINUS Sweet Master Minos, I am forfeited to eternal disgrace if you do not commiserate. Good officer, be not so officious. 25

3.4

[Enter] Tucca [and] Pyrgi

TUCCA Why, how now, my good brace of bloodhounds? Whither do you drag the gent'man? You mongrels, you curs, you bandogs, we are Captain Tucca that talk to you, you inhuman pilchers!

MINOS Sir, he is their prisoner.

TUCCA Their pestilence. What are you, sir? 5

MINOS A citizen of Rome, sir.

TUCCA Then you are not far distant from a fool, sir.

MINOS A 'pothecary, sir.

TUCCA [*sniffing at Minos*] I knew that was not a physician°— faugh! Out of my nostrils, thou stinkst of lotium and the syringe! Away, 10 quack-salver! Follower, my sword.

[1] PYRGUS Here, noble leader. [*Aside*] You'll do no harm with it, I'll trust you.

TUCCA Do you hear, you goodman slave? Hook, ram, rogue, catchpole, loose the gent'man, or by my velvet arms— 15

[1 Lictor strikes up his heels, and takes his sword]

[1] LICTOR What will you do, sir?

TUCCA Kiss thy hand, my honourable active varlet, and embrace thee, thus.

[1] PYRGUS [*aside*] Oh patient metamorphosis!

TUCCA My sword, my tall° rascal. 20

[1] LICTOR Nay, soft, sir. Some wiser than some.

TUCCA What? And a wit, too? By Pluto, thou must be cherished, slave. Here's three drachmas for thee: hold.

[1] PYRGUS [*aside*] There's half his lendings° gone.

TUCCA Give me. 25

[1] LICTOR No, sir, your first word shall stand; I'll hold all.

TUCCA Nay, but rogue—

[1] LICTOR You would make a rescue of our prisoner, sir, you?

TUCCA I, a rescue? Away, inhuman varlet. Come, come, I never relish

above one jest at most; do not disgust me, sirra, do not. Rogue, I tell   30
thee, rogue, do not.

[1] LICTOR How, sir? Rogue?

TUCCA Ay—why, thou art not angry, rascal, art thou?

[1] LICTOR I cannot tell, sir; I am little better upon these terms.

TUCCA Ha! Gods and fiends! Why, dost hear? Rogue, thou, give me   35
thy hand; I say unto thee, thy hand, rogue. What? Dost not thou
know me? Not me, rogue? Not Captain Tucca, rogue?

MINOS Come, pra' surrender the gentleman his sword, officer; we'll
have no fighting here.

TUCCA What's thy name?   40

MINOS Minos, an 't please you.

TUCCA Minos? Come hither, Minos. Thou art a wise fellow, it seems.
Let me talk with thee.

CRISPINUS Was ever wretch so wretched as unfortunate I?

TUCCA Thou art one of the *centumviri*,° old boy, art not?   45

MINOS No, indeed, master captain.

TUCCA Go to, thou shalt be then; I'll ha' thee one, Minos. Take my
sword from those rascals, dost thou see? Go do it; I cannot attempt
with patience. What does this gentleman owe thee, little Minos?

MINOS Fourscore sesterces, sir.   50

TUCCA What? No more? Come, thou shalt release him, Minos. What,
I'll be his bail, thou shalt take my word, old boy, and cashier° these
furies; thou shalt do 't, I say, thou shalt, little Minos, thou shalt.

CRISPINUS Yes, and as I am a gentleman and a reveller, I'll make a
piece of poetry and absolve° all, within these five days.   55

TUCCA Come, Minos is not to learn how to use a gent'man of quality,
I know—my sword.° If he pay thee not, I will, and I must, old boy.
Thou shalt be my 'pothecary, too; hast good eryngoes, Minos?

MINOS The best in Rome, sir.

TUCCA Go to, then. [*To Pyrgus*] Vermin, know the house.   60

[1] PYRGUS I warrant you, colonel.

TUCCA For this gentleman, Minos?

MINOS I'll take your word, captain.

TUCCA Thou hast it—my sword.

MINOS Yes, sir. But you must discharge the arrest,° Master Crispinus.   65

TUCCA How, Minos? Look in the gentleman's face, and but read his
silence. Pay, pay; 'tis honour, Minos.

[*Minos pays Lictors, and they release Crispinus*]

CRISPINUS By Jove, sweet captain, you do most infinitely endear and
oblige me to you.

TUCCA Tut, I cannot compliment, by Mars; but Jupiter love me, as I 70
love good words and good clothes, and there's an end. Thou shalt
give my boy that girdle and hangers° when thou hast worn them a
little more.

CRISPINUS O Jupiter! Captain, he shall have them now, presently.
Please you to be acceptive, young gentleman. 75

[1] PYRGUS Yes, sir, fear not, I shall accept. [*Aside*] I have a pretty
foolish humour of taking,° if you knew all.

TUCCA Not now, you shall not take, boy.

CRISPINUS By my truth and earnest, but a shall, captain, by your
leave. 80

TUCCA Nay, and a swear by his truth, take it, boy; do not make a
gentleman forsworn.

[1] LICTOR Well, sir, there is your sword; but thank Master Minos.
You had not carried it as you do, else.
    [*Lictors begin to leave*]

TUCCA Minos is just, and you are knaves, and— 85

[1] LICTOR [*turning back*] What say you, sir?

TUCCA Pass on, my good scoundrel, pass on, I honour thee.
    [*Lictors move off*]
But that I hate to have action with such base rogues as these, you
should ha' seen me unrip their noses now, and have sent 'em to the
next barber's to stitching,° for, do you see, I am a man of humour— 90
    [*Lictors turn back*]
and I do love the varlets, the honest varlets; they have wit and valour,
and are, indeed, good profitable—
    [*Exeunt Lictors*]
errant rogues, as any live in an empire. [*Aside to Crispinus*] Dost
thou hear, poetaster?° Second me. [*To Minos*] Stand up, Minos,
close, gather, yet—so. Sir—[*aside to Crispinus*] thou shalt have a 95
quarter share, be resolute—[*raising his voice*] you shall at my
request take Minos by the hand here; little Minos, I will have it so.
All friends, and a health; be not inexorable.
    [*They shake hands*]
And thou shalt impart the wine, old boy, thou shalt do 't, little
Minos, thou shalt. Make us pay it in our physic. What? We must 100
live and honour the gods sometimes; now Bacchus, now Comus,
now Priapus°—every god a little.
    [*Enter Histrio*]
What's he that stalks by there? Boy, Pyrgus, you were best let him
pass, sirrah; do, leveret,° let him pass, do.

1 PYRGUS 'Tis a player, sir.   105

TUCCA A player? Call him, call the lousy slave hither; what'll he sail
by, and not once strike, or vail to a man of war?° ha? Do you hear?
You, player, rogue, stalker, come back here. No respect to men of
worship, you slave? What, you are proud, you rascal, are you
proud? ha? You grow rich, do you, and purchase?° You have for-   110
tune° and the good year on your side, you stinkard? You have? You
have?

HISTRIO Nay, sweet captain, be confined to some reason. I protest I
saw you not, sir.

TUCCA You did not? Where was your sight, Oedipus?° You walk with   115
hare's eyes,° do you? I'll ha' 'em glazed,° rogue; and you say the
word, they shall be glazed for you. Come, we must have you turn
fiddler again, slave, get a bass violin° at your back, and march in a
tawny coat with one sleeve to Goose Fair,° and then you'll know us,
you'll see us then; you will, gulch, you will! Then, 'Will't please   120
your worship to have any music, captain?'

HISTRIO [*laughing*] Nay, good captain.

TUCCA What? Do you laugh, Owl-glass?° 'Death, you perstemptu-
ous° varlet, I am none of your fellows; I have commanded a hun-
dred and fifty such rogues, I.   125

1 PYRGUS [*aside*] Ay, and most of that hundred and fifty have been
leaders of a legion.°

HISTRIO If I have exhibited° wrong, I'll tender satisfaction, captain.

TUCCA Say'st thou so, honest vermin? Give me thy hand, thou shalt
make us a supper one of these nights.   130

HISTRIO When you please, by Jove, captain, most willingly.

TUCCA Dost thou swear? Tomorrow, then; say and hold, slave. There
are some of you players honest gent'man-like scoundrels: a man
may skelder ye now and then of half a dozen shillings or so. Dost
thou not know that *capriccio*° there?   135

HISTRIO No, I assure you, captain.

TUCCA Go and be acquainted with him, then; he is a gent'man parcel-
poet,° you slave—his father was a man of worship, I tell thee. Go,
he pens high, lofty, in a new stalking strain, bigger than half the
rhymers i' the town again; he was born to fill thy mouth, Minotau-   140
rus,° he was. He will teach thee to tear and rand,° rascal: to him,
cherish his Muse, go. Thou hast forty—forty shillings, I mean,
stinkard—give him in earnest, do; he shall write for thee, slave.° If
he pen for thee once, thou shalt not need to travel with thy pumps
full of gravel anymore, after a blind jade and a hamper.   145

38

HISTRIO Troth, I think I ha' not so much about me, captain.

TUCCA It's no matter, give him what thou hast, paunch, I'll give my word for the rest; though it lack a shilling or two, it skills not. Go, thou art an honest twenty i' the hundred;° I'll ha' the statute repealed for thee. Minos, I must tell thee, Minos, thou hast dejected 150 yon gent'man's spirit exceedingly.° Dost observe? Dost note, little Minos?

MINOS Yes, sir.

TUCCA Go to then, raise, recover, do—suffer him not to droop in prospect° of a player, a rogue, a stager. Put twenty into his hand, 155 twenty drachmas, I mean, and let nobody see. Go, do it; the work shall commend itself: be Minos, I'll pay.

MINOS Yes, forsooth, captain.

2 PYRGUS [aside to 1 Pyrgus] Do not we serve a notable shark?

TUCCA And what new plays have you now afoot, sirrah? ha? I would 160 fain come with my cockatrice one day and see a play, if I knew when there were a good bawdy one; but they say you ha' nothing but humours, revels, and satires that gird° and fart at the time, you slave.

HISTRIO No, I assure you, captain, not we. They are on the other side of Tiber.° We have as much ribaldry in our plays as can be, as you 165 would wish, captain. All the sinners i' the suburbs come and applaud our action daily.

TUCCA I hear you'll bring me o' the stage there; you'll play me, they say: I shall be presented by a sort of copper-laced scoundrels° of you. Death of Pluto, and you stage me, stinkard, your mansions 170 shall sweat for 't; your tabernacles, varlets; your Globes, and your triumphs!°

HISTRIO Not we, by Phoebus, captain; do not do us imputation without desert.

TUCCA I wou' not, my good twopenny rascal—reach me thy neuf.° 175 Dost hear? What wilt thou give me a week for my brace of beagles here, my little point trussers?° You shall ha' them act among ye. [To 1 Pyrgus] Sirrah, you, pronounce. Thou shalt hear him speak in King Darius' doleful strain.°

1 PYRGUS 'O doleful days! O direful deadly dump! 180
O wicked world! and worldly wickedness!
How can I hold my fist from crying thump,
In rue of this right rascal wretchedness!'

TUCCA In an amorous vein now, sirrah—peace.

1 PYRGUS 'Oh, she is wilder, and more hard withal, 185
Than beast or bird, or tree or stony wall.

Yet might she love me, to uprear her state:
Ay, but perhaps she hopes some nobler mate.
Yet might she love me to content her sire:
Ay, but her reason masters her desire.   190
Yet might she love me as her beauty's thrall:
Ay, but I fear, she cannot love at all.'°

TUCCA Now the 'orrible fierce soldier, you, sirrah.

1 PYRGUS 'What? Will I brave thee? Ay, and beard thee, too.
A Roman spirit scorns to bear a brain   195
So full of base pusillanimity.'°

HISTRIO Excellent!

TUCCA Nay, thou shall see that shall ravish thee anon; prick up thine
ears, stinkard—the ghost, boys.

1 PYRGUS 'Vindicta!'   200

2 PYRGUS 'Timoria!'

1 PYRGUS 'Vindicta!'

2 PYRGUS 'Timoria!'

1 PYRGUS 'Veni!'

2 PYRGUS 'Veni!'°   205

TUCCA Now thunder, sirrah, you, the rumbling player.

2 PYRGUS Ay, but somebody must cry 'Murder' then, in a small
voice.

TUCCA Your fellow sharer there shall do't. Cry, sirrah, cry!

1 PYRGUS 'Murder, murder!'   210

2 PYRGUS 'Who calls out murder? Lady, was it you?'°

HISTRIO Oh, admirable good, I protest.

TUCCA Sirrah, boy, brace your drum a little straighter,° and do the
tother fellow there, he in the—what sha' call him?—and 'yet stay,'°
too.   215

2 PYRGUS 'Nay, and thou dalliest, then I am thy foe,
And fear shall force what friendship cannot win;
Thy death shall bury what thy life conceals—
Villain! Thou diest for more respecting her than me.'

1 PYRGUS 'Oh, stay my lord.'   220

2 PYRGUS 'Yet speak the truth, and I will guerdon thee;
But if thou dally once again, thou diest.'°

TUCCA Enough of this, boy.

2 PYRGUS 'Why then, lament therefore; damned be thy guts
Unto King Pluto's hell, and princely Erebus,   225
For sparrows must have food.'°

HISTRIO Pray, sweet captain, let one of them do a little of a lady.

TUCCA [*indicating 1 Pyrgus*] Oh, he will make thee eternally enamoured of him there. Do, sirrah, do; 'twill allay your fellow's fury
a little.   230

1 PYRGUS 'Master, mock on: the scorn thou givest me,
Pray Jove some lady may return on thee—'°

2 PYRGUS No, you shall see me do the Moor.° Master, lend me your
scarf a little.

TUCCA Here, 'tis at thy service, boy.   235

2 PYRGUS You, Master Minos, hark hither a little.
          [*2 Pyrgus and Minos withdraw to make themselves ready*]

TUCCA How dost like him? Art not rapt? Art not tickled now? Dost
not applaud, rascal, dost not applaud?

HISTRIO Yes—what will you ask for 'em a week, captain?

TUCCA No, you mangonizing° slave, I will not part from 'em; you'll   240
sell 'em for ingles, you. Let's ha' good cheer tomorrow night at
supper, stalker, and then we'll talk. Good capon and plover, do you
hear, sirrah? And do not bring your eating player with you there, I
cannot away with him. He will eat a leg of mutton while I am in my
porridge, the lean Poluphagus;° his belly is like Barathrum,° he   245
looks like a midwife in man's apparel, the slave. Nor the villainous-
out-of-tune fiddler Enobarbus,° bring not him. What hast thou
there? Six and thirty? ha?

HISTRIO No, here's all I have, captain, some five and twenty. Pray, sir,
will you present and accommodate° it unto the gentleman? For mine   250
own part, I am a mere stranger to his humour; besides, I have some
business invites me hence, with Master Asinius Lupus, the tribune.

TUCCA Well, go thy ways, pursue thy projects, let me alone with this
design; my poetaster shall make thee a play, and thou shalt be a man
of good parts in it. But stay, let me see—do not bring your father   255
Aesop, your politician, unless you can ram up his mouth with
cloves: the slave smells ranker than some sixteen dunghills, and is
seventeen times more rotten. Marry, you may bring Friskin, my
zany; he's a good skipping swaggerer; and your fat fool there, my
mango,° bring him, too, but let him not beg rapiers nor scarves in   260
his over-familiar playing face, nor roar out his barren bold jests
with a tormenting laughter, between drunk and dry. Do you hear,
rascal? Give him warning, admonition, to forsake his saucy, glaver-
ing° grace, and his goggle eye; it does not become him, sirrah, tell
him so.°   265

HISTRIO Yes, captain; Jupiter and the rest of the gods confine° your
modern delights, without disgust.

41

TUCCA Stay—thou shalt see the Moor ere thou goest.

    [*Enter Demetrius*]

    What's he with the half arms° there, that salutes us out of his cloak
    like a motion? ha?   270

HISTRIO Oh sir, his doublet's a little decayed; he is otherwise a very
    simple honest fellow, sir: one Demetrius, a dresser° of plays about
    the town here. We have hired him to abuse Horace, and bring him
    in in a play with all his gallants: as Tibullus, Maecenas, Cornelius
    Gallus, and the rest.°   275

TUCCA And why so, stinkard?

HISTRIO Oh, it will get us a huge deal of money, captain, and we
    have need on 't, for this winter has made us all poorer than so
    many starved snakes. Nobody comes at us, not a gentleman nor
    a—°   280

TUCCA But you know nothing by him, do you, to make a play of?

HISTRIO Faith, not much, captain; but our author will devise enough.

TUCCA Why, my Parnassus° here shall help him, if thou wilt. Can thy
    author do it impudently enough?

HISTRIO Oh, I warrant you, captain, and spitefully enough, too; he   285
    has one of the most overflowing, villainous wits in Rome. He will
    slander any man that breathes, if he disgust him.

TUCCA I'll know the poor, egregious, nitty° rascal; an he have such
    commendable qualities, I'll cherish him. Stay, here comes the
    tartar.° I'll make a gathering for him, I, a purse, and put the poor   290
    slave° in fresh rags; tell him so, to comfort him.

    [*The boy comes in on Minos' shoulders, who stalks as he acts*]

    Well said, boy.

2 PYRGUS 'Where art thou, boy? Where is Calipolis?
    Fight, earthquakes, in the entrails of the earth,
    And eastern whirlwinds in the hellish shades;   295
    Some foul contagion of th' infected heavens
    Blast all the trees, and in their cursèd tops
    The dismal night-raven and tragic owl
    Breed and become forerunners of my fall.'°

TUCCA [*to Histrio*] Well, now fare thee well, my honest penny-biter.   300
    Commend me to seven shares and a half,° and remember tomorrow.
    If you lack a service, you shall play in my name, rascals; but you shall
    buy your own cloth, and I'll ha' two shares for my countenance°—
    let thy author stay with me.

    [*Exit Histrio*]

DEMETRIUS Yes, sir.   305

TUCCA 'Twas well done, little Minos, thou didst stalk well; forgive me
that I said thou stunkst, Minos, 'twas the savour of a poet I met
sweating in the street, hangs yet in my nostrils.

CRISPINUS Who? Horace?

TUCCA Ay, he, dost thou know him?   310

CRISPINUS Oh, he forsook me most barbarously, I protest.

TUCCA Hang him, fusty satyr, he smells all goat; he carries a ram
under his armholes, the slave. I am the worse when I see him. [*Aside
to Crispinus*] Did not Minos impart?

CRISPINUS [*aside to Tucca*] Yes, here's twenty drachmas he did   315
convey.°

TUCCA [*aside to Crispinus*] Well said, keep 'em, we'll share anon.
Come, little Minos.

CRISPINUS Faith, captain, I'll be bold to show you a mistress of mine,
a jeweller's wife, a gallant, as we go along.   320

TUCCA There spoke my genius. Minos, some of thy eryngoes, little
Minos—send. [*To Crispinus*] Come hither, Parnassus. I must ha'
thee familiar with my little locust here; 'tis a good vermin, they say.

    Exeunt

4.1

[*Enter*] *Chloë, Cytheris,* [*and Maids*]

CHLOË But sweet lady, say: am I well enough attired for the court, in sadness?

CYTHERIS Well enough? Excellent well, sweet Chloë. This straight bodied city attire, I can tell you, will stir a courtier's blood more than the finest loose sacks the ladies use to be put in. And then you 5
are as well jewelled as any of them; your ruff and linen about you is much more pure than theirs. And for your beauty, I can tell you, there's many of them would defy the painter,° if they could change with you. Marry, the worst is, you must look to be envied, and endure a few court frumps° for it. 10

CHLOË O God! Madam, I shall buy them too cheap. [*To Maids*] Give me my muff, and my dog° there. [*To Cytheris*] And will the ladies be anything familiar with me, think you?

CYTHERIS O Hercules! Why, you shall see 'em flock about you with their puff wings,° and ask you, where you bought your lawn? And 15
what you paid for it? Who starches you? And entreat you to help 'em to some pure laundresses, out of the city.

CHLOË O, Cupid! [*To Maids*] Give me my fan, and my mask, too. [*To Cytheris*] And will the lords and the poets there use one well, too, lady? 20

CYTHERIS Doubt not of that: you shall have kisses from them go pit-pat, pit-pat, pit-pat upon your lips, as thick as stones out of slings at the assault of a city. And then your ears will be so furred with the breath of their compliments, that you cannot catch cold of your head (if you would) in three winters after. 25

CHLOË Thank you, sweet lady. O heaven! And how must one behave herself amongst 'em? You know all.

CYTHERIS Faith, impudently enough, Mistress Chloë, and well enough. Carry not too much underthought betwixt yourself and them; nor your city mannerly word 'forsooth', use it not too often 30
in any case, but plain 'Ay, madam', and 'No, madam'. Nor never say 'Your lordship', nor 'Your honour', but 'You', and 'You, my lord', and 'My lady'. The other they count too simple and minceative. And though they desire to kiss heaven with their titles, yet they will count them fools that give them too humbly. 35

44

CHLOË Oh, intolerable, Jupiter! By my troth, lady, I would not for a
world, but you had lien in my house; and, i' faith, you shall not pay
a farthing for your board, nor your chambers.

CYTHERIS O sweet Mistress Chloë!

CHLOË I' faith, you shall not, lady; nay, good lady, do not offer it.   40

4.2

[Enter] Cornelius Gallus [and] Tibullus

GALLUS Come, where be these ladies? By your leave, bright stars, this
gentleman and I are come to man you to court, where your late kind
entertainment is now to be requited with a heavenly banquet.

CYTHERIS A heavenly banquet, Gallus?

GALLUS No less, my dear Cytheris.   5

TIBULLUS That were not strange, lady, if the epithet were only given
for the company invited thither: yourself, and this fair gentlewoman.

CHLOË Are we invited to court, sir?

TIBULLUS You are, lady, by the great princess Julia, who longs to   10
greet you with any favours that may worthily make you an often
courtier.

CHLOË In sincerity, I thank her, sir. You have a coach, ha' you not?

TIBULLUS The princess hath sent her own, lady.

CHLOË O Venus, that's well! I do long to ride in a coach most   15
vehemently.

CYTHERIS But sweet Gallus, pray you, resolve me why you give that
heavenly praise to this earthly banquet?

GALLUS Because, Cytheris, it must be celebrated by the heavenly
powers. All the gods and goddesses will be there, to two of which,   20
you two must be exalted.

CHLOË A pretty fiction, in truth.

CYTHERIS A fiction, indeed, Chloë, and fit for the fit of a poet.°

GALLUS Why, Cytheris, may not poets, from whose divine spirits all
the honours of the gods have been deduced, entreat so much hon-   25
our of the gods, to have their divine presence at a poetical banquet?

CYTHERIS Suppose that no fiction, yet where are your abilities to
make us two goddesses at your feast?

GALLUS Who knows not, Cytheris, that the sacred breath of a true
poet can blow any virtuous humanity up to deity?   30

45

TIBULLUS To tell you the female truth (which is the simple truth),
ladies, and to show that poets, in spite of the world, are able to deify
themselves, at this banquet, to which you are invited, we intend to
assume the figures of the gods, and to give our several loves the
forms of goddesses. Ovid will be Jupiter, the Princess Julia, Juno;   35
Gallus here, Apollo; you, Cytheris, Pallas; I will be Bacchus, and
my love, Plautia, Ceres. And to install you and your husband, fair
Chloë, in honours equal with ours, you shall be a goddess, and your
husband a god.

CHLOË A god? O my God!   40

TIBULLUS A god, but a lame god, lady, for he shall be Vulcan, and
you, Venus. And this will make our banquet no less than heavenly.

CHLOË In sincerity, it will be sugared. Good Jove, what a pretty,
foolish thing it is to be a poet! But hark you, sweet Cytheris, could
they not possibly leave out my husband? Methinks a body's   45
husband does not so well at court—a body's friend, or so—but
husband, 'tis like your clog to your marmoset° for all the world, and
the heavens.

CYTHERIS Tut, never fear, Chloë; your husband will be left without in
the lobby or the great chamber when you shall be put in i' the   50
closet° by this lord, and by that lady.

CHLOË Nay, then I am certified:° he shall go.

4.3

[*Enter*] *Horace*

GALLUS Horace! Welcome.

HORACE Gentlemen, hear you the news?

TIBULLUS What news, my Quintus?

HORACE Our melancholic friend, Propertius,
Hath closed himself up in his Cynthia's tomb,   5
And will by no entreaties be drawn thence.

[*Enter*] *Albius* [*and*] *Crispinus*, [*followed by*] *Tucca*
[*and*] *Demetrius*

ALBIUS Nay, good Master Crispinus, pray you bring near the
gentleman.

HORACE Crispinus? Hide me, good Gallus—Tibullus, shelter me.

CRISPINUS Make your approach, sweet captain.   10

TIBULLUS What means this, Horace?

46

HORACE I am surprised again! Farewell.

GALLUS   Stay, Horace.

HORACE What, and be tired on by yond vulture? No,°
    Phoebus defend me.

        Exit [Horace]

TIBULLUS   'Slight! I hold my life,
    This same is he met him in Via Sacra.   15

GALLUS Troth, 'tis like enough. This act of Propertius relisheth very
    strange with me.

TUCCA By thy leave, my neat scoundrel, what, is this the mad boy you
    talked on?

CRISPINUS Ay, this is Master Albius, captain.   20

TUCCA Give me thy hand, Agamemnon. We hear abroad thou art the
    Hector of citizens—what sayest thou? Are we welcome to thee,
    noble Pyrrhus?°

ALBIUS Welcome, captain? By Jove, and all the gods i' the Capitol.

TUCCA No more, we conceive thee. Which of these is thy wedlock,   25
    Menelaus—thy Helen, thy Lucrece°—that we may do her honour,
    mad boy?

CRISPINUS She i' the little velvet cap, sir, is my mistress.

ALBIUS For fault of a better, sir.

TUCCA A better, profane rascal? I cry thee mercy, my good scroyle,   30
    was 't thou?

ALBIUS No harm, captain.

TUCCA She is a Venus, a Vesta, a Melpomene. Come hither, Penelope.
    What's thy name, Iris?°
        [Kisses her]

CHLOË My name is Chloë, sir; I am a gentlewoman.   35

TUCCA Thou art in merit to be an empress, Chloë, for an eye and a lip;
    thou hast an emperor's nose. Kiss me again—
        [They kiss]
    —'tis a virtuous punk, so. Before Jove, the gods were a sort of
    goslings when they suffered so sweet a breath to perfume the bed
    of a stinkard; thou hadst ill fortune, Thisbe;° the fates were   40
    infatuate;° they were, punk, they were.

CHLOË That's sure, sir; let me crave your name, I pray you, sir.

TUCCA I am known by the name of Captain Tucca, punk; the noble
    Roman, punk; a gent'man, and a commander, punk.
        [Chloë walks aside]

CHLOË In good time! A gentleman, and a commander? That's as good   45
    as a poet!

CRISPINUS A pretty instrument. It's my cousin Cytheris' viol, this, is't not?

CYTHERIS Nay, play, cousin; it wants but such a voice and hand to grace it as yours is.   50

CRISPINUS Alas, cousin, you are merrily inspired.

CYTHERIS Pray you play, if you love me.

CRISPINUS Yes, cousin; you know I do not hate you.

TIBULLUS A most subtle wench! How she hath baited him with a viol yonder for a song!   55

CRISPINUS Cousin, pray you call Mistress Chloë; she shall hear an essay° of my poetry.

TUCCA I'll call her. Come hither, cockatrice; here's one will set thee up, my sweet punk, set thee up.

CHLOË Are you a pewit° so soon, sir?   60

ALBIUS Wife, mum.

[CRISPINUS (*sings*)]

> Love is blind, and a wanton;
> In the whole world there is scant
>   One such another:
>   No, not his mother.   65
> He hath plucked her doves and sparrows
> To feather his sharp arrows,
>   And alone prevaileth,
>   Whilst sick Venus waileth.
> But if Cypris once recover°   70
> The wag, it shall behove her
>   To look better to him,
>   Or she will undo him.

ALBIUS Oh, most odoriferous music!

TUCCA Aha, stinkard! Another Orpheus,° you slave, another Orpheus! An Arion, riding on the back of a dolphin,° rascal.   75

GALLUS Have you a copy of this ditty, sir?

CRISPINUS Master Albius has.

ALBIUS Ay, but in truth, they are my wife's verses; I must not show 'em.   80

TUCCA Show 'em, bankrupt, show 'em; they have salt in 'em, and will brook the air, stinkard.

GALLUS [*reading*] How? 'To his bright mistress, Canidia?'°

CRISPINUS Ay, sir, that's but a borrowed name, as Ovid's Corinna, or Propertius his Cynthia, or your Nemesis,° or Delia, Tibullus.   85

GALLUS It's the name of Horace his witch, as I remember.

TIBULLUS [*reading*] Why, the ditty's all borrowed—'tis Horace's! Hang him, plagiary!

TUCCA How? He borrow of Horace? He shall pawn himself to ten brokers first. Do you hear, poetasters? I know you to be knights, and men of worship. He shall write with Horace, for a talent, and let Maecenas and his whole College of Critics take his part. Thou shalt do't, young Phoebus, thou shalt, Phaethon,° thou shalt.

DEMETRIUS Alas sir, Horace? He is a mere sponge; nothing but humours and observation; he goes up and down sucking from every society, and when he comes home, squeezes himself dry again. I know him, I.

TUCCA Thou sayest true, my poor poetical fury, he will pen all he knows. A sharp, thorny-toothed, satirical rascal; fly him, he carries hay in his horn:° he will sooner lose his best friend, than his least jest. What he once drops upon paper against a man lives eternally to upbraid him in the mouth of every slave tankard-bearer or water-man; not a bawd or a boy that comes from the bakehouse, but shall point at him. 'Tis all dog and scorpion: he carries poison in his teeth, and a sting in his tail—faugh! Body of Jove! I'll have the slave whipped one of these days for his satires and his humours by one cashiered° clerk or another.

CRISPINUS We'll undertake him, captain.

DEMETRIUS Ay, and tickle him, i' faith, for his arrogancy and his impudence in commending his own things, and for his translating: I can trace him, i'faith. Oh, he is the most open fellow living; I had as lief as a new suit I were at it.

TUCCA Say no more then, but do it; 'tis the only way to get thee a new suit. Sting him, my little newts; I'll give you instructions. I'll be your intelligencer; we'll all join, and hang upon him like so many horseleeches—the players and all. We shall sup together soon, and then we'll conspire, i'faith.

GALLUS [*aside to Tibullus*] Oh, that Horace had stayed still here.

TIBULLUS [*aside to Gallus*] So would not I, for both these would have turned Pythagoreans then.

GALLUS [*aside to Tibullus*] What, mute?°

TIBULLUS [*aside to Gallus*] Ay, as fishes, i'faith. Come, ladies, shall we go?

CYTHERIS We await you, sir. But Mistress Chloë asks if you have not a god to spare for this gentleman.

GALLUS Who, Captain Tucca?

CYTHERIS Ay, he.

GALLUS Yes, if we can invite him along, he shall be Mars.

CHLOË Has Mars anything to do with Venus?

TIBULLUS Oh, most of all, lady.   130

CHLOË Nay then, I pray, let him be invited—and what shall Crispinus
be?

TIBULLUS Mercury, Mistress Chloë.

CHLOË Mercury? That's a poet, is 't?

GALLUS No, lady, but somewhat inclining that way: he is a herald at   135
arms.

CHLOË A herald at arms? Good. And Mercury? Pretty. He has to do
with Venus, too?

TIBULLUS A little with her face, lady, or so.°

CHLOË 'Tis very well; pray, let's go, I long to be at it.   140

CYTHERIS [to Crispinus and Tucca] Gentlemen, shall we pray your
companies along?

CRISPINUS You shall not only pray, but prevail, lady. Come, sweet
captain.

TUCCA Yes, I follow. [Aside to Albius] But thou must not talk of this   145
now, my little bankrupt.

ALBIUS [aside to Tucca] Captain, look here: mum.

DEMETRIUS I'll go write, sir.

TUCCA Do, do—stay, there's a drachma to purchase gingerbread for
thy Muse.   150

  Exeunt

4.4

  [Enter] Lupus, Histrio, [and] Lictors

LUPUS Come, let us talk here; here we may be private. Shut the door,
lictor. You are a player, you say.

HISTRIO Ay, and 't please your worship.

LUPUS Good. And how are you able to give this intelligence?°

HISTRIO Marry, sir, they directed a letter to me and my fellow   5
sharers.

LUPUS Speak lower, you are not now i' your theatre, stager. [To 1
Lictor] My sword, knave. [To Histrio] They directed a letter to you
and your fellow sharers—forward.

HISTRIO Yes, sir, to hire some of our properties, as a sceptre and a   10
crown for Jove, and a caduceus for Mercury, and a petasus—

LUPUS Caduceus? And petasus? Let me see your letter. [Reads] This

is a conjuration;° a conspiracy, this. [*To 1 Lictor*] Quickly, on with
my buskins: I'll act a tragedy, i'faith. Will nothing but our gods
serve these poets to profane? Dispatch! Player, I thank thee. The   15
emperor shall take knowledge of thy good service.
    [*A knocking within*]
Who's there now? [*To 1 Lictor*] Look, knave.
    [*Exit 1 Lictor*]
A crown and a sceptre? This is good—rebellion now!
    [*Enter 1 Lictor*]
[1] LICTOR 'Tis your 'pothecary, sir, Master Minos.
LUPUS What tell'st thou me of 'pothecaries, knave? Tell him I have   20
affairs of state in hand; I can talk to no 'pothecaries now. [*Pauses*]
Heart of me! Stay the 'pothecary there. You shall see, I have fished
out a cunning piece of plot now. They have had some intelligence
that their project is discovered, and now have they dealt with my
'pothecary to poison me—'tis so—knowing that I meant to take   25
physic today. As sure as death, 'tis there. Jupiter, I thank thee, that
thou hast yet made me so much of a politician.°
    [*Enter Minos*]
You are welcome, sir. Take the potion from him there. I have an
antidote more than you wot of, sir. Throw it on the ground there;
so. Now fetch in the dog—and yet we cannot tarry to try experi-   30
ments° now. Arrest him. You shall go with me, sir, I'll tickle you,
'pothecary; I'll give you a clyster, i'faith. Have I the letter? Ay, 'tis
here. Come, your fasces,° lictors. The half-pikes, and the halberds,
take them down from the lares,° there. Player, assist me.
    [*As they are going out, enter Maecenas and Horace*]
MAECENAS Whither now, Asinius Lupus, with this armoury?   35
LUPUS I cannot talk now. I charge you, assist me. Treason, treason!
HORACE How? Treason?
LUPUS Ay—if you love the emperor and the state, follow me.
    Exeunt

4.5

    [*Enter*] *Ovid, Julia, Gallus, Cytheris, Tibullus,*
    Plautia, Albius, Chloë, Tucca, Crispinus, Hermogenes,
    [*and 1*] *Pyrgus* [*dressed as gods and goddesses*]°
OVID Gods and goddesses, take your several° seats. Now, Mercury,
move your caduceus, and in Jupiter's name command silence.

CRISPINUS In the name of Jupiter—silence!

HERMOGENES The crier of the court hath too clarified a voice.

GALLUS Peace, Momus.°   5

OVID Oh, he is the god of reprehension, let him alone; 'tis his office.
    Mercury, go forward, and proclaim after Phoebus our high pleasure
    to all the deities that shall partake this high banquet.

CRISPINUS Yes, sir.

GALLUS The great god Jupiter—   10

CRISPINUS The great god Jupiter—

[GALLUS] Of his licentious goodness—

[CRISPINUS] Of his licentious goodness—

[GALLUS] Willing to make this feast no fast—

[CRISPINUS] Willing to make this feast no fast—   15

[GALLUS] From any manner of pleasure—

[CRISPINUS] From any manner of pleasure—

[GALLUS] Nor to bind any god or goddess—

[CRISPINUS] Nor to bind any god or goddess—

[GALLUS] To be anything the more god or goddess for their names—   20

[CRISPINUS] To be anything the more god or goddess for their
    names—

[GALLUS] He gives them all free licence—

[CRISPINUS] He gives them all free licence—

[GALLUS] To speak no wiser than persons of baser titles—   25

[CRISPINUS] To speak no wiser than persons of baser titles—

[GALLUS] And to be nothing better than common men or women—

[CRISPINUS] And to be nothing better than common men or women—

[GALLUS] And therefore no god—

[CRISPINUS] And therefore no god—   30

[GALLUS] Shall need to keep himself more strictly to his goddess—

[CRISPINUS] Shall need to keep himself more strictly to his goddess—

[GALLUS] Than any man does to his wife—

[CRISPINUS] Than any man does to his wife—

[GALLUS] Nor any goddess—   35

[CRISPINUS] Nor any goddess—

[GALLUS] Shall need to keep herself more strictly to her god—

[CRISPINUS] Shall need to keep herself more strictly to her god—

[GALLUS] Than any woman does to her husband—

[CRISPINUS] Than any woman does to her husband—   40

[GALLUS] But since it is no part of wisdom—

[CRISPINUS] But since it is no part of wisdom—

[GALLUS] In these days to come into bonds—

[CRISPINUS] In these days to come into bonds—
[GALLUS] It shall be lawful for every lover—   45
[CRISPINUS] It shall be lawful for every lover—
[GALLUS] To break loving oaths—
[CRISPINUS] To break loving oaths—
[GALLUS] To change their lovers and make love to others—
[CRISPINUS] To change their lovers and make love to others—   50
[GALLUS] As the heat of everyone's blood—
[CRISPINUS] As the heat of everyone's blood—
[GALLUS] And the spirit of our nectar shall inspire—
[CRISPINUS] And the spirit of our nectar shall inspire—
[GALLUS] And Jupiter save Jupiter!—   55
[CRISPINUS] And Jupiter save Jupiter!
TIBULLUS So now we may play the fools by authority.
HERMOGENES To play the fool by authority is wisdom.
JULIA Away with your mattery sentences, Momus; they are too grave
    and wise for this meeting.   60
OVID [to Crispinus] Mercury, give our jester a stool, let him sit by; and
    reach him of our cates.
TUCCA Dost hear, mad Jupiter? We'll have it enacted: he that speaks
    the first wise word shall be made cuckold. What sayst thou? Is 't not
    a good motion?   65
OVID Deities, are you all agreed?
ALL Agreed, great Jupiter.
ALBIUS I have read in a book, that to play the fool wisely is high
    wisdom.°
GALLUS How now, Vulcan! Will you be the first wizard?°   70
OVID [to Tucca] Take his wife, Mars, and make him cuckold, quickly.
TUCCA Come, cockatrice.
CHLOË No—let me alone with him, Jupiter. I'll make you take heed,
    sir, while you live again, if there be twelve in a company, that you be
    not the wisest of 'em.°   75
ALBIUS No more I will not, indeed, wife; hereafter, I'll be here, mum.
OVID [to 1 Pyrgus] Fill us a bowl of nectar, Ganymede; we will drink
    to our daughter, Venus.
GALLUS [to Albius] Look to your wife, Vulcan; Jupiter begins to court
    her.   80
TIBULLUS Nay, let Mars look to it; Vulcan must do as Venus does—
    bear.°
TUCCA Sirrah, boy—catamite! Look you play Ganymede well now,
    you slave: do not spill your nectar; carry your cup even, so. You

should have rubbed your face with whites of eggs,° you rascal, till   85
your brows had shone like our sooty brother's° here, as sleek as a
horn-book, or ha' steeped your lips in wine, till you made 'em so
plump that Juno might have been jealous of 'em. Punk, kiss me,
punk.°

OVID [*to Chloë*] Here, daughter Venus, I drink to thee.   90

CHLOË Thank you, good father Jupiter.

TUCCA [*to Julia*] Why, mother Juno! Gods and fiends! What, wilt thou
suffer this ocular temptation?

TIBULLUS Mars is enraged: he looks big, and begins to stut° for anger.

HERMOGENES Well played, Captain Mars.   95

TUCCA Well said, minstrel Momus. I must put you in, must I? When
will you be in good fooling of yourself, fiddler? Never?

HERMOGENES Oh, 'tis our fashion to be silent when there is a better
fool in place, ever.

TUCCA Thank you, rascal.   100

OVID [*to 1 Pyrgus*] Fill to our daughter Venus, Ganymede, who fills
her father with affection.

JULIA Wilt thou be ranging, Jupiter, before my face?

OVID Why not, Juno? Why should Jupiter stand in awe of thy face,
Juno?   105

JULIA Because it is thy wife's face, Jupiter.

OVID What, shall a husband be afraid of his wife's face? Will she paint
it so horribly? We are a King, cotquean, and we will reign in
our pleasures, and we will cudgel thee to death if thou find fault
with us.   110

JULIA I will find fault with thee, King Cuckold-Maker! What, shall
the king of gods turn the king of good fellows, and have no
fellow in wickedness? This makes our poets, that know our
profaneness, live as profane as we. By my godhead, Jupiter, I will
join with all the other gods here, bind thee hand and foot, throw   115
thee down into earth, and make a poor poet of thee, if thou abuse
me thus.

GALLUS A good smart-tongued goddess; a right Juno.

OVID Juno, we will cudgel thee, Juno; we told thee so yesterday, when
thou wert jealous of us for Thetis.°   120

[1] PYRGUS Nay, today she had me in inquisition, too.

TUCCA Well said, my fine Phrygian fry:° inform, inform. [*To Crispinus*]
Give me some wine, king of heralds, I may drink to my cockatrice.

OVID No more, Ganymede. We will cudgel thee, Juno; by Styx, we
will.   125

JULIA It's well—gods may grow impudent in iniquity, and they must not be told of it.

OVID Yea, we will knock our chin against our breast, and shake thee out of Olympus° into an oyster boat for thy scolding.

JULIA Your nose is not long enough to do it,° Jupiter, if all thy 130 strumpets thou hast among the stars took thy part. And there is never a star in thy forehead but shall be a horn if thou persist to abuse me.

CRISPINUS A good jest, i' faith.

OVID We tell thee, thou angerst us, cotquean, and we will thunder 135 thee in pieces for thy cotqueanity; we will lay this city desolate and flat as this hand for thy offences. These two fingers are the walls of it; these within, the people; which people shall be all thrown down, thus, and nothing left standing in this city but these walls.°

CRISPINUS Another good jest. 140

ALBIUS O, my hammers and my Cyclops! This boy fills not wine enough to make us kind enough to one another.

TUCCA Nor thou hast not collied° thy face enough, stinkard.

ALBIUS I'll ply the table with nectar, and make them friends.

HERMOGENES Heaven is like to have but a lame skinker° then. 145

ALBIUS 'Wine and good livers, make true lovers.'° I'll sentence them together. Here father, here mother: for shame, drink yourselves drunk, and forget this dissension. You two should cling together before our faces, and give us example of unity.

GALLUS Oh, excellently spoken, Vulcan, on the sudden! 150

TIBULLUS Jupiter may do well to prefer his tongue to some office for his eloquence.

TUCCA His tongue shall be gent'man usher to his wit, and still go before it.

ALBIUS An excellent fit office. 155

CRISPINUS Ay, and an excellent good jest, besides.

HERMOGENES [to Tucca] What, have you hired Mercury to cry your jests you make?

OVID Momus, you are envious.

TUCCA [to Hermogenes] Why, you whoreson blockhead, 'tis your only 160 block of wit in fashion nowadays, to applaud other folks' jests.

HERMOGENES True, with those that are not artificers themselves. Vulcan, you nod, and the mirth of the feast droops.

[1] PYRGUS He has filled nectar so long, till his brain swims in it.

GALLUS What, do we nod, fellow gods? Sound music, and let us 165 startle° our spirits with a song.

55

TUCCA [*to Gallus*] Do, Apollo; thou art a good musician.

GALLUS What says Jupiter?

OVID Ha? Ha?°

GALLUS A song.   170

OVID Why, do, do, sing.

PLAUTIA [*to Tibullus*] Bacchus, what say you?

TIBULLUS Ceres?

PLAUTIA But to this song?

TIBULLUS Sing, for my part.   175

JULIA Your belly weighs down your head, Bacchus; here's a song
    toward.°

TIBULLUS Begin, Vulcan.

ALBIUS What else? What else?

TUCCA Say, Jupiter—   180

OVID Mercury—

CRISPINUS Ay, say, say—

    [*He sings*]°

        Wake, our mirth begins to die,
        Quicken it with tunes and wine;
        Raise your notes, you're out—fie! fie!   185
        This drowsiness is an ill sign.
          We banish him the choir of gods°
            That droops again:
            Then all are men,
          For here's not one, but nods.   190

OVID I like not this sudden and general heaviness amongst our
    godheads; 'tis somewhat ominous. Apollo, command us louder
    music, and let Mercury and Momus contend to please, and revive
    our senses.

    [*Hermogenes and Crispinus sing*]

HERMOGENES   *Then, in a free and lofty strain,*   195
             Our broken tunes we thus repair;

CRISPINUS   *And we answer them again,*
             Running division on the panting air,

BOTH   *To celebrate this feast of sense,*
              As free from scandal, as offence.   200

HERMOGENES   *Here is beauty for the eye;*

CRISPINUS   *For the ear, sweet melody;*

HERMOGENES *Ambrosiac odours for the smell;*

CRISPINUS   *Delicious nectar for the taste;*

BOTH   *For the touch, a lady's waist,*   205

Which doth all the rest excel.

OVID Ay, this hath waked us. [*To Crispinus*] Mercury, our herald, go
from ourself, the great god Jupiter, to the great emperor, Augustus
Caesar, and command him from us—of whose bounty he hath
received his surname, Augustus—that for a thank-offering to our   210
beneficence he presently sacrifice as a dish to this banquet his
beautiful and wanton daughter, Julia. She's a curst quean,° tell him,
and plays the scold behind his back; therefore, let her be sacrificed.
Command him this, Mercury, in our high name of Jupiter
Altitonans.°   215

JULIA Stay, feather-footed Mercury, and tell Augustus from us, the
great Juno Saturnia,° if he think it hard to do as Jupiter hath
commanded him and sacrifice his daughter, that he had better to do
so ten times than suffer her to love the well-nosed poet, Ovid,
whom he shall do well to whip, or cause to be whipped, about the   220
Capitol, for soothing° her in her follies.

4.6

[*Enter*] *Caesar, Maecenas, Horace, Lupus, Histrio,*
Minos, [*and*] *Lictors*

CAESAR What sight is this? Maecenas, Horace, say:
Have we our senses? Do we hear, and see?
Or are these but imaginary objects
Drawn by our fantasy? Why speak you not?
'Let us do sacrifice?' Are they the gods?   5
Reverence, amaze, and fury fight in me.
          [*Ovid and the rest kneel*]
What? Do they kneel? Nay, then I see 'tis true
I thought impossible—Oh impious sight!
Let me divert mine eyes; the very thought
Everts my soul with passion: look not, man.°   10
There is a panther whose unnatural eyes
Will strike thee dead; turn then, and die on her°
With her own death.
          [*He offers° to kill his daughter*]

MAECENAS, HORACE What means imperial Caesar?

CAESAR What, would you have me let the strumpet live,
That for this pageant earns so many deaths?   15

57

TUCCA Boy, slink, boy.

[1] PYRGUS Pray Jupiter we be not followed by the scent, master.

Exeunt [Tucca and 1 Pyrgus unnoticed]

CAESAR Say, sir, what are you?

ALBIUS I play Vulcan, sir.

CAESAR But what are you, sir?   20

ALBIUS Your citizen, and jeweller, sir.

CAESAR And what are you, dame?

CHLOË I play Venus, forsooth.

CAESAR I ask not what you play, but what you are!

CHLOË Your citizen, and jeweller's wife, sir.   25

CAESAR And you, good sir?

CRISPINUS Your gentleman parcel-poet, sir.

CAESAR Oh, that profanèd name!

[*To Julia*] And are these seemly company for thee,
Degenerate monster? All the rest I know,   30
And hate all knowledge, for their hateful sakes.
Are you, that first the deities inspired
With skill of their high natures and their powers,
The first abusers of their useful light,
Profaning thus their dignities in their forms,   35
And making them, like you, but counterfeits?°
Oh, who shall follow Virtue and embrace her,
When her false bosom is found naught but air?
And yet, of those embraces, centaurs spring,
That war with human peace, and poison men.°   40
Who shall, with greater comforts, comprehend°
Her unseen being and her excellence,
When you, that teach and should eternise her,
Live as she were no law unto your lives—
Nor lived herself, but with your idle breaths?   45
If you think gods but feigned, and virtue painted,
Know we sustain an actual residence,
And with the title of an emperor,
Retain his spirit and imperial power;
By which, in imposition too remiss,   50
Licentious Naso, for thy violent wrong
In soothing the declined affections
Of my base daughter, I exile thy feet
From all approach to our imperial court
On pain of death; and thy misgotten love   55

Commit to patronage of iron doors,
Since her soft-hearted sire cannot contain her.
MAECENAS Oh, good my lord; forgive: be like the gods.
HORACE Let royal bounty, Caesar, mediate.
CAESAR There is no bounty to be showed to such   60
    As have no real goodness. Bounty is
    A spice of virtue: and what virtuous act
    Can take effect on them that have no power
    Of equal habitude to apprehend it,°
    But live in worship of that idol, vice,   65
    As if there were no virtue, but in shade
    Of strong imagination, merely enforced?°
    This shows their knowledge is mere ignorance;
    Their far-fetched dignity of soul, a fancy;
    And all their square pretext of gravity,°   70
    A mere vainglory: hence, away with 'em.
    I will prefer for knowledge none but such
    As rule their lives by it, and can becalm
    All sea of humour with the marble trident
    Of their strong spirits. Others fight below   75
    With gnats and shadows; others nothing know.
    Exeunt

4.7

[Enter] Tucca, Crispinus, [and 1] Pyrgus

TUCCA What's become of my little punk, Venus, and the polt-foot
stinkard, her husband, ha?
CRISPINUS Oh, they are rid home i' the coach as fast as the wheels can
run.
TUCCA God Jupiter is banished, I hear, and his cockatrice, Juno,   5
locked up. 'Heart, and all the poetry in Parnassus get me to be a
player again, I'll sell 'em my share for six pence. But this is
humours—Horace, that goat-footed envious slave, he's turned
fawn° now; an informer, the rogue; 'tis he has betrayed us all. Did
you not see him with the emperor, crouching?   10
CRISPINUS Yes.
TUCCA Well, follow me. Thou shalt libel, and I'll cudgel the rascal.
Boy, provide me a truncheon; revenge shall gratulate him: *tam
Marti, quam Mercurio.*°

[1] PYRGUS Ay, but master, take heed how you give this out; Horace is   15
a man of the sword.

CRISPINUS 'Tis true, in troth; they say he's valiant.

TUCCA Valiant? So is mine arse. Gods and fiends! I'll blow him
into air when I meet him next. He dares not fight with a puck-
fist.   20

[1] PYRGUS Master, here he comes.

      [Horace passes by]

TUCCA Where? [To Horace] Jupiter save thee, my good poet, my
prophet, my noble Horace. [To Crispinus and 1 Pyrgus] I scorn to
beat the rogue i' the court, and I saluted him thus fair because he
should suspect nothing, the rascal. Come, we'll go see how forward   25
our journeyman is toward the untrussing° of him.

CRISPINUS Do you hear, captain? I'll write nothing in it but innocence, because I may swear I am innocent.

      Exeunt

4.[8]

      [Enter Horace, Maecenas, Lupus, Histrio, and Lictors]

HORACE Nay, why pursue you not the emperor
For your reward now, Lupus?

MAECENAS   Stay, Asinius,
You and your stager, and your band of lictors:
I hope your service merits more respect
Than thus, without a thanks, to be sent hence?   5

LUPUS Well, well, jest on, jest on.

HORACE Thou base, unworthy groom.

LUPUS   Ay, 'tis good.

HORACE Was this the treason? This, the dangerous plot
Thy clamorous tongue so bellowed through the court?
Hadst thou no other project to increase   10
Thy grace with Caesar but this wolfish train,°
To prey upon the life of innocent mirth
And harmless pleasures, bred of noble wit?
Away—I loath thy presence. Such as thou,
They are the moths and scarabs of a state;   15
The bane of kingdoms, and the dregs of courts;
Who, to endear themselves to any employment,

Care not whose fame they blast, whose life they endanger;
And under a disguised and cobweb mask
Of love unto their sovereign, vomit forth   20
Their own prodigious malice; and pretending
To be the props and columns of his safety,
The guards unto his person and his peace,
Disturb it most, with their false lapwing cries.
LUPUS Good. Caesar shall know of this; believe it.   25
          Exeunt [Lupus, Histrio, and Lictors]
MAECENAS Caesar doth know it, wolf, and to his knowledge,
He will, I hope, reward your base endeavours.
Princes that will but hear, or give access
To such officious spies, can ne'er be safe:
They take in poison with an open ear,   30
And, free from danger, become slaves to fear.°
          Exeunt

4.[9]

          [Enter] Ovid
OVID Banished the court? Let me be banished life,
Since the chief end of life is there concluded.°
Within the court is all the kingdom bounded,
And as her sacred sphere doth comprehend
Ten thousand times so much as so much place   5
In any part of all the empire else,
So every body moving in her sphere
Contains ten thousand times as much in him
As any other her choice orb excludes.
As in a circle, a magician then   10
Is safe against the spirit he excites,
But out of it, is subject to his rage
And loseth all the virtue of his art,
So I, exiled the circle of the court,
Lose all the good gifts that in it I joyed.°   15
No virtue current is, but with her stamp,
Nor no vice vicious, blanched with her white hand.
The court's the abstract of all Rome's desert,
And my dear Julia, the abstract of the court.

Methinks, now I come near her, I respire   20
Some air of that late comfort I received;
And while the evening, with her modest veil,
Gives leave to such poor shadows as myself°
To steal abroad, I, like a heartless ghost,
Without the living body of my love,   25
Will here walk and attend her. For I know
Not far from hence she is imprisonèd,
And hopes, of her strict guardian, to bribe
So much admittance as to speak to me,
And cheer my fainting spirits with her breath.   30

4.[10]

[Enter] Julia. [She appears above, as at her chamber window.]

JULIA Ovid? My love?

OVID   Here, heavenly Julia.

JULIA Here? And not here? Oh, how that word doth play
    With both our fortunes, differing like ourselves;
    Both one, and yet divided, as opposed:
    I high, thou low. Oh, this our plight of place   5
    Doubly presents the two lets of our love,
    Local and ceremonial height and lowness:°
    Both ways I am too high, and thou, too low.
    Our minds are even, yet. Oh, why should our bodies,
    That are their slaves, be so without their rule?   10
    I'll cast myself down to thee: if I die,
    I'll ever live with thee; no height of birth,
    Of place, of duty, or of cruel power,
    Shall keep me from thee. Should my father lock
    This body up within a tomb of brass,   15
    Yet I'll be with thee. If the forms I hold
    Now in my soul be made one substance with it,
    That soul immortal, and the same 'tis now,
    Death cannot raze th' affects she now retaineth;°
    And then may she be anywhere she will.   20
    The souls of parents rule not children's souls
    When death sets both in their dissolved estates;

Then is no child, nor father; then eternity
Frees all from any temporal respect.
I come, my Ovid: take me in thine arms,   25
And let me breathe my soul into thy breast.
OVID   O stay, my love! The hopes thou dost conceive
  Of thy quick death, and of thy future life,
  Are not authentical. Thou choosest death
  So thou mightst joy thy love in th' other life.   30
  But know, my princely love, when thou art dead,
  Thou only must survive in perfect soul,
  And in the soul are no affections;°
  We pour out our affections with our blood,
  And with our blood's affections, fade our loves.   35
  No life hath love in such sweet state as this;
  No essence is so dear to moody sense
  As flesh and blood, whose quintessence is sense.
  Beauty, composed of blood and flesh, moves more,
  And is more plausible to blood and flesh,°   40
  Than spiritual beauty can be to the spirit.
  Such apprehension as we have in dreams,
  When sleep, the bond of senses, locks them up,
  Such shall we have, when death destroys them quite.
  If love be then thy object, change not life: 45
  Live high, and happy still; I still below,
  Close with my fortunes, in thy height shall joy.
JULIA   Ay me, that virtue, whose brave eagle's wings
  With every stroke blow stars in burning heaven,
  Should, like a swallow, preying toward storms,   50
  Fly close to earth, and with an eager plume
  Pursue those objects which none else can see,
  But seem to all the world the empty air.
  Thus thou, poor Ovid, and all virtuous men,
  Must prey like swallows on invisible food,   55
  Pursuing flies, or nothing; and thus love,
  And every worldly fancy, is transposed
  By worldly tyranny to what plight it list.
  O father, since thou gav'st me not my mind,
  Strive not to rule it. Take but what thou gav'st   60
  To thy disposure; thy affections
  Rule not in me. I must bear all my griefs,
  Let me use all my pleasures: virtuous love

Was never scandal to a goddess' state.
But he's inflexible and, my dear love,   65
Thy life may chance be shortened by the length
Of my unwilling speeches to depart.
Farewell, sweet life. Though thou be yet exiled
Th' officious court, enjoy me amply still;
My soul, in this my breath, enters thine ears,   70
And on this turret's floor will I lie dead
Till we may meet again. In this proud height
I kneel beneath thee in my prostrate love,
And kiss the happy sands that kiss thy feet.
Great Jove submits a sceptre to a cell,°   75
And lovers, ere they part, will meet in hell.
OVID Farewell all company, and, if I could,
    All light with thee. Hell's shade should hide my brows
    Till thy dear beauty's beams redeemed my vows.
        [*Ovid turns to leave. She calls him back.*]
JULIA Ovid, my love; alas, may we not stay   80
    A little longer, think'st thou, undiscerned?
OVID For thine own good, fair goddess, do not stay:
    Who would engage a firmament of fires
    Shining in thee, for me, a falling star?
    Be gone, sweet life-blood; if I should discern   85
    Thyself but touched for my sake, I should die.
JULIA I will be gone then, and not heaven itself
    Shall draw me back.
        [*She turns to leave. He calls her back.*]
OVID   Yet Julia, if thou wilt,
    A little longer stay.
JULIA   I am content.
OVID O mighty Ovid! What the sway of heaven   90
    Could not retire, my breath hath turnèd back.°
JULIA Who shall go first, my love? My passionate eyes
    Will not endure to see thee turn from me.
OVID If thou go first, my soul will follow thee.
JULIA Then we must stay.
OVID   Ay me, there is no stay   95
    In amorous pleasures: if both stay, both die.°
    I hear thy father—hence, my deity!
        Exit Julia
Fear forgeth sounds in my deluded ears;

I did not hear him, I am mad with love.
There is no spirit under heaven that works   100
With such illusion; yet such witchcraft kill me
Ere a sound mind, without it, save my life.
Here, on my knees, I worship the blest place
That held my goddess, and the loving air
That closed her body in his silken arms.   105
Vain Ovid—kneel not to the place, nor air:
She's in thy heart. Rise then, and worship there.
The truest wisdom silly men can have°
Is dotage on the follies of their flesh.
    Exit

5.1

[*Enter*] *Caesar, Maecenas, Gallus, Tibullus,*
[*and*] *Horace*°

CAESAR We that have conquered still to save the conquered,°
    And loved to make inflictions feared, not felt,
    Grieved to reprove, and joyful to reward,
    More proud of reconcilement than revenge,
    Resume into the late state of our love,   5
    Worthy Cornelius Gallus, and Tibullus:°
    You both are knights; and you, Cornelius,
    A soldier of renown, and the first provost
    That ever let our Roman eagles fly
    On swarthy Egypt, quarried with her spoils.°   10
    Yet (not to bear cold forms, nor men's out-terms,
    Without the inward fires and lives of men)
    You both have virtues shining through your shapes
    To show your titles are not writ on posts
    Or hollow statues, which the best men are,   15
    Without Promethean stuffings reached from heaven.°
    Sweet poesy's sacred garlands crown your knighthoods,
    Which is, of all the faculties on earth,°
    The most abstract and perfect, if she be
    True born and nursed with all the sciences.   20
    She can so mould Rome and her monuments
    Within the liquid marble of her lines,
    That they shall stand fresh and miraculous,
    Even when they mix with innovating dust;°
    In her sweet streams shall our brave Roman spirits   25
    Chase and swim after death, with their choice deeds
    Shining on their white shoulders; and therein
    Shall Tiber and our famous rivers fall
    With such attraction, that th' ambitious line
    Of the round world shall to her centre shrink   30
    To hear their music. And for these high parts,
    Caesar shall reverence the Pierian arts.°
MAECENAS Your Majesty's high grace to poesy
    Shall stand 'gainst all the dull detractions

Of leaden souls, who (for the vain assumings° 35
Of some, quite worthless of her sovereign wreaths)
Contain her worthiest prophets in contempt.°
GALLUS Happy is Rome of all earth's other states,
To have so true and great a precedent°
For her inferior spirits to imitate 40
As Caesar is; who addeth to the sun
Influence and lustre, in increasing thus
His inspirations, kindling fire in us.
HORACE Phoebus himself shall kneel at Caesar's shrine
And deck it with bay garlands dewed with wine 45
To quit the worship Caesar does to him,°
Where other princes, hoisted to their thrones°
By Fortune's passionate and disordered power,
Sit in their height, like clouds before the sun,
Hind'ring his comforts, and by their excess° 50
Of cold in virtue and cross heat in vice,
Thunder and tempest on those learned heads,
Whom Caesar with such honour doth advance.
TIBULLUS All human business, Fortune doth command
Without all order; and with her blind hand, 55
She, blind, bestows blind gifts, that still have nursed
They see not who, nor how, but still the worst.
CAESAR Caesar, for his rule, and for so much stuff
As Fortune puts in his hand, shall dispose it—
As if his hand had eyes and soul in it— 60
With worth and judgement. Hands that part with gifts,
Or will restrain their use without desert,
Or with a misery numbed to virtue's right,°
Work as they had no soul to govern them,
And quite reject her, severing their estates 65
From human order. Whosoever can
And will not cherish virtue is no man.
          [*Enter one of the Equites Romani*]
[1] EQUES Virgil is now at hand, imperial Caesar.
CAESAR Rome's honour is at hand then. Fetch a chair
And set it on our right hand, where 'tis fit 70
Rome's honour, and our own, should ever sit.
          [*1 Eques sets the chair, and exits*]
Now he is come out of Campania,°
I doubt not he hath finished all his *Aeneids*,

67

Which, like another soul, I long t' enjoy.
   [*To Maecenas, Gallus, and Tibullus*]
What think you three of Virgil, gentlemen,   75
That are of his profession, though ranked higher?°
Or Horace, what sayest thou, that art the poorest,
And likeliest to envy or to detract?°
HORACE Caesar speaks after common men in this,
   To make a difference of me for my poorness;   80
   As if the filth of poverty sunk as deep
   Into a knowing spirit, as the bane
   Of riches doth, into an ignorant soul.
   No, Caesar, they be pathless, moorish minds,°
   That being once made rotten with the dung   85
   Of damnèd riches, ever after sink
   Beneath the steps of any villainy.
   But knowledge is the nectar that keeps sweet
   A perfect soul even in this grave of sin;
   And for my soul, it is as free as Caesar's: 90
   For what I know is due, I'll give to all.
   He that detracts or envies virtuous merit
   Is still the covetous and the ignorant spirit.°
CAESAR Thanks, Horace, for thy free and wholesome sharpness,
   Which pleaseth Caesar more than servile fawns.   95
   A flattered prince soon turns the prince of fools.
   And for thy sake, we'll put no difference more
   'Twixt knights, and knightly spirits, for being poor.
   Say then, loved Horace, thy true thought of Virgil.
HORACE I judge him of a rectified spirit,°   100
   By many revolutions of discourse
   In his bright reason's influence, refined
   From all the tartarous moods of common men;°
   Bearing the nature and similitude
   Of a right heavenly body; most severe   105
   In fashion and collection of himself;
   And then as clear and confident as Jove.
GALLUS And yet so chaste and tender is his ear
   In suffering any syllable to pass
   That he thinks may become the honoured name   110
   Of issue to his so examined self,
   That all the lasting fruits of his full merit
   In his own poems he doth still distaste:

As if his mind's piece, which he strove to paint,
Could not with fleshly pencils have her right.   115
TIBULLUS But to approve his works of sovereign worth,
. This observation, methinks, more than serves,
And is not vulgar: that which he hath writ,
Is with such judgement laboured and distilled
Through all the needful uses of our lives,   120
That could a man remember but his lines,
He should not touch at any serious point,
But he might breathe his spirit out of him.°
CAESAR You mean he might repeat part of his works,
As fit for any conference he can use?°   125
TIBULLUS True, royal Caesar.
CAESAR   'Tis worthily observed,
And a most worthy virtue in his works.
What thinks material Horace of his learning?°
HORACE His learning labours not the school-like gloss
That most consists in echoing words and terms   130
And soonest wins a man an empty name,
Nor any long or far-fetched circumstance
Wrapped in the curious generalties of arts,
But a direct and analytic sum
Of all the worth and first effects of arts.   135
And for his poesy, 'tis so rammed with life
That it shall gather strength of life with being,
And live hereafter more admired, than now.
CAESAR This one consent in all your dooms of him,°
And mutual loves of all your several merits,   140
Argues a truth of merit in you all.

5.2

[*Enter*] *Virgil* [*with*] *Equites Ro*[*mani*]
CAESAR See, here comes Virgil; we will rise and greet him.
Welcome to Caesar, Virgil. Caesar and Virgil
Shall differ but in sound; to Caesar, Virgil
(Of his expressed greatness) shall be made
A second surname; and to Virgil, Caesar.   5
Where are thy famous *Aeneids*? Do us grace

To let us see, and surfeit on their sight.
VIRGIL Worthless they are of Caesar's gracious eyes
   If they were perfect; much more, with their wants,
   Which yet are more than my time could supply;   10
   And could great Caesar's expectation
   Be satisfied with any other service,
   I would not show them.
CAESAR   Virgil is too modest,
   Or seeks, in vain, to make our longings more.
   Show them, sweet Virgil.
VIRGIL   Then, in such due fear   15
   As fits presenters of great works to Caesar,
   I humbly show them—
      [*He gives a copy of the poem to Caesar*]
CAESAR   Let us now behold
   A human soul made visible in life,
   And more refulgent in a senseless paper
   Than in the sensual complement of kings.°   20
   Read, read thyself, dear Virgil, let not me
   Profane one accent with an untuned tongue:
   Best matter, badly shown, shows worse than bad.
   See then this chair, of purpose set for thee
   To read thy poem in: refuse it not.   25
   Virtue, without presumption, place may take
   Above best kings, whom only she should make.
VIRGIL It will be thought a thing ridiculous
   To present eyes, and to all future times
   A gross untruth, that any poet, void   30
   Of birth, or wealth, or temporal dignity,
   Should with decorum transcend Caesar's chair.
   Poor virtue raised, high birth and wealth set under,
   Crosseth heaven's courses, and makes worldlings wonder.
CAESAR The course of heaven and fate itself in this   35
   Will Caesar cross, much more all worldly custom.
HORACE Custom, in course of honour, ever errs;
   And they are best, whom fortune least prefers.°
CAESAR Horace hath, but more strictly, spoke our thoughts.
   The vast rude swinge of general confluence   40
   Is, in particular ends, exempt from sense;°
   And therefore reason (which in right should be
   The special rector of all harmony)

Shall show we are a man, distinct by it,
From those that custom rapteth in her press.   45
Ascend then, Virgil, and where first by chance
We here have turned thy book, do thou first read.
VIRGIL Great Caesar hath his will: I will ascend.
'Twere simple injury to his free hand,
That sweeps the cobwebs from unusèd virtue   50
And makes her shine proportioned to her worth,
To be more nice to entertain his grace,°
Than he is choice and liberal to afford it.
CAESAR Gentlemen of our chamber, guard the doors,°
And let none enter. Peace. Begin, good Virgil.   55
VIRGIL [reads]
Meanwhile the skies 'gan thunder, and in tail
Of that, fell pouring storms of sleet and hail:°
The Tyrian lords and Trojan youth, each where°
With Venus' Dardan nephew, now in fear°
Seek out for several shelter through the plain,   60
Whilst floods come rolling from the hills amain.
Dido a cave, the Trojan prince the same°
Lighted upon. There Earth, and heaven's great dame
That hath the charge of marriage, first gave sign°
Unto this contract; fire and air did shine   65
As guilty of the match; and from the hill,
The nymphs with shriekings do the region fill.
Here first began their bane; this day was ground
Of all their ills. For now, nor rumour's sound,
Nor nice respect of state moves Dido aught;°   70
Her love no longer now by stealth is sought:
She calls this wedlock, and with that fair name
Covers her fault. Forthwith the bruit and fame°
Through all the greatest Lybian towns is gone:
Fame, a fleet evil, than which is swifter none;   75
That moving grows, and flying gathers strength;
Little at first, and fearful, but at length
She dares attempt the skies, and stalking proud
With feet on ground, her head doth pierce a cloud.
This child our parent Earth, stirred up with spite   80
Of all the gods, brought forth; and as some write,
She was last sister of that giant race
That thought to scale Jove's court: right swift of pace,°

And swifter far of wing, a monster vast
And dreadful. Look how many plumes are placed   85
On her huge corpse, so many waking eyes°
Stick underneath; and (which may stranger rise
In the report) as many tongues she bears,
As many mouths, as many listening ears.
Nightly, in midst of all the heaven, she flies,   90
And through the earth's dark shadow, shrieking, cries;
Nor do her eyes once bend to taste sweet sleep:
By day, on tops of houses she doth keep,
Or on high towers, and doth thence affright
Cities and towns of most conspicuous site.   95
As covetous she is of tales and lies,
As prodigal of truth. This monster—
  [*He is interrupted by shouting off-stage*]

5.3

  [*Enter, upstage and unseen by Caesar,*]° *Lupus, Tucca,*
  [*and*] *Lictors,* [*held back by*] *Equites Ro*[*mani*]

LUPUS Come, follow me, assist me, second me! Where's the emperor?
I EQUES Sir, you must pardon us.
2 EQUES Caesar is private now, you may not enter.
TUCCA Not enter? Charge 'em upon their allegiance, cropshin.
I EQUES We have a charge to the contrary, sir.   5
LUPUS I pronounce you all traitors, horrible traitors! What? Do you
  know my affairs? I have matter of danger and state to impart to
  Caesar.
CAESAR What noise is there? Who's that names Caesar?
LUPUS A friend to Caesar! One that for Caesar's good would speak   10
  with Caesar.
CAESAR Who is 't? Look, Cornelius.
I EQUES Asinius Lupus.
CAESAR Oh, bid the turbulent informer hence.
  We have no vacant ear now to receive   15
  The unseasoned fruits of his officious tongue.
MAECENAS [*to I Eques*] You must avoid° him there.
LUPUS I conjure thee, as thou art Caesar, or respect'st thine own
  safety, or the safety of the state, Caesar: hear me, speak with me,

Caesar! 'Tis no common business I come about, but such as, being   20
neglected, may concern the life of Caesar.

CAESAR The life of Caesar? Let him enter. Virgil, keep thy seat.

EQUITES Bear back there—whither will you?° Keep back!
    [*Lupus, Tucca, and Lictors approach*]

TUCCA [*to 1 Eques*] By thy leave, goodman usher; mend thy periwig, so.

LUPUS Lay hold on Horace there, and on Maecenas, lictors. Romans,   25
offer no rescue, upon your allegiance.
    [*Giving Caesar a paper*]
Read, royal Caesar. [*To Horace*] I'll tickle you, satire.

TUCCA He will, humours, he will; he will squeeze you, poet puck-fist.

LUPUS I'll lop you off for an unprofitable branch, you satirical varlet.

TUCCA Ay, and Epaminondas,° your patron here, with his flagon   30
chain. [*To Maecenas*] Come, resign: though 'twere your great
grandfather's, the law has made it mine now, sir.
    [*He takes the chain*]
Look to him, my parti-coloured° rascals; look to him.

CAESAR What is this, Asinius Lupus? I understand it not.

LUPUS Not understand it? A libel,° Caesar. A dangerous, seditious   35
libel. A libel in picture.

CAESAR A libel?

LUPUS Ay, I found it in this Horace his study, in Maecenas his house
here: I challenge the penalty of the laws against 'em.

TUCCA Ay, and remember to beg their land betimes,° before some of   40
these hungry court-hounds scent it out.

CAESAR [*to 1 Eques*] Show it to Horace. Ask him if he know it.

LUPUS Know it? His hand° is at it, Caesar.

CAESAR Then 'tis no libel.

HORACE It is the imperfect body of an emblem,° Caesar, I began for   45
Maecenas.

LUPUS An emblem? Right—that's Greek for a libel. Do but mark how
confident he is.

HORACE A just man cannot fear, thou foolish tribune,
Not though the malice of traducing tongues,   50
The open vastness of a tyrant's ear,
The senseless rigour of the wrested laws,
Or the red eyes of strained authority
Should, in a point, meet all to take his life:
His innocence is armour 'gainst all these.   55

LUPUS Innocence? Oh impudence!
    [*Taking the paper*]

Let me see, let me see. Is not here an eagle? And is not that eagle
meant by Caesar? Ha? Does not Caesar give the eagle? Answer me;
what say'st thou?

TUCCA Hast thou any evasion, stinkard?   60

LUPUS Now he's turned dumb. I'll tickle you, satire.

HORACE Pish. Ha! Ha!°

LUPUS Dost thou pish me? [*To 1 Lictor*] Give me my long sword.

HORACE With reverence to great Caesar, worthy Romans,
Observe but this ridiculous commenter.   65
The soul to my device was in this distich:
> Thus oft the base and ravenous multitude
> Survive to share the spoils of fortitude.

Which in this body I have figured here
A vulture—   70

LUPUS A vulture? Ay, now 'tis a vulture. Oh, abominable! Monstrous!
Monstrous! Has not your vulture a beak? Has it not legs? And
talons? And wings? And feathers?

TUCCA Touch him, old buskins.

HORACE And therefore must it be an eagle?   75

MAECENAS Respect him not, good Horace. Say your device.

HORACE A vulture and a wolf—

LUPUS A wolf? Good. That's I, I am the wolf: my name's Lupus; I am
meant by the wolf. On, on: a vulture and a wolf—

HORACE Preying upon the carcass of an ass—   80

LUPUS An ass? Good still; that's I, too.° I am the ass. You mean me by
the ass.

MAECENAS Pray thee, leave braying then.

HORACE If you will needs take it, I cannot with modesty give it from
you.   85

MAECENAS But by that beast the old Egyptians
Were wont to figure in their hieroglyphics
Patience, frugality, and fortitude,
For none of which we can suspect you, tribune.

CAESAR Who was it, Lupus, that informed you first   90
This should be meant by us? Or was 't your comment?°

LUPUS No, Caesar. A player gave me the first light of it, indeed.

TUCCA Ay, an honest sycophant-like slave, and a politician besides.

CAESAR Where is that player?

TUCCA He is without here.   95

CAESAR Call him in.

TUCCA Call in the player there, Master Aesop,° call him.

EQUITES Player? Where is the player?
    [*Enter Histrio, followed by Crispinus and Demetrius*]
  Bear back! None but the player enter.
TUCCA Yes, this gent'man and his Achates° must.   100
CRISPINUS Pray you, master usher; we'll stand close here.
TUCCA [*indicating Crispinus*] 'Tis a gent'man of quality, this, though
  he be somewhat out of clothes, I tell ye. Come, Aesop, hast a bay-
  leaf i' thy mouth?° Well said; be not out, stinkard. Thou shalt have
  a monopoly of playing confirmed to thee and thy covey under the   105
  emperor's broad seal° for this service.
CAESAR Is this he?
LUPUS Ay, Caesar—this is he.
CAESAR Let him be whipped.° Lictors, go, take him hence.
    [*Exeunt some of the Lictors with Histrio*]
  And Lupus, for your fierce credulity,   110
  One fit him with a pair of larger ears.°
  'Tis Caesar's doom, and must not be revoked.°
  We hate to have our court and peace disturbed
  With these quotidian clamours. [*To 1 Eques*] See it done.
LUPUS Caesar!   115
CAESAR Gag him, we may have his silence.
    [*Equites gag Lupus and exeunt*]
VIRGIL Caesar hath done like Caesar. Fair and just
  Is his award against these brainless creatures.
  'Tis not the wholesome sharp morality
  Or modest anger of a satiric spirit   120
  That hurts or wounds the body of a state,
  But the sinister application
  Of the malicious, ignorant, and base
  Interpreter, who will distort and strain
  The general scope and purpose of an author   125
  To his particular and private spleen.
CAESAR We know it, our dear Virgil, and esteem it
  A most dishonest practice in that man
  Will seem too witty in another's work.
  What would Cornelius Gallus and Tibullus?   130
    [*This while Gallus and Tibullus whisper to Caesar*]
TUCCA [*to Maecenas*] Nay, but as thou art a man, dost hear? A man of
  worship, and honourable: hold, here, take thy chain again. Resume,
  mad Maecenas. What? Dost thou think I meant t' have kept it, old
  boy? No, I did it but to fright thee, I; to try how thou wouldst take

it. What? Will I turn shark upon my friends? Or my friends'   135
friends? I scorn it with my three souls. Come, I love bully Horace as
well as thou dost, I—'tis an honest hieroglyphic. Give me thy wrist,
Helicon. Dost thou think I'll second e'er a rhinoceros of them all
against thee? ha? Or thy noble Hippocrene° here? I'll turn stager
first, and be whipped, too; dost thou see, bully?   140

CAESAR You have your will of Caesar; use it, Romans.
Virgil shall be your praetor, and ourself°
Will here sit by, spectator of your sports,
And think it no impeach of royalty.
[*To Virgil*] Our ear is now too much profaned, grave Maro,°   145
With these distastes, to take thy sacred lines.
Put up thy book till both the time and we
Be fitted with more hallowed circumstance
For the receiving so divine a labour.
[*To Gallus, Tibullus, and Maecenas*]
Proceed with your design.

MAECENAS, GALLUS, TIBULLUS Thanks to great Caesar.   150

GALLUS Tibullus, draw you the indictment then, whilst Horace
arrests them on the statute of calumny. Maecenas and I will take
our places here. Lictors, assist him.

HORACE I am the worst accuser under heaven.

GALLUS Tut, you must do't; 'twill be noble mirth.   155

HORACE I take no knowledge that they do malign me.°

TIBULLUS Ay, but the world takes knowledge.

HORACE   Would the world knew
How heartily I wish a fool should hate me.

TUCCA [*aside*] Body of Jupiter! What, will they arraign my brisk
poetaster and his poor journeyman? ha? Would I were abroad   160
skeldering for twopence, so I were out of this labyrinth again; I do
feel myself turn stinkard already. But I must set the best face I
have upon 't now—Well said, my divine, deft Horace! Bring the
whoreson detracting slaves to the bar, do. Make 'em hold up their
spread golls;° I'll give in evidence for thee, if thou wilt. [*Aside to*   165
Crispinus] Take courage, Crispinus. Would thy man had a clean
band.°

CRISPINUS [*aside to Tucca*] What must we do, captain?

TUCCA [*aside to Crispinus*] Thou shalt see anon. Do not make division
with thy legs so.°   170

CAESAR [*indicating Tucca*] What's he, Horace?

HORACE I only know him for a motion, Caesar.

TUCCA I am one of thy commanders, Caesar; a man of service and
action. My name is Pantilius Tucca: I have served i' thy wars
against Mark Antony, I.   175

CAESAR Do you know him, Cornelius?

GALLUS He's one that hath had the mustering or convoy of a company now and then; I never noted him by any other employment.

CAESAR We will observe him better.

TIBULLUS Lictor, proclaim silence in the court.   180

(1) LICTOR In the name of Caesar: silence!

TIBULLUS Let the parties, the accuser and the accused, present
themselves.

(1) LICTOR The accuser and the accused: present yourselves in court.

CRISPINUS, DEMETRIUS Here.   185

VIRGIL Read the indictment.

TIBULLUS [*reading*] Rufus Laberius Crispinus and Demetrius Fannius, hold up your hands. You are before this time jointly and
severally° indicted, and here presently to be arraigned upon the
statute of calumny, or *lex Remmia*° (the one by the name of Rufus   190
Laberius Crispinus, alias Crispinus, poetaster and plagiary; the
other by the name of Demetrius Fannius, play-dresser and plagiary) that you, not having the fear of Phoebus or his shafts before
your eyes, contrary to the peace of our liege lord, Augustus Caesar,
his crown and dignity, and against the form of a statute in that case   195
made and provided, have most ignorantly, foolishly, and (more like
yourselves) maliciously gone about to deprave° and calumniate the
person and writings of Quintus Horatius Flaccus, here present,
poet, and priest to the Muses. And to that end have mutually conspired and plotted, at sundry times, as by several means, and in   200
sundry places, for the better accomplishing your base and envious
purpose; taxing him falsely of self-love, arrogancy, impudence, railing, filching by translation, etc. Of all which calumnies, and every
of them, in manner and form aforesaid, what answer you? Are you
guilty, or not guilty?   205

TUCCA [*aside to Crispinus and Demetrius*] Not guilty, say.

CRISPINUS, DEMETRIUS Not guilty.

TIBULLUS How will you be tried?

TUCCA [*aside to Crispinus and Demetrius*] By the Roman gods, and the
noblest Romans.   210

CRISPINUS, DEMETRIUS By the Roman gods, and the noblest Romans.

VIRGIL Here sits Maecenas and Cornelius Gallus.
Are you contented to be tried by these?

77

TUCCA [*aside to Crispinus and Demetrius*] Ay, so the noble captain may
be joined with them in commission, say.   215

CRISPINUS, DEMETRIUS Ay, so the noble captain may be joined with
them in commission.

VIRGIL What says the plaintiff?

HORACE I am content.

VIRGIL Captain, then take your place.   220

TUCCA Alas, my worshipful praetor! 'Tis more of thy gent'ness than
of my deserving, iwis. But since it hath pleased the court to make
choice of my wisdom and gravity, come, my calumnious varlets,
let's hear you talk for yourselves now, an hour or two. What can you
say? Make a noise. Act, act!   225

VIRGIL [*to Tucca, Maecenas, and Gallus*] Stay—turn and take
an oath first. You shall swear
By thunder-darting Jove, the king of gods,
And by the genius of Augustus Caesar,°
By your own white and uncorrupted souls,
And the deep reverence of our Roman justice,   230
To judge this case with truth and equity,
As bound by your religion and your laws.
[*They nod assent*]
Now read the evidence; but first demand
Of either prisoner if that writ be theirs.

TIBULLUS [*giving the papers to 1 Lictor*] Show this unto   235
Crispinus. Is it yours?

TUCCA Say ay. What? Dost thou stand upon it, pimp? Do not deny
thine own Minerva, thy Pallas, the issue of thy brain.°

CRISPINUS Yes, it is mine.

TIBULLUS [*to 1 Lictor*] Show that unto Demetrius. Is it yours?   240

DEMETRIUS It is.

TUCCA There's a father will not deny his own bastard now, I warrant
thee.

VIRGIL Read them aloud.

TIBULLUS [*reads*] 'Ramp up, my genius, be not retrograde,   245
    But boldly nominate a spade, a spade.°
    What, shall thy lubrical and glibbery Muse°
    Live as she were defunct, like punk in stews?'

TUCCA [*aside*] Excellent.

TIBULLUS   'Alas! That were no modern consequence,°   250
    To have cothurnal buskins frighted hence.
    No, teach thy incubus to poetize,°

78

And throw abroad thy spurious snotteries°
                Upon that puffed-up lump of barmy froth—'°
TUCCA [*aside*] Ah ha!   255
TIBULLUS 'Or clumsy chilblained judgement, that with oath
                Magnificates his merit, and bespawls°
                The conscious time with humorous foam and brawls,
                As if his organons of sense would crack°
                The sinews of my patience. Break his back,   260
                O poets, all and some: for now we list
                Of strenuous veng-èance to clutch the fist.°
                Subscribed Crispinus; alias, Innocence.'
TUCCA Ay, marry, this was written like a Hercules in poetry, now.
CAESAR Excellently well threatened.   265
VIRGIL Ay, and as strangely worded, Caesar.
CAESAR We observe it.
VIRGIL [*to Tibullus*] The other now.
TUCCA This's a fellow of a good prodigal tongue, too; this'll do well.
TIBULLUS [*reads*] 'Our Muse is in mind for th' untrussing a poet;   270
                I slip by his name, for most men do know it:
                A critic that all the world bescumbers°
                With satirical humours, and lyrical numbers—'
TUCCA [*aside*] Art thou there, boy?
TIBULLUS 'And for the most part, himself doth advance   275
                With much self-love, and more arrogance—'
TUCCA [*aside*] Good again.
TIBULLUS 'And, but that I would not be thought a prater,
                I could tell you he were a translator.°
                I know the authors from whence he has stole,   280
                And could trace him, too, but that I understand
                'em not full and whole.'
TUCCA [*aside*] That line is broke loose from all his fellows; chain him
        up shorter, do.
TIBULLUS 'The best note I can give you to know him by,
                Is that he keeps gallants company;   285
                Whom, I would wish, in time should him fear,
                Lest after they buy repentance too dear.
                Subscribed Demetrius Fannius.'
TUCCA Well said. This carries palm with it.°
HORACE And why, thou motley gull? Why should they fear?   290
        When hast thou known us wrong or tax a friend?
        I dare thy malice to betray it. Speak.

Now thou curl'st up, thou poor and nasty snake,
And shrink'st thy pois'nous head into thy bosom.°
Out, viper, thou that eat'st thy parents, hence!°   295
Rather, such speckled creatures as thyself
Should be eschewed and shunned—such as will bite
And gnaw their absent friends, not cure their fame;°
Catch at the loosest laughters, and affect
To be thought jesters; such, as can devise   300
Things never seen or heard, t' impair men's names
And gratify their credulous adversaries;
Will carry tales, do basest offices,
Cherish divided fires, and increase
New flames out of old embers; will reveal   305
Each secret that's committed to their trust:
These be black slaves. Romans, take heed of these.

TUCCA   Thou twang'st right, little Horace, they be, indeed: a couple of
chap-fallen curs. Come, we of the bench, let's rise to the urn° and
condemn 'em quickly.   310

VIRGIL   Before you go together, worthy Romans,
We are to tender our opinion,
And give you those instructions that may add
Unto your even judgement in the cause,
Which thus we do commence. First, you must know   315
That where there is a true and perfect merit
There can be no dejection; and the scorn°
Of humble baseness oftentimes so works
In a high soul upon the grosser spirit,
That to his blearèd and offended sense,   320
There seems a hideous fault blazed in the object,
When only the disease is in his eyes.°
Here-hence it comes our Horace now stands taxed
Of impudence, self-love, and arrogance
By these who share no merit in themselves,   325
And therefore think his portion is as small.
For they, from their own guilt, assure their souls
If they should confidently praise their works,
In them it would appear inflation;
Which, in a full and well-digested man,°   330
Cannot receive that foul abusive name,
But the fair title of erection.°
And, for his true use of translating men,

It still hath been a work of as much palm
In clearest judgements, as t'invent, or make.   335
His sharpness, that is most excusable,
As being forced out of a suffering virtue
Oppressèd with the licence of the time.
And howsoever fools or jerking pedants,°
Players, or such like buffoonery wits,   340
May with their beggarly and barren trash
Tickle base vulgar ears in their despite,°
This, like Jove's thunder, shall their pride control:
The honest satire hath the happiest soul.°
Now, Romans, you have heard our thoughts. Withdraw when you   345
please.

TIBULLUS Remove the accused from the bar.

TUCCA Who holds the urn to us, ha? [*Aside to Crispinus and Demetrius*]
Fear nothing—I'll quit° you, mine honest pitiful stinkards. I'll do 't.

CRISPINUS [*aside to Tucca*] Captain, you shall eternally girt me to   350
you, as I am generous.

TUCCA [*aside*] Go to.

CAESAR Tibullus, let there be a case of vizards° privately provided;
we have found a subject to bestow them on.

TIBULLUS It shall be done, Caesar.   355

CAESAR Here be words, Horace, able to bastinado a man's ears.

HORACE Ay. Please it, great Caesar, I have pills about me,
Mixed with the whitest kind of hellebore,
Would give him a light vomit that should purge
His brain and stomach of those tumorous heats,°   360
Might I have leave to minister unto him.°

CAESAR O, be as Aesculapius, gentle Horace!
You shall have leave, and he shall be your patient.
Virgil, use your authority, command him forth.

VIRGIL Caesar is careful of your health, Crispinus,   365
And hath himself chose a physician
To minister unto you: take his pills.

HORACE [*giving Crispinus a pill*] They are somewhat bitter,
but wholesome;
Take another yet, so. Stand by, they'll work anon.

TIBULLUS Romans, return to your several seats. Lictors,   370
Bring forward the urn, and set the accused at the bar.

TUCCA Quickly, you whoreson egregious varlets, come forward.
What, shall we sit all day upon you? You make no more haste now

than a beggar upon pattens, or a physician to a patient that has no
money, you pilchers.   375

TIBULLUS Rufus Laberius Crispinus and Demetrius Fannius, hold
up your hands. You have, according to the Roman custom, put
yourselves upon trial to the urn for divers and sundry calumnies,
whereof you have before this time been indicted, and are now presently arraigned. Prepare yourselves to hearken to the verdict of   380
your triers. Caius Cilnius Maecenas pronounceth you, by this
handwriting, guilty. Cornelius Gallus, guilty. Pantilius Tucca—

TUCCA Parcel-guilty,° I.

DEMETRIUS He means himself, for it was he, indeed,
Suborned us to the calumny.   385

TUCCA I, you whoreson *cantharides*?° Was 't I?

DEMETRIUS I appeal to your conscience, captain.

TIBULLUS Then you confess it now.

DEMETRIUS I do, and crave the mercy of the court.

TIBULLUS What saith Crispinus?   390

CRISPINUS [*groaning*] Oh, the captain, the captain.

HORACE My physic begins to work with my patient, I see.

VIRGIL Captain, stand forth and answer.

TUCCA Hold thy peace, poet praetor; I appeal from thee to Caesar, I.
Do me right, royal Caesar.   395

CAESAR Marry, and I will, sir. Lictors, gag him,
And put a case of vizards o'er his head,
That he may look bi-fronted as he speaks.°

TUCCA Gods and fiends! Caesar! Thou wilt not, Caesar, wilt thou?
Away, you whoreson vultures, away. You think I am a dead corpse   400
now, because Caesar is disposed to jest with a man of mark, or so.
Hold your hooked talons out of my flesh, you inhuman Gorboducs.° Go to, do't. What, will the royal Augustus cast away a
gent'man of worship, a captain and a commander, for a couple
of condemned, caitiff, calumnious cargoes?   405

CAESAR Dispatch, lictors.

TUCCA Caesar!
                    [*Lictors place the double-fronted mask over his head*]

CAESAR Forward, Tibullus.

VIRGIL Demand what cause they had to malign Horace.

DEMETRIUS In troth, no great cause, not I, I must confess, but that he   410
kept better company for the most part than I, and that better men
loved him than loved me, and that his writings thrived better than
mine, and were better liked and graced. Nothing else.

VIRGIL Thus envious souls repine at others' good.

HORACE If this be all, faith, I forgive thee freely. 415
    Envy me still—so long as Virgil loves me,
    Gallus, Tibullus, and the best-best Caesar;
    My dear Maecenas; while these, with many more
    (Whose names I wisely slip) shall think me worthy
    Their honoured and adored society, 420
    And read and love, prove and applaud my poems,°
    I would not wish but such as you should spite them.°

CRISPINUS [groaning] Oh—

TIBULLUS How now, Crispinus?

CRISPINUS Oh, I am sick. 425

HORACE A basin, a basin, quickly; our physic works. Faint not, man.
    [Horace holds a basin into which Crispinus appears to vomit his
    words]

CRISPINUS Oh—retrograde—reciprocal—incubus.

CAESAR What's that, Horace?

HORACE Retrograde, reciprocal, and incubus are come up.

GALLUS Thanks be to Jupiter. 430

CRISPINUS Oh—glibbery—lubrical—defunct—Oh—

HORACE Well said; here's some store!°

VIRGIL What are they?

HORACE Glibbery, lubrical, and defunct.

GALLUS Oh, they came up easy. 435

CRISPINUS Oh—Oh—

TIBULLUS What's that?

HORACE Nothing yet.

CRISPINUS Magnificate.

MAECENAS Magnificate? That came up somewhat hard. 440

HORACE Ay. What cheer, Crispinus?

CRISPINUS Oh, I shall cast up my—spurious—snotteries—

HORACE Good. Again.

CRISPINUS Chilblained—Oh—Oh—clumsy—

HORACE That clumsy stuck terribly. 445

MAECENAS What's all that, Horace?

HORACE Spurious, snotteries, chilblained, clumsy.

TIBULLUS Oh, Jupiter!

GALLUS Who would have thought there should ha' been such a deal
    of filth in a poet? 450

CRISPINUS Oh—barmy froth—

CAESAR What's that?

CRISPINUS—*puffy*—*inflate*—*turgidous*°—*ventosity*°.

HORACE *Barmy froth, puffy, inflate, turgidous*, and *ventosity* are come
up.   455

TIBULLUS Oh, terrible windy words!

GALLUS A sign of a windy brain.

CRISPINUS Oh—*oblatrant*°—*obcecate*°—*furibund*°—*fatuate*°—*strenuous*—

HORACE Here's a deal: *oblatrant, obcecate, furibund, fatuate, strenuous*.   460

CAESAR Now all's come up, I trow. What a tumult he had in his belly!

HORACE No, there's the often *conscious* behind still.

CRISPINUS Oh—*conscious*.

HORACE It's come up, thanks to Apollo, and Aesculapius. Yet there's
another: you were best take a pill more?   465

CRISPINUS Oh, no! Oh—Oh—Oh—Oh—

HORACE Force yourself then a little with your finger.

CRISPINUS Oh—Oh—*prorumped*.°

TIBULLUS *Prorumped*? What a noise it made! As if his spirit would
have prorumped with it.   470

CRISPINUS Oh—Oh—Oh—

VIRGIL Help him—it sticks strangely, whatever it is.

CRISPINUS Oh—*clutched*.

HORACE Now it's come—*clutched*.

CAESAR *Clutched*? It's well that's come up. It had but a narrow   475
passage.

CRISPINUS Oh—

VIRGIL Again! Hold him; hold his head there.

CRISPINUS *Tropological—anagogical—loquacity—
pinnosity*.°   480

HORACE How now, Crispinus?

CRISPINUS Oh—*obstupefact*.°

TIBULLUS Nay, that are all we, I assure you.

HORACE How do you feel yourself?

CRISPINUS Pretty and well, I thank you.   485

VIRGIL These pills can but restore him for a time,
Not cure him quite of such a malady
Caught by so many surfeits, which have filled
His blood and brain thus full of crudities;
'Tis necessary, therefore, he observe   490
A strict and wholesome diet. [*To Crispinus*] Look you take
Each morning of old Cato's principles°
A good draught next your heart; that walk upon°

Till it be well digested. Then come home
And taste a piece of Terence; suck his phrase° 495
Instead of licorice; and, at any hand,
Shun Plautus, and old Ennius. They are meats°
Too harsh for a weak stomach. Use to read
(But not without a tutor) the best Greeks:
As Orpheus, Musaeus, Pindarus,° 500
Hesiod, Callimachus, and Theocrite,°
High Homer; but beware of Lycophron,°
He is too dark and dangerous a dish.
You must not hunt for wild, outlandish terms
To stuff out a peculiar dialect, 505
But let your matter run before your words.
And if, at any time, you chance to meet
Some Gallo-Belgic phrase, you shall not straight°
Rack your poor verse to give it entertainment,
But let it pass; and do not think yourself 510
Much damnified if you do leave it out,
When nor your understanding nor the sense
Could well receive it. This fair abstinence,
In time, will render you more sound and clear;
And this have I prescribed to you in place 515
Of a strict sentence. [*To Lictors*] Which till he perform,
Attire him in that robe. [*To Crispinus*] And henceforth learn°
To bear yourself more humbly; not to swell,
Or breathe your insolent and idle spite
On him whose laughter can your worst affright. 520
TIBULLUS [*to Lictors*] Take him away.
CRISPINUS   Jupiter guard Caesar.
VIRGIL And for a week or two, see him locked up
    In some dark place, removed from company;°
    He will talk idly else after his physic.
    [*To Demetrius*] Now to you, sir. Th' extremity of law 525
    Awards you to be branded in the front
    For this your calumny; but, since it pleaseth°
    Horace, the party wronged, t' entreat of Caesar
    A mitigation of that juster doom,
    With Caesar's tongue thus we pronounce your sentence. 530
    Demetrius Fannius, thou shalt here put on
    That coat and cap; and henceforth think thyself
    No other than they make thee. Vow to wear them

85

In every fair and generous assembly,
Till the best sort of minds shall take to knowledge   535
As well thy satisfaction, as thy wrongs.

HORACE Only, grave praetor, here in open court,
I crave the oath for good behaviour
May be administered unto them both.

VIRGIL Horace, it shall. Tibullus, give it them.   540

TIBULLUS Rufus Laberius Crispinus and Demetrius Fannius, lay
your hands on your hearts. You shall here solemnly contest and
swear, that never, after this instant, either at booksellers' stalls, in
taverns, twopenny rooms,° 'tiring houses,° noblemen's butteries,
puisnes' chambers° (the best and farthest places where you are   545
admitted to come) you shall once offer, or dare (thereby to endear
yourself the more to any player, ingle, or guilty gull in your company) to malign, traduce, or detract the person or writings of Quintus Horatius Flaccus, or any other eminent man transcending you
in merit, whom your envy shall find cause to work upon, either for   550
that, or for keeping himself in better acquaintance, or enjoying
better friends. Or if, transported by any sudden and desperate resolution, you do, that then you shall not under the baston, or in the
next presence, being an honorable assembly of his favourers, be
brought as voluntary gentlemen to undertake the forswearing of it. 555
Neither shall you at any time (ambitiously affecting the title of the
untrussers or whippers of the age) suffer the itch of writing to
overrun your performance in libel, upon pain of being taken up for
lepers in wit, and losing both your time and your papers, be
irrecoverably forfeited to the Hospital of Fools. So help you our   560
Roman gods, and the genius of great Caesar.

[*They nod assent*]

VIRGIL So. Now dissolve the court.

HORACE, TIBULLUS, GALLUS, MAECENAS, VIRGIL
                              And thanks to Caesar,
That thus hath exercised his patience.

[*Exeunt Crispinus and Demetrius led out by lictors*]

CAESAR We have, indeed, you worthiest friends of Caesar.
It is the bane and torment of our ears   565
To hear the discords of those jangling rhymers,
That with their bad and scandalous practices,
Bring all true arts and learning in contempt.
But let not your high thoughts descend so low
As these despisèd objects; let them fall   570

With their flat, grovelling souls. Be you yourselves.
And as with our best favours you stand crowned,
So let your mutual loves be still renowned.
Envy will dwell where there is want of merit,
Though the deserving man should crack his spirit.   575

SONG

Blush, folly, blush: here's none that fears
The wagging of an ass's ears,
Although a wolfish case he wears.°
Detraction is but baseness, varlet,
And apes are apes, though clothed in scarlet.   580

Exeunt

Rumpatur quisquis rumpitur invidia.°

TO THE READER.°

Here (reader) in place of the Epilogue, was meant to thee an apology from the author, with his reasons for the publishing of this book; but since he is no less restrained than thou deprived of it by authority, he prays thee to think charitably of what thou hast read, till thou may'st hear him speak what he hath written. 5

ADDITIONAL PASSAGES

PASSAGE A

The folio edition opens with the following dedicatory letter:

To the Virtuous, and My Worthy Friend, Mr Richard Martin.

Sir, a thankful man owes a courtesy ever; the unthankful, but when he needs it. To make mine own mark appear, and show by which of these seals I am known, I send you this piece of what may live of mine; for whose innocence, as for the author's, you were once a noble and timely undertaker, to the greatest   5
justice of this kingdom. Enjoy now the delight of your goodness, which is to see that prosper, you preserved; and posterity to owe the reading of that, without offence to your name, which so much ignorance, and malice of the times, then conspired to have suppressed.

Your true lover,   10
Ben. Jonson

PASSAGE B

In place of Tucca's line (1.2.88), 'Thou speak'st sentences, old Bias,' is printed the following passage in the folio edition:

TUCCA Or purchase him a senator's revenue? Could it?°
OVID SENIOR Ay, or give him place in the commonwealth? Worship or
    attendants? Make him be carried in his litter?
TUCCA Thou speak'st sentences, old Bias.
LUPUS All this the law will do, young sir, if you'll follow it.   5
OVID SENIOR If he be mine, he shall follow and observe what I will
    apt° him to, or I profess here openly and utterly to disclaim in him.
OVID Sir, let me crave you will forgo these moods;
    I will be anything, or study anything:
    I'll prove the unfashioned body of the law   10
    Pure elegance, and make her rugged'st strains
    Run smoothly as Propertius' elegies.
OVID SENIOR Propertius' elegies? Good!

LUPUS Nay, you take him too quickly, Marcus.

OVID SENIOR Why, he cannot speak, he cannot think out of poetry, he   15
is bewitched with it.

LUPUS Come, do not misprize° him.

OVID SENIOR Misprize? Ay, marry, I would have him use some such
words now; they have some touch, some taste of the law. He should
make himself a style out of these, and let his Propertius' elegies   20
go by.

LUPUS Indeed, young Publius, he that will now hit the mark must
shoot through the law; we have no other planet reigns, and in that
sphere you may sit and sing with angels.° Why, the law makes a
man happy, without respecting any other merit; a simple° scholar,   25
or none at all, may be a lawyer.

TUCCA He tells thee true, my noble neophyte, my little grammaticaster, he does. It shall never put thee to thy mathematics,
metaphysics, philosophy, and I know not what supposed sufficien-
cies. If thou canst but have the patience to plod enough, talk, and   30
make noise enough, be impudent enough, and 'tis enough.

LUPUS Three books will furnish you.

TUCCA And the less art, the better; besides when it shall be in the
power of thy cheverel conscience° to do right or wrong at thy
pleasure, my pretty Alcibiades.°   35

LUPUS Ay, and to have better men than himself, by many thousand
degrees, to observe him, and stand bare.

TUCCA True, and he to carry himself proud and stately, and have the
law on his side for't, old boy.

PASSAGE C

*Tucca's speech at 3.4.253–69 concludes in the folio version with the
following lines:*

I have stood up and defended you, I, to gent'men, when you have
been said to prey upon puisnes and honest citizens for socks or
buskins,° or when they ha' called you usurers or brokers, or said
you were able to help to a piece of flesh—I have sworn I did not
think so. Nor that you were the common retreats for punks decayed   5
i' their practice. I cannot believe it of you—

HISTRIO Thank you, captain;

PASSAGE D

Immediately following 3.4 in the folio is printed this scene between Horace and Trebatius:

        [Enter] Horace [and] Trebatius°
[HORACE] There are, to whom I seem excessive sour,
    And past a satire's law t'extend my power;
    Others that think whatever I have writ
    Wants pith and matter to eternize it,
    And that they could, in one day's light, disclose   5
    A thousand verses such as I compose.
    What shall I do, Trebatius? Say.
TREBATIUS   Surcease.°
HORACE And shall my muse admit no more increase?
TREBATIUS So I advise.
HORACE   An ill death let me die
    If 'twere not best; but sleep avoids mine eye,   10
    And I use these lest nights should tedious seem.
TREBATIUS Rather, contend to sleep and live like them
    That holding golden sleep in special price,
    Rubbed with sweet oils, swim silver Tiber thrice,
    And every even with neat wine steeped be;°   15
    Or, if such love of writing ravish thee,
    Then dare to sing unconquered Caesar's deeds,
    Who cheers such actions with abundant meeds.
HORACE That, father, I desire, but when I try,
    I feel defects in every faculty;   20
    Nor is't a labour fit for every pen
    To paint the horrid troops of armèd men,
    The lances burst in Gallia's slaughtered forces,°
    Or wounded Parthians tumbled from their horses—
    Great Caesar's wars cannot be fought with words.   25
TREBATIUS Yet what his virtue in his peace affords,
    His fortitude and justice, thou canst show,
    As wise Lucilius honoured Scipio.°
HORACE Of that, my powers shall suffer no neglect
    When such slight labours may aspire respect.   30
    But if I watch not a most chosen time,
    The humble words of Flaccus cannot climb°

The attentive ear of Caesar; nor must I
With less observance shun gross flattery,
For he, reposèd safe in his own merit,   35
Spurns back the glozes of a fawning spirit.
TREBATIUS But how much better would such accents sound,
  Than with a sad and serious verse to wound
  Pantolabus, railing in his saucy jests?
  Or Nomentanus, spent in riotous feasts?°   40
  In satires, each man (though untouched) complains
  As he were hurt, and hates such biting strains.
HORACE What shall I do? Milonius shakes his heels°
  In ceaseless dances when his brain once feels
  The stirring fervour of the wine ascend,   45
  And that his eyes false number apprehend;
  Castor his horse, Pollux loves handy-fights:°
  A thousand heads, a thousand choice delights.
  My pleasure is in feet my words to close,°
  As, both our better, old Lucilius does.   50
  He, as his trusty friends, his books did trust
  With all his secrets; nor in things unjust
  Or actions lawful, ran to other men.
  So that the old man's life described was seen
  As in a votive table in his lines:°   55
  And to his steps my genius inclines,
  Lucanian or Apulian, I not whether,
  For the Venusian colony plows either,°
  Sent thither when the Sabines were forced thence
  (As old fame sings) to give the place defence   60
  'Gainst such, as seeing it empty, might make road
  Upon the empire, or there fix abode:
  Whether th'Apulian borderer it were,
  Or the Lucanian violence they fear.
  But this my style no living man shall touch,°   65
  If first I be not forced by base reproach;
  But like a sheathèd sword it shall defend
  My innocent life. For why should I contend
  To draw it out when no malicious thief
  Robs my good name, the treasure of my life?   70
  O Jupiter, let it with rust be eaten
  Before it touch or insolently threaten
  The life of any with the least disease;°

So much I love and woo a general peace.
But he that wrongs me, better, I proclaim,   75
He never had assayed to touch my fame,
For he shall weep, and walk with every tongue
Throughout the city, infamously sung.
Servius, the praetor, threats the laws and urn
If any at his deeds repine or spurn;   80
The witch, Canidia, that Albucius got,
Denounceth witchcraft where she loveth not;°
Thurius, the judge, doth thunder worlds of ill
To such as strive with his judicial will:
All men affright their foes in what they may,   85
Nature commands it, and men must obey.
Observe with me: the wolf his tooth doth use,
The bull his horn. And who doth this infuse
But nature? There's luxurious Scaeva. Trust°
His long-lived mother with him: his so just   90
And scrupulous right hand no mischief will;
No more than with his heel a wolf will kill,
Or ox with jaw. Marry, let him alone
With tempered poison to remove the crone.
But briefly: if to age I destined be,   95
Or that quick death's black wings environ me,
If rich or poor, at Rome, or fate command
I shall be banished to some other land,
What hue soever my whole state shall bear,
I will write satires still, in spite of fear.   100
TREBATIUS Horace, I fear thou draw'st no lasting breath,
    And that some great man's friend will be thy death.
HORACE What! When the man that first did satirize°
    Durst pull the skin over the ears of vice,
    And make who stood in outward fashion clear   105
    Give place, as foul within, shall I forbear?
    Did Laelius, or the man so great with fame°
    That from sacked Carthage fetched his worthy name,°
    Storm, that Lucilius did Metellus pierce,
    Or bury Lupus quick in famous verse?°   110
    Rulers and subjects by whole tribes he checked,
    But virtue and her friends did still protect;
    And when from sight, or from the judgement seat,°
    The virtuous Scipio and wise Laelius met

Unbraced, with him in all light sports they shared,   115
Till their most frugal suppers were prepared.
Whate'er I am, though both for wealth and wit
Beneath Lucilius I am pleased to sit,
Yet envy (spite of her empoisoned breast)
Shall say I lived in grace here with the best,   120
And seeking in weak trash to make her wound,
Shall find me solid, and her teeth unsound—
'Less learned Trebatius' censure disagree.
TREBATIUS No, Horace, I of force must yield to thee:
Only take heed, as being advised by me,   125
Lest thou incur some danger. Better pause
Than rue thy ignorance of the sacred laws;°
There's justice, and great action may be sued
'Gainst such as wrong men's fames with verses lewd.
HORACE Ay, with lewd verses, such as libels be,   130
And aimed at persons of good quality.
I reverence and adore that just decree;
But if they shall be sharp yet modest rhymes,
That spare men's persons and but tax their crimes,°
Such shall in open court find current pass,   135
Were Caesar judge, and with the maker's grace.
TREBATIUS Nay, I'll add more: if thou thyself, being clear,
Shalt tax in person a man fit to bear
Shame and reproach, his suit shall quickly be
Dissolved in laughter, and thou thence set free.   140
    [*Exeunt*]

PASSAGE E

In the folio, immediately following the dramatic action, is printed:

TO THE READER

If, by looking on what is past, thou hast deserved that name, I am
willing thou should'st yet know more by that which follows, an apologetical dialogue, which was only once spoken upon the stage,° and all
the answer I ever gave to sundry impotent libels then cast out (and some   5
yet remaining) against me, and this play. Wherein I take no pleasure to

revive the times, but that posterity may make a difference between their manners that provoked me then, and mine that neglected them ever. For in these strifes, and on such persons, were as wretched to affect a victory, as it is unhappy to be committed with them. 10

Non annorum canicies est laudanda, sed morum.°

THE PERSONS

Nasutus
Polyposus°
Author 15

[*Enter Nasutus and Polyposus*]

NASUTUS I pray you, let's go see him, how he looks
    After these libels.

POLYPOSUS   Oh, vexed, vexed, I warrant you.

NASUTUS Do you think so? I should be sorry for him
    If I found that.

POLYPOSUS   Oh, they are such bitter things
    He cannot choose.

NASUTUS   But is he guilty of 'em? 20

POLYPOSUS Faugh! That's no matter.

NASUTUS   No?

POLYPOSUS   No. Here's his lodging;
    We'll steal upon him. Or let's listen; stay.
    He has a humour oft t' talk t' himself.

NASUTUS They are your manners lead me, not mine own.
    [*The Author is discovered in his study*]

AUTHOR The Fates have not spun him the coarsest thread° 25
    That (free from knots of perturbation)
    Doth yet so live, although but to himself,
    As he can safely scorn the tongues of slaves,
    And neglect Fortune, more than she can him.
    It is the happiest thing, this not to be 30
    Within the reach of malice: it provides
    A man so well, to laugh off injuries,
    And never sends him farther for his vengeance
    Than the vexed bosom of his enemy.
    Ay, now, but think how poor their spite sets off,° 35

Who, after all their waste of sulphurous terms,
And burst-out thunder of their chargèd mouths,
Have nothing left but the unsavoury smoke
Of their black vomit to upbraid themselves;
Whilst I, at whom they shot, sit here shot-free,   40
And as unhurt of envy, as unhit.
    [*Polyposus and Nasutus come forward*]
POLYPOSUS Ay, but the multitude, they think not so, sir,
    They think you hit, and hurt; and dare give out
    Your silence argues it, in not rejoining
    To this or that late libel.
AUTHOR   'Las, good rout!   45
    I can afford them leave to err so still,
    And, like the barking students of Bears' College,°
    To swallow up the garbage of the time
    With greedy gullets, whilst myself sit by
    Pleased, and yet tortured, with their beastly feeding.   50
    'Tis a sweet madness runs along with them,
    To think all that are aimed at, still are struck;
    Then, where the shaft still lights, make that the mark:
    And so each fear- or fever-shaken fool
    May challenge Teucer's hand in archery.°   55
    Good troth, if I knew any man so vile
    To act the crimes these whippers reprehend,
    Or what their servile apes gesticulate,°
    I should not then much muse their shreds were liked,
    Since ill men have a lust t' hear other's sins   60
    And good men have a zeal to hear sin shamed.
    But when it is all excrement they vent,
    Base filth and offal, or thefts notable
    As ocean piracies or highway stands,°
    And not a crime there taxed but is their own,   65
    Or what their own foul thoughts suggested to them,
    And that in all their heat of taxing others,
    Not one of them but lives himself, if known,
    Improbior satiram scribente cinaedo,°
    What should I say more? Then turn stone with wonder!   70
NASUTUS I never saw this play bred all this tumult.
    What was there in it could so deeply offend,
    And stir so many hornets?
AUTHOR   Shall I tell you?

NASUTUS Yes, and ingenuously.

AUTHOR   Then, by the hope°
    Which I prefer unto all other objects,   75
    I can profess I never writ that piece
    More innocent, or empty of offence.
    Some salt it had, but neither tooth nor gall,
    Nor was there in it any circumstance
    Which, in the setting down, I could suspect   80
    Might be perverted by an enemy's tongue.
    Only it had the fault to be called mine.
    That was the crime.

POLYPOSUS   No? Why they say you taxed
    The law and lawyers, captains, and the players
    By their particular names.

AUTHOR   It is not so.°   85
    I used no name. My books have still been taught
    To spare the persons, and to speak the vices.
    These are mere slanders, and enforced by such
    As have no safer ways to men's disgraces
    But their own lies, and loss of honesty: 90
    Fellows of practised, and most laxative tongues,°
    Whose empty and eager bellies i' the year
    Compel their brains to many desperate shifts
    (I spare to name 'em, for their wretchedness
    Fury itself would pardon). These, or such,   95
    Whether of malice, or of ignorance,
    Or itch t' have me their adversary (I know not),
    Or all these mixed, but sure I am, three years
    They did provoke me with their petulant styles
    On every stage. And I at last, unwilling,°   100
    But weary, I confess, of so much trouble,
    Thought I would try if shame could win upon 'em.
    And therefore chose Augustus Caesar's times,
    When wit and arts were at their height in Rome,
    To show that Virgil, Horace, and the rest   105
    Of those great master spirits did not want
    Detractors then, or practisers against them.
    And by this line (although no parallel)
    I hoped at last they would sit down and blush.
    But nothing could I find more contrary.   110
    And though the impudence of flies be great,

Yet this hath so provoked the angry wasps,
Or as you said, of the next nest, the hornets,
That they fly buzzing, mad, about my nostrils,
And like so many screaming grasshoppers   115
Held by the wings, fill every ear with noise.
And what? Those former calumnies you mentioned:
First, of the law. Indeed, I brought in Ovid,
Chid by his angry father for neglecting
The study of their laws for poetry;   120
And I am warranted by his own words:
    Saepe pater dixit, 'studium quid inutile tentas?
    Maeonides nullas ipse reliquit opes'.°
And in far harsher terms elsewhere, as these:
     Non me verbosas leges ediscere, non me   125
     Ingrato voces prostituisse foro.°
But how this should relate unto our laws,
Or their just ministers, with least abuse,
I reverence both too much to understand!
Then for the captain, I will only speak   130
An epigram I here have made. It is
'Unto true soldiers.' That's the lemma. Mark it.°
    Strength of my country, whilst I bring to view
    Such as are miscalled captains, and wrong you
    And your high names, I do desire that thence   135
    Be nor put on you, nor you take offence.
    I swear by your true friend, my Muse, I love
    Your great profession, which I once did prove,
    And did not shame it with my actions then,°
    No more than I dare now do with my pen.   140
    He that not trusts me, having vowed thus much,
    But's angry for the captain still, is such.°
Now, for the players, it is true I taxed 'em,
And yet, but some; and those so sparingly,
As all the rest might have sat still, unquestioned,   145
Had they but had the wit, or conscience,
To think well of themselves. But, impotent, they
Thought each man's vice belonged to their whole tribe:
And much good do 't 'em. What th' have done 'gainst me,
I am not moved with. If it gave 'em meat,   150
Or got 'em clothes, 'tis well. That was their end.
Only amongst them I am sorry for

Some better natures, by the rest so drawn,
To run in that vile line.
POLYPOSUS   And is this all?
Will you not answer then the libels?
AUTHOR   No.   155
POLYPOSUS   Nor the untrussers?
AUTHOR   Neither.
POLYPOSUS   You're undone then.°
AUTHOR   With whom?
POLYPOSUS   The world.
AUTHOR   The bawd!
POLYPOSUS   It will be taken
To be stupidity, or tameness in you.
AUTHOR   But they that have incensed me can in soul
Acquit me of that guilt. They know I dare   160
To spurn or baffle 'em, or squirt their eyes°
With ink or urine; or I could do worse,
Armed with Archilochus' fury, write iambics
Should make the desperate lashers hang themselves:°
Rhyme 'em to death, as they do Irish rats   165
In drumming tunes. Or, living, I could stamp°
Their foreheads with those deep and public brands
That the whole company of barber-surgeons
Should not take off, with all their art and plasters.
And these my prints should last, still to be read   170
In their pale fronts, when what they write 'gainst me
Shall, like a figure drawn in water, fleet,
And the poor wretched papers be employed
To clothe tobacco, or some cheaper drug.
This I could do, and make them infamous.   175
But to what end? When their own deeds have marked 'em,
And that I know within his guilty breast
Each slanderer bears a whip that shall torment him
Worse than a million of these temporal plagues;
Which, to pursue, were but a feminine humour,   180
And far beneath the dignity of a man.
NASUTUS   'Tis true, for to revenge their injuries
Were to confess you felt 'em. Let 'em go
And use the treasure of the fool, their tongues,
Who makes his gain by speaking worst, of best.   185
POLYPOSUS   Oh, but they lay particular imputations—

AUTHOR As what?

POLYPOSUS   That all your writing is mere railing.

AUTHOR Ha! If all the salt in the old comedy
    Should be so censured, or the sharper wit
    Of the bold satire termèd scolding rage,   190
    What age could then compare with those for buffoons?
    What should be said of Aristophanes?
    Persius? Or Juvenal? Whose names we now°
    So glorify in schools—at least pretend it.
    Ha' they no other?

POLYPOSUS   Yes, they say you are slow,   195
    And scarce bring forth a play a year.

AUTHOR   'Tis true.
    I would they could not say that I did that:
    There's all the joy that I take i' their trade,
    Unless such scribes as they might be proscribed
    Th' abusèd theatres. They would think it strange now,   200
    A man should take but coltsfoot for one day,
    And between whiles spit out a better poem
    Than e'er the master of art, or giver of wit,
    Their belly, made. Yet this is possible,
    If a free mind had but the patience   205
    To think so much together, and so vile.
    But that these base and beggarly conceits
    Should carry it by the multitude of voices
    Against the most abstracted work, opposed
    To the stuffed nostrils of the drunken rout!°   210
    Oh, this would make a learned and liberal soul
    To rive his stainèd quill up to the back,
    And damn his long-watched labours to the fire—
    Things that were born when none but the still night
    And his dumb candle saw his pinching throes—   215
    Were not his own free merit a more crown
    Unto his travails than their reeling claps.
    This 'tis that strikes me silent, seals my lips,
    And apts me rather to sleep out my time,
    Than I would waste it in contemnèd strifes   220
    With these vile ibides, these unclean birds,
    That make their mouths their clysters, and still purge
    From their hot entrails. But I leave the monsters
    To their own fate. And since the comic Muse

Hath proved so ominous to me, I will try   225
If Tragedy have a more kind aspect.
Her favours in my next I will pursue,°
Where, if I prove the pleasure but of one,
So he judicious be, he shall b' alone
A theatre unto me. Once I'll say°   230
To strike the ear of time in those fresh strains
As shall, beside the cunning of their ground,°
Give cause to some of wonder, some despite,°
And unto more, despair to imitate their sound.
I that spend half my nights and all my days   235
Here in a cell, to get a dark, pale face,
To come forth worth the ivy or the bays,
And in this age can hope no other grace —
Leave me. There's something come into my thought
That must and shall be sung, high and aloof,   240
Safe from the wolf's black jaw, and the dull ass's hoof.
NASUTUS I reverence these raptures, and obey 'em.
  [*Exeunt Nasutus and Polyposus*]

    This comical satire was first acted in the year 1601
    by the then Children of Queen Elizabeth's Chapel.
    The principal comedians were,   245

  Nat[haniel] Field   Joh[n] Underwood
  Sal[amon] Pavy   Will[iam] Ostler
  Tho[mas] Day   Tho[mas] Marton

  With the allowance of the Master of Revels.

SEJANUS HIS FALL

TO THE READERS

The following and voluntary labours of my friends, prefixed to my book, have relieved me in much, whereat without them, I should necessarily have touched. Now I will only use three or four short and needful notes, and so rest.

First, if it be objected that what I publish is no true poem in the strict laws of time,° I confess it: as also in the want of a proper chorus, whose habit and moods° are such, and so difficult, as not any whom I have seen since the ancients—no, not they who have most presently affected laws—have yet come in the way of. Nor is it needful, or almost possible, in these our times, and to such auditors as commonly things are presented, to observe the old state and splendour of dramatic poems with preservation of any popular delight. But of this I shall take more seasonable cause to speak in my observations upon Horace his *Art of Poetry*, which, with the text translated, I intend shortly to publish.° In the meantime, if in truth of argument, dignity of persons, gravity and height of elocution, fullness and frequency of sentence,° I have discharged the other offices of a tragic writer, let not the absence of these forms be imputed to me, wherein I shall give you occasion hereafter (and without my boast) to think I could better prescribe than omit the due use for want of a convenient° knowledge.

The next is, lest in some nice nostril the quotations° might savour affected, I do let you know that I abhor nothing more, and have only done it to show my integrity in the story, and save myself in those common torturers that bring all wit to the rack; whose noses are ever like swine spoiling and rooting up the Muses' gardens, and their whole bodies, like moles, as blindly working under earth to cast any the least hills upon virtue.

Whereas they are in Latin and the work in English, it was presupposed none but the learned would take the pains to confer° them, the authors themselves being all in the learned tongues, save one,° with whose English side I have had little to do; to which it may be required, since I haue quoted the page, to name what editions I followed: *Tacit. Lips.* in 4°. *Antuerp. edit. 600. Dio. Folio. Hen. Step. 92.* For the rest, as *Sueton. Seneca.*° etc, the chapter doth sufficiently direct, or the edition is not varied.

Lastly, I would inform you that this book, in all numbers°, is not the same with that which was acted on the public stage, wherein a second pen had good share;° in place of which I have rather chosen to put weaker—and no doubt less pleasing—of mine own, than to defraud so happy a genius of his right by my loathed usurpation. 40

Fare you well. And if you read farther of me, and like, I shall not be afraid of it though you praise me out.

Neque enim mihi cornea fibra est.°

But that I should plant my felicity in your general saying 'good', or 'well', etc., were a weakness which the better sort of you might 45 worthily contemn, if not absolutely hate, me for.

BEN. JONSON and no such.

Quem palma negata macrum, donata reducit opimum.°

In SEIANVM
BEN. IONSONI
Et Musis, et sibi in Deliciis°

So brings the wealth-contracting jeweller
Pearls and dear stones from richest shores and streams,
As thy accomplished travail doth confer
From skill-enrichèd souls their wealthier gems;°
So doth his hand enchase in amelled gold,   5
Cut and adorned beyond their native merits,
His solid flames, as thine hath here enrolled,
In more than golden verse, those bettered spirits;
So he entreasures princes' cabinets,
As thy wealth will their wishèd libraries;   10
So, on the throat of the rude sea, he sets
His ventrous foot for his illustrous prize;°
And through wild deserts, armed with wilder beasts,
As thou adventur'st on the multitude,
Upon the boggy, and engulfèd breasts   15
Of hirelings, sworn to find most right, most rude;
And he, in storms at sea, doth not endure,
Nor in vast deserts amongst wolves, more danger,
Than we, that would with virtue live secure,
Sustain for her in every vice's anger.   20
Nor is this allegory unjustly racked
To this strange length; only that jewels are,
In estimation merely, so exact;°
And thy work, in itself, is dear and rare.
Wherein Minerva had been vanquishèd,   25
Had she, by it, her sacred looms advanced,
And through thy subject woven her graphic thread,
Contending therein to be more entranced;
For though thy hand was scarce addressed to draw
The semi-circle of Sejanus' life,   30
Thy muse yet makes it the whole sphere, and law
To all state lives, and bounds ambition's strife.
And as a little brook creeps from his spring,
With shallow tremblings, through the lowest vales,

SEJANUS

As if he feared his stream abroad to bring,   35
Lest profane feet should wrong it, and rude gales;
But finding happy channels, and supplies
Of other fords mix with his modest course,
He grows a goodly river, and descries
The strength that manned him since he left his source;   40
Then takes he in delightsome meads and groves,
And with his two-edged waters flourishes
Before great palaces, and all men's loves
Build by his shores, to greet his passages:
So thy chaste muse, by virtuous self-mistrust,   45
Which is a true mark of the truest merit,
In virgin fear of men's illiterate lust,
Shut her soft wings, and durst not show her spirit;
Till, nobly cherished, now thou letst her fly,
Singing the sable orgies of the Muses,°   50
And in the highest pitch of tragedy
Mak'st her command all things thy ground produces.
But as it is a sign of love's first firing,
Not pleasure by a lovely presence taken
And boldness to attempt, but close retiring   55
To places desolate, and fever-shaken;
So when the love of knowledge first affects us,
Our tongues do falter, and the flame doth rove
Through our thin spirits, and of fear detects us
T' attain her truth, whom we so truly love.   60
Nor can (saith Aeschylus) a fair young dame,°
Kept long without a husband, more contain
Her amorous eye from breaking forth in flame
When she beholds a youth that fits her vein,
Than any man's first taste of knowledge truly   65
Can bridle the affection she inspireth,
But let it fly on men that most unduly
Haunt her with hate, and all the loves she fireth.
If our teeth, head, or but our finger ache,
We straight seek the physician; if a fever,   70
Or any cureful malady we take,
The grave physician is desirèd ever;
But if proud melancholy, lunacy,
Or direct madness overheat our brains,
We rage, beat out, or the physician fly,   75

107

Losing with vehemence even the sense of pains.
So of offenders, they are past recure
That with a tyrannous spleen their stings extend
'Gainst their reprovers; they that will endure
All discreet discipline are not said t' offend.   80
Though others qualified, then, with natural skill
(More sweet-mouthed, and affecting shrewder wits)
Blanch coals, call illness good, and goodness ill,
Breathe thou the fire that true-spoke knowledge fits.
Thou canst not then be great? Yes! Who is he,   85
Said the good Spartan king, greater than I,
That is not likewise juster? No degree
Can boast of eminence or empery
(As the great Stagirite held) in any one°
Beyond another whose soul farther sees,   90
And in whose life the gods are better known:
Degrees of knowledge difference all degrees.
Thy poem, therefore, hath this due respect,
That it lets pass nothing without observing
Worthy instruction, or that might correct   95
Rude manners, and renown the well-deserving;
Performing such a lively evidence
In thy narrations, that thy hearers still
Thou turnst to thy spectators; and the sense
That thy spectators have of good or ill,   100
Thou injectst jointly to thy readers' souls.
So dear is held, so decked thy numerous task,
As thou putst handles to the Thespian bowls,
Or stuckst rich plumes in the Palladian casque.°
All thy worth, yet, thyself must patronize,   105
By quaffing more of the Castalian head;°
In expiscation of whose mysteries
Our nets must still be clogged with heavy lead
To make them sink and catch: for cheerful gold
Was never found in the Pierian streams,   110
But wants, and scorns, and shames for silver sold.
What, what shall we elect in these extremes?
Now by the shafts of the great Cyrrhan poet,°
That bear all light that is about the world,
I would have all dull poet-haters know it,   115
They shall be soul-bound and in darkness hurled

A thousand years (as Satan was, their sire)
Ere any worthy the poetic name
(Might I that warm but at the Muses' fire
Presume to guard it) should let deathless Fame   120
Light half a beam of all her hundred eyes
At his dim taper in their memories.
Fly, fly, you are too near; so odorous flowers,
Being held too near the sensor of our sense,
Render not pure, nor so sincere their powers   125
As being held a little distance thence,
Because much-troubled earthy parts improve them,
Which mixèd with the odours we exhale,
Do vitiate what we draw in. But remove them
A little space, the earthy parts do fall,   130
And what is pure and hot by his tenuity
Is to our powers of savour purely borne.
But fly or stay, use thou the assiduity
Fit for a true contemner of their scorn.
Our Phoebus may, with his exampling beams.°   135
Burn out the webs from their Arachnean eyes,°
Whose knowledge—day-star to all diadems—
Should banish knowledge-hating policies.
So others, great in the sciential grace:
His Chancellor, fautor of all human skills;°   140
His Treasurer, taking them into his place;
Northumber, that, with them, his crescent fills;
Grave Worcester, in whose nerves they guard their fire;
Northampton, that to all his height in blood
Heightens his soul with them; and Devonshire,   145
In whom their streams, ebbed to their spring, are flood;
Oraculous Salisbury, whose inspirèd voice,
In state proportions, sings their mysteries;
And (though last named) first, in whom they rejoice,
To whose true worth they vow most obsequies,   150
Most noble Suffolk, who by nature noble,
And judgement virtuous, cannot fall by fortune,
Who when our herd came not to drink, but trouble
The Muses' waters, did a wall importune,
Midst of assaults, about their sacred river;   155
In whose behalfs, my poor soul (consecrate
To poorest virtue) to the longest liver

His name, in spite of death, shall propagate.
O, could the world but feel how sweet a touch
A good deed hath in one in love with goodness   160
(If poesy were not ravishèd so much,
And her composed rage held the simplest woodness,
Though of all heats that temper human brains
Hers ever was most subtle, high, and holy,
First binding savage lives in civil chains: 165
Solely religious, and adorèd solely,
If men felt this) they would not think a love
That gives itself in her did vanities give;
Who is, in earth though low, in worth above,
Most able t' honour life, though least to live.   170
And so, good friend, safe passage to thy freight,
To thee a long peace through a virtuous strife,
In which, let's both contend to virtue's height,
Not making fame our object, but good life.

Come forth, Sejanus, fall before this book,   175
And of thy fall's reviver ask forgiveness,
That thy low birth and merits durst to look
A fortune in the face of such unevenness;
For so his fervent love to virtue hates
That her plucked plumes should wing vice to such calling,   180
That he presents thee to all marking states
As if thou hadst been all this while in falling;
His strong arm plucking from the middle world
Fame's brazen house, and lays her tower as low
As Homer's Barathrum; that, from heaven hurled,°   185
Thou might'st fall on it: and thy ruins grow
To all posterities, from his work, the ground,
And under heav'n, nought but his song might sound.

Haec commentatus est
Georgius Chapmannus°   190

For his worthy friend, the Author

In that this book doth deign Sejanus' name,
Him unto more than Caesar's love it brings;
For where he could not with ambition's wings,
One quill doth heave him to the height of fame.
Ye great ones, though (whose ends may be the same),   5
Know that however we do flatter kings,
Their favours (like themselves) are fading things,
With no less envy had, than lost with shame.
Nor make yourselves less honest than you are,
To make our author wiser than he is;°   10
Ne of such crimes accuse him, which I dare
By all his muses swear be none of his.
The men are not, some faults may be these times';
He acts those men, and they did act these crimes.

                              Hugh Holland°   15

To the deserving Author

When I respect thy argument, I see°
An image of those times; but when I view
The wit, the workmanship, so rich, so true,
The times themselves do seem retrieved to me.
And as Sejanus in thy tragedy   5
Falleth from Caesar's grace, even so the crew
Of common playwrights, whom opinion blew
Big with false greatness, are disgraced by thee.
Thus, in one tragedy, thou makest twain;
And since fair works of justice fit the part   10
Of tragic writers, muses do ordain
That all tragedians, masters of their art,
Who shall hereafter follow on this tract,
In writing well, thy tragedy shall act.

                              Cygnus°   15

To his learned and beloved Friend,
upon his equal work

Sejanus, great and eminent in Rome,
Raised above all the Senate, both in grace
Of prince's favour, authority, place,
And popular dependence; yet how soon,°
Even with the instant of his overthrow,   5
Is all this pride and greatness now forgot—
Only that in former grace he stood not—
By them which did his state, not treason, know!
His very flatterers, that did adorn
Their necks with his rich medals, now in flame   10
Consume them, and would lose even his name,
Or else recite it with reproach or scorn!
This was his Roman fate. But now thy muse,
To us that neither knew his height nor fall,
Hath raised him up with such memorial,   15
All future states and times his name shall use.
What not his good nor ill could once extend
To the next age, thy verse, industrious
And learned friend, hath made illustrious
To this. Nor shall his or thy fame have end.   20

Th. R.°

Amicis, amici nostri dignissimi, dignissimis,
Epigramma.
D.
Iohannes Marstonivs°

Ye ready friends, spare your unneedful bays;
This work despairful envy must even praise.

Phoebus hath voiced it loud through echoing skies,°
'Sejanus' Fall shall force thy merit rise;
For never English shall, or hath before,   5
Spoke fuller graced.' He could say much, not more.

Upon Sejanus

How high a poor man shows in low estate,
Whose base is firm, and whole frame competent,
That sees this cedar made the shrub of fate:
Th' one's little, lasting; th' other's confluence spent.°
And as the lightning comes behind the thunder   5
From the torn cloud, yet first invades our sense,
So every violent fortune, that to wonder
Hoists men aloft, is a clear evidence
Of a vaunt-curring blow the Fates have given°
To his forced state: swift lightning blinds his eyes,   10
While thunder from comparison-hating heaven
Dischargeth on his height, and there it lies.
If men will shun swol'n Fortune's ruinous blasts,
Let them use temperance. Nothing violent lasts.

William Strachey°   15

To him that hath so excelled on this excellent subject

Thy poem (pardon me) is mere deceit;
Yet such deceit, as thou that dost beguile,
Are juster far than they who use no wile;
And they who are deceivèd by this feat,
More wise than such who can eschew thy cheat.   5
For thou hast given each part so just a style
That men suppose the action now on file;
And men suppose, who are of best conceit.
Yet some there be that are not moved hereby,
And others are so quick that they will spy   10
Where later times are in some speech enweaved;°
Those wary simples, and these simple elves:
They are so dull, they cannot be deceived,
These so unjust, they will deceive themselves.

ΦΙΛΟΣ°   15

To the most understanding Poet

When in the Globe's fair ring, our world's best stage,
I saw *Sejanus*, set with that rich foil,°
I looked the author should have borne the spoil
Of conquest from the writers of the age;
But when I viewed the people's beastly rage,   5
Bent to confound thy grave and learned toil
That cost thee so much sweat and so much oil,
My indignation I could hardly assuage.
And many there, in passion, scarce could tell
Whether thy fault or theirs deserved most blame—   10
Thine, for so showing, theirs, to wrong the same;
But both they left within that doubtful hell.
From whence, this publication sets thee free;
They, for their ignorance, still damnèd be.

                                    Ev. B.°   15

THE ARGUMENT

Aelius Sejanus, son to Seius Strabo, a gentleman of Rome, and born at Vulsinium, after his long service in court, first under Augustus, afterward Tiberius,° grew into that favour with the latter, and won him by those arts, as there wanted nothing but the name to make him a copartner of the Empire. Which greatness of his, Drusus, the Emperor's son, not brooking, after many smothered dislikes, it one day breaking out, the prince struck him publicly on the face. To revenge which disgrace, Livia—the wife of Drusus, being before corrupted by him to her dishonour, and the discovery of her husband's counsels—Sejanus practiseth° with, together with her physician, called Eudemus, and one Lygdus, an eunuch, to poison Drusus. This, their inhuman act, having successful and unsuspected passage, it emboldeneth Sejanus to farther and more insolent projects, even the ambition of the Empire: where finding the lets° he must encounter to be many and hard in respect of the issue of Germanicus° (who were next in hope), he deviseth to make Tiberius' self his means, and instils into his ears many doubts and suspicions both against the princes and their mother Agrippina, which Caesar jealously° hearkening to, as covetously consenteth to their ruin, and their friends'. In this time, the better to mature and strengthen his design, he labours to marry Livia, and worketh (with all his engine) to remove Tiberius from the knowledge of public business with allurements of a quiet and separated life; the latter of which Tiberius, out of a proneness to lust, and a desire to hide these unnatural pleasures which he could not so publicly practise, embraceth. The former enkindleth his fears, and there gives him first cause of doubt or suspect toward Sejanus, against whom he raiseth in private a new instrument, one Sertorius Macro, and by him underworketh, discovers the other's counsels, his means, his ends, sounds the affections of the senators, divides, distracts them; at last, when Sejanus least looketh, and is most secure, with pretext of doing him an unwonted honour in the Senate, he trains° him from his guards; with one letter, and in one day, hath him suspected, accused, condemned, and torn in pieces by the rage of the people.

This do we advance as a mark of terror to all traitors and treasons, to show how just the heavens are in pouring and thundering down a weighty vengeance on their unnatural intents, even to the worst princes: much more to those for guard of whose piety and virtue the angels are in continual watch, and God himself miraculously working.

Tiberius [Emperor of Rome]
[Aelius] Sejanus [favourite of the
  emperor]°
Drusus Se[nior, son of
  Tiberius]°
[Marcus] Lepidus [senator]
Cotta [senator]
Sanquinius [senator]
Afer [orator]°
Haterius [senator]
[Cremutius] Cordus [historian]
[Sertorius] Macro [prefect]°
[Gracinus] Laco [commander of
  the night-wardens]°

[*Those loyal to Sejanus*]
Terentius
Minutius
Satrius [Secundus]
[Pinnarius] Natta
Latiaris [senator]°
[Pomponius, senator]
Rufus
Opsius
Varro [consul in AD 24]°
[Julius] Posthumus [senator]
[Fulcinius] Trio [suffect consul
  in AD 31]°
Livia [wife of Drusus Senior, and
  Sejanus' lover]
Eudemus [physician]

[*Of the Germanican faction*]
Agrippina [widow of
  Germanicus]
Nero [eldest son of Agrippina]°
Drusus Ju[nior son of
  Agrippina]°
[Caius] Caligula [son of
  Agrippina]°
[Lucius] Arruntius [senator]°
[Caius] Silius [senator]°
Sosia [wife of Silius]°
[Titius] Sabinus [nobleman]
[Memmius] Regulus [suffect
  consul in AD 31]°
[Asinius] Gallus [senator]°

[*Unnamed parts*]
Praecones° [heralds]
Flamen [priest]
Ministers [attendants to the
  priest]
Trumpeters
Flautists
[Fortune]
Nuntius [messenger]
Tribunes
Lictors, [attendants to
  magistrates]
[Praetor, one of twelve officials
  beneath the consuls]
Servants°

1.[1]

*[Enter] Sabinus [and] Silius. Satrius [and] Natta [enter
separately, and stand aside]*

SABINUS Hail, Caius Silius!

SILIUS   Titius Sabinus, hail!
   You're rarely met in court!

SABINUS   Therefore, well met.

SILIUS 'Tis true; indeed, this place is not our sphere.

SABINUS No, Silius, we are no good engineers;
   We want the fine arts, and their thriving use   5
   Should make us graced or favoured of the times:
   We have no shift of faces, no cleft tongues,
   No soft and glutinous bodies that can stick
   Like snails on painted walls, or on our breasts
   Creep up, to fall from that proud height to which   10
   We did by slavery, not by service, climb.°
   We are no guilty men, and then no great;
   We have nor place in court, office in state,
   That we can say we owe unto our crimes;
   We burn with no black secrets which can make   15
   Us dear to the pale authors, or live feared
   Of their still-waking jealousies, to raise°
   Ourselves a fortune by subverting theirs.
   We stand not in the lines that do advance
   To that so courted point.

SILIUS   But yonder lean   20
   A pair that do.

     [Enter Latiaris, who walks over to join Satrius and Natta]

SABINUS *[to Latiaris as he passes]* Good cousin Latiaris.

SILIUS Satrius Secundus and Pinnarius Natta,
   The great Sejanus' clients. There be two°
   Know more than honest counsels; whose close breasts,
   Were they ripped up to light, it would be found   25
   A poor and idle sin to which their trunks
   Had not been made fit organs. These can lie,°
   Flatter, and swear; forswear, deprave, inform;

Smile, and betray; make guilty men, then beg
The forfeit lives to get the livings; cut°   30
Men's throats with whisp'rings; sell to gaping suitors
The empty smoke that flies about the palace;
Laugh when their patron laughs; sweat when he sweats;
Be hot and cold with him; change every mood,
Habit, and garb as often as he varies;   35
Observe him, as his watch observes his clock;
And, true as turquoise in the dear lord's ring,°
Look well or ill with him—ready to praise
His lordship if he spit, or but piss fair,
Have an indifferent stool, or break wind well: 40
Nothing can scape their catch.
SABINUS   Alas! These things
Deserve no note, conferred with other vile°
And filthier flatteries that corrupt the times.
When not alone our gentry's chief are fain
To make their safety from such sordid acts,   45
But all our consuls, and no little part°
Of such as have been praetors—yea, the most
Of senators, that else not use their voices,
Start up in public Senate, and there strive
Who shall propound most abject things and base,   50
So much, as oft Tiberius hath been heard,
Leaving the court, to cry, 'O race of men,
Prepared for servitude!'—which showed that he,
Who least the public liberty could like,
As loathly brooked their flat servility.   55
SILIUS Well, all is worthy of us were it more,
Who with our riots, pride, and civil hate
Have so provoked the justice of the gods.
We that (within these fourscore years) were born
Free, equal lords of the triumphèd world,   60
And knew no masters but affections,
To which betraying first our liberties,
We since became the slaves to one man's lusts,
And now to many. Every ministering spy°
That will accuse and swear is lord of you,   65
Of me, of all: our fortunes, and our lives.
Our looks are called to question, and our words,
How innocent soever, are made crimes;

We shall not shortly dare to tell our dreams,
Or think, but 'twill be treason.
SABINUS   Tyrants' arts   70
Are to give flatterers grace, accusers power,
That those may seem to kill whom they devour.
        [*Enter Cordus and Arruntius*]
Now, good Cremutius Cordus.
CORDUS   Hail to your lordship!
        [*They walk aside*]°
NATTA Who's that salutes your cousin?
LATIARIS   'Tis one Cordus,
A gentleman of Rome; one that has writ   75
Annals of late, they say, and very well.
NATTA Annals? Of what times?
LATIARIS   I think of Pompey's,
And Caius Caesar's, and so down to these.°
NATTA How stands h' affected to the present state?
Is he or Drusian, or Germanican?°   80
Or ours, or neutral?
LATIARIS   I know him not so far.
NATTA Those times are somewhat queasy to be touched.
Have you or seen or heard part of his work?
LATIARIS Not I; he means they shall be public shortly.
NATTA Oh. Cordus do you call him?
LATIARIS   Ay.
        [*Exeunt Satrius, Natta, and Latiaris*]
SABINUS   But these our times   85
Are not the same, Arruntius.
ARRUNTIUS   Times? The men,
The men are not the same: 'tis we are base,
Poor, and degenerate from th' exalted strain°
Of our great fathers. Where is now the soul
Of god-like Cato? He that durst be good,°   90
When Caesar durst be evil; and had power,
As not to live his slave, to die his master.
Or where the constant Brutus that (being proof°
Against all charm of benefits) did strike
So brave a blow into the monster's heart   95
That sought unkindly to captive his country?°
Oh, they are fled the light. Those mightly spirits
Lie raked up with their ashes in their urns,

And not a spark of their eternal fire
Glows in a present bosom. All's but blaze,   100
Flashes, and smoke wherewith we labour so.
There's nothing Roman in us; nothing good,
Gallant, or great. 'Tis true, that Cordus says:
'Brave Cassius was the last of all that race.'°
SABINUS Stand by! Lord Drusus.
     Drusus passeth by [attended by Haterius]°
HATERIUS   Th' emperor's son, give place!   105
SILIUS I like the Prince well.
ARRUNTIUS   A riotous youth,
There's little hope of him.
SABINUS   That fault his age
Will, as it grows, correct. Methinks he bears
Himself each day more nobly than other,
And wins no less on men's affections   110
Than doth his father lose. Believe me, I love him;
And chiefly for opposing to Sejanus.
SILIUS And I for gracing his young kinsmen so,
The sons of Prince Germanicus. It shows
A gallant clearness in him, a straight mind,   115
That envies not in them their father's name.
ARRUNTIUS His name was, while he lived, above all envy;°
And being dead, without it. Oh that man!
If there were seeds of the old virtue left,
They lived in him.
SILIUS   He had the fruits, Arruntius,   120
More than the seeds; Sabinus and myself
Had means to know him within, and can report him.
We were his followers; he would call us friends.
He was a man most like to virtue; in all,
And every action, nearer to the gods   125
Than men in nature; of a body as fair
As was his mind; and no less reverend
In face than fame. He could so use his state,
Temp'ring his greatness with his gravity,
As it avoided all self-love in him,°   130
And spite in others. What his funerals lacked
In images and pomp, they had supplied°
With honourable sorrow, soldiers' sadness,
A kind of silent mourning such as men

Who know no tears but from their captives use   135
    To show in so great losses.
CORDUS   I thought once,
    Considering their forms, age, manner of deaths,
    The nearness of the places where they fell,
    T' have paralleled him with great Alexander:°
    For both were of best feature, of high race,   140
    Yeared but to thirty, and in foreign lands,
    By their own people, alike made away.
SABINUS I know not for his death how you might wrest it,
    But for his life, it did as much disdain
    Comparison with that voluptuous, rash,   145
    Giddy, and drunken Macedon's, as mine
    Doth with my bondman's. All the good in him°
    (His valour and his fortune) he made his;°
    But he had other touches of late Romans
    That more did speak him: Pompey's dignity,   150
    The innocence of Cato, Caesar's spirit,
    Wise Brutus' temperance, and every virtue
    Which, parted unto others, gave them name,
    Flowed mixed in him. He was the soul of goodness,°
    And all our praises of him are like streams   155
    Drawn from a spring, that still rise full, and leave
    The part remaining greatest.
ARRUNTIUS   I am sure
    He was too great for us, and that they knew
    Who did remove him hence.
SABINUS   When men grow fast
    Honoured and loved, there is a trick in state   160
    (Which jealous princes never fail to use)
    How to decline that growth with fair pretext°
    And honourable colours of employment,
    Either by embassy, the war, or such,
    To shift them forth into another air   165
    Where they may purge and lessen; so was he:
    And had his seconds there sent by Tiberius
    And his more subtle dam to discontent him;°
    To breed and cherish mutinies; detract°
    His greatest actions; give audacious check   170
    To his commands; and work to put him out
    In open act of treason. All which snares

When his wise cares prevented, a fine poison
Was thought on to mature their practices.
CORDUS Here comes Sejanus.
SILIUS   Now observe the stoops,   175
The bendings, and the falls.
ARRUNTIUS   Most creeping base!
        [*Enter*] *Sejanus, Satrius, Terentius, with others*. [*They pass over
        the stage*]
SEJANUS I note 'em well—no more. Say you.
SATRIUS   My lord,
There is a gentleman of Rome would buy—
SEJANUS How call you him you talked with?
SATRIUS   Please your lordship,
It is Eudemus, the physician   180
To Livia, Drusus' wife.
SEJANUS   On with your suit.
Would buy, you said.
SATRIUS   A tribune's place, my lord.°
SEJANUS What will he give?
SATRIUS   Fifty sestertia.°
SEJANUS Livia's physician, say you, is that fellow?
SATRIUS It is, my lord. Your lordship's answer?
SEJANUS   To what?   185
SATRIUS The place, my lord. 'Tis for a gentleman
Your lordship will well like of when you see him;
And one you may make yours by the grant.
SEJANUS Well, let him bring his money, and his name.
SATRIUS Thank your lordship. He shall, my lord.
SEJANUS   Come hither.°   190
Know you this same Eudemus? Is he learned?
SATRIUS Reputed so, my lord, and of deep practice.
SEJANUS Bring him in to me in the gallery,
And take you cause to leave us there together:
I would confer with him about a grief.—On!   195
        [*Exeunt Sejanus, Satrius, Terentius, with others; some of
        Sejanus' clients remain behind*]
ARRUNTIUS So, yet! Another, yet? Oh, desperate state
Of grov'ling honour! Seest thou this, O sun,
And do we see thee after? Methinks day
Should lose his light when men do lose their shames,
And for the empty circumstance of life   200

123

Betray their cause of living.

SILIUS   Nothing so.
Sejanus can repair, if Jove should ruin.
He is the now court-god, and well applied
With sacrifice of knees, of crooks, and cringe,
He will do more than all the house of heaven   205
Can for a thousand hecatombs. 'Tis he
Makes us our day or night; Hell and Elysium
Are in his look: we talk of Rhadamanth,
Furies, and firebrands, but 'tis his frown
That is all these, where, on the adverse part,   210
His smile is more than e'er (yet) poets feigned
Of bliss and shades, nectar—

ARRUNTIUS   A serving boy.
I knew him at Caius' trencher when for hire°
He prostituted his abused body
To that great gourmand, fat Apicius,°   215
And was the noted pathic of the time.°

SABINUS And now, the second face of the whole world.
The partner of the empire, hath his image
Reared equal with Tiberius, borne in ensigns;
Commands, disposes every dignity;   220
Centurions, tribunes, heads of provinces,
Praetors, and consuls, all that heretofore
Rome's general suffrage gave, is now his sale.°
The gain, or rather spoil, of all the earth,
One, and his house, receives.

SILIUS   He hath of late   225
Made him a strength, too, strangely, by reducing°
All the praetorian bands into one camp
Which he commands; pretending that the soldier
By living loose and scattered fell to riot;°
And that if any sudden enterprise   230
Should be attempted, their united strength
Would be far more than severed; and their life
More strict, if from the city more removed.

SABINUS Where now he builds what kind of forts he please,
Is hard to court the soldier by his name,°   235
Woos, feasts the chiefest men of action,
Whose wants, not loves, compel them to be his.
And though he ne'er were liberal by kind,°

124

Yet to his own dark ends he's most profuse,
Lavish, and letting fly he cares not what   240
To his ambition.
ARRUNTIUS   Yet hath he ambition?
Is there that step in state can make him higher?
Or more? Or anything he is, but less?
SILIUS Nothing, but emperor.
ARRUNTIUS   The name Tiberius,
I hope, will keep, howe'er he hath forgone   245
The dignity and power.
SILIUS   Sure, while he lives.
ARRUNTIUS And dead, it comes to Drusus. Should he fail,
To the brave issue of Germanicus,
And they are three: too many—ha?—for him°
To have a plot upon?
SABINUS   I do not know   250
The heart of his designs; but sure, their face
Looks farther than the present.
ARRUNTIUS   By the gods,
If I could guess he had but such a thought,
My sword should cleave him down from head to heart
But I would find it out; and with my hand   255
I'd hurl his panting brain about the air°
In mites as small as atomi, to undo
The knotted bed—
SABINUS   You are observed, Arruntius.°
ARRUNTIUS Death! I dare tell him so, and all his spies:
        [*He turns to Sejanus' clients*]
You, sir, I would, do you look? And you!
SABINUS   Forbear.   260
        [*Enter*] Satrius [*and*] Eudemus [*who stand apart*]
SATRIUS Here he will instant be; let's walk a turn.
You're in a muse, Eudemus?
EUDEMUS   Not I, sir.
I wonder he should mark me out so. Well,
Jove and Apollo form it for the best.
SATRIUS Your fortune's made unto you now, Eudemus,   265
If you can but lay hold upon the means.
Do but observe his humour, and—believe it—
He is the noblest Roman, where he takes—
Here comes his lordship.

[Enter Sejanus]

SEJANUS   Now, good Satrius.

SATRIUS This is the gentleman, my lord.

SEJANUS   Is this?   270
  Give me your hand, we must be more acquainted.
  Report, sir, hath spoke out your art and learning,
  And I am glad I have so needful cause
  (However in itself painful and hard)
  To make me known to so great virtue. Look,°   275
  Who's that? Satrius—
     [Exit Satrius]
                 I have a grief, sir,
  That will desire your help. Your name's Eudemus?

EUDEMUS Yes.

SEJANUS   Sir?

EUDEMUS   It is, my lord.

SEJANUS   I hear you are
  Physician to Livia, the princess?

EUDEMUS I minister unto her, my good lord.   280

SEJANUS You minister to a royal lady, then.

EUDEMUS She is, my lord, and fair.

SEJANUS   That's understood
  Of all their sex, who are, or would be so:
  And those that would be, physic soon can make 'em;
  For those that are, their beauties fear no colours.°   285

EUDEMUS Your lordship is conceited.

SEJANUS   Sir, you know it.°
  And can, if need be, read a learnèd lecture
  On this, and other secrets. Pray you, tell me,
  What more of ladies besides Livia
  Have you your patients?

EUDEMUS   Many, my good lord.   290
  The great Augusta, Urgulania,
  Mutilia Prisca, and Plancina, divers—°

SEJANUS And all these tell you the particulars
  Of every several grief? How first it grew,
  And then increased, what action causèd that,   295
  What passion that; and answer to each point
  That you will put 'em?

EUDEMUS   Else, my lord, we know not
  How to prescribe the remedies.

SEJANUS   Go to,
   You're a subtle nation, you physicians,
   And grown the only cabinets in court°   300
   To ladies' privacies! Faith—which of these
   Is the most pleasant lady in her physic?°
   Come, you are modest now.
EUDEMUS   'Tis fit, my lord.
SEJANUS Why sir, I do not ask you of their urines,
   Whose smells most violet, or whose siege is best?°   305
   Or who makes hardest faces on the stool?
   Which lady sleeps with her own face a-nights?
   Which puts her teeth off, with her clothes, in court?
   Or which her hair? Which her complexion,
   And in which box she puts it? These were questions   310
   That might, perhaps, have put your gravity
   To some defence of blush. But I inquired
   Which was the wittiest? Merriest? Wantonest?
   Harmless intergatories, but conceits.°
   Methinks Augusta should be most perverse   315
   And froward in her fit?
EUDEMUS   She is so, my lord.
SEJANUS I knew it. And Mutilia the most jocund?
EUDEMUS 'Tis very true, my lord.
SEJANUS   And why would you
   Conceal this from me now? Come, what's Livia?
   I know she's quick, and quaintly spirited,°   320
   And will have strange thoughts when she's at leisure.
   She tells 'em all to you?
EUDEMUS   My noblest lord,
   He breathes not in the Empire, or the earth,
   Whom I would be ambitious to serve—
   In any act that may preserve mine honour—   325
   Before your lordship.
SEJANUS   Sir, you can lose no honour
   By trusting aught to me. The coarsest act
   Done to my service I can so requite
   As all the world shall style it honourable;
   Your idle, virtuous definitions   330
   Keep honour poor, and are as scorned, as vain:
   Those deeds breathe honour, that do suck in gain.
EUDEMUS But, good my lord, if I should thus betray

The counsels of my patient, and a lady's
Of her high place and worth, what might your lordship,   335
Who presently are to trust me with your own,
Judge of my faith?
SEJANUS   Only the best, I swear.
   Say now, that I should utter you my grief;
   And with it, the true cause—that it were love,
   And love to Livia: you should tell her this?   340
   Should she suspect your faith? I would you could
   Tell me as much from her; see, if my brain
   Could be turned jealous.
EUDEMUS   Happily, my lord,°
   I could in time tell you as much, and more;
   So I might safely promise but the first   345
   To her from you.
SEJANUS   As safely, my Eudemus
   (I now dare call thee so), as I have put
   The secret into thee.
EUDEMUS   My lord—
SEJANUS   Protest not.
   Thy looks are vows to me, use only speed,
   And but affect her with Sejanus' love.°   350
   Thou art a man made to make consuls. Go.
EUDEMUS My lord, I'll promise you a private meeting
   This day, together.
SEJANUS   Canst thou?
EUDEMUS   Yes.
SEJANUS   The place?
EUDEMUS My gardens, whither I shall fetch your lordship.
SEJANUS Let me adore my Aesculapius.   355
   Why, this indeed is physic, and outspeaks
   The knowledge of cheap drugs, or any use
   Can be made out of it; more comforting
   Than all your opiates, juleps, apozems,
   Magistral syrups, or—Begone, my friend,°   360
   Not barely stylèd, but created so;
   Expect things greater than thy largest hopes
   To overtake thee. Fortune shall be taught
   To know how ill she hath deserved thus long,
   To come behind thy wishes. Go, and speed.   365
      [*Exit Eudemus*]

Ambition makes more trusty slaves than need.
These fellows, by the favour of their art,
Have still the means to tempt, oft-times, the power.°
If Livia will be now corrupted, then
Thou hast the way, Sejanus, to work out   370
His secrets, who (thou knowest) endures thee not,
Her husband, Drusus—and to work against them.
Prosper it, Pallas, thou that betterst wit;
For Venus hath the smallest share in it.

> [*Enter*] *Tiberius* [*and*] *Drusus* [*attended by Haterius,*
> *Latiaris, Satrius, and Natta;*° *they stand apart from*
> *Arruntius, Cordus, Silius, and Sabinus. One kneels to*
> *Tiberius*]

TIBERIUS We not endure these flatteries; let him stand.   375
Our Empire, ensigns, axes, rods, and state°
Take not away our human nature from us:
Look up on us, and fall before the gods.
SEJANUS How like a god speaks Caesar!
ARRUNTIUS   There, observe.
He can endure that second, that's no flattery.   380
Oh, what is it proud slime will not believe
Of his own worth, to hear it equal praised
Thus with the gods?
CORDUS   He did not hear it, sir.
ARRUNTIUS He did not? Tut, he must not, we think meanly.
'Tis your most courtly, known confederacy   385
To have your private parasite redeem
What he, in public subtlety, will lose
To making him a name.
HATERIUS [*gives Tiberius letters*] Right mighty lord.
TIBERIUS We must make up our ears 'gainst these assaults
Of charming tongues; we pray you use no more   390
These contumelies to us. Style not us
Or lord, or mighty, who profess ourself
The servant of the Senate, and are proud
T' enjoy them, our good, just, and favouring lords.°
CORDUS Rarely dissembled.
ARRUNTIUS   Prince-like, to the life.   395
SABINUS When power, that may command, so much descends,
Their bondage, whom it stoops to, it intends.
TIBERIUS Whence are these letters?

HATERIUS   From the Senate.
TIBERIUS   So.
    [Latiaris gives him letters]
    Whence these?
LATIARIS   From thence, too.
TIBERIUS   Are they sitting now?
LATIARIS They stay thy answer, Caesar.
SILIUS   If this man   400
    Had but a mind allied unto his words,
    How blest a fate were it to us and Rome?
    We could not think that state for which to change,
    Although the aim were our old liberty:
    The ghosts of those that fell for that would grieve   405
    Their bodies lived not now, again to serve.
    Men are deceived who think there can be thrall
    Beneath a virtuous prince. Wished liberty
    Ne'er lovelier looks than under such a crown.
    But when his grace is merely but lip-good,   410
    And that no longer than he airs himself
    Abroad in public, there to seem to shun°
    The strokes and stripes of flatterers which within
    Are lechery unto him, and so feed
    His brutish sense with their afflicting sound,   415
    As (dead to virtue) he permits himself
    Be carried like a pitcher, by the ears,
    To every act of vice, this is a case
    Deserves our fear, and doth presage the nigh
    And close approach of blood and tyranny.   420
    Flattery is midwife unto princes' rage;
    And nothing sooner doth help forth a tyrant
    Than that, and whisperers' grace, who have the time,
    The place, the power to make all men offenders.
ARRUNTIUS He should be told this, and be bid dissemble   425
    With fools and blind men. We that know the evil
    Should hunt the palace rats, or give them bane;
    Fright hence these worse than ravens that devour
    The quick, where they but prey upon the dead.°
    He shall be told it.
SABINUS   Stay, Arruntius,   430
    We must abide our opportunity,
    And practise what is fit, as what is needful.

It is not safe t' enforce a sovereign's ear:
Princes hear well, if they at all will hear.°

ARRUNTIUS Ha? Say you so? Well. In the meantime, Jove—   435
Say not, but I do call upon thee now—
Of all wild beasts, preserve me from a tyrant;
And of all tame, a flatterer.

SILIUS   'Tis well prayed.

TIBERIUS Return the lords this voice: we are their creature;°
And it is fit a good and honest prince   440
Whom they, out of their bounty, have instructed°
With so dilate and absolute a power,
Should owe the office of it to their service,
And good of all and every citizen.
Nor shall it e'er repent us to have wished   445
The Senate just and favouring lords unto us,
Since their free loves do yield no less defence
To a prince's state than his own innocence.
Say then, there can be nothing in their thought
Shall want to please us that hath pleasèd them;°   450
Our suffrage rather shall prevent than stay°
Behind their wills: 'tis empire to obey
Where such, so great, so grave, so good determine.
Yet, for the suit of Spain, t' erect a temple
In honour of our mother and ourself,   455
We must—with pardon of the Senate—not
Assent thereto. Their lordships may object
Our not denying the same late request
Unto the Asian cities; we desire°
That our defence for suffering that be known   460
In these brief reasons, with our after-purpose.
Since deified Augustus hindered not
A temple to be built at Pergamum°
In honour of himself and sacred Rome,
We, that have all his deeds and words observed   465
Ever in place of laws, the rather followed
That pleasing precedent because, with ours,
The Senate's reverence also there was joined.
But as t' have once received it may deserve
The gain of pardon, so to be adored   470
With the continued style and note of gods
Through all the provinces were wild ambition,

And no less pride: yea, ev'n Augustus' name
Would early vanish, should it be profaned
With such promiscuous flatteries. For our part,   475
We here protest it, and are covetous
Posterity should know it, we are mortal,
And can but deeds of men: 'twere glory enough,°
Could we be truly a prince. And they shall add
Abounding grace unto our memory   480
That shall report us worthy our forefathers,
Careful of your affairs, constant in dangers,
And not afraid of any private frown
For public good. These things shall be to us
Temples and statues rearèd in your minds,   485
The fairest and most during imagery;°
For those of stone or brass, if they become
Odious in judgement of posterity,
Are more contemned as dying sepulchres
Than ta'en for living monuments. We then   490
Make here our suit, alike to gods and men,
The one, until the period of our race,°
T' inspire us with a free and quiet mind,
Discerning both divine and human laws;
The other, to vouchsafe us after death   495
An honourable mention and fair praise
T' accompany our actions and our name.
The rest of greatness princes may command,
And, therefore, may neglect; only a long,
A lasting, high, and happy memory   500
They should, without being satisfied, pursue.
Contempt of fame begets contempt of virtue.
NATTA Rare!
SATRIUS   Most divine!
SEJANUS   The oracles are ceased,
That only Caesar, with their tongue, might speak.
ARRUNTIUS Let me be gone—most felt and open, this!°   505
CORDUS Stay.
ARRUNTIUS   What? To hear more cunning and fine
     words,
With their sound flattered, ere their sense be meant?
TIBERIUS Their choice of Antium, there to place the gift
     Vowed to the goddess for our mother's health,
     We will the Senate know, we fairly like;   510

As also of their grant to Lepidus,
For his repairing the Aemilian place,
And restauration of those monuments;°
Their grace, too, in confining of Silanus
To th' other isle Cythera at the suit   515
Of his religious sister much commends
Their policy, so tempered with their mercy.°
But for the honours which they have decreed
To our Sejanus, to advance his statue
In Pompey's theatre (whose ruining fire   520
His vigilance and labour kept restrained
In that one loss), they have therein outgone
Their own great wisdoms by their skilful choice
And placing of their bounties on a man
Whose merit more adorns the dignity   525
Than that can him, and gives a benefit
In taking, greater than it can receive.
Blush not, Sejanus, thou great aid of Rome,
Associate of our labours, our chief helper;
Let us not force thy simple modesty   530
With offering at thy praise, for more we cannot,
Since there's no voice can take it. No man here°
Receive our speeches as hyperboles;
For we are far from flattering our friend
(Let envy know) as from the need to flatter.   535
Nor let them ask the causes of our praise;
Princes have still their grounds reared with themselves
Above the poor, low flats of common men,
And who will search the reasons of their acts,
Must stand on equal bases. Lead, away.   540
Our loves unto the Senate.
     [*Exeunt Tiberius, Sejanus, Haterius, Latiaris, Satrius, and*
     Natta]
ARRUNTIUS   Caesar!
SABINUS   Peace.
CORDUS Great Pompey's theatre was never ruined
    Till now, that proud Sejanus hath a statue
    Reared on his ashes.
ARRUNTIUS   Place the shame of soldiers
    Above the best of generals? Crack the world,   545
    And bruise the name of Romans into dust
    Ere we behold it.

SILIUS   Check your passion;
  Lord Drusus tarries.
DRUSUS   Is my father mad?
  Weary of life and rule, lords? Thus to heave
  An idol up with praise? Make him his mate?   550
  His rival in the Empire?
ARRUNTIUS   Oh good prince!°
DRUSUS Allow him statues? Titles? Honours? Such
  As he himself refuseth?
ARRUNTIUS   Brave, brave Drusus!
DRUSUS The first ascents to sovereignty are hard,
  But entered once, there never wants or means   555
  Or ministers, to help th' aspirer on.°
ARRUNTIUS True, gallant Drusus.
DRUSUS   We must shortly pray
  To modesty that he will rest contented.
ARRUNTIUS Ay, where he is, and not write emperor.°
          [*Enter*] *Sejanus,* [*Latiaris, and clients*]
SEJANUS There is your bill, and yours; bring you your
      man.°   560
  I have moved for you, too, Latiaris.
DRUSUS   What?
  Is your vast greatness grown so blindly bold
  That you will over us?
SEJANUS   Why, then give way.
DRUSUS Give way, Colossus? Do you lift? Advance you?°
  Take that!
          [*Strikes him*]
ARRUNTIUS Good! Brave! Excellent brave prince!   565
DRUSUS Nay, come, approach.
          [*Draws his sword*]
                    What, stand you off? At gaze?
  It looks too full of death for thy cold spirit.
  Avoid mine eye, dull camel, or my sword°
  Shall make thy bravery fitter for a grave
  Than for a triumph. I'll advance a statue   570
  O' your own bulk—but 't shall be on the cross,
  Where I will nail your pride at breadth and length,
  And crack those sinews which are yet but stretched
  With your swollen fortune's rage.
ARRUNTIUS   A noble prince!

ALL A Castor! A Castor! A Castor!°   575
      [Exeunt all but] Sejanus
SEJANUS He that with such wrong moved can bear it through
    With patience and an even mind, knows how
    To turn it back. Wrath, covered, carries fate:
    Revenge is lost if I profess my hate.
    What was my practice late, I'll now pursue°   580
    As my fell justice. This hath styled it new.
      [Exit]
      [Chorus of musicians]°

2.1

[Enter] Sejanus, Livia, [and] Eudemus

SEJANUS Physician, thou art worthy of a province
   For the great favours done unto our loves;
   And but that greatest Livia bears a part
   In the requital of thy services,
   I should alone despair of aught like means   5
   To give them worthy satisfaction.
LIVIA Eudemus, I will see it, shall receive
   A fit and full reward for his large merit.
   But for this potion we intend to Drusus
   (No more our husband now), whom shall we choose   10
   As the most apt and abled instrument
   To minister it to him?
EUDEMUS   I say Lygdus.
SEJANUS Lygdus? What's he?
LIVIA   An eunuch Drusus loves.
EUDEMUS Ay, and his cup-bearer.
SEJANUS   Name not a second.
   If Drusus love him, and he have that place,   15
   We cannot think a fitter.
EUDEMUS   True, my lord,
   For free access and trust are two main aids.
SEJANUS Skilful physician!
LIVIA   But he must be wrought
   To th' undertaking with some laboured art.
SEJANUS Is he ambitious?
LIVIA   No.
SEJANUS   Or covetous?   20
LIVIA Neither.
EUDEMUS   Yet gold is a good general charm.
SEJANUS What is he then?
LIVIA   Faith, only wanton, light.
SEJANUS How! Is he young and fair?
EUDEMUS   A delicate youth.
SEJANUS Send him to me, I'll work him. Royal lady,°
   Though I have loved you long, and with that height   25

136

Of zeal and duty, like the fire, which more
It mounts, it trembles, thinking nought could add
Unto the fervour which your eye had kindled,
Yet now I see your wisdom, judgement, strength,
Quickness, and will to apprehend the means   30
To your own good and greatness, I protest
Myself through rarefied, and turned all flame°
In your affection. Such a spirit as yours
Was not created for the idle second°
To a poor flash as Drusus, but to shine   35
Bright, as the moon among the lesser lights,
And share the sovereignty of all the world.
Then Livia triumphs in her proper sphere
When she and her Sejanus shall divide
The name of Caesar, and Augusta's star   40
Be dimmed with glory of a brighter beam;
When Agrippina's fires are quite extinct,
And the scarce-seen Tiberius borrows all
His little light from us, whose folded arms°
Shall make one perfect orb.
     [*Knocking within*]
                  Who's that? Eudemus,   45
Look, 'tis not Drusus?
     [*Exit Eudemus*]
              Lady, do not fear.
LIVIA Not I, my lord. My fear and love of him
   Left me at once.
SEJANUS   Illustrous lady! Stay—°
EUDEMUS [*within*] I'll tell his lordship.
     [*Enter Eudemus*]
SEJANUS   Who is 't, Eudemus?
EUDEMUS One of your lordship's servants brings you word   50
   The emperor hath sent for you.
SEJANUS   Oh! Where is he?
   With your fair leave, dear princess. I'll but ask
   A question, and return.
     [*Exit Sejanus*]
EUDEMUS   Fortunate princess!
   How are you blest in the fruition°
   Of this unequalled man, this soul of Rome,   55
   The Empire's life, and voice of Caesar's world!

LIVIA So blessèd, my Eudemus, as to know
  The bliss I have, with what I ought to owe
  The means that wrought it. How do I look today?
EUDEMUS Excellent clear, believe it. This same fucus   60
  Was well laid on.
LIVIA   Methinks 'tis here not white.
EUDEMUS Lend me your scarlet, lady. 'Tis the sun
  Hath given some little taint unto the ceruse;
  You should have used of the white oil I gave you.
   [*He paints her cheeks*]
  Sejanus for your love? His very name   65
  Commandeth above Cupid, or his shafts—
LIVIA Nay, now you've made it worse.
EUDEMUS   I'll help it straight—
  And, but pronounced, is a sufficient charm
  Against all rumour; and of absolute power
  To satisfy for any lady's honour—   70
LIVIA What do you now, Eudemus?
EUDEMUS   Make a light fucus
  To touch you o'er withal.—Honoured Sejanus!
  What act, though ne'er so strange and insolent,
  But that addition will at least bear out,
  If 't do not expiate?
LIVIA   Here, good physician.   75
EUDEMUS I like this study to preserve the love
  Of such a man, that comes not every hour
  To greet the world.—'Tis now well, lady, you should
  Use of the dentifrice I prescribed you, too,
  To clear your teeth, and the prepared pomatum,   80
  To smooth the skin.—A lady cannot be
  Too curious of her form that still would hold°
  The heart of such a person made her captive,
  As you have his; who, to endear him more
  In your clear eye, hath put away his wife,   85
  The trouble of his bed and your delights,
  Fair Apicata, and made spacious room
  To your new pleasures.
LIVIA   Have not we returned
  That with our hate of Drusus, and discovery
  Of all his counsels?
EUDEMUS   Yes, and wisely, lady;   90

The ages that succeed, and stand far off
To gaze at your high prudence, shall admire
And reckon it an act without your sex,°
It hath that rare appearance. Some will think
Your fortune could not yield a deeper sound°   95
Than mixed with Drusus; but when they shall hear
That and the thunder of Sejanus meet,
Sejanus, whose high name doth strike the stars
And rings about the concave, great Sejanus,°
Whose glories, style, and titles are himself,   100
The often iterating of Sejanus—
They then will lose their thoughts, and be ashamed
To take acquaintance of them.
    [*Enter Sejanus*]
SEJANUS   I must make
A rude departure, lady. Caesar sends
With all his haste both of command and prayer.   105
Be resolute in our plot; you have my soul
As certain yours, as it is my body's.
And wise physician, so prepare the poison
As you may lay the subtle operation
Upon some natural disease of his.   110
Your eunuch send to me. I kiss your hands,
Glory of ladies, and commend my love
To your best faith and memory.
LIVIA   My lord,
I shall but change your words. Farewell. Yet this°
Remember for your heed: he loves you not.   115
You know what I have told you. His designs
Are full of grudge and danger; we must use
More than a common speed.
SEJANUS   Excellent lady,
How you do fire my blood!
LIVIA   Well, you must go?
The thoughts be best are least set forth to show.   120
    [*Exit Sejanus*]
EUDEMUS When will you take some physic, lady?
LIVIA   When°
I shall, Eudemus; but let Drusus' drug
Be first prepared.
EUDEMUS   Were Lygdus made, that's done;

I have it ready. And tomorrow morning
I'll send you a perfume, first to resolve   125
And procure sweat, and then prepare a bath°
To cleanse and clear the cutis; against when
I'll have an excellent new fucus made,
Resistive 'gainst the sun, the rain, or wind,
Which you shall lay on with a breath or oil,   130
As you best like, and last some fourteen hours.
This change came timely, lady, for your health
And the restoring your complexion,
Which Drusus' choler had almost burnt up;°
Wherein your fortune hath prescribed you better   135
Than art could do.
LIVIA   Thanks, good physician,
I'll use my fortune (you shall see) with reverence.
Is my coach ready?
EUDEMUS   It attends your highness.
        [*Exeunt*]

2.2

[*Enter*] *Sejanus*

SEJANUS If this be not revenge when I have done
And made it perfect, let Egyptian slaves,
Parthians, and barefoot Hebrews brand my face
And print my body full of injuries.
Thou lost thyself, child Drusus, when thou thoughtst   5
Thou couldst outskip my vengeance, or outstand
The power I had to crush thee into air:
Thy follies now shall taste what kind of man
They have provoked, and this thy father's house
Crack in the flame of my incensèd rage,   10
Whose fury shall admit no shame or mean.
Adultery? It is the lightest ill
I will commit. A race of wicked acts
Shall flow out of my anger and o'er-spread
The world's wide face, which no posterity   15
Shall e'er approve, nor yet keep silent; things
That for their cunning, close, and cruel mark

Thy father would wish his—and shall perhaps
Carry the empty name, but we the prize.
On then, my soul, and start not in thy course;° 20
Though heaven drop sulphur, and hell belch out fire,
Laugh at the idle terrors. Tell proud Jove,
Between his power and thine there is no odds.
'Twas only fear first in the world made gods.
        [*Enter*] *Tiberius* [*and Attendants*]
TIBERIUS Is yet Sejanus come?
SEJANUS   He's here, dread Caesar. 25
TIBERIUS Let all depart that chamber, and the next.
        [*Exeunt Attendants*]
    Sit down, my comfort. When the master prince
    Of all the world, Sejanus, saith he fears,
    Is it not fatal?
SEJANUS   Yes, to those are feared.
TIBERIUS And not to him?
SEJANUS   Not if he wisely turn 30
    That part of fate he holdeth first on them.
TIBERIUS That nature, blood, and laws of kind forbid.°
SEJANUS Do policy and state forbid it?
TIBERIUS   No.°
SEJANUS The rest of poor respects then let go by:
    State is enough to make th' act just, them guilty. 35
TIBERIUS Long hate pursues such acts.
SEJANUS   Whom hatred frights,
    Let him not dream on sovereignty.
TIBERIUS   Are rites
    Of faith, love, piety, to be trod down?
    Forgotten, and made vain?
SEJANUS   All for a crown.
    The prince who shames a tyrant's name to bear 40
    Shall never dare do anything but fear;
    All the command of sceptres quite doth perish
    If it begin religious thoughts to cherish:°
    Whole empires fall, swayed by those nice respects.°
    It is the licence of dark deeds protects 45
    Ev'n states most hated, when no laws resist
    The sword, but that it acteth what it list.
TIBERIUS Yet so, we may do all things cruelly,
    Not safely—

SEJANUS   Yes, and do them throughly.°
TIBERIUS Knows yet, Sejanus, whom we point at?
SEJANUS   Ay,   50
    Or else my thought, my sense, or both do err:
    'Tis Agrippina?
TIBERIUS   She; and her proud race.°
SEJANUS Proud? Dangerous, Caesar. For in them apace
    The father's spirit shoots up. Germanicus
    Lives in their looks, their gait, their form, t' upbraid us   55
    With his close death, if not revenge the same.°
TIBERIUS The act's not known.
SEJANUS   Not proved. But whispering fame°
    Knowledge and proof doth to the jealous give,
    Who, than to fail, would their own thought believe:°
    It is not safe the children draw long breath,   60
    That are provokèd by a parent's death.
TIBERIUS It is as dangerous to make them hence,
    If nothing but their birth be their offence.
SEJANUS Stay till they strike at Caesar, then their crime
    Will be enough, but late, and out of time   65
    For him to punish.
TIBERIUS   Do they purpose it?
SEJANUS You know, sir, thunder speaks not till it hit.°
    Be not secure: none swiftlier are oppressed
    Than they whom confidence betrays to rest.
    Let not your daring make your danger such;   70
    All power's to be feared, where 'tis too much.
    The youths are (of themselves) hot, violent,
    Full of great thought; and that male-spirited dame,
    Their mother, slacks no means to put them on
    By large allowance, popular presentings,°   75
    Increase of train and state, suing for titles,
    Hath them commended with like prayers, like vows,
    To the same gods, with Caesar; days and nights
    She spends in banquets and ambitious feasts
    For the nobility, where Caius Silius,   80
    Titius Sabinus, old Arruntius,
    Asinius Gallus, Furnius, Regulus,°
    And others of that discontented list
    Are the prime guests. There, and to these, she tells
    Whose niece she was, whose daughter, and whose wife,°   85

And then must they compare her with Augusta,°
Ay, and prefer her, too, commend her form,
Extol her fruitfulness; at which a shower
Falls for the memory of Germanicus,
Which they blow over straight with windy praise   90
And puffing hopes of her aspiring sons;
Who, with these hourly ticklings, grow so pleased,
And wantonly conceited of themselves,
As now they stick not to believe they are such
As these do give 'em out—and would be thought   95
(More than competitors) immediate heirs;
Whilst to their thirst of rule they win the rout
(That's still the friend of novelty) with hope
Of future freedom, which on every change,
That greedily, though emptily, expects.   100
Caesar, 'tis age in all things breeds neglects,
And princes that will keep old dignity
Must not admit too youthful heirs stand by—
Not their own issue, but so darkly set
As shadows are in picture, to give height   105
And lustre to themselves.
TIBERIUS   We will command°
Their rank thoughts down, and with a stricter hand°
Than we have yet put forth, their trains must bate,°
Their titles, feasts, and factions.
SEJANUS   Or your state.°
But how, sir, will you work?
TIBERIUS   Confine 'em.
SEJANUS   No.   110
They are too great, and that too faint a blow
To give them now: it would have served at first,
When with the weakest touch their knot had burst.
But now your care must be not to detect
The smallest chord or line of your suspect,°   115
For such, who know the weight of princes' fear,
Will, when they find themselves discovered, rear
Their forces like seen snakes, that else would lie
Rolled in their circles, close. Nought is more high,°
Daring, or desperate, than offenders found;   120
Where guilt is, rage and courage both abound.
The course must be to let 'em still swell up,

Riot, and surfeit on blind Fortune's cup;
Give 'em more place, more dignities, more style,
Call 'em to court, to Senate: in the while,°   125
Take from their strength some one or twain, or more,
Of the main fautors—it will fright the store—
And by some by-occasion. Thus with sleight
You shall disarm them first, and they, in night
Of their ambition, not perceive the train°   130
Till in the engine they are caught and slain.
TIBERIUS We would not kill, if we knew how to save;
    Yet, than a throne, 'tis cheaper give a grave.
    Is there no way to bind them by deserts?
SEJANUS Sir, wolves do change their hair, but not their hearts.   135
    While thus your thought unto a mean is tied,
    You neither dare enough, nor do provide.
    All modesty is fond; and chiefly where°
    The subject is no less compelled to bear
    Than praise his sovereign's acts.
TIBERIUS   We can no longer   140
    Keep on our mask to thee, our dear Sejanus;
    Thy thoughts are ours in all, and we but proved°
    Their voice in our designs, which by assenting
    Hath more confirmed us than if heart'ning Jove
    Had from his hundred statues bid us strike,   145
    And at the stroke clicked all his marble thumbs.°
    But who shall first be struck?
SEJANUS   First, Caius Silius.
    He is the most of mark, and most of danger:
    In power and reputation equal strong,
    Having commanded an imperial army   150
    Seven years together, vanquished Sacrovir
    In Germany, and thence obtained to wear
    The ornaments triumphal. His steep fall,°
    By how much it doth give the weightier crack,
    Will send more wounding terror to the rest,   155
    Command them stand aloof, and give more way
    To our surprising of the principal.
TIBERIUS But what Sabinus?
SEJANUS   Let him grow awhile,
    His fate is not yet ripe: we must not pluck
    At all together, lest we catch ourselves.   160

And there's Arruntius, too, he only talks.
But Sosia, Silius' wife, would be wound in
Now, for she hath a fury in her breast
More than hell ever knew, and would be sent
Thither in time. Then is there one Cremutius   165
Cordus, a writing fellow they have got
To gather notes of the precedent times
And make them into annals; a most tart
And bitter spirit, I hear, who under colour
Of praising those, doth tax the present state,   170
Censures the men, the actions, leaves no trick,
No practice unexamined, parallels
The times, the governments; a pròfessed champion
For the old liberty—
TIBERIUS   A perishing wretch.
As if there were that chaos bred in things,°   175
That laws and liberty would not rather choose
To be quite broken, and ta'en hence by us,
Than have the stain to be preserved by such.
Have we the means to make these guilty first?
SEJANUS Trust that to me; let Caesar, by his power,   180
But cause a formal meeting of the Senate,
I will have matter and accusers ready.
TIBERIUS But how? Let us consult.
SEJANUS   We shall misspend
The time of action. Counsels are unfit
In business where all rest is more pernicious   185
Than rashness can be. Acts of this close kind
Thrive more by execution than advice:
There is no ling'ring in that work begun,
Which cannot praisèd be, until through done.
TIBERIUS Our edict shall forthwith command a court.   190
While I can live, I will prevent earth's fury:°
Emou thanontos gaia michtheto puri.°
        [*Exit Tiberius. Enter*] *Posthumus*
POSTHUMUS My lord Sejanus?
SEJANUS   Julius Posthumus,
Come with my wish! What news from Agrippina's?
POSTHUMUS Faith, none. They all lock up themselves o' late,   195
Or talk in character. I have not seen°
A company so changed, except they had

Intelligence by augury of our practice.
SEJANUS When were you there?
POSTHUMUS   Last night.
SEJANUS   And what guests found you?
POSTHUMUS Sabinus, Silius—the old list—Arruntius,   200
  Furnius, and Gallus.
SEJANUS   Would not these talk?
POSTHUMUS   Little.
  And yet we offered choice of argument.
  Satrius was with me.
SEJANUS   Well, 'tis guilt enough
  Their often meeting. You forgot t' extol
  The hospitable lady?
POSTHUMUS   No, that trick   205
  Was well put home, and had succeeded, too,
  But that Sabinus coughed a caution out,
  For she began to swell—
SEJANUS   And may she burst.
  Julius, I would have you go instantly
  Unto the palace of the great Augusta,   210
  And, by your kindest friend, get swift access;
  Acquaint her with these meetings. Tell the words°
  You brought me th' other day of Silius;
  Add somewhat to 'em. Make her understand
  The danger of Sabinus, and the times,   215
  Out of his closeness. Give Arruntius words°
  Of malice against Caesar; so, to Gallus:
  But above all, to Agrippina. Say
  (As you may truly) that her infinite pride,
  Propped with the hopes of her too-fruitful womb,   220
  With popular studies gapes for sovereignty,°
  And threatens Caesar. Pray Augusta then,
  That for her own, great Caesar's, and the pub-
  Lic safety, she be pleased to urge these dangers.°
  Caesar is too secure—he must be told,   225
  And best he'll take it from a mother's tongue.
  Alas! What is 't for us to sound, t' explore,°
  To watch, oppose, plot, practise, or prevent,
  If he, for whom it is so strongly laboured,
  Shall, out of greatness and free spirit, be   230
  Supinely negligent? Our city's now

Divided, as in time o' th' civil war,
And men forbear not to declare themselves
Of Agrippina's party. Every day
The faction multiplies; and will do more   235
If not resisted—you can best enlarge it
As you find audience. Noble Posthumus,
Commend me to your Prisca; and pray her
She will solicit this great business
To earnest and most present execution,°   240
With all her utmost credit with Augusta.

POSTHUMUS I shall not fail in my instructions.
        [*Exit Posthumus*]

SEJANUS This second, from his mother, will well urge°
    Our late design, and spur on Caesar's rage,
    Which else might grow remiss. The way to put   245
    A prince in blood is to present the shapes
    Of dangers greater than they are, like late
    Or early shadows, and sometimes to feign
    Where there are none, only to make him fear;
    His fear will make him cruel; and once entered,   250
    He doth not easily learn to stop or spare
    Where he may doubt. This have I made my rule,
    To thrust Tiberius into tyranny,
    And make him toil to turn aside those blocks
    Which I alone could not remove with safety.   255
    Drusus once gone, Germanicus' three sons
    Would clog my way, whose guards have too much faith
    To be corrupted; and their mother known
    Of too too unreproved a chastity
    To be attempted as light Livia was.   260
    Work then, my art, on Caesar's fears, as they
    On those they fear, till all my lets be cleared,
    And he in ruins of his house, and hate
    Of all his subjects, bury his own state—
    When, with my peace and safety, I will rise   265
    By making him the public sacrifice.
        [*Exit*]

2.3

[*Enter*] *Satrius* [*and*] *Natta*°

SATRIUS They are grown exceeding circumspect and wary.

NATTA They have us in the wind—and yet Arruntius
Cannot contain himself.

SATRIUS   Tut, he's not yet
Looked after; there are others more desired
That are more silent.

NATTA   Here he comes. Away.   5

[*Exeunt Satrius and Natta. Enter*] *Sabinus, Arruntius,* [*and*]
Cordus

SABINUS How is it that these beagles haunt the house
Of Agrippina?

ARRUNTIUS   Oh, they hunt, they hunt.
There is some game here lodged which they must rouse
To make the great ones sport.

CORDUS   Did you observe
How they inveighed 'gainst Caesar?

ARRUNTIUS   Ay, baits, baits   10
For us to bite at; would I have my flesh
Torn by the public hook, these qualified hangmen°
Should be my company.

CORDUS   Here comes another.

[*Afer passeth by*]°

ARRUNTIUS Ay, there's a man, Afer the orator:
One that hath phrases, figures, and fine flowers°   15
To strew his rhetoric with, and doth make haste
To get him note or name by any offer
Where blood or gain be objects; steeps his words,
When he would kill, in artificial tears—
The crocodile of Tiber! Him I love,   20
That man is mine. He hath my heart and voice
When I could curse, he, he!

SABINUS   Contemn the slaves,
Their present lives will be their future graves.

[*Exeunt*]

2.4

[*Enter*] *Silius, Agrippina, Nero,* [*and*] *Sosia*

SILIUS May 't please your highness not forget yourself,
   I dare not, with my manners, to attempt
   Your trouble farther.
AGRIPPINA   Farewell, noble Silius.
SILIUS Most royal princess.
AGRIPPINA   Sosia stays with us?
SILIUS She is your servant, and doth owe your grace   5
   An honest, but unprofitable, love.°
AGRIPPINA How can that be, when there's no gain but virtue's?
SILIUS You take the moral, not the politic, sense.
   I meant, as she is bold and free of speech,
   Earnest to utter what her zealous thought   10
   Travails withal in honour of your house;°
   Which act, as it is simply borne in her,°
   Partakes of love and honesty, but may
   By th' over-often and unseasoned use°
   Turn to your loss and danger. For your state   15
   Is waited on by envies, as by eyes;
   And every second guest your tables take
   Is a fee'd spy, t' observe who goes, who comes,
   What conference you have, with whom, where, when,
   What the discourse is, what the looks, the thoughts   20
   Of every person there they do extract
   And make into a substance.
AGRIPPINA   Hear me, Silius,
   Were all Tiberius' body stuck with eyes,
   And every wall and hanging in my house
   Transparent as this lawn I wear, or air;   25
   Yea, had Sejanus both his ears as long
   As to my inmost closet, I would hate°
   To whisper any thought, or change an act,
   To be made Juno's rival. Virtue's forces
   Show ever noblest in conspicuous courses.   30
SILIUS 'Tis great, and bravely spoken, like the spirit

Of Agrippina. Yet your highness knows
There is nor loss, nor shame, in providence:°
Few can, what all should do, beware enough.
You may perceive with what officious face   35
Satrius and Natta, Afer, and the rest
Visit your house of late t' enquire the secrets;
And with what bold and privileged art they rail
Against Augusta, yea, and at Tiberius,
Tell tricks of Livia and Sejanus, all   40
T' excite and call your indignation on,
That they might hear it at more liberty.
AGRIPPINA You're too suspicious, Silius.
SILIUS   Pray the gods
I be so, Agrippina. But I fear
Some subtle practice. They, that durst to strike   45
At so exampless and unblamed a life
As that of the renowned Germanicus,
Will not sit down with that exploit alone:
He threatens many, that hath injured one.
NERO 'Twere best rip forth their tongues, sear out their eyes,   50
When next they come.
SOSIA   A fit reward for spies.
        [*Enter*] *Drusus Junior*
DRUSUS JUNIOR Hear you the rumour?
AGRIPPINA   What?
DRUSUS JUNIOR   Drusus is dying.
AGRIPPINA Dying?
NERO   That's strange!
AGRIPPINA   You were with him yesternight.
DRUSUS JUNIOR One met Eudemus the physician,
Sent for but now, who thinks he cannot live.   55
SILIUS Thinks? If 't be arrived at that, he knows,
Or none.
AGRIPPINA This's quick! What should be his disease?
SILIUS Poison, poison.
AGRIPPINA   How, Silius!
NERO   What's that?
SILIUS Nay, nothing. There was—late—a certain blow°
Given o' the face.

NERO   Ay, to Sejanus?
SILIUS   True.   60
DRUSUS JUNIOR And what of that?
SILIUS   I am glad I gave it not.
NERO But there is somewhat else?
SILIUS   Yes, private meetings,
    With a great lady, at a physician's,
    And a wife turned away.
NERO   Ha!
SILIUS   Toys, mere toys.
    What wisdom's now i' th' streets? I' th' common mouth?   65
DRUSUS JUNIOR Fears, whisp'rings, tumults, noise, I know not what—
    They say the Senate sit.
SILIUS   I'll thither straight,
    And see what's in the forge.
AGRIPPINA   Good Silius, do.
    Sosia and I will in.
SILIUS   Haste you, my lords,
    To visit the sick prince; tender your loves   70
    And sorrows to the people. This Sejanus—
    Trust my divining soul—hath plots on all:
    No tree that stops his prospect but must fall.
            [*Exeunt*]
            [*Chorus of musicians*]

3.1

The Senate°

[*Enter*] *Praecones, Lictors, Varro, Sejanus, Latiaris, Cotta,* [*and*]
Afer

SEJANUS 'Tis only you must urge against him, Varro,
    Nor I, nor Caesar, may appear therein
    Except in your defence, who are the consul,°
    And under colour of late enmity
    Between your father and his may better do it,°   5
    As free from all suspicion of a practice.
    Here be your notes, what points to touch at—read.
    Be cunning in them. Afer has them, too.
VARRO But is he summoned?
SEJANUS   No. It was debated
    By Caesar, and concluded as most fit   10
    To take him unprepared.
AFER   And prosecute
    All under name of treason.
VARRO   I conceive.

[*Enter Sabinus,*] *Gallus, Lepidus,* [*and*] *Arruntius*

SABINUS Drusus being dead, Caesar will not be here.
GALLUS What should the business of this Senate be?
ARRUNTIUS That can my subtle whisperers tell you. We,   15
    That are the good–dull–noble lookers-on,
    Are only called to keep the marble warm.
    What should we do with those deep mysteries,
    Proper to these fine heads? Let them alone.
    Our ignorance may perchance help us be saved   20
    From whips and furies.
GALLUS   See, see, see, their action!°
ARRUNTIUS Ay, now their heads do travail, now they work;
    Their faces run like shuttles, they are weaving
    Some curious cobweb to catch flies.
SABINUS   Observe,
    They take their places.
ARRUNTIUS   What, so low?
GALLUS   Oh yes,   25

They must be seen to flatter Caesar's grief,
Though but in sitting.
VARRO   Bid us silence.
PRAECO   Silence!
VARRO   Fathers conscript, may this our present meeting
     Turn fair and fortunate to the commonwealth.
        [*Enter*] *Silius* [*and other Senators*]
SEJANUS   See, Silius enters.
SILIUS   Hail, grave fathers!
LICTOR   Stand.   30
     Silius, forbear thy place.
SENATORS   How!
PRAECO   Silius, stand forth,
     The consul hath to charge thee.
LICTOR   Room for Caesar!
ARRUNTIUS   Is he come, too? Nay then, expect a
     trick.
SABINUS   Silius accused? Sure he will answer nobly.
        [*Enter*] *Tiberius* [*and Attendants*]
TIBERIUS   We stand amazèd, fathers, to behold   35
     This general dejection. Wherefore sit
     Rome's consuls thus dissolved, as they had lost°
     All the remembrance both of style and place?
     It not becomes. No woes are of fit weight
     To make the honour of the Empire stoop;   40
     Though I, in my peculiar self, may meet
     Just reprehension, that so suddenly,
     And in so fresh a grief, would greet the Senate,°
     When private tongues of kinsmen and allies,
     Inspired with comforts, loathly are endured,   45
     The face of men not seen, and scarce the day,
     To thousands that communicate our loss.°
     Nor can I argue these of weakness, since
     They take but natural ways; yet I must seek
     For stronger aids, and those fair helps draw out   50
     From warm embraces of the commonwealth.
     Our mother, great Augusta, is struck with time,
     Ourself impressed with agèd characters;°
     Drusus is gone, his children young, and babes.
     Our aims must now reflect on those that may   55
     Give timely succour to these present ills,

And are our only glad-surviving hopes,
The noble issue of Germanicus,
Nero and Drusus. Might it please the consul
Honour them in (they both attend without)   60
I would present them to the Senate's care,
And raise those springs of joy that should exhaust
These floods of sorrow in your drownèd eyes.
ARRUNTIUS [*aside*] By Jove, I am not Oedipus enough
    To understand this Sphinx.
SABINUS   The princes come.°   65
        [*Enter*] *Nero* [*and*] *Drusus Junior*
TIBERIUS Approach you, noble Nero, noble Drusus.
    These princes, fathers, when their parent died,
    I gave unto their uncle with this prayer,°
    That though he had proper issue of his own,
    He would no less bring up and foster these,   70
    Than that self blood; and by that act confirm
    Their worths to him, and to posterity.
    Drusus ta'en hence, I turn my prayers to you,
    And 'fore our country and our gods, beseech
    You take and rule Augustus' nephew's sons,   75
    Sprung of the noblest ancestors; and so
    Accomplish both my duty, and your own.
    Nero and Drusus, these shall be to you
    In place of parents, these your fathers, these,
    And not unfitly: for you are so born   80
    As all your good or ill's the commonwealth's.
    Receive them, you strong guardians; and blest gods,
    Make all their actions answer to their bloods;
    Let their great titles find increase by them,
    Not they by titles; set them, as in place,   85
    So in example, above all the Romans;
    And may they know no rivals but themselves.
    Let Fortune give them nothing, but attend
    Upon their virtue—and that still come forth
    Greater than hope, and better than their fame.   90
    Relieve me, fathers, with your general voice.°
SENATORS May all the gods consent to Caesar's wish,
    And add to any honours that may crown
    The hopeful issue of Germanicus.
TIBERIUS We thank you, reverend fathers, in their right.   95

ARRUNTIUS [*aside*] If this were true now! But the space, the space
    Between the breast and lips—Tiberius' heart°
    Lies a thought farther than another man's.
TIBERIUS My comforts are so flowing in my joys
    As in them all my streams of grief are lost,   100
    No less than are land-waters in the sea
    Or showers in rivers, though their cause was such°
    As might have sprinkled even the gods with tears.
    Yet since the greater doth embrace the less,
    We covetously obey.
ARRUNTIUS [*aside*]   Well acted, Caesar.°   105
TIBERIUS And now I am the happy witness made
    Of your so much desired affections
    To this great issue, I could wish the Fates
    Would here set peaceful period to my days;
    However, to my labours I entreat,   110
    And beg it of this Senate, some fit ease—
ARRUNTIUS [*aside*] Laugh, fathers, laugh! Ha' you no spleens
    about you?
TIBERIUS The burden is too heavy I sustain
    On my unwilling shoulders; and I pray
    It may be taken off, and reconferred   115
    Upon the consuls, or some other Roman,
    More able, and more worthy.
ARRUNTIUS [*aside*]   Laugh on, still!
SABINUS Why this doth render all the rest suspected!°
GALLUS It poisons all.
ARRUNTIUS   Oh, do you taste it then?
SABINUS It takes away my faith to anything   120
    He shall hereafter speak.
ARRUNTIUS   Ay, to pray that,°
    Which would be to his head as hot as thunder
    ('Gainst which he wears that charm) should but the court°
    Receive him at his word.
GALLUS   Hear!
TIBERIUS   For myself,
    I know my weakness, and so little covet—   125
    Like some gone past—the weight that will oppress me,
    As my ambition is the counterpoint.°
ARRUNTIUS [*aside*] Finely maintained; good still.
SEJANUS   But Rome, whose blood

155

Whose nerves, whose life, whose very frame relies
On Caesar's strength, no less than heaven on Atlas,   130
Cannot admit it but with general ruin.°
ARRUNTIUS [*aside*] Ah! Are you there to bring him off?
SEJANUS   Let Caesar
No more then urge a point so contrary
To Caesar's greatness, the grieved Senate's vows,
Or Rome's necessity.
GALLUS [*aside*]   He comes about.   135
ARRUNTIUS [*aside*] More nimbly than Vertumnus.
TIBERIUS   For the public,°
I may be drawn to show I can neglect
All private aims, though I affect my rest;
But if the Senate still command me serve,
I must be glad to practise my obedience.   140
ARRUNTIUS [*aside*] You must, and will, sir. We do know it.
SENATORS   Caesar,
Live long and happy, great and royal Caesar;
The gods preserve thee and thy modesty,
Thy wisdom and thy innocence.
ARRUNTIUS [*aside*]   Where is 't?
The prayer's made before the subject.
SENATORS   Guard   145
His meekness, Jove, his piety, his care,
His bounty—
ARRUNTIUS [*aside*] And his subtlety, I'll put in—
Yet he'll keep that himself, without the gods.
All prayers are vain for him.
TIBERIUS   We will not hold
Your patience, fathers, with long answer; but   150
Shall still contend to be what you desire,
And work to satisfy so great a hope.
Proceed to your affairs.
ARRUNTIUS [*aside*]   Now, Silius, guard thee;
The curtain's drawing. Afer advanceth.
PRAECO   Silence!
AFER Cite Caius Silius.
PRAECO   Caius Silius!
SILIUS   Here.   155
AFER The triumph that thou hadst in Germany
For thy late victory on Sacrovir,

Thou hast enjoyed so freely, Caius Silius,
As no man it envied thee; nor would Caesar
Or Rome admit that thou wert then defrauded   160
Of any honours thy deserts could claim
In the fair service of the commonwealth.
But now if, after all their loves and graces—
Thy actions and their courses being discovered—
It shall appear to Caesar and this Senate   165
Thou hast defiled those glories with thy crimes—
SILIUS Crimes?
AFER   Patience, Silius.
SILIUS   Tell thy mule of patience,
I am a Roman. What are my crimes? Proclaim them.
Am I too rich? Too honest for the times?
Have I or treasure, jewels, land, or houses   170
That some informer gapes for? Is my strength
Too much to be admitted? Or my knowledge?
These now are crimes.
AFER   Nay, Silius, if the name
Of crime so touch thee, with what impotence
Wilt thou endure the matter to be searched?   175
SILIUS I tell thee, Afer, with more scorn than fear.
Employ your mercenary tongue and art.
Where's my accuser?
VARRO   Here.
ARRUNTIUS [*aside*]   Varro? The consul?
Is he thrust in?
VARRO   'Tis I accuse thee, Silius.
Against the majesty of Rome and Caesar,°   180
I do pronounce thee here a guilty cause:
First, of beginning and occasioning,
Next, drawing out, the war in Gallia
For which thou late triumph'st; dissembling long
That Sacrovir to be an enemy,   185
Only to make thy entertainment more
Whilst thou and thy wife Sosia polled the province;°
Wherein, with sordid-base desire of gain,
Thou hast discredited thy action's worth
And been a traitor to the state.
SILIUS   Thou liest.   190
ARRUNTIUS [*aside*] I thank thee, Silius, speak so still, and often.

VARRO If I not prove it, Caesar, but injustly
  Have called him into trial, here I bind
  Myself to suffer what I claim 'gainst him,
  And yield to have what I have spoke confirmed   195
  By judgement of the court, and all good men.
SILIUS Caesar, I crave to have my cause deferred
  Till this man's consulship be out.
TIBERIUS   We cannot,
  Nor may we grant it.
SILIUS   Why? Shall he design
  My day of trial? Is he my accuser?   200
  And must he be my judge?
TIBERIUS   It hath been usual,
  And is a right that custom hath allowed
  The magistrate, to call forth private men,
  And to appoint their day: which privilege
  We may not in the consul see infringed,   205
  By whose deep watches and industrious care
  It is so laboured, as the commonwealth
  Receive no loss, by any oblique course.
SILIUS Caesar, thy fraud is worse than violence.
TIBERIUS Silius, mistake us not, we dare not use   210
  The credit of the consul to thy wrong,
  But only do preserve his place and power
  So far as it concerns the dignity
  And honour of the state.
ARRUNTIUS   Believe him, Silius.
COTTA Why so he may, Arruntius.
ARRUNTIUS   I say so.   215
  And he may choose to.
TIBERIUS   By the Capitol,
  And all our gods, but that the dear republic,
  Our sacred laws, and just authority
  Are interested therein, I should be silent.
AFER Please Caesar to give way unto his trial.   220
  He shall have justice.
SILIUS   Nay, I shall have law;
  Shall I not, Afer? Speak.
AFER   Would you have more?
SILIUS No, my well-spoken man, I would no more—
  Nor less—might I enjoy it natural,

Not taught to speak unto your present ends,   225
Free from thine, his, and all your unkind handling,°
Furious enforcing, most unjust presuming,
Malicious and manifold applying,
Foul wresting, and impossible construction.
AFER He raves, he raves.
SILIUS   Thou durst not tell me so,   230
  Hadst thou not Caesar's warrant. I can see
  Whose power condemns me.
VARRO   This betrays his spirit.
  This doth enough declare him what he is.
SILIUS What am I? Speak.
VARRO   An enemy to the state.
SILIUS Because I am an enemy to thee,   235
  And such corrupted ministers of the state,
  That here art made a present instrument°
  To gratify it with thine own disgrace.
SEJANUS This, to the consul, is most insolent!
  And impious!
SILIUS   Ay, take part. Reveal yourselves.   240
  Alas, I scent not your confederacies?
  Your plots and combinations? I not know°
  Minion Sejanus hates me; and that all
  This boast of law, and law, is but a form,
  A net of Vulcan's filing, a mere engine,°   245
  To take that life by a pretext of justice
  Which you pursue in malice? I want brain
  Or nostril to persuade me that your ends
  And purposes are made to what they are
  Before my answer? Oh you equal gods,   250
  Whose justice not a world of wolf-turned men
  Shall make me to accuse—howe'er provoke—
  Have I for this so oft engaged myself?
  Stood in the heat and fervour of a fight,
  When Phoebus sooner hath forsook the day   255
  Than I the field against the blue-eyed Gauls,
  And crispèd Germans? When our Roman eagles°
  Have fanned the fire with their labouring wings,
  And no blow dealt that left not death behind it?
  When I have charged, alone, into the troops   260
  Of curled Sicambrians, routed them, and came°

Not off with backward ensigns of a slave,
But forward marks, wounds on my breast and face,°
Were meant to thee, O Caesar, and thy Rome?
And have I this return? Did I, for this,   265
Perform so noble and so brave defeat
On Sacrovir? O Jove, let it become me
To boast my deeds when he, whom they concern,
Shall thus forget them.
AFER   Silius, Silius,
These are the common customs of thy blood°   270
When it is high with wine, as now with rage.
This well agrees with that intemperate vaunt
Thou lately mad'st at Agrippina's table,
That when all other of the troops were prone
To fall into rebellion, only thine   275
Remained in their obedience. Thou wert he
That saved'st the Empire; which had then been lost,
Had but thy legions there rebelled or mutined.°
Thy virtue met and fronted every peril.
Thou gav'st to Caesar and to Rome their surety.   280
Their name, their strength, their spirit, and their state,
Their being was a donative from thee.
ARRUNTIUS [aside] Well worded, and most like an orator.
TIBERIUS Is this true, Silius?
SILIUS   Save thy question, Caesar.
Thy spy of famous credit hath affirmed it.°   285
ARRUNTIUS [aside] Excellent Roman!
SABINUS [aside]   He doth answer stoutly.
SEJANUS If this be so, there needs no farther cause
Of crime against him.
VARRO   What can more impeach°
The royal dignity and state of Caesar,
Than to be urgèd with a benefit   290
He cannot pay?
COTTA   In this, all Caesar's fortune
Is made unequal to the courtesy.
LATIARIS His means are clean destroyed that should requite.
GALLUS Nothing is great enough for Silius' merit.
ARRUNTIUS [aside] Gallus o' that side, too?
SILIUS   Come, do not hunt   295
And labour so about for circumstance

To make him guilty whom you have foredoomed;
Take shorter ways, I'll meet your purposes.
The words were mine; and more I now will say:
Since I have done thee that great service, Caesar,   300
Thou still hast feared me; and in place of grace,
Returned me hatred. So soon all best turns
With princes do convert to injuries
In estimation, when they greater rise
Than can be answered. Benefits with you   305
Are of no longer pleasure than you can
With ease restore them; that transcended once,°
Your studies are not how to thank, but kill.
It is your nature to have all men slaves
To you, but you acknowledging to none.   310
The means that make your greatness must not come
In mention of it; if it do, it takes
So much away, you think; and that which helped
Shall soonest perish, if it stand in eye
Where it may front, or but upbraid the high.°   315

COTTA Suffer him speak no more.
VARRO   Note but his spirit.
AFER This shows him in the rest.
LATIARIS   Let him be censured.
SEJANUS He hath spoke enough to prove him Caesar's foe.
COTTA His thoughts look through his words.
SEJANUS   A censure.
SILIUS   Stay,
    Stay, most officious Senate, I shall straight   320
    Delude thy fury. Silius hath not placed°
    His guards within him against Fortune's spite
    So weakly but he can escape your gripe
    That are but hands of Fortune; she herself,
    When virtue doth oppose, must lose her threats.   325
    All that can happen in humanity,
    The frown of Caesar, proud Sejanus' hatred,
    Base Varro's spleen, and Afer's bloodying tongue,
    The Senate's servile flattery, and these
    Mustered to kill, I am fortified against   330
    And can look down upon: they are beneath me.
    It is not life whereof I stand enamoured;
    Nor shall my end make me accuse my fate.

The coward and the valiant man must fall,
Only the cause and manner how discerns them—   335
Which then are gladdest, when they cost us dearest.°
Romans, if any here be in this Senate,
Would know to mock Tiberius' tyranny,
Look upon Silius, and so learn to die.
          [*Stabs himself*]
VARRO Oh desperate act!
ARRUNTIUS [*aside*]   An honourable hand!   340
TIBERIUS Look, is he dead?
SABINUS [*aside*]   'Twas nobly struck, and home.
ARRUNTIUS [*aside*] My thought did prompt him to it. Farewell,
     Silius.
Be famous ever for thy great example.
TIBERIUS We are not pleased in this sad accident
     That thus hath stallèd and abused our mercy,   345
     Intended to preserve thee, noble Roman,
     And to prevent thy hopes.
ARRUNTIUS [*aside*]   Excellent wolf!
     Now he is full, he howls.
SEJANUS   Caesar doth wrong
     His dignity and safety thus to mourn
     The deserved end of so professed a traitor,   350
     And doth, by this his lenity, instruct
     Others as factious to the like offence.
TIBERIUS The confiscation merely of his state
     Had been enough.
ARRUNTIUS [*aside*]   Oh, that was gaped for then?
VARRO Remove the body.
          [*Lictors exit with body*]
SEJANUS   Let citation   355
     Go out for Sosia.
GALLUS   Let her be proscribed.°
     And for the goods, I think it fit that half
     Go to the treasure, half unto the children.°
LEPIDUS With leave of Caesar, I would think that fourth,
     The which the law doth cast on the informers,   360
     Should be enough; the rest go to the children:
     Wherein the prince shall show humanity
     And bounty, not to force them by their want
     (Which in their parents' trespass they deserved)

To take ill courses.

TIBERIUS   It shall please us.

ARRUNTIUS [*aside*]   Ay,   365
    Out of necessity. This Lepidus
    Is grave and honest, and I have observed
    A moderation still in all his censures.

SABINUS [*aside*] And bending to the better—
    [*Enter*] Cordus [*with*] Satrius [*and*] Natta°
                        Stay, who's this?
    Cremutius Cordus? What? Is he brought in?   370

ARRUNTIUS More blood unto the banquet? Noble Cordus,
    I wish thee good: be as thy writings, free
    And honest.

TIBERIUS   What is he?

SEJANUS   For th' annals, Caesar.°

PRAECO Cremutius Cordus!

CORDUS   Here.

PRAECO   Satrius Secundus,
    Pinnarius Natta, you are his accusers.   375

ARRUNTIUS [*aside*] Two of Sejanus' bloodhounds, whom he breeds
    With human flesh to bay at citizens.

AFER Stand forth before the Senate, and confront him.

SATRIUS I do accuse thee here, Cremutius Cordus,
    To be a man factious and dangerous,   380
    A sower of sedition in the state,
    A turbulent and discontented spirit,
    Which I will prove from thine own writings here,
    The annals thou last published; where thou bit'st
    The present age, and with a viper's tooth,   385
    Being a member of it, dar'st that ill
    Which never yet degenerous bastard did
    Upon his parent.

NATTA   To this I subscribe;°
    And, forth a world of more particulars,
    Instance in only one. Comparing men   390
    And times, thou praisest Brutus, and affirmst
    That 'Cassius was the last of all the Romans.'

COTTA How! What are we then?

VARRO   What is Caesar? Nothing?

AFER My lords, this strikes at every Roman's private,°
    In whom reigns gentry and estate of spirit,   395

To have a Brutus brought in parallel,
A parricide, an enemy of his country,°
Ranked and preferred to any real worth
That Rome now holds. This is most strangely invective;
Most full of spite and insolent upbraiding.   400
Nor is 't the time alone is here disprized,
But the whole man of time, yea, Caesar's self°
Brought in disvalue; and he aimed at most
By oblique glance of his licentious pen.°
Caesar, if Cassius were the last of Romans,   405
Thou hast no name.
TIBERIUS   Let's hear him answer. Silence.
CORDUS So innocent I am of fact, my lords°
As but my words are argued; yet those words
Not reaching either prince, or prince's parent,
The which your law of treason comprehends.   410
Brutus and Cassius I am charged t' have praised,
Whose deeds, when many more besides myself
Have writ, not one hath mentioned without honour.
Great Titus Livius, great for eloquence°
And faith amongst us, in his history   415
With so great praises Pompey did extol,
As oft Augustus called him a Pompeian:
Yet this not hurt their friendship. In his book
He often names Scipio, Afranius,°
Yea, the same Cassius, and this Brutus, too,   ⟨420
As worthiest men; not thieves and parricides,
Which notes upon their fames are now imposed.
Asinius Pollio's writings quite throughout°
Give them a noble memory; so Messalla°
Renowned his general Cassius—yet both these   425
Lived with Augustus, full of wealth and honours.
To Cicero's book, where Cato was heaved up
Equal with heaven, what else did Caesar answer,
Being then dictator, but with a penned oration,
As if before the judges? Do but see   430
Antonius' letters; read but Brutus' pleadings,°
What vile reproach they hold against Augustus—
False, I confess, but with much bitterness.
The epigrams of Bibaculus and Catullus°
Are read, full stuffed with spite of both the Caesars;   435

Yet deifièd Julius, and no less Augustus,
Both bore them, and contemned them (I not know
Promptly to speak it, whether done with more
Temper or wisdom), for such obloquies,°
If they despisèd be, they die suppressed,   440
But if with rage acknowledged, they are confessed.
The Greeks I slip, whose licence not alone,
But also lust did scape unpunishèd:
Or where someone (by chance) exception took,
He words with words revenged. But in my work,   445
What could be aimed more free, or farther off
From the time's scandal, than to write of those
Whom death from grace or hatred had exempted?
Did I, with Brutus and with Cassius,
Armed, and possessed of the Philippi fields,   450
Incense the people in the civil cause
With dangerous speeches? Or do they, being slain
Seventy years since, as by their images—
Which not the conqueror hath defaced—appears,°
Retain that guilty memory with writers?   455
Posterity pays every man his honour.
Nor shall there want, though I condemnèd am,°
That will not only Cassius well approve,
And of great Brutus' honour mindful be,
But that will also mention make of me.°   460
ARRUNTIUS [*aside*] Freely and nobly spoken.
SABINUS [*aside*]   With good temper.
   I like him, that he is not moved with passion.
ARRUNTIUS [*aside*] He puts 'em to their whisper.
TIBERIUS   Take him hence.
   We shall determine of him at next sitting.
         [*Exit Cordus, guarded*]
COTTA Meantime, give order that his books be burned   465
   To the aediles.
SEJANUS   You have well advised.°
AFER It fits not such licentious things should live
   T' upbraid the age.
ARRUNTIUS [*aside*]   If th' age were good they might.
LATIARIS Let 'em be burnt.
GALLUS   All sought and burnt. Today.
PRAECO The court is up. Lictors, resume the fasces.   470

165

[*Exeunt all but*] *Arruntius, Sabinus,* [*and*] *Lepidus*

ARRUNTIUS Let 'em be burnt? Oh how ridiculous
    Appears the Senate's brainless diligence,
    Who think they can with present power extinguish
    The memory of all succeeding times.

SABINUS 'Tis true, when contrary, the punishment   475
    Of wit doth make th' authority increase.
    Nor do they aught that use this cruelty
    Of interdiction, and this rage of burning,
    But purchase to themselves rebuke and shame,
    And to the writers an eternal name.   480

LEPIDUS It is an argument the times are sore,
    When virtue cannot safely be advanced,
    Nor vice reproved.

ARRUNTIUS   Ay, noble Lepidus.
    Augustus well foresaw what we should suffer
    Under Tiberius when he did pronounce   485
    The Roman race most wretched, that should live
    Between so slow jaws, and so long a-bruising.
        [*Exeunt*]

3.2

[*Enter*] *Tiberius* [*and*] *Sejanus*

TIBERIUS This business hath succeeded well, Sejanus,
    And quite removed all jealousy of practice°
    'Gainst Agrippina and our nephews. Now
    We must bethink us how to plant our engines
    For th' other pair, Sabinus and Arruntius,   5
    And Gallus, too—howe'er he flatter us,
    His heart we know.

SEJANUS   Give it some respite, Caesar.
    Time shall mature and bring to perfect crown
    What we with so good vultures have begun.
    Sabinus shall be next.

TIBERIUS   Rather Arruntius.   10

SEJANUS By any means, preserve him. His frank tongue
    Being lent the reins, will take away all thought
    Of malice in your course against the rest.

We must keep him to stalk with.

TIBERIUS   Dearest head,°
    To thy most fortunate design I yield it.   15

SEJANUS Sir—I have been so long trained up in grace,
    First with your father, great Augustus, since,
    To your most happy bounties so inured,
    As I not sooner would commit my hopes
    Or wishes to the gods than to your ears.   20
    Nor have I ever yet been covetous
    Of overbright and dazzling honours, rather
    To watch and travail in great Caesar's safety,
    With the most common soldier.

TIBERIUS   'Tis confessed.

SEJANUS The only gain, and which I count most fair   25
    Of all my fortunes, is that mighty Caesar
    Hath thought me worthy his alliance. Hence
    Begin my hopes.

TIBERIUS   H'mh?

SEJANUS   I have heard Augustus,
    In the bestowing of his daughter, thought
    But even of gentlemen of Rome. If so—   30
    I know not how to hope so great a favour—
    But if a husband should be sought for Livia,
    And I be had in mind, as Caesar's friend,
    I would but use the glory of the kindred;°
    It should not make me slothful, or less caring   35
    For Caesar's state—it were enough to me
    It did confirm and strengthen my weak house
    Against the now unequal opposition
    Of Agrippina; and for dear regard
    Unto my children, this I wish. Myself   40
    Have no ambition farther than to end
    My days in service of so dear a prince.

TIBERIUS We cannot but commend thy piety,
    Most loved Sejanus, in acknowledging
    Those—bounties—which we, faintly, such remember.   45
    But to thy suit. The rest of mortal men,
    In all their drifts and counsels, pursue profit;
    Princes alone are of a different sort,
    Directing their main actions still to fame.
    We therefore will take time to think, and answer.   50

For Livia, she can best herself resolve
If she will marry after Drusus, or
Continue in the family; besides,
She hath a mother and a grandam yet,
Whose nearer counsels she may guide her by—   55
But I will simply deal. That enmity°
Thou fearst in Agrippina would burn more
If Livia's marriage should, as 'twere in parts,
Divide th' imperial house; an emulation°
Between the women might break forth, and discord   60
Ruin the sons and nephews on both hands.
What if it cause some present difference?
Thou art not safe, Sejanus, if thou prove it.
Canst thou believe that Livia, who was wife
To Caius Caesar, then to Drusus, now°   65
Will be contented to grow old with thee,
Born but a private gentleman of Rome?
And raise thee with her loss, if not her shame?
Or say that I should wish it, canst thou think
The Senate, or the people—who have seen   70
Her brother, father, and our ancestors
In highest place of Empire—will endure it?
The state, thou hold'st already, is in talk;
Men murmur at thy greatness; and the nobles
Stick not, in public, to upbraid thy climbing   75
Above our father's favours, or thy scale,
And dare accuse me, from their hate to thee.
Be wise, dear friend. We would not hide these things
For friendship's dear respect. Nor will we stand
Adverse to thine or Livia's designments.   80
What we had purposed to thee in our thought,
And with what near degrees of love to bind thee,
And make thee equal to us, for the present
We will forbear to speak. Only thus much
Believe, our loved Sejanus, we not know   85
That height in blood or honour which thy virtue
And mind to us may not aspire with merit;
And this we'll publish, on all watched occasion
The Senate or the people shall present.
SEJANUS I am restored, and to my sense again,   90
    Which I had lost in this so blinding suit.

Caesar hath taught me better to refuse,
Than I knew how to ask. How pleaseth Caesar
T' embrace my late advice, for leaving Rome?
TIBERIUS We are resolved.
SEJANUS [*giving him a paper*] Here are some motives more   95
Which I have thought on since, may more confirm.
TIBERIUS Careful Sejanus! We will straight peruse them.
Go forward in our main design, and prosper.
      [*Exit Tiberius*]
SEJANUS If those but take, I shall. Dull, heavy Caesar!
Wouldst thou tell me thy favours were made crimes?   100
And that my fortunes were esteemed thy faults?
That thou, for me, wert hated? And not think
I would with wingèd haste prevent that change
When thou mightst win all to thyself again,
By forfeiture of me? Did those fond words   105
Fly swifter from thy lips than this my brain,
This sparkling forge, created me an armour
T' encounter chance, and thee? Well, read my charms,
And may they lay that hold upon thy senses,
As thou hadst snuffed up hemlock, or ta'en down   110
The juice of poppy and of mandrakes. Sleep,°
Voluptuous Caesar, and security
Seize on thy stupid powers, and leave them dead°
To public cares, awake but to thy lusts,
The strength of which makes thy libidinous soul   115
Itch to leave Rome—and I have thrust it on,
With blaming of the city business,
The multitude of suits, the confluence
Of suitors, then their importunacies,
The manifold distractions he must suffer,   120
Besides ill rumours, envies, and reproaches,
All which, a quiet and retirèd life
(Larded with ease and pleasure) did avoid;
And yet, for any weighty and great affair,
The fittest place to give the soundest counsels.   125
By this shall I remove him both from thought
And knowledge of his own most dear affairs;
Draw all dispatches through my private hands;
Know his designments, and pursue mine own;
Make mine own strengths by giving suits and places,   130

Conferring dignities and offices:
And these that hate me now, wanting access
To him, will make their envy none, or less.
For when they see me arbiter of all,
They must observe; or else, with Caesar, fall.   135
     [*Exit*]

3.3

     [*Enter*] *Tiberius*
TIBERIUS   To marry Livia? Will no less, Sejanus,
   Content thy aims? No lower object? Well.
   Thou knowst how thou art wrought into our trust,
   Woven in our design; and thinkst we must
   Now use thee, whatsoe'er thy projects are.   5
   'Tis true. But yet with caution, and fit care.
   And, now we better think—Who's there, within?
     [*Enter Servant*]
SERVANT   Caesar?
TIBERIUS   To leave our journey off were sin
   'Gainst our decreed delights, and would appear
   Doubt—or, what less becomes a prince, low fear.   10
   Yet doubt hath law, and fears have their excuse
   Where princes' states plead necessary use,
   As ours doth now: more in Sejanus' pride,
   Than all fell Agrippina's hates beside.
   They are the dreadful enemies we raise   15
   With favours, and make dangerous with praise.
   The injured by us may have will alike,
   But 'tis the favourite hath the power to strike;
   And fury ever boils more high and strong,
   Heat with ambition, than revenge of wrong.°   20
   'Tis then a part of supreme skill to grace
   No man too much, but hold a certain space
   Between th' ascender's rise and thine own flat
   Lest, when all rounds be reached, his aim be that.°
   'Tis thought. [*To Servant*] Is Macro in the palace? See.   25
   If not, go seek him to come to us.
     [*Exit Servant*]

He
Must be the organ we must work by now;
Though none less apt for trust: need doth allow
What choice would not. I have heard that aconite,
Being timely taken, hath a healing might   30
Against the scorpion's stroke; the proof we'll give:
That while two poisons wrestle, we may live.
He hath a spirit too working to be used°
But to th' encounter of his like. Excused
Are wiser sovereigns then, that raise one ill   35
Against another, and both safely kill.
The prince that feeds great natures, they will sway him;
Who nourisheth a lion, must obey him.
      [*Enter*] *Macro* [*and Servant*]
Macro, we sent for you.
MACRO   I heard so, Caesar.
TIBERIUS [*to Servant*] Leave us a while.
      [*Exit Servant*]
                              When you shall know, good Macro,   40
The causes of our sending, and the ends,
You then will hearken nearer, and be pleased
You stand so high, both in our choice, and trust.
MACRO The humblest place in Caesar's choice or trust
May make glad Macro proud; without ambition,   45
Save to do Caesar service—
TIBERIUS   Leave our courtings.
We are in purpose, Macro, to depart
The city for a time and see Campania;°
Not for our pleasures, but to dedicate
A pair of temples, one to Jupiter   50
At Capua, th' other at Nola, to Augustus;°
In which great work perhaps our stay will be
Beyond our will produced. Now since we are
Not ignorant what danger may be born
Out of our shortest absence in a state   55
So subject unto envy and embroiled
With hate and faction, we have thought on thee,
Amongst a field of Romans, worthiest Macro,
To be our eye and ear; to keep strict watch
On Agrippina, Nero, Drusus—ay,   60
And on Sejanus. Not that we distrust

His loyalty, or do repent one grace
Of all that heap we have conferred on him
(For that were to disparage our election,°
And call that judgement now in doubt, which then   65
Seemed as unquestioned as an oracle).
But greatness hath his cankers. Worms and moths
Breed out of too much humour in the things°
Which after they consume, transferring quite
The substance of their makers int' themselves.   70
Macro is sharp, and apprehends. Besides,
I know him subtle, close, wise, and well-read
In man and his large nature; he hath studied
Affections, passions, knows their springs, their ends,
Which way, and whither they will work: 'tis proof°   75
Enough of his great merit that we trust him.
Then, to a point, because our conference
Cannot be long without suspicion.
Here, Macro, we assign thee both to spy,
Inform, and chastise; think, and use thy means,   80
Thy ministers, what, where, on whom thou wilt;
Explore, plot, practise: all thou dost in this°
Shall be as if the Senate or the laws
Had giv'n it privilege, and thou thence styled
The saviour both of Caesar, and of Rome.   85
We will not take thy answer, but in act;
Whereto, as thou proceedst, we hope to hear
By trusted messengers. If 't be enquired
Wherefore we called you, say you have in charge
To see our chariots ready, and our horse.   90
Be still our loved, and (shortly) honoured Macro.
    [*Exit Tiberius*]
MACRO I will not ask why Caesar bids do this;
But joy that he bids me. It is the bliss
Of courts to be employed, no matter how:
A prince's power makes all his actions virtue.   95
We, whom he works by, are dumb instruments
To do, but not enquire; his great intents
Are to be served, not searched. Yet as that bow
Is most in hand whose owner best doth know
T' effect his aims, so let that statesman hope   100
Most use, most price, can hit his prince's scope.°

Nor must he look at what, or whom to strike,
But loose at all; each mark must be alike.
Were it to plot against the fame, the life,
Of one with whom I twinned; remove a wife   105
From my warm side, as loved as is the air;
Practise away each parent; draw mine heir
In compass, though but one; work all my kin
To swift perdition; leave no untrained engine,°
For friendship or for innocence; nay, make   110
The gods all guilty: I would undertake
This, being imposed me, both with gain and ease.
The way to rise is to obey and please.
He that will thrive in state, he must neglect
The trodden paths that truth and right respect,   115
And prove new, wilder ways; for virtue, there,
Is not that narrow thing she is elsewhere.
Men's fortune there is virtue; reason, their will;
Their licence, law; and their observance, skill.°
Occasion is their foil; conscience, their stain;   120
Profit, their lustre; and what else is, vain.°
If then it be the lust of Caesar's power
T' have raised Sejanus up, and in an hour
O'erturn him, tumbling down from height of all,
We are his ready engine—and his fall   125
May be our rise. It is no uncouth thing°
To see fresh buildings from old ruins spring.
        [*Exit*]
        [*Chorus of musicians*]

4.1

[*Enter*] *Gallus* [*and*] *Agrippina*

GALLUS You must have patience, royal Agrippina.

AGRIPPINA I must have vengeance first—and that were nectar
    Unto my famished spirits. O my fortune,
    Let it be sudden thou prepar'st against me;
    Strike all my powers of understanding blind   5
    And ignorant of destiny to come.
    Let me not fear, that cannot hope.

GALLUS   Dear princess,
    These tyrannies on yourself are worse than Caesar's.

AGRIPPINA Is this the happiness of being born great?
    Still to be aimed at? Still to be suspected?   10
    To live the subject of all jealousies?
    At least the colour made, if not the ground,
    To every painted danger? Who would not
    Choose once to fall, than thus to hang forever?

GALLUS You might be safe, if you would—

AGRIPPINA   What, my Gallus?   15
    Be lewd Sejanus' strumpet? Or the bawd
    To Caesar's lusts, he now is gone to practise?
    Not these are safe, where nothing is. Yourself,
    While thus you stand but by me, are not safe.
    Was Silius safe? Or the good Sosia safe?   20
    Or was my niece, dear Claudia Pulchra, safe?
    Or innocent Furnius? They that latest have,
    By being made guilty, added reputation
    To Afer's eloquence? O foolish friends,
    Could not so fresh example warn your loves,   25
    But you must buy my favours with that loss
    Unto yourselves—and when you might perceive
    That Caesar's cause of raging must forsake him
    Before his will? Away, good Gallus, leave me.
    Here to be seen is danger; to speak, treason: 30
    To do me least observance is called faction.
    You are unhappy in me, and I in all.°
    Where are my sons, Nero and Drusus? We

Are they be shot at. Let us fall apart;
Not, in our ruins, sepulchre our friends.   35
Or shall we do some action like offence°
To mock their studies that would make us faulty,
And frustrate practice by preventing it?
The danger's like: for what they can contrive,°
They will make good. No innocence is safe   40
When power contests. Nor can they trespass more,
Whose only being was all crime before.

      [Enter] Nero, Drusus Junior, [and] Caligula

NERO You hear Sejanus is come back from Caesar?
GALLUS No, how? Disgraced?
DRUSUS JUNIOR   More gracèd now than ever.
GALLUS By what mischance?
CALIGULA   A fortune, like enough   45
  Once to be bad.
DRUSUS JUNIOR But turned to good to both.°
GALLUS What was 't?
NERO   Tiberius sitting at his meat°
  In a farmhouse they call Spelunca, sited
  By the seaside among the Fundane Hills
  Within a natural cave, part of the grot   50
  (About the entry) fell, and overwhelmed°
  Some of the waiters; others ran away.
  Only Sejanus, with his knees, hands, face
  O'erhanging Caesar, did oppose himself
  To the remaining ruins, and was found   55
  In that so labouring posture by the soldiers
  That came to succour him. With which adventure
  He hath so fixed himself in Caesar's trust
  As thunder cannot move him, and is come
  With all the height of Caesar's praise to Rome.   60
AGRIPPINA And power to turn those ruins all on us,
  And bury whole posterities beneath them.
  Nero, and Drusus, and Caligula,
  Your places are the next, and therefore most°
  In their offence. Think on your birth and blood,   65
  Awake your spirits, meet their violence;
  'Tis princely when a tyrant doth oppose,
  And is a fortune sent to exercise
  Your virtue, as the wind doth try strong trees,

Who by vexation grow more sound and firm.   70
After your father's fall, and uncle's fate,
What can you hope but all the change of stroke
That force or sleight can give? Then stand upright;
And though you do not act, yet suffer nobly:
Be worthy of my womb, and take strong cheer.   75
What we do know will come, we should not fear.
    [*Exeunt*]

4.2

    [*Enter*] *Macro*
MACRO Returned so soon? Renewed in trust and grace?
Is Caesar then so weak? Or hath the place
But wrought this alteration with the air;
And he, on next remove, will all repair?
Macro, thou art engaged; and what before   5
Was public, now must be thy private, more.
The weal of Caesar fitness did imply;
But thine own fate confers necessity
On thy employment: and the thoughts borne nearest
Unto ourselves move swiftest still and dearest.   10
If he recover, thou art lost; yea, all
The weight of preparation to his fall
Will turn on thee, and crush thee. Therefore, strike
Before he settle, to prevent the like
Upon thyself. He doth his vantage know,   15
That makes it home, and gives the foremost blow.
    [*Exit*]

4.3

    [*Enter*] *Latiaris, Rufus,* [*and*] *Opsius*
LATIARIS It is a service lord Sejanus will
See well requited, and accept of nobly.
Here place yourselves, between the roof and ceiling,

And when I bring him to his words of danger,
Reveal yourselves, and take him.
RUFUS   Is he come?   5
LATIARIS I'll now go fetch him.
          [*Exit Latiaris*]
OPSIUS   With good speed. I long
    To merit from the state in such an action.
RUFUS I hope it will obtain the consulship
    For one of us.
OPSIUS   We cannot think of less,
    To bring in one so dangerous as Sabinus.   10
RUFUS He was a follower of Germanicus,
    And still is an observer of his wife
    And children, though they be declined in grace;
    A daily visitant, keeps them company
    In private and in public; and is noted   15
    To be the only client of the house—°
    Pray Jove he will be free to Latiaris.°
OPSIUS He is allied to him, and doth trust him well.
RUFUS And he'll requite his trust?
OPSIUS   To do an office
    So grateful to the state, I know no man   20
    But would strain nearer bands than kindred.
RUFUS   List,
    I hear them come.
OPSIUS   Shift to our holes with silence.
          [*They retire.° Enter*] Latiaris [*and*] Sabinus
LATIARIS It is a noble constancy you show
    To this afflicted house, that not like others—
    The friends of season—you do follow fortune,   25
    And in the winter of their fate, forsake
    The place whose glories warmed you. You are just,
    And worthy such a princely patron's love,
    As was the world's renowned Germanicus—
    Whose ample merit when I call to thought,   30
    And see his wife and issue objects made
    To so much envy, jealousy, and hate,°
    It makes me ready to accuse the gods
    Of negligence, as men of tyranny.
SABINUS They must be patient, so must we.
LATIARIS   Oh Jove!   35

What will become of us, or of the times,
When to be high or noble are made crimes?
When land and treasure are most dangerous faults?
SABINUS Nay, when our table, yea, our bed, assaults
 Our peace and safety? When our writings are,   40
By any envious instruments that dare°
Apply them to the guilty, made to speak
What they will have, to fit their tyrannous wreak?
When ignorance is scarcely innocence,
And knowledge made a capital offence?   45
When not so much but the bare empty shade°
Of liberty is reft us? And we made
The prey to greedy vultures, and vile spies,
That first transfix us with their murdering eyes?°
LATIARIS Methinks the genius of the Roman race°   50
 Should not be so extinct, but that bright flame
Of liberty might be revived again
(Which no good man but with his life should lose),
And we not sit like spent and patient fools
Still puffing in the dark at one poor coal,   55
Held on by hope, till the last spark is out.
The cause is public, and the honour, name,
The immortality of every soul
That is not bastard or a slave in Rome,
Therein concerned—whereto, if men would change 60
The wearied arm, and for the weighty shield
So long sustained, employ the facile sword,°
We might have some assurance of our vows.°
This ass's fortitude doth tire us all.
It must be active valour must redeem   65
Our loss, or none. The rock and our hard steel
Should meet, t' enforce those glorious fires again
Whose splendour cheered the world, and heat gave life
No less than doth the sun's.
SABINUS   'Twere better stay
 In lasting darkness and despair of day.   70
No ill should force the subject undertake
Against the sovereign, more than hell should make
The gods do wrong. A good man should, and must,
Sit rather down with loss, than rise unjust.°
Though, when the Romans first did yield themselves 75

To one man's power, they did not mean their lives,
Their fortunes, and their liberties should be
His absolute spoil, as purchased by the sword.
LATIARIS Why, we are worse, if to be slaves, and bond
    To Caesar's slave be such, the proud Sejanus?   80
    He that is all, does all, gives Caesar leave
    To hide his ulcerous and anointed face
    With his bald crown at Rhodes, while he here stalks°
    Upon the heads of Romans and their princes,
    Familiarly to empire.
SABINUS   Now you touch°   85
    A point, indeed, wherein he shows his art,
    As well as power.
LATIARIS   And villainy in both.
    Do you observe where Livia lodges? How
    Drusus came dead? What men have been cut off?
SABINUS Yes, those are things removed: I nearer looked°   90
    Into his later practice, where he stands
    Declared a master in his mystery.°
    First, ere Tiberius went, he wrought his fear
    To think that Agrippina sought his death,
    Then put those doubts in her; sent her oft word   95
    Under the show of friendship to beware
    Of Caesar, for he laid to poison her:
    Drove them to frowns, to mutual jealousies,
    Which now in visible hatred are burst out.
    Since, he hath had his hirèd instruments   100
    To work on Nero, and to heave him up;
    To tell him Caesar's old; that all the people,
    Yea, all the army, have their eyes on him;
    That both do long to have him undertake
    Something of worth to give the world a hope;   105
    Bids him to court their grace. The easy youth
    Perhaps gives ear, which straight he writes to Caesar,
    And with this comment: 'See yond dangerous boy,
    Note but the practice of the mother there;
    She's tying him, for purposes at hand,   110
    With men of sword.' Here's Caesar put in fright
    'Gainst son and mother. Yet he leaves not thus.
    The second brother, Drusus—a fierce nature,
    And fitter for his snares because ambitious

And full of envy—him he clasps and hugs,   115
Poisons with praise, tells him what hearts he wears,
How bright he stands in popular expectance;
That Rome doth suffer with him in the wrong
His mother does him by preferring Nero—
Thus sets he them asunder, each 'gainst other,   120
Projects the course that serves him to condemn,°
Keeps in opinion of a friend to all,
And all drives on to ruin.
LATIARIS   Caesar sleeps,
And nods at this?
SABINUS   Would he might ever sleep,
Bogged in his filthy lusts.
        [*Opsius and Rufus rush in*]
OPSIUS   Treason to Caesar!   125
RUFUS Lay hands upon the traitor, Latiaris,
Or take the name thyself.
LATIARIS   I am for Caesar.
SABINUS Am I then catched?
RUFUS   How think you, sir? You are.
SABINUS Spies of this head! So white! So full of years!
Well, my most reverend monsters, you may live   130
To see yourselves thus snared.
OPSIUS   Away with him.
LATIARIS Hale him away.
RUFUS   To be a spy for traitors
Is honourable vigilance.
SABINUS   You do well,
My most officious instruments of state,
Men of all uses. Drag me hence, away.   135
The year is well begun, and I fall fit
To be an offering to Sejanus. Go.°
OPSIUS Cover him with his garments, hide his face.
SABINUS It shall not need. Forbear your rude assault:
The fault's not shameful villainy makes a fault.   140
        [*Exeunt*]

4.4

[Enter] Macro [and] Caligula

MACRO Sir, but observe how thick your dangers meet
In his clear drifts. Your mother and your brothers
Now cited to the Senate. Their friend, Gallus,
Feasted today by Caesar, since committed.
Sabinus here we met, hurried to fetters.   5
The senators all struck with fear and silence,
Save those whose hopes depend not on good means,
But force their private prey from public spoil.
And you must know, if here you stay, your state
Is sure to be the subject of his hate,   10
As now the object.
CALIGULA   What would you advise me?
MACRO To go for Capreae presently; and there
Give up yourself entirely to your uncle.
Tell Caesar, since your mother is accused
To fly for succours to Augustus' statue°   15
And to the army with your brethren, you
Have rather chose to place your aids in him
Than live suspected, or in hourly fear
To be thrust out by bold Sejanus' plots—
Which you shall confidently urge to be   20
Most full of peril to the state and Caesar,
As being laid to his peculiar ends,
And not to be let run with common safety.°
All which, upon the second, I'll make plain,
And both shall love and trust with Caesar gain.   25
CALIGULA Away then, let's prepare us for our journey.
  [Exeunt]

4.5

[Enter] Arruntius

ARRUNTIUS Still dost thou suffer, heaven? Will no flame,
No heat of sin, make thy just wrath to boil
In thy distempered bosom, and o'erflow

The pitchy blazes of impiety
Kindled beneath thy throne? Still canst thou sleep,   5
Patient, while vice doth make an antic face
At thy dread power, and blow dust and smoke
Into thy nostrils? Jove, will nothing wake thee?
Must vile Sejanus pull thee by the beard
Ere thou wilt open thy black-lidded eye,   10
And look him dead? Well. Snore on, dreaming gods,
And let this last of that proud giant race
Heave mountain upon mountain 'gainst your state—°
Be good unto me, Fortune, and you powers
Whom I, expostulating, have profaned.°   15
I see (what's equal with a prodigy)
A great, a noble Roman, and an honest,
Live an old man.
          [*Enter*] *Lepidus*
                    O Marcus Lepidus,
When is our turn to bleed? Thyself and I,
Without our boast, are almost all the few   20
Left to be honest in these impious times.
LEPIDUS What we are left to be, we will be, Lucius,
Though tyranny did stare as wide as death
To fright us from it.
ARRUNTIUS   'T hath so, on Sabinus!°
LEPIDUS I saw him now drawn from the Gemonies,°   25
And, what increased the direness of the fact,
His faithful dog, upbraiding all us Romans,
Never forsook the corpse, but seeing it thrown
Into the stream, leaped in, and drowned with it—
ARRUNTIUS O act! To be envied him of us men!   30
We are the next the hook lays hold on, Marcus.
What are thy arts—good patriot, teach them me—
That have preserved thy hairs to this white dye,
And kept so reverend and so dear a head
Safe on his comely shoulders?
LEPIDUS   Arts, Arruntius?   35
None but the plain and passive fortitude
To suffer, and be silent; never stretch
These arms against the torrent; live at home,
With my own thoughts and innocence about me,
Not tempting the wolf's jaws: these are my arts.   40

ARRUNTIUS I would begin to study 'em, if I thought
    They would secure me. May I pray to Jove
    In secret, and be safe? Ay, or aloud?
    With open wishes, so I do not mention
    Tiberius or Sejanus? Yes, I must,   45
    If I speak out. 'Tis hard, that. May I think,
    And not be racked? What danger is 't to dream?
    Talk in one's sleep? Or cough? Who knows the law?
    May I shake my head, without a comment? Say
    It rains, or it holds up, and not be thrown   50
    Upon the Gemonies? These now are things
    Whereon men's fortune, yea, their fate depends.
    Nothing hath privilege 'gainst the violent ear.
    No place, no day, no hour, we see, is free—
    Not our religious and most sacred times—   55
    From some one kind of cruelty. All matter,
    Nay, all occasion, pleaseth. Madmen's rage,
    The idleness of drunkards, women's nothing,
    Jesters' simplicity, all, all is good
    That can be catched at. Nor is now th' event   60
    Of any person, or for any crime,
    To be expected, for 'tis always one:°
    Death, with some little difference of place
    Or time—what's this? Prince Nero? Guarded?
        [Enter] Laco [and] Nero, [with Lictors]

LACO On, lictors, keep your way. My lords, forbear.   65
    On pain of Caesar's wrath, no man attempt
    Speech with the prisoner.

NERO   Noble friends, be safe:
    To lose yourselves for words were as vain hazard,
    As unto me small comfort. Fare you well.
    Would all Rome's suff'rings in my fate did dwell.   70

LACO Lictors, away.
        [Exit Nero, guarded]

LEPIDUS   Where goes he, Laco?

LACO   Sir,
    He's banished into Pontia by the Senate.°

ARRUNTIUS Do I see? And hear? And feel? May I trust sense?
    Or doth my fant'sy form it?

LEPIDUS   Where's his brother?°

LACO Drusus is prisoner in the palace.

ARRUNTIUS   Ha?
   I smell it now—'tis rank. Where's Agrippina?
LACO The princess is confined to Pandataria.°
ARRUNTIUS Bolts, Vulcan, bolts for Jove; Phoebus, thy bow;
   Stern Mars, thy sword; and blue-eyed maid, thy spear;°
   Thy club, Alcides! All the armoury   80
   Of heaven is too little—Ha? To guard
   The gods, I meant. Fine, rare dispatch! This same°
   Was swiftly borne! Confined? Imprisoned? Banished?
   Most tripartite! The cause, sir?
LACO   Treason.
ARRUNTIUS   Oh?
   The complement of all accusings? That°   85
   Will hit when all else fails.
LEPIDUS   This turn is strange!
   But yesterday, the people would not hear,
   Far less objected, but cried Caesar's letters
   Were false and forged; that all these plots were malice;
   And that the ruin of the princes' house   90
   Was practised 'gainst his knowledge. Where are now
   Their voices? Now that they behold his heirs
   Locked up, disgraced, led into exile?
ARRUNTIUS   Hushed.
   Drowned in their bellies. Wild Sejanus' breath
   Hath, like a whirlwind, scattered that poor dust   95
   With this rude blast.
     [*He turns to Laco, and the rest*]
           We'll talk no treason, sir,
   If that be it you stand for? Fare you well.
   We have no need of horse-leeches. Good spy,
   Now you are spied, be gone.
     [*Exeunt Laco, and Lictors*]
LEPIDUS   I fear you wrong him.
   He has the voice to be an honest Roman.°   100
ARRUNTIUS And trusted to this office? Lepidus,
   I'd sooner trust Greek Sinon than a man°
   Our state employs. He's gone; and being gone,
   I dare tell you (whom I dare better trust)
   That our night-eyed Tiberius doth not see°   105
   His minion's drifts. Or if he do, he's not
   So arrant subtle as we fools do take him—°

To breed a mongrel up, in his own house,
With his own blood, and, if the good gods please,
At his own throat train him to take a leap.   110
I do not beg it, heav'n; but if the Fates
Grant it these eyes, they must not wink.
LEPIDUS   They must°
    Not see it, Lucius.
ARRUNTIUS   Who should let 'em?
LEPIDUS   Zeal°
    And duty; with the thought, he is our prince.
ARRUNTIUS He is our monster: forfeited to vice   115
    So far, as no racked virtue can redeem him;
    His loathèd person fouler than all crimes;
    An emperor only in his lusts. Retired
    (From all regard of his own fame, or Rome's)
    Into an obscure island, where he lives—   120
    Acting his tragedies with a comic face—
    Amidst his rout of Chaldees; spending hours,°
    Days, weeks, and months in the unkind abuse
    Of grave astrology, to the bane of men,
    Casting the scope of men's nativities,°   125
    And having found aught worthy in their fortune,
    Kill, or precipitate them in the sea,
    And boast he can mock fate. Nay, muse not: these
    Are far from ends of evil, scarce degrees.
    He hath his slaughterhouse at Capreae   130
    Where he doth study murder as an art;
    And they are dearest in his grace that can
    Devise the deepest tortures. Thither, too,
    He hath his boys and beauteous girls ta'en up
    Out of our noblest houses, the best formed,   135
    Best nurtured, and most modest: what's their good
    Serves to provoke his bad. Some are allured,
    Some threatened; others, by their friends detained,
    Are ravished hence like captives, and in sight
    Of their most grievèd parents, dealt away   140
    Unto his spintries, sellaries, and slaves,
    Masters of strange and new-commented lusts,
    For which wise nature hath not left a name.
    To this (what most strikes us, and bleeding Rome)
    He is, with all his craft, become the ward   145

To his own vassal, a stale catamite,°
Whom he, upon our low and suffering necks,
Hath raised from excrement to side the gods,
And have his proper sacrifice in Rome—°
Which Jove beholds, and yet will sooner rive   150
A senseless oak with thunder than his trunk.
    [*Enter*] *Laco, Pomponius, Minutius, and others*
LACO These letters make men doubtful what t' expect,
    Whether his coming, or his death.
POMPONIUS   Troth, both—
    And which comes soonest, thank the gods for.
ARRUNTIUS [*aside to Lepidus*]   List,
    Their talk is Caesar, I would hear all voices.   155
MINUTIUS One day he's well, and will return to Rome;
    The next day sick, and knows not when to hope it.
LACO True, and today, one of Sejanus' friends
    Honoured by special writ; and on the morrow
    Another punished—
POMPONIUS   By more special writ.   160
MINUTIUS This man receives his praises of Sejanus;
    A second, but slight mention; a third, none;
    A fourth, rebukes. And thus he leaves the Senate
    Divided and suspended, all uncertain.
LACO These forkèd tricks, I understand 'em not.°   165
    Would he would tell us whom he loves or hates,
    That we might follow, without fear or doubt.
ARRUNTIUS [*aside to Lepidus*] Good heliotrope! Is this
    your honest man?
    Let him be yours so still. He is my knave.
POMPONIUS I cannot tell; Sejanus still goes on,   170
    And mounts, we see. New statues are advanced,
    Fresh leaves of titles, large inscriptions read,°
    His fortune sworn by, himself new gone out
    Caesar's colleague in the fifth consulship;°
    More altars smoke to him than all the gods.   175
    What would we more?
ARRUNTIUS [*aside*]   That the dear smoke would choke him.°
LACO But there are letters come, they say, ev'n now,
    Which do forbid that last.
MINUTIUS   Do you hear so?
LACO   Yes.

POMPONIUS By Castor, that's the worst.

ARRUNTIUS [*aside*]   By Pollux, best.°   180

MINUTIUS I did not like the sign when Regulus—
      Whom all we know no friend unto Sejanus—
      Did, by Tiberius' so precise command,
      Succeed a fellow in the consulship:
      It boded somewhat.

POMPONIUS   Not a mote. His partner,   185
      Fulcinius Trio, is his own; and sure.
      Here comes Terentius. He can give us more.
            [*Enter Terentius. They whisper with him.*]

LEPIDUS I'll ne'er believe but Caesar hath some scent
      Of bold Sejanus' footing. These cross-points
      Of varying letters and opposing consuls,   190
      Mixing his honours and his punishments,
      Feigning now ill, now well, raising Sejanus,
      And then depressing him—as now of late
      In all reports we have it—cannot be
      Empty of practice. 'Tis Tiberius' art.   195
      For, having found his favourite grown too great,
      And with his greatness, strong; that all the soldiers
      Are, with their leaders, made at his devotion;
      That almost all the Senate are his creatures,
      Or hold on him their main dependences   200
      Either for benefit, or hope, or fear;
      And that himself hath lost much of his own
      By parting unto him, and by th' increase°
      Of his rank lusts and rages quite disarmed
      Himself of love or other public means   205
      To dare an open contestation,
      His subtlety hath chose this doubling line
      To hold him even in—not so to fear him
      As wholly put him out, and yet give check
      Unto his farther boldness. In meantime,   210
      By his employments makes him odious
      Unto the staggering rout, whose aid, in fine,°
      He hopes to use, as sure who, when they sway,
      Bear down, o'erturn all objects in their way.

ARRUNTIUS You may be a Lynceus, Lepidus, yet I°   215
      See no such cause but that a politic tyrant
      (Who can so well disguise it) should have ta'en

A nearer way: feigned honest, and come home
To cut his throat by law.
LEPIDUS   Ay, but his fear
  Would ne'er be masked, albe his vices were.   220
POMPONIUS His lordship then is still in grace?
TERENTIUS   Assure you,
  Never in more, either of grace or power.
POMPONIUS The gods are wise and just.
ARRUNTIUS [*aside*]   The fiends they are.
  To suffer thee belie 'em?
TERENTIUS   I have here
  His last and present letters, where he writes him   225
  The 'partner of his cares', and 'his Sejanus'—
LACO But is that true, it is prohibited
  To sacrifice unto him?
TERENTIUS   Some such thing
  Caesar makes scruple of, but forbids it not,
  No more than to himself; says he could wish   230
  It were forborne to all.
LACO   Is it no other?
TERENTIUS No other, on my trust. For your more surety,
  Here is that letter, too.
ARRUNTIUS [*aside to Lepidus*] How easily
  Do wretched men believe what they would have!
  Looks this like plot?
LEPIDUS [*aside to Arruntius*] Noble Arruntius, stay.   235
LACO He names him here without his titles.
LEPIDUS [*aside to Arruntius*]   Note.
ARRUNTIUS [*aside to Lepidus*] Yes, and come off your notable
      fool. I will.
LACO No other than 'Sejanus'.
POMPONIUS   That's but haste
  In him that writes. Here he gives large amends.
MINUTIUS And with his own hand written?
POMPONIUS   Yes.
LACO   Indeed?   240
TERENTIUS Believe it, gentlemen, Sejanus' breast
  Never received more full contentments in
  Than at this present.
POMPONIUS   Takes he well th' escape
  Of young Caligula with Macro?

TERENTIUS   Faith,
  At the first air, it somewhat mated him.°   245
LEPIDUS [*aside to Arruntius*] Observe you?
ARRUNTIUS [*aside to Lepidus*]   Nothing. Riddles. Till
  I see Sejanus struck, no sound thereof strikes me.
POMPONIUS I like it not. I muse h' would not attempt
  Somewhat against him in the consulship,
  Seeing the people 'gin to favour him.°   250
TERENTIUS He doth repent it now; but h' has employed
  Pagonianus after him: and he holds
  That correspondence there with all that are
  Near about Caesar, as no thought can pass
  Without his knowledge thence in act to front him.   255
POMPONIUS I gratulate the news.
LACO   But how comes Macro
  So in trust and favour with Caligula?
POMPONIUS Oh sir, he has a wife, and the young prince
  An appetite—he can look up and spy
  Flies in the roof when there are fleas i' bed,   260
  And hath a learnèd nose to assure his sleeps.
  Who, to be favoured of the rising sun,
  Would not lend little of his waning moon?
  'Tis the saf'st ambition. Noble Terentius.
TERENTIUS The night grows fast upon us. At your service.   265
    [*Exeunt*]°
    [*Chorus of musicians*]

5.1

[*Enter*] *Sejanus*

SEJANUS Swell, swell, my joys, and faint not to declare
    Yourselves as ample as your causes are.
    I did not live till now. This my first hour,
    Wherein I see my thoughts reached by my power:
    But this, and gripe my wishes. Great and high,   5
    The world knows only two: that's Rome, and I.
    My roof receives me not; 'tis air I tread:
    And at each step, I feel my advanced head°
    Knock out a star in heaven. Reared to this height,
    All my desires seem modest, poor, and slight,   10
    That did before sound impudent. 'Tis place,
    Not blood, discerns the noble and the base.°
    Is there not something more than to be Caesar?
    Must we rest there? It irks t' have come so far,
    To be so near a stay. Caligula,   15
    Would thou stood'st stiff, and many, in our way.
    Winds lose their strength when they do empty fly,
    Unmet of woods or buildings; great fires die
    That want their matter to withstand them. So
    It is our grief, and will be our loss, to know   20
    Our power shall want opposites; unless
    The gods, by mixing in the cause, would bless
    Our fortune with their conquest. That were worth°
    Sejanus' strife, durst Fates but bring it forth.
    [*Enter*] *Terentius* [*and Servant*]

TERENTIUS Safety to great Sejanus!

SEJANUS   Now, Terentius?   25

TERENTIUS Hears not my lord the wonder?

SEJANUS   Speak it, no.

TERENTIUS I meet it violent in the people's mouths,
    Who run in routs to Pompey's theatre
    To view your statue, which, they say, sends forth
    A smoke as from a furnace, black and dreadful.   30

SEJANUS Some traitor hath put fire in. [*To Servant*] You, go see.
    And let the head be taken off to look

What 'tis.
    [*Exit Servant*]
        Some slave hath practised an imposture
To stir the people.
    [*Enter*] *Satrius, Natta,* [*and Servant*]
           How now? [*To Servant*] Why return you?
SATRIUS The head, my lord, already is ta'en off,   35
  I saw it; and at opening there leapt out
  A great and monstrous serpent.
SEJANUS   Monstrous! Why?
  Had it a beard? And horns? No heart? A tongue
  Forkèd as flattery? Looked it of the hue
  To such as live in great men's bosoms? Was   40
  The spirit of it Macro's?
NATTA   May it please
  The most divine Sejanus, in my days
  (And by his sacred fortune I affirm it)
  I have not seen a more extended, grown,
  Foul, spotted, venomous, ugly—
SEJANUS   Oh, the Fates!   45
  What a wild muster's here of attributes,
  T' express a worm, a snake?
TERENTIUS   But how that should
  Come there, my lord?
SEJANUS   What! And you, too, Terentius?
  I think you mean to make 't a prodigy
  In your reporting?
TERENTIUS   Can the wise Sejanus   50
  Think heaven hath meant it less?
SEJANUS   O superstition!
  Why, then the falling of our bed that broke
  This morning, burdened with the populous weight°
  Of our expecting clients to salute us,°
  Or running of the cat betwixt our legs   55
  As we set forth unto the Capitol,
  Were prodigies.
TERENTIUS   I think them ominous—
  And would they had not happened. As today
  The fate of some your servants, who, diverting
  Their way, not able for the throng to follow,   60
  Slipped down the Gemonies and broke their necks.

Besides, in taking your last augury,
No prosperous bird appeared, but croaking ravens
Flagged up and down; and from the sacrifice°
Flew to the prison where they sat all night,   65
Beating the air with their obstreperous beaks.
I dare not counsel, but I could entreat
That great Sejanus would attempt the gods
Once more with sacrifice.

SEJANUS   What excellent fools
Religion makes of men! Believes Terentius   70
(If these were dangers, as I shame to think them)
The gods could change the certain course of fate?
Or if they could, they would—now, in a moment—
For a beef's fat, or less, be bribed t' invert
Those long decrees? Then think the gods, like flies,   75
Are to be taken with the steam of flesh°
Or blood diffused about their altars; think
Their power as cheap, as I esteem it small.
Of all the throng that fill th' Olympian hall,
And, without pity, lade poor Atlas' back,°   80
I know not that one deity but Fortune
To whom I would throw up, in begging smoke,
One grain of incense, or whose ear I'd buy
With thus much oil. Her, I indeed adore;
And keep her grateful image in my house,°   85
Sometimes belonging to a Roman king,°
But now called mine, as by the better style.
To her I care not if, for satisfying
Your scrupulous fancies, I go offer. Bid°
Our priest prepare us honey, milk, and poppy,   90
His masculine odours, and night vestments. Say°
Our rites are instant, which performed, you'll see
How vain and worthy laughter your fears be.
    [*Exeunt*]

5.2

[*Enter*] *Cotta* [*and*] *Pomponius*
COTTA Pomponius! Whither in such speed?
POMPONIUS   I go
   To give my lord Sejanus notice—
COTTA   What?
POMPONIUS Of Macro.
COTTA   Is he come?
POMPONIUS   Entered but now
   The house of Regulus.
COTTA   The opposite consul?°
POMPONIUS Some half hour since.
COTTA   And by night, too? Stay, sir;   5
   I'll bear you company.
POMPONIUS   Along then—
        [*Exeunt*]

5.3

[*Enter*] *Macro, Regulus,* [*and Servant*]
MACRO 'Tis Caesar's will to have a frequent Senate.°
   And therefore must your edict lay deep mulct
   On such as shall be absent.
REGULUS   So it doth.
   [*To Servant*] Bear it my fellow consul to ascribe.
MACRO And tell him it must early be proclaimed;   5
   The place, Apollo's temple.
        [*Exit Servant*]
REGULUS   That's remembered.
MACRO And at what hour?
REGULUS   Yes.
MACRO   You do forget
   To send one for the provost of the watch?
REGULUS I have not—here he comes.
        [*Enter Laco*]
MACRO   Gracinus Laco,
   You are a friend most welcome. By and by   10

I'll speak with you. [*To Regulus*] You must procure this list
Of the praetorian cohorts, with the names°
Of the centurions, and their tribunes.
REGULUS   Ay.
MACRO I bring you letters, and a health from Caesar.
LACO Sir, both come well.
MACRO [*to Regulus*]   And hear you, with your note,   15
Which are the eminent men, and most of action.
REGULUS That shall be done you, too.
            [*Exit Regulus*]
MACRO   Most worthy Laco,
Caesar salutes you. Consul—death and furies!
Gone now? [*To Laco*] The argument will please you, sir.
Ho, Regulus! [*Aside*] The anger of the gods   20
Follow your diligent legs, and overtake 'em
In likeness of the gout.
            [*Enter Regulus*]
                            Oh, good my lord,
We lacked you present; I would pray you send
Another to Fulcinius Trio straight,
To tell him you will come and speak with him—   25
The matter we'll devise—to stay him there
While I, with Laco, do survey the watch.
            [*Exit Regulus*]
What are your strengths, Gracinus?
LACO   Seven cohorts.
MACRO You see what Caesar writes, and—[*aside*] Gone again?
H' has sure a vein of Mercury in his feet.   30
[*To Laco*] Know you what store of the praetorian soldiers
Sejanus holds about him for his guard?
LACO I cannot the just number—but I think°
Three centuries.
MACRO   Three? Good.
LACO   At most, not four.°
MACRO And who be those centurions?
LACO   That the consul   35
Can best deliver you.
MACRO [*aside*]   When he's away—
Spite on his nimble industry. [*To Laco*] Gracinus,°
You find what place you hold there in the trust
Of royal Caesar?

LACO   Ay, and I am—
MACRO   Sir,
  The honours there proposed are but beginnings   40
  Of his great favours.
LACO   They are more—
MACRO   I heard him
  When he did study what to add—
LACO   My life,
  And all I hold—
MACRO   You were his own first choice,
  Which doth confirm as much as you can speak;
  And will, if we succeed, make more. Your guards   45
  Are seven cohorts, you say?
LACO   Yes.
MACRO   Those we must
  Hold still in readiness, and undischarged.
LACO I understand so much. But how it can—
MACRO Be done without suspicion, you'll object?
    [Enter Regulus]
REGULUS What's that?
LACO   The keeping of the watch in arms   50
  When morning comes.
MACRO   The Senate shall be met, and set
  So early in the temple, as all mark
  Of that will be avoided.
REGULUS   If we need,
  We have commission to possess the palace,
  Enlarge Prince Drusus, and make him our chief—   55
MACRO *[aside]* That secret would have burnt his reverend
    mouth,
  Had he not spit it out now. *[To Regulus]* By the gods,
  You carry things, too—let me borrow a man
  Or two to bear these.
    [Exit Regulus]
            That of freeing Drusus
  Caesar projected as the last, and utmost;   60
  Not else to be remembered.
    [Enter Regulus and Servants]
REGULUS   Here are servants.
MACRO *[giving them letters]* These to Arruntius, these to Lepidus,
  This bear to Cotta, this to Latiaris.

If they demand you of me, say I have ta'en
Fresh horse, and am departed.
    [*Exit Servants*]
                      You, my lord,   65
To your colleague; and be you sure to hold him
With long narration of the new fresh favours
Meant to Sejanus, his great patron; I,
With trusted Laco here, are for the guards—
Then, to divide. For night hath many eyes,   70
Whereof, though most do sleep, yet some are spies.
    [*Exeunt*]

5.4

    [*Enter*] *Trumpeters, Flautists, Praecones, Flamen, Ministers,*
    Sejanus, Terentius, Satrius, [*Natta,*] *etc.*

PRAECO Be all profane far hence; fly, fly, far off;
  Be absent far; far hence be all profane.
    Trumpeters [*and*] *Flautists. These sound while the Flamen*
    washeth

FLAMEN We have been faulty, but repent us now;
  And bring pure hands, pure vestments, and pure minds.

[1] MINISTER Pure vessels.

[2] MINISTER   And pure off'rings.

[3] MINISTER   Garlands pure.   5

FLAMEN Bestow your garlands; and with reverence place
  The vervain on the altar.

PRAECO   Favour your tongues.°

FLAMEN Great mother Fortune, queen of human state,
  Rectress of action, arbitress of fate,
  To whom all sway, all power, all empire bows,   10
  Be present and propitious to our vows.

PRAECO Favour it with your tongues.

MINISTERS Be present and propitious to our vows.

    Trumpeters [*and*] *Flautists. While they sound again, the*
    Flamen takes of the honey with his finger and tastes, then
    ministers to all the rest; so of the milk, in an earthen vessel, he
    deals about. Which done, he sprinkleth upon the altar milk,
    then imposeth the honey, and kindleth his gums,° *and after*

censing about the altar, placeth his censer thereon, into which
they put several branches of poppy, and the music ceasing,
say all:

ALL Accept our off'ring, and be pleased, great goddess.

TERENTIUS See, see, the image stirs!

SATRIUS   And turns away!   15

NATTA Fortune averts her face!

FLAMEN   Avert, you gods,°
The prodigy. Still! Still! Some pious rite
We have neglected. Yet! Heaven, be appeased.
And be all tokens false, or void, that speak
Thy present wrath.

SEJANUS   Be thou dumb, scrupulous priest,   20
And gather up thyself, with these thy wares,
Which I, in spite of thy blind mistress, or
Thy juggling mystery, religion, throw°
Thus scornèd on the earth.
        [*Sweeps the altar clean*]
                    Nay, hold thy look
Averted till I woo thee turn again,   25
And thou shalt stand to all posterity
Th' eternal game and laughter, with thy neck°
Writhed to thy tail like a ridiculous cat.
Avoid these fumes, these superstitious lights,°
And all these cozening ceremonies—you!   30
Your pure and spicèd conscience.
        [*Exeunt all but Sejanus, Terentius, Satrius, and Natta*]
                    I, the slave°
And mock of fools—scorn on my worthy head—
That have been titled and adored a god,
Yea, sacrificed unto, myself, in Rome
No less than Jove: and I be brought to do   35
A peevish giglot rites? Perhaps the thought
And shame of that made Fortune turn her face,
Knowing herself the lesser deity,
And but my servant. Bashful queen, if so,
Sejanus thanks thy modesty. Who's that?   40
        [*Enter*] Pomponius [*and*] Minutius

POMPONIUS His fortune suffers, till he hears my news;
I have waited here too long. Macro, my lord—

SEJANUS Speak lower, and withdraw.

[*Takes him aside*]

TERENTIUS   Are these things true?

MINUTIUS Thousands are gazing at it in the streets.

SEJANUS What's that?

TERENTIUS   Minutius tells us here, my lord,   45
    That, a new head being set upon your statue,
    A rope is since found wreathed about it. And
    But now, a fiery meteor in the form
    Of a great ball was seen to roll along
    The troubled air, where yet it hangs, unperfect,°   50
    The amazing wonder of the multitude.

SEJANUS No more. That Macro's come is more than all.

TERENTIUS Is Macro come?

POMPONIUS   I saw him.

TERENTIUS   Where? With whom?

POMPONIUS With Regulus.

SEJANUS   Terentius—

TERENTIUS   My lord?

SEJANUS Send for the tribunes, we will straight have up   55
    More of the soldiers for our guard.

      [*Exit Terentius*]

                     Minutius,
    We pray you go for Cotta, Latiaris,
    Trio the consul, or what senators
    You know are sure, and ours.

      [*Exit Minutius*]

                 You, my good Natta,
    For Laco, provost of the watch.

      [*Exit Natta*]

                 Now, Satrius,   60
    The time of proof comes on. Arm all our servants,
    And without tumult.

      [*Exit Satrius*]

             You, Pomponius,
    Hold some good correspondence with the consul;
    Attempt him, noble friend.

      [*Exit Pomponius*]

              These things begin
    To look like dangers now, worthy my fates.   65
    Fortune, I see thy worst. Let doubtful states,
    And things uncertain hang upon thy will:

Me surest death shall render certain still.
Yet why is now my thought turned toward death,
Whom Fates have let go on so far in breath,   70
Unchecked, or unreproved? I, that did help
To fell the lofty cedar of the world,
Germanicus; that at one stroke cut down
Drusus, that upright elm; withered his vine;
Laid Silius and Sabinus, two strong oaks,   75
Flat on the earth; besides those other shrubs,
Cordus and Sosia, Claudia Pulchra,
Furnius and Gallus, which I have grubbed up;
And since have set my axe so strong and deep
Into the root of spreading Agrippine,   80
Lopped off and scattered her proud branches, Nero,
Drusus, and Caius, too, although replanted—°
If you will, destinies, that after all
I faint now ere I touch my period,
You are but cruel, and I already have done   85
Things great enough. All Rome hath been my slave.
The Senate sat an idle looker-on
And witness of my power, when I have blushed
More to command, than it to suffer. All
The fathers have sat ready and prepared   90
To give me empire, temples, or their throats
When I would ask 'em. And, what crowns the top,
Rome, Senate, people, all the world have seen
Jove, but my equal; Caesar, but my second.
'Tis then your malice, Fates, who (but your own)   95
Envy and fear t' have any power long known.
       [*Exit*]

5.5

       [*Enter*] *Terentius* [*and*] *Tribunes*
TERENTIUS Stay here. I'll give his lordship you are come.
       [*Enter*] *Minutius, Cotta,* [*and*] *Latiaris*
MINUTIUS Marcus Terentius, pray you tell my lord,
    Here's Cotta and Latiaris.
TERENTIUS   Sir, I shall.

[Exit Terentius. Cotta and Latiaris confer their letters]
COTTA My letter is the very same with yours;
    Only requires me to be present there,   5
    And give my voice to strengthen his design.
LATIARIS Names he not what it is?
COTTA   No, nor to you.
LATIARIS 'Tis strange, and singular doubtful.
COTTA   So it is.
    It may be all is left to lord Sejanus.
        [Enter] Natta [and] Laco
NATTA Gentlemen, where's my lord?
TRIBUNE   We wait him here.   10
COTTA The provost Laco? What's the news?
LATIARIS   My lord—
        [Enter] Sejanus [and] Terentius
SEJANUS Now, my right dear, noble, and trusted friends;
    How much I am a captive to your kindness!
    Most worthy Cotta, Latiaris; Laco,
    Your valiant hand; and gentlemen, your loves.   15
    I wish I could divide myself unto you;
    Or that it lay within our narrow powers
    To satisfy for so enlargèd bounty.
    Gracinus, we must pray you hold your guards
    Unquit when morning comes. Saw you the consul?   20
MINUTIUS Trio will presently be here, my lord.
COTTA They are but giving order for the edict,
    To warn the Senate.
SEJANUS   How! The Senate?
LATIARIS   Yes.°
    This morning, in Apollo's temple.
COTTA   We
    Are charged by letter to be there, my lord.   25
SEJANUS By letter? Pray you, let's see.
LATIARIS   Knows not his lordship?
COTTA It seems so.
SEJANUS   A Senate warned? Without my knowledge?
    And on this sudden? Senators by letters
    Requirèd to be there? Who brought these?
COTTA   Macro.
SEJANUS Mine enemy. And when?
COTTA   This midnight.

SEJANUS   Time,   30
    With every other circumstance, doth give
    It hath some strain of engine in 't.
       [*Enter*] *Satrius*
                     How now?
SATRIUS My lord, Sertorius Macro is without,
    Alone, and prays t' have private conference
    In business of high nature with your lordship,   35
    He says to me; and which regards you much.
SEJANUS Let him come here.
SATRIUS   Better, my lord, withdraw;
    You will betray what store and strength of friends
    Are now about you, which he comes to spy.
SEJANUS Is he not armed?
SATRIUS   We'll search him.
SEJANUS   No, but take   40
    And lead him to some room where you, concealed,
    May keep a guard upon us.
       [*Exit Satrius*]
               Noble Laco,
    You are our trust; and till our own cohorts
    Can be brought up, your strengths must be our guard.
    Now, good Minutius, honoured Latiaris,   45
    Most worthy, and my most unwearied friends,
    I return instantly.
       [*Exit Sejanus*]
LATIARIS   Most worthy lord!
COTTA His lordship is turned instant kind, methinks;
    I have not observed it in him heretofore.
1 TRIBUNE 'Tis true, and it becomes him nobly.
1 MINUTIUS   I   50
    Am rapt withal.
2 TRIBUNE   By Mars, he has my lives,
    Were they a million, for this only grace.
LACO Ay, and to name a man?
LATIARIS   As he did me!
MINUTIUS And me!
LATIARIS   Who would not spend his life and fortunes
    To purchase but the look of such a lord?   55
LACO [*aside*] He that would nor be lord's fool, nor the world's.
       [*Exeunt*]

5.6

[*Enter*] *Sejanus, Macro,* [*and Satrius*]

SEJANUS Macro! Most welcome, as most coveted friend,
  Let me enjoy my longings. When arrived you?
MACRO About the noon of night.
SEJANUS   Satrius, give leave.
          [*Exit Satrius*]
MACRO I have been, since I came, with both the consuls,
  On a particular design from Caesar.   5
SEJANUS How fares it with our great and royal master?
MACRO Right plentifully well. As with a prince,
  That still holds out the great proportion
  Of his large favours where his judgement hath
  Made once divine election; like the god   10
  That wants not, nor is wearied to bestow
  Where merit meets his bounty, as it doth
  In you, already the most happy, and ere
  The sun shall climb the south, most high Sejanus.
  Let not my lord be amused. For to this end   15
  Was I by Caesar sent for to the isle°
  With special caution to conceal my journey;
  And thence had my dispatch as privately
  Again to Rome; charged to come here by night;
  And only to the consuls make narration   20
  Of his great purpose—that the benefit
  Might come more full and striking, by how much
  It was less looked for or aspired by you,
  Or least informèd to the common thought.
SEJANUS What may this be? Part of myself, dear Macro!   25
  If good, speak out, and share with your Sejanus.
MACRO If bad, I should forever loathe myself
  To be the messenger to so good a lord.
  I do exceed m' instructions to acquaint
  Your lordship with thus much; but 'tis my venture   30
  On your retentive wisdom, and because°
  I would no jealous scruple should molest
  Or rack your peace of thought. For I assure
  My noble lord, no senator yet knows
  The business meant; though all, by several letters,°   35

Are warnèd to be there and give their voices,
Only to add unto the state and grace
Of what is purposed.
SEJANUS   You take pleasure, Macro,
Like a coy wench, in torturing your lover.
What can be worth this suffering?
MACRO   That which follows—   40
The tribunicial dignity and power:°
Both which Sejanus is to have this day
Conferred upon him, and by public Senate.
SEJANUS Fortune, be mine again—thou hast satisfied
For thy suspected loyalty.
MACRO   My lord,   45
I have no longer time, the day approacheth,
And I must back to Caesar.
SEJANUS   Where's Caligula?
MACRO That I forgot to tell your lordship. Why,
He lingers yonder, about Capreae,
Disgraced. Tiberius hath not seen him yet.   50
He needs would thrust himself to go with me,
Against my wish or will, but I have quitted°
His forward trouble with as tardy note
As my neglect or silence could bestow.
Your lordship cannot now command me aught,   55
Because I take no knowledge that I saw you,
But I shall boast to live to serve your lordship,
And so take leave.
SEJANUS   Honest and worthy Macro,
Your love and friendship. Who's there?
        [*Enter Satrius*]
                              Satrius,
Attend my honourable friend forth.
        [*Exeunt Macro and Satrius*]
                              Oh!   60
How vain and vile a passion is this fear?
What base, uncomely things it makes men do!
Suspect their noblest friends—as I did this—
Flatter poor enemies, entreat their servants,
Stoop, court, and catch at the benevolence   65
Of creatures unto whom, within this hour,
I would not have vouchsafed a quarter-look,

Or piece of face! By you, that fools call gods,
Hang all the sky with your prodigious signs,
Fill earth with monsters, drop the scorpion down   70
Out of the zodiac, or the fiercer lion,
Shake off the loosened globe from her long hinge,°
Roll all the world in darkness, and let loose
Th' enragèd winds to turn up groves and towns.
When I do fear again, let me be struck   75
With forkèd fire and unpitied die:°
Who fears, is worthy of calamity.
        [*Exit*]

5.7

[*Enter Terentius, Minutius, Laco, Cotta, Latiaris, Tribunes,
and others. Enter separately*] *Pomponius, Regulus,* [*and*] *Trio.*
POMPONIUS Is not my lord here?
TERENTIUS   Sir, he will be straight.
COTTA What news, Fulcinius Trio?
TRIO   Good, good tidings.
    But keep it to yourself. My lord Sejanus
    Is to receive this day, in open Senate,
    The tribunicial dignity.
COTTA   Is 't true?   5
TRIO No words—not to your thought—but sir, believe it.
LATIARIS What says the consul?
COTTA   Speak it not again—
    He tells me that today my lord Sejanus—
TRIO I must entreat you, Cotta, on your honour,
    Not to reveal it.
COTTA   On my life, sir.
LATIARIS   Say.   10
COTTA Is to receive the tribunicial power.
    But as you are an honourable man
    Let me conjure you not to utter it,
    For it is trusted to me with that bond.
LATIARIS I am Harpocrates.
TERENTIUS   Can you assure it?°   15
POMPONIUS The consul told it me, but keep it close.

MINUTIUS Lord Latiaris, what's the news?
LATIARIS   I'll tell you,
    But you must swear to keep it secret—
        [*Enter*] *Sejanus*
SEJANUS I knew the Fates had on their distaff left
    More of our thread than so.
REGULUS   Hail, great Sejanus!°   20
TRIO Hail, the most honoured—
COTTA   Happy—
LATIARIS   High Sejanus!
SEJANUS Do you bring prodigies, too?
TRIO   May all presage
    Turn to those fair effects, whereof we bring
    Your lordship news.
REGULUS   May 't please my lord withdraw?
SEJANUS Yes. [*To some that stand by*] I will speak with you anon.
TERENTIUS   My lord,   25
    What is your pleasure for the tribunes?
SEJANUS   Why,
    Let 'em be thanked, and sent away.
MINUTIUS   My lord—
LACO Will 't please your lordship to command me—
SEJANUS   No.
    You are troublesome.
        [*Exit Sejanus*]
MINUTIUS   The mood is changed.
[1] TRIBUNE   Not speak?
[2] TRIBUNE Nor look?
LACO   Ay. He is wise will make him friends°   30
    Of such, who never love but for their ends.
        [*Exeunt*]

5.8

    [*Enter*] *Arruntius* [*and*] *Lepidus*, [*divers other senators passing
    by them*]
ARRUNTIUS Ay, go, make haste. Take heed you be not last
    To tender your 'All hail' in the wide hall
    Of huge Sejanus. Run a lictor's pace;°

Stay not to put your robes on, but away,
With the pale troubled ensigns of great friendship   5
Stamped i' your face. Now, Marcus Lepidus,
You still believe your former augury?
Sejanus must go downward? You perceive
His wane approaching fast?

LEPIDUS   Believe me, Lucius,
    I wonder at this rising!

ARRUNTIUS   Ay, and that we   10
    Must give our suffrage to it? You will say
    It is to make his fall more steep and grievous?
    It may be so. But think it they that can
    With idle wishes 'say to bring back time;°
    In cases desperate, all hope is crime.   15
    See, see! What troops of his officious friends
    Flock to salute my lord! And start before°
    My great, proud lord to get a lord-like nod!
    Attend my lord unto the Senate house!
    Bring back my lord! Like servile ushers, make   20
    Way for my lord! Proclaim his idol lordship
    More than ten criers, or six noise of trumpets!
    Make legs, kiss hands, and take a scattered hair
    From my lord's excellent shoulder. See Sanquinius,
    With his slow belly and his dropsy! Look°   25
    What toiling haste he makes! Yet here's another,°
    Retarded with the gout, will be afore him.
    Get thee Liburnian porters, thou gross fool,°
    To bear thy obsequious fatness, like thy peers.
    They are met. The gout returns, and his great carriage.° 30
        Lictors, Consuls,° Sejanus, etc. [*pass over the stage*]

LICTOR Give way, make place! Room for the consul!

SATRIUS   Hail,
    Hail, great Sejanus!

HATERIUS   Hail, my honoured lord!

ARRUNTIUS We shall be marked anon for our not-hail.

LEPIDUS That is already done.

ARRUNTIUS   It is a note
    Of upstart greatness to observe and watch   35
    For these poor trifles, which the noble mind
    Neglects and scorns.

LEPIDUS   Ay, and they think themselves

Deeply dishonoured where they are omitted,
As if they were necessities that helped
To the perfection of their dignities,   40
And hate the men that but refrain 'em.
ARRUNTIUS   Oh,
There is a farther cause of hate. Their breasts
Are guilty that we know their obscure springs
And base beginnings. Thence the anger grows. On. Follow.
    [*Exeunt*]

5.9

    [*Enter*] *Macro* [*and*] *Laco*
MACRO When all are entered, shut the temple doors,
And bring your guards up to the gate.
LACO   I will.
MACRO If you shall hear commotion in the Senate,
Present yourself; and charge on any man
Shall offer to come forth.
LACO   I am instructed.   5
    [*Exeunt*]

5.10

The Senate

    [*Enter*] *Praecones, Lictors, Regulus, Sejanus, Trio, Haterius,
    Sanquinius, Cotta, Pomponius, Latiaris, Lepidus, Arruntius,
    [Praetor, and other Senators*]
HATERIUS How well his lordship looks today!
TRIO   As if
He had been born, or made for this hour's state.
COTTA Your fellow consul's come about, methinks?
TRIO Ay, he is wise.
SANQUINIUS   Sejanus trusts him well.
TRIO Sejanus is a noble, bounteous lord.   5
HATERIUS He is so, and most valiant.

LATIARIS   And most wise.
[1] SENATOR He's everything.
LATIARIS   Worthy of all, and more
    Than bounty can bestow.
TRIO   This dignity
    Will make him worthy.
POMPONIUS   Above Caesar.
SANQUINIUS   Tut,
    Caesar is but the rector of an isle,°   10
    He of the Empire.
TRIO   Now he will have power
    More to reward than ever.
COTTA   Let us look
    We be not slack in giving him our voices.
LATIARIS Not I.
SANQUINIUS   Nor I.
COTTA   The readier we seem
    To propagate his honours, will more bind   15
    His thought to ours.
HATERIUS   I think right with your lordship.
    It is the way to have us hold our places.
SANQUINIUS Ay, and get more.
LATIARIS   More office, and more titles.
POMPONIUS I will not lose the part I hope to share
    In these his fortunes, for my patrimony.   20
LATIARIS See how Arruntius sits, and Lepidus.
TRIO Let 'em alone, they will be marked anon.
[1] SENATOR I'll do with others.
[2] SENATOR   So will I.
[3] SENATOR   And I.
    Men grow not in the state, but as they are planted
    Warm in his favours.
COTTA   Noble Sejanus!   25
HATERIUS Honoured Sejanus!
LATIARIS   Worthy, and great Sejanus!
ARRUNTIUS Gods! How the sponges open, and take in,
    And shut again! Look, look! Is not he blest
    That gets a seat in eye-reach of him? More,
    That comes in ear- or tongue-reach? Oh, but most,   30
    Can claw his subtle elbow, or with a buzz
    Fly-blow his ears.

PRAETOR   Proclaim the Senate's peace;
And give last summons by the edict.
PRAECO   Silence!
In name of Caesar, and the Senate. Silence!
[*Reads*] 'Memmius Regulus and Fulcinius Trio, consuls, these   35
present calends of June,° with the first light, shall hold a Senate
in the temple of Apollo Palatine. All that are fathers,° and are
registered fathers, that have right of entering the Senate, we warn
or command you be frequently present.° Take knowledge the
business is the commonwealth's. Whosoever is absent, his fine or   40
mulct will be taken. His excuse will not be taken.'°
TRIO Note who are absent, and record their names.
REGULUS Fathers conscript. May what I am to utter
Turn good and happy for the commonwealth.
And thou, Apollo, in whose holy house   45
We here are met, inspire us all with truth,
And liberty of censure to our thought.°
The majesty of great Tiberius Caesar
Propounds to this grave Senate the bestowing
Upon the man he loves, honoured Sejanus,   50
The tribunicial dignity and power.
Here are his letters, signèd with his signet.
What pleaseth now the fathers to be done?
SENATORS Read, read 'em, open, publicly! Read 'em!
COTTA Caesar hath honoured his own greatness much,   55
In thinking of this act.
TRIO   It was a thought
Happy, and worthy Caesar.
LATIARIS   And the lord
As worthy it, on whom it is directed.
HATERIUS Most worthy.
SANQUINIUS   Rome did never boast the virtue
That could give envy bounds, but his: Sejanus—   60
[1] SENATOR Honoured, and noble!
[2] SENATOR   Good and great Sejanus!
ARRUNTIUS [*aside*] Oh most tame slavery, and fierce flattery!
PRAECO   Silence!
[*Reads*] 'Tiberius Caesar to the Senate, greeting.
If you, conscript fathers, with your children, be in health, it is
abundantly well; we with our friends here, are so. The care of the   65
commonwealth, howsoever we are removed in person, cannot be

absent to our thought; although oftentimes, even to princes most
present, the truth of their own affairs is hid; than which, nothing
falls out more miserable to a state, or makes the art of governing
more difficult. But since it hath been our easeful happiness to enjoy   70
both the aids and industry of so vigilant a Senate, we profess to
have been the more indulgent to our pleasures, not as being careless
of our office, but rather secure of the necessity.° Neither do these
common rumours of many and infamous libels published against
our retirement at all afflict us, being born more out of men's ignor-   75
ance, than their malice; and will, neglected, find their own grave
quickly, whereas too sensibly° acknowledged, it would make their
obloquy ours. Nor do we desire their authors, though found, be
censured, since in a free state (as ours) all men ought to enjoy both
their minds and tongues free.'   80

ARRUNTIUS [*aside*] The lapwing, the lapwing.

PRAECO [*reads*] 'Yet in things which shall worthily, and more near
concern the majesty of a prince, we shall fear to be so unnaturally
cruel to our own fame as to neglect them. True it is, conscript
fathers, that we have raised Sejanus from obscure, and almost   85
unknown gentry—'

SENATORS How! How!

PRAECO [*reads*] '—to the highest, and most conspicuous point of
greatness, and, we hope, deservingly; yet not without danger, it
being a most bold hazard in that sovereign who, by his particular   90
love to one, dares adventure the hatred of all his other subjects.'

ARRUNTIUS [*aside*] This touches, the blood turns.

PRAECO [*reads*] 'But we affy in your loves and understandings, and do
no way suspect the merit of our Sejanus to make our favours offensive to any.'   95

SENATORS Oh, good, good.

PRAECO [*reads*] 'Though we could have wished his zeal had run a
calmer course against Agrippina and our nephews, howsoever the
openness of their actions declared them delinquents; and that he
would have remembered no innocence is so safe, but it rejoiceth to   100
stand in the sight of mercy. The use of which in us, he hath so quite
taken away toward them by his loyal fury, as now our clemency
would be thought but wearied cruelty, if we should offer to exercise
it.'

ARRUNTIUS [*aside*] I thank him, there I looked for 't. A good fox!   105

PRAECO [*reads*] 'Some there be, that would interpret this his public
severity to be particular° ambition, and that, under a pretext of

service to us, he doth but remove his own lets—alleging the
strengths he hath made to himself by the praetorian soldiers, by his
faction in court and Senate, by the offices he holds himself and   110
confers on others, his popularity and dependents, his urging—and
almost driving—us to this our unwilling retirement, and lastly, his
aspiring to be our son-in-law.'

SENATORS This's strange.

ARRUNTIUS [*aside to Lepidus*] I shall anon believe your vultures,
  Marcus.   115

PRAECO [*reads*] 'Your wisdoms, conscript fathers, are able to examine
  and censure° these suggestions. But were they left to our absolving
  voice, we durst pronounce them as we think them, most malicious.'

SENATORS Oh, he has restored all, list.

PRAECO [*reads*] 'Yet are they offered to be averred,° and on the lives   120
  of the informers. What we should say, or rather what we should not
  say, lords of the Senate, if this be true, our gods and goddesses
  confound us if we know! Only, we must think we have placed our
  benefits ill; and conclude that in our choice, either we were wanting
  to the gods, or the gods to us.'   125

ARRUNTIUS [*aside*] The place grows hot, they shift.

PRAECO [*reads*] 'We have not been covetous, honourable fathers, to
  change; neither is it now any new lust that alters our affection, or
  old loathing, but those needful jealousies of state that warn wiser
  princes hourly to provide their safety; and do teach them how   130
  learned a thing it is to beware of the humblest enemy—much more
  of those great ones, whom their own employed° favours have made
  fit for their fears.'

[1] SENATOR Away.

[2] SENATOR   Sit farther.

COTTA   Let's remove—

ARRUNTIUS [*aside*] Gods! How the leaves drop off, this little wind!   135

PRAECO [*reads*] 'We therefore desire that the offices he holds be first
  seized by the Senate; and himself suspended from all exercise of
  place, or power—'

SENATORS How!

SANQUINIUS [*thrusting by*] By your leave.

ARRUNTIUS   Come, porpoise—where's
  Haterius?   140
  His gout keeps him most miserably constant.
  Your dancing shows a tempest.

SEJANUS   Read no more.°

REGULUS Lords of the Senate, hold your seats. Read on.
SEJANUS These letters, they are forged.
REGULUS   A guard! Sit still.
    [Laco enters with the guards]
ARRUNTIUS *[aside]* Here's change.
REGULUS   Bid silence, and read forward.
PRAECO   Silence!   145
    [Reads] '—and himself suspended from all exercise of place, or
power, but till due and mature trial be made of his innocency,
which yet we can faintly apprehend the necessity to doubt. If,
conscript fathers, to your more searching wisdoms there shall
appear farther cause—or of farther proceeding, either to seizure of   150
lands, goods, or more—it is not our power that shall limit your
authority, or our favour that must corrupt your justice: either were
dishonourable in you, and both uncharitable to ourself. We would
willingly be present with your counsels in this business, but the
danger of so potent a faction (if it should prove so) forbids our   155
attempt—except one of the consuls would be entreated for our
safety to undertake the guard of us home; then we should most
readily adventure. In the meantime, it shall not be fit for us to
importune so judicious a Senate, who know how much they hurt
the innocent that spare the guilty, and how grateful a sacrifice to the   160
gods is the life of an ingrateful person. We reflect not in this on
Sejanus—notwithstanding, if you keep an eye upon him—and
there is Latiaris, a senator, and Pinnarius Natta, two of his most
trusted ministers, and so professed,° whom we desire not to have
apprehended, but as the necessity of the cause exacts it.'   165
REGULUS A guard on Latiaris.
ARRUNTIUS   Oh, the spy!
  The reverend spy is caught! Who pities him?
  Reward, sir, for your service; now you ha' done
  Your property, you see what use is made?°
  Hang up the instrument.
    [Exeunt Latiaris and Natta, guarded]
SEJANUS   Give leave.
LACO   Stand, stand!°   170
  He comes upon his death that doth advance
  An inch toward my point.
SEJANUS   Have we no friend here?
ARRUNTIUS Hushed. Where now are all the hails and acclamations?
    [Enter] Macro

MACRO Hail to the consuls, and this noble Senate!

SEJANUS [*aside*] Is Macro here? Oh, thou art lost, Sejanus.   175

MACRO Sit still, and unaffrighted, reverend fathers.
    Macro, by Caesar's grace the new-made provost,
    And now possessed of the praetorian bands
    (An honour late belonged to that proud man)
    Bids you be safe; and to your constant doom°   180
    Of his deservings, offers you the surety
    Of all the soldiers, tribunes, and centurions
    Received in our command.

REGULUS   Sejanus, Sejanus!
    Stand forth, Sejanus!

SEJANUS   Am I called?

MACRO   Ay, thou,
    Thou insolent monster, art bid stand.

SEJANUS   Why, Macro,   185
    It hath been otherwise between you and I!
    This court, that knows us both, hath seen a difference,
    And can (if it be pleased to speak) confirm
    Whose insolence is most.

MACRO   Come down, Typhoeus!°
    If mine be most, lo, thus I make it more—   190
    Kick up thy heels in air, tear off thy robe,
    Play with thy beard and nostrils. Thus 'tis fit—°
    And no man take compassion of thy state—
    To use th' ingrateful viper, tread his brains
    Into the earth.

REGULUS   Forbear.

MACRO   If I could lose   195
    All my humanity now, 'twere well to torture
    So meriting a traitor. Wherefore, fathers,
    Sit you amazed and silent, and not censure°
    This wretch, who in the hour he first rebelled
    'Gainst Caesar's bounty, did condemn himself?   200
    Phlegra, the field where all the sons of earth°
    Mustered against the gods, did ne'er acknowledge
    So proud and huge a monster.

REGULUS   Take him hence!
    And all the gods guard Caesar!

TRIO   Take him hence!

HATERIUS Hence!

COTTA   To the dungeon with him!
SANQUINIUS   He deserves it.   205
[I] SENATOR Crown all our doors with bays!
SANQUINIUS   And let an ox,°
   With gilded horns and garlands, straight be led
   Unto the Capitol—
HATERIUS   And sacrificed
   To Jove, for Caesar's safety.
TRIO   All our gods
   Be present still to Caesar!
COTTA   Phoebus!
SANQUINIUS   Mars!   210
HATERIUS Diana!
SANQUINIUS   Pallas!
[I] SENATOR   Juno, Mercury,
   All guard him!
MACRO   Forth, thou prodigy of men.
        [*Exit Sejanus guarded*]
COTTA Let all the traitor's titles be defaced!
TRIO His images and statues be pulled down!
HATERIUS His chariot wheels be broken!
ARRUNTIUS   And the legs   215
   Of the poor horses, that deservèd naught,
   Let them be broken too.
LEPIDUS   Oh violent change,
   And whirl of men's affections!
ARRUNTIUS   Like as both
   Their bulks and souls were bound on Fortune's wheel,°
   And must act only with her motion.   220
        [*Exeunt all but*] Lepidus *and* Arruntius
LEPIDUS Who would depend upon the popular air,°
   Or voice of men, that have today beheld
   (That which if all the gods had foredeclared,
   Would not have been believed) Sejanus' fall?
   He that this morn rose proudly as the sun,   225
   And breaking through a mist of clients' breath,
   Came on as gazed at and admired as he
   When superstitious Moors salute his light!
   That had our servile nobles waiting him°
   As common grooms, and hanging on his look,   230
   No less than human life on destiny!

That had men's knees as frequent as the gods;
And sacrifices, more than Rome had altars—
And this man fall! Fall? Ay, without a look
That durst appear his friend, or lend so much   235
Of vain relief to his changed state as pity!
ARRUNTIUS They that before, like gnats, played in his beams,
And thronged to circumscribe him, now not seen!
Nor deign to hold a common seat with him!
Others, that waited him unto the Senate,   240
Now inhumanely ravish him to prison!°
Whom (but this morn) they followed as their lord,
Guard through the streets, bound like a fugitive.
Instead of wreaths, give fetters; strokes, for stoops;°
Blind shame, for honours; and black taunts, for titles. 245
Who would trust slippery Chance?
LEPIDUS   They that would make
Themselves her spoil, and foolishly forget,
When she doth flatter, that she comes to prey.
Fortune, thou hadst no deity, if men
Had wisdom—we have placèd thee so high,   250
By fond belief in thy felicity.
[SENATORS] [shout within] The gods guard Caesar! All
        the gods guard Caesar!
        [Enter] Macro, Regulus, [and] Senators
MACRO Now, great Sejanus, you that awed the state,
And sought to bring the nobles to your whip;
That would be Caesar's tutor, and dispose   255
Of dignities and offices; that had
The public head still bare to your designs,
And made the general voice to echo yours;
That looked for salutations twelve score off,°
And would have pyramids, yea, temples, reared   260
To your huge greatness—now you lie as flat
As was your pride advanced.
REGULUS   Thanks to the gods!
SENATORS And praise to Macro, that hath savèd Rome!
Liberty, liberty, liberty! Lead on,
And praise to Macro, that hath savèd Rome!   265
        [Exeunt all but] Arruntius [and] Lepidus
ARRUNTIUS I prophesy, out of this Senate's flattery,
That this new fellow, Macro, will become

A greater prodigy in Rome than he
That now is fall'n.
        [*Enter Terentius*]
TERENTIUS   Oh you whose minds are good,
And have not forced all mankind from your breasts;°   270
That yet have so much stock of virtue left
To pity guilty states when they are wretched:
Lend your soft ears to hear, and eyes to weep,°
Deeds done by men beyond the acts of furies.
The eager multitude, who never yet   275
Knew why to love or hate, but only pleased
T' express their rage of power, no sooner heard
The murmur of Sejanus in decline,
But with that speed and heat of appetite
With which they greedily devour the way   280
To some great sports or a new theatre,
They filled the Capitol and Pompey's Cirque—°
Where, like so many mastiffs biting stones,
As if his statues now were sensitive
Of their wild fury, first they tear them down;°   285
Then fastening ropes, drag them along the streets,
Crying in scorn, 'This, this was that rich head
Was crowned with garlands and with odours; this,°
That was in Rome so reverencèd. Now
The furnace and the bellows shall to work,   290
The great Sejanus crack, and piece by piece,
Drop i' the founder's pit.'
LEPIDUS   O popular rage!°
TERENTIUS The whilst the Senate, at the temple of Concord,
Make haste to meet again, and thronging, cry,
'Let us condemn him, tread him down in water   295
While he doth lie upon the bank! Away!'
Where some, more tardy, cry unto their bearers,
'He will be censured ere we come—run, knaves!'
And use that furious diligence, for fear
Their bondmen should inform against their slackness,   300
And bring their quaking flesh unto the hook.
The rout, they follow with confusèd voice,
Crying, they are glad, say they could ne'er abide him;
Enquire, what man he was? What kind of face?
What beard he had? What nose? What lips? Protest   305

They ever did presage h' would come to this—
They never thought him wise, nor valiant. Ask
After his garments when he dies? What death?
And not a beast of all the herd demands,
What was his crime? Or who were his accusers? 310
Under what proof or testimony he fell?
'There came,' says one, 'a huge, long, worded letter
From Capreae against him.' 'Did there so?
Oh!' They are satisfied; no more.
LEPIDUS   Alas!
They follow Fortune, and hate men condemned, 315
Guilty or not.
ARRUNTIUS   But had Sejanus thrived
In his design, and prosperously oppressed
The old Tiberius, then in that same minute
These very rascals that now rage like furies
Would have proclaimed Sejanus emperor. 320
LEPIDUS But what hath followed?
TERENTIUS   Sentence, by the Senate,
To lose his head—which was no sooner off,
But that, and th' unfortunate trunk were seized
By the rude multitude; who, not content
With what the forward justice of the state° 325
Officiously had done, with violent rage°
Have rent it limb from limb. A thousand heads,
A thousand hands, ten thousand tongues and voices,
Employed at once in several acts of malice.
Old men not staid with age, virgins with shame,° 330
Late wives with loss of husbands, mothers of children,
Losing all grief in joy of his sad fall,
Run quite transported with their cruelty;
These mounting at his head, these at his face,
These digging out his eyes, those with his brain, 335
Sprinkling themselves, their houses, and their friends.
Others are met, have ravished thence an arm,
And deal small pieces of the flesh for favours;
These with a thigh; this hath cut off his hands,
And this his feet; these fingers, and these toes; 340
That hath his liver; he, his heart: there wants
Nothing but room for wrath, and place for hatred.°
What cannot oft be done, is now o'erdone.

The whole and all of what was great Sejanus,
And next to Caesar did possess the world,   345
Now torn, and scattered, as he needs no grave;
Each little dust covers a little part.
So lies he nowhere, and yet often buried.
          [*Enter*] *Nuntius*°
ARRUNTIUS More of Sejanus?
NUNTIUS   Yes.
LEPIDUS   What can be added?
  We know him dead.
NUNTIUS   Then there begin your pity: 350
  There is enough behind to melt ev'n Rome
  And Caesar into tears, though never slave
  Could yet so highly offend, but tyranny
  In torturing him would make him worth lamenting.
  A son and daughter to the dead Sejanus—   355
  Of whom there is not now so much remaining
  As would give fastening to the hangman's hook—
  Have they drawn forth for farther sacrifice;
  Whose tenderness of knowledge, unripe years,
  And childish silly innocence was such°   360
  As scarce would lend them feeling of their danger.
  The girl so simple, as she often asked,°
  Where they would lead her? For what cause they dragged her?
  Cried, she would do no more, that she could take
  Warning with beating. And because our laws   365
  Admit no virgin immature to die,°
  The wittily and strangely cruel Macro°
  Delivered her to be deflowered and spoiled
  By the rude lust of the licentious hangman,
  Then to be strangled with her harmless brother.   370
LEPIDUS O act, most worthy hell and lasting night
  To hide it from the world!
NUNTIUS   Their bodies thrown
  Into the Gemonies—I know not how,
  Or by what accident returned—the mother,
  Th' expulsèd Apicata, finds them there;   375
  Whom, when she saw lie spread on the degrees,°
  After a world of fury on herself,
  Tearing her hair, defacing of her face,
  218

Beating her breasts and womb, kneeling amazed,
Crying to heaven, then to them; at last,   380
Her drownèd voice got up above her woes,
And with such black and bitter execrations
As might affright the gods, and force the sun
Run backward to the east—nay, make the old°
Deformèd Chaos rise again t' o'erwhelm°   385
Them, us, and all the world—she fills the air,
Upbraids the heavens with their partial dooms,°
Defies their tyrannous powers, and demands
What she and those poor innocents have transgressed,
That they must suffer such a share in vengeance,   390
Whilst Livia, Lygdus, and Eudemus live,
Who—as she says, and firmly vows to prove it
To Caesar and the Senate—poisoned Drusus.
LEPIDUS Confederates with her husband?
NUNTIUS   Ay.
LEPIDUS   Strange act!
ARRUNTIUS And strangely opened. What says now my monster,   395
    The multitude? They reel now, do they not?
NUNTIUS Their gall is gone, and now they 'gin to weep
    The mischief they have done.
ARRUNTIUS   I thank 'em, rogues!
NUNTIUS Part are so stupid, or so flexible,°
    As they believe him innocent. All grieve;   400
    And some, whose hands yet reek with his warm blood,
    And gripe the part which they did tear of him,
    Wish him collected, and created new.
LEPIDUS How Fortune plies her sports when she begins
    To practise 'em! Pursues, continues, adds;   405
    Confounds, with varying her impassioned moods!
ARRUNTIUS Dost thou hope, Fortune, to redeem thy crimes?
    To make amends for thy ill-placèd favours
    With these strange punishments? Forbear, you things°
    That stand upon the pinnacles of state,   410
    To boast your slippery height; when you do fall,
    You pash yourselves in pieces, ne'er to rise,
    And he that lends you pity is not wise.
TERENTIUS Let this example move th' insolent man
    Not to grow proud, and careless of the gods.   415

It is an odious wisdom to blaspheme,
Much more to slighten or deny their powers.
For whom the morning saw so great and high,
Thus low, and little, 'fore the even doth lie.
    [*Exeunt*]

ADDITIONAL PASSAGE A

Preceding the preliminary material in the folio is the following dedicatory letter:

TO THE NO LESS
NOBLE BY VIRTUE
THAN BLOOD:

Esmé
L. Aubigny.°   5

My Lord,

If ever any ruin were so great as to survive, I think this be one I send you: The
Fall of Sejanus. It is a poem that, if I well remember, in your lordship's sight
suffered no less violence from our people here than the subject of it did from
the rage of the people of Rome; but with a different fate, as (I hope) merit: for   10
this hath outlived their malice, and begot itself a greater favour than he lost,
the love of good men. Amongst whom, if I make your lordship the first it
thanks, it is not without a just confession of the bond your benefits have, and
ever shall hold upon me.

Your lordship's most faithful honourer,   15

BEN. JONSON.

ADDITIONAL PASSAGE B

*Immediately following the action of the play in the folio is this note about
the original performance of* Sejanus:

This tragedy was first acted in the year 1603 by the King's Majesty's
Servants.
The principal tragedians were

Richard Burbage	William Shakespeare
Augustine Phillips	John Hemminges
William Sly	Henry Condell
John Lowin	Alexander Cooke

With the allowance of the Master of Revels.

THE DEVIL IS AN ASS

THE PERSONS OF THE PLAY

Satan, the great devil
Pug,° the less devil [assumes the
   name Devil when in human
   form]
Iniquity, the Vice
Fitzdottrel,° a squire of
   Norfolk
Mistress Frances, his wife
Merecraft, the projector°
Everill, his champion°
Wittipol, a young gallant
Manly, his friend
Engine,° a broker
Trains, the projector's man
[Tom] Gilthead,° a goldsmith

Plutarchus,° his son
Sir Paul Eitherside,° a lawyer and
   justice
Lady Eitherside, his wife
Lady Tailbush, the lady
   projectress
Pitfall,° her woman
Ambler, her gentleman usher
Sledge, a smith, the constable
Shackles, Keeper of Newgate
[Prologue]
[Epilogue]
[Four Keepers at Newgate]
Sergeants
[Attendants]

THE SCENE

London

The Prologue

'The Devil is an Ass.' That is, today,
The name of what you are met for, a new play.
Yet, grandees, would you were not come to grace
Our matter with allowing us no place.°
Though you presume Satan a subtle thing,   5
And may have heard he's worn in a thumb-ring,
Do not on these presumptions force us act
In compass of a cheese trencher. This tract°
Will ne'er admit our vice, because of yours.
Anon, who worse than you the fault endures   10
That yourselves make? When you will thrust and spurn,
And knock us o' the elbows, and bid turn,
As if, when we had spoke, we must be gone,
Or till we speak, must all run in to one,
Like the young adders at the old one's mouth?°   15
Would we could stand due north, or had no south,
If that offend—or were Muscovy glass,
That you might look our scenes through as they pass.°
We know not how to affect you. If you'll come
To see new plays, pray you afford us room,   20
And show this but the same face you have done
Your dear delight, 'The Devil of Edmonton.'°
Or if for want of room it must miscarry,
'Twill be but justice that your censure tarry
Till you give some. And when six times you ha' seen 't,°   25
If this play do not like, the devil is in 't.°

1.1

[Enter Satan and] Pug

[SATAN] Ho, ho, ho, ho, ho, ho, ho, ho!°
To earth? And why to earth, thou foolish spirit?
What wouldst thou do on earth?

PUG   For that, great chief,
As time shall work! I do but ask my month,
Which every petty puny devil has;°   5
Within that term the Court of Hell will hear
Something may gain a longer grant perhaps.

SATAN For what? The laming a poor cow or two?
Entering a sow to make her cast her farrow?°
Or crossing of a market-woman's mare   10
'Twixt this and Tottenham? These were wont to be°
Your main achievements, Pug. You have some plot now
Upon a tunning of ale to stale the yeast,
Or keep the churn so that the butter come not,
Spite o' the housewife's cord or her hot spit?°   15
Or some good ribibe about Kentish Town
Or Hoxton you would hang now for a witch°
Because she will not let you play round robin,
And you'll go sour the citizens' cream 'gainst Sunday°
That she may be accused for 't, and condemned   20
By a Middlesex jury, to the satisfaction
Of their offended friends, the Londoners' wives,
Whose teeth were set on edge with it? Foolish fiend,
Stay i' your place, know your own strengths, and put not
Beyond the sphere of your activity.   25
You are too dull a devil to be trusted°
Forth in those parts, Pug, upon any affair
That may concern our name on earth. It is not
Everyone's work. The state of Hell must care
Whom it employs, in point of reputation,   30
Here about London. You would make, I think,
An agent to be sent for Lancashire
Proper enough; or some parts of Northumberland,
So you'd good instructions, Pug.

PUG   O chief!°
    You do not know, dear chief, what there is in me.   35
    Prove me but for a fortnight—for a week—°
    And lend me but a Vice to carry with me
    To practise there with any playfellow,°
    And you will see there will come more upon 't
    Than you'll imagine, precious chief.
SATAN   What Vice?   40
    What kind wouldst th' have it of?
PUG   Why, any—Fraud,
    Or Covetousness, or Lady Vanity,
    Or old Iniquity. I'll call him hither.°
    [*Enter Iniquity*]
INIQUITY What is he calls upon me and would seem to lack a Vice?
    Ere his words be half spoken, I am with him in a trice;   45
    Here, there, and everywhere, as the cat is with the mice:
    True *vetus Iniquitas*. Lack'st thou cards, friend, or dice?°
    I will teach thee cheat, child, to cog, lie, and swagger,
    And ever and anon to be drawing forth thy dagger;
    To swear by Gog's nowns, like a Lusty Juventus,°   50
    In a cloak to thy heel, and a hat like a penthouse,
    Thy breeches of three fingers, and thy doublet all belly,°
    With a wench that shall feed thee with cock-stones and jelly.
PUG Is it not excellent, chief? How nimble he is!
INIQUITY Child of Hell, this is nothing! I will fetch thee a leap   55
    From the top of Paul's steeple to the Standard in Cheap,°
    And lead thee a dance through the streets without fail,
    Like a needle of Spain, with a thread at my tail.
    We will survey the suburbs, and make forth our sallies
    Down Petticoat Lane and up the Smock Alleys,   60
    To Shoreditch, Whitechapel, and so to Saint Kather'n's,°
    To drink with the Dutch there, and take forth their patterns.°
    From thence we will put in at Custom House Quay there,°
    And see how the factors and prentices play there°
    False with their masters, and geld many a full pack,   65
    To spend it in pies at the Dagger and the Woolsack.°
PUG Brave, brave, Iniquity! Will not this do, chief?
INIQUITY Nay, boy, I will bring thee to the bawds and the roisters
    At Billingsgate, feasting with claret wine and oysters,
    From thence shoot the bridge, child, to the Cranes i' the Vintry,° 70
    And see there the gimlets, how they make their entry!

Or if thou hadst rather, to the Strand down to fall,
'Gainst the lawyers come dabbled from Westminster Hall,°
And mark how they cling with their clients together,
Like ivy to oak, so velvet to leather—°   75
Ha, boy, I would show thee!

PUG   Rare, rare!
SATAN   Peace, dotard.
And thou more ignorant thing that so admir'st,
Art thou the spirit thou seem'st? So poor? To choose
This for a Vice t' advance the cause of Hell
Now? As Vice stands this present year? Remember   80
What number it is: six hundred and sixteen.°
Had it but been five hundred—though some sixty
Above, that's fifty years agone, and six—
When every great man had his Vice stand by him
In his long coat, shaking his wooden dagger,°   85
I could consent that then this your grave choice
Might have done that with his lord chief, the which°
Most of his chamber can do now. But Pug,
As the times are, who is it will receive you?
What company will you go to? Or whom mix with?   90
Where canst thou carry him, except to taverns?
To mount up on a joint-stool with a Jew's trump
To put down Cokeley, and that must be to citizens?°
He ne'er will be admitted there where Vennar comes.°
He may perchance, in tail of a sheriff's dinner,   95
Skip with a rhyme o' the table from new nothing,
And take his Almain-leap into a custard,°
Shall make my Lady Mayoress and her sisters
Laugh all their hoods over their shoulders. But°
This is not that will do; they are other things   100
That are received now upon earth for Vices:
Stranger and newer, and changed every hour.
They ride 'em like their horses off their legs,
And here they come to Hell, whole legions of 'em,
Every week, tired. We still strive to breed°   105
And rear 'em up new ones, but they do not stand
When they come there: they turn 'em on our hands.
And it is feared they have a stud o' their own
Will put down ours. Both our breed and trade
Will suddenly decay, if we prevent not.°   110

Unless it be a Vice of quality
Or fashion now, they take none from us. Carmen
Are got into the yellow starch, and chimney-sweepers°
To their tobacco and strong waters, hum,
Mead, and obarni. We must therefore aim   115
At extraordinary subtle ones now
When we do send, to keep us up in credit,
Not old Iniquities. [*To Iniquity*] Get you e'en back, sir,
To making of your rope of sand again.°
You are not for the manners, nor the times.   120
They have their Vices there most like to Virtues;
You cannot know 'em apart by any difference:
They wear the same clothes, eat the same meat,°
Sleep i' the self-same beds, ride i' those coaches,
Or very like, four horses in a coach,   125
As the best men and women. Tissue gowns,
Garters and roses, fourscore pound a pair,
Embroidered stockings, cut-work smocks and shirts,
More certain marks of lechery now, and pride,
Than ere they were of true nobility!°   130
       [*Exit Iniquity*]
But Pug, since you do burn with such desire
To do the commonwealth of Hell some service,
I am content, assuming of a body,
You go to earth and visit men a day.
But you must take a body ready made, Pug,   135
I can create you none; nor shall you form
Yourself an airy one, but become subject
To all impression of the flesh you take
So far as human frailty. So this morning
There is a handsome cutpurse hanged at Tyburn,°   140
Whose spirit departed, you may enter his body.
For clothes, employ your credit with the hangman,
Or let our tribe of brokers furnish you.°
And look how far your subtlety can work
Thorough those organs; with that body, spy   145
Amongst mankind—you cannot there want Vices,
And therefore the less need to carry 'em wi' you.
But as you make your soon at night's relation,
And we shall find it merits from the state,
You shall have both trust from us, and employment.   150

PUG Most gracious chief!
SATAN   Only thus more I bind you,
     To serve the first man that you meet; and him
     I'll show you now. Observe him. Yon is he
     You shall see first, after your clothing.
              [*Enter Fitzdottrel. Satan*] *shows Fitzdottrel to* [*Pug*]
                                   Follow him.
     But once engaged, there you must stay and fix;   155
     Not shift, until the midnight's cock do crow.
PUG Any conditions to be gone.
SATAN   Away then.
          [*Exeunt*]

1.2

[FITZDOTTREL] Ay, they do now name Bretnor, as before
     They talked of Gresham and of Doctor Forman,
     Franklin, and Fiske, and Savory (he was in, too),°
     But there's not one of these that ever could
     Yet show a man the devil in true sort.   5
     They have their crystals, I do know, and rings,
     And virgin parchment, and their dead men's skulls,
     Their ravens' wings, their lights, and pentacles
     With characters; I ha' seen all these. But—°
     Would I might see the devil. I would give   10
     A hundred o' these pictures to see him
     Once out of picture. May I prove a cuckold°
     (And that's the one main mortal thing I fear),
     If I begin not now to think the painters
     Have only made him. 'Slight, he would be seen°   15
     One time or other else. He would not let
     An ancient gentleman of a good house—°
     As most are now in England—the Fitzdottrels,°
     Run wild and call upon him thus in vain,
     As I ha' done this twelvemonth. If he be not   20
     At all, why are there conjurers? If they be not,
     Why are there laws against 'em? The best artists
     Of Cambridge, Oxford, Middlesex and London,
     Essex and Kent, I have had in pay to raise him

These fifty weeks, and yet h' appears not. 'Sdeath,°   25
I shall suspect they can make circles only
Shortly, and know but his hard names. They do say
He'll meet a man (of himself) that has a mind to him.
If he would so, I have a mind and a half for him:
He should not be long absent. Pray thee, come,   30
I long for thee.
              He expresses a longing to see the devil°
                       An I were with child by him,°
And my wife, too, I could not more. Come yet,
Good Beelzebub. Were he a kind devil°
And had humanity in him, he would come, but
To save one's longing. I should use him well,   35
I swear, and with respect (would he would try me);
Not as the conjurers do, when they ha' raised him,
Get him in bonds and send him post on errands
A thousand miles—it is preposterous, that,
And, I believe, is the true cause he comes not.   40
And he has reason. Who would be engaged
That might live freely, as he may do? I swear,
They are wrong all. The burnt child dreads the fire.
They do not know to entertain the devil.
I would so welcome him, observe his diet,   45
Get him his chamber hung with arras, two of 'em,
I' my own house; lend him my wife's wrought pillows—
And as I am an honest man, I think
If he had a mind to her, too, I should grant him,
To make our friendship perfect. So I would not   50
To every man. If he but hear me now!
And should come to me in a brave young shape
And take me at my word! Ha! Who is this?

1.3

[Enter] Pug

[PUG] Sir, your good pardon that I thus presume
        Upon your privacy. I am born a gentleman,
        A younger brother, but in some disgrace
        Now with my friends, and want some little means°

To keep me upright while things be reconciled.   5
Please you to let my service be of use to you, sir.

FITZDOTTREL Service? 'Fore hell, my heart was at my mouth
Till I had viewed his shoes well, for those roses
Were big enough to hide a cloven foot.

He looks and surveys his feet, over and over°

No, friend, my number's full. I have one servant   10
Who is my all, indeed, and from the broom
Unto the brush—for just so far I trust him.
He is my wardrobe man, my cater, cook,
Butler, and steward; looks unto my horse;
And helps to watch my wife. H' has all the places   15
That I can think on, from the garret downward,
E'en to the manger and the curry-comb.

PUG Sir, I shall put your worship to no charge
More than my meat, and that but very little;
I'll serve you for your love.

FITZDOTTREL   Ha? Without wages?   20
I'd hearken o' that ear, were I at leisure.
But now I'm busy. Prithee, friend, forbear me;
An thou hadst been a devil I should say
Somewhat more to thee. Thou dost hinder now
My meditations.

PUG   Sir, I am a devil.   25

FITZDOTTREL How!

PUG   A true devil, sir.

FITZDOTTREL   Nay, now you lie—
Under your favour, friend, for I'll not quarrel.
I looked o' your feet afore; you cannot cozen me,
Your shoe's not cloven, sir, you are whole hoofed.

He views his feet again

PUG Sir, that's a popular error, deceives many.   30
But I am that I tell you.

FITZDOTTREL   What's your name?

PUG My name is Devil, sir.

FITZDOTTREL   Say'st thou true?

PUG   Indeed, sir.

FITZDOTTREL 'Slid! There's some omen i' this! What countryman?°

PUG Of Derbyshire, sir, about the Peak.

FITZDOTTREL   That hole
Belonged to your ancestors?

232

PUG   Yes, Devil's Arse, sir.° 35
FITZDOTTREL I'll entertain him for the namesake. Ha?
    And turn away my tother man? And save
    Four pound a year by that! There's luck, and thrift, too!
    The very devil may come hereafter as well.
    Friend, I receive you: but withal I acquaint you 40
    Aforehand—if yo' offend me, I must beat you.
    It is a kind of exercise I use,
    And cannot be without.
PUG   Yes, if I do not
    Offend, you can, sure.
FITZDOTTREL   Faith, Devil, very hardly:
    I'll call you by your surname, 'cause I love it. 45

1.4

    [Enter] Engine [carrying a cloak], Wittipol, [and] Manly
[ENGINE] Yonder he walks, sir. I'll go lift him for you.°
WITTIPOL To him, good Engine, raise him up by degrees
    Gently, and hold him there, too, you can do it.
    Show yourself now a mathematical broker.°
ENGINE I'll warrant you for half a piece.
WITTIPOL   'Tis done, sir.° 5
    [Engine and Fitzdottrel walk aside]
MANLY Is't possible there should be such a man?
WITTIPOL You shall be your own witness, I'll not labour
    To tempt you past your faith.
MANLY   And is his wife
    So very handsome, say you?
WITTIPOL   I ha' not seen her
    Since I came home from travel, and they say 10
    She is not altered. Then, before I went,
    I saw her once; but so as she hath stuck
    Still i' my view, no object hath removed her.
MANLY 'Tis a fair guest, friend, beauty; and once lodged
    Deep in the eyes, she hardly leaves the inn. 15
    How does he keep her?
WITTIPOL   Very brave. However
    Himself be sordid, he is sensual that way.

In every dressing he does study her.

MANLY And furnish forth himself so from the brokers?

WITTIPOL Yes, that's a hired suit he now has on,   20
    To see *The Devil is an Ass* today in;
    This Engine gets three or four pound a week by him.
    He dares not miss a new play or a feast,
    What rate soever clothes be at; and thinks
    Himself still new, in other men's old.

MANLY   But stay,   25
    Does he love meat so?

WITTIPOL   Faith, he does not hate it.
    But that's not it. His belly and his palate
    Would be compounded with for reason. Marry,
    A wit he has, of that strange credit with him,
    'Gainst all mankind, as it doth make him do   30
    Just what it list. It ravishes him forth,
    Whither it please, to any assembly or place,
    And would conclude him ruined should he scape
    One public meeting, out of the belief
    He has of his own great and catholic strengths°   35
    In arguing and discourse.

        Engine hath won Fitzdottrel to 'say° on the cloak
                It takes, I see:
    H' has got the cloak upon him.

FITZDOTTREL   A fair garment,
    By my faith, Engine!

ENGINE   It was never made, sir,
    For threescore pound, I assure you. 'Twill yield thirty.
    The plush, sir, cost three pound ten shillings a yard!   40
    And then the lace and velvet.

FITZDOTTREL   I shall, Engine,°
    Be looked at prettily in it! Art thou sure
    The play is played today?

ENGINE   O, here's the bill, sir.
    I had forgot to gi't you.

        He gives him the playbill

FITZDOTTREL   Ha? *The Devil!*
    I will not lose you, sirrah! But Engine, think you   45
    The gallant is so furious in his folly?
    So mad upon the matter that he'll part
    With's cloak upo' these terms?

ENGINE   Trust not your Engine,
   Break me to pieces else, as you would do
   A rotten crane or an old rusty jack   50
   That has not one true wheel in him. Do but talk with him.°
FITZDOTTREL I shall do that to satisfy you, Engine,
   And myself, too.
        He turns to Wittipol.
               With your leave, gentlemen.
   Which of you is it, is so mere idolater°
   To my wife's beauty, and so very prodigal   55
   Unto my patience, that for the short parley
   Of one swift hour's quarter with my wife
   He will depart with, let me see, this cloak here,
   The price of folly? Sir, are you the man?
WITTIPOL I am that venturer, sir.
FITZDOTTREL   Good time! Your name   60
   Is Wittipol?
WITTIPOL   The same, sir.
FITZDOTTREL   And 'tis told me
   You've travelled lately?
WITTIPOL   That I have, sir.
FITZDOTTREL   Truly,
   Your travels may have altered your complexion,°
   But sure, your wit stood still.
WITTIPOL   It may well be, sir.
   All heads ha' not like growth.
FITZDOTTREL   The good man's gravity   65
   That left you land, your father, never taught you
   These pleasant matches?
WITTIPOL   No, nor can his mirth
   With whom I make 'em, put me off.
FITZDOTTREL   You are
   Resolved then?
WITTIPOL   Yes, sir.
FITZDOTTREL   Beauty is the saint
   You'll sacrifice yourself into the shirt to?   70
WITTIPOL So I may still clothe and keep warm your wisdom.
FITZDOTTREL You lade me, sir!
WITTIPOL   I know what you will bear, sir.°
FITZDOTTREL Well, to the point. 'Tis only, sir, you say,
   To speak unto my wife?

WITTIPOL	Only to speak to her.
FITZDOTTREL	And in my presence?
WITTIPOL	In your very presence. 75
FITZDOTTREL	And in my hearing?
WITTIPOL	In your hearing—so

   You interrupt us not.
FITZDOTTREL   For the short space
   You do demand, the fourth part of an hour,
   I think I shall, with some convenient study,
   And this good help to boot, bring myself to 't.   80
      He shrugs himself up in the cloak
WITTIPOL I ask no more.
FITZDOTTREL   Please you, walk to'ard my house.
   Speak what you list; that time is yours: my right
   I have departed with. But not beyond,
   A minute, or a second, look for. Length,
   And drawing out, ma' advance much to these matches.   85
   And I except all kissing. Kisses are
   Silent petitions still with willing lovers.
WITTIPOL Lovers? How falls that o' your fant'sy?
FITZDOTTREL   Sir.°
   I do know somewhat; I forbid all lip-work.
WITTIPOL I am not eager at forbidden dainties.   90
   Who covets unfit things, denies himself.
FITZDOTTREL You say well, sir. 'Twas prettily said that same,
   He does indeed. I'll have no touches, therefore,
   Nor takings by the arms, nor tender circles
   Cast 'bout the waist, but all be done at distance.   95
   Love is brought up with those soft migniard handlings;
   His pulse lies in his palm: and I defend°
   All melting joints and fingers—that's my bargain—
   I do defend 'em, anything like action.
   But talk, sir, what you will. Use all the tropes   100
   And schemes that Prince Quintilian can afford you:°
   And much good do your rhetoric's heart. You are welcome, sir.
   Engine, God b' wi' you.
WITTIPOL   Sir, I must condition
   To have this gentleman by, a witness.
FITZDOTTREL   Well,
   I am content, so he be silent.
MANLY   Yes, sir.   105

FITZDOTTREL Come, Devil, I'll make you room straight. But I'll
  show you
First to your mistress, who's no common one,
You must conceive, that brings this gain to see her.
I hope thou'st brought me good luck.
PUG   I shall do 't, sir.
      [*Exeunt*]°

1.5

  [*Enter Wittipol, Manly, and Engine*]
[WITTIPOL] Engine, you hope o' your half piece?
  [*Gives Engine money*]
                                  'Tis there, sir.
Be gone.
  [*Exit Engine*]
      Friend Manly, who's within here? Fixed?
  Wittipol knocks his friend o' the breast
MANLY I am directly in a fit of wonder
What'll be the issue of this conference!
WITTIPOL For that, ne'er vex yourself till the event.   5
How like yo' him?
MANLY   I would fain see more of him.
WITTIPOL What think you of this?
MANLY   I am past degrees of thinking.
Old Afric, and the new America,
With all their fruit of monsters, cannot show°
So just a prodigy.
WITTIPOL   Could you have believed,   10
Without your sight, a mind so sordid inward
Should be so specious, and laid forth abroad,
To all the show that ever shop or ware was?°
MANLY I believe anything now, though I confess
His vices are the most extremities   15
I ever knew in nature. But why loves he
The devil so?
WITTIPOL   O sir! For hidden treasure
He hopes to find; and has proposed himself°
So infinite a mass, as to recover,

He cares not what he parts with of the present   20
To his men of art, who are the race may coin him.°
Promise gold mountains, and the covetous
Are still most prodigal.
MANLY   But ha' you faith
    That he will hold his bargain?
WITTIPOL   Oh dear sir!
    He will not off on 't. Fear him not. I know him.   25
    One baseness still accompanies another.
    See! He is here already, and his wife too.
MANLY A wondrous handsome creature, as I live!

1.6

[*Enter*] *Fitzdottrel* [*and*] *Mistress Fitzdottrel*
[FITZDOTTREL] Come, wife, this is the gentleman. Nay, blush not.
MISTRESS FITZDOTTREL Why, what do you mean, sir? Ha' you your
    reason?
FITZDOTTREL Wife,
    I do not know that I have lent it forth
    To anyone, at least, without a pawn, wife;
    Or that I have eat or drunk the thing of late   5
    That should corrupt it. Wherefore, gentle wife,
    Obey, it is thy virtue; hold no acts
    Of disputation.
MISTRESS FITZDOTTREL Are you not enough
    The talk of feasts and meetings, but you'll still
    Make argument for fresh?
FITZDOTTREL   Why, careful wedlock,   10
    If I have a longing to have one tale more
    Go of me, what is that to thee, dear heart?
    Why shouldst thou envy my delight? Or cross it
    By being solicitous, when it not concerns thee?
MISTRESS FITZDOTTREL Yes, I have share in this. The scorn will fall 15
    As bitterly on me, where both are laughed at.
FITZDOTTREL Laughed at, sweet bird? Is that the scruple? Come,
    come,
    Thou art a nyas. Which of your great houses°
    (I will not mean at home here, but abroad),

Your families in France, wife, send not forth   20
Something within the seven year may be laughed at?°
I do not say seven months, nor seven weeks,
Nor seven days, nor hours—but seven year, wife.
I give 'em time. Once, within seven year,
I think they may do something may be laughed at   25
In France, I keep me there still. Wherefore, wife,
Let them that list, laugh still, rather than weep
For me. Here is a cloak cost fifty pound, wife,
Which I can sell for thirty, when I ha' seen
All London in 't, and London has seen me.   30
Today I go to the Blackfriars Playhouse,°
Sit i' the view, salute all my acquaintance,
Rise up between the acts, let fall my cloak,
Publish a handsome man, and a rich suit°
(As that's a special end why we go thither,   35
All that pretend to stand for 't o' the stage).
The ladies ask, who's that? (For they do come
To see us, love, as we do to see them.)
Now I shall lose all this for the false fear
Of being laughed at? Yes, wusse. Let 'em laugh, wife.°   40
Let me have such another cloak tomorrow,
And let 'em laugh again, wife, and again,
And then grow fat with laughing, and then fatter,
All my young gallants, let 'em bring their friends, too:
Shall I forbid 'em? No, let heaven forbid 'em—   45
Or wit, if 't have any charge on 'em. Come, thy ear, wife,
Is all I'll borrow of thee. Set your watch, sir.
Thou only art to hear, not speak a word, dove,
To aught he says. That I do gi' you in precept,°
No less than counsel, on your wifehood, wife,   50
Not though he flatter you, or make court or love
(As you must look for these), or say he rail;
Whate'er his arts be, wife, I will have thee
Delude 'em with a trick, thy obstinate silence:
I know advantages, and I love to hit   55
These pragmatic young men at their own weapons.°
Is your watch ready? Here my sail bears for you.
Tack toward him, sweet pinnace. Where's your watch?°
        He disposes his wife to her place and sets his watch
WITTIPOL   I'll set it, sir, with yours.

MISTRESS FITZDOTTREL   I must obey.

MANLY Her modesty seems to suffer with her beauty,   60
    And so, as if his folly were away,
    It were worth pity.

FITZDOTTREL   Now they're right, begin, sir.°
    But first, let me repeat the contract briefly.°
    I am, sir, to enjoy this cloak I stand in
    Freely, and as your gift, upon condition   65
    You may as freely speak here to my spouse
    Your quarter of an hour, always keeping
    The measured distance of your yard or more°
    From my said spouse, and in my sight and hearing.
    This is your covenant?

WITTIPOL   Yes, but you'll allow   70
    For this time spent now?

FITZDOTTREL   Set 'em so much back.

WITTIPOL I think I shall not need it.

FITZDOTTREL   Well, begin, sir.
    There is your bound, sir. Not beyond that rush.°

WITTIPOL If you interrupt me, sir, I shall discloak you.

    Wittipol begins

    The time I have purchased, lady, is but short;   75
    And therefore if I employ it thriftily,
    I hope I stand the nearer to my pardon.
    I am not here to tell you, you are fair,
    Or lovely, or how well you dress you, lady;
    I'll save myself that eloquence of your glass°   80
    Which can speak these things better to you than I.
    And 'tis a knowledge wherein fools may be
    As wise as a court parliament. Nor come I°
    With any prejudice or doubt that you
    Should, to the notice of your own worth, need   85
    Least revelation. She's a simple woman
    Knows not her good—whoever knows her ill—
    And at all carats. That you are the wife°
    To so much blasted flesh as scarce hath soul
    Instead of salt to keep it sweet, I think   90
    Will ask no witnesses to prove. The cold
    Sheets that you lie in, with the watching candle,
    That sees how dull to any thaw of beauty,
    Pieces and quarters, half, and whole nights sometimes,°

The devil-given elfin squire, your husband,   95
Doth leave you, quitting here his proper circle°
For a much worse i' the walks of Lincoln's Inn°
Under the elms, t' expect the fiend in vain there,
Will confess for you.
FITZDOTTREL   I did look for this gear.°
WITTIPOL And what a daughter of darkness he does make you,   100
Locked up from all society or object,
Your eye not let to look upon a face
Under a conjurer's (or some mould for one,
Hollow and lean like his) but by great means
As I now make, your own too sensible sufferings,   105
Without the extraordinary aids
Of spells or spirits may assure you, lady.
For my part, I protest 'gainst all such practice;
I work by no false arts, medicines, or charms
To be said forward and backward.
FITZDOTTREL   No, I except—   110
WITTIPOL Sir, I shall ease you.
          He offers° to discloak him
FITZDOTTREL   Mum.
WITTIPOL   Nor have I ends, lady,
Upon you more than this: to tell you how Love,
Beauty's good angel, he that waits upon her
At all occasions, and no less than Fortune,
Helps th' adventurous, in me makes that proffer   115
Which never fair one was so fond to lose°
Who could but reach a hand forth to her freedom.
On the first sight I loved you, since which time,
Though I have travelled, I have been in travail°
More for this second blessing of your eyes   120
Which now I have purchased, than for all aims else.
Think of it, lady; be your mind as active
As is your beauty: view your object well.
Examine both my fashion, and my years.
Things that are like are soon familiar,   125
And Nature joys still in equality.°
Let not the sign o' the husband fright you, lady.
But ere your spring be gone, enjoy it. Flowers,
Though fair, are oft but of one morning. Think,
All beauty doth not last until the autumn.   130

You grow old while I tell you this. And such
As cannot use the present are not wise.
If Love and Fortune will take care of us,
Why should our will be wanting? This is all.
What do you answer, lady?

     She stands mute

FITZDOTTREL   Now the sport comes.   135
Let him still wait, wait, wait, while the watch goes,
And the time runs. Wife!

WITTIPOL   How! Not any word?°
Nay then, I taste a trick in 't. Worthy lady,
I cannot be so false to mine own thoughts
Of your presumed goodness, to conceive   140
This as your rudeness, which I see's imposed.
Yet since your cautelous jailer here stands by you,
And you're denied the liberty o' the house,
Let me take warrant, lady, from your silence
(Which ever is interpreted consent)   145
To make your answer for you—which shall be
To as good purpose as I can imagine,
And what I think you'd speak.

     He sets Master Manly, his friend, in his place°

FITZDOTTREL   No, no, no, no!

WITTIPOL I shall resume, sir.

MANLY   Sir, what do you mean?

WITTIPOL [*to Fitzdottrel*] One interruption more, sir, and
    you go   150
Into your hose and doublet, nothing saves you.
And therefore hearken. This is for your wife.

MANLY You must play fair, sir.

WITTIPOL   Stand for me, good friend.

     And [Wittipol] speaks for her

Troth, sir, 'tis more than true that you have uttered
Of my unequal, and so sordid match here,   155
With all the circumstances of my bondage.
I have a husband, and a two-legged one,
But such a moonling, as no wit of man
Or roses can redeem from being an ass.°
He's grown too much the story of men's mouths   160
To scape his lading; should I make 't my study,
And lay all ways, yea, call mankind to help

To take his burden off, why, this one act
Of his, to let his wife out to be courted,
And at a price, proclaims his asinine nature   165
So loud, as I am weary of my title to him.
But, sir, you seem a gentleman of virtue,
No less than blood, and one that every way
Looks as he were of too good quality
To entrap a credulous woman, or betray her.   170
Since you have paid thus dear, sir, for a visit,
And made such venture on your wit and charge
Merely to see me, or at most to speak to me,
I were too stupid, or (what's worse) ingrate,
Not to return your venture. Think but how   175
I may with safety do it; I shall trust
My love and honour to you, and presume
You'll ever husband both against this husband;
Who, if we chance to change his liberal ears
To other ensigns, and with labour make°   180
A new beast of him, as he shall deserve,
Cannot complain he is unkindly dealt with.
This day he is to go to a new play, sir,
From whence no fear, no, nor authority,
Scarcely the King's command, sir, will restrain him,   185
Now you have fitted him with a stage garment,
For the mere name's sake, were there nothing else;°
And many more such journeys he will make,
Which, if they now, or any time hereafter,
Offer us opportunity, you hear, sir,   190
Who'll be as glad, and forward to embrace,
Meet, and enjoy it cheerfully as you.
    He shifts to his own place again
I humbly thank you, lady.
FITZDOTTREL   Keep your ground, sir.
WITTIPOL Will you be lightened?
FITZDOTTREL   Mum.
WITTIPOL   And but I am,
By the sad contract, thus to take my leave of you   195
At this so envious distance, I had taught
Our lips ere this to seal the happy mixture
Made of our souls. But we must both now yield
To the necessity. Do not think yet, lady,

But I can kiss, and touch, and laugh, and whisper,   200
And do those crowning courtships, too, for which
Day and the public have allowed no name,
But now my bargain binds me. 'Twere rude injury
T' importune more, or urge a noble nature
To what of its own bounty it is prone to,   205
Else I should speak—But, lady, I love so well,
As I will hope, you'll do so to. I have done, sir.

FITZDOTTREL Well then, I ha' won?

WITTIPOL   Sir. And I may win, too.

FITZDOTTREL Oh yes! No doubt on 't. I'll take careful order
That she shall hang forth ensigns at the window   210
To tell you when I am absent. Or I'll keep
Three or four footmen, ready still of purpose,
To run and fetch you at her longings, sir.
I'll go bespeak me straight a gilt caroche
For her and you to take the air in—yes,   215
Into Hyde Park, and thence into Blackfriars;
Visit the painters, where you may see pictures,°
And note the properest limbs, and how to make 'em.
Or what do you say unto a middling gossip?°
To bring you aye together at her lodging,   220
Under pretext of teaching o' my wife
Some rare receipt of drawing almond milk? ha?
It shall be a part of my care. Good sir, God b' wi' you.
I ha' kept the contract, and the cloak is mine.

WITTIPOL Why, much good do 't you, sir; it may fall out   225
That you ha' bought it dear, though I ha' not sold it.

FITZDOTTREL A pretty riddle! Fare you well, good sir.
        He turns his wife about
Wife, your face this way, look on me; and think
You've had a wicked dream, wife, and forget it.

MANLY This is the strangest motion I e'er saw.°   230
        [*Exeunt Manly and Wittipol*]

FITZDOTTREL Now, wife, sits this fair cloak the worse upon me
For my great sufferings, or your little patience? ha?
They laugh, you think?

MISTRESS FITZDOTTREL Why, sir, and you might see 't.
What thought they have of you may be soon collected
By the young gentleman's speech.

FITZDOTTREL   Young gentleman?   235

244

Death! You are in love with him, are you? Could he not
Be named the gentleman, without the young?
Up to your cabin again.

MISTRESS FITZDOTTREL My cage, yo' were best
To call it!

FITZDOTTREL Yes, sing there. You'd fain be making
Blanc-manger with him at your mother's! I know you.   240
Go, get you up.

   [*Exit Mistress Fitzdottrel*]
     How now! What say you, Devil?

1.7

  [*Enter Pug*]

[PUG] Here is one Engine, sir, desires to speak with you.

FITZDOTTREL I thought he brought some news of a broker! Well,
Let him come in, good Devil; fetch him else.
   [*Exit Pug. Enter Engine*]
O, my fine Engine! What's th' affair? More cheats?

ENGINE No, sir—the wit, the brain, the great projector   5
I told you of, is newly come to town.

FITZDOTTREL Where, Engine?

ENGINE   I ha' brought him (he's without),
Ere he pulled off his boots, sir, but so followed
For businesses—

FITZDOTTREL   But what is a projector?
I would conceive.

ENGINE   Why, one, sir, that projects   10
Ways to enrich men, or to make 'em great,
By suits, by marriages, by undertakings,
According as he sees they humour it.

FITZDOTTREL Can he not conjure at all?

ENGINE   I think he can, sir,
To tell you true, but you do know of late   15
The state hath ta'en such note of 'em, and compelled 'em
To enter such great bonds, they dare not practise.°

FITZDOTTREL 'Tis true, and I lie fallow for 't the while!

ENGINE O sir! You'll grow the richer for the rest.

FITZDOTTREL I hope I shall—but Engine, you do talk   20

Somewhat too much o' my courses. My cloak customer°
Could tell me strange particulars.

ENGINE   By my means?

FITZDOTTREL How should he have 'em else?

ENGINE   You do not know, sir,
What he has—and by what arts. A moneyed man, sir,
And is as great with your almanac-men as you are.   25

FITZDOTTREL That gallant?

ENGINE   You make the other wait too long here,
And he is extreme punctual.

FITZDOTTREL   Is he a gallant?

ENGINE Sir, you shall see: he is in his riding suit,
As he comes now from Court. But hear him speak;
Minister matter to him, and then tell me.°   30

2.1

[Enter] Merecraft, Trains, [and three Waiters]
[MERECRAFT] Sir, money's a whore, a bawd, a drudge,
  Fit to run out on errands. Let her go.°
  Via pecunia! When she's run and gone,°
  And fled and dead, then will I fetch her again
  With aqua-vitae out of an old hogshead!   5
  While there are lees of wine or dregs of beer,
  I'll never want her! Coin her out of cobwebs,
  Dust, but I'll have her! Raise wool upon eggshells,
  Sir, and make grass grow out o' marrowbones
  To make her come. (*To a Waiter*) Commend me to your mistress,°   10
  Say, let the thousand pound but be had ready,
  And it is done.
          [Exit Waiter]
                  I would but see the creature
  Of flesh and blood, the man, the prince, indeed,
  That could employ so many millions
  As I would help him to.
FITZDOTTREL   How talks he? Millions?   15
MERECRAFT (*to another*) I'll give you an account of this tomorrow.
          [Exit second Waiter]
  Yes, I will talk no less, and do it, too,
  If they were myriads—and without the devil,
  By direct means; it shall be good in law.
ENGINE   Sir.
MERECRAFT (*to a third*) Tell Master Woodcock I'll not fail to meet
      him°   20
  Upon th' Exchange at night. Pray him to have°
  The writings there, and we'll dispatch it.
          [Exit third Waiter.] He turns to Fitzdottrel
                                    Sir,
  You are a gentleman of a good presence,
  A handsome man—I have considered you
  As a fit stock to graft honours upon: 25
  I have a project to make you a duke now.
  That you must be one, within so many months

    As I set down, out of true reason of state,
    You sha' not avoid it. But you must hearken then.

ENGINE Hearken? Why, sir, do you doubt his ears? Alas!   30
    You do not know Master Fitzdottrel.

FITZDOTTREL He does not know me indeed. I thank you, Engine,
    For rectifying him.

MERECRAFT   Good!

    He turns to Engine

                   Why, Engine, then
    I'll tell it you—I see you ha' credit here,
    And that you can keep counsel, I'll not question.   35
    He shall but be an undertaker with me°
    In a most feasible business. It shall cost him
    Nothing.

ENGINE   Good, sir.

MERECRAFT   Except he please, but's countenance°
    (That I will have) t' appear in 't to great men,
    For which I'll make him one. He shall not draw   40
    A string of's purse. I'll drive his patent for him.
    We'll take in citizens, commoners, and aldermen
    To bear the charge, and blow 'em off again,
    Like so many dead flies, when 'tis carried.
    The thing is for recovery of drowned land,   45
    Whereof the Crown's to have his moiety°
    If it be owner; else, the Crown and owners
    To share that moiety, and the recoverers
    T' enjoy the tother moiety for their charge.

ENGINE Throughout England?

MERECRAFT   Yes, which will arise   50
    To eighteen millions, seven the first year;
    I have computed all, and made my survey
    Unto an acre. I'll begin at the pan,°
    Not at the skirts, as some ha' done, and lost
    All that they wrought, their timber-work, their trench,   55
    Their banks all borne away, or else filled up
    By the next winter. Tut, they never went
    The way—I'll have it all.

ENGINE   A gallant tract
    Of land it is!

MERECRAFT 'Twill yield a pound an acre.
    We must let cheap, ever, at first. But sir,   60

This looks too large for you, I see. Come hither,
We'll have a less. Here's a plain fellow, you see him,
   [*He points to Trains*]
Has his black bag of papers there, in buckram,
Wi' not be sold for th' earldom of Pancridge. Draw,°
Gi' me out one by chance.
   [*Trains plucks a paper from the bag*]°
                   'Project 4: dog-skins.'   65
Twelve thousand pound! The very worst, at first.

FITZDOTTREL Pray you let's see 't, sir.

MERECRAFT   'Tis a toy, a trifle!

FITZDOTTREL Trifle! Twelve thousand pound for dogs' skins?

MERECRAFT   Yes,
But by my way of dressing, you must know, sir,°
And med'cining the leather to a height   70
Of improved ware, like your borachio
Of Spain, sir, I can fetch nine thousand for 't—°

ENGINE Of the King's glover?

MERECRAFT   Yes, how heard you that?

ENGINE Sir, I do know you can.

MERECRAFT   Within this hour—
And reserve half my secret. Pluck another;   75
See if thou hast a happier hand.
    He plucks out the second [*paper*]: *bottle-ale*
                  I thought so.
The very next worse to it! Bottle-ale.
Yet, this is two and twenty thousand. Prithee
Pull out another, two or three.

FITZDOTTREL   Good, stay, friend,
By bottle-ale, two and twenty thousand pound?   80

MERECRAFT Yes, sir, it's cast to penny-halfpenny-farthing
O' the backside; there you may see it, read:°
I will not bate a harrington o' the sum.°
I'll win it i' my water and my malt,
My furnaces, and hanging o' my coppers,   85
The tunning, and the subtlety o' my yeast;
And then the earth of my bottles, which I dig,
Turn up, and steep, and work, and neal myself
To a degree of porcelain. You will wonder
At my proportions, what I will put up   90
In seven years! For so long time I ask

For my invention. I will save in cork,
In my mere stoppling, 'bove three thousand pound;°
Within that term, by gouging of 'em out
Just to the size of my bottles, and not slicing.   95
There's infinite loss i' that. What hast thou there?
    He draws out another [paper]: raisins
O' making wine of raisins; this is in hand now.

ENGINE Is not that strange, sir, to make wine of raisins?

MERECRAFT Yes, and as true a wine as th' wines of France,
    Or Spain, or Italy. Look of what grape   100
    My raisin is, that wine I'll render perfect,
    As of the muscatel grape, I'll render muscatel;
    Of the canary, his; the claret, his;
    So of all kinds—and bate you of the prices
    Of wine throughout the kingdom, half in half.   105

ENGINE But how, sir, if you raise the other commodity,
    Raisins?

MERECRAFT Why, then I'll make it out of blackberries,
    And it shall do the same. 'Tis but more art,
    And the charge less. Take out another.

FITZDOTTREL   No, good sir.
    Save you the trouble, I'll not look nor hear   110
    Of any but your first there, the drowned land—
    If 't will do as you say.

MERECRAFT   Sir, there's not place
    To gi' you demonstration of these things.
    They are a little too subtle. But I could show you
    Such a necessity in 't, as you must be   115
    But what you please, against the received heresy
    That England bears no dukes. Keep you the land, sir,°
    The greatness of th' estate shall throw 't upon you.
    If you like better turning it to money,
    What may not you, sir, purchase with that wealth?   120
    Say you should part with two o' your millions
    To be the thing you would, who would not do 't?
    As I protest I will, out of my dividend,
    Lay for some pretty principality
    In Italy, from the Church. Now you perhaps   125
    Fancy the smoke of England, rather? But—
    Ha' you no private room, sir, to draw to
    T' enlarge ourselves more upon?

FITZDOTTREL   O yes—Devil!

MERECRAFT These, sir, are businesses ask to be carried
    With caution, and in cloud.

FITZDOTTREL   I apprehend;°   130
    They do so, sir.
        [*Enter Pug*]
             Devil, which way is your mistress?

PUG Above, sir, in her chamber.

FITZDOTTREL   Oh, that's well.
    Then this way, good sir.

MERECRAFT   I shall follow you. Trains,
    Gi' me the bag and go you presently,°
    Commend my service to my Lady Tailbush.   135
    Tell her I am come from Court this morning; say
    I have got our business moved, and well. Entreat her
    That she give you the fourscore angels, and see 'em
    Disposed of to my counsel, Sir Paul Eitherside.
    Sometime today I'll wait upon her ladyship   140
    With the relation.
        [*Exit Trains*]

ENGINE   Sir, of what dispatch
    He is! Do you mark?

MERECRAFT   Engine, when did you see
    My cousin Everill? Keeps he still your quarter
    I' the Bermudas?

ENGINE   Yes, sir, he was writing°
    This morning, very hard.

MERECRAFT   Be not you known to him°   145
    That I am come to town; I have effected
    A business for him, but I would have it take him
    Before he thinks for 't.

ENGINE   Is it past?

MERECRAFT   Not yet.
    'Tis well o' the way.

ENGINE   O sir! Your worship takes
    Infinite pains.

MERECRAFT   I love friends to be active;   150
    A sluggish nature puts off man and kind.°

ENGINE And such a blessing follows it.

MERECRAFT   I thank
    My fate. Pray you, let's be private, sir?

FITZDOTTREL   In here.
MERECRAFT Where none may interrupt us.
        [*Exit Merecraft with Engine*]
FITZDOTTREL   You hear, Devil,
    Lock the street doors fast and let no one in   155
    (Except they be this gentleman's followers)
    To trouble me. Do you mark? You've heard and seen
    Something today; and by it, you may gather
    Your mistress is a fruit that's worth the stealing,
    And therefore worth the watching. Be you sure now   160
    You've all your eyes about you; and let in
    No lace-woman, nor bawd that brings French masks
    And cut-works. See you? Nor old crones with wafers
    To convey letters. Nor no youths, disguised°
    Like country wives, with cream and marrow puddings.   165
    Much knavery may be vented in a pudding,°
    Much bawdy intelligence: they are shrewd ciphers.°
    Nor turn the key to any neighbour's need,
    Be 't but to kindle fire or beg a little;
    Put it out, rather—all out, to an ash—   170
    That they may see no smoke. Or water, spill it.
    Knock o' the empty tubs, that by the sound
    They may be forbid entry. Say we are robbed
    If any come to borrow a spoon, or so.
    I wi' not have good fortune or God's blessing   175
    Let in while I am busy.
PUG   I'll take care, sir:
    They sha' not trouble you, if they would.
FITZDOTTREL   Well, do so.
        [*Exit Fitzdottrel*]

2.2

[PUG] I have no singular service of this now,
    Nor no superlative master! I shall wish°
    To be in hell again, at leisure. Bring
    A Vice from thence? That had been such a subtlety°
    As to bring broadcloths hither, or transport   5
    Fresh oranges into Spain. I find it now;

My chief was i' the right. Can any fiend
Boast of a better Vice than here by nature
And art they're owners of? Hell ne'er own me
But I am taken—the fine tract of it°   10
Pulls me along! To hear men such professors
Grown in our subtlest sciences! My first act now
Shall be to make this master of mine cuckold;
The primitive work of darkness I will practise.
I will deserve so well of my fair mistress   15
By my discoveries first, my counsels after,
And keeping counsel after that, as who
Soever is one, I'll be another sure;
I'll ha' my share. Most delicate damned flesh
She will be! Oh that I could stay time now;   20
Midnight will come too fast upon me, I fear,
To cut my pleasure—
        [*Enter Mistress Fitzdottrel*]
MISTRESS FITZDOTTREL Look at the back door.
    One knocks, see who it is.
            She sends Devil out
PUG (*aside*)   Dainty she-devil!
        [*Exit Pug*]
MISTRESS FITZDOTTREL I cannot get this venture of the cloak
    Out of my fancy; nor the gentleman's way   25
    He took, which though 'twere strange, yet 'twas handsome,
    And had a grace withal beyond the newness.
    Sure he will think me that dull stupid creature
    He said, and may conclude it, if I find not
    Some thought to thank th' attempt. He did presume,   30
    By all the carriage of it, on my brain
    For answer; and will swear 'tis very barren
    If it can yield him no return.
        [*Enter Pug*]
                        Who is it?
PUG Mistress, it is—but first, let me assure
    The excellence of mistresses, I am,   35
    Although my master's man, my mistress' slave,
    The servant of her secrets and sweet turns,
    And know what fitly will conduce to either.
MISTRESS FITZDOTTREL What's this? I pray you come to yourself
    and think

What your part is: to make an answer. Tell,   40
Who is it at the door?
PUG   The gentleman, mistress,
Who was at the cloak-charge to speak with you
This morning, who expects only to take
Some small commandments from you, what you please,
Worthy your form, he says, and gentlest manners.   45
MISTRESS FITZDOTTREL Oh! You'll anon prove his hired man, I fear.
What has he giv'n you for this message? Sir,
Bid him put off his hopes of straw, and leave
To spread his nets in view, thus. Though they take
Master Fitzdottrel, I am no such foul   50
Nor fair one, tell him, will be had with stalking.°
And wish him to forbear his acting to me
At the gentleman's chamber window in Lincoln's Inn there
That opens to my gallery; else, I swear
T' acquaint my husband with his folly, and leave him   55
To the just rage of his offended jealousy.
Or if your master's sense be not so quick
To right me, tell him I shall find a friend
That will repair me. Say I will be quiet°
In mine own house! Pray you, in those words give it him.   60
PUG This is some fool turned!
     [Exit Pug]
MISTRESS FITZDOTTREL   If he be the master
Now of that state and wit which I allow him,
Sure he will understand me; I durst not
Be more direct. For this officious fellow,
My husband's new groom, is a spy upon me   65
I find already. Yet if he but tell him
This in my words, he cannot but conceive
Himself both apprehended and requited.
I would not have him think he met a statue,
Or spoke to one not there, though I were silent.   70
     [Enter Pug]
How now? Ha' you told him?
PUG   Yes.
MISTRESS FITZDOTTREL   And what says he?
PUG Says he? That which myself would say to you, if I durst.
That you are proud, sweet mistress! And withal
A little ignorant to entertain

254

The good that's proffered; and (by your beauty's leave)   75
Not all so wise as some true politic wife
Would be, who having matched with such a nupson
(I speak it with my master's peace) whose face
Hath left t' accuse him now, for 't doth confess him
What you can make him, will yet (out of scruple   80
And a spiced conscience) defraud the poor gentleman,°
At least delay him in the thing he longs for,
And makes it his whole study, how to compass
Only a title. Could but he write cuckold,
He had his ends. For, look you—
MISTRESS FITZDOTTREL   This can be   85
None but my husband's wit.
PUG   My precious mistress—
MISTRESS FITZDOTTREL It creaks his engine; the groom never durst
Be else so saucy.
PUG   If it were not clearly
His worshipful ambition, and the top of it—
The very forked top, too—why should he°   90
Keep you thus mured up in a backroom, mistress,
Allow you ne'er a casement to the street,
Fear of engendering by the eyes with gallants,
Forbid you paper, pen, and ink, like ratsbane,
Search your half pint of muscatel lest a letter   95
Be sunk i' the pot, and hold your new-laid egg
Against the fire, lest any charm be writ there?
Will you make benefit of truth, dear mistress,
If I do tell it you? I do 't not often.
I am set over you, employed, indeed,   100
To watch your steps, your looks, your very breathings,
And to report them to him. Now if you
Will be a true, right, delicate sweet mistress,
Why, we will make a cokes of this wise master,
We will, my mistress, an absolute fine cokes,   105
And mock to air all the deep diligences
Of such a solemn and effectual ass,
An ass to so good purpose as we'll use him.
I will contrive it so that you shall go
To plays, to masques, to meetings, and to feasts.   110
For why is all this rigging and fine tackle, mistress,
If you neat handsome vessels of good sail

Put not forth ever and anon with your nets
Abroad into the world? It is your fishing.
There you shall choose your friends, your servants, lady,   115
Your squires of honour; I'll convey your letters,
Fetch answers, do you all the offices
That can belong to your blood and beauty. And,
For the variety, at my times, although
I am not in due symmetry the man   120
Of that proportion, or in rule
Of physic of the just complexion,°
Or of that truth of piccadill in clothes°
To boast a sovereignty o'er ladies, yet
I know to do my turns, sweet mistress. Come, kiss—   125
MISTRESS FITZDOTTREL How now!
PUG   Dear delicate mistress, I am your slave,
Your little worm that loves you; your fine monkey;
Your dog, your jack, your Pug, that longs to be°
Styled o' your pleasures.
        She thinks her husband watches
MISTRESS FITZDOTTREL   Hear you all this? Sir, pray you,
Come from your standing, do; a little spare   130
Yourself, sir, from your watch, t' applaud your squire,
That so well follows your instructions!

2.3

        [*Enter Fitzdottrel*]
[FITZDOTTREL] How now, sweetheart? What's the matter?
MISTRESS FITZDOTTREL   Good!
You are a stranger to the plot! You set not
Your saucy Devil here to tempt your wife
With all the insolent uncivil language
Or action he could vent?
FITZDOTTREL   Did you so, Devil?   5
MISTRESS FITZDOTTREL Not you? You were not planted i' your hole
    to hear him
Upo' the stairs? Or here, behind the hangings?°
I do not know your qualities? He durst do it,
And you not give directions?

FITZDOTTREL   You shall see, wife,
  Whether he durst or no, and what it was   10
  I did direct.
PUG   Sweet mistress, are you mad?
         [*Exit Fitzdottrel, who*] *enters presently with a cudgel upon him*
FITZDOTTREL You most mere rogue! You open, manifest villain!
  You fiend apparent, you! You declared hellhound!
PUG Good sir!
FITZDOTTREL   Good knave, good rascal, and good traitor!
  Now I do find you parcel devil, indeed.°   15
  Upo' the point of trust? I' your first charge?
  The very day o' your probation,
  To tempt your mistress?
         [*Beats Pug*]
                    You do see, good wedlock,
  How I directed him.
MISTRESS FITZDOTTREL Why, where, sir, were you?
FITZDOTTREL (*after a pause*) Nay, there is one blow more for
     exercise: 20
         [*Strikes him again*]
  I told you I should do it.
PUG   Would you had done, sir.
FITZDOTTREL O wife, the rarest man! [*To Pug*] Yet there's another
  To put you in mind o' the last.
         He strikes him again
                         Such a brave man, wife!
  Within, he has his projects, and does vent 'em,
  The gallantest! [*To Pug*] Were you tentiginous? ha?   25
         And again
  Would you be acting of the incubus?
  Did her silks rustling move you?
PUG   Gentle sir.
FITZDOTTREL Out of my sight. If thy name were not Devil
  Thou shouldst not stay a minute with me. In,
  Go, yet stay—yet go, too. I am resolved   30
  What I will do, and you shall know 't aforehand;
  Soon as the gentleman is gone, do you hear?
  I'll help your lisping.
         [*Exit Pug*]
                  Wife, such a man, wife!°
  He has such plots! He will make me a duke,

No less, by heaven! Fix mares to your coach, wife,   35
That's your proportion! And your coachman bald,
Because he shall be bare enough. Do not you laugh,°
We are looking for a place and all i' the map
What to be of. Have faith, be not an infidel.
You know I am not easy to be gulled.   40
I swear, when I have my millions, else, I'll make
Another duchess, if you ha' not faith.

MISTRESS FITZDOTTREL You'll ha' too much, I fear, in these false
    spirits.

FITZDOTTREL Spirits? Oh, no such thing! Wife! Wit, mere wit!
This man defies the devil and all his works!   45
He does 't by engine and devices, he.
He has his winged ploughs that go with sails,
Will plough you forty acres at once. And mills,
Will spout you water ten miles off. All Crowland°
Is ours, wife; and the fens, from us in Norfolk°   50
To the utmost bound of Lincolnshire. We have viewed it
And measured it within, all by the scale.
The richest tract of land, love, i' the kingdom!
There will be made seventeen or eighteen millions;
Or more, as 't may be handled! Wherefore think,   55
Sweetheart, if th' hast a fancy to one place
More than another to be duchess of,
Now, name it; I will ha't, whate'er it cost
(If 'twill be had for money) either here,
Or 'n France or Italy.

MISTRESS FITZDOTTREL You ha' strange fantasies!   60

2.4

    [*Enter*] *Merecraft* [*and*] *Engine*

[MERECRAFT] Where are you, sir?

FITZDOTTREL   I see thou hast no talent
This way, wife. Up to thy gallery; do, chuck,
Leave us to talk of it who understand it.
    [*Exit Mistress Fitzdottrel*]

MERECRAFT I think we ha' found a place to fit you now, sir.
Gloucester.

FITZDOTTREL Oh no, I'll none!

MERECRAFT;   Why, sir?

FITZDOTTREL   'Tis fatal.   5

MERECRAFT That you say right in. Spenser, I think, the younger,
　　Had his last honour thence. But he was but Earl.°

FITZDOTTREL I know not that, sir. But Thomas of Woodstock,
　　I'm sure, was Duke, and he was made away
　　At Calais; as Duke Humphrey was at Bury;   10
　　And Richard the Third, you know what end he came to.°

MERECRAFT By m' faith, you are cunning i' the chronicle, sir.°

FITZDOTTREL No, I confess I ha't from the playbooks,
　　And think they are more authentic.

ENGINE   That's sure, sir.

MERECRAFT What say you to this then?

　　　　He whispers him of a place

FITZDOTTREL   No, a noble house   15
　　Pretends to that. I will do no man wrong.°

MERECRAFT Then take one proposition more, and hear it
　　As past exception.

FITZDOTTREL   What's that?

MERECRAFT   To be
　　Duke of those lands you shall recover. Take
　　Your title thence, sir: Duke of the Drowned-lands,   20
　　Or Drowned-land.

FITZDOTTREL   Ha? That last has a good sound!
　　I like it well. The Duke of Drowned-land?

ENGINE   Yes:
　　It goes like Greenland, sir, if you mark it.

MERECRAFT   Ay,
　　And drawing thus your honour from the work,
　　You make the reputation of that greater,   25
　　And stay 't the longer i' your name.

FITZDOTTREL   'Tis true.
　　Drowned-lands will live in Drowned-land!

MERECRAFT   Yes, when you
　　Ha' no foot left, as that must be, sir, one day.
　　And though it tarry in your heirs some forty,
　　Fifty descents, the longer liver at last yet   30
　　Must thrust 'em out on 't, if no quirk in law
　　Or odd vice o' their own not do it first.°
　　We see those changes daily: the fair lands

That were the client's, are the lawyer's now;
And those rich manors there of goodman tailor's   35
Had once more wood upon 'em than the yard
By which th' were measured out for the last purchase.
Nature hath these vicissitudes. She makes
No man a state of perpetuity, sir.
FITZDOTTREL You're i' the right. Let's in then, and conclude.   40
        He spies Devil, [who enters]
I' my sight again? I'll talk with you anon.
        [*Exeunt Fitzdottrel, Merecraft, and Engine*]

2.5

[PUG] Sure he will geld me if I stay, or worse,
        Pluck out my tongue—one o' the two. This fool,
        There is no trusting of him; and to quit him
        Were a contempt against my chief, past pardon.
        It was a shrewd disheartening this, at first!   5
        Who would ha' thought a woman so well harnessed,
        Or rather well caparisoned, indeed,
        That wears such petticoats and lace to her smocks,
        Broad seaming laces (as I see 'em hang there),°
        And garters which are lost, if she can show 'em,°   10
        Could ha' done this? Hell! Why is she so brave?
        It cannot be to please Duke Dottrel, sure,
        Nor the dull pictures in her gallery,
        Nor her own dear reflection in her glass.
        Yet that may be. I have known many of 'em   15
        Begin their pleasure, but none end it, there.
        (That I consider, as I go along with it.)
        They may, for want of better company,
        Or that they think the better, spend an hour,
        Two, three, or four, discoursing with their shadow;   20
        But sure they have a farther speculation.°
        No woman dressed with so much care and study
        Doth dress herself in vain. I'll vex this problem
        A little more before I leave it, sure.
            [*Exit*]

2.6

[*Enter*] *Wittipol* [*and*] *Manly,* [*at a window opposite Mistress
Fitzdottrel's gallery*]°

[WITTIPOL] This was a fortune happy above thought,
That this should prove thy chamber, which I feared
Would be my greatest trouble! This must be
The very window, and that the room.

MANLY   It is.
I now remember I have often seen there   5
A woman, but I never marked her much.

WITTIPOL Where was your soul, friend?

MANLY   Faith, but now and then
Awake unto those objects.

WITTIPOL   You pretend so.
Let me not live if I am not in love
More with her wit for this direction now   10
Than with her form, though I ha' praised that prettily
Since I saw her and you today. Read those.

> *He gives him a paper, wherein is the copy of a song*

They'll go unto the air you love so well.
Try 'em unto the note, maybe the music
Will call her sooner.

> [*Enter Mistress Fitzdottrel in her gallery*]

                  'Slight, she's here! Sing quickly.   15

MISTRESS FITZDOTTREL Either he understood him not, or else
The fellow was not faithful in delivery
Of what I bade. And I am justly paid,
That might have made my profit of his service,
But, by mistaking, have drawn on his envy°   20
And done the worse defeat upon myself.

> *Manly sings. Pug enters,* [*and*] *perceives it*

How! Music? Then he may be there—and is, sure.

PUG [*aside*] Oh, is it so? Is there the interview?
Have I drawn to you at last, my cunning lady?
The devil is an ass! Fooled off and beaten!   25
Nay, made an instrument, and could not scent it!
Well, since you've shown the malice of a woman,
No less than her true wit and learning, mistress,

I'll try if little Pug have the malignity
To recompense it and so save his danger.   30
'Tis not the pain, but the discredit of it,
The devil should not keep a body entire.°
    [Exit Pug]
WITTIPOL Away, fall back, she comes.
MANLY   I'll leave you, sir,
The master of my chamber. I have business.
    [Exit Manly]
WITTIPOL Mistress!
MISTRESS FITZDOTTREL You make me paint, sir.
WITTIPOL   They're fair colours,° 35
Lady, and natural! I did receive
Some commands from you lately, gentle lady,
But so perplexed and wrapped in the delivery,°
As I may fear t' have misinterpreted,
But must make suit still to be near your grace.   40
    This scene is acted at two windows, as out of two contiguous
    buildings
MISTRESS FITZDOTTREL Who is there with you, sir?
WITTIPOL   None but myself.
It falls out, lady, to be a dear friend's lodging.
Wherein there's some conspiracy of fortune
With your poor servant's blessed affections.
MISTRESS FITZDOTTREL Who was it sung?
WITTIPOL   He, lady, but he's gone 45
Upon my entreaty of him, seeing you
Approach the window. Neither need you doubt him
If he were here. He is too much a gentleman.
MISTRESS FITZDOTTREL Sir, if you judge me by this simple action,
And by the outward habit, and complexion°   50
Of easiness it hath to your design,
You may with justice say I am a woman;
And a strange woman. But when you shall please
To bring but that concurrence of my fortune
To memory which today yourself did urge,   55
It may beget some favour like excuse,
Though none like reason.
WITTIPOL   No, my tuneful mistress?
Then surely Love hath none; nor Beauty, any;
Nor Nature violenced in both these:°

With all whose gentle tongues you speak at once.   60
I thought I had enough removed already
That scruple from your breast and left yo' all reason,
When, through my morning's perspective, I showed you°
A man so above excuse, as he is the cause
Why anything is to be done upon him,   65
And nothing called an injury, misplaced.
I rather now had hope to show you how Love,
By his accesses, grows more natural;
And what was done this morning with such force
Was but devised to serve the present, then.   70

     He grows more familiar in his courtship, plays with her paps,
     kisseth her hands, etc.°

That since Love hath the honour to approach
These sister-swelling breasts, and touch this soft
And rosy hand, he hath the skill to draw
Their nectar forth with kissing; and could make
More wanton salts, from this brave promontory°   75
Down to this valley, than the nimble roe;°
Could play the hopping sparrow 'bout these nets,
And sporting squirrel in these crispèd groves;
Bury himself in every silkworm's kell°
Is here unravelled; run into the snare,   80
Which every hair is, cast into a curl
To catch a Cupid flying; bathe himself
In milk and roses here, and dry him there;
Warm his cold hands to play with this smooth, round,
And well-turned chin as with the billiard ball;   85
Roll on these lips, the banks of love, and there
At once both plant, and gather kisses. Lady,
Shall I, with what I have made today here, call
All sense to wonder, and all faith to sign
The mysteries revealed in your form?   90
And will Love pardon me the blasphemy
I uttered when I said a glass could speak
This beauty, or that fools had power to judge it?
    [*Sings*]
       Do but look on her eyes! They do light—
        All that Love's world compriseth!   95
       Do but look on her hair! It is bright
        As Love's star when it riseth!

> Do but mark, her forehead's smoother
> Than words that soothe her!
> And from her arched brows, such a grace   100
> Sheds itself through the face,
> As alone there triumphs to the life
> All the gain, all the good, of the elements' strife!

> Have you seen but a bright lily grow
> Before rude hands have touched it?   105
> Have you marked but the fall of the snow,
> Before the soil hath smutched it?°
> Have you felt the wool o' the beaver?
> Or swansdown, ever?
> Or have smelt o' the bud o' the briar?   110
> Or the nard i' the fire?
> Or have tasted the bag o' the bee?
> Oh, so white! Oh, so soft! Oh, so sweet is she!

2.7

[*Enter*] *Fitzdottrel* [*behind his wife*]
[FITZDOTTREL] Is she so, sir? And I will keep her so,
  If I know how, or can; that wit of man
  Will do 't, I'll go no farther. At this window
  She shall no more be buzzed at. Take your leave on 't.°
  If you be sweetmeats, wedlock, or sweet flesh,   5
  All's one; I do not love this hum about you.
  A fly-blown wife is not so proper. In.°
      He speaks out of his wife's window
  For you, sir, look to hear from me.
WITTIPOL   So I do, sir.
FITZDOTTREL No, but in other terms. There's no man offers
  This to my wife, but pays for 't.
WITTIPOL   That have I, sir.   10
FITZDOTTREL Nay then, I tell you, you are—
WITTIPOL   What am I, sir?
FITZDOTTREL Why, that I'll think on, when I ha' cut your throat.
WITTIPOL Go, you are an ass.
FITZDOTTREL   I am resolved on 't, sir.

WITTIPOL I think you are.
FITZDOTTREL   To call you to a reckoning.°
WITTIPOL Away, you broker's block, you property.°   15
        [*Wittipol strikes Fitzdottrel*]
FITZDOTTREL 'Slight, if you strike me, I'll strike your mistress.
        [*Fitzdottrel*] strikes his wife
WITTIPOL Oh! I could shoot mine eyes at him for that now;
    Or leave my teeth in him, were they cuckold's bane
    Enough to kill him. What prodigious,
    Blind, and most wicked change of fortune's this?   20
    I ha' no air of patience; all my veins
    Swell, and my sinews start at iniquity of it.
    I shall break, break.
        [*Exit Wittipol. Enter Pug on the main stage*] below
PUG   This for the malice of it,
    And my revenge may pass! But now my conscience
    Tells me I have profited the cause of Hell   25
    But little in the breaking off their loves,
    Which, if some other act of mine repair not,
    I shall hear ill of in my account.
        Fitzdottrel enters with his wife as come down°
FITZDOTTREL   Oh, bird!
    Could you do this? 'Gainst me? And at this time, now?
    When I was so employed wholly for you,   30
    Drowned i' my care (more than the land, I swear,
    I have hope to win) to make you peerless? Studying
    For footmen for you, fine-paced ushers, pages,
    To serve you o' the knee; with what knight's wife
    To bear your train, and sit with your four women   35
    In council, and receive intelligences
    From foreign parts to dress you at all pieces!°
    You've almost turned my good affection to you;
    Soured my sweet thoughts, all my pure purposes.
    I could now find i' my very heart to make   40
    Another lady Duchess, and depose you.
    Well, go your ways in.
        [*Exit Mistress Fitzdottrel*]
                    Devil, you have redeemed all.
    I do forgive you. And I'll do you good.
        [*Exit Pug*]

2.8

[Enter] Merecraft [and] Engine
[MERECRAFT] Why ha' you these excursions? Where ha' you been, sir?
FITZDOTTREL Where I ha' been vexed a little with a toy.
MERECRAFT O sir! No toys must trouble your grave head,
    Now it is growing to be great. You must
    Be above all those things.
FITZDOTTREL   Nay, nay, so I will.   5
MERECRAFT Now you are to'ard the lord, you must put off
    The man, sir.
ENGINE   He says true.
MERECRAFT   You must do nothing
    As you ha' done it heretofore; not know,
    Or salute any man.
ENGINE   That was your bedfellow°
    The other month.
MERECRAFT   The other month? The week.   10
    Thou dost not know the privileges, Engine,
    Follow that title, nor how swift. Today,
    When he has put on his lord's face once, then—
FITZDOTTREL Sir, for these things I shall do well enough,
    There is no fear of me. But then my wife is   15
    Such an untoward thing! She'll never learn
    How to comport with it. I am out of all
    Conceit on her behalf.
MERECRAFT   Best have her taught, sir.°
FITZDOTTREL Where? Are there any schools for ladies? Is there
    An academy for women? I do know   20
    For men there was; I learned in it myself
    To make my legs, and do my postures.
        Engine whispers [to] Merecraft
ENGINE   Sir.°
    Do you remember the conceit you had
    O' the Spanish gown, at home?
MERECRAFT   Ha! I do thank thee
    With all my heart, dear Engine.
        Merecraft turns to Fitzdottrel
                Sir, there is   25

A certain lady here about the town,
An English widow, who hath lately travelled,
But she's called the Spaniard, 'cause she came
Latest from thence, and keeps the Spanish habit.
Such a rare woman! All our women here   30
That are of spirit and fashion flock unto her
As to their president, their law, their canon,°
More than they ever did to oracle Forman.
Such rare receipts she has, sir, for the face;
Such oils, such tinctures, such pomatums,   35
Such perfumes, med'cines, quintessences, etc.°
And such a mistress of behaviour—
She knows, from the duke's daughter to the doxy,
What is their due just, and no more!

FITZDOTTREL   O sir!
You please me i' this more than mine own greatness.   40
Where is she? Let us have her.

MERECRAFT   By your patience,
We must use means; cast how to be acquainted—

FITZDOTTREL Good sir, about it.

MERECRAFT   We must think how, first.

FITZDOTTREL   Oh!
I do not love to tarry for a thing
When I have a mind to 't. You do not know me,   45
If you do offer it.

MERECRAFT   Your wife must send
Some pretty token to her, with a compliment,
And pray to be received in her good graces;
All the great ladies do 't.

FITZDOTTREL   She shall, she shall.
What were it best to be?

MERECRAFT   Some little toy,   50
I would not have it any great matter, sir.
A diamond ring of forty or fifty pound
Would do it handsomely, and be a gift
Fit for your wife to send, and her to take.

FITZDOTTREL I'll go and tell my wife on 't straight.
        [Exit] Fitzdottrel

MERECRAFT   Why, this   55
Is well! The clothes we have now—but where's this lady?
If we could get a witty boy now, Engine,

267

That were an excellent crack. I could instruct him°
To the true height. For anything takes this dottrel.
ENGINE Why, sir, your best will be one o' the players.   60
MERECRAFT No, there's no trusting them. They'll talk on 't,
And tell their poets.
ENGINE   What if they do? The jest
Will brook the stage. But there be some of 'em
Are very honest lads. There's Dick Robinson,°
A very pretty fellow, and comes often   65
To a gentleman's chamber, a friend's of mine. We had°
The merriest supper of it there one night—
The gentleman's landlady invited him
To a gossip's feast. Now he, sir, brought Dick Robinson°
Dressed like a lawyer's wife amongst 'em all   70
(I lent him clothes), but to see him behave it,
And lay the law, and carve, and drink unto 'em,°
And then talk bawdy, and send frolics! Oh!°
It would have burst your buttons, or not left you
A seam.
MERECRAFT They say he's an ingenious youth.   75
ENGINE O sir! And dresses himself the best! Beyond
Forty o' your very ladies. Did you ne'er see him?
MERECRAFT No, I do seldom see those toys. But think you
That we may have him?
ENGINE   Sir, the young gentleman
I tell you of, can command him. Shall I attempt it?   80
MERECRAFT Yes, do it.
          [*Enter Fitzdottrel*]
FITZDOTTREL   'Slight, I cannot get my wife
To part with a ring on any terms, and yet
The sullen monkey has two.
MERECRAFT   It were 'gainst reason
That you should urge it. Sir, send to a goldsmith,
Let not her lose by 't.
FITZDOTTREL   How does she lose by 't?   85
Is 't not for her?
MERECRAFT   Make it your own bounty,
It will ha' the better success; what is a matter
Of fifty pound to you, sir?
FITZDOTTREL   I have but a hundred
Pieces to show here, that I would not break—

MERECRAFT You shall ha' credit, sir. I'll send a ticket   90
    Unto my goldsmith. Here my man comes, too,
    To carry it fitly.
        [*Enter*] *Trains*
                        How now, Trains? What birds?°
TRAINS Your Cousin Everill met me, and has beat me
    Because I would not tell him where you were;
    I think he has dogged me to the house, too.
FITZDOTTREL   Well—   95
    You shall go out at the backdoor then, Trains.
    You must get Gilthead hither by some means.
TRAINS 'Tis impossible!
FITZDOTTREL   Tell him we have venison;
    I'll gi' him a piece, and send his wife a pheasant.
        [*Exit Fitzdottrel*]
TRAINS A forest moves not till that forty pound°   100
    Yo' had of him last be paid. He keeps more stir
    For that same petty sum than for your bond
    Of six, and statute of eight hundred!
MERECRAFT   Tell him°
    We'll hedge in that. Cry up Fitzdottrel to him,°
    Double his price. Make him a man of metal.°   105
TRAINS That will not need, his bond is current enough.
        [*Exeunt*]

3.1

[Enter] Gilthead *[and]* Plutarchus

[GILTHEAD] All this is to make you a gentleman,
    I'll have you learn, son. Wherefore have I placed you
    With Sir Paul Eitherside, but to have so much law
    To keep your own? Besides, he is a justice
    Here i' the town; and dwelling, son, with him,   5
    You shall learn that in a year, shall be worth twenty
    Of having stayed you at Oxford or at Cambridge,
    Or sending you to the Inns of Court or France.
    I am called for now in haste by Master Merecraft
    To trust Master Fitzdottrel, a good man —   10
    I have enquired him, eighteen hundred a year,
    His name is current—for a diamond ring
    Of forty, shall not be worth thirty (that's gained).
    And this is to make you a gentleman!
PLUTARCHUS Oh, but good father, you trust too much!
GILTHEAD   Boy, boy,   15
    We live by finding fools out to be trusted.
    Our shop-books are our pastures, our corn-grounds,
    We lay 'em op'n for them to come into;
    And when we have 'em there, we drive 'em up
    Int' one of our two pounds, the Counters, straight,°   20
    And this is to make you a gentleman!
    We citizens never trust, but we do cozen:
    For if our debtors pay, we cozen them;
    And if they do not, then we cozen ourselves.
    But that's a hazard everyone must run   25
    That hopes to make his son a gentleman!
PLUTARCHUS I do not wish to be one, truly, father.
    In a descent or two, we come to be°
    Just i' their state, fit to be cozened like 'em.
    And I had rather ha' tarried i' your trade—   30
    For since the gentry scorn the city so much,
    Methinks we should in time, holding together,
    And matching in our own tribes, as they say,
    Have got an Act of Common Council for it,

That we might cozen them out of *rerum natura*.°   35
GILTHEAD Ay, if we had an Act first to forbid
   The marrying of our wealthy heirs unto 'em,
   And daughters, with such lavish portions.
   That confounds all.
PLUTARCHUS   And makes a mongrel breed, father.°
   And when they have your money, then they laugh at you,   40
   Or kick you down the stairs. I cannot abide 'em.
   I would fain have 'em cozened, but not trusted.

3.2

[Enter] Merecraft [and] Fitzdottrel
[MERECRAFT] Oh, is he come! I knew he would not fail me.
   Welcome, good Gilthead, I must ha' you do
   A noble gentleman a courtesy here
   In a mere toy (some pretty ring or jewel)
   Of fifty or threescore pound. *[Aside to Gilthead]* Make it a hundred,   5
   And hedge in the last forty that I owe you,
   And your own price for the ring. *[Aloud]* He's a good man, sir,
   And you may hap see him a great one! He°
   Is likely to bestow hundreds and thousands
   Wi' you, if you can humour him. A great prince   10
   He will be shortly. What do you say?
GILTHEAD   In truth, sir,
   I cannot. 'T has been a long vacation with us—
FITZDOTTREL Of what, I pray thee? of wit? or honesty?
   Those are your citizens' long vacations.
PLUTARCHUS Good father, do not trust 'em.
MERECRAFT   Nay, Tom Gilthead,   15
   He will not buy a courtesy and beg it:
   He'll rather pay than pray. If you do for him,
   You must do cheerfully. His credit, sir,
   Is not yet prostitute! Who's this? Thy son?
   A pretty youth, what's his name?
PLUTARCHUS   Plutarchus, sir.   20
MERECRAFT Plutarchus! How came that about?
GILTHEAD   That year, sir,
   That I begot him, I bought Plutarch's *Lives*,°

And fell s' in love with the book, as I called my son
By his name, in hope he should be like him,
And write the lives of our great men.

MERECRAFT   I' the city?   25
And you do breed him there?

GILTHEAD   His mind, sir, lies
Much to that way.

MERECRAFT   Why then, he is i' the right way.

GILTHEAD But now I had rather get him a good wife,
And plant him i' the country, there to use
The blessing I shall leave him—

MERECRAFT   Out upon 't!   30
And lose the laudable means thou hast at home here,
T' advance and make him a young alderman?
Buy him a captain's place, for shame; and let him
Into the world early, and with his plume
And scarves march through Cheapside, or along Cornhill,°   35
And by the virtue of those draw down a wife
There from a window, worth ten thousand pound!
Get him the posture book and's leaden men°
To set upon a table, 'gainst his mistress
Chance to come by, that he may draw her in,   40
And show her Finsbury battles.

GILTHEAD   I have placed him°
With Justice Eitherside, to get so much law—

MERECRAFT As thou hast conscience. Come, come, thou dost wrong
Pretty Plutarchus, who had not his name
For nothing, but was born to train the youth   45
Of London in the military truth—
That way his genius lies. My cousin Everill!

3.3

[*Enter*] *Everill*

[EVERILL] Oh, are you here, sir? Pray you let us whisper.
        [*Takes Merecraft aside*]

PLUTARCHUS Father, dear father, trust him if you love me.

GILTHEAD Why, I do mean it, boy; but what I do
Must not come easily from me. We must deal

With courtiers, boy, as courtiers deal with us.   5
If I have a business there with any of them,
Why, I must wait, I am sure on 't, son; and though
My lord dispatch me, yet his worshipful man
Will keep me for his sport a month or two,
To show me with my fellow citizens.   10
I must make his train long and full, one quarter,°
And help the spectacle of his greatness. There
Nothing is done at once but injuries, boy—
And they come headlong! All their good turns move not,
Or very slowly.
PLUTARCHUS   Yet, sweet father, trust him.   15
GILTHEAD Well, I will think.
          [*Gilthead and Plutarchus walk aside*]
EVERILL   Come, you must do 't, sir.
I am undone else, and your Lady Tailbush
Has sent for me to dinner, and my clothes
Are all at pawn. I had sent out this morning,
Before I heard you were come to town, some twenty   20
Of my epistles, and no one return—°
MERECRAFT Why, I ha' told you o' this. This comes of wearing
Scarlet, gold lace, and cut-works! Your fine gartering,
With your blown roses, cousin! And your eating
Pheasant and godwit here in London! Haunting   25
The Globes and Mermaids, wedging in with lords°
Still at the table, and affecting lechery
In velvet! Where, could you ha' contented yourself
With cheese, salt-butter, and a pickled herring
I' the Low Countries, there worn cloth and fustian,°   30
Been satisfied with a leap o' your host's daughter
In garrison, a wench of a stooter, or°
Your sutler's wife i' the leaguer of two blanks,°
You never then had run upon this flat,
To write your letters missive and send out   35
Your privy seals, that thus have frighted off°
All your acquaintance, that they shun you at a distance
Worse than you do the bailies!
EVERILL   Pox upon you.°
I come not to you for counsel, I lack money.
MERECRAFT You do not think what you owe me already?
EVERILL   I?   40

273

They owe you, that mean to pay you. I'll be sworn,
I never meant it. Come, you will project.
I shall undo your practice for this month else—
You know me.
MERECRAFT   Ay, you're a right sweet nature.
EVERILL Well, that's all one.
MERECRAFT   You'll leave this empire one day?°   45
You will not ever have this tribute paid,
Your sceptre o' the sword?
EVERILL   Tie up your wit,
Do, and provoke me not—
MERECRAFT   Will you, sir, help
To what I shall provoke another for you?
EVERILL I cannot tell—try me. I think I am not   50
So utterly of an ore un-to-be-melted,
But I can do myself good on occasions.
MERECRAFT Strike in then, for your part. Master Fitzdottrel,°
If I transgress in point of manners, afford me
Your best construction; I must beg my freedom   55
From your affairs this day.
          Merecraft pretends business°
FITZDOTTREL   How, sir!
MERECRAFT   It is
In succour of this gentleman's occasions,
My kinsman—
FITZDOTTREL   You'll not do me that affront, sir.
MERECRAFT I am sorry you should so interpret it,
But, sir, it stands upon his being invested   60
In a new office he has stood for long:
Master of the Dependences! A place°
Of my projection, too, sir, and hath met
Much opposition; but the state now sees
That great necessity of it, as after all   65
Their writing and their speaking against duels,
They have erected it. His book is drawn—°
For since there will be differences daily
'Twixt gentlemen, and that the roaring manner
Is grown offensive, that those few we call   70
The civil men o' the sword abhor the vapours,°
They shall refer now hither for their process,
And such as trespass 'gainst the rule of court

Are to be fined—
FITZDOTTREL   In troth, a pretty place!
MERECRAFT A kind of arbitrary court 'twill be, sir.°   75
FITZDOTTREL I shall have matter for it, I believe,
    Ere it be long; I had a distaste.
MERECRAFT   But now, sir,°
    My learned counsel, they must have a feeling;
    They'll part, sir, with no books without the hand-gout
    Be oiled, and I must furnish. If 't be money,   80
    To me straight. I am mine, mint, and exchequer,
    To supply all. What is 't? A hundred pound?
EVERILL No, th' harpy now stands on a hundred pieces.°
MERECRAFT Why, he must have 'em, if he will. Tomorrow, sir,
    Will equally serve your occasions,   85
    And therefore let me obtain that you will yield
    To timing a poor gentleman's distresses,
    In terms of hazard—
FITZDOTTREL   By no means!
MERECRAFT   I must
    Get him this money, and will—
FITZDOTTREL   Sir, I protest
    I'd rather stand engaged for it myself,   90
    Than you should leave me.
MERECRAFT   O good sir, do you think
    So coarsely of our manners, that we would,
    For any need of ours, be pressed to take it,
    Though you be pleased to offer it?
FITZDOTTREL   Why, by heaven,
    I mean it!
MERECRAFT I can never believe less.   95
    But we, sir, must preserve our dignity,
    As you do publish yours. By your fair leave, sir.
            He offers to be gone
FITZDOTTREL As I am a gentleman, if you do offer
    To leave me now, or if you do refuse me,
    I will not think you love me.
MERECRAFT   Sir, I honour you.   100
    And with just reason, for these noble notes
    Of the nobility you pretend to! But sir—°
    I would know why? A motive (he a stranger)
    You should do this?

EVERILL [*aside to Merecraft*] You'll mar all with your fineness.

FITZDOTTREL Why, that's all one if 'twere, sir, but my fancy.   105
　　But I have a business that perhaps I'd have
　　Brought to his office.

MERECRAFT　　　　　O sir! I have done then,
　　If he can be made profitable to you.

FITZDOTTREL Yes, and it shall be one of my ambitions
　　To have it the first business. May I not?   110

EVERILL So you do mean to make 't a perfect business.

FITZDOTTREL Nay, I'll do that, assure you; show me once.

MERECRAFT Sir, it concerns the first be a perfect business°
　　For his own honour.

EVERILL　　　　　Ay, and th' reputation,
　　Too, of my place.

FITZDOTTREL　　　Why, why do I take this course else?   115
　　I am not altogether an ass, good gentlemen.
　　Wherefore should I consult you, do you think?
　　To make a song on 't? How's your manner? Tell us.

MERECRAFT Do, satisfy him; give him the whole course.

EVERILL First, by request, or otherwise, you offer   120
　　Your business to the court, wherein you crave
　　The judgement of the master and the assistants.

FITZDOTTREL Well, that's done, now what do you upon it?

EVERILL We straight, sir, have recourse to the spring-head;
　　Visit the ground, and so disclose the nature,°   125
　　If it will carry, or no. If we do find
　　By our proportions it is like to prove°
　　A sullen and black business, that it be
　　Incorrigible, and out of treaty, then
　　We file it a dependence.

FITZDOTTREL　　　　So, 'tis filed.   130
　　What follows? I do love the order of these things.

EVERILL We then advise the party, if he be
　　A man of means and havings, that forthwith
　　He settle his estate; if not, at least
　　That he pretend it. For by that the world   135
　　Takes notice that it now is a dependence.
　　And this we call, sir, publication.

FITZDOTTREL Very sufficient! After publication, now?

EVERILL Then we grant out our process, which is divers;
　　Either by cartel, sir, or *ore-tenus*,   140

Wherein the challenger and challengee,
Or (with your Spaniard) your *provocador*
And *provocado*, have their several courses—

FITZDOTTREL I have enough on 't! For an hundred pieces?
Yes, for two hundred underwrite me, do.   145
Your man will take my bond?

MERECRAFT   That he will, sure,
But these same citizens, they are such sharks!

He whispers [to] Fitzdottrel aside
There's an old debt of forty, I ga' my word
For one is run away to the Bermudas,°
And he will hook in that, or he wi' not do.   150

FITZDOTTREL Why, let him. That and the ring, and a hundred pieces,
Will all but make two hundred?

MERECRAFT   No, no more, sir.
What ready arithmetic you have!

And then [he whispers to] Gilthead
                               Do you hear?
A pretty morning's work for you, this. Do it,
You shall ha' twenty pound on 't.

GILTHEAD   Twenty pieces?   155

PLUTARCHUS [*aside*] Good father, do 't.

MERECRAFT   You will hook still? Well,
Show us your ring. You could not ha' done this now
With gentleness, at first, we might ha' thanked you?
But groan, and ha' your courtesies come from you
Like a hard stool, and stink? A man may draw   160
Your teeth out easier than your money! Come,
Were little Gilthead here no better a nature
I should ne'er love him, that could pull his lips off, now!

He pulls Plutarchus by the lips
Was not thy mother a gentlewoman?

PLUTARCHUS   Yes, sir.

MERECRAFT And went to the Court at Christmas and St George's
tide,°   165
And lent the lords' men chains?

PLUTARCHUS   Of gold and pearl, sir.

MERECRAFT I knew thou must take after somebody!
Thou couldst not be else. This was no shop-look.
I'll ha' thee Captain Gilthead, and march up,
And take in Pimlico, and kill the bush   170

At every tavern! Thou shalt have a wife,°
If smocks will mount, boy.
　　　　He turns to old Gilthead, [who offers him a jewel]
　　　　　　　　　How now? You ha' there now
Some Bristol-stone, or Cornish counterfeit°
You'd put upon us.

GILTHEAD　　　　　No, sir, I assure you—
Look on his lustre! He will speak himself!　　　　　　　　175
I'll gi' you leave to put him i' the mill.°
He's no great, large stone, but a true paragon,°
H' has all his corners, view him well.

MERECRAFT　　　　　　　　　He's yellow.

GILTHEAD Upo' my faith, sir, o' the right black water,°
And very deep! He's set without a foil, too.　　　　　　180
Here's one o' the yellow water I'll sell cheap.

MERECRAFT And what do you value this at? Thirty pound?

GILTHEAD No, sir, he cost me forty ere he was set.

MERECRAFT Turnings, you mean? I know your equivokes;°
You are grown the better fathers of 'em o' late.　　　　185
Well, where 't must go, 'twill be judged, and therefore
Look you 't be right. You shall have fifty pound for 't.
Not a denier more! (*To Fitzdottrel*) And because you would
Have things dispatched, sir, I'll go presently
Enquire out this lady. If you think good, sir,　　　　　190
Having an hundred pieces ready, you may
Part with those now to serve my kinsman's turns,
That he may wait upon you anon the freer,
And take 'em when you ha' sealed again of Gilthead.

FITZDOTTREL I care not if I do!

MERECRAFT　　　　　　　　And dispatch all　　　　　195
Together.

FITZDOTTREL There, they're just: a hundred pieces!°
I' ha' told 'em over twice a day these two months.

MERECRAFT Well, go and seal then, sir, make your return
As speedy as you can.
　　　　He turns [Fitzdottrel, Gilthead, and Plutarchus] out together.
　　　　And Everill and he fall to share.

EVERILL　　　　　　Come, gi' me.

MERECRAFT　　　　　　　　　Soft, sir.

EVERILL Marry, and fair, too, then. I'll no delaying, sir.　　　200

MERECRAFT But you will hear?

EVERILL   Yes, when I have my dividend.

MERECRAFT There's forty pieces for you.

EVERILL   What is this for?

MERECRAFT Your half. You know that Gilthead must ha' twenty.

EVERILL And what's your ring there? Shall I ha' none o' that?

MERECRAFT Oh, that's to be given to a lady!   205

EVERILL Is 't so?

MERECRAFT   By that good light, it is.

EVERILL   Come, gi' me
   Ten pieces more then.

MERECRAFT   Why?

EVERILL   For Gilthead. Sir,
   Do you think I'll 'low him any such share?

MERECRAFT   You must.

EVERILL Must I? Do you your musts, sir, I'll do mine.
   You wi' not part with the whole, sir, will you? Go to—   210
   Gi' me ten pieces!

MERECRAFT   By what law do you this?

EVERILL E'en lion-law, sir; I must roar else.

MERECRAFT   Good!

EVERILL You've heard how th' ass made his divisions wisely?°

MERECRAFT And I am he. I thank you.

EVERILL   Much good do you, sir.

MERECRAFT I shall be rid o' this tyranny one day?

EVERILL   Not   215
   While you do eat and lie about the town here,
   And cozen i' your bullions, and I stand°
   Your name of credit, and compound your business,
   Adjourn your beatings every term, and make
   New parties for your projects. I have now   220
   A pretty task of it, to hold you in
   Wi' your Lady Tailbush; but the toy will be
   How we shall both come off?

MERECRAFT   Leave you your doubting.
   And do your portion, what's assigned you. I
   Never failed yet.

EVERILL   With reference to your aids?   225
   You'll still be unthankful. Where shall I meet you, anon?
   You ha' some feat to do alone now, I see;
   You wish me gone. Well, I will find you out,
   And bring you after to the audit.

[*Exit Everill*]

MERECRAFT   'Slight!
There's Engine's share, too, I had forgot! This reign   230
Is too-too-unsupportable! I must
Quit myself of this vassalage! Engine! Welcome.

3.4

[*Enter*] *Engine* [*followed by*] *Wittipol*

[MERECRAFT] How goes the cry?
ENGINE   Excellent well!
MERECRAFT   Will 't do?
Where's Robinson?
ENGINE   Here is the gentleman, sir,
Will undertake 't himself. I have acquainted him.
MERECRAFT Why did you so?
ENGINE   Why, Robinson would ha' told him,
You know. And he's a pleasant wit! Will hurt   5
Nothing you purpose. Then, he is of opinion
That Robinson might want audacity,
She being such a gallant. Now he has been
In Spain and knows the fashions there, and can
Discourse; and being but mirth, he says, leave much   10
To his care.
MERECRAFT   But he is too tall!
ENGINE   For that°
He has the bravest device—you'll love him for 't—
To say he wears cioppinos, and they do so
In Spain! And Robinson's as tall as he.
MERECRAFT Is he so?
ENGINE   Every jot.
MERECRAFT   Nay, I had rather°   15
To trust a gentleman with it, o' the two.
ENGINE Pray you go to him then, sir, and salute him.
MERECRAFT Sir, my friend, Engine, has acquainted you
With a strange business here.
WITTIPOL   A merry one, sir.
The Duke of Drowned-land, and his Duchess?
MERECRAFT   Yes, sir.   20

Now that the conjurers ha' laid him by,
I ha' made bold to borrow him a while.
WITTIPOL With purpose yet to put him out, I hope,
To his best use?
MERECRAFT   Yes, sir.
WITTIPOL   For that small part
That I am trusted with, put off your care;   25
I would not lose to do it for the mirth
Will follow of it—and, well, I have a fancy.
MERECRAFT Sir, that will make it well.
WITTIPOL   You will report it so.
Where must I have my dressing?
ENGINE   At my house, sir.
MERECRAFT You shall have caution, sir, for what he yields,   30
To sixpence.
WITTIPOL   You shall pardon me. I will share, sir,°
I' your sports only; nothing i' your purchase.°
But you must furnish me with complements
To th' manner of Spain: my coach, my guarda-duennas—°
MERECRAFT Engine's your *provedore*. But, sir, I must,°   35
Now I have entered trust wi' you thus far,
Secure still i' your quality, acquaint you°
With somewhat beyond this. The place designed
To be the scene for this our merry matter,
Because it must have countenance of women°   40
To draw discourse and offer it, is hereby,
At the Lady Tailbush's.
WITTIPOL   I know her, sir,
And her gentleman usher.
MERECRAFT   Master Ambler?
WITTIPOL   Yes, sir.
MERECRAFT Sir, it shall be no shame to me to confess
To you that we poor gentlemen that want acres,   45
Must for our needs turn fools up, and plough ladies
Sometimes, to try what glebe they are; and this
Is no unfruitful piece. She and I now
Are on a project for the fact and venting°
Of a new kind of fucus (paint, for ladies)   50
To serve the kingdom; wherein she herself
Hath travailed specially, by way of service
Unto her sex, and hopes to get the monopoly

As the reward of her invention.
WITTIPOL What is her end in this?
MERECRAFT   Merely ambition,   55
Sir, to grow great and court it with the secret,
Though she pretend some other. For she's dealing
Already upon caution for the shares,°
And Master Ambler, is he named examiner
For the ingredients, and the register   60
Of what is vented, and shall keep the office.
Now if she break with you of this (as I°
Must make the leading thread to your acquaintance,
That how experience gotten i' your being
Abroad will help our business) think of some   65
Pretty additions but to keep her floating;
It may be she will offer you a part.
Any strange names of —
WITTIPOL   Sir, I have my instructions.
Is it not high time to be making ready?
MERECRAFT Yes, sir.
ENGINE   The fool's in sight, Dottrel.
MERECRAFT   Away, then.   70
        [*Exeunt Wittipol and Engine*]

3.5

        [*Enter*] *Fitzdottrel*
[MERECRAFT] Returned so soon?
FITZDOTTREL   Yes, here's the ring; I ha' sealed.
But there's not so much gold in all the Row, he says,°
Till 't come fro' the Mint. 'Tis ta'en up for the gamesters.
MERECRAFT There's a shop-shift! Plague on 'em.
FITZDOTTREL   He does swear it.
MERECRAFT He'll swear, and forswear, too, it is his trade;   5
You should not have left him.
FITZDOTTREL   'Slid, I can go back
And beat him yet.
MERECRAFT   No, now let him alone.
FITZDOTTREL I was so earnest after the main business,
To have this ring gone.

MERECRAFT   True, and 'tis time.
    I have learned, sir, sin' you went, her ladyship eats°   10
    With the Lady Tailbush here, hard by.
FITZDOTTREL   I' the lane here?
MERECRAFT Yes—if you had a servant now of presence,
    Well clothed, and of an airy voluble tongue,
    Neither too big or little for his mouth,°
    That could deliver your wife's compliment,   15
    To send along withal.
FITZDOTTREL   I have one, sir,
    A very handsome, gentleman-like fellow
    That I do mean to make my duchess' usher—
    I entertained him but this morning, too.
    I'll call him to you. The worst of him is his name.   20
MERECRAFT She'll take no note of that, but of his message.
FITZDOTTREL Devil!
        [Enter] Pug. [Fitzdottrel] shows [Merecraft] his Pug
                    How like you him, sir? Pace, go a little.
    Let's see you move.
MERECRAFT   He'll serve, sir, give it him;
    And let him go along with me, I'll help
    To present him, and it.
FITZDOTTREL   Look you do, sirrah,   25
    Discharge this well, as you expect your place.
    Do you hear? Go on, come off with all your honours.°
    I would fain see him do it.
MERECRAFT   Trust him with it.°
FITZDOTTREL Remember kissing of your hand, and answering
    With the French-time, in flexure of your body.°   30
    I could now so instruct him—and for his words—
MERECRAFT I'll put them in his mouth.
FITZDOTTREL   Oh, but I have 'em
    O' the very academies.
MERECRAFT   Sir, you'll have use for 'em
    Anon yourself, I warrant you, after dinner
    When you are called.
FITZDOTTREL   'Slight, that'll be just play-time.°   35
    It cannot be, I must not lose the play!
MERECRAFT Sir, but you must, if she appoint to sit.
    And she's president.
FITZDOTTREL   'Slid, it is *The Devil*!

MERECRAFT And 'twere his dam, too, you must now apply
    Yourself, sir, to this wholly—or lose all.   40
FITZDOTTREL If I could but see a piece—
MERECRAFT   Sir, never think on 't.
FITZDOTTREL Come but to one act, and I did not care;
    But to be seen to rise, and go away,
    To vex the players and to punish their poet—
    Keep him in awe!
MERECRAFT   But say that he be one   45
    Wi' not be awed, but laugh at you. How then?
FITZDOTTREL Then he shall pay for his dinner himself.
MERECRAFT   Perhaps
    He would do that twice, rather than thank you.
    Come, get *The Devil* out of your head, my lord
    (I'll call you so in private still), and take   50
    Your lordship i' your mind. You were, sweet lord,
    In talk to bring a business to the office.
FITZDOTTREL   Yes.°
MERECRAFT Why should not you, sir, carry it o' yourself,
    Before the office be up? And show the world
    You had no need of any man's direction;   55
    In point, sir, of sufficiency. I speak
    Against a kinsman, but as one that tenders
    Your grace's good.
FITZDOTTREL   I thank you; to proceed—°
MERECRAFT To publications; ha' your deed drawn presently.
    And leave a blank to put in your feoffees,   60
    One, two, or more, as you see cause—
FITZDOTTREL   I thank you
    Heartily, I do thank you. Not a word more,
    I pray you, as you love me. Let me alone.
        He is angry with himself
    That I could not think o' this as well as he?
    Oh, I could beat my infinite blockhead—   65
        [*Exit Fitzdottrel*]
MERECRAFT Come, we must this way.
PUG   How far is 't?
MERECRAFT   Hard by here
    Over the way. [*Aside*] Now, to achieve this ring
    From this same fellow that is to assure it,°
    Before he give it.

284

He thinks how to cozen the bearer of the ring
    Though my Spanish lady
Be a young gentleman of means, and scorn 70
To share, as he doth say, I do not know
How such a toy may tempt his ladyship;
And therefore I think best it be assured.
PUG Sir, be the ladies brave we go unto?
MERECRAFT Oh, yes.
PUG   And shall I see 'em, and speak to 'em? 75
MERECRAFT What else?
 [*Enter Trains. Merecraft*] *questions his man* [*aside*].
    Ha' you your false beard about you, Trains?
TRAINS Yes.
MERECRAFT And is this one of your double cloaks?°
TRAINS The best of 'em.
MERECRAFT   Be ready then.
 [*Exit Trains*]
     Sweet Pitfall!

3.6

 [*Enter*] *Pitfall*
[MERECRAFT] Come, I must buss—
 Offers to kiss [*Pitfall*]
PITFALL   Away.
MERECRAFT   I'll set thee up again,
 Never fear that; canst thou get ne'er a bird?
 No thrushes hungry? Stay till cold weather come,
 I'll help thee to an ouzel, or a fieldfare.°
 Who's within with madam?
PITFALL   I'll tell you straight. 5
 [*Exit Pitfall, who*] *runs in, in haste*
MERECRAFT Please you stay here a while, sir, I'll go in.
 [*Exit Merecraft*]
PUG I do so long to have a little venery
 While I am in this body! I would taste
 Of every sin a little, if it might be
 After the manner of man!
 [*Enter Pitfall.*] *Pug leaps at Pitfall's coming in.*

Sweetheart!

PITFALL   What would you, sir?   10

PUG   Nothing but fall into you; be your blackbird,
    My pretty pit (as the gentleman said, your throstle);
    Lie tame and taken with you—here is gold
    To buy you so much new stuffs from the shop,
    As I may take the old up—
        [*Enter*] *Trains in his false cloak,* [*who*] *brings a false message,*
        and gets the ring

TRAINS   You must send, sir,   15
    The gentleman the ring.

PUG   There 'tis.
        [*Exit Trains*]

                              Nay look,
    Will you be foolish, Pit?

PITFALL   This is strange rudeness.

PUG   Dear Pit.

PITFALL   I'll call, I swear.
        [*Exit Pitfall. Enter*] *Merecraft presently, and asks for* [*the ring*]

MERECRAFT   Where are you, sir?
    Is your ring ready? Go with me.

PUG   I sent it you.

MERECRAFT   Me? When? By whom?

PUG   A fellow here, e'en now,   20
    Came for it i' your name.

MERECRAFT   I sent none, sure.
    My meaning ever was you should deliver it
    Yourself. So was your master's charge, you know.
    What fellow was it, do you know him?

PUG   Here,
    But now, he had it.
        Ent[*er*] *Trains as himself again*

MERECRAFT   Saw you any, Trains?   25

TRAINS   Not I.

PUG   The gentlewoman saw him.

MERECRAFT   Enquire.
        [*Exit Trains*]

PUG   I was so earnest upon her, I marked not!°
    My devilish chief has put me here in flesh
    To shame me! This dull body I am in,
    I perceive nothing with! I offer at nothing   30

That will succeed!
  [*Enter Trains*]
TRAINS   Sir, she saw none, she says.
PUG Satan himself has ta'en a shape t' abuse me.
  It could not be else!
MERECRAFT   This is above strange,
  That you should be so reckless. What'll you do, sir?°
  How will you answer this when you are questioned?°   35
PUG Run from my flesh, if I could: put off mankind!
  This's such a scorn! And will be a new exercise
  For my archduke! Woe to the several cudgels
  Must suffer on this back! Can you no succours? Sir?
MERECRAFT Alas! The use of it is so present.
PUG   I ask,°   40
  Sir, credit for another but till tomorrow?
MERECRAFT There is not so much time, sir. But, however,
  The lady is a noble lady and will
  (To save a gentleman from check) be entreated
  To say she has received it.
PUG   Do you think so?   45
  Will she be won?
MERECRAFT   No doubt, to such an office,
  It will be a lady's bravery and her pride.°
PUG And not be known on 't after unto him?
MERECRAFT That were a treachery! Upon my word,
  Be confident. Return unto your master: 50
  My lady president sits this afternoon,
  Has ta'en the ring, commends her services
  Unto your lady duchess. You may say
  She's a civil lady, and does give her
  All her respects already; bade you tell her   55
  She lives but to receive her wished commandments,
  And have the honour here to kiss her hands,
  For which she'll stay this hour yet. Hasten you
  Your prince, away.
PUG   And sir, you will take care
  Th' excuse be perfect?
MERECRAFT   You confess your fears°   60
  Too much.
PUG   The shame is more, I'll quit you of either.
    [*Exeunt*]

4.1

[Enter] Tailbush [and] Merecraft

[TAILBUSH] A pox upo' referring to commissioners,
    I had rather hear that it were past the seals;
    Your courtiers move so snail-like i' your business.
    Would I had not begun wi' you.
MERECRAFT   We must move,
    Madam, in order, by degrees: not jump.   5
TAILBUSH Why, there was Sir John Moneyman could jump
    A business quickly.
MERECRAFT   True, he had great friends.
    But because some, sweet madam, can leap ditches,
    We must not all shun to go over bridges.
    The harder parts, I make account, are done,   10
    Now 'tis referred.
              He flatters her
              You are infinitely bound
    Unto the ladies, they ha' so cried it up!
TAILBUSH Do they like it then?
MERECRAFT   They ha' sent the Spanish lady,
    To gratulate with you—
TAILBUSH   I must send 'em thanks,
    And some remembrances.
MERECRAFT   That you must, and visit 'em.   15
    Where's Ambler?
TAILBUSH   Lost, today we cannot hear of him.
MERECRAFT Not, madam?
TAILBUSH   No, in good faith. They say he lay not
    At home tonight. And here has fall'n a business
    Between your cousin and Master Manly has
    Unquieted us all.
MERECRAFT   So I hear, madam.   20
    Pray you, how was it?
TAILBUSH   Troth, it but appears
    Ill o' your kinsman's part. You may have heard
    That Manly is a suitor to me, I doubt not—
MERECRAFT I guessed it, madam.

TAILBUSH   And it seems he trusted
  Your cousin to let fall some fair reports   25
  Of him unto me.
MERECRAFT   Which he did.
TAILBUSH   So far
  From it, as he came in and took him railing
  Against him.
MERECRAFT   How! And what said Manly to him?
TAILBUSH Enough, I do assure you—and with that scorn
  Of him and the injury, as I do wonder   30
  How Everill bore it! But that guilt undoes
  Many men's valours.
MERECRAFT   Here comes Manly.
    [*Enter Manly*]
MANLY   Madam,
  I'll take my leave—
    Manly offers to be gone
TAILBUSH   You sha' not go, i' faith.
  I'll ha' you stay and see this Spanish miracle
  Of our English lady.
MANLY   Let me pray your ladyship,   35
  Lay your commands on me some other time.
TAILBUSH Now, I protest; and I will have all pieced°
  And friends again.
MANLY   It will be but ill soldered.
TAILBUSH You are too much affected with it.
MANLY   I cannot,
  Madam, but think on 't for th' injustice.
TAILBUSH   Sir,   40
  His kinsman here is sorry.
MERECRAFT   Not I, madam,°
  I am no kin to him, we but call cousins,
  And if we were, sir, I have no relation
  Unto his crimes.
MANLY   You are not urged with 'em.°
  I can accuse, sir, none but mine own judgement,   45
  For though it were his crime so to betray me,
  I am sure 'twas more mine own, at all to trust him.
  But he therein did use but his old manners,
  And savour strongly what he was before.
TAILBUSH Come, he will change!

MANLY   Faith, I must never think it.   50
   Nor were it reason in me to expect
   That for my sake he should put off a nature
   He sucked in with his milk. It may be, madam,°
   Deceiving trust is all he has to trust to;
   If so, I shall be loath that any hope   55
   Of mine should bate him of his means.
TAILBUSH   You're sharp, sir.
   This act may make him honest.
MANLY   If he were
   To be made honest by an act of parliament,
   I should not alter i' my faith of him.
      [*Tailbush*] *spies the Lady Eitherside*
TAILBUSH   Eitherside!
   Welcome, dear Eitherside! How hast thou done, good wench?   60
   Thou hast been a stranger! I ha' not seen thee this week.

4.2

   [*Enter Lady*] *Eitherside*
[EITHERSIDE] Ever your servant, madam.
TAILBUSH   Where ha' thou been?
   I did so long to see thee.
EITHERSIDE   Visiting, and so tired!
   I protest, madam, 'tis a monstrous trouble.
TAILBUSH And so it is. I swear I must tomorrow
   Begin my visits (would they were over) at Court.   5
   It tortures me to think on 'em.
EITHERSIDE   I do hear°
   You ha' cause, madam, your suit goes on.
TAILBUSH   Who told thee?
EITHERSIDE One that can tell: Master Eitherside.
TAILBUSH   Oh, thy husband!
   Yes, faith, there's life in 't now. It is referred.
   If we once see it under the seals, wench, then   10
   Have with 'em for the great caroche, six horses,
   And the two coachmen, with my Ambler bare,
   And my three women; we will live, i' faith,
   The examples o' the town, and govern it.
   I'll lead the fashion still.

EITHERSIDE   You do that now,   15
Sweet madam.
TAILBUSH   Oh, but then, I'll every day
Bring up some new device. Thou and I, Eitherside,
Will first be in it, I will give it thee;
And they shall follow us. Thou shalt, I swear,
Wear every month a new gown out of it.   20
EITHERSIDE Thank you, good madam.
TAILBUSH   Pray thee, call me Tailbush,
As I thee, Eitherside; I not love this 'madam'.
EITHERSIDE Then I protest to you, Tailbush, I am glad
Your business so succeeds.
TAILBUSH   Thank thee, good Eitherside.
EITHERSIDE But Master Eitherside tells me that he likes   25
Your other business better.
TAILBUSH   Which?
EITHERSIDE   O' the toothpicks.
TAILBUSH I never heard on 't.
EITHERSIDE   Ask Master Merecraft.
        Merecraft hath whispered with [Manly] the while
MERECRAFT Madam? He's one, in a word, I'll trust his malice
With any man's credit I would have abused.°
MANLY Sir, if you think you do please me in this,   30
You are deceived.
MERECRAFT   No, but because my lady
Named him my kinsman, I would satisfy you
What I think of him—and pray you, upon it
To judge me.
MANLY   So I do: that ill men's friendship
Is as unfaithful as themselves.
TAILBUSH   Do you hear?   35
Ha' you a business about toothpicks?
MERECRAFT   Yes, madam.
Did I ne'er tell 't you? I meant to have offered it
Your ladyship on the perfecting the patent.
TAILBUSH How is 't?
MERECRAFT   For serving the whole state with toothpicks;°
Somewhat an intricate business to discourse, but—   40
I show how much the subject is abused
First in that one commodity. Then what diseases
And putrefactions in the gums are bred
By those are made of adult'rate and false wood.°

My plot for reformation of these follows: 45
To have all toothpicks brought unto an office,
There sealed; and such as counterfeit 'em, mulcted.
And last, for venting 'em, to have a book
Printed to teach their use, which every child
Shall have throughout the kingdom that can read,   50
And learn to pick his teeth by. Which beginning
Early to practise, with some other rules,
Of never sleeping with the mouth open, chawing°
Some grains of mastic, will preserve the breath
Pure, and so free from taint—
    [*Enter Trains*]
                        Ha? What is 't? Say'st thou?   55
    Trains his man whispers [to] him
TAILBUSH Good faith, it sounds a very pretty business!
EITHERSIDE So Master Eitherside says, madam.
MERECRAFT   The lady is come.
TAILBUSH Is she? Good, wait upon her in.
    [*Exit Merecraft and Trains*]
                       My Ambler
Was never so ill absent. Eitherside,
How do I look today? Am I not dressed   60
Spruntly?
    She looks in her glass
EITHERSIDE Yes, verily, madam.
TAILBUSH   Pox o' madam,
Will you not leave that?
EITHERSIDE   Yes, good Tailbush.
TAILBUSH   So?
Sounds not that better? What vile fucus is this
Thou hast got on?
EITHERSIDE   'Tis pearl.
TAILBUSH   Pearl? Oyster-shells,
As I breathe, Eitherside, I know 't. Here comes,   65
They say, a wonder, sirrah, has been in Spain,
Will teach us all! She's sent to me from Court
To gratulate with me! Prithee, let's observe her,
What faults she has, that we may laugh at 'em
When she is gone.
EITHERSIDE   That we will heartily, Tailbush.   70
TAILBUSH O me! The very infanta of the giants!°

4.3

*[Enter] Merecraft [and] Wittipol; Wittipol is dressed like a
Spanish lady*

MERECRAFT Here is a noble lady, madam, come
From your great friends at Court to see your ladyship,
And have the honour of your acquaintance.

TAILBUSH   Sir,
She does us honour.

[Wittipol] excuses himself for not kissing

WITTIPOL   Pray you, say to her ladyship
It is the manner of Spain to embrace only,   5
Never to kiss. She will excuse the custom.

TAILBUSH Your use of it is law. Please you, sweet madam,
To take a seat.

WITTIPOL   Yes, madam. I have had
The favour through a world of fair report
To know your virtues, madam; and in that   10
Name, have desired the happiness of presenting
My service to your ladyship.

TAILBUSH   Your love, madam,
I must not own it else.

WITTIPOL   Both are due, madam,
To your great undertakings.

TAILBUSH   Great? In troth, madam,
They are my friends that think 'em anything;   15
If I can do my sex by 'em any service,
I have my ends, madam.

WITTIPOL   And they are noble ones,
That make a multitude beholden, madam:
The commonwealth of ladies must acknowledge from you.

EITHERSIDE Except some envious, madam.

WITTIPOL   You're right in that, madam,   20
Of which race I encountered some but lately,
Who, 't seems, have studied reasons to discredit
Your business.

TAILBUSH   How, sweet madam?

WITTIPOL   Nay, the parties
Wi' not be worth your pause—most ruinous things, madam,

That have put off all hope of being recovered   25
To a degree of handsomeness.
TAILBUSH   But their reasons, madam?
I would fain hear.
WITTIPOL   Some, madam, I remember.
They say that painting quite destroys the face—
EITHERSIDE Oh, that's an old one, madam.
WITTIPOL   There are new ones, too:°
Corrupts the breath, hath left so little sweetness   30
In kissing, as 'tis now used but for fashion
And shortly will be taken for a punishment;
Decays the foreteeth that should guard the tongue,
And suffers that run riot everlasting,
And (which is worse) some ladies when they meet   35
Cannot be merry and laugh, but they do spit
In one another's faces!
MANLY   I should know
This voice, and face, too.
WITTIPOL   Then they say, 'tis dangerous°
To all the fallen, yet well disposed, Madames°
That are industrious, and desire to earn   40
Their living with their sweat. For any distemper
Of heat and motion may displace the colours;
And if the paint once run about their faces,
Twenty to one they will appear so ill-favoured
Their servants run away, too, and leave the pleasure° · 45
Imperfect, and the reckoning als' unpaid.°
EITHERSIDE Pox, these are poets' reasons.
TAILBUSH   Some old lady
That keeps a poet has devised these scandals.
EITHERSIDE Faith, we must have the poets banished, madam,
As Master Eitherside says.
          [*Enter Trains, who whispers to Merecraft*]
MERECRAFT   Master Fitzdottrel   50
And his wife? Where? Madam, the Duke of Drowned-land,
That will be shortly.
WITTIPOL   Is this my lord?
MERECRAFT   The same.

4.4

[Enter] Fitzdottrel, Mistress Fitzdottrel, [and] Pug
[FITZDOTTREL] Your servant, madam!
    Wittipol whispers with Manly
WITTIPOL   How now, friend? Offended
    That I have found your haunt here?
MANLY   No, but wondering
    At your strange-fashioned venture hither.
WITTIPOL   It is
    To show you what they are you so pursue.
MANLY I think 'twill prove a med'cine against marriage   5
    To know their manners.
WITTIPOL   Stay and profit then.
MERECRAFT The lady, madam, whose prince has brought her here
    To be instructed.
    He presents Mistress Fitzdottrel
WITTIPOL   Please you sit with us, lady.
MERECRAFT That's lady-president.
FITZDOTTREL   A goodly woman!
    I cannot see the ring, though.
MERECRAFT   Sir, she has it.   10
TAILBUSH But, madam, these are very feeble reasons!
WITTIPOL So I urged, madam, that the new complexion°
    Now to come forth in name o' your ladyship's fucus
    Had no ingredient—
TAILBUSH   But I durst eat, I assure you.
WITTIPOL So do they in Spain.
TAILBUSH   Sweet madam, be so liberal   15
    To give us some o' your Spanish fucuses!
WITTIPOL They are infinite, madam.
TAILBUSH   So I hear. They have
    Water of gourds, of radish, the white beans,
    Flowers of glass, of thistles, rosmarine,°
    Raw honey, mustard-seed, and bread dough-baked,   20
    The crumbs o' bread, goat's milk, and whites of eggs,
    Camphor, and lily roots, the fat of swans,
    Marrow of veal, white pigeons, and pine kernels,
    The seeds of nettles, purslane, and hare's gall,
    Lemons, thin-skinned—

EITHERSIDE   How her ladyship has studied°   25
  All excellent things!
WITTIPOL   But ordinary, madam.
  No, the true rarities are th' *alvagada*,
  And *argentata* of Queen Isabella.°
TAILBUSH Ay, what are their ingredients, gentle madam?
WITTIPOL Your *allum scagliola*, or *pol di pedra*;°   30
  And *zuccarino*; turpentine of Abezzo,°
  Washed in nine waters; *soda di levante*,°
  Or your fern ashes; *benjamin di gotta*;°
  Grasso di serpe; *porcelletto marino*;°
  Oils of *lentisco*, *zucche*, *mugia* make°   35
  The admirable varnish for the face,
  Gives the right lustre—but two drops rubbed on
  With a piece of scarlet makes a lady of sixty
  Look at sixteen. But, above all, the water°
  Of the white hen of the Lady Estifania's!°   40
TAILBUSH Oh, ay, that same, good madam, I have heard of!
  How is it done?
WITTIPOL   Madam, you take your hen,
  Plume it and skin it, cleanse it o' the inwards;°
  Then chop it, bones and all; add to four ounces
  Of *carrnuacins*, *pipitas*, soap of Cyprus;°   45
  Make the decoction, strain it. Then distil it,
  And keep it in your gallipot well gliddered.°
  Three drops preserves from wrinkles, warts, spots, moles,
  Blemish, or sun-burnings, and keeps the skin
  In decimo sexto, ever bright and smooth°   50
  As any looking-glass; and indeed, is called
  The virgin's milk for the face, *oglio reale*.°
  A ceruse, neither cold or heat will hurt;
  And mixed with oil of myrrh, and the red gillyflower
  Called *cataputia*, and flowers of *rovistico*,°   55
  Makes the best *muta*, or dye, of the whole world.°
TAILBUSH Dear madam, will you let us be familiar?
WITTIPOL Your ladyship's servant.
MERECRAFT   How do you like her?
FITZDOTTREL   Admirable!
  But yet I cannot see the ring.
PUG   Sir.
MERECRAFT [*aside*]   I must

Deliver it, or mar all. This fool's so jealous.   60
     [*Fitzdottrel*] *is jealous about his ring, and Merecraft delivers it*
Madam—[*whispering to Wittipol*] Sir, wear this ring, and pray you
  take knowledge
'Twas sent you by his wife. And give her thanks.
  [*To Pug*] Do not you dwindle, sir, bear up.
PUG   I thank you, sir.
TAILBUSH But for the manner of Spain! Sweet madam, let us
  Be bold, now we are in—are all the ladies   65
  There i' the fashion?
WITTIPOL   None but grandees, madam,
  O' the clasped train, which may be worn at length, too,
  Or thus, upon my arm.
TAILBUSH   And do they wear°
  Cioppinos all?
WITTIPOL   If they be dressed *in punto*, madam.°
EITHERSIDE Gilt as those are, madam?
WITTIPOL   Of goldsmith's work, madam,   70
  And set with diamonds; and their Spanish pumps°
  Of perfumed leather.
TAILBUSH   I should think it hard
  To go in 'em, madam.
WITTIPOL   At the first it is, madam.
TAILBUSH Do you never fall in 'em?
WITTIPOL   Never.
EITHERSIDE   I swear, I should
  Six times an hour.
TAILBUSH   But you have men at hand still   75
  To help you, if you fall?
WITTIPOL   Only one, madam,
  The guarda-duennas [*indicating Trains*], such a little old man
  As this.
EITHERSIDE Alas, he can do nothing! This!
WITTIPOL I'll tell you, madam, I saw i' the Court of Spain once,
  A lady fall i' the King's sight, along.   80
  And there she lay, flat spread as an umbrella,
  Her hoop here cracked; no man durst reach a hand°
  To help her till the guarda-duennas came,
  Who is the person onl' allowed to touch
  A lady there—and he but by this finger.°   85
EITHERSIDE Ha' they no servants, madam, there? Nor friends?

WITTIPOL An escudero or so, madam, that waits
　Upon 'em in another coach at distance,
　And when they walk or dance, holds by a handkercher,
　Never presumes to touch 'em.
EITHERSIDE　　　　　　　This's scurvy!　　　　90
　And a forced gravity! I do not like it.
　I like our own much better.
TAILBUSH　　　　　　　'Tis more French,
　And courtly ours.
EITHERSIDE　　　And tastes more liberty.
　We may have our dozen of visitors at once
　Make love t' us.
TAILBUSH　　　And before our husbands!
EITHERSIDE　　　　　　　Husband?°　　　　95
　As I am honest, Tailbush, I do think
　If nobody should love me but my poor husband,
　I should e'en hang myself.
TAILBUSH　　　　　　Fortune forbid, wench,
　So fair a neck should have so foul a necklace.
EITHERSIDE 'Tis true, as I am handsome!
WITTIPOL　　　　　　　I received, lady,　　　100
　A token from you which I would not be
　Rude to refuse, being your first remembrance.
FITZDOTTREL [*aside to Merecraft*] Oh, I am satisfied now!
MERECRAFT　　　　　　　Do you see it, sir?
WITTIPOL But since you come to know me nearer, lady,
　I'll beg the honour you will wear it for me,　　105
　It must be so.
　　　Wittipol gives it [to] Mistress Fitzdottrel
MISTRESS FITZDOTTREL Sure I have heard this tongue.
MERECRAFT [*aside to Wittipol*] What do you mean, sir?
WITTIPOL [*aside to Merecraft*]　　Would you ha' me mercenary?°
　We'll recompense it anon in somewhat else.
FITZDOTTREL I do not love to be gulled, though in a toy.°
　Wife, do you hear? You're come into the school, wife,　　110
　Where you may learn, I do perceive it, anything!
　How to be fine, or fair, or great, or proud,
　Or what you will, indeed, wife; here 'tis taught.
　And I am glad on 't, that you may not say
　Another day, when honours come upon you,　　115
　You wanted means.

He upbraids her with his bill of costs
                 I ha' done my parts—been
Today at fifty pound charge, first, for a ring
To get you entered. Then left my new play
To wait upon you here to see 't confirmed,
That I may say, both to mine own eyes and ears,   120
'Senses, you are my witness, she hath enjoyed
All helps that could be had for love or money—'
MISTRESS FITZDOTTREL   To make a fool of her.
FITZDOTTREL   Wife, that's your malice,
The wickedness o' your nature, to interpret
Your husband's kindness thus. But I'll not leave   125
Still to do good for your depraved affections:
Intend it. Bend this stubborn will: be great.
TAILBUSH   Good madam, whom do they use in messages?
WITTIPOL   They commonly use their slaves, madam.
TAILBUSH   And does your ladyship
Think that so good, madam?
WITTIPOL   No, indeed, madam; I   130
Therein prefer the fashion of England far,
Of your young delicate page, or discreet usher.
FITZDOTTREL   And I go with your ladyship in opinion
Directly for your gentleman-usher;
There's not a finer officer goes on ground.   135
WITTIPOL   If he be made and broken to his place, once.
FITZDOTTREL   Nay, so I presuppose him.
WITTIPOL   And they are fitter
Managers, too, sir, but I would have 'em called°
Our escuderos.
FITZDOTTREL   Good.
WITTIPOL   Say I should send
To your ladyship who (I presume) has gathered   140
All the dear secrets to know how to make
Pastillos of the duchess of Braganza,°
Coquettas, almojavanas, mantecadas,°
Alcoreas, mustaccioli; or say it were°
The *peladore* of Isabella, or balls°   145
Against the itch, or *aqua nanfa*; or oil°
Of jessamine for gloves of the Marquess Muja,°
Or for the head and hair. Why, these are offices—
FITZDOTTREL   Fit for a gentleman, not a slave.

WITTIPOL   They only
    Might ask for your *piveti*, Spanish coal,°   150
    To burn and sweeten a room; but the arcana
    Of ladies' cabinets—
FITZDOTTREL   Should be elsewhere trusted.
    You're much about the truth.
                He enters himself with the ladies
                                    Sweet honoured ladies,
    Let me fall in wi' you. I ha' my female wit,
    As well as my male. And I do know what suits   155
    A lady of spirit, or a woman of fashion!
WITTIPOL And you would have your wife such.
FITZDOTTREL   Yes, madam, airy,
    Light; not to plain dishonesty, I mean,
    But somewhat o' this side.
WITTIPOL   I take you, sir.
    H' has reason, ladies. I'll not give this rush   160
    For any lady that cannot be honest
    Within a thread.
TAILBUSH   Yes, madam, and yet venture°
    As far for th' other, in her fame—
WITTIPOL   As can be.°
    Coach it to Pimlico; dance the saraband;
    Hear and talk bawdy; laugh as loud as a larum;   165
    Squeak, spring, do anything.
EITHERSIDE   In young company, madam.
TAILBUSH Or afore gallants. If they be brave, or lords,
    A woman is engaged.
FITZDOTTREL   I say so, ladies,°
    It is civility to deny us nothing.
PUG [*aside*] You talk of a university! Why, Hell is   170
    A grammar school to this!
EITHERSIDE   But then,°
    She must not lose a look on stuffs or cloth, madam.
TAILBUSH Nor no coarse fellow.
WITTIPOL   She must be guided, madam,
    By the clothes he wears, and company he is in,
    Whom to salute, how far—
FITZDOTTREL   I ha' told her this.   175
    And how that bawdry, too, upo' the point,
    Is (in itself) as civil a discourse—

        300

WITTIPOL As any other affair of flesh, whatever.

FITZDOTTREL But she will ne'er be capable, she is not
So much as coming, madam; I know not how   180
She loses all her opportunities
With hoping to be forced. I have entertained
A gentleman, a younger brother here,
Whom I would fain breed up her escudero
Against some expectations that I have,°   185
And she'll not countenance him.
          He shows his Pug

WITTIPOL   What's his name?

FITZDOTTREL Devil, o' Derbyshire.

EITHERSIDE   Bless us from him!

TAILBUSH   Devil?
Call him De-vile, sweet madam.

MISTRESS FITZDOTTREL   What you please, ladies.

TAILBUSH De-vile's a prettier name!

EITHERSIDE   And sounds, methinks,
As it came in with the Conqueror—

MANLY   Over smocks!°   190
What things they are! That nature should be at leisure
Ever to make 'em! My wooing is at an end.
          [*Exit*] *Manly,* [*in*] *indignation*

WITTIPOL What can he do?

EITHERSIDE   Let's hear him.

TAILBUSH   Can he manage?

FITZDOTTREL Please you to try him, ladies. Stand forth, Devil.

PUG [*aside*] Was all this but the preface to my torment?   195

FITZDOTTREL Come, let their ladyships see your honours.

EITHERSIDE   Oh,°
He makes a wicked leg.

TAILBUSH   As ever I saw!

WITTIPOL Fit for a devil.

TAILBUSH   Good madam, call him De-vile.
          They begin their catechism

WITTIPOL De-vile, what property is there most required,
I' your conceit now, in the escudero?   200

FITZDOTTREL Why do you not speak?

PUG   A settled discreet pace, madam.

WITTIPOL I think a barren head, sir, mountain-like,°
To be exposed to the cruelty of weathers—

FITZDOTTREL Ay, for his valley is beneath the waste, madam,°
    And to be fruitful there, it is sufficient.   205
    [*To Pug*] Dullness upon you! Could not you hit this?
       He strikes him
PUG Good sir—
WITTIPOL   He then had had no barren head.
    You daw him too much, in troth, sir.
FITZDOTTREL   I must walk
    With the French stick, like an old verger, for you.°
       The devil prays
PUG O chief, call me to Hell again, and free me.   210
FITZDOTTREL Do you murmur now?
PUG   Not I, sir.
WITTIPOL   What do you take,
    Master De-vile, the height of your employment
    In the true perfect escudero?
FITZDOTTREL   When?
    What do you answer?
PUG   To be able, madam,
    First to enquire, then report the working   215
    Of any lady's physic, in sweet phrase.
WITTIPOL Yes, that's an act of elegance and importance.
    But what above?
FITZDOTTREL   Oh, that I had a goad for him.
PUG To find out a good corn-cutter.
TAILBUSH   Out on him!
EITHERSIDE Most barbarous!
FITZDOTTREL   Why did you do this, now?   220
    Of purpose to discredit me? You damned devil.
PUG [*aside*] Sure if I be not yet, I shall be. All
    My days in Hell were holidays to this!
TAILBUSH 'Tis labour lost, madam!
EITHERSIDE   He's a dull fellow
    Of no capacity!
TAILBUSH   Of no discourse!   225
    Oh, if my Ambler had been here!
EITHERSIDE   Ay, madam;
    You talk of a man, where is there such another?
WITTIPOL Master De-vile, put case one of my ladies here
    Had a fine brach, and would employ you forth
    To treat 'bout a convenient match for her.   230

What would you observe?

PUG   The colour and the size, madam.

WITTIPOL And nothing else?

FITZDOTTREL   The moon, you calf, the moon!°

WITTIPOL Ay, and the sign.

TAILBUSH   Yes, and receipts for proneness.°

WITTIPOL Then when the puppies came, what would you do?

PUG Get their nativities cast!

WITTIPOL   This's well. What more?   235

PUG Consult the almanac-man which would be least?
    Which cleanliest?

WITTIPOL   And which silentest? This's well, madam!
    And while she were with puppy?

PUG   Walk her out,°
    And air her every morning.

WITTIPOL   Very good!
    And be industrious to kill her fleas?

PUG   Yes!   240

WITTIPOL He will make a pretty proficient.

PUG [*aside*]   Who,°
    Coming from Hell, could look for such catechising?
    The devil is an ass. I do acknowledge it.

FITZDOTTREL The top of woman! All her sex in abstract!°
    I love her to each syllable falls from her.   245

TAILBUSH Good madam, give me leave to go aside with him,
    And try him a little!

WITTIPOL   Do, and I'll withdraw, madam,
    With this fair lady; read to her the while.

TAILBUSH Come, sir.

          The devil prays again

PUG   Dear chief, relieve me, or I perish.

WITTIPOL Lady, we'll follow.

          [*Exeunt Tailbush, Pug, and Eitherside*]
                          You are not jealous, sir?   250

FITZDOTTREL Oh, madam! You shall see.

          He gives his wife to him, taking him to be a lady
                          Stay wife, behold,
    I give her up here absolutely to you,
    She is your own. Do with her what you will!
    Melt, cast, and form her as you shall think good.
    Set any stamp on! I'll receive her from you   255

As a new thing, by your own standard.
WITTIPOL   Well, sir!
    [*Exeunt Mistress Fitzdottrel and Wittipol*]

4.5

[MERECRAFT] But what ha' you done i' your dependence since?
FITZDOTTREL Oh, it goes on. I met your cousin, the Master—
MERECRAFT You did not acquaint him, sir?
FITZDOTTREL   Faith, but I did, sir.
  And upon better thought, not without reason!
  He, being chief officer, might ha' ta'en it ill else,   5
  As a contempt against his place, and that
  In time, sir, ha' drawn on another dependence.
  No, I did find him in good terms, and ready
  To do me any service.
MERECRAFT   So he said, to you!
  But, sir, you do not know him.
FITZDOTTREL   Why, I presumed   10
  Because this business of my wife's required me,
  I could not ha' done better. And he told
  Me that he would go presently to your counsel,
  A knight here i' the lane—
MERECRAFT   Yes, Justice Eitherside.
FITZDOTTREL And get the feoffment drawn, with a letter of attorney   15
  For livery and seisin!
MERECRAFT   That I know's the course.°
  But, sir, you mean not to make him feoffee?
FITZDOTTREL Nay, that I'll pause on.
    [*Enter Pitfall*]
MERECRAFT   How now, little Pitfall!
PITFALL Your cousin, Master Everill, would come in—
  But he would know if Master Manly were here.   20
MERECRAFT No—tell him if he were, I ha' made his peace!
    [*Exit Pitfall.*] Merecraft *whispers against* [*Everill*]
  He's one, sir, has no state, and a man knows not
  How such a trust may tempt him.
FITZDOTTREL   I conceive you.
    [*Enter Everill and Plutarchus*]

EVERILL Sir, this same deed is done here.

MERECRAFT   Pretty Plutarchus!
    Art thou come with it? And has Sir Paul viewed it?   25

PLUTARCHUS His hand is to the draft.

MERECRAFT   Will you step in, sir,
    And read it?

FITZDOTTREL Yes.

EVERILL   I pray you a word wi' you.
       Everill whispers against Merecraft
    Sir Paul Eitherside willed me gi' you caution
    Whom you did make feoffee, for 'tis the trust
    O' your whole state; and though my cousin here   30
    Be a worthy gentleman, yet his valour has
    At the tall board been questioned, and we hold°
    Any man so impeached of doubtful honesty.
    I will not justify this, but give it you
    To make your profit of it; if you utter it,   35
    I can forswear it.

FITZDOTTREL   I believe you, and thank you, sir.
      [*Exeunt*]

4.6

    [*Enter*] *Wittipol, Mistress Fitzdottrel,* [*and*] *Manly,* [*hidden*]

[WITTIPOL] Be not afraid, sweet lady; you're trusted
    To love, not violence, here. I am no ravisher,
    But one whom you, by your fair trust again,
    May of a servant make a most true friend.°

MISTRESS FITZDOTTREL And such a one I need, but not this way.   5
    Sir, I confess me to you, the mere manner
    Of your attempting me this morning took me,
    And I did hold m' invention and my manners
    Were both engaged to give it a requital,
    But not unto your ends. My hope was then—   10
    Though interrrupted, ere it could be uttered—
    That whom I found the master of such language,
    That brain and spirit, for such an enterprise,
    Could not but, if those succours were demanded
    To a right use, employ them virtuously,   15

And make that profit of his noble parts
Which they would yield. Sir, you have now the ground
To exercise them in. I am a woman
That cannot speak more wretchedness of myself
Than you can read; matched to a mass of folly   20
That every day makes haste to his own ruin;
The wealthy portion that I brought him, spent;
And (through my friends' neglect) no jointure made me.
My fortunes standing in this precipice,
'Tis counsel that I want, and honest aids: 25
And in this name I need you for a friend!
Never in any other; for his ill
Must not make me, sir, worse.

      Manly, concealed this while, shows himself

MANLY   O friend! Forsake not
The brave occasion virtue offers you
To keep you innocent. I have feared for both,   30
And watched you, to prevent the ill I feared.
But since the weaker side hath so assured me,
Let not the stronger fall by his own vice,
Or be the less a friend, 'cause virtue needs him.

WITTIPOL Virtue shall never ask my succours twice;   35
Most friend, most man, your counsels are commands.
Lady, I can love goodness in you more
Than I did beauty, and do here entitle
Your virtue to the power upon a life
You shall engage in any fruitful service,   40
Even to forfeit.

      [*Enter Merecraft*]

MERECRAFT   Madam.

      *Merecraft takes Wittipol aside and moves a project for
      himself*

                   Do you hear, sir,°
We have another leg strained for this dottrel.°
He has a quarrel to carry, and has caused
A deed of feoffment of his whole estate
To be drawn yonder; h' has 't within. And you   45
Only he means to make feoffee. He's fallen
So desperately enamoured on you, and talks
Most like a madman—you did never hear
A frantic so in love with his own favour!°

Now, you do know 'tis of no validity   50
In your name, as you stand; therefore, advise him
To put in me—he's come here—you shall share, sir.

4.7

[Enter] Fitzdottrel, Everill, [and] Plutarchus
FITZDOTTREL Madam, I have a suit to you, and aforehand
  I do bespeak you; you must not deny me,
  I will be granted.
WITTIPOL   Sir, I must know it, though.
FITZDOTTREL No, lady, you must not know it—yet you must,
    too,
  For the trust of it, and the fame indeed,   5
  Which else were lost me. I would use your name
  But in a feoffment; make my whole estate
  Over unto you: a trifle, a thing of nothing,
  Some eighteen hundred.
WITTIPOL   Alas! I understand not
  Those things, sir. I am a woman, and most loath   10
  To embark myself—
FITZDOTTREL   You will not slight me, madam?
WITTIPOL Nor you'll not quarrel me?
FITZDOTTREL   No, sweet madam, I have
  Already a dependence, for which cause
  I do this. Let me put you in, dear madam,
  I may be fairly killed.
WITTIPOL   You have your friends, sir,   15
  About you here for choice.
EVERILL   She tells you right, sir.°
FITZDOTTREL Death, if she do, what do I care for that?
  Say I would have her tell me wrong.
WITTIPOL   Why, sir,
  If for the trust, you'll let me have the honour
  To name you one.
FITZDOTTREL   Nay, you do me the honour, madam.   20
  Who is 't?
WITTIPOL This gentleman.
    She designs Manly

FITZDOTTREL   Oh no, sweet madam,
   He's friend to him with whom I ha' the dependence.
WITTIPOL Who might he be?
FITZDOTTREL   One Wittipol—do you know him?
WITTIPOL Alas, sir, he? A toy. This gentleman
   A friend to him? No more than I am, sir!   25
FITZDOTTREL But will your ladyship undertake that, madam?°
WITTIPOL Yes, and what else for him you will engage me.
FITZDOTTREL What is his name?
WITTIPOL   His name is Eustace Manly.
FITZDOTTREL Whence does he write himself?
WITTIPOL   Of Middlesex,
   Esquire.
FITZDOTTREL Say nothing, madam. Clerk, come hither.   30
   Write Eustace Manly, squire o' Middlesex.
MERECRAFT [*aside to Wittipol*] What ha' you done, sir?
WITTIPOL [*aside to Merecraft*]   Named a gentleman
   That I'll be answerable for to you, sir.
   Had I named you, it might ha' been suspected:
   This way 'tis safe.
FITZDOTTREL   Come, gentlemen, your hands   35
   For witness.
       Everill applauds it
MANLY   What is this?
EVERILL   You ha' made election
   Of a most worthy gentleman!
MANLY   Would one
   Of worth had spoke it; whence it comes, it is
   Rather a shame to me than a praise.
EVERILL Sir, I will give you any satisfaction.   40
MANLY Be silent then: falsehood commends not truth.°
PLUTARCHUS You do deliver this, sir, as your deed,
   To th' use of Master Manly?
FITZDOTTREL   Yes. And sir,
   When did you see young Wittipol? I am ready
   For process now; sir, this is publication.   45
   He shall hear from me; he would needs be courting
   My wife, sir.
MANLY   Yes: so witnesseth his cloak there.
FITZDOTTREL Nay, good sir—madam, you did undertake—°
WITTIPOL What?

FITZDOTTREL   That he was not Wittipol's friend.

WITTIPOL   I hear,
    Sir, no confession of it.

FITZDOTTREL   Oh, she knows not;   50
    Now I remember, madam! This young Wittipol
    Would ha' debauched my wife and made me cuckold
    Through a casement; he did fly her home
    To mine own window, but I think I soused him
    And ravished her away out of his pounces.°   55
    I ha' sworn to ha' him by the ears. I fear°
    The toy wi' not do me right.

WITTIPOL   No? That were pity!
    What right do you ask, sir? Here he is will do 't you!
       Wittipol discovers himself

FITZDOTTREL Ha? Wittipol?

WITTIPOL   Ay, sir, no more lady now,
    Nor Spaniard!

MANLY   No, indeed, 'tis Wittipol!   60

FITZDOTTREL Am I the thing I feared?

WITTIPOL   A cuckold? No, sir,
    But you were late in possibility,
    I'll tell you so much.

MANLY   But your wife's too virtuous!

WITTIPOL We'll see her, sir, at home, and leave you here°
    To be made Duke o' Shoreditch with a project.°   65

FITZDOTTREL Thieves, ravishers!

WITTIPOL   Cry but another note, sir,
    I'll mar the tune o' your pipe!

FITZDOTTREL   Gi' me my deed then!
       [*Fitzdottrel snatches at*] *his deed*

WITTIPOL Neither; that shall be kept for your wife's good,
    Who will know better how to use it.

FITZDOTTREL   Ha!
    To feast you with my land?

WITTIPOL   Sir, be you quiet,   70
    Or I shall gag you ere I go; consult
    Your Master of Dependences how to make this
    A second business, you have time, sir.
       Wittipol baffles° him and [*exits with Manly and Mistress*
       Fitzdottrel]

FITZDOTTREL   Oh!

What will the ghost of my wise grandfather,
My learned father, with my worshipful mother   75
Think of me now, that left me in this world
In state to be their heir? That am become
A cuckold, and an ass, and my wife's ward;
Likely to lose my land; ha' my throat cut—
All by her practice!

MERECRAFT   Sir, we are all abused!   80

FITZDOTTREL And be so still! Who hinders you? I pray you,
    Let me alone, I would enjoy myself,
    And be the Duke o' Drowned-land you ha' made me.

MERECRAFT Sir, we must play an after-game o' this.

FITZDOTTREL But I am not in case to be a gamester:°   85
    I tell you once again—

MERECRAFT   You must be ruled,
    And take some counsel.

FITZDOTTREL   Sir, I do hate counsel,
    As I do hate my wife, my wicked wife!

MERECRAFT But we may think how to recover all,
    If you will act.

FITZDOTTREL   I will not think, nor act,   90
    Nor yet recover; do not talk to me!
    I'll run out o' my wits rather than hear;
    I will be what I am, Fabian Fitzdottrel,
    Though all the world say nay to 't!
        [*Exit Fitzdottrel*]

MERECRAFT   Let's follow him.
        [*Exeunt*]

5.1

[*Enter*] *Ambler* [*and*] *Pitfall*

[AMBLER] But has my lady missed me?

PITFALL   Beyond telling!
Here has been that infinity of strangers!
And then she would ha' had you to ha' sampled you°
With one within that they are now a-teaching,
And does pretend to your rank.

AMBLER   Good fellow Pitfall,   5
Tell Master Merecraft I entreat a word with him.
        [*Exit*] *Pitfall*
This most unlucky accident will go near
To be the loss o' my place, I am in doubt!
        [*Enter Merecraft*]

MERECRAFT With me? What say you, Master Ambler?

AMBLER   Sir,
I would beseech your worship stand between   10
Me and my lady's displeasure for my absence.

MERECRAFT Oh, is that all? I warrant you.

AMBLER   I would tell you, sir,
But how it happened.

MERECRAFT   Brief, good Master Ambler,
Put yourself to your rack, for I have task°
Of more importance.
        Merecraft seems full of business

AMBLER   Sir, you'll laugh at me!   15
But (so is truth) a very friend of mine,
Finding by conference with me that I lived
Too chaste for my complexion (and indeed°
Too honest for my place, sir) did advise me
If I did love myself (as that I do,   20
I must confess)—

MERECRAFT   Spare your parenthesis.

AMBLER To gi' my body a little evacuation—

MERECRAFT Well, and you went to a whore?

AMBLER   No, sir. I durst not
(For fear it might arrive at somebody's ear

It should not) trust myself to a common house,   25
    Ambler tells this with extraordinary speed
But got the gentlewoman to go with me,
And carry her bedding to a conduit-head°
Hard by the place toward Tyburn which they call
My Lord Mayor's Banqueting House. Now, sir, this morning°
Was execution, and I ne'er dreamt on 't   30
Till I heard the noise o' the people and the horses;
And neither I nor the poor gentlewoman
Durst stir till all was done and past: so that
I' the interim we fell asleep again.
    He flags
MERECRAFT Nay, if you fall from your gallop I am gone, sir.   35
AMBLER But when I waked to put on my clothes, a suit
I made new for the action, it was gone,
And all my money, with my purse, my seals,
My hard wax and my table-books, my studies,
And a fine new device I had to carry   40
My pen and ink, my civet, and my toothpicks,
All under one. But that which grieved me was
The gentlewoman's shoes (with a pair of roses
And garters I had given her for the business),
So as that made us stay till it was dark;   45
For I was fain to lend her mine, and walk
In a rug by her barefoot to Saint Giles's.°
MERECRAFT A kind of Irish penance! Is this all, sir?°
AMBLER To satisfy my lady.
MERECRAFT   I will promise you, sir.
AMBLER I ha' told the true disaster.
MERECRAFT   I cannot stay wi' you,   50
Sir, to condole, but gratulate your return.
    [*Exit Merecraft*]
AMBLER An honest gentleman, but he's never at leisure
To be himself; he has such tides of business.
    [*Exit*]

5.2

[*Enter*] *Pug*

[PUG] Oh call me home again, dear chief, and put me
    To yoking foxes, milking of he-goats,
    Pounding of water in a mortar, laving°
    The sea dry with a nutshell, gathering all
    The leaves are fallen this autumn, drawing farts   5
    Out of dead bodies, making ropes of sand,
    Catching the winds together in a net,
    Must'ring of ants, and numb'ring atoms; all°
    That Hell and you thought exquisite torments, rather
    Than stay me here a thought more: I would sooner   10
    Keep fleas within a circle, and be accountant
    A thousand year which of 'em and how far
    Out-leaped the other, than endure a minute
    Such as I have within. There is no Hell
    To a lady of fashion. All your tortures there   15
    Are pastimes to it. 'Twould be a refreshing
    For me to be i' the fire again, from hence.
        [*Enter*] *Ambler,* [*who*] *surveys him*
AMBLER This is my suit, and those the shoes and roses!
PUG They've such impertinent vexations,
    A general council o' devils could not hit—°   20
        Pug perceives it, and starts
    Ha! This is he I took asleep with his wench,
    And borrowed his clothes. What might I do to balk him?
AMBLER Do you hear, sir?
PUG   Answer him, but not to th' purpose.
AMBLER What is your name, I pray you, sir?
        He answers quite from the purpose
PUG   Is 't so late, sir?
AMBLER I ask not o' the time, but of your name, sir.   25
PUG I thank you, sir. Yes it does hold, sir, certain.
AMBLER Hold, sir? What holds? I must both hold, and talk to you
    About these clothes.
PUG   A very pretty lace!
    But the tailor cozened me.
AMBLER   No, I am cozened
    By you! Robbed!

PUG   Why, when you please, sir, I am   30
  For threepenny gleek, your man.
AMBLER   Pox o' your gleek,°
  And threepence. Give me an answer.
PUG   Sir,
  My master is the best at it.
AMBLER   Your master!
  Who is your master?
PUG   Let it be Friday night.
AMBLER What should be then?
PUG   Your best song's 'Tom o' Bedlam'.°   35
AMBLER I think you are he. Does he mock me, trow, from purpose?
  Or do not I speak to him what I mean?
  Good sir, your name.
PUG   Only a couple o' cocks, sir,
  If we can get a widgeon, 'tis in season.
AMBLER He hopes to make one o' these Sciptics o' me°   40
  (I think I name 'em right) and does not fly me.
  I wonder at that! 'Tis a strange confidence!
  I'll prove another way to draw his answer.
            [*Exit Ambler*]°

5.3

        [*Enter*] *Merecraft, Fitzdottrel,* [*and*] *Everill*
[MERECRAFT] It is the easiest thing, sir, to be done.
  As plain as fizzling: roll but wi' your eyes,°
  And foam at th' mouth. A little castle-soap
  Will do 't, to rub your lips; and then a nutshell
  With tow and touchwood in it to spit fire.°   5
  Did you ne'er read, sir, little Darrel's tricks,
  With the boy o' Burton, and the seven in Lancashire,
  Sommers at Nottingham? All these do teach it.°
  And we'll give out, sir, that your wife has bewitched you—
EVERILL And practised with those two as sorcerers.   10
MERECRAFT And ga' you potions, by which means you were
  Not *compos mentis* when you made your feoffment.°
  There's no recovery o' your state but this:
  This, sir, will sting.

EVERILL   And move in a court of equity.
MERECRAFT For it is more than manifest that this was   15
    A plot o' your wife's to get your land.
FITZDOTTREL   I think it.
EVERILL Sir, it appears.
MERECRAFT   Nay, and my cousin has known
    These gallants in these shapes.
EVERILL   T' have done strange things, sir.
    One as the lady, the other as the squire.
MERECRAFT How a man's honesty may be fooled! I thought him   20
    A very lady.
FITZDOTTREL So did I—renounce me else.
MERECRAFT But this way, sir, you'll be revenged at height.
EVERILL Upon 'em all.
MERECRAFT   Yes, faith, and since your wife
    Has run the way of woman thus, e'en give her—
FITZDOTTREL Lost, by this hand, to me; dead to all joys   25
    Of her dear Dottrel. I shall never pity her,
    That could pity herself.
MERECRAFT   Princely resolved, sir,
    And like yourself still, *in potentia*.°

5.4

    [*Enter*] *Gilthead, Plutarchus, Sledge,* [*and*] *Sergeants*
[MERECRAFT] Gilthead, what news?
    Fitzdottrel asks [*Gilthead*] *for his money*
FITZDOTTREL   Oh sir, my hundred pieces!
    Let me ha' them yet.
GILTHEAD   Yes, sir—officers,
    Arrest him.
FITZDOTTREL Me?
SERGEANT   I arrest you.
SLEDGE   Keep the peace,
    I charge you, gentlemen.
FITZDOTTREL   Arrest me? Why?
GILTHEAD For better security, sir. My son, Plutarchus,   5
    Assures me you're not worth a groat.
PLUTARCHUS   Pardon me, father,

I said his worship had no foot of land left;
And that I'll justify, for I writ the deed.°
FITZDOTTREL Ha' you these tricks i' the city?
GILTHEAD   Yes, and more.
  [*Indicating Merecraft*] Arrest this gallant, too, here, at my suit.   10
SLEDGE Ay, and at mine. He owes me for his lodging
    Two year and a quarter.
MERECRAFT   Why, Master Gilthead, landlord,
    Thou art not mad, though th' art constable,
    Puffed up with th' pride of the place? Do you hear, sirs?
    Have I deserved this from you two for all   15
    My pains at Court to get you each a patent?
GILTHEAD For what?
MERECRAFT   Upo' my project o' the forks.°
SLEDGE Forks? What be they?
MERECRAFT   The laudable use of forks,
    Brought into custom here, as they are in Italy,
    To th' sparing o' napkins. That, that should have made   20
    Your bellows go at the forge, as his at the furnace.
    I ha' procured it, ha' the signet for it,°
    Dealt with the linen-drapers on my private,°
    By cause I feared they were the likeliest ever
    To stir against, to cross it, for 'twill be   25
    A mighty saver of linen through the kingdom
    (As that is one o' my grounds, and to spare washing).
    Now on you two had I laid all the profits.
    Gilthead to have the making of all those
    Of gold and silver for the better personages;   30
    And you, of those of steel for the common sort.
    And both by patent. I had brought you your seals in,
    But now you have prevented me, and I thank you.
        Sledge is brought about
SLEDGE Sir, I will bail you, at mine own apperil.
MERECRAFT Nay, choose.
PLUTARCHUS   Do you so, too, good father.   35
        And Gilthead comes
GILTHEAD I like the fashion o' the project well,
    The forks. It may be a lucky one. And is not
    Intricate, as one would say, but fit for
    Plain heads as ours to deal in. Do you hear,
    Officers, we discharge you.

[*Exeunt Sergeants*]

MERECRAFT   Why, this shows   40
A little good nature in you, I confess,
But do not tempt your friends thus. Little Gilthead,
Advise your sire, great Gilthead, from these courses;
And here to trouble a great man in reversion,°
For a matter o' fifty on a false alarm—   45
Away, it shows not well. Let him get the pieces
And bring 'em. You'll hear more else.

PLUTARCHUS   Father.

[*Exit Plutarchus with Gilthead*]

5.5

[*Enter*] *Ambler*

[AMBLER] Oh, Master Sledge, are you here? I ha' been to seek you.
   You are the constable, they say. Here's one
   That I do charge with felony for the suit
   He wears, sir.

MERECRAFT   Who? Master Fitzdottrel's man?
   'Ware what you do, Master Ambler.

AMBLER   Sir, these clothes,   5
   I'll swear, are mine, and the shoes the gentlewoman's
   I told you of—and ha' him afore a Justice,
   I will.

PUG   My master, sir, will pass his word for me.

AMBLER   Oh, can you speak to purpose now?

   Fitzdottrel disclaims him

FITZDOTTREL   Not I.
   If you be such a one, sir, I will leave you   10
   To your godfathers in law. Let twelve men work.°

PUG   Do you hear, sir; pray, in private.

FITZDOTTREL   Well, what say you?
   Brief, for I have no time to lose.

PUG   Truth is, sir,
   I am the very devil, and had leave
   To take this body I am in to serve you,   15
   Which was a cutpurse's, and hanged this morning.
   And it is likewise true I stole this suit

To clothe me with. But, sir, let me not go
To prison for it. I have hitherto
Lost time, done nothing; shown, indeed, no part   20
O' my devil's nature. Now I will so help
Your malice 'gainst these parties, so advance
The business that you have in hand of witchcraft
And your possession, as myself were in you.
Teach you such tricks to make your belly swell   25
And your eyes turn, to foam, to stare, to gnash
Your teeth together and to beat yourself,
Laugh loud, and feign six voices—

FITZDOTTREL   Out, you rogue!
   You most infernal counterfeit wretch! Avaunt!
   Do you think to gull me with your Aesop's fables?   30
   Here, take him to you, I ha' no part in him.

PUG   Sir!

FITZDOTTREL Away, I do disclaim; I will not hear you.
       And [Fitzdottrel] sends [Pug] away [with Sledge]

MERECRAFT What said he to you, sir?

FITZDOTTREL   Like a lying rascal
   Told me he was the devil.

MERECRAFT   How! A good jest!

FITZDOTTREL And that he would teach me such fine devil's
       tricks   35
   For our new resolution.

EVERILL   A pox on him!
   'Twas excellent wisely done, sir, not to trust him.

MERECRAFT Why, if he were the devil, we sha' not need him,
   If you'll be ruled.
       Merecraft gives the instructions to [Fitzdottrel and Everill]
                  Go throw yourself on a bed, sir,
   And feign you ill. We'll not be seen wi' you   40
   Till after that you have a fit, and all
   Confirmed within. [*To Everill*] Keep you with the two ladies
   And persuade them. I'll to Justice Eitherside,
   And possess him with all. Trains shall seek out Engine,
   And they two fill the town with 't; every cable   45
   Is to be veered. We must employ out all°
   Our emissaries now. Sir, I will send you°
   Bladders and bellows. Sir, be confident,°
   'Tis no hard thing t' outdo the devil in:

A boy o' thirteen year old made him an ass   50
But tother day.

FITZDOTTREL   Well, I'll begin to practise,°
And scape the imputation of being cuckold
By mine own act.

MERECRAFT   You're right.

    [*Exit Fitzdottrel*]

EVERILL   Come, you ha' put
Yourself to a simple coil here, and your friends,°
By dealing with new agents in new plots.   55

MERECRAFT No more o' that, sweet cousin.

EVERILL   What had you
To do with this same Wittipol, for a lady?

MERECRAFT Question not that; 'tis done.

EVERILL   You had some strain
'Bove ela?

MERECRAFT I had indeed.

EVERILL   And now you crack for 't.°

MERECRAFT Do not upbraid me.

EVERILL   Come, you must be told on 't;   60
You are so covetous still to embrace
More than you can, that you lose all.

MERECRAFT   'Tis right.
What would you, more than guilty? Now, your succours.

    [*Exeunt*]

5.6

    [*Enter*] *Shackles* [*and*] *Pug. Pug is brought to Newgate*°

[SHACKLES] Here you are lodged, sir; you must send your garnish°
If you'll be private.

PUG   There it is, sir, leave me.

    [*Exit Shackles*]

To Newgate brought? How is the name of devil
Discredited in me! What a lost fiend
Shall I be on return! My chief will roar   5
In triumph now, that I have been on earth
A day and done no noted thing but brought
That body back here, was hanged out this morning.

Well! Would it once were midnight, that I knew
My utmost. I think Time be drunk and sleeps,   10
He is so still, and moves not. I do glory
Now i' my torment. Neither can I expect it,
I have it with my fact.
    Enter Iniquity the Vice
INIQUITY   Child of Hell, be thou merry;°
Put a look on as round, boy, and red as a cherry.
Cast care at thy posterns, and firk i' thy fetters,   15
They are ornaments, baby, have graced thy betters.
Look upon me, and hearken. Our chief doth salute thee,
And lest the cold iron should chance to confute thee,°
H' hath sent thee grant-parole by me to stay longer
A month here on earth against cold, child, or hunger—   20
PUG How? Longer here a month?
INIQUITY   Yes, boy, till the session,°
That so thou mayest have a triumphal egression.
PUG In a cart, to be hanged.
INIQUITY   No, child, in a car,°
The chariot of triumph, which most of them are.
And in the meantime to be greasy and bousy,   25
And nasty and filthy, and ragged and lousy,
With damn me, renounce me, and all the fine phrases
That bring unto Tyburn the plentiful gazes.
PUG He is a devil! And may be our chief!°
The great superior devil for his malice—   30
Arch-devil! I acknowledge him. He knew
What I would suffer when he tied me up thus
In a rogue's body, and he has (I thank him)
His tyrannous pleasure on me, to confine me
To the unlucky carcass of a cutpurse,   35
Wherein I could do nothing.
    Enter [Satan, who] upbraids [Pug] with all his day's work
SATAN   Impudent fiend,
Stop thy lewd mouth. Dost thou not shame and tremble
To lay thine own dull damned defects upon
An innocent case there? Why, thou heavy slave!°
The spirit that did possess that flesh before,   40
Put more true life in a finger and a thumb
Than thou in the whole mass. Yet thou rebell'st
And murmur'st! What one proffer hast thou made,°

Wicked enough this day, that might be called
Worthy thine own, much less the name that sent thee?   45
First, thou didst help thyself into a beating
Promptly, and with 't endangered'st, too, thy tongue—
A devil, and could not keep a body entire
One day! That, for our credit. And, to vindicate it,°
Hinder'dst (for aught thou know'st) a deed of darkness: 50
Which was an act of that egregious folly,
As no one to'ard the devil could ha' thought on.°
This for your acting! But for suffering! Why,
Thou hast been cheated on with a false beard
And a turned cloak. Faith, would your predecessor,   55
The cutpurse, think you, ha' been so? Out upon thee!
The hurt th' hast done, to let men know their strength,
And that they're able to outdo a devil
Put in a body, will forever be
A scar upon our name. Whom hast thou dealt with,   60
Woman or man, this day, but have outgone thee
Some way, and most have proved the better fiends?
Yet you would be employed! Yes, Hell shall make you
Provincial o' the cheaters, or bawd-ledger°
For this side o' the town! No doubt you'll render   65
A rare account of things. Bane o' your itch
And scratching for employment! I'll ha' brimstone
To allay it sure, and fire to singe your nails off.
But that I would not such a damned dishonour
Stick on our state, as that the devil were hanged,   70
And could not save a body that he took
From Tyburn, but it must come thither again,
You should e'en ride. But up, away with him—°
        Iniquity takes [Pug] on his back
INIQUITY Mount, darling of darkness, my shoulders are broad:
He that carries the fiend is sure of his load.   75
The devil was wont to carry away the evil;
But now the evil out-carries the devil.°
        [*Exeunt*]

5.7

A great noise is heard in Newgate. [Enter Shackles and] the
Keepers, affrighted

[SHACKLES] Oh me!

1 KEEPER   What's this?

2 KEEPER   A piece of Justice Hall°
Is broken down.

3 KEEPER   Faugh! What a steam of brimstone
Is here!

4 KEEPER The prisoner's dead, came in but now!°

SHACKLES Ha? Where?

4 KEEPER   Look here.

1 KEEPER   'Slid, I should know his countenance!°
It is Gil Cutpurse, was hanged out this morning!   5

SHACKLES 'Tis he!

2 KEEPER   The devil, sure, has a hand in this!

3 KEEPER What shall we do?

SHACKLES   Carry the news of it
Unto the sheriffs.

1 KEEPER   And to the Justices.

4 KEEPER This's strange!

3 KEEPER   And savours of the devil strongly!

2 KEEPER I ha' the sulphur of hell-coal i' my nose.   10

1 KEEPER Faugh!

SHACKLES   Carry him in.

1 KEEPER   Away!

2 KEEPER   How rank it is!

[*Exeunt with the body*]

5.8

[*Enter*] *Sir Paul Eitherside, Merecraft, Everill,* [*Lady Tailbush,*
Lady Eitherside], *Trains, Pitfall,* [*Ambler, and*] *Fitzdottrel*
[*lying on a bed*]. *The Justice comes out wondering, and the rest*
informing him.

[SIR PAUL] This was the notablest conspiracy
   That e'er I heard of.

MERECRAFT   Sir, they had giv'n him potions
   That did enamour him on the counterfeit lady—

EVERILL Just to the time o' delivery o' the deed—

MERECRAFT And then the witchcraft 'gan t' appear, for straight   5
   He fell into his fit.

EVERILL   Of rage at first, sir,
   Which since has so increased.

TAILBUSH   Good Sir Paul, see him,
   And punish the impostors.

SIR PAUL   Therefore I come, madam.

EITHERSIDE Let Master Eitherside alone, madam.

SIR PAUL [*to Ambler*]   Do you hear?
   Call in the constable, I will have him by;   10
  He's the King's officer. And some citizens
   Of credit. I'll discharge my conscience clearly.

MERECRAFT Yes, sir, and send for his wife.

EVERILL   And the two sorcerers,
   By any means!
      [*Exit Ambler*]

TAILBUSH   I thought one a true lady,
   I should be sworn. So did you, Eitherside!   15

EITHERSIDE Yes, by that light, would I might ne'er stir else, Tailbush.

TAILBUSH And the other a civil gentleman.

EVERILL   But, madam,
   You know what I told your ladyship.

TAILBUSH   I now see it.
   I was providing of a banquet for 'em,
   After I had done instructing o' the fellow   20
   De-vile, the gentleman's man.

MERECRAFT   Who's found a thief, madam,

And to have robbed your usher, Master Ambler,
This morning.
TAILBUSH   How?
MERECRAFT   I'll tell you more anon.
    [*Fitzdottrel on the bed*] *begins his fit*
FITZDOTTREL Gi' me some garlic, garlic, garlic, garlic!
MERECRAFT Hark the poor gentleman, how he is tormented!   25
FITZDOTTREL My wife is a whore, I'll kiss her no more, and why?
    Mayst not thou be a cuckold as well as I?
    Ha, ha, ha, ha, ha, ha, ha, ha, etc.°
      The Justice interprets all
SIR PAUL That is the devil speaks and laughs in him.
MERECRAFT Do you think so, sir?
SIR PAUL   I discharge my conscience.   30
FITZDOTTREL And is not the devil good company? Yes, wis.
EVERILL How he changes, sir, his voice!
FITZDOTTREL   And a cuckold is—
    Where e'er he put his head, with a wanion,°
    If his horns be forth—the devil's companion!
    Look, look, look, else.
MERECRAFT   How he foams!
EVERILL   And swells!   35
TAILBUSH Oh, me! What's that there rises in his belly?
EITHERSIDE A strange thing! Hold it down!
TRAINS, PITFALL   We cannot, madam.°
SIR PAUL 'Tis too apparent this!
    Enter Wittipol, Manly and Mistress Fitzdottrel
FITZDOTTREL   Wittipol, Wittipol!
WITTIPOL How now, what play ha' we here?
MANLY   What fine new matters?
WITTIPOL *The Coxcomb and the Coverlet.*
MERECRAFT   Oh, strange impudence!°   40
    That these should come to face their sin!
EVERILL   And outface°
    Justice! They are the parties, sir.
SIR PAUL   Say nothing.
MERECRAFT Did you mark, sir, upon their coming in,
    How he called Wittipol?
EVERILL   And never saw 'em.
SIR PAUL I warrant you did I; let 'em play a while.   45
FITZDOTTREL Buzz, buzz, buzz, buzz.

TAILBUSH   'Las, poor gentleman!
    How he is tortured!
MISTRESS FITZDOTTREL Fie, Master Fitzdottrel!
    What do you mean to counterfeit thus?
            [*Mistress Fitzdottrel*] *goes to him*
FITZDOTTREL   Oh, Oh,
    She comes with a needle, and thrusts it in,
    She pulls out that, and she puts in a pin,   50
    And now, and now, I do not know how, nor where,
    But she pricks me here, and she pricks me there! Oh, Oh—
SIR PAUL Woman, forbear.
WITTIPOL   What, sir?
SIR PAUL   A practice foul
    For one so fair.
WITTIPOL   Hath this then credit with you?
MANLY Do you believe in 't?
SIR PAUL   Gentlemen, I'll discharge   55
    My conscience. 'Tis a clear conspiracy!
    A dark and devilish practice! I detest it.
WITTIPOL The Justice, sure, will prove the merrier man!
MANLY This is most strange, sir!
SIR PAUL   Come not to confront
    Authority with impudence. I tell you,   60
    I do detest it.
            [*Enter Ambler, with Sledge and Gilthead*]
                    Here comes the King's constable,
    And with him a right worshipful commoner—
    My good friend, Master Gilthead! I am glad
    I can, before such witnesses, profess
    My conscience, and my detestation of it.   65
    Horrible! Most unnatural! Abominable!
            [*Merecraft and Everill*] *whisper* [*to Fitzdottrel,*] *and give him*
            soap to act with
EVERILL You do not tumble enough.
MERECRAFT   Wallow! Gnash!
TAILBUSH Oh, how he is vexed!
SIR PAUL   'Tis too manifest.
EVERILL Give him more soap to foam with—now lie still.
MERECRAFT And act a little.
TAILBUSH   What does he now, sir?
SIR PAUL   Show   70

The taking of tobacco, with which the devil
Is so delighted.
FITZDOTTREL   Hum!
SIR PAUL   And calls for hum.°
You takers of strong waters and tobacco,
Mark this.
FITZDOTTREL Yellow, yellow, yellow, yellow, etc.
SIR PAUL That's starch! The devil's idol of that colour.   75
He ratifies it with clapping of his hands.
The proofs are pregnant.
GILTHEAD   How the devil can act!
SIR PAUL He is the master of players, Master Gilthead,°
And poets, too—you heard him talk in rhyme!
I had forgot to observe it to you, erewhile.   80
TAILBUSH See, he spits fire!
SIR PAUL   Oh no, he plays at figgum,°
The devil is the author of wicked figgum—
MANLY Why speak you not unto him?
WITTIPOL   If I had
All innocence of man to be endangered,
And he could save or ruin it, I'd not breathe   85
A syllable in request to such a fool
He makes himself.
FITZDOTTREL   Oh they whisper, whisper, whisper!
We shall have more, of devils a score,
To come to dinner in me the sinner.
EITHERSIDE Alas, poor gentleman!
SIR PAUL   Put 'em asunder.   90
Keep 'em one from the other.
MANLY   Are you frantic, sir,
Or what grave dotage moves you to take part
With so much villainy? We are not afraid
Either of law or trial; let us be
Examined what our ends were, what the means   95
To work by, and possibility of those means.
Do not conclude against us ere you hear us.
SIR PAUL I will not hear you, yet I will conclude
Out of the circumstances.
MANLY   Will you so, sir?°
SIR PAUL Yes, they are palpable—
MANLY   Not as your folly.   100

SIR PAUL I will discharge my conscience, and do all
　　To the meridian of justice.
GILTHEAD　　　　　　　　You do well, sir.°
FITZDOTTREL Provide me to eat, three or four dishes o' good
　　meat;
　　I'll feast them and their trains: a Justice' head and brains°
　　Shall be the first.
SIR PAUL　　　　　　The devil loves not justice,　　　　　　105
　　There you may see.
FITZDOTTREL　　　　A spare-rib o' my wife,
　　And a whore's purt'nance! A gilthead whole.°
SIR PAUL Be not you troubled, sir, the devil speaks it.
FITZDOTTREL Yes, wusse, knight, shite, Paul, jowl, owl, foul, trull,
　　bowl.°
SIR PAUL Crambe, another of the devil's games!　　　　　　110
MERECRAFT [aside] Speak, sir, some Greek if you can. Is not the
　　Justice°
　　A solemn gamester?
EVERILL [aside]　　　　Peace.
FITZDOTTREL　　　　　　Oimoi, kakodaimon,
　　Kai triskakodaimon, kai tetrakis, kai pentakis,
　　Kai dodekakis, kai muriakis.
SIR PAUL　　　　　　　He curses°
　　In Greek, I think.
EVERILL [aside]　　Your Spanish that I taught you.　　　　　　115
FITZDOTTREL Quebremos el ojo de burlas.
EVERILL　　　　　　　　How? Your rest—°
　　Let's break his neck in jest, the devil says.
FITZDOTTREL Di grazia, signor mio se havete denari fatamene
　　parte.°
MERECRAFT What, would the devil borrow money?
FITZDOTTREL　　　　　　　　　Oui,
　　Oui, monsieur, un pauvre diable! Diabletin!°　　　　　　120
SIR PAUL It is the devil, by his several languages.
　　　　Enter [Shackles,] the Keeper of Newgate
SHACKLES Where's Sir Paul Eitherside?
SIR PAUL　　　　　　　Here, what's the matter?
SHACKLES Oh! Such an accident fallen out at Newgate, sir—
　　A great piece of the prison is rent down!°
　　The devil has been there, sir, in the body　　　　　　125
　　Of the young cutpurse was hanged out this morning,

But in new clothes, sir; everyone of us know him.
These things were found in his pocket.

AMBLER   Those are mine, sir.°

SHACKLES I think he was committed on your charge, sir,
For a new felony.

AMBLER   Yes.

SHACKLES   He's gone, sir, now,   130
And left us the dead body. But withal, sir,°
Such an infernal stink and steam behind,
You cannot see St Pulchre's steeple yet.°
They smell 't as far as Ware as the wind lies°
By this time, sure.

FITZDOTTREL   Is this upon your credit, friend?   135

SHACKLES Sir, you may see, and satisfy yourself.

           Fitzdottrel leaves counterfeiting

FITZDOTTREL Nay then, 'tis time to leave off counterfeiting.
Sir, I am not bewitched, nor have a devil,
No more than you. I do defy him, I,
And did abuse you. These two gentlemen   140
Put me upon it. (I have faith against him.)
They taught me all my tricks. I will tell truth
And shame the fiend. See, here, sir, are my bellows,°
And my false belly, and my mouse, and all
That should ha' come forth!

MANLY   Sir, are not you ashamed   145
Now of your solemn, serious vanity?

SIR PAUL I will make honourable amends to truth.

FITZDOTTREL And so will I. But these are cozeners still,
And ha' my land, as plotters with my wife—
Who, though she be not a witch, is worse: a whore.   150

MANLY Sir, you belie her. She is chaste and virtuous,
And we are honest. I do know no glory
A man should hope by venting his own follies,
But you'll still be an ass, in spite of providence.
[*To Sir Paul*] Please you go in, sir, and hear truths, then judge 'em,   155
And make amends for your late rashness, when
You shall but hear the pains and care was taken
To save this fool from ruin—his Grace of Drowned-land.

FITZDOTTREL My land is drowned indeed—

SIR PAUL   Peace.

MANLY   And how much

His modest, and too worthy wife hath suffered   160
By misconstruction from him, you will blush,
First, for your own belief, more for his actions.
His land is his, and never, by my friend
Or by myself, meant to another use
But for her succours, who hath equal right.   165
If any other had worse counsels in 't
(I know I speak to those can apprehend me)°
Let 'em repent 'em, and be not detected.
It is not manly to take joy or pride
In human errors. We do all ill things: 170
They do 'em worst that love 'em, and dwell there
Till the plague comes. The few that have the seeds
Of goodness left will sooner make their way
To a true life by shame, than punishment.

    [*Exeunt*]

The Epilogue

Thus the projector here is overthrown.
But I have now a project of mine own,
If it may pass: that no man would invite
The poet from us to sup forth tonight
If the play please. If it displeasant be,   5
We do presume that no man will—nor we.

THE NEW INN
Or, The Light Heart
A Comedy

THE DEDICATION TO THE READER

If thou be such, I make thee my patron and dedicate the piece to thee. If not so much, would I had been at the charge° of thy better literature. Howsoever, if thou canst but spell and join my sense, there is more hope of thee than of a hundred fastidious impertinents who were there present the first day, yet never made piece of their prospect° the 5 right way. 'What did they come for, then?' thou wilt ask me. I will as punctually answer, to see and to be seen. To make a general muster of themselves in their clothes of credit, and possess the stage against the play.° To dislike all, but mark nothing. And by their confidence of rising between the acts in oblique lines,° make affidavit to the whole 10 house of their not understanding one scene. Armed with this prejudice,° as° the stage furniture or arras cloths, they were there, as spectators, away. For the faces in the hangings and they beheld alike. So I wish they may do ever. And do trust myself and my book rather to thy rustic candour, than all the pomp of their pride, and solemn ignorance 15 to boot. Fare thee well, and fall to. Read.

BEN JONSON.

But first, the argument.

[Editor's Note: *There are some unexpected twists in the fifth act, and readers unfamiliar with the plot of* The New Inn *are advised not to read the argument and character list before reading the play.*]

THE ARGUMENT

The Lord Frampul, a noble gentleman, well educated and bred a scholar in Oxford, was married young to a virtuous gentlewoman, Sylly's daughter of the south,° whose worth, though he truly enjoyed, he never could rightly value, but as many green husbands, given over to their extravagant° delights and some peccant humours of their own, 5 occasioned in his over-loving wife so deep a melancholy by his leaving her in the time of her lying-in of her second daughter, she having brought him only two daughters, Frances and Laetitia, and (out of her

hurt fancy), interpreting that to be a cause of her husband's coldness
in affection—her not being blessed with a son—took a resolution with   10
herself, after her month's time and thanksgiving ritely in the church,°
to quit her home with a vow never to return, till by reducing° her lord
she could bring a wished happiness to the family.

He, in the meantime, returning and hearing of this departure of his
lady, began, though over-late, to resent° the injury he had done her,   15
and out of his cock-brained resolution entered into as solemn a quest
of her. Since when, neither of them had been heard of. But the eldest
daughter, Frances, by the title of Lady Frampul, enjoyed the state, her
sister being lost young, and is the sole relict of the family.

Act 1   20

Here begins our comedy.

This lady, being a brave, bountiful lady, and enjoying this free and
plentiful estate, hath an ambitious disposition to be esteemed the mistress of many servants,° but loves none. And hearing of a famous new
inn that is kept by a merry host called Goodstock, in Barnet,° invites   25
some lordsand gentlemen to wait on her thither, as well to see the
fashions of the place, as to make themselves merry with the accidents
on the by. It happens there is a melancholic gentleman, one Master
Lovel, hath been lodged there some days before in the inn, who
(unwilling to be seen) is surprised by the lady and invited by Pru-   30
dence, the lady's chambermaid, who is elected governess of the sports
in the inn for that day, and installed their sovereign. Lovel is persuaded by the host, and yields to the lady's invitation, which concludes
the first Act. Having revealed his quality before to the host.

[Act 2]   35

In the second Act.

Prudence and her lady express their anger conceived at the tailor
who had promised to make Prudence a new suit and bring it home, on
the eve, against this day.° But, he failing of his word, the lady had
commanded a standard of her own best apparel to be brought down   40
and Prudence is so fitted. The lady, being put in mind that she is there
alone without other company of women, borrows, by the advice of

Pru, the host's son of the house, whom they dress with the host's
consent like a lady, and send out the coachman with the empty coach
as for a kinswoman of her ladyship's, Mistress Laetitia Sylly, to bear   45
her company. Who, attended with his nurse, an old charwoman in the
inn, dressed oddly° by the host's counsel, is believed to be a lady of
quality, and so received, entertained, and love made to her° by the
young Lord Beaufort, etc. In the meantime, the fly of the inn° is
discovered to Colonel Glorious, with the militia of the house below the   50
stairs, in the drawer, tapster, chamberlain, and ostler, inferior officers,
with the coachman Trundle, Ferret, etc. And the preparation is made
to the lady's design upon Lovel, his upon her, and the sovereign's
upon both.

[Act 3]   55

Here begins, at the third Act, the epitasis or business of the play.

Lovel, by the dexterity and wit of the sovereign of the sports,
Prudence, having two hours assigned him of free colloquy and love-
making to his mistress—one after dinner, the other after supper—the
court being set, is demanded by the Lady Frampul what love is, as   60
doubting if there were any such power or no. To whom he first by
definition, and after by argument answers, proving, and describing the
effects of love so vively, as she, who had derided the name of love
before, hearing his discourse, is now so taken both with the man and
his matter as she confesseth herself enamoured of him and, but for the   65
ambition she hath to enjoy the other hour, had presently° declared
herself, which gives both him and the spectators occasion to think she
yet dissembles, notwithstanding the payment of her kiss, which he
celebrates. And the court dissolves upon a news brought of a new lady,
a newer coach, and a new coachman called Barnaby.   70

Act 4

The house being put into a noise with the rumour of this new lady, and
there being drinking below in the court,° the colonel, Sir Glorious,
with Bat° Burst, a broken° citizen, and Hodge Huffle, his champion,
she falls into their hands, and being attended but with one footman, is   75
uncivilly entreated° by them and a quarrel commenced, but is rescued

by the valour of Lovel; which beheld by the Lady Frampul from the
window, she is invited up for safety, where coming and conducted by
the host, her gown is first discovered to be the same with the whole
suit which was bespoken for Pru, and she herself, upon examination,   80
found to be Pinnacia Stuff,° the tailor's wife, who was wont to be
preoccupied in° all his customer's best clothes by the footman her
husband. They are both condemned and censured, she stripped like a
doxy and sent home afoot. In the interim the second hour goes on, and
the question, at suit of the Lady Frampul, is changed from love to   85
valour; which ended, he receives his second kiss, and by the rigour of
the sovereign falls into a fit of melancholy worse or more desperate
than the first.

[Act 5]

The fifth and last act is the catastrophe, or knitting up of all, where Fly   90
brings word to the host of the Lord Beaufort's being married privately
in the new stable to the supposed lady, his son, which the host receives
as an omen of mirth; but complains that Lovel is gone to bed melancholic, when Prudence appears dressed in the new suit, applauded by
her lady, and employed to retrieve Lovel. The host encounters them   95
with this relation of Lord Beaufort's marriage, which is seconded by
the Lord Latimer and all the servants of the house. In this while, Lord
Beaufort comes in and professes it, calls for his bed and bride-bowl to
be made ready, the host forbids both, shows whom he hath married,
and discovers him to be his son, a boy. The lord bridegroom con-   100
founded, the nurse enters like a frantic bedlam, cries out on Fly, says
she is undone in her daughter, who is confessed to be the Lord Frampul's child, sister to the other lady, the host to be their father, she his
wife. He, finding his children, bestows them one on Lovel, the other
on the Lord Beaufort, the inn upon Fly who had been a gypsy with   105
him, offers a portion° with Prudence for her wit, which is refused, and
she taken by the Lord Latimer to wife for the crown of her virtue and
goodness. And all are contented.

THE PERSONS OF THE PLAY

With some short characterism of the chief actors.

GOODSTOCK. The HOST (played well), alias, the LORD FRAMPUL.°
He pretends to be a gentleman and a scholar neglected by the times,
turns host and keeps an inn, the sign of the Light Heart in Barnet: 5
is supposed to have one only son but is found to have none, but two
daughters, Frances and Laetitia, who was lost young, etc.

LOVEL. A complete° gentleman, a soldier and a scholar, is a melancholy guest in the inn; first quarrelled, after much honoured and
beloved by the host. He is known to have been page to the old Lord   10
Beaufort, followed him in the French wars, after, a companion of his
studies, and left guardian to his son. He is assisted in his love to the
Lady Frampul by the host and the chambermaid, Prudence. He was
one that acted well, too.

FERRET. Who is also called STOAT and VERMIN, is Lovel's servant; a   15
fellow of a quick, nimble wit, knows the manners and affections° of
people, and can make profitable and timely discoveries of them.

FRANK. Supposed a boy and the host's son, borrowed to be dressed for
a lady, and set up as a stale° by Prudence to catch Beaufort or
Latimer, proves to be LAETITIA, sister to Frances, and Lord Fram-   20
pul's younger daughter, stolen by a beggar-woman,° shorn, put into
boy's apparel, sold to the host, and brought up by him as his son.

NURSE. A poor charwoman in the inn, with one eye, that tends the
boy, is thought the Irish beggar that sold him, but is truly the LADY
FRAMPUL, who left her home melancholic and jealous° that her   25
lord loved her not because she brought him none but daughters, and
lives unknown to her husband, as he to her.

FRANCES. Supposed the LADY FRAMPUL, being reputed his sole
daughter and heir, the barony descending upon her, is a lady of
great fortunes and beauty, but fantastical;° thinks nothing a felicity,   30
but to have a multitude of servants and be called mistress by them,
comes to the inn to be merry with a chambermaid only, and her
servants her guests, etc.

PRUDENCE. The chambermaid, is elected sovereign of the sports in
the inn, governs all, commands, and so orders as the Lord Latimer   35

is exceedingly taken with her, and takes her to his wife in
conclusion.

LORD LATIMER and LORD BEAUFORT are a pair of young lords,
servants and guests to the Lady Frampul, but as Latimer falls
enamoured of Prudence, so doth Beaufort on the boy, the host's
son, set up for Laetitia, the younger sister, which she proves to be,
indeed.

SIR GLORIOUS TIPTO.° A knight and colonel, hath the luck to think
well of himself, without a rival, talks gloriously of anything, but very
seldom is in the right. He is the lady's guest, and her servant, too,
but this day utterly neglects his service, or that him.° For he is so
enamoured on the fly of the inn, and the militia below stairs, with
Hodge Huffle and Bat Burst, guests that come in, and Trundle,
Barnaby, etc. as no other society relisheth with him.

FLY. Is the parasite of the inn, visitor-general of the house,° one that
had been a strolling gypsy, but now is reclaimed to be inflamer of
the reckonings.°

PIERCE. The drawer, knighted by the colonel, styled SIR PIERCE and
young ANON,° one of the chief of the infantry.

JORDAN.° The chamberlain, another of the militia and an officer,
commands the tertia° of the beds.

JUG. The tapster, a thoroughfare of news.

PECK.° The ostler.

BAT BURST. A broken citizen, an in-and-in man.°

HODGE HUFFLE.° A cheater, his champion.

NICK STUFF. The lady's tailor.

PINNACIA STUFF. His wife.

TRUNDLE. A coachman.

BARNABY. A hired coachman.

[PROLOGUE]

[EPILOGUE]

STAGGERS. The smith; TREE. The saddler—only talked on.°

40

45

50

55

60

65

The Prologue

You are welcome, welcome all, to the new inn;
Though the old house, we hope our cheer will win°
Your acceptation. We ha' the same cook
Still, and the fat, who says you sha' not look°
Long for your bill of fare, but every dish   5
Be served in, i' the time, and to your wish:
If anything be set to a wrong taste,
'Tis not the meat there, but the mouth's displaced;°
Remove but that sick palate, all is well.
For this the secure dresser bad me tell,°   10
Nothing more hurts just meetings than a crowd;
Or, when the expectation's grown too loud,°
That the nice stomach would ha' this or that,°
And being asked or urged, it knows not what;
When sharp or sweet have been too much a feast,   15
And both outlived the palate of the guest.
Beware to bring such appetites to the stage,
They do confess a weak, sick, queasy age,
And a shrewd grudging, too, of ignorance,°
When clothes and faces 'bove the men advance.   20
Hear for your health then. But at any hand,
Before you judge, vouchsafe to understand;
Concoct, digest; if then it do not hit,
Some are in a consumption of wit
Deep, he dares say—he will not think that all—   25
For hectics are not epidemical.°

1.1

[Enter] Host [and] Ferret

[HOST] I am not pleased, indeed, you are i' the right;
Nor is my house pleased, if my sign could speak,
The sign o' the Light Heart. There you may read it;°
So may your master, too, if he look on 't.
A heart weighed with a feather, and outweighed, too:°   5
A brain-child o' mine own, and I am proud on 't.
And if his worship think here to be melancholy
In spite of me or my wit, he is deceived;
I will maintain the rebus 'gainst all humours,
And all complexions i' the body of man,°   10
That's my word, or i' the isle of Britain!
FERRET You have reason, good mine host.
HOST Sir, I have rhyme, too:
Whether it be by chance or art,
A heavy purse makes a light heart.°   15
There 'tis expressed—first, by a purse of gold,
'A heavy purse', and then two turtles, 'makes',°
A heart with a light stuck in 't, 'a light heart'!
Old Abbot Islip could not invent better,
Or Prior Bolton with his 'bolt' and 'ton'.°   20
I am an innkeeper, and know my grounds°
And study 'em; brain o' man, I study 'em.
I must ha' jovial guests to drive my ploughs,
And whistling boys to bring my harvest home,
Or I shall hear no flails thwack. Here your master°   25
And you ha' been this fortnight, drawing fleas
Out of my mats, and pounding 'em in cages°
Cut out of cards, and those roped round with packthread
Drawn thorough bird-lime. A fine subtlety!°
Or poring through a multiplying glass   30
Upon a captived crab-louse, or a cheese-mite,
To be dissected as the sports of nature
With a neat Spanish needle. Speculations°
That do become the age, I do confess!
As measuring an ant's eggs with the silkworm's   35

By a fantastic instrument of thread,
Shall give you their just difference to a hair.°
Or else recovering o' dead flies with crumbs—
Another quaint conclusion i' the physics—°
Which I ha' seen you busy at through the keyhole,   40
But never had the fate to see a fly
    Enter Lovel
Alive i' your cups, or once heard, 'Drink, mine host',
Or such a cheerful chirping charm come from you.

1.2

[LOVEL] What's that? What's that?
FERRET   A buzzing of mine host
  About a fly! A murmur that he has.
HOST Sir, I am telling your stoat here, Monsieur Ferret—
  For that I hear's his name—and dare tell you, sir,
  If you have a mind to be melancholy and musty,   5
  There's Footman's Inn at the town's end, the stocks,°
  Or Carrier's Place at sign o' the Broken Wain,°
  Mansions of state! Take up your harbour there;
  There are both flies and fleas, and all variety
  Of vermin for inspection or dissection.   10
LOVEL We ha' set our rest up here, sir, i' your Heart.
HOST Sir, set your heart at rest, you shall not do it,
  Unless you can be jovial. Brain o' man,
  Be jovial first, and drink, and dance, and drink.
  Your lodging here, and wi' your daily dumps,   15
  Is a mere libel 'gain' my house and me;°
  And then, your scandalous commons—
LOVEL   How, mine host?°
HOST Sir, they do scandal me upo' the road here.
  A poor quotidian rack o' mutton, roasted
  Dry to be grated! And that driven down   20
  With beer and buttermilk mingled together,
  Or clarified whey instead of claret!
  It is against my freehold, my inheritance,
  My *magna charta, cor laetificat,*°
  To drink such balderdash, or bonny-clabber!   25

Gi' me good wine, or catholic or christian:
Wine is the word that glads the heart of man,
And mine's the house of wine. 'Sack', says my bush,°
'Be merry, and drink sherry': that's my poesy!°
For I shall never joy i' my Light Heart,   30
So long as I conceive a sullen guest,
Or anything that's earthy.

LOVEL   Humorous host.°

HOST I care not if I be.

LOVEL   But airy also.°
Not to defraud you of your rights, or trench
Upo' your privileges or great charter°   35
(For those are every ostler's language now),
Say you were born beneath those smiling stars
Have made you lord and owner of the Heart,
Of the Light Heart in Barnet, suffer us
Who are more saturnine t' enjoy the shade   40
Of your round roof yet.

HOST   Sir, I keep no shades°
Nor shelters, I, for either owls or reremice.

1.3

[FERRET] He'll make you a bird of night, sir.
          Enter Frank

HOST   Bless you, child.°
     [*To Lovel and Ferret*] You'll make yourselves such.
          The Host speaks to his child o' the by°

LOVEL   That your son, mine
     host?

HOST He's all the sons I have, sir.

LOVEL   Pretty boy!
     Goes he to school?

FERRET   Oh Lord, sir, he prates Latin
     An 'twere a parrot or a play-boy.

LOVEL   Thou—°   5
     Commend'st him fitly.

FERRET   To the pitch he flies, sir.°
     He'll tell you what is Latin for a looking-glass,

A beard-brush, rubber, or quick warming-pan.°

LOVEL What's that?

FERRET   A wench, i' the inn-phrase, is all these:

A looking-glass in her eye,   10

A beard-brush with her lips,

A rubber with her hand,

And a warming-pan with her hips.

HOST This in your scurril dialect. But my inn

Knows no such language.   That's because, mine host,   15

FERRET

You do profess the teaching him yourself.

HOST Sir, I do teach him somewhat. By degrees

And with a funnel, I make shift to fill

The narrow vessel; he is but yet a bottle.

LOVEL Oh let him lose no time, though.

HOST   Sir, he does not.   20

LOVEL And less his manners.

HOST   I provide for those, too.

Come hither, Frank, speak to the gentleman

In Latin. He is melancholy; say,

'I long to see him merry, and so would treat him.'

FRANK *Subtristis visu'es esse aliquantulum patri,*   25

Qui te laute excipere, atque etiam tractare gestit.

LOVEL   *Pulchrè.*°

HOST Tell him, 'I fear it bodes us some ill luck,

His too reservedness.'

FRANK   *Veretur pater,*

Ne quid nobis mali ominis apportet iste

Nimis praeclusus vultus.

LOVEL   *Bellè.* A fine child!°   30

You wou' not part with him, mine host?

HOST   Who told you

I would not?

LOVEL   I but ask you.

HOST   And I answer.

To whom? For what?

LOVEL   To me, to be my page.

HOST I know no mischief yet the child hath done

To deserve such a destiny.

LOVEL   Why?

HOST   Go down, boy,   35

342

And get your breakfast.
　　[*Exeunt Frank and Ferret*]
　　　　　　　　　Trust me, I had rather
Take a fair halter, wash my hands, and hang him
Myself, make a clean riddance of him, than—
LOVEL   What?
HOST Than damn him to that desperate course of life.
LOVEL Call you that desperate, which by a line   40
　　Of institution from our ancestors°
　　Hath been derived down to us, and received
　　In a succession for the noblest way
　　Of breeding up our youth in letters, arms,
　　Fair mien, discourses, civil exercise,   45
　　And all the blazon of a gentleman?
　　Where can he learn to vault, to ride, to fence,
　　To move his body gracefuller? To speak
　　His language purer? Or to tune his mind
　　Or manners more to the harmony of Nature   50
　　Than in these nurseries of nobility—
HOST Ay, that was when the nursery's self was noble,
　　And only virtue made it, not the market,
　　That titles were not vented at the drum
　　Or common outcry; goodness gave the greatness,°   55
　　And greatness worship: every house became
　　An academy of honour, and those parts—
　　We see departed in the practice now,
　　Quite from the institution.
LOVEL   Why do you say so?
　　Or think so enviously? Do they not still   60
　　Learn there the centaurs' skill, the art of Thrace,°
　　To ride? Or Pollux' mystery, to fence?°
　　The Pyrrhic gestures, both to dance and spring°
　　In armour, to be active for the wars?
　　To study figures, numbers, and proportions,°   65
　　May yield 'em great in counsels, and the arts
　　Grave Nestor and the wise Ulysses practised?°
　　To make their English sweet upon their tongue,
　　As rev'rend Chaucer says?
HOST   Sir, you mistake:°
　　To play Sir Pandarus, my copy hath it,   70
　　And carry messages to Madam Cressid.°

343

Instead of backing the brave steed o' mornings,
To mount the chambermaid; and for a leap
O' the vaulting horse, to ply the vaulting house;°
For exercise of arms, a bale of dice°   75
Or two or three packs of cards to show the cheat
And nimbleness of hand; mistake a cloak
From my lord's back and pawn it; ease his pockets
Of a superfluous watch, or geld a jewel
Of an odd stone or so; twinge three or four buttons°   80
From off my lady's gown. These are the arts,
Or seven liberal deadly sciences
Of pagery, or rather paganism,°
As the tides run. To which, if he apply him,°
He may perhaps take a degree at Tyburn°   85
A year the earlier; come to read a lecture
Upon Aquinas at St Thomas a Waterings,°
And so go forth a laureate in hemp circle.°

LOVEL You're tart, mine host, and talk above your seasoning,   •
    O'er what you seem: it should not come, methinks,   90
    Under your cap, this vein of salt and sharpness,°
    These strikings upon learning now and then.
    How long have you (if your dull guest may ask it)
    Drove this quick trade of keeping the Light Heart,°
    Your mansion, palace here, or hostelry?   95

HOST Troth, I was born to somewhat, sir, above it.

LOVEL I easily suspect that. Mine host, your name?

HOST They call me Goodstock.

LOVEL   Sir, and you confess it,
    Both i' your language, treaty, and your bearing.

HOST Yet all, sir, are not sons o' the white hen,°   100
    Nor can we, as the songster says, come all
    To be wrapped soft and warm in Fortune's smock
    When she is pleased to trick or trump mankind;
    Some may be coats, as in the cards, but then°
    Some must be knaves, some varlets, bawds, and ostlers,   105
    As aces, deuces, cards o' ten, to face it
    Out i' the game which all the world is.

LOVEL   But°
    It being i' your freewill (as 'twas), to choose
    What parts you would sustain, methinks a man
    Of your sagacity and clear nostril should°   110

344

Have made another choice than of a place
So sordid as the keeping of an inn,
Where every jovial tinker, for his chink,
May cry, 'Mine host, to crambe! Give us drink!
And do not slink, but skink, or else you stink.'   115
Rogue, bawd, and cheater call you by the surnames
And known synonyma of your profession.°
HOST But if I be no such, who then's the rogue,
In understanding, sir, I mean? Who errs?
Who tinkleth then, or personates Tom Tinker?°   120
Your weasel here may tell you I talk bawdy
And teach my boy it, and you may believe him;
But sir, at your own peril if I do not,
And at his, too, if he do lie and affirm it.
No slander strikes, less hurts, the innocent.   125
If I be honest, and that all the cheat°
Be of myself in keeping this Light Heart,
Where I imagine all the world's a play;
The state and men's affairs, all passages
Of life to spring new scenes, come in, go out,   130
And shift and vanish; and if I have got
A seat to sit at ease here i' mine inn
To see the comedy, and laugh and chuck°
At the variety and throng of humours
And dispositions that come justling in   135
And out still, as they one drove hence another—°
Why, will you envy me my happiness
Because you are sad and lumpish; carry a loadstone
I' your pocket to hang knives on, or jet rings
T'entice light straws to leap at 'em; are not taken°   140
With the alacrities of an host? 'Tis more,
And justlier, sir, my wonder, why you took
My house up, Fiddlers' Hall, the seat of noise
And mirth, an inn here, to be drowsy in,
And lodge your lethargy in the Light Heart,   145
As if some cloud from court had been your harbinger,
Or Cheapside debtbooks, or some mistress charge,°
Seeing your love grow corpulent, gi' it a diet
By absence, some such mouldy passion!
LOVEL [aside] 'Tis guessed unhappily.
        [Enter Ferret]

345

FERRET   Mine host, you're called.   150
HOST I come, boys.
        [*Exit Host*]
LOVEL   Ferret, have not you been ploughing
    With this mad ox, mine host? Nor he with you?°
FERRET For what, sir?
LOVEL   Why, to find my riddle out.
FERRET I hope you do believe, sir, I can find
    Other discourse to be at than my master   155
    With hosts and ostlers.
LOVEL   If you can, 'tis well.
    Go down and see who they are come in, what guests,
    And bring me word.
        [*Exit Ferret*]

1.4

LOVEL   O love, what passion art thou!
    So tyrannous and treacherous! First, t' enslave,
    And then betray all that in truth do serve thee,
    That not the wisest nor the wariest creature
    Can more dissemble thee than he can bear   5
    Hot burning coals in his bare palm or bosom,
    And less conceal or hide thee, than a flash
    Of inflamed powder, whose whole light doth lay it
    Open to all discovery, even of those
    Who have but half an eye, and less of nose!   10
    An host to find me! Who is commonly
    The log, a little o' this side the signpost!
    Or at the best, some round grown thing; a jug,
    Faced with a beard, that fills out to the guests,°
    And takes in fro' the fragments o' their jests!   15
    But I may wrong this out of sullenness,°
    Or my mistaking humour. Pray thee, fant'sy,°
    Be laid again. And, gentle melancholy,
    Do not oppress me. I will be as silent
    As the tame lover should be, and as foolish.°   20

1.5

[*Enter*] *Host*

[HOST] My guest, my guest, be jovial, I beseech thee.
    I have fresh golden guests, guests o' the game:°
    Three coachful! Lords and ladies, new come in.
    And I will cry them to thee, and thee to them,°
    So I can spring a smile but i' this brow,   5
    That like the rugged Roman alderman,
    Old master Gross, surnamed Agelastos,
    Was never seen to laugh, but at an ass.°
    Enter Ferret

FERRET Sir, here's the Lady Frampul.

LOVEL   How!

FERRET   And her train:
    Lord Beaufort and Lord Latimer, the Colonel   10
    Tipto, with Mistress Pru, the chambermaid,°
    Trundle, the coachman—

LOVEL   Stop! Discharge the house°
    And get my horses ready; bid the groom
    Bring 'em to the back gate.
    [*Exit Ferret*]

HOST   What mean you, sir?

LOVEL To take fair leave, mine host.

HOST   I hope, my guest,   15
    Though I have talked somewhat above my share,
    At large, and been i' the altitudes, th' extravagants,
    Neither myself nor any of mine have gi'n you
    The cause to quit my house thus on the sudden.

LOVEL No, I affirm it, on my faith. Excuse me   20
    From such a rudeness; I was now beginning
    To taste and love you, and am heartily sorry
    Any occasion should be so compelling
    To urge my abrupt departure thus. But—
    Necessity's a tyrant, and commands it.   25

HOST She shall command me first to fire my bush,
    Then break up house; or if that will not serve,
    To break with all the world; turn country bankrupt
    I' mine own town upo' the market-day,
    And be protested for my butter and eggs°   30

To the last bodge of oats and bottle of hay;
Ere you shall leave me, I will break my Heart:
Coach and coach-horses, lords and ladies, pack!
All my fresh guests shall stink! I'll pull my sign down,
Convert mine inn to an almshouse or a spital   35
For lazars or switch-sellers! Turn it to
An academy o' rogues! Or gi' it away
For a free school to breed up beggars in,
And send 'em to the canting universities,°
Before you leave me.

LOVEL   Troth, and I confess   40
I am loath, mine host, to leave you: your expressions
Both take and hold me. But in case I stay,
I must enjoin you and your whole family°
To privacy, and to conceal me. For
The secret is I would not willingly   45
See or be seen to any of this ging,
Especially the lady.

HOST   Brain o' man,
What monster is she, or cockatrice in velvet,
That kills thus?

LOVEL   Oh good words, mine host. She is
A noble lady, great in blood and fortune;   50
Fair, and a wit! But of so bent a fant'sy°
As she thinks nought a happiness but to have
A multitude of servants. And to get them,
Though she be very honest, yet she ventures
Upon these precipices that would make her°   55
Not seem so to some prying, narrow natures.
We call her, sir, the Lady Frances Frampul,
Daughter and heir to the Lord Frampul.

HOST   Who?
He that did live in Oxford, first, a student,
And after married with the daughter of—

LOVEL   Sylly.   60

HOST Right; of whom the tale went to turn puppet-master.

LOVEL And travel with young Goose, the motion-man.°

HOST And lie and live with the gypsies half a year
Together, from his wife.

LOVEL   The very same:
The mad Lord Frampul! And this same is his daughter,   65

348

But as cock-brained as e'er the father was.
There were two of 'em, Frances and Laetitia,
But Laetice was lost young, and, as the rumour
Flew then, the mother upon it lost herself.°
A fond, weak woman, went away in a melancholy;°   70
Because she brought him none but girls, she thought
Her husband loved her not. And he, as foolish,
Too late resenting the cause given, went after
In quest of her, and was not heard of since.
HOST   A strange division of a family!   75
LOVEL   And scattered, as i' the great confusion.°
HOST   But yet the lady, th' heir, enjoys the land.
LOVEL   And takes all lordly ways how to consume it
    As nobly as she can; if clothes, and feasting,
    And the authorized means of riot will do it.°   80
        Enter Ferret
HOST   She shows her extract, and I honour her for it.

1.6

[FERRET]   Your horses, sir, are ready, and the house
    Dis—
LOVEL   Pleased, thou think'st?
FERRET   I cannot tell; discharged
    I am sure it is.
LOVEL   Charge it again, good Ferret,
    And make unready the horses: thou knowst how.
    Chalk, and renew the rondels. I am now°   5
    Resolved to stay.
FERRET   I easily thought so,
    When you should hear what's purposed.
LOVEL   What?
FERRET   To throw
    The house out o' the window!
HOST   Brain o' man,°
    I shall ha' the worst o' that! Will they not throw
    My household stuff out first? Cushions and carpets,   10
    Chairs, stools, and bedding? Is not their sport my ruin?
LOVEL   Fear not, mine host, I am not o' the fellowship.

FERRET I cannot see, sir, how you will avoid it:
  They know already, all, you are i' the house.
LOVEL Who know?
FERRET   The lords: they have seen me, and inquired it.   15
LOVEL Why were you seen?
FERRET   Because, indeed, I had
  No med'cine, sir, to go invisible;
  No fern-seed in my pocket, nor an opal
  Wrapped in a bayleaf i' my left fist°
  To charm their eyes with.
HOST   He does give you reasons   20
  As round as Gyges' ring; which, say the ancients,°
  Was a hoop-ring: and that is, round as a hoop!°
LOVEL You will ha' your rebus still, mine host.
HOST   I must.
FERRET My lady, too, looked out o' the window and called me.
    [*Enter Prudence*]
  And see where Secretary Pru comes from her,°   25
  Employed upon some embassy unto you—
HOST I'll meet her, if she come upon employment.
  Fair lady, welcome, as your host can make you.
PRUDENCE Forbear, sir, I am first to have mine audience
  Before the compliment. This gentleman   30
  Is my address to.
HOST   And it is in state.°
PRUDENCE My lady, sir, as glad o' the encounter
  To find a servant here, and such a servant
  Whom she so values, with her best respects,
  Desires to be remembered; and invites   35
  Your nobleness to be a part today
  Of the society and mirth intended
  By her and the young lords, your fellow-servants,
  Who are alike ambitious of enjoying
  The fair request; and to that end have sent   40
  Me, their imperfect orator, to obtain it:
  Which if I may, they have elected me,
  And crowned me with the title of a sovereign
  Of the day's sports devisèd i' the inn,
  So you be pleased to add your suffrage to it.°   45
LOVEL So I be pleased, my gentle mistress Prudence?
  You cannot think me of that coarse condition

T' envy you anything.

HOST   That's nobly said,°
  And like my guest!

LOVEL   I gratulate your honour,
  And should with cheer lay hold on any handle   50
  That could advance it. But for me to think
  I can be any rag or particle
  O' your lady's care, more than to fill her list,
  She being the lady that professeth still
  To love no soul or body, but for ends   55
  Which are her sports—and is not nice to speak this,°
  But doth proclaim it in all companies—
  Her ladyship must pardon my weak counsels,
  And weaker will, if it decline t' obey her.

PRUDENCE O Master Lovel, you must not give credit   60
  To all that ladies publicly profess,
  Or talk o' th' volley unto their servants:°
  Their tongues and thoughts oft-times lie far asunder.
  Yet, when they please, they have their cabinet-counsels,
  And reserved thoughts, and can retire themselves   65
  As well as others.

HOST   Ay, the subtlest of us!°
  All that is born within a lady's lips—

PRUDENCE Is not the issue of their hearts, mine host.

HOST Or kiss, or drink afore me.

PRUDENCE   Stay, excuse me;°
  Mine errand is not done. Yet if her ladyship's   70
  Slighting or disesteem, sir, of your service
  Hath formerly begot any distaste
  Which I not know of, here I vow unto you,
  Upon a chambermaid's simplicity,
  Reserving still the honour of my lady,°   75
  I will be bold to hold the glass up to her,
  To show her ladyship where she hath erred
  And how to tender satisfaction,
  So you vouchsafe to prove but the day's venture.°

HOST What say you, sir? Where are you? Are you within?   80
      [*Strikes Lovel on the chest*]°

LOVEL Yes—I will wait upon her and the company.

HOST It is enough, Queen Prudence; I will bring him,
  And o' this kiss.

[*Kisses her. Exit Prudence*]
                    I longed to kiss a queen!
LOVEL There is no life on earth but being in love!
    There are no studies, no delights, no business,   85
    No intercourse, or trade of sense or soul,
    But what is love! I was the laziest creature,
    The most unprofitable sign of nothing,
    The veriest drone, and slept away my life
    Beyond the dormouse, till I was in love.   90
    And now, I can outwake the nightingale,
    Outwatch an usurer, and outwalk him, too,
    Stalk like a ghost that haunted 'bout a treasure,
    And all that fancied treasure, it is love!
HOST But is your name Love-ill, sir, or Love-well?   95
    I would know that.
LOVEL   I do not know 't myself,
    Whether it is. But it is love hath been°
    The hereditary passion of our house,°
    My gentle host, and, as I guess, my friend;
    The truth is, I have loved this lady long   100
    And impotently, with desire enough,°
    But no success: for I have still forborne
    To express it in my person to her.
HOST   How then?
LOVEL I ha' sent her toys, verses, and anagrams,
    Trials o' wit, mere trifles she has commended,   105
    But knew not whence they came, nor could she guess.
HOST This was a pretty riddling way of wooing!
LOVEL I oft have been, too, in her company,
    And looked upon her a whole day; admired her;
    Loved her, and did not tell her so; loved still,   110
    Looked still, and loved; and loved, and looked, and sighed;
    But, as a man neglected, I came off,°
    And unregarded—
HOST   Could you blame her, sir,
    When you were silent, and not said a word?
LOVEL Oh but I loved the more; and she might read it   115
    Best in my silence, had she been—
HOST   As melancholic
    As you are. Pray you, why would you stand mute, sir?
LOVEL Oh thereon hangs a history, mine host.

Did you ever know, or hear, of the Lord Beaufort,
Who served so bravely in France? I was his page   120
And, ere he died, his friend. I followed him
First i' the wars; and i' the times of peace
I waited on his studies, which were right.
He had no Arthurs, nor no Rosicleers,
No Knights o' the Sun, nor Amadis de Gauls,   125
Primalions, and Pantagruels, public nothings;°
Abortives of the fabulous dark cloister°
Sent out to poison courts and infest manners:°
But great Achilles', Agamemnon's acts,
Sage Nestor's counsels, and Ulysses' sleights,   130
Tydides' fortitude, as Homer wrought them
In his immortal fant'sy for examples°
Of the heroic virtue. Or as Virgil,°
That master of the epic poem, limned
Pious Aeneas, his religious prince,°   135
Bearing his aged parent on his shoulders,
Rapt from the flames of Troy, with his young son.°
And these he brought to practice and to use.
He gave me first my breeding, I acknowledge,
Then showered his bounties on me, like the Hours,°   140
That open-handed sit upon the clouds
And press the liberality of heaven
Down to the laps of thankful men. But then!
The trust committed to me at his death
Was above all, and left so strong a tie   145
On all my powers as time shall not dissolve
Till it dissolve itself, and bury all:
The care of his brave heir and only son!
Who being a virtuous, sweet, young, hopeful lord,°
Hath cast his first affections on this lady.   150
And though I know, and may presume her such
As, out of humour, will return no love,
And therefore might indifferently be made
The courting-stock for all to practise on°
As she doth practise on all us, to scorn,   155
Yet out of a religion to my charge°
And debt professed, I ha' made a self-decree
Ne'er to express my person, though my passion
Burn me to cinders.

HOST   Then you're not so subtle
  Or half so read in love-craft as I took you.   160
  Come, come, you are no phoenix: an you were,
  I should expect no miracle from your ashes.°
  Take some advice. Be still that rag of love
  You are. Burn on till you turn tinder.
  This chambermaid may hap to prove the steel   165
  To strike a spark out o' the flint, your mistress,
  May beget bonfires yet. You do not know
  What light may be forced out, and from what darkness.
LOVEL Nay, I am so resolved, as still I'll love,
  Though not confess it.
HOST   That's, sir, as it chances.   170
  We'll throw the dice for it: cheer up.
LOVEL   I do.
      [*Exeunt*]

2.1

[Enter] Lady *[Frampul and]* Prudence

[LADY FRAMPUL] Come, wench, this suit will serve; dispatch, make
    ready.
    It was a great deal with the biggest for me,°
    Which made me leave it off after once wearing.
    How does it fit? Will 't come together?
PRUDENCE   Hardly.
LADY FRAMPUL Thou must make shift with it. Pride feels no pain.   5
    Girt thee hard, Pru. Pox o' this errant tailor,°
    He angers me beyond all mark of patience.
    These base mechanics never keep their word
    In anything they promise.
PRUDENCE   'Tis their trade, madam,
    To swear and break, they all grow rich by breaking   10
    More than their words: their honesties and credits
    Are still the first commodity they put off.°
LADY FRAMPUL And worst, it seems, which makes 'em do 't so often.
    If he had but broke with me, I had not cared,
    But with the company, the body politic—   15
PRUDENCE Frustrate our whole design, having that time,
    And the materials in so long before?
LADY FRAMPUL And he to fail in all and disappoint us?
    The rogue deserves a torture—
PRUDENCE   To be cropped
    With his own scissors.°
LADY FRAMPUL   Let's devise him one.   20
PRUDENCE And ha' the stumps seared up with his own cering
    candle.°
LADY FRAMPUL Close to his head, to trundle on his pillow.°
    I'll ha' the lease of his house cut out in measures.°
PRUDENCE And he be strangled with 'em?
LADY FRAMPUL   No, no life
    I would ha' touched, but stretched on his own yard   25
    He should be a little, ha' the strappado.
PRUDENCE   Or an ell of taffeta
    Drawn through his guts by way of clyster, and fired
    With *aqua-vitae.*

LADY FRAMPUL   Burning i' the hand°
  With the pressing iron cannot save him.
PRUDENCE   Yes.°
  Now I have got this on, I do forgive him°   30
  What robes he should ha' brought.
LADY FRAMPUL   Thou art not cruel,
  Although strait-laced, I see, Pru!
PRUDENCE   This is well.°
LADY FRAMPUL 'Tis rich enough. But 'tis not what I meant thee.
  I would ha' had thee braver than myself,
  And brighter far. 'Twill fit the players yet   35
  When thou hast done with it, and yield thee somewhat.°
PRUDENCE That were illiberal, madam, and mere sordid°
  In me, to let a suit of yours come there.
LADY FRAMPUL Tut, all are players, and but serve the scene. Pru,
  Dispatch; I fear thou dost not like the province,°   40
  Thou art so long a-fitting thyself for it.
  Here is a scarf to make thee a knot finer.
PRUDENCE You send me a-feasting, madam.
LADY FRAMPUL   Wear it, wench.
PRUDENCE Yes. But, with leave o' your ladyship, I would tell you
  This can but bear the face of an odd journey.   45
LADY FRAMPUL Why, Pru?
PRUDENCE   A lady of your rank and quality
  To come to a public inn, so many men,
  Young lords, and others i' your company,
  And not a woman but myself, a chambermaid.
LADY FRAMPUL Thou doubtst to be overlaid, Pru? Fear it not,°   50
  I'll bear my part, and share with thee i' the venture.
PRUDENCE Oh but the censure, madam, is the main:
  What will they say of you? Or judge of me,
  To be translated thus, 'bove all the bound°
  Of fitness or decorum?
LADY FRAMPUL   How now, Pru!   55
  Turned fool upo' the sudden, and talk idly
  I' thy best clothes? Shoot bolts and sentences°
  T'affright babies with? As if I lived
  To any other scale than what's my own,
  Or sought myself, without myself, from home?°   60
PRUDENCE Your ladyship will pardon me my fault:
  If I have overshot, I'll shoot no more.

LADY FRAMPUL Yes, shoot again, good Pru, I'll ha' thee shoot,
    And aim, and hit; I know 'tis love in thee,
    And so I do interpret it.
PRUDENCE   Then, madam,   65
    I'd crave a farther leave.
LADY FRAMPUL   Be it to license,
    It sha' not want an ear, Pru. Say, what is it?
PRUDENCE A toy I have, to raise a little mirth
    To the design in hand.
LADY FRAMPUL   Out with it, Pru,
    If it but chime of mirth.
PRUDENCE   Mine host has, madam,   70
    A pretty boy i' the house, a dainty child,
    His son, and is o' your ladyship's name, too, Frances,
    Whom if your ladyship would borrow of him,
    And give me leave to dress him as I would,
    Should make the finest lady and kinswoman   75
    To keep you company, and deceive my lords
    Upo' the matter, with a fountain o' sport.
LADY FRAMPUL I apprehend thee, and the source of mirth
    That it may breed, but is he bold enough,
    The child? And well assured?
PRUDENCE   As I am, madam;   80
    Have him in no suspicion more than me.
    Here comes mine host: will you but please to ask him,
    Or let me make the motion?
LADY FRAMPUL   Which thou wilt, Pru.

2.2

    [*Enter*] *Host*
[HOST] Your ladyship and all your train are welcome.
LADY FRAMPUL I thank my hearty host.
HOST   So is your sovereignty:
    Madam, I wish you joy o' your new gown.
LADY FRAMPUL It should ha' been, my host, but Stuff, our tailor,
    Has broke with us; you shall be o' the counsel.   5
PRUDENCE He will deserve it, madam. My lady has heard
    You have a pretty son, mine host; she'd see him.

LADY FRAMPUL Ay, very fain; I prithee let me see him.
HOST Your ladyship shall presently. [*Calling offstage*] Ho!
PIERCE [*within*]   Anon!
HOST Bid Frank come hither, Anon, unto my lady.   10
    It is a bashful child, homely brought up
    In a rude hostelry. But the Light Heart
    It is his father's, and it may be his.
       [*Enter Frank*]
    Here he comes. Frank, salute my lady.
FRANK   I do°
    What, madam, I am designed to by my birthright   15
    As heir of the Light Heart, bid you most welcome.
LADY FRAMPUL And I believe your 'most', my pretty boy,
    Being so emphased by you.
FRANK   Your ladyship,
    If you believe it such, are sure to make it.
LADY FRAMPUL Prettily answered! Is your name Francis?
FRANK   Yes.   20
LADY FRAMPUL I love mine own the better.
FRANK   If I knew yours,
    I should make haste to do so, too, good madam.
LADY FRAMPUL It is the same with yours.
FRANK   Mine then acknowledgeth
    The lustre it receives, by being named after.
LADY FRAMPUL You will win upon me in compliment.
FRANK   By silence.   25
LADY FRAMPUL A modest, and a fair well-spoken child.
HOST Her ladyship shall have him, sovereign Pru,
    Or what I have beside—divide my Heart
    Between you and your lady. Make your use of it:
    My house is yours, my son is yours. Behold,   30
    I tender him to your service: Frank, become
    What these brave ladies would ha' you. Only this,
    There is a charwoman i' the house, his nurse,
    An Irish woman I took in, a beggar
    That waits upon him; a poor silly fool,°   35
    But an impertinent and sedulous one
    As ever was: will vex you on all occasions,
    Never be off, or from you, but in her sleep,
    Or drink, which makes it. She doth love him so,
    Or rather dote on him. Now, for her, a shape,°   40

As we may dress her (and I'll help) to fit her
With a tuftaffeta cloak, an old French hood,°
And other pieces, heterogene enough.
PRUDENCE We ha' brought a standard of apparel down,
Because this tailor failed us i' the main. 45
HOST She shall advance the game.
PRUDENCE   About it then.
And send but Trundle hither, the coachman, to me.
HOST I shall. [*Aside*] But Pru, let Lovel ha' fair quarter.
PRUDENCE The best.
        [*Exit Host*]
LADY FRAMPUL   Our host, methinks, is very gamesome.
PRUDENCE How like you the boy?
LADY FRAMPUL   A miracle!
PRUDENCE   Good madam, 50
But take him in, and sort a suit for him;
I'll give our Trundle his instructions,
And wait upon your ladyship i' the instant.
LADY FRAMPUL But Pru, what shall we call him when we ha' dressed
    him?
PRUDENCE My Lady Nobody, anything, what you will. 55
LADY FRAMPUL Call him Laetitia, by my sister's name,
And so 'twill mind our mirth, too, we have in hand.°
        [*Exit Lady Frampul with Frank*]

2.3

        [*Enter*] *Trundle*
[PRUDENCE] Good Trundle, you must straight make ready the coach,
And lead the horses out but half a mile
Into the fields, whither you will, and then
Drive in again with the coach-leaves put down
At the back gate, and so to the back stairs, 5
As if you brought in somebody to my lady,
A kinswoman that she sent for. Make that answer
If you be asked, and give it out i' the house so.
TRUNDLE What trick is this, good mistress secretary,
You'd put upon us?

PRUDENCE   Us? Do you speak plural?   10
TRUNDLE Me and my mares are us.
PRUDENCE   If you so join 'em,
    Elegant Trundle, you may use your figures.°
    I can but urge, it is my lady's service.
TRUNDLE Good Mistress Prudence, you can urge enough.
    I know you are secretary to my lady,   15
    And mistress steward.
PRUDENCE   You'll still be trundling,°
    And ha' your wages stopped now at the audit.
TRUNDLE 'Tis true, you are gentlewoman o' the horse, too,
    Or what you will beside, Pru. I do think it
    My best to obey you.
PRUDENCE   And I think so, too, Trundle.   20
       [*Exeunt*]

2.4

     [*Enter*] *Beaufort* [*and*] *Latimer*
[BEAUFORT] Why, here's return enough of both our ventures,
    If we do make no more discovery.
LATIMER   What°
    Then o' this parasite?
BEAUFORT   Oh he's a dainty one:°
    The parasite o' the house.
       [*Enter Host*]
LATIMER   Here comes mine host.
HOST My lords, you both are welcome to the Heart.   5
BEAUFORT To the Light Heart, we hope.
LATIMER   And merry, I swear.
    We never yet felt such a fit of laughter
    As your glad Heart hath offered us sin' we entered.
BEAUFORT How came you by this property?
HOST   Who? My Fly?°
BEAUFORT Your Fly if you call him so.
HOST   Nay, he is that,   10
    And will be still.
BEAUFORT   In every dish and pot?
HOST In every cup and company, my lords;

A creature of all liquors, all complexions:
Be the drink what it will, he'll have his sip.
LATIMER He is fitted with a name.
HOST   And he joys in 't.   15
I had him when I came to take the inn here,
Assigned me over in the inventory
As an old implement, a piece of household-stuff,
And so he doth remain.
BEAUFORT   Just such a thing°
We thought him.
LATIMER   Is he a scholar?
HOST   Nothing less.°   20
But colours for it, as you see: wears black,
And speaks a little tainted, fly-blown Latin
After the School.
BEAUFORT   Of Stratford o' the Bow:°
'For Lily's Latin is to him unknow'.°
LATIMER What calling has he?
HOST   Only to call in,   25
Inflame the reckoning, bold to charge a bill,
Bring up the shot i' the rear, as his own word is.°
BEAUFORT And does it in the discipline of the house
As corporal o' the field, *maestro del campo?*°
HOST And visitor-general of all the rooms.   30
He has formed a fine militia for the inn, too.
BEAUFORT And means to publish it?
HOST   With all his titles.°
Some call him Deacon Fly, some Doctor Fly,
Some Captain, some Lieutenant; but my folks
Do call him Quartermaster Fly, which he is.   35

2.5

        [*Enter*] *Tipto* [*and*] *Fly*°
[TIPTO] Come, Quartermaster Fly.
HOST   Here's one already
Hath got his titles.
TIPTO   Doctor!
FLY   Noble colonel!

No doctor, yet a poor professor of ceremony
Here i' the inn, retainer to the host,
I discipline the house.

TIPTO   Thou readst a lecture   5
Unto the family here, when is thy day?

FLY This is the day.

TIPTO   I'll hear thee, and ha' thee a doctor.
Thou shalt be one, thou hast a doctor's look;
A face disputative, of Salamanca.°

HOST Who's this?

LATIMER   The glorious Colonel Tipto, host.   10

BEAUFORT One talks upon his tiptoes, if you'll hear him.

TIPTO Thou hast good learning in thee, *macte* Fly.°

FLY And I say *macte* to my colonel.

HOST Well *macted* of 'em both.

BEAUFORT   They are matched, i'faith.

TIPTO But Fly, why *macte*?

FLY   *Quasi magis aucte*,°   15
My honourable colonel.

TIPTO   What, a critic?

HOST There's another accession: critic Fly.°

LATIMER I fear a taint here i' the mathematics.
They say lines parallel do never meet;
He has met his parallel in wit and schoolcraft.   20

BEAUFORT They side, not meet, man; mend your metaphor,°
And save the credit of your mathematics.

TIPTO But Fly, how cam'st thou to be here, committed°
Unto this inn?

FLY   Upon suspicion o' drink, sir,
I was taken late one night here with the tapster   25
And the under-officers, and so deposited.°

TIPTO I will redeem thee, Fly, and place thee better,
With a fair lady.

FLY   A lady, sweet Sir Glorious!

TIPTO A sovereign lady. Thou shalt be the bird
To Sovereign Pru, queen of our sports, her fly,   30
The fly in household and in ordinary;°
Bird of her ear, and she shall wear thee there!
A fly of gold, enamelled, and a school-fly.

HOST The school, then, are my stables or the cellar,
Where he doth study deeply at his hours   35

Cases of cups (I do not know how spiced
With conscience) for the tapster and the ostler: as°
Whose horses may be cosened? Or what jugs
Filled up with froth? That is his way of learning.

TIPTO What antiquated feather's that, that talks?°   40

FLY The worshipful host, my patron, Master Goodstock:
    A merry Greek, and cants in Latin comely,
    Spins like the parish-top.

TIPTO   I'll set him up, then.°
    Art thou the dominus?

HOST   Factotum here, sir.°

TIPTO Host real o' the house, and cap of maintenance?°   45

HOST The lord o' the Light Heart, sir, cap-à-pie,
    Whereof the feather is the emblem, colonel,
    Put up with the ace of hearts.

TIPTO   But why *in cuerpo*?°
    I hate to see an host, and old, *in cuerpo*.

HOST *Cuerpo*? What's that?

TIPTO   Light, skipping hose and doublet—   50
    The horse boy's garb! Poor blank and half-blank *cuerpo*,°
    They relish not the gravity of an host,°
    Who should be king-at-arms and ceremonies
    In his own house; know all, to the gold-weights.°

BEAUFORT Why, that his fly doth for him here, your bird.   55

TIPTO But I would do it myself, were I my host;
    I would not speak unto a cook of quality,
    Your lordship's footman, or my lady's Trundle
    In cuerpo. If a dog but stayed below
    That were a dog of fashion, and well-nosed,   60
    And could present himself, I would put on
    The Savoy chain about my neck, the ruff°
    And cuffs of Flanders, then the Naples hat,°
    With the Rome hatband and the Florentine agate,
    The Milan sword, the cloak of Genoa set   65
    With Brabant buttons, all my given pieces—
    Except my gloves, the natives of Madrid—°
    To entertain him in, and compliment
    With a tame cony, as with a prince that sent it.

HOST The same deeds, though, become not every man;   70
    What fits a colonel will not fit an host.

TIPTO Your Spanish host is never seen *in cuerpo*,

Without his *paramentos*, cloak, and sword.
FLY   Sir,°
He has the father of swords within, a long sword,°
Blade Cornish, styled of Sir Rud Hudibras.°   75
TIPTO And why a long sword, bully bird? Thy sense?
FLY To note him a tall man, and a master of fence.°
TIPTO But doth he teach the Spanish way of Don Lewis?°
FLY No, the Greek master he.
TIPTO   What call you him?
FLY   Euclid.
TIPTO Fart upon Euclid, he is stale and antique.   80
Gi' me the moderns.
FLY   Sir, he minds no moderns—
Go by, Hieronimo!
TIPTO   What was he?
FLY   The Italian°
That played with Abbot Antony i' the Friars,°
And Blinkinsops the bold.
TIPTO   Ay, marry, those°
Had fencing names, what are become o' them?   85
HOST They had their times, and we can say they were.
So had Carranza his, so hath Don Lewis.
TIPTO Don Lewis of Madrid is the sole master
Now of the world.
HOST   But this o' the other world.°
Euclid demonstrates! He, he's for all: 90
The only fencer of name now in Elysium.
FLY He does it all by lines and angles, colonel,
By parallels and sections, has his diagrams.
BEAUFORT Wilt thou be flying, Fly?
LATIMER   At all; why not?
The air's as free for a fly as for an eagle.   95
BEAUFORT A buzzard! He is in his contemplation.
TIPTO Euclid a fencer, and in the Elysium!
HOST He played a prize last week with Archimedes°
And beat him, I assure you.
TIPTO   Do you assure me?°
For what?
HOST   For four i' the hundred. Gi' me five,   100
And I assure you again.
TIPTO   Host peremptory,

364

You may be ta'en. But where? Whence had you this?
HOST Upo' the road. A post that came from thence
    Three days ago, here, left it with the tapster.
FLY Who is indeed a thoroughfare of news,   105
    Jack Jug with the great belly, a witty fellow!
HOST Your bird here heard him.
TIPTO   Did you hear him, bird?
HOST Speak i' the faith of a fly.
    [Exit Host]
FLY   Yes, and he told us
    Of one that was the Prince of Orange's fencer.
TIPTO Stevinus?
FLY   Sir, the same, had challenged Euclid°   110
    At thirty weapons, more than Archimedes
    E'er saw, and engines: most of his own invention.°
TIPTO This may have credit, and chimes reason, this.
    If any man endanger Euclid, bird,
    Observe (that had the honour to quit Europe   115
    This forty year), 'tis he. He put down Scaliger.°
FLY And he was a great master.
BEAUFORT   Not of fence, Fly.
TIPTO Excuse him, lord, he went o' the same grounds.
BEAUFORT On the same earth, I think, with other mortals?
TIPTO I mean, sweet lord, the mathematics. *Basta!*°   120
    When thou know'st more, thou wilt take less green honour.
    He had his circles, semicircles, quadrants—
FLY He writ a book o' the quadrature o' the circle.°
TIPTO *Cyclometría*, I read—
BEAUFORT   The title only.
LATIMER And indice.
BEAUFORT   If it had one: of that, *quaere*.°   125
    What insolent, half-witted things these are?
LATIMER So are all smatterers insolent and impudent.
BEAUFORT They lightly go together.
LATIMER   'Tis my wonder°
    Two animals should hawk at all discourse thus!°
    Fly every subject to the mark, or retrieve—   130
BEAUFORT And never ha' the luck to be i' the right.
LATIMER 'Tis some folk's fortune.
BEAUFORT   Fortune's a bawd
    And a blind beggar; 'tis their vanity,

And shows most vilely.

TIPTO   I could take the heart now
  To write unto Don Lewis into Spain,   135
  To make a progress to the Elysian fields
  Next summer—

BEAUFORT   And persuade him die for fame
  Of fencing with a shadow! Where's mine host?°
  I would he had heard this bubble break, i' faith.

2.6

[Enter] Host [with] Prudence, Frank [as a woman], Nurse, [and]
Lady [Frampul]

[HOST] Make place, stand by for the queen regent, gentlemen.

TIPTO This is thy queen that shall be, bird, our sovereign.

BEAUFORT Translated Prudence!

PRUDENCE   Sweet my lord, hand off:°
  It is not now as when plain Prudence lived,
  And reached her ladyship—

HOST   The chamberpot.   5

PRUDENCE The looking-glass, mine host, lose your house metaphor.
  You have a negligent memory, indeed;
  Speak the host's language. Here's a young lord°
  Will make 't a precedent else.

LATIMER   Well acted, Pru.

HOST First minute of her reign! What will she do   10
  Forty year hence? God bless her!

PRUDENCE   If you'll kiss°
  Or compliment, my lord, behold a lady,
  A stranger, and my lady's kinswoman.

BEAUFORT I do confess my rudeness, that had need
  To have mine eye directed to this beauty.   15

FRANK It was so little as it asked a perspicil.

BEAUFORT Lady, your name?

FRANK   My lord, it is Laetitia.

BEAUFORT Laetitia! A fair omen! And I take it:°
  Let me have still such lettuce for my lips—°
  But that o' your family, lady?

FRANK   Sylly, sir.   20

BEAUFORT My lady's kinswoman?
FRANK   I am so honoured.
HOST [*aside*] Already it takes!
LADY FRAMPUL   An excellent fine boy.
NURSE He is descended of a right good stock, sir.
BEAUFORT What's this? An antiquary?
HOST   An antiquity
  By th' dress, you'd swear! An old Welsh herald's widow: 25
  She's a wild Irish born, sir, and a hybrid,
  That lives with this young lady a mile off here,
  And studies Vincent against York.
BEAUFORT   She'll conquer°
  If she read Vincent. Let me study her.
HOST She's perfect in most pedigrees, most descents.   30
BEAUFORT [*aside*] A bawd, I hope, and knows to blaze a coat.°
HOST And judgeth all things with a single eye.°
  Fly, come you hither. [*Aside to Fly*] No discovery
  Of what you see to your Colonel Toe, or Tip, here,
  But keep all close, though you stand i' the way o' preferment,   35
  Seek it off from the road; no flattery for 't,°
  No lick-foot, pain of losing your proboscis,
  My lickerish Fly.
TIPTO   What says old velvet-head?°
FLY He will present me himself, sir, if you will not.
TIPTO Who? He present? What? Whom? An host? A groom?   40
  Divide the thanks with me? Share in my glories?
  Lay up. I say no more.
HOST   Then silence, sir,
  And hear the sovereign.
TIPTO   Ostlers to usurp
  Upon my Sparta, or province, as they say?
  No broom but mine?
HOST   Still, colonel, you mutter!°   45
TIPTO I dare speak out, as *cuerpo*.
FLY   Noble colonel—°
TIPTO And carry what I ask—
HOST   Ask what you can, sir,
  So 't be i' the house.
TIPTO   I ask my rights and privileges,
  And though for form I please to call 't a suit,
  I have not been accustomed to repulse.   50

PRUDENCE No, sweet Sir Glorious, you may still command—
HOST And go without.
PRUDENCE   But yet, sir, being the first,
    And called a suit, you'll look it shall be such
    As we may grant.
LADY FRAMPUL   It else denies itself.
PRUDENCE You hear the opinion of the court.
TIPTO   I mind   55
    No court opinions.
PRUDENCE   'Tis my lady's, though.
TIPTO My lady is a spinster at the law,°
    And my petition is of right.
PRUDENCE   What is it?
TIPTO It is for this poor learned bird.
HOST   The fly?
TIPTO Professor in the inn, here, of small matters.   60
LATIMER How he commends him!
HOST   As to save himself in him.
LADY FRAMPUL So do all politics in their commendations.
HOST This is a state-bird, and the verier fly!
TIPTO Hear him problematize.
PRUDENCE   Bless us, what's that?
TIPTO Or syllogize, elenchize.
LADY FRAMPUL   Sure, petards   65
    To blow us up.
LATIMER   Some enginous strong words!°
HOST He means to erect a castle i' the air,
    And make his fly an elephant to carry it.°
TIPTO Bird of the arts he is, and Fly by name.
PRUDENCE Buzz!
HOST   Blow him off, good Pru, they'll mar all else.°   70
TIPTO The sovereign's honour is to cherish learning.
PRUDENCE What, in a fly?
TIPTO   In anything industrious.
PRUDENCE But flies are busy!
LADY FRAMPUL   Nothing more troublesome,°
    Or importune.
TIPTO   There's nothing more domestic,
    Tame, or familiar, than your fly *in cuerpo*.   75
HOST That is when his wings are cut, he is tame, indeed, else
    Nothing more impudent and greedy, licking—

LADY FRAMPUL Or saucy, good Sir Glorious.
PRUDENCE   Leave your advocateship,
    Except that we shall call you orator Fly,
    And send you down to the dresser and the dishes.°   80
HOST A good flap, that!
PRUDENCE   Commit you to the steam!°
LADY FRAMPUL Or else condemn you to the bottles.
PRUDENCE   And pots.
    There is his quarry.
HOST   He will chirp far better,
    Your bird, below.
LADY FRAMPUL   And make you finer music.
PRUDENCE His buzz will there become him.
TIPTO   Come away.   85
    Buzz in their faces. Give 'em all the buzz,
    Dor in their ears and eyes: hum, dor, and buzz!°
    I will statuminate and under-prop thee.
    If they scorn us, let us scorn them—we'll find
    The thoroughfare below, and *quaere* him.°   90
    Leave these relics, Buzz; they shall see that I,°
    Spite of their jeers, dare drink, and with a fly.
       [Exeunt Tipto and Fly]
LATIMER A fair remove at once of two impertinents!
    Excellent Pru! I love thee for thy wit,
    No less than state.
PRUDENCE   One must preserve the other.   95
       [Enter Lovel]
LADY FRAMPUL Who's here?
PRUDENCE   Oh Lovel, madam, your sad servant.
LADY FRAMPUL Sad? He is sullen still and wears a cloud
    About his brows; I know not how to approach him.
PRUDENCE I will instruct you, madam, if that be all:
    Go to him and kiss him.
LADY FRAMPUL   How, Pru?
PRUDENCE   Go and kiss him,   100
    I do command it.
LADY FRAMPUL   Th'art not wild, wench?
PRUDENCE   No,
    Tame, and exceeding tame, but still your sovereign.
LADY FRAMPUL Hath too much bravery made thee mad?
PRUDENCE   Nor proud.°

Do what I do enjoin you. No disputing
Of my prerogative with a front or frown;   105
Do not detrect: you know th' authority
Is mine, and I will exercise it swiftly
If you provoke me.

LADY FRAMPUL   I have woven a net
To snare myself in. Sir, I am enjoined
To tender you a kiss, but do not know   110
Why, or wherefore, only the pleasure royal
Will have it so, and urges. Do not you
Triumph on my obedience, seeing it forced thus.
There 'tis.
          [*She kisses Lovel*]

LOVEL   And welcome. [*Aside*] Was there ever kiss
That relished thus, or had a sting like this;   115
Of so much nectar, but with aloes mixed?°

PRUDENCE No murmuring nor repining, I am fixed.

LOVEL [*aside*] It had, methinks, a quintessence of either,°
But that which was the better, drowned the bitter.
How soon it passed away! How unrecovered!   120
The distillation of another soul°
Was not so sweet. And till I meet again
That kiss, those lips like relish, and this taste,
Let me turn all consumption, and here waste.

PRUDENCE The royal assent is passed, and cannot alter.   125

LADY FRAMPUL You'll turn a tyrant.

PRUDENCE   Be not you a rebel,
It is a name is alike odious.

LADY FRAMPUL You'll hear me?

PRUDENCE   No, not o' this argument.
Would you make laws, and be the first that break 'em?
The example is pernicious in a subject,   130
And of your quality, most.

LATIMER   Excellent princess!

HOST Just queen!

LATIMER   Brave sovereign!

HOST   A she-Trajan, this!°

BEAUFORT What is 't? Proceed, incomparable Pru!°
I am glad I am scarce at leisure to applaud thee.

LATIMER It's well for you, you have so happy expressions.   135

LADY FRAMPUL Yes, cry her up with acclamations, do,

And cry me down, run all with sovereignty:
Prince Power will never want her parasites.
PRUDENCE Nor Murmur her pretences: Master Lovel,°
For so your libel here or bill of complaint,°   140
Exhibited in our high court of sovereignty
At this first hour of our reign, declares
Against this noble lady a disrespect
You have conceived, if not received, from her.
HOST Received, so the charge lies in our bill.   145
PRUDENCE We see it, his learned counsel, leave your plaining.
We that do love our justice above all
Our other attributes, and have the nearness
To know your extraordinary merit,
As also to discern this lady's goodness,   150
And find how loath she'd be to lose the honour
And reputation she hath had in having
So worthy a servant, though but for few minutes,
Do here enjoin—
HOST   Good!
PRUDENCE   Charge, will, and command
Her ladyship, pain of our high displeasure   155
And the committing an extreme contempt
Unto the court, our crown and dignity—
HOST Excellent sovereign, and egregious Pru!
PRUDENCE To entertain you for a pair of hours
(Choose when you please, this day) with all respects,   160
And valuation of a principal servant,
To give you all the titles, all the privileges,
The freedoms, favours, rights, she can bestow—
HOST Large, ample words, of a brave latitude!°
PRUDENCE Or can be expected, from a lady of honour   165
Or quality, in discourse, access, address—
HOST   Good.
PRUDENCE Not to give ear, or admit conference
With any person but yourself; nor there,
Of any other argument but love,
And the companion of it, gentle courtship.°   170
For which your two hours' service, you shall take
Two kisses.
HOST   Noble!
PRUDENCE   For each hour, a kiss

To be ta'en freely, fully, and legally,
Before us, in the court here and our presence.

HOST   Rare!

PRUDENCE But those hours past, and the two kisses paid,   175
The binding caution is never to hope
Renewing of the time, or of the suit,
On any circumstance.

HOST   A hard condition!

LATIMER Had it been easier, I should have suspected
The sovereign's justice.

HOST   Oh you are servant,   180
My lord, unto the lady, and a rival:
In point of law, my lord, you may be challenged.

LATIMER I am not jealous!

HOST   Of so short a time
Your lordship needs not, and being done *in foro*.°

PRUDENCE What is the answer?

HOST   He craves respite, madam,   185
To advise with his learned counsel.

PRUDENCE   Be you he,
And go together quickly.

          [*Lovel and Host walk aside*]

LADY FRAMPUL   You are no tyrant?

PRUDENCE If I be, madam, you were best appeal me.

LATIMER Beaufort—

BEAUFORT   I am busy, prithee let me alone;
I have a cause in hearing, too.

LATIMER   At what bar?   190

BEAUFORT Love's court o' requests.

LATIMER   Bring 't into the sovereignty;°
It is the nobler court, afore Judge Pru,
The only learned mother of the law,
And lady o' conscience, too.

BEAUFORT   'Tis well enough
Before this Mistress of Requests, where it is.   195

HOST Let 'em not scorn you. Bear up, Master Lovel,
And take your hours and kisses. They are a fortune.

LOVEL Which I cannot approve, and less make use of.°

HOST Still i' this cloud! Why cannot you make use of?

LOVEL Who would be rich to be so soon undone?   200
The beggar's best is wealth he doth not know,

And but to show it him, inflames his want.

HOST Two hours at height?

LOVEL   That joy is too, too narrow
    Would bound a love so infinite as mine;
    And being past, leaves an eternal loss.   205
    Who so prodigiously affects a feast
    To forfeit health and appetite to see it?
    Or but to taste a spoonful, would forgo
    All gust of delicacy ever after?

HOST These yet are hours of hope.

LOVEL   But all hours following   210
    Years of despair, ages of misery!
    Nor can so short a happiness but spring
    A world of fear with thought of losing it;
    Better be never happy, than to feel
    A little of it, and then lose it ever.   215

HOST I do confess it is a strict injunction;
    But then the hope is it may not be kept.
    A thousand things may intervene. We see
    The wind shift often, thrice a day sometimes;
    Decrees may alter upon better motion,   220
    And riper hearing. The best bow may start,°
    And th' hand may vary. Pru may be a sage
    In law, and yet not sour. Sweet Pru, smooth Pru,°
    Soft, debonair, and amiable Pru,
    May do as well as rough and rigid Pru;   225
    And yet maintain her venerable Pru,
    Majestic Pru, and serenissimous Pru.
    Try but one hour first, and as you like
    The loose o' that, draw home and prove the other.°

LOVEL If one hour could the other happy make,   230
    I should attempt it.

HOST   Put it on, and do.

LOVEL Or in the blest attempt that I might die!

HOST Ay, marry, there were happiness, indeed,
    Transcendent to the melancholy meant.°
    It were a fate above a monument   235
    And all inscription to die so; a death
    For emperors to enjoy, and the kings
    Of the rich East to pawn their regions for,
    To sow their treasure, open all their mines,

Spend all their spices to embalm their corps,°   240
And wrap the inches up in sheets of gold,
That fell by such a noble destiny!
And for the wrong to your friend, that fear's away,
He rather wrongs himself, following fresh light,
New eyes to swear by. If Lord Beaufort change,   245
It is no crime in you to remain constant.
And upon these conditions, at a game
So urged upon you.
PRUDENCE   Sir, your resolution—
HOST How is the lady affected?
PRUDENCE   Sovereigns use not
To ask their subjects' suffrage where 'tis due,   250
But where conditional.
HOST   A royal sovereign!°
LATIMER And a rare stateswoman. I admire her bearing
In her new regiment.
HOST   Come, choose your hours:°
Better be happy for a part of time,
Than not the whole, and a short part, than never.   255
Shall I appoint 'em, pronounce for you?
LOVEL   Your pleasure.
HOST Then he designs his first hour after dinner,
His second after supper. Say ye? Content?
PRUDENCE Content.
LADY FRAMPUL   I am content.
LATIMER   Content.
FRANK   Content.
BEAUFORT What's that? I am content, too.
LATIMER   You have reason,   260
You had it on the by, and we observed it.
NURSE Trot' I am not content: in fait' I am not.
HOST Why art not thou content, good Shelee-nien?°
NURSE He tauk so desperate, and so debausht,
So bawdy like a courtier and a lord,   265
God bless him, one that taketh tobacco.
HOST   Very well mixed.
What did he say?
NURSE   Nay, nothing to the purposh,
Or very little, nothing at all to purposh.
HOST Let him alone, nurse.

NURSE   I did tell him of Serly
Was a great family come out of Ireland,   270
Descended of O'Neill, Mac Con, Mac Dermot,
Mac Murrogh, but he marked not.
HOST   Nor do I.°
Good queen of heralds, ply the bottle, and sleep.
        [*Exeunt*]

3.1

[Enter] Tipto, Fly, [and] Jug

[TIPTO] I like the plot of your militia well.°
It is a fine militia, and well ordered,
And the division's neat! 'Twill be desired
Only the expressions were a little more Spanish:
For there's the best militia o' the world!   5
To call 'em tertias—tertia of the kitchen,
The tertia of the cellar, tertia of the chamber,
And tertia of the stables.

FLY   That I can, sir,
And find out very able, fit commanders
In every tertia.

TIPTO   Now you are i' the right!   10
As i' the tertia o' the kitchen, yourself
Being a person elegant in sauces,
There to command as prime *maestro del campo*,
Chief master of the palate, for that tertia;
Or the cook under you, 'cause you are the marshal,   15
And the next officer i' the field to the host.
Then for the cellar, you have young Anon,
Is a rare fellow—what's his other name?

FLY Pierce, sir.

TIPTO   Sir Pierce, I'll ha' him a cavalier.
Sir Pierce Anon will pierce us a new hogshead!   20
And then your thoroughfare, Jug here, his *alferez*:°
An able officer. Gi' me thy beard, round Jug,
I take thee by this handle, and do love
One of thy inches! I' the chambers, Jordan here!°
He is the *don del campo* o' the beds.°   25
And for the stables, what's his name?

FLY   Old Peck.

TIPTO *Maestro del campo* Peck! His name is curt,
A monosyllabe, but commands the horse well.°

FLY Oh, in an inn, sir, we have other horse,°
Let those troops rest a while. Wine is the horse   30
That we must charge with here.

TIPTO   Bring up the troops,
  Or call, sweet Fly; 'tis an exact militia,°
  And thou an exact professor. Lipsius Fly
  Thou shalt be called, and Jouse—
     [*Enter Ferret and Trundle*]
                       Jack Ferret! Welcome,°
  Old trenchmaster, and colonel o' the pioneers!   35
  What canst thou bolt us now? A cony or two°
  Out of Tom Trundle's burrow here, the coach?
  This is the master of the carriages!
  How is thy driving, Tom, good as 'twas?
TRUNDLE It serves my lady, and our officer Pru.   40
  Twelve mile an hour! Tom has the old trundle still.
TIPTO I am taken with the family here, fine fellows,
  Viewing the muster-roll.
TRUNDLE   They are brave men.
FERRET And of the fly-blown discipline all, the quartermaster!
TIPTO The Fly's a rare bird in his profession.   45
  Let's sip a private pint with him. I would have him
  Quit this light sign of the Light Heart, my bird,
  And lighter house. It is not for his tall°
  And growing gravity, so cedar-like,
  To be the second to an host *in cuerpo*   50
  That knows no elegancies. Use his own
  Dictamen and his genius, I would have him
  Fly high, and strike at all.
     [*Enter Pierce*]
                 Here's young Anon, too.
PIERCE What wine is 't, gentlemen, white or claret?
TIPTO   White,
  My brisk Anon.
PIERCE   I'll draw you Juno's milk   55
  That dyed the lilies, colonel.
TIPTO   Do so, Pierce.°
    [*Exit Pierce. Enter Peck*]
PECK A plague of all jades, what a clap he has gi'en me!
FLY Why, how now, cousin?
    [*Fly takes Peck aside*]°
TIPTO   Who's that?
FERRET   The ostler.
FLY What ail'st thou, cousin Peck?

PECK   O me, my haunches!°
 As sure as you live, sir, he knew perfectly   60
 I meant to cozen him. He did leer so on me,
 And then he sneered, as who would say, 'Take heed,
  sirrah.'
 And when he saw our half-peck, which you know
 Was but an old court-dish, lord, how he stamped!°
 I thought 't had been for joy. When suddenly   65
 He cuts me a back caper with his heels,
 And takes me just o' the crupper. Down come I
 And my whole ounce of oats! Then he neighed out,
 As if he had a mare by the tail.
FLY   Troth, cousin,
 You are to blame to use the poor dumb Christians   70
 So cruelly, defraud 'em o' their *dimensum*.°
 Yonder's the colonel's horse (there I looked in)
 Keeping Our Lady's Eve! The devil a bit°
 He has got, sin' he came in yet. There he stands,
 And looks and looks, but 'tis your pleasure, coz,   75
 He should look lean enough.
PECK   He has hay before him.
FLY Yes, but as gross as hemp, and as soon will choke him
 Unless he eat it buttered. He'd four shoes,°
 And good ones, when he came in: it is a wonder
 With standing still he should cast three.
PECK   Troth, quartermaster,   80
 This trade is a kind of mystery that corrupts°
 Our standing manners quickly; once a week
 I meet with such a brush to mollify me,
 Sometimes a brace, to awake my conscience,
 Yet still I sleep securely.
FLY   Cousin Peck,   85
 You must use better dealing, faith, you must.
PECK Troth, to give good example to my successors,
 I could be well content to steal but two girths,
 And now and then a saddle-cloth, change a bridle
 For exercise, and stay there.
FLY   If you could,   90
 There were some hope on you, coz. But the fate is
 You are drunk so early you mistake whole saddles—°
 Sometimes a horse.

PECK   Ay, there's—
    [*Enter Pierce with wine*]
FLY   The wine. Come, coz,
  I'll talk with you anon.
PECK   Do, lose no time,
  Good quartermaster.
TIPTO   There are the horse come, Fly.   95
FLY Charge in, boys, in.
    [*Enter Jordan*]
        Lieutenant o' the ordnance,°
  Tobacco and pipes.
TIPTO   Who's that? Old Jordan, good!
  A comely vessel, and a necessary.
  New-scoured he is. Here's to thee, marshal Fly;
  In milk, my young Anon says.
PIERCE   Cream o' the grape   100
  That dropped from Juno's breasts and sprung the lily.
  I can recite your fables, Fly. Here is, too,
  The blood of Venus, mother o' the rose.°
    [*Music within*]
JORDAN The dinner is gone up.
JUG   I hear the whistle.
JORDAN Ay, and the fiddlers. We must all go wait.   105
PIERCE Pox o' this waiting, quartermaster Fly.
FLY When chambermaids are sovereigns, wait their ladies;
  Fly scorns to breathe—
PECK   Or blow upon them, he.
PIERCE Old Parcel Peck! Art thou there? How now,
   lame?°
PECK Yes, faith: it is ill halting afore cripples;°   110
  I ha' got a dash of a jade here will stick by me.
PIERCE Oh you have had some fant'sy, fellow Peck,
  Some revelation—
PECK   What?
PIERCE   To steal the hay
  Out o' the racks again.
FLY   I told him so,
  When the guests' backs were turned.
PIERCE   Or bring his peck   115
  The bottom upwards, heaped with oats, and cry,
  'Here's the best measure upon all the road!' When,

You know, the guest put in his hand to feel
And smell to the oats, that grated all his fingers
Upo' the wood—
PECK   Mum!
PIERCE   And found out your cheat.   120
PECK I ha' been i' the cellar, Pierce.
PIERCE   You were then there
Upo' your knees, I do remember it,
To ha' the fact concealed. I could tell more:
Soaping of saddles, cutting of horse tails,
And cropping—pranks of ale and hostelry—   125
FLY Which he cannot forget, he says, young knight:
No more than you can other deeds of darkness
Done i' the cellar.
TIPTO   Well said, bold professor.
FERRET We shall ha' some truth explained.
PIERCE   We are all mortal,
And have our visions.
PECK   Truly, it seems to me   130
That every horse has his whole peck, and tumbles
Up to the ears in litter.
FLY   When, indeed,°
There's no such matter; not a smell of provender.
FERRET Not so much straw as would tie up a horse-tail.
FLY Nor anything i' the rack but two old cobwebs,   135
And so much rotten hay as had been a hen's nest.
TRUNDLE And yet he's ever apt to sweep the mangers!
FERRET But puts in nothing.
PIERCE   These are fits and fancies
Which you must leave, good Peck.
FLY   And you must pray
It may be revealed to you at some times   140
Whose horse you ought to cozen; with what conscience;
The how, and when. A parson's horse may suffer—
PIERCE Whose master's double beneficed, put in that.°
FLY A little greasing i' the teeth; 'tis wholesome,°
And keeps him in a sober shuffle.
PIERCE   His saddle, too,   145
May want a stirrup.
FLY   And it may be sworn°
His learning lay o' one side, and so broke it.
PECK They have ever oats i' their cloak-bags to affront us.

FLY And therefore 'tis an office meritorious
　　To tithe such soundly.
PIERCE　　　　　　　　And a grazier's may—　　　　　　　150
FERRET Oh they are pinching puckfists!
TRUNDLE　　　　　　　　　　　And suspicious.
PIERCE Suffer before the master's face, sometimes.
FLY He shall think he sees his horse eat half a bushel—
PIERCE When the sleight is, rubbing his gums with salt
　　Till all the skin come off, he shall but mumble　　　155
　　Like an old woman that were chewing brawn,
　　And drop 'em out again.
TIPTO　　　　　　　　Well argued, cavalier.
FLY It may do well, and go for an example.
　　But, coz, have care of understanding horses,
　　Horses with angry heels, nobility horses,　　　　　160
　　Horses that know the world; let them have meat
　　Till their teeth ache, and rubbing till their ribs
　　Shine like a wench's forehead. They are devils else,
　　Will look into your dealings.
PECK　　　　　　　　　For mine own part,
　　The next I cozen o' the pampered breed,　　　　　165
　　I wish he may be foundered.
FLY　　　　　　　　　Foun-der-ed:°
　　Prolate it right.
PECK　　　　　And of all four, I wish it;°
　　I love no crupper compliments.
PIERCE　　　　　　　　Whose horse was it?
PECK Why, Master Burst's.
PIERCE　　　　　　Is Bat Burst come?
PECK　　　　　　　　　　An hour
　　He has been here.
TIPTO　　　　　What Burst?
PIERCE　　　　　　　　Mass, Bartolmew Burst.°　　170
　　One that hath been a citizen, since a courtier,
　　And now a gamester. Hath had all his whirls
　　And bouts of fortune, as a man would say,
　　Once a bat and ever a bat! A reremouse°
　　And bird o' twilight, he has broken thrice.　　　175
TIPTO Your better man, the Genoway proverb says,°
　　Men are not made of steel.
PIERCE　　　　　　　　Nor are they bound
　　Always to hold.

FLY   Thrice honourable colonel!°
    Hinges will crack—
TIPTO   Though they be Spanish iron.
PIERCE He is a merchant still, adventurer,   180
    At in-and-in, and is our thoroughfare's friend.°
TIPTO Who, Jug's?
PIERCE   The same; and a fine gentleman
    Was with him!
PECK   Master Huffle.
PIERCE   Who, Hodge Huffle?
TIPTO What's he?
PIERCE   A cheater, and another fine gentleman,
    A friend o' the chamberlain's Jordan's. Master Huffle,   185
    He is Burst's Protection.
FLY   Fights and vapours for him.°
PIERCE He will be drunk so civilly—
FLY   So discreetly—
PIERCE And punctually! Just at his hour.
FLY   And then
    Call for his jordan with that hum and state,
    As if he pissed the *Politics*.
PIERCE   And sup°   190
    With his tuftaffeta night-gear here so silently.°
FLY Nothing but music.
PIERCE   A dozen of bawdy songs.
TIPTO And knows the general this?
FLY   Oh no, sir, *dormit*,
    Dormit patronus still; the master sleeps,°
    They'll steal to bed.
PIERCE   In private, sir, and pay   195
    The fiddlers with that modesty next morning.°
FLY Take a disjune of muscadel and eggs.°
PIERCE And pack away i' their trundling cheats like gypsies.°
TRUNDLE Mysteries, mysteries, Ferret.
FERRET   Ay, we see, Trundle,
    What the great officers in an inn may do;   200
    I do not say the officers of the Crown,°
    But the Light Heart.
TIPTO   I'll see the Bat and Huffle.
FERRET I ha' some business, sir, I crave your pardon—
TIPTO What?

382

FERRET   To be sober.
     [*Exit Ferret*]
TIPTO   Pox, go get you gone then.
     Trundle shall stay.
TRUNDLE   No, I beseech you, colonel,   205
     Your lordship has a mind to be drunk private
     With these brave gallants; I will step aside
     Into the stables and salute my mares.
          [*Exit Trundle*]
PIERCE Yes, do, and sleep with 'em. Let him go—base whipstock.
     He's as drunk as a fish now, almost as dead.   210
TIPTO Come, I will see the flickermouse, my Fly.
          [*Exeunt*]

3.2

     [*Musicians enter and play. Enter*] Prudence, *ushered by the Host,*
     [*who*] *takes her seat of judicature. Enter Nurse, Frank, the two*
     lords Beaufort and Latimer, [*Jug, Trundle, Ferret, and Jordan,*
     who] *assist of the bench*°
PRUDENCE Here set the hour; but first produce the parties,°
     And clear the court. The time is now of price.
HOST Jug, get you down, and Trundle, get you up,
     You shall be crier. Ferret here, the clerk.
     Jordan, smell you without till the ladies call you;°   5
     Take down the fiddlers, too, silence that noise
     Deep i' the cellar, safe.
          [*Exeunt Jug, Jordan, and Musicians*]
PRUDENCE   Who keeps the watch?
HOST Old Shelee-nien here is the Madam Tell-Clock.
NURSE No, fait' and trot', sweet maister, I shall sleep,
     I' fait', I shall.
BEAUFORT   I prithee do then, screech-owl.   10
     She brings to mind the fable o' the dragon
     That kept the Hesperian fruit. Would I could charm her.°
HOST Trundle will do it with his hum. Come, Trundle.
     Precede him, Ferret, i' the form.
FERRET Oyez, oyez, oyez—   15
TRUNDLE Oyez, oyez, oyez—

[FERRET] Whereas there hath been awarded—
[TRUNDLE] Whereas there hath been awarded—
[FERRET] By the queen regent of love—
[TRUNDLE] By the queen regent of love—   20
[FERRET] In this high court of sovereignty—
[TRUNDLE] In this high court of sovereignty—
[FERRET] Two special hours of address—
[TRUNDLE] Two special hours of address—
[FERRET] To Herbert Lovel, appellant—   25
[TRUNDLE] To Herbert Lovel, appellant—
[FERRET] Against the Lady Frampul, defendant—
[TRUNDLE] Against the Lady Frampul, defendant—
[FERRET] Herbert Lovel, come into the court—
[TRUNDLE] Herbert Lovel, come into the court—   30
[FERRET] Make challenge to thy first hour—°
[TRUNDLE] Make challenge to thy first hour—
[FERRET] And save thee and thy bail—°
[TRUNDLE] And save thee and thy bail.
          [*Enter Lovel, who sits at one side of the stage*]
HOST Lo, louting, where he comes into the court.   35
     Clerk of the sovereignty, take his appearance,
     And how accoutred, how designed he comes.°
FERRET 'Tis done. Now, crier, call the Lady Frampul,
     And by the name of Frances, Lady Frampul, defendant—
TRUNDLE Frances, Lady Frampul, defendant—   40
[FERRET] Come into the court—
[TRUNDLE] Come into the court—
[FERRET] Make answer to the award—
[TRUNDLE] Make answer to the award—
[FERRET] And save thee and thy bail—   45
[TRUNDLE] And save thee and thy bail.
          Enter Lady [Frampul, who sits on the opposite side of the stage,
          confronting Lovel]
HOST She makes a noble and a just appearance.
     Set it down likewise, and how armed she comes.
PRUDENCE Usher of Love's court, give 'em their oath
     According to the form, upon Love's missal.   50
HOST Arise, and lay your hands upon the book.
     Herbert Lovel, appellant, and Lady Frances Frampul, defendant,
     you shall swear upon the liturgy of love, Ovid *De Arte Amandi*,° that
     you neither have, ne will have, nor in any wise bear about you, thing

or things, pointed or blunt, within these lists, other than what are   55
natural and allowed by the court: no enchanted arms or weapons,
stones of virtue,° herb of grace,° charm, character,° spell, philtre,
or other power than Love's only, and the justness of your cause. So
help you Love, his mother, and the contents of this book. Kiss it.°   60
    [*Lovel and Lady Frampul kiss the book*]
Return unto your seats. Crier, bid silence.

TRUNDLE Oyez, oyez, oyez.

FERRET I' the name o' the sovereign of love—

TRUNDLE I' the name o' the sovereign of love—   65

[FERRET] Notice is given by the court—

[TRUNDLE] Notice is given by the court—

[FERRET] To the appellant and defendant—

[TRUNDLE] To the appellant and defendant—

[FERRET] That the first hour of address proceeds—   70

[TRUNDLE] That the first hour of address proceeds—

[FERRET] And love save the sovereign—

[TRUNDLE] And love save the sovereign. Every man or woman keep
    silence, pain of imprisonment.

PRUDENCE Do your endeavours, in the name of love.   75

LOVEL To make my first approaches, then, in love.

LADY FRAMPUL Tell us what love is, that we may be sure
    There's such a thing, and that it is in nature.

LOVEL Excellent lady, I did not expect
    To meet an infidel, much less an atheist   80
    Here in Love's lists! Of so much unbelief
    To raise a question of his being—

HOST   Well charged!

LOVEL I rather thought, and with religion think,
    Had all the character of love been lost,
    His lines, dimensions, and whole signature°   85
    Razed and defaced with dull humanity,
    That both his nature and his essence might
    Have found their mighty instauration here,
    Here where the confluence of fair and good
    Meets to make up all beauty. For what else   90
    Is love, but the most noble, pure affection
    Of what is truly beautiful and fair?
    Desire of union with the thing beloved?°

BEAUFORT Have the assistants of the court their votes
    And writ of privilege to speak them freely?°   95

PRUDENCE Yes, to assist, but not to interrupt.

BEAUFORT Then I have read somewhere, that man and woman
    Were in the first creation both one piece,
    And being cleft asunder, ever since
    Love was an appetite to be rejoined.°   100
    As for example—
        [*Kisses Frank*]

NURSE   *Cra-mo-cree*! What mean'sh 'tou?°

BEAUFORT Only to kiss and part.

HOST   So much is lawful.

LATIMER And stands with the prerogative of Love's court.

LOVEL It is a fable of Plato's in his *Banquet*,
    And uttered there by Aristophanes.   105

HOST 'Twas well remembered here, and to good use.
    But on with your description what love is:
    'Desire of union with the thing beloved'—

LOVEL I meant a definition. For I make
    The efficient cause, what's beautiful and fair;   110
    The formal cause, the appetite of union;
    The final cause, the union itself.°
    But larger, if you'll have it, by description:°
    It is a flame and ardour of the mind,
    Dead in the proper corpse, quick in another's,°   115
    Transfers the lover into the loved.
    The he or she that loves, engraves or stamps
    Th' idea of what they love, first in themselves—
    Or, like to glasses, so their minds take in
    The forms of their beloved, and them reflect.°   120
    It is the likeness of affections
    Is both the parent and the nurse of love.
    Love is a spiritual coupling of two souls,
    So much more excellent, as it least relates
    Unto the body; circular, eternal,°   125
    Not feigned or made, but born; and then, so precious
    As nought can value it but itself; so free
    As nothing can command it but itself;
    And in itself so round and liberal
    As where it favours, it bestows itself.   130

BEAUFORT And that do I. [*To Frank*] Here my whole self I tender,
    According to the practice o' the court.

NURSE Ay, 'tish a naughty practish, a lewd practish;

Be quiet, man, dou shalt not leip her here.°
BEAUFORT Leap her! I lip her, foolish queen-at-arms,°   135
  Thy blazon's false: wilt thou blaspheme thine office?
LOVEL But we must take and understand this love
  Along still as a name of dignity,°
  Not pleasure.
HOST [*to Beaufort*] Mark you that, my light young lord?
LOVEL True love hath no unworthy thought, no light,   140
  Loose, unbecoming appetite or strain,
  But fixèd, constant, pure, immutable.
BEAUFORT I relish not these philosophical feasts.
  Give me a banquet o' sense, like that of Ovid:°
  A form to take the eye; a voice, mine ear;   145
  Pure aromatics, to my scent; a soft,
  Smooth, dainty hand to touch; and for my taste,
  Ambrosiac kisses to melt down the palate.
LOVEL They are the earthly, lower form of lovers
  Are only taken with what strikes the senses,   150
  And love by that loose scale. Although I grant
  We like what's fair and graceful in an object,
  And, true, would use it in the all we tend to,
  Both of our civil and domestic deeds:
  In ordering of an army, in our style,°   155
  Apparel, gesture, building, or what not.
  All arts and actions do affect their beauty.
  But put the case: in travel I may meet
  Some gorgeous structure, a brave frontispiece.°
  Shall I stay captive i' the outer court,   160
  Surprised with that, and not advance to know°
  Who dwells there, and inhabiteth the house?
  There is my friendship to be made within,
  With what can love me again, not with the walls,
  Doors, windows, architrabes, the frieze, and coronice.   165
  My end is lost in loving of a face,
  An eye, lip, nose, hand, foot, or other part,
  Whose all is but a statue, if the mind
  Move not, which only can make the return.
  The end of love is to have two made one   170
  In will and in affection, that the minds
  Be first inoculated, not the bodies.°
BEAUFORT Gi' me the body, if it be a good one.

[*He kisses Frank*]

FRANK Nay, sweet my lord, I must appeal the sovereign
    For better quarter, if you hold your practice.   175
TRUNDLE Silence, pain of imprisonment! Hear the court.
LOVEL The body's love is frail, subject to change,
    And alters still with it; the mind's is firm,
    One and the same, proceedeth first from weighing
    And well examining what is fair and good,   180
    Then what is like in reason, fit in manners:
    That breeds good will, good will desire of union.
    So knowledge first begets benevolence,
    Benevolence breeds friendship, friendship love.
    And where it starts or steps aside from this,°   185
    It is a mere degenerous appetite,
    A lost, oblique, depraved affection,°
    And bears no mark or character of love.
LADY FRAMPUL How am I changed! By what alchemy
    Of love or language am I thus translated?   190
    His tongue is tipped with the philosophers' stone,°
    And that hath touched me through every vein.
    I feel that transmutation o' my blood,
    As I were quite become another creature,
    And all he speaks, it is projection!°   195
PRUDENCE Well feigned, my lady—now her parts begin.°
LATIMER And she will act 'em subtly.
PRUDENCE   She fails me else.
LOVEL Nor do they trespass within bounds of pardon,
    That, giving way and licence to their love,
    Divest him of his noblest ornaments,   200
    Which are his modesty and shamefacedness;
    And so they do that have unfit designs
    Upon the parties they pretend to love.
    For what's more monstrous, more a prodigy,
    Than to hear me protest truth of affection   205
    Unto a person that I would dishonour?
    And what's a more dishonour than defacing
    Another's good with forfeiting mine own,
    And drawing on a fellowship of sin?
    From note of which, though for a while we may   210
    Be both kept safe by caution, yet the conscience
    Cannot be cleansed. For what was hitherto

Called by the name of love becomes destroyed
Then with the fact; the innocency lost,°
The bating of affection soon will follow;   215
And love is never true that is not lasting,
No more than any can be pure or perfect
That entertains more than one object. *Dixi.*°
LADY FRAMPUL Oh speak, and speak forever! Let mine ear
Be feasted still, and filled with this banquet!   220
No sense can ever surfeit on such truth:
It is the marrow of all lovers' tenents!
Who hath read Plato, Heliodore, or Tatius,
Sidney, d'Urfé, or all Love's fathers, like him?°
He is there the Master of the Sentences,°   225
Their school, their commentary, text, and gloss,
And breathes the true divinity of Love!
PRUDENCE Excellent actor! How she hits this passion!
LADY FRAMPUL Where have I lived in heresy, so long
Out o' the congregation of Love,   230
And stood irregular, by all his canons?°
LATIMER But do you think she plays?
PRUDENCE   Upo' my sovereignty,
Mark her anon.
LATIMER   I shake and am half jealous.
LADY FRAMPUL What penance shall I do to be received
And reconcilèd to the church of Love?   235
Go on procession, barefoot, to his image,
And say some hundred penitential verses
There out of Chaucer's *Troilus and Cressid*?°
Or to his mother's shrine vow a wax candle°
As large as the town maypole is, and pay it?   240
Enjoin me anything this court thinks fit,
For I have trespassed and blasphemèd Love.°
I have, indeed, despised his deity,
Whom, till this miracle wrought on me, I knew not.
Now I adore Love, and would kiss the rushes   245
That bear this reverend gentleman, his priest,
If that would expiate—but I fear it will not.
For though he be somewhat struck in years, and old
Enough to be my father, he is wise,
And only wise men love, the other covet.   250
I could begin to be in love with him,

But will not tell him yet because I hope
T' enjoy the other hour with more delight,
And prove him farther.
PRUDENCE   Most Socratic lady,°
  Or, if you will, ironic! Gi' you joy°   255
  O' your Platonic love here, Master Lovel.
  But pay him his first kiss yet, i' the court,
  Which is a debt and due, for the hour's run.
LADY FRAMPUL How swift is time, and slyly steals away
  From them would hug it, value it, embrace it?   260
  I should have thought it scarce had run ten minutes,
  When the whole hour is fled. Here, take your kiss, sir,
  Which I most willing tender you in court.
        [*She kisses Lovel*]
BEAUFORT And we do imitate—
        [*He kisses Frank*]
LADY FRAMPUL   And I could wish
  It had been twenty—so the sovereign's   265
  Poor narrow nature had decreed it so—
  But that is past, irrevocable, now:
  She did her kind according to her latitude—
PRUDENCE Beware you do not conjure up a spirit
  You cannot lay.
LADY FRAMPUL I dare you, do your worst,°   270
  Show me but such an injustice: I would thank you
  To alter your award.
LATIMER   Sure she is serious!
  I shall have another fit of jealousy,
  I feel a grudging!
HOST   Cheer up, noble guest,
  We cannot guess what this may come to yet;   275
  The brain of man, or woman, is uncertain.
LOVEL Tut, she dissembles. All is personated°
  And counterfeit comes from her. If it were not,
  The Spanish monarchy, with both the Indies,
  Could not buy off the treasure of this kiss,   280
  Or half give balance for my happiness.
HOST Why, as it is yet, it glads my Light Heart
  To see you roused thus from a sleepy humour
  Of drowsy, accidental melancholy,°
  And all those brave parts of your soul awake   285

That did before seem drowned and buried in you.
That you express yourself as you had backed
The Muses' horse! Or got Bellerophon's arms!°
    [*Enter Fly*]
—What news with Fly?

FLY   News of a newer lady,
A finer, fresher, braver, bonnier beauty;   290
A very *bona-roba*, and a bouncer°
In yellow, glistering, golden satin!

LADY FRAMPUL   Pru,
Adjourn the court.

PRUDENCE   Cry, Trundle—

TRUNDLE Oyez, any man or woman that hath any personal attendance
to give unto the court: keep the second hour, and Love save the   295
sovereign.
    [*Exeunt*]

4.1

[*Enter*] *Jug, Barnaby,* [*and*] *Jordan*

[JUG] Oh Barnaby!

JORDAN   Welcome, Barnaby! Where hast thou been?

BARNABY I' the foul weather.

JUG   Which has wet thee, Ban.

BARNABY As dry as a chip. Good Jug, a cast o' thy name,°
  As well as thy office: two jugs!

JUG   By and by.°

      [*Exit Jug*]

JORDAN What lady's this thou hast brought here?

BARNABY   A great lady!   5
  I know no more; one that will try you, Jordan.
  She'll find your gauge, your circle, your capacity.°
  How does old Staggers, the smith? And Tree, the saddler?
  Keep they their penny-club still?

JORDAN   And th' old catch, too,°
  Of 'Whoop Barnaby—'

BARNABY   Do they sing at me?   10

JORDAN They are reeling at it in the parlour now.

      [*Enter Jug with drink*]

BARNABY I'll to 'em—gi' me a drink first.

JORDAN   Where's thy hat?

BARNABY I lost it by the way—gi' me another.

JUG A hat?

BARNABY A drink.

JUG   Take heed of taking cold, Ban—

BARNABY The wind blew 't off at Highgate, and my lady°   15
  Would not endure me 'light to take it up,
  But made me drive bareheaded i' the rain.

JORDAN That she might be mistaken for a countess?°

BARNABY Troth, like enough! She might be an o'er-grown duchess,°
  For aught I know.

JUG   What! With one man!

BARNABY   At a time;   20
  They carry no more, the best of 'em.

JORDAN   Nor the bravest.

392

BARNABY And she is very brave.

JORDAN   A stately gown
And petticoat she has on.

BARNABY   Ha' you spied that, Jordan?
You are a notable peerer, an old rabbi°
At a smock's hem, boy.

JUG   As he is chamberlain,   25
He may do that by his place.

JORDAN   What's her squire?

BARNABY A toy that she allows eight-pence a day,
A slight man-net, to port her up and down.°
Come, show me to my playfellows, old Staggers,
And Father Tree.

JORDAN   Here, this way, Barnaby.   30
          [*Exeunt*]

4.2

          [*Enter*] *Tipto, Burst, Huffle, Fly,* [*and Pierce*]

[TIPTO] Come, let us take in fresco here one quart.°

BURST [*to Pierce*] Two quarts, my man-of-war, let us not be stinted.

HUFFLE Advance three jordans, varlet o' the house.
          Exit Pierce

TIPTO I do not like your Burst, bird; he is saucy.
Some shopkeeper he was?

FLY   Yes, sir.

TIPTO   I knew it.   5
A broke-winged shopkeeper? I nose 'em straight.°
He had no father, I warrant him, that durst own him;
Some foundling in a stall, or the church-porch;
Brought up i' the Hospital; and so bound prentice;°
Then master of a shop; then one o' the Inquest;°   10
Then breaks out bankrupt, or starts alderman:
The original of both is a church-porch—

FLY Of some, my colonel.

TIPTO   Good faith, of most
O' your shop citizens, they're rude animals!
And let 'em get but ten mile out o' town,   15
Th' out-swagger all the wapentake.

FLY   What's that?
TIPTO A Saxon word to signify the hundred.
       [*Enter Pierce, who sets down the drink and exits*]
BURST Come, let us drink, Sir Glorious, some brave
    health
    Upon our tiptoes.
TIPTO   To the health o' the Bursts.
BURST Why Bursts?
TIPTO   Why Tiptos?
BURST   Oh, I cry you mercy!   20
TIPTO It is sufficient.
HUFFLE   What is so sufficient?
TIPTO To drink to you is sufficient.
HUFFLE   On what terms?
TIPTO That you shall give security to pledge me.°
HUFFLE So you will name no Spaniard, I will pledge you.
TIPTO I rather choose to thirst—and will thirst ever,   25
    Than leave that cream of nations uncried up.
    Perish all wine and gust of wine!
             [*Throws the drink at Huffle*]
HUFFLE   How, spill it?
    Spill it at me?
TIPTO   I reck not, but I spilt it.
FLY Nay, pray you be quiet, noble bloods.
BURST   No Spaniards,
    I cry, with my cousin Huffle.
HUFFLE   Spaniards? Pilchers!   30
TIPTO Do not provoke my patient blade; it sleeps,
    And would not hear thee. Huffle, thou art rude,
    And dost not know the Spanish composition.°
BURST What is the recipe? Name the ingredients.
TIPTO Valour.
BURST   Two ounces!
TIPTO   Prudence.
BURST   Half a dram!   35
TIPTO Justice.
BURST   A pennyweight!
TIPTO   Religion.
BURST Three scruples!
TIPTO   And of *gravedàd*—
BURST   A face-full!°
TIPTO He carries such a dose of it in his looks,

Actions, and gestures, as it breeds respect
To him from savages, and reputation   40
With all the sons of men.
BURST   Will it give him credit
    With gamesters, courtiers, citizens, or tradesmen?
TIPTO He'll borrow money on the stroke of his beard,
    Or turn of his *mustaccio*! His mere *cuello*,°
    Or ruff about his neck, is a bill of exchange   45
    In any bank in Europe! Not a merchant
    That sees his gait but straight will furnish him
    Upon his pace!
HUFFLE   I have heard the Spanish name
    Is terrible to children in some countries,
    And used to make them eat—their bread and butter,°   50
    Or take their wormseed.
TIPTO   Huffle, you do shuffle.
        [*Enter*] *Stuff* [*and*] *Pinnacia* [*richly dressed*]
BURST 'Slid, here's a lady!
HUFFLE   And a lady gay!°
TIPTO A well-trimmed lady!
HUFFLE   Let's lay her aboard.°
BURST Let's hail her first.
TIPTO   By your sweet favour, lady.
STUFF Good gentlemen, be civil; we are strangers.   55
BURST And you were Flemings, sir!
HUFFLE   Or Spaniards!
TIPTO They're here have been at Seville i' their days,°
    And at Madrid, too.
PINNACIA   He is a foolish fellow,
    I pray you mind him not, he is my Protection.
TIPTO In your protection he is safe, sweet lady.   60
    So shall you be in mine.
HUFFLE   A share, good colonel.
TIPTO Of what?
HUFFLE   Of your fine lady! I am Hodge,
    My name is Huffle.
TIPTO   Huffling Hodge, be quiet.
BURST And I pray you, be you so, glorious colonel;
    Hodge Huffle shall be quiet.
HUFFLE [*singing*]   65
        A lady gay, gay;
        For she is a lady gay, gay, gay. For she's a lady gay.

TIPTO Bird o' the vespers, *vespertilio* Burst,°
　　You are a gentleman o' the first head,°
　　But that head may be broke as all the body is,
　　Burst, if you tie not up your Huffle, quickly.　　　　　　　70
HUFFLE Tie dogs, not man.
BURST　　　　　　　　　　Nay, pray thee, Hodge, be still.
TIPTO This steel here rides not on this thigh in vain.
HUFFLE Show'st thou thy steel and thigh, thou glorious dirt?
　　Then Hodge sings *Sampson*, and no ties shall hold!°
　　　　[They fight. Enter] Pierce, Jug, [and] Jordan
PIERCE Keep the peace, gentlemen! What do you mean?　　　75
TIPTO I will not discompose myself for Huffle.
　　　　[Exeunt all but Stuff and Pinnacia, fighting]
PINNACIA You see what your entreaty and pressure still
　　Of gentlemen to be civil doth bring on?
　　A quarrel, and perhaps manslaughter! You
　　Will carry your goose about you still, your planing-iron,°　80
　　Your tongue to smooth all! Is not here fine stuff?
STUFF Why, wife?
PINNACIA　　　　　　Your wife? Ha' not I forbidden you that?
　　Do you think I'll call you husband i' this gown,
　　Or anything, in that jacket, but Protection?°
　　Here, tie my shoe, and show my vellute petticoat　　　　85
　　And my silk stocking! Why do you make me a lady,
　　If I may not do like a lady in fine clothes?
STUFF Sweetheart, you may do what you will with me.
PINNACIA Ay, I knew that at home, what to do with you.
　　But why was I brought hither? To see fashions?°　　　　　90
STUFF And wear them, too, sweetheart, but this wild company—
PINNACIA Why do you bring me in wild company?
　　You'd ha' me tame and civil in wild company?
　　I hope I know wild company are fine company,
　　And in fine company, where I am fine myself,　　　　　　95
　　A lady may do anything, deny nothing
　　To a fine party, I have heard you say 't.°
　　　　[Enter] Pierce
PIERCE There are a company of ladies above
　　Desire your ladyship's company, and to take
　　The surety of their lodgings from the affront°　　　　　100
　　Of these half-beasts were here e'en now, the Centaurs.°
PINNACIA Are they fine ladies?

PIERCE   Some very fine ladies.

PINNACIA As fine as I?

PIERCE   I dare use no comparisons,
  Being a servant, sent—

PINNACIA   Spoke like a fine fellow!
  I would thou wert one: I'd not then deny thee.   105
  But thank thy lady.

          [*Exit Pierce. Enter*] Host

HOST   Madam, I must crave you
  To afford a lady a visit, would excuse
  Some harshness o' the house you have received
  From the brute guests.

PINNACIA   This's a fine old man!
  I'd go with him an he were a little finer.   110

STUFF You may, sweetheart, it is mine host.

PINNACIA   Mine host!

HOST Yes, madam, I must bid you welcome.

PINNACIA   Do, then.

STUFF But do not stay.

PINNACIA   I'll be advised by you, yes!

          [*Exeunt*]

4.3

      [*Enter*] Latimer, Beaufort, Lady [*Frampul*], Prudence, Frank
      [*and Nurse*]

[LATIMER] What more than Thracian barbarism was this?°

BEAUFORT The battle o' the Centaurs with the Lapiths!

LADY FRAMPUL There is no taming o' the monster drink.

LATIMER But what a glorious beast our Tipto showed!
  He would not discompose himself, the don!   5
  Your Spaniard ne'er doth discompose himself.

BEAUFORT Yet how he talked and roared i' the beginning!

PRUDENCE And ran as fast as a knocked marrowbone.°

BEAUFORT So they did all at last, when Lovel went down
  And chased 'em 'bout the court.

LATIMER   For all's Don Lewis,   10
  Or fencing after Euclid!

LADY FRAMPUL   I ne'er saw

A lightning shoot so as my servant did:
His rapier was a meteor, and he waved it
Over 'em like a comet as they fled him!
I marked his manhood; every stoop he made   15
Was like an eagle's at a flight of cranes
(As I have read somewhere).

BEAUFORT   Bravely expressed.°

LATIMER And like a lover.

LADY FRAMPUL   Of his valour, I am.
He seemed a body rarefied to air,
Or that his sword and arm were of a piece,   20
They went together so!
            [*Enter Host with Pinnacia*]
                            Here comes the lady.

BEAUFORT A bouncing *bona-roba*, as the Fly said.

FRANK She is some giantess! I'll stand off
For fear she swallow me.

LADY FRAMPUL   Is not this our gown, Pru,
That I bespoke of Stuff?

PRUDENCE   It is the fashion.   25

LADY FRAMPUL Ay, and the silk! Feel, sure it is the same!

PRUDENCE And the same petticoat, lace, and all!

LADY FRAMPUL   I'll swear it.
How came it hither? Make a bill of enquiry.°

PRUDENCE You've a fine suit on, madam, and a rich one.

LADY FRAMPUL And of a curious making.

PRUDENCE   And a new.°   30

PINNACIA As new as day.

LATIMER   She answers like a fishwife.°

PINNACIA I put it on since noon, I do assure you.

PRUDENCE Who is your tailor?

LADY FRAMPUL   Pray you, your fashioner's name?

PINNACIA My fashioner is a certain man o' mine own,
He is i' the house: no matter for his name.   35

HOST Oh, but to satisfy this bevy of ladies,
Of which a brace here longed to bid you welcome.

PINNACIA He is one, in truth, I title my Protection.
Bid him come up.

HOST [*calls*]   Our new lady's Protection!
What is your ladyship's style?

PINNACIA   Countess Pinnacia.°   40

HOST Countess Pinnacia's man, come to your lady.
    [*Enter Stuff*]
PRUDENCE Your ladyship's tailor! Master Stuff!
LADY FRAMPUL   How, Stuff?
    He the Protection?
HOST   Stuff looks like a remnant.
STUFF [*falling on his knees*] I am undone, discovered!
PRUDENCE   'Tis the suit, madam,
    Now without scruple! And this some device°   45
    To bring it home with.
PINNACIA   Why upon your knees?
    Is this your lady godmother?
STUFF   Mum, Pinnacia,
    It is the Lady Frampul, my best customer.
LADY FRAMPUL What show is this that you present us with?
STUFF I do beseech your ladyship, forgive me.   50
    She did but say the suit on.
LADY FRAMPUL   Who? Which she?°
STUFF My wife, forsooth.
LADY FRAMPUL   How? Mistress Stuff? Your wife!
    Is that the riddle?
PRUDENCE   We all looked for a lady,
    A duchess or a countess at the least.
STUFF She is my own lawfully begotten wife°   55
    In wedlock. We ha' been coupled now seven years.
LADY FRAMPUL And why thus masked? You like a footman, ha!
    And she your countess!
PINNACIA   To make a fool of himself,
    And of me, too.
STUFF   I pray thee, Pinnace, peace.
PINNACIA Nay, it shall out since you have called me wife   60
    And openly dis-ladied me! Though I am dis-countessed,
    I am not yet dis-countenanced. These shall see.
HOST   Silence!
PINNACIA It is a foolish trick, madam, he has;
    For though he be your tailor, he is my beast.
    I may be bold with him and tell his story.   65
    When he makes any fine garment will fit me,
    Or any rich thing that he thinks of price,
    Then must I put it on and be his countess
    Before he carry it home unto the owners.

A coach is hired, and four horse; he runs   70
   In his velvet jacket thus to Romford, Croydon,
   Hounslow, or Barnet, the next bawdy road;°
   And takes me out, carries me up, and throws me
   Upon a bed—
LADY FRAMPUL Peace, thou immodest woman!
   She glories in the bravery o' the vice.   75
LATIMER 'Tis a quaint one!
BEAUFORT   A fine *species*°
   Of fornicating with a man's own wife,
   Found out by—what's his name?
LATIMER   Master Nick Stuff.
HOST The very figure of preoccupation°
   In all his customer's best clothes.
LATIMER   He lies   80
   With his own succuba in all your names.
BEAUFORT And all your credits.
HOST   Ay, and at all their costs.°
LATIMER This gown was then bespoken for the sovereign?
BEAUFORT Ay, marry, was it.
LADY FRAMPUL   And a main offence
   Committed 'gainst the sovereignty, being not brought   85
   Home i' the time; beside, the profanation,
   Which may call on the censure of the court.°
HOST Let him be blanketed. Call up the quartermaster.°
   Deliver him o'er to Fly.
          [*Enter Fly*]
STUFF   Oh good my lord!
HOST Pillage the pinnace.
LADY FRAMPUL   Let his wife be stripped.°   90
BEAUFORT Blow off her upper deck.
LATIMER   Tear all her tackle.
LADY FRAMPUL Pluck the polluted robes over her ears,
   Or cut them all to pieces, make a fire o' them.
PRUDENCE To rags and cinders, burn th' idolatrous vestures.
HOST Fly and your fellows, see that the whole censure   95
   Be throughly executed.
FLY   We'll toss him bravely
   Till the stuff stink again.
HOST   And send her home,
   Divested to her flannel, in a cart.

400

LATIMER And let her footman beat the basin afore her.°
FLY The court shall be obeyed.
HOST   Fly and his officers   100
    Will do it fiercely.
STUFF   Merciful Queen Pru!
PRUDENCE I cannot help you.
        [*Exit Fly, with Stuff and Pinnacia*]
BEAUFORT   Go thy ways, Nick Stuff,
    Thou hast nicked it for a fashioner of venery.°
LATIMER For his own hell, though he run ten mile for 't.
PRUDENCE Oh, here comes Lovel for his second hour.   105
BEAUFORT And after him, the type of Spanish valour.°

4.4

    [*Enter*] *Lovel* [*with a paper, followed by*] *Tipto*
[LADY FRAMPUL] Servant, what have you there?
LOVEL   A meditation,
    Or rather a vision, madam, and of beauty,
    Our former subject.
LADY FRAMPUL   Pray you, let us hear it.
LOVEL   It was a beauty that I saw,
        So pure, so perfect, as the frame   5
        Of all the universe was lame°
        To that one figure, could I draw
        Or give least line of it a law!

        A skein of silk without a knot,
        A fair march made without a halt,   10
        A curious form without a fault,°
        A printed book without a blot:
        All beauty, and without a spot.

LADY FRAMPUL They are gentle words, and would deserve a note°
    Set to 'em as gentle.
LOVEL   I have tried my skill   15
    To close the second hour, if you will hear them;
    My boy by that time will have got it perfect.

LADY FRAMPUL Yes, gentle servant. [*Aside*] In what calm he speaks
    After this noise and tumult, so unmoved,
    With that serenity of countenance   20
    As if his thoughts did acquiesce in that°
    Which is the object of the second hour,
    And nothing else.
PRUDENCE   Well then, summon the court.
LADY FRAMPUL I have a suit to the sovereign of Love,
    If it may stand with the honour of the court,   25
    To change the question but from love to valour,
    To hear it said but what true valour is,
    Which oft begets true love.
LATIMER   It is a question
    Fit for the court to take true knowledge of,
    And hath my just assent.
PRUDENCE   Content.
BEAUFORT   Content.   30
FRANK Content. I am content, give him his oath.
HOST Herbert Lovel, thou shalt swear upon *The Testament of Love*° to
    make answer to this question propounded to thee by the court,
    what true valour is; and therein to tell the truth, the whole truth,
    and nothing but the truth. So help thee Love, and thy bright sword
    at need.   35
LOVEL So help me Love, and my good sword at need.
    It is the greatest virtue, and the safety
    Of all mankind; the object of it is danger.°
    A certain mean 'twixt fear and confidence:
    No inconsiderate rashness, or vain appetite°   40
    Of false encount'ring formidable things;°
    But a true science of distinguishing
    What's good or evil. It springs out of reason,
    And tends to perfect honesty; the scope°
    Is always honour and the public good: 45
    It is no valour for a private cause.
BEAUFORT No? Not for reputation?
LOVEL   That's man's idol
    Set up 'gainst God, the maker of all laws,
    Who hath commanded us we should not kill;
    And yet we say we must for reputation.   50
    What honest man can either fear his own,°
    Or else will hurt another's reputation?

Fear to do base, unworthy things is valour;
If they be done to us, to suffer them
Is valour, too. The office of a man   55
That's truly valiant is considerable°
Three ways: the first is in respect of matter,
Which still is danger; in respect of form,
Wherein he must preserve his dignity;
And in the end, which must be ever lawful.   60
LATIMER But men, when they are heated and in passion,
   Cannot consider.
LOVEL   Then it is not valour.
   I never thought an angry person valiant:
   Virtue is never aided by a vice.
   What need is there of anger and of tumult   65
   When reason can do the same things, or more?
BEAUFORT Oh yes, 'tis profitable, and of use:
   It makes us fierce and fit to undertake.°
LOVEL Why, so will drink make us both bold and rash,
   Or frenzy if you will: do these make valiant?°   70
   They are poor helps, and virtue needs them not.
   No man is valianter by being angry,
   But he that could not valiant be without;
   So that it comes not in the aid of virtue,
   But in the stead of it.
LATIMER   He holds the right.   75
LOVEL And 'tis an odious kind of remedy,
   To owe our health to a disease.
TIPTO   If man
   Should follow the dictamen of his passion,
   He could not 'scape—
BEAUFORT   To discompose himself.
LATIMER According to Don Lewis!
HOST   Or Carranza!   80
LOVEL Good Colonel Glorious, whilst we treat of valour,
   Dismiss yourself.
LATIMER   You are not concerned.
LOVEL   Go drink,
   And congregate the ostlers and the tapsters,°
   The under-officers o' your regiment;
   Compose with them, and be not angry valiant.°   85
      Tipto goes out

BEAUFORT How does that differ from true valour?
LOVEL   Thus:°
    In the efficient, or that which makes it,
    For it proceeds from passion, not from judgement;
    Then brute beasts have it, wicked persons—there
    It differs in the subject; in the form,   90
    'Tis carried rashly and with violence;
    Then i' the end, where it respects not truth°
    Or public honesty, but mere revenge.
    Now confident and undertaking valour°
    Sways from the true two other ways, as being   95
    A trust in our own faculties, skill, or strength,
    And not the right, or conscience o' the cause
    That works it; then i' the end, which is the victory,
    And not the honour.
BEAUFORT   But the ignorant valour
    That knows not why it undertakes, but doth it   100
    T'escape the infamy merely—
LOVEL   Is worst of all:
    That valour lies i' the eyes o' the lookers on,
    And is called valour with a witness.
BEAUFORT   Right.
LOVEL The things true valour is exercised about
    Are poverty, restraint, captivity,   105
    Banishment, loss of children, long disease:
    The least is death. Here valour is beheld,
    Properly seen; about these it is present;
    Not trivial things which but require our confidence.
    And yet to those we must object ourselves°   110
    Only for honesty: if any other
    Respect be mixed, we quite put out her light.°
    And as all knowledge, when it is removed
    Or separate from justice, is called craft
    Rather than wisdom, so a mind affecting   115
    Or undertaking dangers for ambition
    Or any self pretext, not for the public,°
    Deserves the name of daring, not of valour,
    And over-daring is as great a vice
    As over-fearing.
LATIMER   Yes, and often greater.   120
LOVEL But as it is not the mere punishment

But cause that makes a martyr, so it is not
Fighting or dying, but the manner of it
Renders a man himself. A valiant man
Ought not to undergo or tempt a danger   125
But worthily and by selected ways:
He undertakes with reason, not by chance.
His valour is the salt to his other virtues,
They are all unseasoned without it. The waiting-maids,
Or the concomitants of it, are his patience,   130
His magnanimity, his confidence,
His constancy, security, and quiet;°
He can assure himself against all rumour,
Despairs of nothing, laughs at contumelies,
As knowing himself advanced in a height   135
Where injury cannot reach him, nor aspersion°
Touch him with soil.
LADY FRAMPUL   Most manly uttered all!
    As if Achilles had the chair in valour,
    And Hercules were but a lecturer.
    Who would not hang upon those lips forever   140
    That strike such music? I could run on them;°
    But modesty is such a schoolmistress
    To keep our sex in awe.
PRUDENCE   Or you can feign,
    My subtle and dissembling lady mistress!
LATIMER I fear she means it, Pru, in too good earnest!   145
LOVEL The purpose of an injury 'tis to vex
    And trouble me. Now, nothing can do that
    To him that's valiant. He that is affected
    With the least injury is less than it.
    It is but reasonable to conclude,   150
    That should be stronger still which hurts than that
    Which is hurt. Now, no wickedness is stronger
    Than what opposeth it: not Fortune's self,
    When she encounters virtue, but comes off
    Both lame and less. Why should a wise man, then,   155
    Confess himself the weaker, by the feeling
    Of a fool's wrong? There may an injury
    Be meant me. I may choose if I will take it.
    But we are now come to that delicacy
    And tenderness of sense, we think an insolence   160

Worse than an injury, bear words worse than deeds;
We are not so much troubled with the wrong,
As with the opinion of the wrong. Like children,
We are made afraid with visors. Such poor sounds
As is the lie or common words of spite,°   165
Wise laws thought never worthy a revenge;
And 'tis the narrowness of human nature,
Our poverty and beggary of spirit,
To take exception at these things. He laughed at me!
He broke a jest! A third took place of me!   170
How most ridiculous quarrels are all these?
Notes of a queasy and sick stomach, labouring
With want of a true injury. The main part
Of the wrong is our vice of taking it.
LATIMER Or our interpreting it to be such.   175
LOVEL You take it rightly. If a woman or child
Give me the lie, would I be angry? No,
Not if I were i' my wits, sure I should think it
No spice of a disgrace. No more is theirs,°
If I will think it, who are to be held   180
In as contemptible a rank or worse.
I am kept out a masque, sometime thrust out,
Made wait a day, two, three, for a great word,
Which, when it comes forth, is all frown and forehead:°
What laughter should this breed, rather than anger!   185
Out of the tumult of so many errors,°
To feel, with contemplation, mine own quiet.
If a great person do me an affront,
A giant of the time, sure I will bear it
Or out of patience or necessity.°   190
Shall I do more for fear than for my judgement?
For me now to be angry with Hodge Huffle,
Or Burst, his broken charge, if he be saucy,
Or our own type of Spanish valour, Tipto—
Who, were he now necessited to beg,   195
Would ask an alms like Conde Olivares—°
Were just to make myself such a vain animal
As one of them. If light wrongs touch me not,
No more shall great; if not a few, not many.
There's nought so sacred with us but may find   200
A sacrilegious person, yet the thing is

No less divine 'cause the profane can reach it.
He is shot-free in battle is not hurt,
Not he that is not hit. So he is valiant
That yields not unto wrongs, not he that scapes 'em.   205
They that do pull down churches, and deface
The holiest altars, cannot hurt the godhead.
A calm wise man may show as much true valour
Amidst these popular provocations
As can an able captain show security°   210
By his brave conduct through an enemy's country.
A wise man never goes the people's way,
But as the planets still move contrary
To the world's motion, so doth he to opinion.
He will examine if those accidents   215
(Which common fame calls injuries) happen to him
Deservedly or no: come they deservedly,
They are no wrongs then, but his punishments;
If undeservedly, and he not guilty,
The doer of them first should blush, not he.   220

LATIMER Excellent!
BEAUFORT   Truth, and right!
FRANK   An oracle
Could not have spoken more!
LADY FRAMPUL   Been more believed!
PRUDENCE The whole court runs into your sentence, sir!°
And see, your second hour is almost ended.
LADY FRAMPUL It cannot be! Oh, clip the wings of Time,   225
Good Pru, or make him stand still with a charm:
Distil the gout into it, cramps, all diseases
T' arrest him in the foot and fix him here.
O for an engine to keep back all clocks,°
Or make the sun forget his motion!   230
If I but knew what drink the time now loved,
To set my Trundle at him, mine own Barnaby!
PRUDENCE Why, I'll consult our Shelee-nien Thomas.
      [*She shakes the Nurse*]
NURSE *Er grae Chreest.*
BEAUFORT   Wake her not.
NURSE   *Tower een cuppan*°
D'usque bagh doone.
PRUDENCE   *Usque bagh*'s her drink,°   235

But 'twi' not make the time drunk.

HOST   As 't hath her.
Away with her, my lord, but marry her first.
        [*Exeunt Lord Beaufort and Frank*]
PRUDENCE Ay, that'll be sport anon, too, for my lady,
But she hath other game to fly at yet.
The hour is come, your kiss.
LADY FRAMPUL   My servant's song first.   240
PRUDENCE I say the kiss first, and I so enjoined it:
At your own peril do make the contempt.
LADY FRAMPUL Well, sir, you must be paid, and legally.
        [*She kisses Lovel*]
PRUDENCE Nay nothing, sir, beyond.
LOVEL   One more—I except!°
This was but half a kiss, and I would change it.   245
PRUDENCE The court's dissolved, removed, and the play ended.
No sound or air of love more, I decree it.
LOVEL From what a happiness hath that one word
Thrown me, into the gulf of misery?°
To what a bottomless despair? How like   250
A court removing, or an ended play,
Shows my abrupt precipitate estate;°
By how much more my vain hopes were increased
By these false hours of conversation!
Did not I prophesy this of myself,   255
And gave the true prognostics? O my brain!°
How art thou turned, and my blood congealed,
My sinews slackened, and my marrow melted,
That I remember not where I have been,
Or what I am? Only my tongue's on fire,   260
And burning downward, hurls forth coals and cinders
To tell this temple of love will soon be ashes!
Come, Indignation, now, and be my mistress:
No more of Love's ingrateful tyranny,
His wheel of torture, and his pits of bird-lime,   265
His nets of nooses, whirlpools of vexation,
His mills to grind his servants into powder—
I will go catch the wind first in a sieve,
Weigh smoke and measure shadows, plough the water,
And sow my hopes there, ere I stay in love.°   270
LATIMER [*aside*] My jealousy is off, I am now secure.

[*Exit Latimer*]

LOVEL Farewell the craft of crocodiles, women's piety°
And practice of it, in this art of flattering
And fooling men. I ha' not lost my reason,
Though I have lent myself out for two hours,   275
Thus to be baffled by a chambermaid°
And the good actor, her lady, afore mine host
Of the Light Heart here that hath laughed at all—

HOST Who, I?

LOVEL   Laugh on, sir, I'll to bed and sleep,
And dream away the vapour of love, if th' house   280
And your leer drunkards let me.

          [*Exeunt all but Lady Frampul, Prudence, and Nurse*]

LADY FRAMPUL   Pru.

PRUDENCE   Sweet madam.°

LADY FRAMPUL Why would you let him go thus?

PRUDENCE   In whose power
Was it to stay him, prop'rer than my lady's?

LADY FRAMPUL Why in her lady's? Are not you the sovereign?

PRUDENCE Would you in conscience, madam, ha' me vex   285
His patience more?

LADY FRAMPUL   Not but apply the cure,
Now it is vexed.

PRUDENCE   That's but one body's work:
Two cannot do the same thing handsomely.

LADY FRAMPUL But had not you the authority absolute?

PRUDENCE And were not you i' rebellion, Lady Frampul,   290
From the beginning?

LADY FRAMPUL   I was somewhat froward,
I must confess, but frowardness sometime
Becomes a beauty, being but a visor
Put on. You'll let a lady wear her mask, Pru.

PRUDENCE But how do I know when her ladyship is pleased   295
To leave it off, except she tell me so?

LADY FRAMPUL You might ha' known that by my looks and language,
Had you been or regardant or observant.°
One woman reads another's character
Without the tedious trouble of deciphering   300
If she but give her mind to 't; you knew well
It could not sort with any reputation
Of mine to come in first, having stood out

So long without conditions for mine honour.

PRUDENCE I thought you did expect none, you so jeered him   305
And put him off with scorn—

LADY FRAMPUL   Who, I? With scorn?
I did express my love to idolatry rather,
And so am justly plagued, not understood.

PRUDENCE I swear I thought you had dissembled, madam,
And doubt you do so yet.

LADY FRAMPUL   Dull, stupid, wench!°   310
Stay i' thy state of ignorance still, be damned,
An idiot chambermaid! Hath all my care,
My breeding thee in fashion, thy rich clothes,
Honours, and titles wrought no brighter effects
On thy dark soul than thus? Well! Go thy ways—   315
Were not the tailor's wife to be demolished,
Ruined, uncased, thou should'st be she, I vow.°

PRUDENCE [tearing off her gown] Why, take your spangled properties,
    your gown,°
And scarves.

LADY FRAMPUL Pru, Pru, what dost thou mean?

PRUDENCE I will not buy this play-boy's bravery   320
At such a price, to be upbraided for it
Thus every minute.

LADY FRAMPUL   Take it not to heart so.

PRUDENCE The tailor's wife? There was a word of scorn!

LADY FRAMPUL It was a word fell from me, Pru, by chance.

PRUDENCE Good madam, please to undeceive yourself.   325
I know when words do slip, and when they are darted
With all their bitterness. Uncased? Demolished?
An idiot chambermaid, stupid and dull?
Be damned for ignorance? I will be so.
And think I do deserve it—that, and more,   330
Much more I do.

LADY FRAMPUL   Here comes mine host. No crying,
Good Pru.
        [Enter Host]
            Where is my servant Lovel, host?

HOST You ha' sent him up to bed, would you would follow him
And make my house amends!

LADY FRAMPUL   Would you advise it?

HOST I would I could command it. My Light Heart   335

    Should leap till midnight.

LADY FRAMPUL   Pray thee be not sullen,
    I yet must ha' thy counsel. Thou shalt wear, Pru,
    The new gown yet.

PRUDENCE   After the tailor's wife?

LADY FRAMPUL Come, be not angry or grieved: I have a project.
        [*Exeunt Lady Frampul and Prudence*]

HOST Wake, Shelee-nien Thomas! Is this your heraldry   340
    And keeping of records, to lose the main?
    Where is your charge?

NURSE   *Gra Chreest*!

HOST   Go ask th'oracle
    O' the bottle at your girdle, there you lost it:
    You are a sober setter of the watch.
        [*Exeunt*]

5.1

[Enter] Host [and] Fly°

[HOST] Come, Fly, and legacy, the bird o' the Heart,
　Prime insect of the inn, professor, quartermaster,
　As ever thou deservedst thy daily drink,
　Paddling in sack and licking i' the same,
　Now show thyself an implement of price　　　　　　　　　　　5
　And help to raise a nap to us out of nothing.°
　Thou sawst 'em married?
FLY　　　　　　　　　　　I do think I did,
　And heard the words, 'I Philip, take thee Laetice.'
　I gave her, too, was then the father Fly,
　And heard the priest do his part far as five nobles　　　　　10
　Would lead him i' the lines of matrimony.
HOST Where were they married?
FLY　　　　　　　　　　　　　I' th' new stable.
HOST　　　　　　　　　　　　　　　　Ominous!
　I ha' known many a church been made a stable,
　But not a stable made a church till now.
　I wish 'em joy. Fly, was he a full priest?　　　　　　　　　15
FLY He bellied for it, had his velvet sleeves°
　And his branched cassock, a side sweeping gown,°
　All his formalities, a good crammed divine!°
　I went not far to fetch him, the next inn
　Where he was lodged, for the action.
HOST　　　　　　　　　　　　　Had they a licence?　　　20
FLY Licence of love, I saw no other; and purse
　To pay the duties both of church and house,
　The angels flew about.
HOST　　　　　　　　Those birds send luck,°
　And mirth will follow. I had thought to ha' sacrificed
　To merriment tonight i' my Light Heart, Fly,　　　　　　　25
　And like a noble poet to have had
　My last act best; but all fails i' the plot.
　Lovel is gone to bed; the Lady Frampul
　And sovereign Pru fall'n out; Tipto and his regiment
　Of mine-men all drunk dumb, from his whoop Barnaby°　　30

To his hoop Trundle: they are his two tropics.°
No project to rear laughter on but this,
The marriage of Lord Beaufort with Laetitia.
Stay, what's here? The satin gown redeemed,°
And Pru restored in 't to her lady's grace!   35
FLY She is set forth in 't, rigged for some employment!
HOST An embassy at least!
FLY   Some treaty of state!
HOST 'Tis a fine tack about, and worth the observing.
       [*They stand aside*]

5.2

       [*Enter*] *Lady* [*Frampul and*] *Prudence* [*magnificently dressed*]
[LADY FRAMPUL] Sweet Pru, aye, now thou art a queen, indeed!
    These robes do royally, and thou becom'st 'em,
    So they do thee. Rich garments only fit
    The parties they are made for; they shame others.
    How did they show on Goody Tailor's back?   5
    Like a caparison for a sow, God save us!
    Thy putting 'em on hath purged and hallowed 'em
    From all pollution meant by the mechanics.
PRUDENCE Hang him, poor snip, a secular shop-wit!°
    H' hath nought but his shears to claim by, and his measures:°   10
    His prentice may as well put in for his needle,
    And plead a stitch.
LADY FRAMPUL   They have no taint in 'em°
    Now o' the tailor.
PRUDENCE   Yes, of his wife's haunches,
    Thus thick of fat; I smell 'em, o' the say.°
LADY FRAMPUL It is restorative, Pru! With thy but chafing it,   15
    A barren hind's grease may work miracles.°
    Find but his chamber door and he will rise
    To thee! Or if thou pleasest, feign to be
    The wretched party herself, and com'st unto him
    In forma pauperis to crave the aid°   20
    Of his knight-errant valour to the rescue
    Of thy distressed robes! Name but thy gown,
    And he will rise to that.

PRUDENCE   I'll fire the charm first.°
　　I had rather die in a ditch with Mistress Shore,
　　Without a smock, as the pitiful matter has it,°   25
　　Than owe my wit to clothes, or ha' it beholden.
HOST Still spirit of Pru!
FLY   And smelling o' the sovereign!
PRUDENCE No, I will tell him as it is, indeed.
　　I come from the fine, froward, frampul lady,°
　　One was run mad with pride, wild with self-love,   30
　　But late encount'ring a wise man who scorned her,
　　And knew the way to his own bed without
　　Borrowing her warming-pan, she hath recovered
　　Part of her wits: so much as to consider
　　How far she hath trespassed, upon whom, and how.   35
　　And now sits penitent and solitary,
　　Like the forsaken turtle, in the volary
　　Of the Light Heart, the cage she hath abused,
　　Mourning her folly, weeping at the height
　　She measures with her eye from whence she is fall'n   40
　　Since she did branch it on the top o' the wood.°
LADY FRAMPUL I prithee, Pru, abuse me enough, that's use me
　　As thou thinkest fit, any coarse way, to humble me,
　　Or bring me home again, or Lovel on.
　　Thou dost not know my suff'rings, what I feel,   45
　　My fires and fears are met: I burn and freeze,
　　My liver's one great coal, my heart shrunk up
　　With all the fibres, and the mass of blood
　　Within me is a standing lake of fire
　　Curled with the cold wind of my gelid sighs   50
　　That drive a drift of sleet through all my body,
　　And shoot a February through my veins.
　　Until I see him, I am drunk with thirst,
　　And surfeited with hunger of his presence.
　　I know not whe'r I am, or no, or speak,°   55
　　Or whether thou dost hear me.
PRUDENCE   Spare expressions.
　　I'll once more venture for your ladyship,
　　So you will use your fortunes reverently.
LADY FRAMPUL Religiously, dear Pru; Love and his mother,
　　I'll build them several churches, shrines, and altars,   60
　　And overhead I'll have, in the glass windows,

The story of this day be painted round
For the poor laity of love to read;
I'll make myself their book, nay their example,
To bid them take occasion by the forelock,   65
And play no after-games of love hereafter.
HOST [*coming forward with Fly*] And here your host and's Fly
    witness your vows.
And like two lucky birds, bring the presage
Of a loud jest: Lord Beaufort married is.
LADY FRAMPUL   Ha!
FLY All-to-be married.
PRUDENCE   To whom? Not your son?°   70
HOST The same, Pru. If her ladyship could take truce
    A little with her passion, and give way
    To their mirth now running—
LADY FRAMPUL   Runs it mirth, let 't come,
    It shall be well received, and much made of it.
PRUDENCE We must of this, it was our own conception.   75

5.3

[*Enter*] *Latimer*
[LATIMER] Room for green rushes, raise the fiddlers, chamberlain,
    Call up the house in arms!
HOST   This will rouse Lovel.
FLY And bring him on, too.
LATIMER   Shelee-nien Thomas
    Runs like a heifer bitten with the breeze
    About the court, crying on Fly and cursing.   5
FLY For what, my lord?
LATIMER   Yo' were best hear that from her,
    It is no office, Fly, fits my relation.
    Here come the happy couple! Joy, Lord Beaufort!
FLY And my young lady, too!
HOST   Much joy, my lord!

5.4

[Enter] Beaufort, Frank, [Ferret, Jordan, Pierce, Jug, Fiddlers,
and] a Servant°

[BEAUFORT] I thank you all, I thank thee, father Fly.
    Madam, my cousin, you look discomposed,
    I have been bold with a salad after supper
    O' your own lettuce here.

LADY FRAMPUL   You have, my lord.
    But laws of hospitality and fair rites   5
    Would have made me acquainted.

BEAUFORT   I' your own house,
    I do acknowledge; else I much had trespassed.
    But in an inn, and public, where there is licence
    Of all community, a pardon o' course°
    May be sued out.

LADY FRAMPUL   It will, my lord, and carry it.   10
    I do not see how any storm or tempest
    Can help it now.

PRUDENCE   The thing being done and past,
    You bear it wisely, and like a lady of judgement.

BEAUFORT She is that, secretary Pru.

PRUDENCE   Why secretary,
    My wise lord? Is your brain lately married?   15

BEAUFORT Your reign is ended, Pru, no sovereign now;
    Your date is out and dignity expired.

PRUDENCE I am annulled; how can I treat with Lovel
    Without a new commission?

LADY FRAMPUL   Thy gown's commission.

HOST Have patience, Pru, expect, bid the lord joy.°   20

PRUDENCE And this brave lady, too. I wish them joy.

PIERCE Joy!

JORDAN   Joy!

JUG   All joy!

HOST   Ay, the house full of joy.

FLY Play the bells; fiddlers, crack your strings with joy!
       [Music plays]

PRUDENCE But, Lady Laetice, you showed a neglect
    Un-to-be-pardoned to'ards my lady, your kinswoman,   25
    Not to advise with her.

BEAUFORT   Good politic Pru,
    Urge not your state advice, your after-wit;
    'Tis near upbraiding. Get our bed ready, chamberlain,
    And host, a bride-cup; you have rare conceits°
    And good ingredients; ever an old host   30
    Upo' the road has his provocative drinks.°
LATIMER He is either a good bawd or a physician.
BEAUFORT 'Twas well he heard you not, his back was turned.
    A bed, the genial bed! A brace of boys°
    Tonight I play for.
PRUDENCE   Give us points, my lord.°   35
BEAUFORT Here, take 'em, Pru, my codpiece point and all,°
    I ha' clasps, my Laetice' arms—here, take 'em, boys!
        [*Throws off his doublet*]
    What, is the chamber ready? Speak! Why stare you
    On one another?
JORDAN   No, sir.
BEAUFORT   And why no?
JORDAN My master has forbid it. He yet doubts   40
    That you are married.
BEAUFORT   Ask his vicar-general,
    His Fly here.
FLY   I must make that good, they are married.
HOST But I must make it bad, my hot young lord.
    Gi' him his doublet again, the air is piercing;
    You may take cold, my lord. See whom you ha' married,   45
    Your host's son, and a boy!
        [*Pulls off Frank's head-dress*]
FLY   You are abused!
LADY FRAMPUL Much joy, my lord!
PRUDENCE   If this be your Laetitia,
    She'll prove a counterfeit mirth, and a clipped lady.°
SERVANT A boy, a boy—my lord has married a boy!
LATIMER Raise all the house in shout and laughter, a boy!   50
HOST Stay, what is here? Peace, rascals, stop your throats.

5.5

[Enter] Nurse

[NURSE] That maggot, worm, that insect! Oh my child,
　My daughter! Where's that Fly? I'll fly in his face,
　The vermin, let me come to him.

FLY　　　　　　　　　　　Why, Nurse Shelee?

NURSE Hang thee, thou parasite, thou son of crumbs
　And orts, thou hast undone me and my child,　　　　　　5
　My daughter, my dear daughter!

HOST　　　　　　　　　　What means this?

NURSE O sir, my daughter, my dear child, is ruined
　By this your Fly here, married in a stable,
　And sold unto a husband.

HOST　　　　　　　　Stint thy cry,
　Harlot, if that be all; didst thou not sell him　　　　　10
　To me for a boy? And broughtst him in boy's rags
　Here to my door to beg an alms of me?

NURSE I did, good master, and I crave your pardon.
　But 'tis my daughter, and a girl.

HOST　　　　　　　　　　　Why saidst thou
　It was a boy, and soldst him then to me　　　　　　15
　With such entreaty for ten shillings, carline?

NURSE Because you were a charitable man,
　I heard, good master, and would breed him well;
　I would ha' giv'n him you for nothing, gladly.
　Forgive the lie o' my mouth, it was to save　　　　　20
　The fruit o' my womb. A parent's needs are urgent,
　And few do know that tyrant o'er good natures.
　But you relieved her, and me, too, the mother,
　And took me into your house to be the nurse,
　For which heaven heap all blessings on your head　　　25
　Whilst there can one be added.

HOST　　　　　　　　　Sure thou speakst
　Quite like another creature than th' hast lived
　Here i' the house, a Shelee-nien Thomas,
　An Irish beggar.

NURSE　　　　So I am, God help me.

HOST What art thou? Tell. The match is a good match   30
    For aught I see—ring the bells once again.
        [*Music plays*]
BEAUFORT Stint, I say, fiddlers.
LADY FRAMPUL   No going off, my lord.
BEAUFORT Nor coming on, sweet lady, things thus standing!
FLY But what's the heinousness of my offence,
    Or the degrees of wrong you suffered by it?   35
    In having your daughter matched thus happily
    Into a noble house, a brave young blood,
    And a prime peer o' the realm?
BEAUFORT   Was that your plot, Fly?
    Gi' me a cloak, take her again among you.
    I'll none of your Light Heart fosterlings, no inmates,°   40
    Supposititious fruits of an host's brain
    And his Fly's hatching, to be put upon me.
    There is a royal court o' the Star Chamber
    Will scatter all these mists, disperse these vapours,
    And clear the truth. Let beggars match with beggars.°   45
    That shall decide it, I will try it there.
NURSE Nay then, my lord, it's not enough, I see,
    You are licentious, but you will be wicked.
    You're not alone content to take my daughter
    Against the law, but having taken her,   50
    You would repudiate and cast her off
    Now at your pleasure, like a beast of power,
    Without all cause, or colour of a cause
    That or a noble or an honest man
    Should dare t' except against, her poverty.   55
    Is poverty a vice?
BEAUFORT   Th' age counts it so.
NURSE God help your lordship and your peers that think so,
    If any be; if not, God bless them all,
    And help the number o' the virtuous,
    If poverty be a crime. You may object   60
    Our beggary to us as an accident,
    But never deeper, no inherent baseness.
    And I must tell you now, young lord of dirt,
    As an incensèd mother, she hath more
    And better blood, running i' those small veins,   65
    Than all the race of Beauforts have in mass,

Though they distil their drops from the left rib
Of John o' Gaunt.
HOST   Old mother o' records,°
Thou knowst her pedigree, then. Whose daughter is she?
NURSE The daughter and co-heir to the Lord Frampul,   70
This lady's sister.
LADY FRAMPUL   Mine? What is her name?
NURSE Laetitia.
LADY FRAMPUL That was lost?
NURSE   The true Laetitia.
LADY FRAMPUL Sister, oh gladness! Then you are our mother?
NURSE I am, dear daughter.
LADY FRAMPUL   On my knees I bless
The light I see you by.
NURSE   And to the author   75
Of that blest light, I ope my other eye,
Which hath almost now seven year been shut
Dark, as my vow was never to see light
Till such a light restored it as my children
Or your dear father, who, I hear, is not.   80
BEAUFORT Give me my wife, I own her now, and will have her.
HOST But you must ask my leave first, my young lord,
Leave is but light. Ferret, go bolt your master,°
Here's gear will startle him.
        [*Exit Ferret*]
                        I cannot keep
The passion in me, I am e'en turned child   85
And I must weep. Fly, take away mine host,
My beard and cap here from me, and fetch my lord.
        [*Exit Fly*]
I am her father, sir, and you shall now
Ask my consent before you have her. Wife!
My dear and loving wife! My honoured wife!   90
Who here hath gained but I? I am Lord Frampul,
The cause of all this trouble. I am he
Have measured all the shires of England over,
Wales, and her mountains, seen those wilder nations
Of people in the Peak and Lancashire;   95
Their pipers, fiddlers, rushers, puppet-masters,
Jugglers, and gypsies, all the sorts of canters
And colonies of beggars, tumblers, ape-carriers,

For to these savages I was addicted,
To search their natures, and make odd discoveries.   100
And here my wife, like a she-Mandeville,°
Ventured in disquisition after me.°
     [Enter Fly with robes, and dresses Lord Frampul]°
NURSE I may look up, admire, I cannot speak°
  Yet to my lord.
HOST   Take heart and breath, recover;
  Thou hast recovered me, who here had coffined   105
  Myself alive in a poor hostelry
  In penance of my wrongs done unto thee,
  Whom I long since gave lost.
NURSE   So did I you,
  Till stealing mine own daughter from her sister,
  I lighted on this error hath cured all.   110
BEAUFORT And in that cure include my trespass, mother
  And father, for my wife—
HOST   No, the Star Chamber.
BEAUFORT Away with that, you sour the sweetest lettuce
  Was ever tasted.
HOST   Gi' you joy, my son,
  Cast her not off again.
     [Enter Lovel]
              O call me father,   115
  Lovel, and this your mother, if you like.
  But take your mistress first, my child; I have power
  To give her now, with her consent. Her sister
  Is given already to your brother Beaufort.
LOVEL Is this a dream now, after my first sleep?   120
  Or are these fancies made i' the Light Heart,
  And sold i' the New Inn?
HOST   Best go to bed
  And dream it over all. Let's all go sleep,
  Each with his turtle. Fly, provide us lodgings,
  Get beds prepared: you're master now o' the inn,   125
  The lord o' the Light Heart, I give it you.
  Fly was my fellow gypsy. All my family,
  Indeed, were gypsies, tapsters, ostlers, chamberlains,
  Reducèd vessels of civility.
  But here stands Pru, neglected, best deserving   130
  Of all that are i' the house, or i' my Heart,

Whom though I cannot help to a fit husband,
I'll help to that will bring one, a just portion:
I have two thousand pound in bank for Pru,
Call for it when she will.

BEAUFORT   And I as much.   135

HOST There's somewhat yet, four thousand pound! That's better
    Than sounds the proverb, 'four bare legs in a bed'.°

LOVEL Me and her mistress she hath power to coin
    Up into what she will.

LADY FRAMPUL   Indefinite Pru!°

LATIMER But I must do the crowning act of bounty.   140

HOST What's that, my lord?

LATIMER   Give her my self, which here
    By all the holy vows of love I do.
    Spare all your promised portions, she is a dowry
    So all-sufficient in her virtue and manners
    That fortune cannot add to her.

PRUDENCE   My lord,   145
    Your praises are instructions to mine ears,
    Whence you have made your wife to live your servant.

HOST Lights, get us several lights!

LOVEL   Stay, let my mistress°
    But hear my vision sung, my dream of beauty,
    Which I have brought, prepared, to bid us joy   150
    And light us all to bed; 'twill be instead
    Of airing of the sheets with a sweet odour.

HOST 'Twill be an incense to our sacrifice
    Of love tonight, where I will woo afresh,
    And like Maecenas, having but one wife,°   155
    I'll marry her every hour of life hereafter.

       They go out with a song

Epilogue

Plays in themselves have neither hopes nor fears,
 Their fate is only in their hearers' ears;
If you expect more than you had tonight,
 The maker is sick and sad. But do him right:
He meant to please you, for he sent things fit   5
 In all the numbers, both of sense and wit,°
If they ha' not miscarried! If they have,
 All that his faint and falt'ring tongue doth crave
Is that you not impute it to his brain.
 That's yet unhurt, although set round with pain;   10
It cannot long hold out. All strength must yield.°
 Yet judgement would the last be i' the field
With a true poet. He could have haled in
 The drunkards and the noises of the inn
In his last act, if he had thought it fit   15
 To vent you vapours in the place of wit.
But better 'twas that they should sleep or spew
 Than in the scene to offend or him or you.
This he did think, and this do you forgive:
 Whene'er the carcass dies, this art will live.   20
And had he lived the care of King and Queen,
 His art in something more yet had been seen;°
But mayors and shrives may yearly fill the stage,
 A king's or poet's birth do ask an age.

423

*Another Epilogue there was, made for the play in the poet's
defence, but the play lived not in opinion to have it spoken*

EPILOGUE

A jovial host and lord of the New Inn
    Clept the Light Heart, with all that passed therein,
Hath been the subject of our play tonight,
    To give the King and Queen and Court delight.
But then we mean the Court above the stairs   5
    And past the guard; men that have more of ears
Than eyes to judge us: such as will not hiss
    Because the chambermaid was namèd Cis.°
We think it would have served our scene as true,
    If, as it is, at first we had called her Pru,   10
For any mystery we there have found,
    Or magic in the letters or the sound.
She only meant was for a girl of wit,
    To whom her lady did a province fit;°
Which she would have discharged and done as well,   15
    Had she been christened Joyce, Grace, Doll, or Nell.

The just indignation the author took at the vulgar censure
of his play by some malicious spectators begat this following
ode to himself

Come, leave the loathèd stage,
And the more loathsome age,
Where pride and impudence, in faction knit,
Usurp the chair of wit,
Indicting and arraigning every day   5
Something they call a play.
Let their fastidious, vain°
Commission of the brain
Run on and rage, sweat, censure, and condemn:
They were not made for thee, less thou for them.   10

Say that thou pourst them wheat,
And they will acorns eat;
'Twere simple fury still thyself to waste°
On such as have no taste,
To offer them a surfeit of pure bread   15
Whose appetites are dead.
No, give them grains their fill,
Husks, draff to drink, and swill;
If they love lees, and leave the lusty wine,
Envy them not, their palate's with the swine.   20

No doubt some mouldy tale
Like *Pericles*, and stale°
As the shrive's crusts, and nasty as his fish-
Scraps out of every dish,
Thrown forth, and raked into the common tub,   25
May keep up the play-club:
There sweepings do as well
As the best ordered meal.
For who the relish of these guests will fit,
Needs set them but the alms-basket of wit.   30

And much good do't you then:
Brave plush and velvet men
Can feed on orts; and safe in your stage-clothes
    Dare quit, upon your oaths,°
The stagers and the stage-wrights, too (your peers)   35
    Of larding your large ears°
    With their foul comic socks,°
    Wrought upon twenty blocks:
Which, if they are torn and turned and patched enough,
The gamesters share your guilt, and you their stuff.°   40

    Leave things so prostitute,
    And take the Alcaic lute,°
Or thine own Horace, or Anacreon's lyre;°
    Warm thee by Pindar's fire:°
And though thy nerves be shrunk and blood be cold   45
    Ere years have made thee old,
    Strike that disdainful heat
    Throughout, to their defeat:
As curious fools, and envious of thy strain,
May, blushing, swear no palsy's in thy brain.   50

    But when they hear thee sing
    The glories of thy king,
His zeal to God, and his just awe o'er men,
    They may, blood-shaken, then
Feel such a flesh-quake to possess their powers,   55
    As they shall cry, 'Like ours
    In sound of peace or wars
    No harp e'er hit the stars,
In tuning forth the acts of his sweet reign,
And raising Charles his chariot 'bove his wain.'°   60

EXPLANATORY NOTES

The following abbreviations are used in the Explanatory Notes: 'Tilley' = Morris Palmer Tilley, *A Dictionary of Proverbs in England in the Sixteenth and Seventeenth Centuries* (Ann Arbor, 1950): 'Dent' = R. W. Dent, *Proverbial Language in English Drama Exclusive of Shakespeare, 1495–1616* (Berkeley and London, 1984).

Poetaster

PERSONS THAT ACT

The . . . Act: a dedicatory letter precedes the cast list in the folio; see Additional Passage A.

Augustus Caesar: the historical figure lived from 63 BC to AD 14.

Julia: Jonson confuses this woman with her daughter, also called Julia, banished for adultery in AD 8; it is possible that Ovid's banishment was the result of an illicit relationship with the latter.

Maecenas: Gaius Maecenas (d. 8 BC). Historically, his literary circle included such writers as Virgil, Horace, and Propertius.

Virgil: Publius Vergilius Maro (70–19 BC), patronized by Maecenas and Augustus.

Horace: Quintus Horatius Flaccus (65–8 BC). This character is identified with Jonson.

Tibullus: The historical Albius Tibullus lived from *c*.55 to 19 BC, and was not amongst Maecenas' circle.

Cor[nelius] Gallus: this historical figure (70?-26 BC), credited with the creation of the genre of love-elegy, was significantly older than Tibullus, Propertius, and Ovid.

Pub[lius] Ovid: Publius Ovidius Naso (43 BC–AD 17).

Propertius: Sextus Propertius (born *c*.54 BC), introduced into Maecenas' circle early in his career.

Hermogenes: criticized in Horace's *Satires* as inconstant and vain.

Mar[cus] Ovid: father of the poet, Publius Ovid.

Tucca: Pantilius Tucca features in Horace's *Satires* as a 'louse'.

[Rufus Laberius] Crispinus: Commonly considered a satirical portrait of the playwright John Marston (1576–1634).

De[metrius] Fannius: the name derives from two characters in Horace's *Satires*: the musician, Demetrius, is a backbiter, and Fannius is an inept poet. The character is generally identified with the playwright Thomas Dekker (*c*.1572–1632).

Lupus: Latin for 'wolf'; the name is suggestive of his character.

Histrio: Latin for 'actor'. It is unclear if the speech prefix should be read as a character name, or if the character is identified only by his profession.

Pyrgi: wooden towers on the side of a gaming board through which dice were rolled; ironically used to designate Tucca's (short) pages. The quarto prints the singular form, 'Pyrgus'.

Equites Romani: the equites were a wealthy, but heterogeneous, social group making up the officer corps of the army and holding a variety of posts in the civil administration.

Livor: Envy (Latin). The form of the name in English is printed in the folio.

DEDICATION

Ad Lectorem: 'To the Reader'. The lines which follow have been slightly adapted from Martial, and read: 'We play with harmless words: I swear by the genius of mighty Fame, and the Castalian choir, and by your ears, which are to me as a great deity, O reader, who art free from ungentle envy' (VII. xii. 9–12). This passage is only printed in the quarto.

Prologue S.D. *after . . . stage*: i.e. rising up from the trapdoor in the stage after the second sounding of the trumpets announcing the beginning of the play. These stage directions are printed only in the folio.

3 *What's . . . Arraignment*: Livor turns to read the title of the play posted on a signboard or playbill at the back of the stage.

10 *maliced*: regarded with malice, threatened.

11–13 *The . . . first*: Poetaster was first performed at Blackfriars, an indoor playhouse lit by candlelight, and Livor, rising from hell and blinded by the brightness of the artificial lighting, resolves to plunge the theatre into darkness. 'Shine' also refers metaphorically to the illustriousness of the audience.

14 *fifteen weeks*: i.e. the length of time Jonson took to write the play. It was not unusual for Jonson to take a year to complete a new play (see Additional Passage E, 94).

22 *ris*: risen. This obsolete form of the past participle preserves the metre.

26 *promoting*: helping.

28 *Crack eyestrings*: the muscles holding the eyeball in place (eyestrings) were thought to break or crack at death or loss of sight.

34–5 *Rome . . . state*: Livor believes this foreign setting forestalls efforts to

428

draw disruptive parallels between the action of the play and early modern London politics.

35 *poet-apes*: rhymesters who ape poets of quality; poetasters.

47 *rusty*: surly, churlish.

57 *calm troop*: i.e. the audience.

78 *argue*: accuse.

1.1.1–2 *Then . . . aspire*: these lines are slightly adapted from Marlowe's translation of Ovid, *Amores*, I. xv; the elegy is quoted in full at the end of the scene. Some critics have argued that Ovid's early entrance misleads an audience into assuming he is the eponymous poetaster, but as Livor indicates, the play was originally performed under the title of *The Arraignment* (Prologue, 3).

4 *God sa' me*: i.e. God save me; a mild oath.

7 *presently*: immediately.

8 *cast*: vomit.

17 *buskins*: tragic actors in ancient drama wore a thick-soled boot, or cothurnus, to confer upon them added dignity and physical height. Tucca applies the term to Lupus in the next scene, glancing at the tribune's self-important sense of himself as a man of state (1.2.142).

22 *skeldering*: sponging, especially by passing oneself off as a disbanded soldier.

23 *velvet arms*: i.e. weapons (arms) encased in velvet scabbards.

33 *Castalian mad*: i.e. made insane with poetic inspiration. The spring into which the nymph Castalia threw herself was consecrated to Apollo and the Muses.

46–7 *Thy . . . name*: the following lines praise classical writers whose fame, according to Ovid, will endure forever; particular references are traced below.

48–9 *Homer . . . slide*: i.e. Homer's fame is as lasting as these geographical landmarks which feature in his work. Tenedos is an Aegean island, while Ide and Simois refer respectively to a mountain and river near Troy.

50–1 *Hesiod . . . ear*: Hesiod is often compared with Homer as one of the oldest-known Greek poets. The agricultural references point to his most-read poem, *Works and Days*.

52–3 *Callimachus . . . flow*: Greek poet and scholar (285–246 BC). Ovid's ambiguous praise results from his reputation as a skilful, but not inspired, writer.

54 *Sophocles*: Athenian tragic playwright (c.496–406 BC).

55 *Aratus*: third-century BC poet born at Soloi in Cilicia, a district of southern Asia Minor.

57 *Menander*: Greek comic playwright (c.344–c.292 BC).

58 *Ennius*: Roman dramatist and poet (239–169 BC).

rude: uneducated, unlearned

Accius: Roman tragic dramatist known for his grandeur of style (170–*c*.86 BC).

60 *Varro*: Roman scholar and politician (116–27 BC). The next line is an allusion to his lost *Argonautica*.

62 *Lucretius*: Epicurean poet (*c*.94–55 BC), author of *De rerum natura* (*On the Nature of Things*).

64 *Tityrus . . . Aenee*: references to three works of Virgil. Tityrus is one of the narrators of the *Eclogues*, while Tillage alludes to the discussions of farming found in the *Georgics*; 'Aenee' is not a recognized variant form of *Aeneid*, but this spelling, reprinted in the folio, is necessary for the line to scan.

67–9 *Tibullus . . . best*: Ovid includes amongst those whose names will not be forgotten two of his friends and fellow poets. Lycoris is the name by which Gallus refers in his poetry to his lover, Cytheris (see 1.3.29–34).

73 *Tagus*: river dividing Spain and Portugal, given by poets the epithet 'aurifer' (Latin for 'gold-bearing').

74 *hinds*: boors.

76 *frost-dread*: i.e. frightened of frost.

impale: encircle.

78–9 *Envy . . . right*: these lines are marked in the early quarto with gnomic pointing (diples, or raised commas, in the margin of the page) to mark them out to the reader as particularly significant.

1.2.11 *Medea*: only two verses of this tragedy survive.

14–16 *An . . . first*: Ovid's father historically disapproved of his son's inclinations to poetry, but the arguments presented in this scene in opposition to acting would have pointed resonance for an Elizabethan audience accustomed to the rhetoric of anti-theatrical polemic.

22 *roll poll*: rascal, worthless person. The more usual form is 'roly poly'.

23 *knight of worship*: Ovid's family was of the equestrian order. All references to knights were revised out of the play when it was reprinted in the 1616 folio, possibly as an act of self-censorship designed to forestall controversy of the sort generated by Jonson's attack on actors, soldiers, and lawyers.

48 *wormwood*: bitter, tart.

49–51 *They . . . tricked*: statutes passed during the reign of Elizabeth I made actors who were not formally patronized by a noble of the realm liable to prosecution as rogues and vagabonds; 'tricked' = drawn in outline, a metaphor from heraldry.

430

58–9 *They . . . reports*: the contrast between Ovid's poetic nature and the others' pragmatism is highlighted throughout the scene by the shift from verse to prose.

71 *exhibition*: maintenance.

80 *booths*: temporary dwellings.

88 *Thou . . . Bias*: a satirical commentary on the law profession, omitted from the printed quarto playtext as controversial and offensive, appears in place of this line in the folio and is included in this edition as Additional Passage B. Jonson's discussion of the uproar caused by the play's satire in the 'Apological Dialogue' (see Additional Passage E) indicates that the passage had been performed on stage. A similarly sharp attack on players was omitted in the third act; see 3.4.262–5 n.

Bias: Greek sage; sentences = sententia, maxims.

91–2 *Send . . . again*: this Roman god, traditionally depicted as double-faced and looking in both directions at the same time, controlled new beginnings; Ovid Senior is telling his son to turn over a new leaf, leaving poetry behind.

96 *drop*: i.e. drop tears.

102 *Cothurnus*: Tucca glances at Lupus' sense of himself as a man of state.

112 *Lucullus*: Licinius Lucullus, a successful warrior and wealthy patron of the arts.

114 *man . . . Maecenas*: alluding to Maecenas' reputation as patron of poets.

126 *yellows*: jaundice.

127 *foundered*: lamed.

128–9 *Then . . . mules*: this line suggests that the character of Tucca is played in performance with a stammer.

130 *talent*: there were approximately 6,000 drachmas in a talent, so Tucca is claiming that Agrippa owes him one thousand times what he goes on to borrow from Ovid Senior.

135 *setter . . . tumbler*: slang terms to describe someone who abets a swindler in a confidence trick. Tucca claims that his page is acting on behalf of Agrippa, but as Luscus' asides indicate, it is Ovid Senior who is being stung.

142 *chain*: worn either as jewellery or as a symbol of office; Tucca removes from Maecenas his 'flagon chain' at 5.3.30–1.

158 *tell*: count.

161 *balk*: avoid, shun.

191 *dudgeon*: spiteful, ill-humoured. Dudgeon as a noun signifies the shaft of a dagger, and the adjective thus anticipates the knifing metaphor introduced later in the line with the verb 'stab'.

1.3.3–4 *Let's . . . away?*: in the folio this passage reads, 'Let's see, what's here? | Nay, I will see it! | OVID. Pray thee away.' *Numa in decimo nono* (Latin) refers to laws passed in the nineteenth year of the rule of Pompilius Numa, legendary second king of Rome; Ovid is studying Roman law.

9 *abroad*: out of doors.

11 *in case*: prepared, ready.

13 *in . . . case*: Tibullus puns on 'case' to mean law cases.

31–2 *Plautia . . . Corinna*: Tibullus wrote of his love, Plautia, by the name Delia, while Ovid wrote love poetry to Julia using the name Corinna.

43–4 *the . . . only*: i.e. only he could hear the music of the spheres, the harmonious music thought by early astrologers to be caused by the motion of the planets around the earth; zenith = expanse of sky.

73 *heart strings*: the tendons or nerves thought to brace and sustain the heart

74 *prove*: try.

2.1.16 *savour . . . felt*: stink . . . smelled.

18 *well said*: well done

20 *Vulcan*: cuckolded by his wife, Venus, with Mars, god of war. This mythology is alluded to again at 4.3.128–9 and 4.5.70–1.

23 *fulsome*: offensive, both in manners and smell.

24 *Gods . . . body*: shortened form of 'God save my body'.

31–3 *which . . . her*: this line might be prompted in performance by Chloë hitting her husband over the head at some point in her previous speech.

44–5 *pack-needles . . . candlesticks*: Albius does not trade solely in jewellery, and Chloë ridicules him for this less prestigious side of his business practice.

47–50 *O . . . barrel*: his wisdom is proverbial (Tilley G3), and derives from Juvenal (xiv. 203–5); respects = expects, anticipates.

56–8 *Nor you . . . bodies*: Chloë figures her fall from the status of gentlewoman to merchant's wife through costume. A French hood is an elaborate headdress which was fixed to the back of the head with a flap of cloth extending down the back; a farthingale was a huge hooped skirt; a bumroll consisted of padded rolls worn around the hips over which a skirt was draped; and whalebone bodies refers to a bodice ('a pair of bodies') stiffened with whalebone; disbased = debased.

59 *Look . . . mum*: the comic effect of Albius' repeated promises of silence might be reinforced with a visual gesture such as putting his finger to his lips.

60 *my . . . of—*: the audience is left to complete Albius' coarse pun—'my very city of sperm'. The wordplay is flagged in the quarto, where 'spermaceti' is spelled as two words ('Sperma Cete').

63 *participate*: partake, enjoy.

432

66 *'Sbody*: God's body.

73 *for . . . better*: he affects and misapplies this polite formulaic tag, inadvertently insulting his cousin. Crispinus is a thinly veiled caricature of John Marston, and throughout this scene and the play, Jonson mocks his pretensions to gentility and his affected and ostentatious language (see, for example, 'strenuously well' at 12, and 'vehemently desire to participate' at 62–3).

77 *you . . . arms*: there might be a pun on 'arms', Crispinus offering in performance to embrace Chloë.

80 *for . . . born*: mocking Marston's short legs; the description of the coat-of-arms which follows is a weak parody of his family crest.

84 *in chief*: occupying the upper part of the shield.

85 *pungent*: sharp-pointed.

89 *flat-cap*: one who wears a flat cap, a London citizen. The word was revised in the folio to 'tradesman', Crispinus going on to add: 'No doubt of that, sweet feature, your carriage shows it in any man's eye that is carried upon you with judgement.'

103 *City-sin*: a disparaging and weak pun on 'citizen', reinforcing the presentation of this character as a snob of limited intellect.

110 *corrigible*: corrective.

2.2.2 *prefer*: give preference to.

8 *approve*: make good, demonstrate.

29 *character*: token, distinctive mark.

60 *It . . . face*: i.e. it is a love which will not be separated from its object.

78–9 *yet . . . do*: this continues Jonson's personal attack on his fellow-dramatist, Marston, who had red hair, a hair colour associated with Judas, and hence deceit.

99 *are . . . him*: i.e. do you have influence or power over him?

113 *do it*: i.e. persuade him.

114 *cunning*: ability, skill.

121 *passingly*: exceedingly.

148–57 *If I . . . barred*: the songs in this play, both in this scene and in 4.5, may have been accompanied by music in the earliest productions.

172 *delicates*: delights, charms.

192 *good legs*: bows.

198 *design*: project.

201–2 *relinquish*: disappear, leave. This verb, along with 'expiate' in the next line (used incorrectly), is typical of Crispinus' overblown and pseudo-courtly manner of speaking.

206 *broker*: pawnbroker, one who deals in second-hand goods.

3.1.7 *Lyaeus*: epithet of Dionysus, god of wine.

10 *sprite*: spirit.

11 *Minerva . . . Muses*: patron goddess of arts and poetry, and the goddesses of inspiration; Crispinus attempts to interact with Horace as a fellow poet.

18–19 *we . . . satirist*: Crispinus became a poet to attract the attentions of Chloë, but this detail further connects him to Marston, who published two books of satirical verse in 1598.

20 *odes . . . sermons*: Horace's major works include the *Odes*, a collection of lyric poetry, and the *Satires*, also called *Sermones*, or conversations.

23 *To . . . beard*: the Greeks associated wisdom with the growth of a beard, but the beard worn by the boy actor playing Crispinus would be false; the implication is that his stoicism is similarly superficial.

28 *prospective*: i.e. built in such a way as to provide a good view or prospect.

32 *Muses—*: the quarto punctuation suggests that Crispinus searches for a suitably poetic manner in which to describe the women sitting in their windows.

33 *Castalian . . . liquors*: water from Castalia, one of the Muses' springs, and liquor of Thespis, the father of ancient Greek tragedy.

39 *tire*: woman's head-dress.

41 *bodkin*: a long pin used to fasten up the hair.

43–5 *high . . . pyramids*: elaborate styles of dressing women's hair popular in early seventeenth-century London.

48 *remitted*: put off, postponed.

57–8 *your . . . it*: i.e. the expensive satin overlay is wearing away to reveal the lining made of frieze, a rough woollen material (rug).

58–9 *And . . . naturally*: Crispinus is wearing grubby breeches (hose) stained by recent sexual activity, which indicates a lustful (hot) temperament.

65 *For . . . think*: merchants would record their clients' debts and strike out their names as the debt was paid; the joke is that Horace—unlike the debt-book of Crispinus' tailor—has been 'crossed'.

74 *hap*: chance, fortune.

76 *smack*: kiss loudly.

91 *with . . . teeth*: i.e. before he is an old man.

94 *stalls*: stables.

95 *lewd solecisms*: referring both to Crispinus' verses, unlearned and ungrammatical, and to his bad manners.

96 *Bolanus*: this historical person is similarly mentioned in the Satire by Horace on which this scene is based (i. ix. 11); nothing more is known of him but that he was a friend of Cicero.

105 *prove*: attempt, try.

128 *divers*: various, diverse.

132 *Rhadamanthys*: one of the three judges of the living and the dead in the lower world; another one of the three, mentioned at 143, was his brother, Minos.

148 *Varius*: Rufus Varius, poet and close friend of Virgil. He introduced Horace to Maecenas.

157–8 *cloth . . . stocking*: i.e. his party clothes; cloth of silver was an expensive fabric woven with silver thread, and long stockings were conventionally worn by dancers.

164 *You . . . you*: with a pun on 'the mother' to mean hysteria.

173 *cunning woman*: soothsayer.

Sabella: Horace speaks of 'a Sabine dame' in the original Satire, which in Latin is rendered 'Sabella'.

179 *hectic fever*: consumption.

181 *surprised*: taken unawares.

197 *loud*: this is the folio reading. The quarto prints two parenthetical brackets, perhaps indicating a hesitation on the actor's part, a censored word, or the compositor's inability to read the copy.

233 *There's no man*: i.e. in the house of Maecenas is no man.

247 *extrude*: thrust out, expel.

250–1 *'Man . . . labour.'*: the quotation-marks printed in the quarto perhaps suggest that the actor delivers this line in a sententious manner.

254–5 *Archer . . . python*: according to ancient mythology, Phoebus (Apollo) killed with arrows the monstrous serpent that guarded Delphi for its patron goddess, Earth, thus assuming sole control of the Delphic oracle.

3.2.4 *land-remora*: a remora is a type of sucking fish thought to be able to stay the progress of any ship to which it attached itself; the expression 'land-remora' is figurative.

6 *Alcides' shirt*: alluding to the poisoned robe sent to Hercules by his wife, Deianira; once put on, the robe stuck to his skin and killed him.

3.3.6 *slip*: neglect, overlook.

18 *vulgarly*: publicly.

22 *exhale me*: drag me away.

3.4.9 *I . . . physician*: i.e. I knew that [smell] was not [that of] a physician. The folio substitutes 'thou wast' for 'that was'.

20 *tall*: brave, valiant.

24 *lendings*: borrowed money.

45 *centumviri*: prestigious panel of men from which a Roman civil court was

selected. The Latin translates as 'one hundred men', but the panel consisted of 180 men at the time of empire.

52 *cashier*: dismiss, discharge.

55 *absolve*: discharge, clear off.

57 *my sword*: Tucca once again asks the lictors to return his sword to him.

65 *discharge . . . arrest*: pay the officers' fees.

72 *girdle . . . hangers*: belt around the waist, with often richly ornamented loops attached to it (hangers), from which one would hang weapons.

77 *taking*: stealing.

90 *barber's to stitching*: early modern barbers also served as surgeons and dentists.

94 *poetaster*: writer of trashy verse, paltry poet.

101–2 *Bacchus . . . Priapus*: i.e. gods of wine, revelling, and procreation.

104 *leveret*: young hare. This word was revised in the folio to 'ferret', emphasizing the servant's cunning and enterprising spirit; Lovel's servant is named Ferret in *The New Inn*.

107 *strike . . . war*: salute a powerful warship by lowering a sail. Tucca is irritated by the actor's failure to doff his hat to him.

110 *purchase*: acquire possessions, become rich.

110–11 *fortune*: with a pun on the Fortune Theatre, opened in 1600.

115 *Oedipus*: alluding to the eponymous hero of Sophocles' tragedy who stabs his own eyes.

115–16 *walk . . . eyes*: sleepwalk; hares were thought to sleep with their eyes open.

116 *glazed*: the pun is on the senses of 'provided with spectacles to amend short-sightedness', and 'covered with a film of tears' as a consequence of the beating Histrio will receive.

118 *bass violin*: the quarto spelling, 'Base Violin', does not indicate whether Tucca is referring to a violoncello or describing a violin in disparaging terms; the ambiguity will be present to an audience's ears in performance.

118–19 *march . . . Fair*: i.e. march to Green Goose Fair in a minstrel's costume; the fair was held annually in Bow, a suburb of London.

123 *Owl-glass*: jester, buffoon; the name is the English rendering of 'Eulenspiegel', the hero of a widely known German jest-book.

123–4 *perstemptuous*: a nonce word, perhaps confused for 'presumptuous'.

126–7 *Ay . . . legion*: i.e. of lice. Tucca's page comically undercuts his master's inference that he has commanded an infantry company of 150 men.

128 *exhibited*: presented.

135 *capriccio*: whimsical or capricious character (from the Italian, meaning 'whim'). The folio reads 'Pantolabus', originally the name of a parasitical character in one of Horace's *Satires* (I. viii. 11), but which by Jonson's time meant simply 'one who takes all'.

137–8 *parcel-poet*: i.e. partly poet; compare Tucca's description of Crispinus as 'poetaster' at 94.

140–1 *Minotaurus*: Minotaur, the monster from Greek mythology with the body of a man and head of a bull; Tucca's suggestion is that the actor bellows like a bull.

141 *rand*: rant, rave.

142–3 *Thou . . . slave*: this detail is typical not of ancient Rome, but Elizabethan London, where it was usual for playwrights to be advanced between 5 shillings and £2 on a new play; in earnest = as an advance on the full fee.

149 *honest . . . hundred*: i.e. an honest cheat; usurers were not permitted legally to charge more than 10 per cent interest. The folio reads 'shifter', meaning trickster or cozener.

150–1 *Minos . . . exceedingly*: Crispinus does not overhear, or in performance might feign not to overhear, this exchange.

155 *prospect*: sight, view.

163 *gird*: sneer, scoff.

164–5 *They . . . Tiber*: i.e. referring to the satirical drama performed by children's companies of Elizabethan England, in theatres north of the Thames.

169 *sort . . . scoundrels*: i.e. by a group (sort) of counterfeiting rogues; copper lace would be used in place of the much more expensive gold lace.

170–2 *mansions . . . triumphs*: Tucca threatens the players by claiming that the very structures in which they perform will feel the force of his anger. Beyond the reference to the Globe Theatre, the terminology is unspecific; there may once have been a 'Triumph' theatre about which we now know nothing, but it seems more likely that Tucca is alluding generally to theatrical pageants.

175 *neuf*: erroneous form of 'nieve', meaning fist.

177 *point trussers*: literally, those who tie (truss) points, laces used to fasten men's hose to their doublets.

179 *King . . . strain*: the lines which follow have not been traced, and may simply parody an overblown dramatic rhetoric; a similar passage is found in Shakespeare's *1 Henry IV*, where Falstaff claims, 'I must speak in passion, and I will do it in King Cambyses' vein' (2.4.381–2).

180–92 *O . . . all*: a condensed and slightly garbled rendition of a speech in which Balthazar protests love for Bel-Imperia in Kyd's *The Spanish Tragedy* (2.1.9–28).

194–6 *What ... pusillanimity*: the source of these lines, if one exists, is untraced.

200–5 *Vindicta ... Veni*: 'Revenge!' 'Terror!' 'Revenge!' 'Terror!' 'I come!' 'I come!' (Latin) The source of this passage is unidentified, but it is in the manner of a Senecan revenge tragedy.

210–11 *Murder ... you?*: this exchange appears in George Chapman's *Blind Beggar of Alexandria* (scene 9.48–9).

213 *brace ... straighter*: it is unlikely that Tucca's servant would happen to have an actual drum to hand as a prop; the expression refers metaphorically to the actor's chest or voice.

214 *'yet stay'*: Tucca is trying to remember the character of Lorenzo from *The Spanish Tragedy*.

216–22 *Nay ... diest*: a slightly condensed rendition of the exchange between Lorenzo and Pedringano from *The Spanish Tragedy* (2.1.67–75); respecting = regarding.

224–6 *Why ... food*: a histrionic, blustering speech which may parody the language of the Moor, Muly Mahomet, in Peele's *Battle of Alcazar* (4.2); a similar speech is delivered by Pistol in *1 Henry IV* (5.3.105). Erebus = the underworld darkness below Hades.

231–2 *Master ... thee—*: the source of this speech is unknown.

233 *the Moor*: i.e. Muly Mahomet, from *The Battle of Alcazar*.

240 *mangonizing*: trafficking in slaves, with overtones of pimping.

245 *Poluphagus*: 'one who eats to excess' (Greek). Tucca alludes throughout this passage to contemporary London actors; although the clues might have been sufficient at the time of the play's earliest performances to identify the actors, the allusions cannot be traced now with certainty.

Barathrum: originally, a deep pit into which Athenian criminals condemned to death were thrown, but the word came to mean in English an insatiable glutton.

247 *Enobarbus*: red-beard (Latin).

250 *accommodate*: supply, furnish.

260 *mango*: bawd, pimp. Tucca perhaps uses the word as a nonce proper name.

263–4 *glavering*: flattering, deceitful.

262–5 *Do ... so*: the extended folio version of this speech describing at length the supposed corruptions of players while ostensibly defending them from criticism (included in this edition as Additional Passage C), was omitted from the printed playtext after the earliest performances; Histrio's response was slightly revised to accommodate the shortened speech.

266 *confine*: enclose within limits.

438

269 *half arms*: the sense is obscure—he might be carrying just a dagger, rather than a sword and dagger, or his doublet might be badly worn out at the elbows. Either way, the effect is ridiculous, and Tucca contemptuously describes him as a 'puppet' (motion); the character is commonly thought to parody Thomas Dekker, another London playwright.

272 *dresser*: i.e. he adapts or otherwise modifies plays; Dekker frequently collaborated with other writers.

273–5 *We . . . rest*: Dekker was hired by the Chamberlain's Men to write *Satiromastix*, a play in which Jonson is ridiculed in the person of Horace; Jonson pre-empted this satirical piece by writing *Poetaster* in fifteen weeks.

279–80 *nor a—*: the quarto punctuation indicates that Tucca interrupts the player.

283 *Parnassus*: mountain sacred to the Dorians; Tucca uses it to mean 'poet'.

288 *nitty*: infested with nits.

290 *tartar*: thief, beggar (cant slang).

290–1 *poor slave*: i.e. Demetrius.

293–9 *'Where . . . fall'*: a slightly conflated version of a speech from *The Battle of Alcazar* delivered by Muly Mahomet (2.3.1–10).

301 *seven . . . half*: i.e. the major shareholder; precisely who Jonson has in mind is uncertain.

303 *countenance*: patronage.

316 *convey*: transfer furtively.

4.1.8 *defy the painter*: i.e. defy him to do his worst in painting their likeness. 'Painter' might also refer to the person who applies a woman's cosmetics (see *Sejanus*, 2.1.62 ff.).

10 *frumps*: flouts, jeers.

12 *muff . . . dog*: along with a fan and mask (mentioned at 20), these were the usual appurtenances of the fashionable lady.

15 *puff wings*: decorative pieces of material hiding the join between the sleeve and body of a garment; the adjective probably refers to the practice of slashing the top layer of material and pulling through the underlying fabric to form 'puffs'.

4.2.23 *fit . . . poet*: with a pun on 'fit' to mean a period of lunacy and a section of a poem.

47 *clog . . . marmoset*: a monkey's (marmoset's) freedom of movement would be limited by a clog tied around its leg or neck.

51 *closet*: private inner chamber.

52 *certified*: assured.

4.3.13 *tired on*: torn at, as by a bird of prey

21–3 *Agamemnon . . . Pyrrhus*: Agamemnon, Hector, and Pyrrhus were heroes of the Trojan war; 'Pyrrhus' was revised in the folio to 'Neoptolemus', both of which names were used of the son of Achilles.

26 *Menelaus . . . Lucrece*: Menelaus was married to Helen, the woman whose abduction by Paris was the supposed cause of the Trojan war; Lucrece, married to Collatinus, was raped by Sextus, the son of Tarquinius Superbus. Tucca's nicknames indicate that Crispinus has told him of his intentions to seduce Chloë.

33–4 *Venus . . . Iris*: Venus is the goddess of love; Vesta, goddess of the hearth and fire; Melpomene, the Muse of tragedy; Penelope, the faithful wife of Odysseus; and Iris is a virgin goddess and the personification of the rainbow which unites heaven and earth. Such elaborate epithets are typical of Tucca's manner of address.

40 *Thisbe*: tragic lover of Pyramus, from Ovid's *Metamorphoses*, iv. 55 ff.

41 *infatuate*: infatuated, foolish.

57 *essay*: sample, example.

60 *pewit*: common name for the lapwing, pronounced either 'puet' or 'pee-wit'. Chloë misuses it for 'poet'.

70 *Cypris*: Venus.

75 *Orpheus*: mythical poet and musician, son of Apollo and a Muse.

76 *Arion . . . dolphin*: Arion was a Greek poet and musician who was reputed to have been thrown overboard by sailors and saved by a dolphin.

83 *Canidia*: a sorceress who features in Horace's *Satires* (I. viii; II. i. 48).

85 *Nemesis*: one of the women to whom Tibullus addressed his love-poetry.

93 *Phaethon*: son of Apollo, who was granted the privilege of driving the chariot of the sun for a day; unable to control the horses, he plunged to earth and was killed.

99–100 *he . . . horn*: hay was twisted around the horn of a mad bull as a warning to passers-by, and the meaning of this proverbial expression is that ill-tempered people are best avoided (Tilley, H233).

107 *cashiered*: dismissed, discharged.

120–1 *Pythagoreans . . . mute*: the Pythagorean society imposed a rule of silence on its novices.

139 *A . . . so*: mercury was a common ingredient in women's cosmetics.

4.4.4 *intelligence*: information, news.

13 *conjuration*: conspiracy.

27 *politician*: politic, or shrewd, person.

30–1 *try experiments*: i.e. do something to see what will come of it; Lupus plans to investigate the effect of the potion on the dog.

33 *fasces*: bundles of rods 1.5 metres long and topped with an axe were borne by lictors in front of magistrates as a symbol of their authority; the number of fasces increased according to the importance of the magistrate, with the emperor having the most.

34 *lares*: i.e. lararium, or household shrine, at which the spirits of dead ancestors (*lares*) were worshipped.

4.5 S.D. *Enter . . . goddesses*: the precise visual effect of this banquet scene will vary as a consequence of each production's use of scenery and staging, but the dialogue requires as a minimum the provision of jugs of wine, wine-glasses, and chairs—or perhaps cushions—on which the characters recline.

1 *several*: various, sundry.

5 *Momus*: Greek god of ridicule; hence, a fault-finder.

68–9 *I . . . wisdom*: this piece of commonplace wisdom is mentioned in Erasmus's *Praise of Folly* (ch. 52).

70 *wizard*: philosopher, sage.

74–5 *if . . . 'em*: referring literally to the twelve characters on stage in this scene.

82 *bear*: with a pun on the senses of 'put up with it' and 'carry the weight of her lover'.

85 *whites of eggs*: make-up was fixed with the application of a glaze made of egg-whites; Tucca suggests that such a glaze would have given his page's face added lustre.

86 *sooty brother's*: Vulcan, god of fire and the forge.

88–9 *Punk . . . punk*: Tucca has previously addressed Chloë with this term (4.3.43–4), but having just drawn attention to the seductive power of his page's face, he might in performance turn instead to the boy to demand a kiss.

94 *stut*: stutter. The likelihood that Tucca's character is played with a stammer is first raised at 1.2.128–9.

120 *Thetis*: sea-nymph and mother of Achilles, courted by Jupiter.

122 *Phrygian fry*: Ganymede, abducted by the gods for his beauty, was the son of the king of Phrygia, an ancient country of Asia Minor.

128–9 *Yea . . . Olympus*: a burlesque of the passage from the *Iliad* in which Jupiter agrees to protect the son of Thetis, despite risking the anger of Juno: 'The son of Cronos spake, and bowed his dark brow in assent, and the ambrosial locks waved from the king's immortal head; and he made great Olympus to quake' (i. 528–30). Trans. A. T. Murray, Loeb Classical Library (London, 1965).

130 *Your . . . it*: mocking Jupiter's sexual prowess (nose is a bawdy reference

441

to penis), with a pun on Ovid's surname, Naso, which translates from the Latin as 'large nosed'.

135–9 *We . . . walls*: this passage only appears in the quarto.

143 *collied*: begrimed, blackened.

145 *lame skinker*: i.e. because Vulcan was portrayed as a lame god; a skinker is a drawer, one who serves drink.

146 *'Wine . . . lovers'*: the liver was regarded as the seat of love and violent passion, and the idea that 'good wine makes a merry heart' is proverbial (Tilley, W460). The quotation-mark printed in the quarto perhaps draws attention to the line as a platitude; note the other gods' ironic praise.

166 *startle*: rouse, excite.

169 *Ha? Ha?*: most of the characters are so drunk they keep falling asleep, and consequently have trouble following what is happening around them when they are unexpectedly prodded awake.

177 *toward*: imminent, impending

183 S.D. *He sings*: the singer is not specified in the early quarto, but it would probably be Crispinus or, in light of Tibullus' direction at 179, Albius.

187 *choir*: company.

212 *curst quean*: shrewish, disagreeable strumpet.

215 *Altitonans*: 'thundering from on high' (Greek).

217 *Saturnia*: Juno was the daughter of Saturn.

221 *soothing*: encouraging, humouring.

4.6.10 *Everts*: upsets, turns upside down

12 *die on*: i.e. die while fighting as an enemy.

13 S.D. *offers*: attempts.

32–6 *Are . . . counterfeits*: although Caesar is angered to find his daughter associating with low-ranking company (29–30), his principal criticism of their entertainment rests on a mistrust of theatre as a 'counterfeit' practice having no true substance or foundation, which is therefore unworthy of poets; skill = knowledge, understanding.

39–40 *And . . . men*: the victim of Ixion's intended rape was replaced by a cloud-image, and the child of the liaison went on to father the centaurs; centaurs, through their drunken lust and violence, were regarded as a threat to human civilization.

41 *comforts*: support, succours.

64 *habitude*: disposition, moral constitution.

66–7 *but . . . imagination*: i.e. except in the unreal products (shade) of their imagination.

70 *square*: solemn, prim.

4.7.9 *fawn*: fawner, toady. Fawn/faun may also carry a pun on 'satyr' (and hence, with particular relevance to Horace, satire, satirist) picking up the reference to 'goat-footed . . . slave' in the previous line; satyrs were classically represented as woodland gods who were half human, half goat or horse.

13–14 *tam . . . Mercurio*: 'both with the cudgel and with a libel' (Latin). The source of the quotation is unknown.

26 *untrussing*: exposing, revealing. Tucca is speaking of Demetrius, employed by the players to satirize Horace (3.4.272–5). Dekker (figured in the character of Demetrius) was working at the time of the earliest performances of *Poetaster* on a satire of Jonson called *Satiromastix*, also known as *The Untrussing of the Humorous Poet*; Dekker's play is alluded to again at 5.3.271.

4.[8].11 *wolfish train*: malicious sequence of actions, punning on Lupus' name.

28–31 *Princes . . . fear*: this passage is highlighted in the quarto and folio with gnomic pointing.

4.[9].2 *concluded*: enclosed, confined.

15 *joyed*: enjoyed.

23 *shadows*: ghosts.

4.[10].5–7 *Oh . . . lowness*: i.e. this insurmountable distance between us represents the two impediments (lets) to our love: our relative positions in space (local height and lowness) and the differences between our social degrees (ceremonial height and lowness).

16–19 *If . . . retaineth*: i.e. if the forms [of love] which I hold in my soul be made one with my soul, and that soul is immortal, then my death cannot erase the desire (affects) my soul now possesses.

33 *affections*: emotions, feelings.

40 *plausible*: acceptable, agreeable.

75 *Great . . . cell*: i.e. her high birth has become a prison cell; *submits* = reduces.

91 *retire*: draw or pull back.

96 *if . . . die*: the wordplay offers two different meanings: 'if both remain, both cease living', and 'if both appease our sexual appetite (stay), both orgasm (die)'.

108 *silly*: deserving of compassion, sympathy.

5.1 s.d. *Enter . . . Horace*: the stage in performance is dominated by Caesar's throne, beside which Virgil's chair of honour is set.

1 *still*: always.

6 *Cornelius . . . Tibullus*: Gallus lost favour with Augustus after proudly

boasting of his military achievements, and, historically, committed suicide after an indictment in the senate; Tibullus felt the force of the emperor's anger at Ovid's banquet (4.5).

10 *quarried*: a term from falconry, referring to the flesh (quarry) with which a bird of prey is rewarded.

16 *Promethean . . . heaven*: Prometheus is credited in classical mythology with infusing life into humans and providing them with fire stolen from heaven.

18 *faculties*: branches of knowledge.

24 *innovating*: changing into something new, altering.

32 *Pierian arts*: i.e. poetry. Pieria, a district in North Thessaly, was thought to be the home of the Muses.

35 *assumings*: pretensions, presumptions.

37 *Contain*: hold (in a certain estimation).

39 *precedent*: the quarto and folio spelling is 'president', a common variant form; the sense of 'governor', however, may also be implicit.

46 *quit*: requite, reward.

47 *Where*: whereas.

49–50 *like . . . comforts*: Horace's metaphor derives from the dual responsibilities of Phoebus as sun-god, and god of poetry.

63 *misery*: miserliness.

72 *Campania*: region of west central Italy.

76 *ranked higher*: i.e. in the social order. Virgil's background is uncertain, but the legend is that his father was a potter or courier who married the boss's daughter.

77–8 *Or . . . detract*: this passage develops the play's attack on Elizabethan dramatists; Jonson, whose stepfather was a bricklayer, gives himself the opportunity to set out the difference between himself and lesser poets such as Marston and Dekker.

84 *pathless, moorish*: untrodden, swampy; describing barren and uncivilized minds.

92–3 *He . . . spirit*: marked as a key point with gnomic pointing in the quarto and folio.

100 *rectified*: refined.

101–3 *By . . . men*: Horace employs a complex astrological metaphor to the effect that Virgil's spirit has been purified of the unrefined (tartarous) moods of ordinary people as the result of his thoughts (discourse) continually revolving around the fixed planet of his reason.

121–3 *That . . . him*: a commonplace about the writing of Virgil, mentioned, for instance, by Francis Bacon in *The Advancement of Learning* (1605).

444

125 *conference*: conversation, discourse.

128 *material*: full of matter or sense; compare Julia's description of Hermogenes as 'mattery' at 4.5.59.

139 *dooms*: judgements, opinions.

5.2.19–20 *And . . . kings*: i.e. the human soul is more radiant (refulgent) in this piece of paper incapable of sense than in the sensuous or luxurious ceremony (complement) of kings.

37–8 *Custom . . . prefers*: the rhyming couplets with which three of the previous four speeches conclude are given added weight with gnomic pointing (26–7, 33–4, 37–8); the danger in performance of such heavy pointing is that the exchange might seem stilted or affected.

40–1 *The . . . sense*: i.e. the vast, uneducated power (rude swinge) of the common mob (confluence) is incapable of discriminating the merit of the particular instance. Caesar is reiterating Horace's point that custom is not a fit guide in every case.

52 *nice*: reluctant, unwilling.

54 *guard . . . doors*: the Equites Romani stand at the doors at the back of the stage, or perhaps exeunt.

56–7 *Meanwhile . . . hail*: this passage, which continues to the end of the scene, is taken from the *Aeneid*, iv. 160–88, and relates the consummation of Dido's sexual desire for Aeneas when they take shelter from a storm in a cave.

58 *each where*: everywhere, on every side.

59 *Venus' . . . nephew*: Ascanius, son of Aeneas, and grandson of Venus; nephew = grandson (from the Latin *nepos*).

62 *Trojan prince*: Aeneas.

63–4 *heaven's . . . marriage*: Juno, goddess of marriage.

70 *nice*: careful, strict.

73 *bruit . . . fame*: rumour, gossip.

82–3 *She . . . court*: according to Greek mythology, Gaia, or Earth, was one of the primordial gods; her children (the Giants) by her brother, Uranus, attempted to overthrow the Olympian gods.

86 *corpse*: body.

5.3 S.D. *[Enter . . . Caesar]*: the original staging is difficult to determine with certainty. Lupus and his fellow informers are unseen by Caesar until they are allowed to enter to him at 23, but it seems dramatically ineffective to have their long exchange with the guards conducted entirely off-stage. Lupus and his men might enter behind Caesar where they are intercepted by the guards, leaving the audience to imagine that the two parts of the stage are separate spaces within the palace.

17 *avoid*: get rid of, dismiss.

23 *whither . . . you*: Tucca pushes past the guards to enter with Lupus.

30 *Epaminondas*: Theban general with a reputation for nobility of character. As with many of Tucca's nicknames, the relevance is unclear.

33 *parti-coloured*: i.e. variously coloured, referring to the lictors' uniforms which are evidently more Elizabethan than Roman.

35 *libel*: seditious or treasonous writing.

40 *remember . . . betimes*: in ancient Rome and Elizabethan England, the wealth of a party found guilty of certain crimes such as treason was handed over to the person(s) who brought the crime to light; Tucca, removing Maecenas' chain at 30–2, has already begun claiming his reward.

43 *hand*: signature.

45 *imperfect . . . emblem*: incomplete emblem, which would consist of a picture followed by a short explanatory verse.

62 *Ha! Ha!*: this should be interpreted in performance not as discrete words, but as a cue for Horace to begin laughing at Lupus; compare the scripting of Satan's roar at the beginning of *The Devil is an Ass*.

81 *Good . . . too*: 'Ass' in Latin is *asinus*, and the tribune's full name is Asinius Lupus.

91 *comment*: explanation, interpretation.

97 *Master Aesop*: referring to the player. Tucca refers to one of the players at 3.4.255–6 as 'father Aesop', which introduces the possibility that it is not Histrio, but another actor named Aesop, who enters here. In light of his characteristic predilection for epithets, however, it seems more likely that Aesop is Tucca's way of designating Histrio.

100 *Achates*: faithful lieutenant of Aeneas in Virgil's *Aeneid*. Tucca is speaking of Demetrius.

103–4 *hast . . . mouth*: i.e. to make his breath sweet, perhaps disguising the smell of alcohol.

106 *broad seal*: engraved stamp used to authorize documents issued in the name of the sovereign.

109 *Let . . . whipped*: this choice of punishment represents Jonson's attempt to have the final word against his rival playwright, Marston, who previously attacked Jonson in a play titled, *Histriomastix, or The Player Whipped*.

111 *pair . . . ears*: i.e. ass's ears.

112 *doom*: sentence.

139 *Hippocrene*: the fountain of the Muses at Mount Helicon. Tucca implicitly likens the close relation of Horace to his benefactor to that of the spring to the mountain.

142 *praetor*: subordinate magistrate.

145 *Maro*: his full name was Publius Vergilius Maro.

156 *knowledge*: cognizance, notice.

164–5 *hold . . . golls*: alluding to the practice of holding up one's hand to take an oath; golls = hands.

167 *band*: collar or ruff worn around the neck.

169–70 *Do . . . so*: Tucca likens Crispinus' legs to a musician's fingers in the execution of a rapid melodic passage (division); his knees are knocking.

189 *severally*: separately, individually.

190 *lex Remmia*: Roman defamation law.

197 *deprave*: vilify, defame.

228 *genius . . . Caesar*: the divine spirit (genius) of the head of the household was invoked when family members took an oath; Augustus encouraged Romans to develop a similar relationship to him as father of the country.

238 *Minerva . . . brain*: Athena (also known as Minerva and Pallas), the patron goddess of arts and poetry, was born out of Zeus' head, fully formed.

245–6 *Ramp . . . spade*: Crispinus' poem is filled with what Jonson considers pretentious and modish words, many of which have been taken from, or are in the manner of, Marston's drama; ramp up = rear up (like a horse).

247 *lubrical*: slippery.

  glibbery: shifty, untrustworthy.

250 *modern*: everyday, commonplace.

252 *incubus*: evil spirit thought to descend on people in their sleep.

253 *throw abroad*: scatter.

  snotteries: snot; hence, filth.

254 *barmy*: covered with barm, frothy.

257 *Magnificates*: magnifies.

  bespawls: splatters with saliva.

259 *organons of sense*: sensory organs.

262 *veng-èance*: Jonson's hyphen draws attention to the fact that the word was usually trisyllabic in Marston's verse.

272 *that . . . bescumbers*: i.e. that shits on all the world.

279 *translator*: the accusation is that Horace tries to pass off translations as his own invention.

289 *carries palm with it*: the palm leaf was carried or worn in the ancient world as a symbol of victory, hence, used emblematically here to mean 'is of supreme excellence'.

293–4 *Now . . . bosom*: Demetrius apparently hangs his head in guilty silence in response to Horace's questioning.

295 *viper . . . parents*: alluding to the popular belief that vipers eat their way through the mother's body at birth, killing her in the process.

298 *cure . . . fame*: care for their reputation.

309 *rise . . . urn*: i.e. vote. The procedure in Roman lawcourts was that after hearing the evidence each juror would cast his ballot, and sentence would be immediately passed.

317 *dejection*: humiliation, abasement.

322 *the . . . eyes*: i.e. a lack of [false] modesty in the high soul (here, the true poet) has a particular effect on the undiscerning sense of the vulgar spirit (the poetaster), making the former's accurate estimation of himself seem a hideous fault, when in fact the fault is in the perception of the latter.

330 *well-digested*: well-disposed.

332 *erection*: fitting self-advancement.

339 *jerking*: scourging or lashing with ridicule. Alternatively, 'jerking pedant' could refer to a schoolmaster who beats his students.

342 *despite*: outrage, contumely.

344 *The honest . . . soul*: this line is marked in the quarto with gnomic pointing.

349 *quit*: acquit, absolve.

353 *case of vizards*: pair of masks.

360 *tumorous*: swollen and inflated, referring in particular to his bombastic language, but also to his pride.

357–61 *Please . . . unto him*: the comic action surrounding the ministration of a purgative that causes Crispinus to vomit his words is based on a similar episode in Lucian's *Lexiphanes*.

383 *Parcel-guilty*: partly guilty. This interjection may be interpreted in two ways since we are never told how Tucca voted: either he voted guilty with the others and now tries to qualify it in order to pacify the accused, or he voted not guilty, and is trying to reinterpret his vote to bring it more into conformity with the other jurors' decisions.

386 *cantharides*: type of beetle which blisters the skin; Tucca implies that Demetrius is blistering his reputation.

398 *look bi-fronted*: i.e. one mask faces forward and the other backward as an emblem of Tucca's two-faced duplicity.

402–3 *Gorboducs*: Gorboduc was a legendary king of Britain whose decision to divide his kingdom led to civil war; the history was popularly known through the play by Thomas Norton and Thomas Sackville called *The*

Tragedy of Gorboduc (1562). The word was revised in the folio to 'harpies'.

421 *prove*: approve, commend.

422 *spite*: regard with contempt or spite.

432 *store*: abundance, large quantity.

453 *turgidous*: turgid, swollen.

ventosity: flatulence and pompous conceit; the folio reads 'ventositous'.

458 *oblatrant*: railing, reviling.

obcecate: mental or spiritual blindness.

furibund: furious, raging.

fatuate: to speak or act foolishly.

468 *prorumped*: to burst forth.

479–80 *Tropological . . . pinnosity*: the folio reads 'Snarling gusts—quaking custard.' 'Pinnosity' is a nonce word which Jonson has invented for the occasion.

482 *obstupefact*: stupefied, stupid.

492 *Cato's principles*: Porcius Cato, known as 'the Censor', who is said to have written in a summary manner (thus an appropriate remedy to Crispinus' overblown style).

493 *next . . . heart*: i.e. on an empty stomach.

495 *Terence*: Publius Terentius Afer, Roman comic playwright.

497 *Plautus . . . Ennius*: early Latin writers; Virgil tells Crispinus to avoid them because their style is in places self-consciously florid.

500 *Musaeus*: mythical singer, closely connected to Orpheus.

Pindarus: Pindar, Greek lyric poet, probably born 518 BC.

501 *Theocrite*: Theocritus, third-century BC Greek pastoral poet.

502 *Lycophron*: Greek playwright of the early third century BC, to whom is attributed *Alexandra*, a dramatic monologue notorious for its laboured style and obscure vocabulary .

508 *Gallo-Belgic phrase*: alluding to a news register published at Cologne called *Mercurii Gallo Belgici*, renowned for its Latinate vocabulary.

517 *that robe*: i.e. the costume of a fool. This staging is supported by a reference in *Satiromastix* to the 'fool's cap' in which Horace dressed his poetasters (4.3.247–8). Demetrius is forced to wear a similar outfit at 533.

522–3 *see . . . company*: the usual treatment imposed on people thought to be insane.

526–7 *branded . . . calumny*: according to early modern commentaries on Roman law, Romans found to have slandered another were branded in the forehead.

544 *twopenny rooms*: areas in the galleries of the public playhouses to which admission would be twopence.

'tiring houses: dressing rooms at the theatres.

545 *puisnes' chambers*: i.e. the chambers of junior judges.

578 *case*: body, exterior.

581 *Rumpatur . . . invidia*: 'Let anyone, whoever he is, who is bursting with envy, burst!' (Latin). The quotation is taken from Martial, IX. xcvii. 12.

TO THE READER

A different letter is printed in the folio, followed by an Apologetical Dialogue which Jonson claims was 'once spoken upon the stage', but which was censored from the quarto. See Additional Passage E.

ADDITIONAL PASSAGE B

1 *Or . . . it*: Additional Passages B and C offer controversial attacks on actors and lawyers, and were suppressed from the first printing of the play. While it seems most likely that these excisions were indicated and required by the Master of the Revels, Edmund Tilney, Jonson may have deleted the passages himself as part of a process of self-censorship. See Additional Passage E, 4 n.

7 *apt*: suitably prepare, make fit.

17 *misprize*: fail to appreciate the good qualities of.

24 *sing . . . angels*: punning on 'angel' to refer to a gold coin worth 10 shillings.

25 *simple*: deficient in knowledge or learning.

34 *cheverel conscience*: of the nature of cheverel leather, pliable, flexible; the expression was proverbially used to describe unscrupulous people (Tilley, C608).

35 *Alcibiades*: Athenian politician, and close friend of Socrates (451–404 BC); an epithet typical of Tucca's over-familiar manner of speech.

ADDITIONAL PASSAGE C

2–3 *prey . . . buskins*: i.e. distract apprentices (puisnes) and citizens from their afternoon labour to see comedies (socks, from *socci*, the slippers worn by ancient Roman comic actors) and tragedies (buskins). This was a complaint frequently made against the theatres by polemical writers.

450

S.D. *Trebatius*: there is no mention of this character in the cast list since he does not appear in the quarto version of the play; historically he was a lawyer, and close friend of both Cicero and Augustus.

1–7 *There . . . Say*: this scene is a free translation of one of Horace's *Satires* (II. i).

15 *even*: evening.

23 *burst*: broken.

28 *Lucilius . . . Scipio*: Gaius Lucilius was a close personal friend of the Roman military leader Scipio Aemilianus Africanus, and was regarded by other satirists as the founder and master of the genre.

32 *Flaccus*: i.e. Horace, whose full name was Quintus Horatius Flaccus.

40 *Nomentanus*: mentioned by Horace in *Satires*, I. i. 102, as a name synonymous with the spendthrift type.

43 *Milonius*: this name is unidentified.

47 *Castor . . . fights*: Castor and Polydeuces were twins, the sons of Zeus; the association of the one with horses and of the other with boxing (handy-fights) derives from the *Iliad*, iii. 237.

49 *in feet*: i.e. in metrical feet, verse.

55 *votive table*: painted tablet consecrated to the gods which hung on temple walls

56–8 *And . . . either*: Venusia, where Horace was born, is situated in the region of Apulia; the Lucanians were a neighbouring warlike people. Horace compares his characteristic disposition (genius) to his birthplace, saying he is uncertain whether he is a defensive or aggressive writer (Apulian settler of a Roman outpost or Lucanian invader); not = ne wot, meaning 'know not'.

65 *my . . . touch*: i.e. my pen (style) shall not attack anyone.

73 *disease*: discomfort, trouble.

82 *Denounceth*: i.e. threatens [to use].

89 *Scaeva*: along with Thurius and Albucius, the identity of this character is unknown; Servius (79) is mentioned by Cicero as an informer, while Horace refers repeatedly to Canidia as a witch.

103 *the man . . . satirize*: i.e. Lucilius.

107 *Laelius*: Roman orator, and Scipio's closest friend.

107–8 *the man . . . name*: i.e. Scipio Aemilianus Africanus, who conquered Carthage in 146 BC.

109–10 *Metellus . . . Lupus*: Roman politicians contemporary with Scipio; quick = alive.

113 *from . . . seat*: an alternative translation of the original line as written by Horace ('a volgo et scaena') is 'from the throng and theatre of life'.

451

127   *sacred laws*: i.e. referring, in particular, to the Roman defamation laws.

134   *That . . . crimes*: this line derives from Martial (x. xxxiii. 9–10). The same defence is used in the Apologetical Dialogue (Additional Passage E, 86–7).

ADDITIONAL PASSAGE E

4   *only . . . stage*: if *Poetaster* remained in the company's repertory after Jonson wrote the Apologetical Dialogue, this claim that his defence of the play was performed only once suggests that the dialogue was prohibited on stage. The Apologetical Dialogue was suppressed from the quarto.

11   *Non . . . morum*: quoting Ambrose, *Epistles* i. 18: 'not the grey hairs of the years deserve praise, but those of character.'

13–14   *Nasutus, Polyposus*: these character names derive from a line in an epigram by Martial: 'nasutum volo, nolo polyposum', which translates as, 'I approve of a man with a nose: I object to one with a polypus' (xii. xxxvii. 2). The phrase 'with a nose' meant to be an excellent critic; hence, Nasutus is a worthy critic, while the judgements of Poluposus are ill-informed and malevolent.

25   *The Fates . . . thread*: the Fates were pictured as three women spinning thread; the point at which the thread was cut marked the end of one's life.

35   *sets off*: appears.

47   *barking . . . College*: i.e. the dogs used to bait bears; they were fed on the garbage and offal provided by the butchers of the city of London.

55   *Teucer's hand*: Teucer, half-brother to Ajax, is portrayed in the *Iliad* as a valiant archer.

58   *servile . . . gesticulate*: actors perform.

64   *stands*: robberies.

69   *Improbior . . . cinaedo*: taken from one of Juvenal's *Satires*: 'More shameless than a sodomite who should write satire' (iv. 106).

74   *ingenuously*: frankly, candidly.

85   *players . . . names*: the players, it could be argued, are 'named' at 3.4.255–75, where Tucca describes individual actors accurately enough for them to be identified by Jonson's audience.

91   *laxative*: i.e. unable to be contained.

98–100   *three . . . stage*: alluding to productions of *Histriomastix*, *Jack Drum's Entertainment*, and *What You Will*; petulant styles = insolent, rude pens.

122–3   *Saepe . . . opes*: quoting Ovid, *Tristia*, iv. x. 21–2: 'Often my father said, "Why do you try a profitless pursuit? Even the Maeonian left no wealth."'

125–6 *Non . . . foro*: quoting Ovid, *Amores*, I. xv. 5–6: 'Nor learning garrulous legal lore, not set my voice for common case in the ungrateful forum.'

132 *lemma*: subject of a literary composition, title.

138–9 *which . . . then*: Jonson fought in the Netherlands in the early 1590s, challenging and killing another soldier in hand-to-hand combat.

133–42 *Strength . . . such*: reprinted in *Epigrams* (1616) as Epigram 108, 'To True Soldiers'; is such = is such as Tucca.

156 *untrussers*: another allusion to Dekker's satire on Jonson, *Satiromastix*, also known as *The Untrussing of the Humorous Poet*.

161 *spurn or baffle*: kick or disgrace.

163–4 *Armed . . . themselves*: Archilochus was a Greek iambic and elegiac poet who reputedly attacked so viciously the reputation of one Lycambes in verse that the latter committed suicide.

165–6 *Rhyme . . . tunes*: the belief that the Irish rhymed rats to death was proverbial (Tilley, D158).

192–3 *Aristophanes . . . Juvenal*: the first is an ancient Greek comic dramatist, and the other two are Roman satirists.

210 *stuffed nostrils*: i.e. undiscerning sensibilities; compare the note on Nasutus' name at lines 13–14.

227 *my next*: i.e. *Sejanus* (1603).

230 *say*: assay, try.

232 *ground*: basis of argument, subject-matter.

233 *despite*: contempt, scorn.

Sejanus

TO THE READERS

6 *strict . . . time*: i.e. the unity of time, which dictates that the events of a play should take place over the span of one day.

7 *moods*: demeanour and modes, referring to movement and music.

13–15 *my . . . publish*: Jonson's translation of Horace was published in 1640, but his commentary was lost in a fire in 1623.

16 *sentence*: i.e. aphorism, sententia. A number of passages in the quarto are marked for special notice with gnomic pointing (diples or raised commas in the margin).

20 *convenient*: suitable, appropriate.

21 *quotations*: Jonson documents his Latin sources in the margins of the

play; these notes have not been reproduced (see Introduction, p. xvi and Note on the Text).

29 *confer*: compare, collate.

30 *authors . . . one*: i.e. Richard Greneway's translation of *The annales of Cornelius Tacitus*, first published in 1598. Jonson occasionally did make use of this source; see Names of the Actors, note on 'Latiaris'.

32–4 *Tacit. . . . Seneca*: i.e. the edition of Tacitus' *Annals* prepared by Justus Lipsius and published in Antwerp in 1600; Dio Cassius' *Roman History*, published by Henri Estienne in 1592; Gaius Suetonius' *Lives of the Caesars*; and the works of Seneca.

36 *numbers*: lines.

37–8 *second . . . share*: probably referring to George Chapman, but Shakespeare has also been suggested as a possible candidate since he was the resident dramatist of the King's Men, the theatrical company that first performed the play.

43 *Neque . . . est*: quoting from Persius, *Satires*, i. 45: 'My heart is not made of horn' (i.e. he is only human in enjoying praise). The next sentence derives from the same passage in Persius.

48 *Quem . . . opimum*: quoting from Horace, *Epistles*, II. i. 181, '[whom] denial of the palm sends home lean, its bestowal plump!'

COMMENDATORY POEMS

In SEIANVM BEN. IONSONI

[Title]: 'On Ben Jonson's *Sejanus*, his own and the muses' favourite' (Latin).

3–4 *confer . . . souls*: i.e. gather from understanding ('skill-enrichéd') classical writers.

12 *ventrous*: adventurous, bold.

23 *exact*: perfect, consummate.

50 *orgies*: rites, ceremonies.

61 *saith Aeschylus*: referring to the *Toxotides*, now extant in fragments; Chapman gets the quotation second-hand from his source text, Plutarch's *Moralia*, 81d.

89 *great Stagirite*: Aristotle, born in Stagira.

103–4 *As . . . casque*: alluding to the bowls out of which water sacred to the Muses was drunk, and the helmet of Athena; the implication is that Jonson makes even better things that are excellent already.

106 *Castalian head*: the spring at Delphi, sacred to Apollo and the Muses.

113 *great Cyrrhan poet*: Apollo.

454

135 *Our Phoebus*: i.e. James I.

136 *Arachnean*: Arachne challenged Athena to a weaving contest, and was transformed into a spider, condemned to weave webs forever.

140 *His Chancellor*: Sir Thomas Egerton, privy counsellor and lord chancellor (1540?–1617). The following is a roll-call of eminent noblemen, all of whom were privy counsellors and known to have an interest in the arts and sciences: Thomas Sackville, first Earl of Dorset, and lord treasurer (1536–1608); Henry Percy, ninth earl of Northumberland (1564–1632); Edward Somerset, fourth earl of Worcester (1553–1628); Henry Howard, earl of Northampton (1540–1614); Charles Blount, earl of Devonshire (1563–1606); Robert Cecil, first earl of Salisbury (1563?–1612); and Thomas Howard, first earl of Suffolk and lord chamberlain (1561–1626).

185 *Barathrum*: the pit into which condemned Athenian criminals were thrown; hence, hell.

189–90 *Haec ... Chapmannus*: 'This was written by George Chapman' (Latin). Chapman was a fellow dramatist, and may have been Jonson's collaborator on the earliest version of *Sejanus*.

For his worthy friend, the Author

9–10 *Nor ... is*: Jonson was brought before the Privy Council for treason in connection with *Sejanus*, and Holland warns the reader not to read elaborate hidden meanings into the play by drawing parallels between Jacobean England and the author's representation of ancient Rome. Since *Sejanus* was revised before going to press, it is impossible to judge the potential subversiveness of the earliest text, but certainly the treatment of power politics found in the play as it exists today would have been considered politically sensitive.

15 *Hugh Holland*: poet (d. 1633).

To the deserving Author

1 *respect*: consider.

15 *Cygnus*: 'swan' (Latin). The identity of this poet is unknown.

To his learned and beloved Friend

4 *popular dependence*: i.e. dependence of the populace on him.

21 *Th. R.*: perhaps Sir Thomas Roe, but the identity of the poet is uncertain.

Amicis, amici nostri dignissimi, dignissimis ... Marstonivs

[Title]: 'To the most worthy friends of our most worthy friend, John

455

Marston presents an epigram' (Latin). Marston was a fellow dramatist, and the object of Jonson's satire (as Crispinus) in *Poetaster*.

3 *Phoebus*: Apollo.

Upon Sejanus

3–4 *That ... spent*: the sentiment is proverbial (Tilley, C208); 'this cedar' = Sejanus.

9 *vaunt-curring blow*: warning blow

15 *William Strachey*: the identity of this writer is uncertain, but he may be the colonist and writer on Virginia who flourished 1609–18.

To him that hath so excelled ... subject

10–11 *And ... enweaved*: see 'For his worthy friend, the Author', 9–10 n.

15 *ΦΙΛΟΣ*: 'A friend' (Greek)

To the most understanding Poet

1–2 *When ... foil*: Sejanus was written in 1603, but almost certainly not performed at the Globe playhouse by the King's Men until 1604, since the theatres were closed in the spring after the death of Queen Elizabeth and remained closed on account of the plague throughout the rest of the year. The poet imagines the play as a rich jewel set in a ring.

15 *Ev. B.*: the identity of this writer is uncertain.

THE ARGUMENT

2–3 *Augustus ... Tiberius*: i.e. Augustus Caesar (63 BC–AD 14), and Tiberius Augustus (b. 42 BC), the first and second emperors of Rome.

10 *practiseth*: plots, conspires.

14 *lets*: obstructions, impediments.

15 *issue ... Germanicus*: Germanicus, a popular politician and military leader, was the nephew and adopted son of Tiberius; he died in suspicious circumstances in AD 19, leaving a wife and nine children.

18 *jealously*: suspiciously, distrustfully.

31 *trains*: lures; the image is taken from falconry, where hawks are enticed by small live birds.

THE NAMES OF THE ACTORS

The order of the characters' names is not identical to that printed in the quarto, as the list has been arranged in such a way as to clarify the factionalism underpinning the play. The main groups may be described as those who are loyal to Sejanus, and those who are loyal to the family of Germanicus; characters who do not fall into either of these factions have been listed separately.

Sejanus: son of a Roman knight, and sole commander of the Praetorian Guard, an elite troop of soldiers; he was killed in AD 31.

Drusus Senior: next in line for succession; married to Livia Julia and poisoned in AD 23. This character is designated with the speech prefix 'Drusus'.

Afer: prosecutor in the trial against Agrippina's cousin, Claudia Pulchra, in AD 26. Jonson modifies the historical record to make him also play an important part in the trial of Silius.

Macro: the agent by whom Tiberius overthrows Sejanus. Tiberius secretly appoints him commander of the Praetorian Guard, giving him the power and authority by which to engineer Sejanus' downfall.

Laco: loyal to Macro in the overthrow of Sejanus.

Latiaris: portrayed as related to Sabinus, a historical error Jonson perpetuated from Greneway's translation of *The annales of Cornelius Tacitus*.

Varro: instrumental in the downfall of Silius during his consulship.

Trio: professional informer. He and Regulus were suffect consuls (i.e. they took over from the original consuls in the middle of the year) at the time of Sejanus' downfall in AD 31.

Nero: Tiberius' grandson, and Drusus Senior's nephew.

Drusus Junior: Tiberius' grandson, and Drusus Senior's nephew.

Caligula: Tiberius' grandson, and Drusus Senior's nephew. 'Caligula' (little-boots) was a nickname; his personal name was 'Gaius', which was conventionally written as 'Caius', the form Jonson uses.

Arruntius: figure of moral integrity in the play and Jonson's spokesperson.

Silius: previously commanded an army in Germany where he served with victory under Germanicus; committed suicide in AD 24.

Sosia: close friend of Agrippina. She was driven into exile after her husband's trial in AD 24.

Regulus: suffect consul with Trio during the period of Sejanus' overthrow in AD 31; known for his independent mind and integrity.

Gallus: on poor relations with the emperor, and married to the emperor's former wife. As his contributions during the trial of Silius suggest, he is not invariably aligned with the Germanicans.

Praecones: Jonson's cast list and scene entrances call for the presence of more than one herald, but the singular form (Praeco) is used as a speech prefix throughout this edition.

Servants: the quarto specifies a single servant, but the action requires more than one in places.

1.[1].5–11 *We . . . climb*: Sabinus disparages the attributes of the parasitical court flatterer who is two-faced, speaks with a forked tongue (proverbially indicative of deceit), and creeps up the career ladder like a snail up a wall. The sharp opposition between the characters who either support or mistrust Sejanus is visually represented in this opening scene by the two groups of Romans ranged on either side of the stage.

15–17 *We . . . jealousies*: i.e. we know no secrets with which we can threaten and frighten others, and which would in turn make us fear their suspicion of us, with a pun on 'dear' to refer to close friendship and blackmail; jealousies = suspicions, mistrust.

23 *clients*: dependents, hangers-on.

24–7 *whose . . . organs*: i.e. if their consciences were subject to an autopsy, it would be revealed there was hardly a sin they had not committed.

29–30 *beg . . . livings*: i.e. beg that their lives are forfeit to the law in order to take over their estates and possessions. See *Poetaster*, 5.3.40 n.

37 *true . . . ring*: turquoise was thought to change colour according to the wearer's mood.

42 *conferred*: compared.

46 *consuls*: two consuls, the chief civil and military magistrates of Rome, were appointed annually by the emperor; these posts would be passed on to the suffect consuls part-way through the year.

63–4 *We . . . many*: Augustus was made the first emperor of Rome in 27 BC, and Tiberius, his heir, succeeded to power in AD 14; although legally the emperors were merely the first amongst equals, in practice their powers were far greater. Silius looks back to the period when Rome was a republic, governed, in effect, by an oligarchy; affections = passions, lusts.

73 S.D. *They . . . aside*: the audience's attention shifts between the two on-stage groupings, from those critical of Tiberius to those who have been careful to curry favour with the current administration.

77–8 *I . . . these*: the period about which Cordus has written, essentially Rome's transition from republic to empire, was marked by political upheaval and turmoil, the ramifications of which were still being felt during the rule of Augustus; Pompey the Great joined Julius Caesar in open alliance to rule Rome in 58 BC.

80 *Drusian . . . Germanican*: according to one of Jonson's sources, Tacitus' *Annals*, the court was divided between those who favoured the emperor and his son, Drusus, and those who favoured the family of Germanicus (Agrippina and her sons). As Silius and Sabinus make clear at 107 ff., disapproval of Tiberius does not necessarily imply a desire to prevent his son from succeeding to power.

88 *degenerate*: i.e. fallen away.

90 *Cato*: Porcius Cato (95–46 BC), ally of Pompey the Great, and long-time opponent of Julius Caesar; he was temporarily imprisoned for his political views in 59. His suicide following the final defeat of the forces opposing Caesar made him a Republican martyr.

93 *Brutus*: Brutus (b. *c.*85 BC) conspired the assassination of Julius Caesar.

96 *captive*: bring into captivity.

104 '*Brave . . . race*': this quotation is offered as evidence of sedition during the trial of Cordus (3.1.392). Cassius was one of Brutus' fellow-conspirators in the murder of Julius Caesar.

105 S.D. *attended . . . Haterius*: neither the quarto nor folio specifies who enters with Drusus, and Haterius is the only one to speak. In performance, Drusus might be accompanied by an entourage of attendants.

117 *His name*: i.e. that of Germanicus.

130 *avoided*: emptied out, cleared away.

131–2 *What . . . pomp*: pictures of the deceased and his ancestors were traditionally carried before the corpse in Roman funerals; since Germanicus died away from home, near Antioch, this ceremony was not performed.

139 *Alexander*: Alexander the Great of Macedon, 356–323 BC, thought to have been poisoned.

147 *him*: i.e. Alexander.

148 *he*: i.e. Germanicus.

152–4 *every . . . him*: i.e. those virtues which, divided amongst them, made each of them famous, were all found in Germanicus.

162 *decline*: bring low, debase.

168 *his . . . dam*: i.e. Tiberius' mother, Livia Drusilla, not to be confused with the wife of Drusus, also called Livia, who appears as a character in the play.

169 *detract*: disparage, belittle.

182 *tribune's place*: tribunes had very little real power by the time of Augustus, but attaining the post was an important career move.

183 *Fifty sestertia*: Jonson notes in the margins, '£375 of our money', indicating to his reader that the bribe was huge.

190 *Come hither*: Sejanus draws Satrius apart from the rest to speak to him privately.

213 *Caius' trencher*: i.e. the table of Caius Julius Caesar, adopted son of Augustus, who died in AD 4.

215 *Apicius*: M. Gavius Apicius, one who famously lived in the height of luxury.

212–16 *A . . . time*: Arruntius' assertion of sexual debauchery lends a sense of urgency to the threat of disorder implicit in the senators' discussion of Sejanus' upstart greatness; pathic = passive partner in male homosexual intercourse, catamite.

223 *general suffrage*: collective vote.

226 *reducing*: bringing or drawing together.

229 *riot*: debauchery, wasteful living.

235 *Is . . . court*: i.e. earnestly courts. Some editors unnecessarily emend 'hard' to 'heard'.

238 *kind*: nature.

249 *they . . . three*: i.e. Nero, Drusus Junior, and Caligula.

256 *panting*: throbbing, pulsing.

258 *knotted bed*: i.e. of Sejanus' designs.

275 *virtue*: ability, excellence.

285 *fear . . . colours*: the phrase usually means 'fear no foes'; colours = military flag. Sejanus appropriates it to mean that naturally beautiful women do not use cosmetics, and therefore need not worry about their make-up running.

286 *conceited*: witty, amusing.

291–2 *Augusta . . . Plancina*: i.e. Tiberius' mother (Augusta), and her close friends.

300 *cabinets*: secret receptacles, storehouses.

302 *pleasant*: ridiculous, laughable.

305 *smells . . . violet*: i.e. which of them has been treated with violets for constipation.

314 *conceits*: whims, fancies.

320 *quaintly*: cleverly, ingeniously.

343 *Happily*: perchance, haply.

350 *affect*: infect, act upon contagiously in the manner of a disease, glancing at the fact that Eudemus is Livia's physician.

360 *Magistral syrups*: syrups specially concocted to remedy a particular ailment.

368 *still*: always.

374 S.D. *attended . . . Natta*: These directions include those characters who speak; in performance, non-speaking actors might also enter in attendance on Tiberius.

376 *axes, rods*: see *Poetaster*, 4.4.33 n.

394 *enjoy*: have the benefit of.

412 *Abroad*: out of doors.

429 *quick*: living.

433–4 *It . . . hear*: this rhyming couplet is marked with gnomic pointing.

439 *creature*: instrument, one willing to do the bidding of another.

441 *instructed*: furnished, equipped.

450 *want*: fail.

451 *suffrage*: approval, consent.
    prevent: anticipate.

459 *Asian cities*: i.e. the self-governing cities of Asia, a Roman province from AD 133.

463 *Pergamum*: located in Mysia, near the Aegean, and one of the three leading cities of provincial Asia.

478 *can*: can do.

486 *during*: lasting, continuing.

492 *period . . . race*: i.e. completion of my life.

505 *felt*: perceived.

511–13 *As . . . monuments*: Jonson's source for this passage, Tacitus' *Annals*, clarifies that Lepidus had 'asked permission to strengthen and decorate . . . a monument of the Aemilian house, at his own expense' (ii. 52); grant = consent, permission.

517 *Their . . . mercy*: Tiberius agrees that Silanus' punishment should be commuted to exile on the island, Cythnus ('Cythera'), as requested by the condemned's sister.

532 *take*: undertake.

551 *rival*: partner.

555–6 *or . . . Or*: either . . . or.

559 *write*: i.e. [aim to] style or designate [himself].

560 *bill*: written petition.

564 *Colossus*: huge statue of the human form.

568 *Avoid*: depart, quit.

575 *Castor*: name of a famous Roman gladiator.

580 *practice*: treachery.

581 S.D. *Chorus of musicians*: the entr'acte, consisting of a performance of music, separates each of the five acts.

2.1.24 *Send . . . him*: the rumour at the time, as noted by Tacitus and cited by Jonson in his marginalia, was that Sejanus corrupted Lygdus by means of 'an indecent connection'.

32 *through rarefied*: thoroughly purified.

34 *second*: one who renders support.

44 *folded*: embracing; i.e. Sejanus and Livia clasped in each other's arms.

48 *at once*: i.e. at the same time.

Illustrous: illustrious. This obsolete form of the adjective has been kept to preserve the metre.

54 *fruition*: possession, enjoyment.

82 *curious*: particular, fastidious.

93 *without*: beyond the scope of.

95 *sound*: sounding (in the sense of measuring the depth of water).

99 *concave*: vault of heaven.

114 *change*: exchange.

121 *physic*: medicine.

125–6 *perfume . . . sweat*: i.e. she is first to dissolve the perfume [in a liquid or oil], which will make her sweat.

130–4 *Which . . . up*: Drusus was known to have a hot temper, as suggested when he strikes Sejanus at the end of Act 1; choler = bile, one of the four humours of early physiology thought to cause irascibility.

2.2.20 *start*: flinch, recoil.

32 *kind*: kindred.

33 *policy . . . state*: synonyms referring to the politics of government; more specifically, cunning or crafty statecraft.

43 *religious*: scrupulous, conscientious.

44 *nice respects*: careful, strict considerations.

49 *throughly*: thoroughly. The folio revises to 'thoroughly', thus improving the line's metre, but the quarto reading has been retained in this edition to preserve the rhyme with 'cruelly' in the previous line.

52 *race*: children, descendants.

56 *close*: hidden, secret.

57 *fame*: rumour.

59 *than*: i.e. rather than.

67 *thunder . . . hit*: i.e. one does not hear the thunder until after the lightning has struck.

74–5 *slacks . . . presentings*: i.e. she makes all efforts to increase popular support for their faction by giving her children financial support and encouraging them to make public appearances.

82 *Furnius*: historically, he was condemned with Agrippina's second cousin, Claudia Pulchra, for adultery; Agrippina, describing Claudia as her niece, alludes to this event as a past occurrence at 4.1.21–2. Unlike the

other names mentioned in this passage, Furnius does not appear as a character in the play.

85 *Whose . . . wife*: Agrippina was the grand-daughter ('niece', from the Latin *neptis*) of the emperor Augustus; her mother was Augustus' daughter, Julia (who appears as a character in *Poetaster*), and her father was Augustus' close friend and ally Vipsanius Agrippa; she was Germanicus' widow.

86 *compare . . . Augusta*: i.e. as the mother of an emperor. Sejanus is exacerbating Tiberius' fears that Agrippina intends to set her sons on the throne.

104–6 *so . . . themselves*: i.e. heirs should have the same function as the areas of a picture set in shadow which serve to draw the viewer's eye to the central focus of attention, the emperor; darkly = obscurely.

107 *rank*: proud, rebellious.

108 *their . . . bate*: i.e. we must must reduce or constrain (bate) their retinues.

109 *Or . . . state*: i.e. or else it will be at the price of your state.

114–15 *detect . . . suspect*: expose the least indication of your suspicion.

119 *high*: overbearing, wrathful.

125 *in . . . while*: in the meantime.

129–30 *in . . . ambition*: i.e. blinded by their ambition.

    train: stratagem, scheme.

138 *fond*: foolish.

142 *proved*: made trial of, tested.

146 *And . . . thumbs*: i.e. and had confirmed their course of action by means of the hand gesture (thumbs up or down) used by Roman audiences to indicate approval or disapproval.

151–3 *vanquished . . . triumphal*: Silius earned great honour and prestige by putting down a dangerous rebellion instigated by Julius Sacrovir in Gaul in AD 21; the 'ornaments triumphal' refer to the insignia conferred by the emperor and worn by the general on his triumphal procession.

175 *chaos . . . things*: confusion.

191 *prevent*: outrun, outstrip.

192 *Emou . . . puri*: 'When I am dead, let fire o'erwhelm the earth', quoted verbatim from Dio's *Roman History*; this line, printed in the quarto in Greek characters, has been transliterated. Dio claims this was a sentiment frequently voiced by Tiberius.

196 *character*: cipher.

209–12 *Julius . . . meetings*: Posthumus not only keeps Sejanus informed about opinions voiced in Agrippina's home, but through Mutilia Prisca, an intimate of Augusta with whom he is having an adulterous affair (his 'kindest friend'), he poisons relations between Agrippina and Tiberius' mother.

216 *closeness*: secrecy, reticence.

221 *popular studies*: partisan sympathy (from the Latin *studium*, meaning zeal, partisanship) of the populace.

223–4 *pub–Lic*: this unusual lineation is a classicism (synaphea) found in the writings of Horace, and occasionally used in early modern drama.

227 *sound*: search into something by indirect questioning.

240 *present*: immediate, urgent.

243 *second*: aid, assistance.

2.3 S.D. *Enter ... Natta*: as the dialogue suggests, these are the first guests to depart from the home of Agrippina; the others follow in two separate groups.

12 *public hook*: a hook (*uncus*) was used to drag the bodies of condemned criminals to the Tarpeian Rock, from which they were thrown.

13 S.D. *passeth by*: Afer enters and crosses the stage to exit on the other side; the direction was first printed in the folio.

15 *flowers*: choice phrases, embellishments of speech.

2.4.5–6 *She ... love*: Tacitus notes that Sosia's overt friendship with Agrippina had earned her the emperor's hatred; Tiberius and Sejanus have already plotted the deaths of Sosia and her husband, Silius (2.2.147–65).

11 *withal*: with.

12 *simply*: unaffectedly, artlessly.

14 *unseasoned*: unseasonable, inopportune.

27 *closet*: private inner chamber.

33 *providence*: foresight, prudent management.

59 *late*: recently, not long since.

3.1 S.D. *The Senate*: it is rare to see a scene's location designated in the stage directions; this heading is indicative of Jonson's tendency to present his drama as a reading, rather than performance, text.

3 *who ... consul*: the trial of Silius took place in AD 24, during the period of Varro's consulship; Sejanus' fall from power (5.10) occurred in AD 31, during the consulship of Trio and Regulus.

4–5 *late ... his*: the conflict occurred between Varro's father and Silius (not Silius' father) during the campaign against Sacrovir. In Roman courts the prosecutor's allegation was held to be more convincing if supported by a strong personal motive.

21 *From ... furies*: i.e. from retribution exacted by the powers of the underworld (known as the Furies).

37 *dissolved*: broken up, dispersed. Tiberius is referring to the lack of customary order and ceremony observed by the grieving consuls.

41–3 *Though . . . Senate*: Jonson builds on the unsubstantiated rumour that Tiberius was not unhappy to see his son die because Sejanus had convinced him that Drusus was plotting against his life; peculiar = particular, individual.

47 *communicate*: share in, partake of.

53 *impressed . . . characters*: stamped with the signs of old age.

64–5 *Oedipus . . . Sphinx*: Oedipus saved the city of Thebes by answering the riddle of the monster (Sphinx).

67–8 *parent . . . uncle*: i.e. Germanicus . . . Drusus.

91 *general*: collective.

96–7 *But . . . lips*: i.e. there is a huge gap between what Tiberius says and what he thinks or intends.

101–2 *No . . . rivers*: i.e. the smaller is swallowed up in the larger; landwaters = any water which flows over land, such as streams or brooks.

105 *covetously*: eagerly.

118 *Why . . . suspected*: i.e. this disingenuous request to surrender his primacy in Rome undermines the apparent sincerity of the appeal he made on behalf of his grandsons.

121 *to pray that*: i.e. to pray [for] a restoration of the republic, or renunciation of his imperial power.

123 *that charm*: Tiberius believed that wearing laurel leaves would protect him from being struck by lightning.

127 *counterpoint*: the exact opposite (of a public life).

131 *admit*: allow, permit.

136 *For . . . public*: i.e. for the well-being of the community.

180 *Against*: in front of, in full view of.

184–7 *dissembling . . . province*: the charge is that Silius and his wife extended the war in order to obtain more provisions and revenue from the state (entertainment) while extorting (polling) money from the territories they were occupying. Tacitus notes there may have been some truth behind this claim, but Varro falsely presents it as treason.

226 *unkind*: unnatural, wicked.

237 *present*: immediately accessible, ready at hand.

242 *combinations*: conspiracies, self-interested confederacies.

245 *net . . . filing*: i.e. a trap smoothed or elaborated to perfection by Vulcan, the Roman god of fire and metal-working.

257 *Roman eagles*: ensign of the Roman army.

261 *curled Sicambrians*: i.e. with their hair twined in a knot. Jonson's marginal note explains that this race of people lived between the Meuse and the Rhine.

262–3 *Not . . . face*: his point is that he never dishonourably fled from battle.

270 *blood*: passion, temper.

278 *mutined*: rose in revolt, mutinied.

285 *famous credit*: notorious reputation.

288 *impeach*: challenge, discredit.

307 *restore*: return.

314–15 *in . . . front*: i.e. in sight where it may confront.

321 *Delude*: frustrate, elude.

336 *gladdest*: most welcome, most acceptable.

356 *proscribed*: condemned to death, her property confiscated.

358 *treasure*: treasury.

369 S.D. *Enter . . . Natta*: it could be dramatically effective for Cordus to enter guarded by lictors.

373 *What . . . Caesar*: Tiberius, unaware of Sejanus' decision to have Cordus tried in the senate, is momentarily at a loss; this brief exchange makes apparent the power and influence exerted by the emperor's subordinate in affairs of state.

384–8 *where . . . parent*: see *Poetaster*, 5.3.297 n.; degenerous = degenerate.

394 *private*: personal interest.

397 *parricide*: one who murders the ruler of a nation, hence, a traitor.

402 *the . . . time*: an obscure phrase which might refer to Tiberius, or, more generally, to all of history (as opposed to their particular age, mentioned in the previous line).

404 *licentious*: unrestrained by law or morality.

407 *fact*: crime.

414 *Titus Livius*: Roman historian (59 BC–AD 17). Although his political views were not always in harmony with those of the emperor, he and Augustus remained personal friends.

419 *Scipio, Afranius*: Caecilius Metellus Pius Scipio and Lucius Afranius served under Pompey the Great and were defeated in battle by Julius Caesar; Scipio was Pompey's father-in-law.

423 *Asinius Pollio's . . . writings*: poet and historian noted for independent political views (76 BC–AD 4).

424 *Messalla*: Marcus Valerius Messalla Corvinus (64 BC–AD 8) fought with Cassius and Brutus at Philippi, eventually transferring his allegiance to Augustus; later in his career he became a writer and orator.

431 *Antonius' letters*: i.e. the letters of Mark Antony, Roman statesman and general (83–31 BC), which are now lost.

434 *Bibaculus*: M. Furius Bibaculus (b. 103? BC), Latin poet.

Catullus: Gaius Valerius Catullus (84?–54? BC), Latin poet.

439 *Temper*: forbearance, mental composure.

454 *conqueror*: i.e. Augustus.

457 *want*: i.e. lack writers; the object of the sentence is implicit.

407–60 *So . . . me*: this speech is translated in its entirety from Tacitus' *Annals*.

466 *aediles*: Roman magistrates.

3.2.2 *jealousy of practice*: suspicion of intrigue, conspiracy.

14 *stalk with*: i.e. as a stalking-horse.

34 *use*: observe, pursue.

56 *simply*: in simple language, plainly.

59 *emulation*: ambitious rivalry for power.

65 *Caius Caesar*: i.e. the grandson of Augustus and brother of Agrippina, who died in AD 4 as a result of battle wounds.

110–11 *hemlock . . . mandrakes*: all of these plants are powerful narcotics.

113 *stupid*: deadened, in a state of stupor.

3.3.20 *Heat*: heated.

24 *rounds*: rungs of a ladder.

33 *working*: energetic, operative.

48 *Campania*: region of west central Italy.

51 *Capua . . . Nola*: prosperous cities near Rome, in Campania.

64 *election*: choice, preference.

68 *too much humour*: too much moisture. His suggestion is that the environment is too conducive to their successful propagation. This passage was revised in the folio to 'too fit matter'.

75 *whither*: to what end, result.

82 *practise*: scheme, conspire.

101 *scope*: mark for shooting or aiming at.

109 *untrained engine*: snare unset.

119 *observance*: dutiful service.

115–21 *The . . . vain*: court corruption and the ruthlessness of ambitious courtiers are highlighted as key themes through the gnomic pointing of this passage.

126 *uncouth*: unknown.

4.1.32 *unhappy*: unfortunate, ill-fated.

467

36 *like offence*: i.e. similar to the offence with which we are falsely accused.

39 *like*: i.e. the same.

46 *to good to both*: the quarto spelling ('too good to both') is ambiguous, and the intended sense may not be that the calamity turned, but that it turned too much, to their mutual benefit.

47 *meat*: food.

51 *overwhelmed*: buried completely.

64 *Your . . . next*: i.e. you are next in succession.

4.3.16 *client*: one who pays court to an influential person as a patron.

17 *free to*: i.e. free of speech to.

22 S.D. *They retire*: in the earliest productions Opsius and Rufus probably crouched on the balcony where they could be seen by the audience, but not by Sabinus; if an upper playing space is not available in modern performance, however, they could exit the stage with the intent to enter their hiding space, re-entering at 217.

32 *envy*: malice, enmity.

41 *envious*: malicious, spiteful.

46 *shade*: shadow, unsubstantial image.

49 *transfix . . . eyes*: Sabinus implicitly likens spies to basilisks, able to kill with a glance, or to the mythical figure of Medusa, whose look turned humans to stone.

50 *genius*: distinctive character or spirit.

62 *facile*: unconstrained, ready. This adjective was revised in the folio to 'ready'.

63 *vows*: earnest wishes, desires.

71–4 *No . . . unjust*: this sentiment is more Jacobean than Roman, echoing the *Homily on Obedience and Rebellion* which preaches that no one should take arms against a prince, even if the prince is unjust. Jonson is treading a potentially explosive political tightrope in dramatizing challenges to state authority; an anachronistic passage such as this may have been included to clear the play with the censor.

82–3 *ulcerous . . . crown*: Jonson's marginalia refers the reader to Tacitus, who notes that Tiberius 'possessed . . . a head without a trace of hair, and an ulcerous face generally variegated with plasters'.

Rhodes: Tiberius has retired to Capri; his exile to Rhodes took place during the reign of Augustus.

85 *Familiarly to empire*: i.e. freely to rule with the absolute authority of an emperor.

90 *removed*: remote (in time).

92 *mystery*: profession, calling.

121 *Projects*: devises, designs.

136–7 *The . . . Sejanus*: offerings were made to Janus on the first day of the new year, and Sabinus presents himself with grim humour as a fit sacrifice to (Se)janus.

4.4.15 *To . . . succours*: i.e. for fleeing for help.

22–3 *peculiar . . . common*: particular . . . public.

4.5.12–13 *last . . . state*: Arruntius compares Sejanus to the Giants, ultimately defeated by Jove at the fields of Phlegra, who rebelled against the Olympian gods by piling up mountains in an effort to scale the heavens.

15 *expostulating*: complaining of.

24 *on Sabinus*: i.e. tell me what has happened to Sabinus.

25 *Gemonies*: steps on the Aventine Hill leading down to the Tiber; the bodies of executed criminals were thrown into the river from there.

60–2 *Nor . . . expected*: i.e. nor do we have to await (expect) the outcome (event) of any trial.

72 *Pontia*: islands west of Naples; he died there of starvation.

74 *fant'sy*: imagination, especially delusory or extravagant.

77 *Pandataria*: island west of Naples; she died there of starvation.

79 *blue-eyed maid*: i.e. Pallas Athena.

81–2 *Ha? . . . meant*: Arruntius only just stops himself from uttering in public treasonous words against the state.

85 *complement*: completing accessory.

100 *voice*: that which is generally or commonly said, report.

102 *Greek Sinon*: a counter-spy who brought about the sack of Troy by convincing the Trojans to bring the Trojan Horse within the city walls.

105 *night-eyed Tiberius*: according to Dio, Tiberius could see extremely well at night, but was short-sighted during the day.

107 *arrant subtle*: thoroughly cunning.

112 *wink*: shut, close.

113 *let*: hinder, prevent.

122 *Chaldees*: natives of Chaldea; renowned for occult learning, astrology, and soothsaying.

125 *nativities*: horoscopes.

146 *his . . . vassal*: i.e. Sejanus.

stale: having lost the vigour or attractiveness of youth.

149 *proper*: own individual.

165 *forkèd*: ambiguous, equivocal.

172 *leaves of titles*: permissions granted for (further) titles.

174 *Caesar's . . . consulship*: Jonson's source, Suetonius, notes that this offer to share the highest office of state was an early move in Tiberius' destruction of Sejanus.

176 *That . . . him*: in the folio an extra line shared between Arruntius and Lepidus immediately follows:

That would I more.
LEPIDUS.   Peace, good Arruntius.

180 *By Castor . . . Pollux*: 'Pollux' and 'Hercules' were substituted in the folio for 'Castor' and 'Pollux' respectively after Jonson discovered that only Roman women swore by Castor.

203 *parting unto*: sharing with.

212 *in fine*: in the end.

215 *Lynceus*: one of the Argonauts, known for his excellent sight.

245 *mated*: put [Sejanus] out of countenance. The folio reads 'troubled'.

250 *Seeing . . . him*: Dio, cited by Jonson in the margin, notes that Caligula's increasing support amongst the populace made Sejanus regret not having taken action against him when he had the opportunity as consul earlier in the year.

265 S.D. *Exeunt*: an exit is not specified for Arruntius and Lepidus in the early printed texts. In this edition, Arruntius and Lepidus eavesdrop to the end of the scene and exit with the others; alternatively, they could leave after their final aside at 247, an interpretation which underscores Arruntius' impatience with Tiberius' 'riddles'.

5.1.8 *advanced*: playing on the senses of physically lifted up, and promoted in rank.

12 *discerns*: distinguishes between.

23 *their conquest*: i.e. Sejanus' conquest of the gods.

53 *populous weight*: i.e. weight of the common people.

54 *expecting*: waiting.

64 *Flagged*: flew unsteadily.

76 *steam of flesh*: smell of cooked meat.

80 *lade*: burden, load oppressively.

85 *grateful*: acceptable, welcome.

86 *Sometimes*: once, in the past.

89 *scrupulous fancies*: anxious or fearful imaginings.

91 *masculine odours*: the best-quality frankincense, taken from the male plant, commonly used in religious ceremonies.

5.2.4 *opposite*: i.e. factionally opposed to Sejanus.

5.3.1 *frequent*: full, crowded.

12 *praetorian cohorts*: imperial bodyguard consisting of select military troops.

33 *I . . . number*: i.e. I do not know the exact number (can = know).

34 *Three centuries*: i.e. about 300 men. The precise size of a century varied, but originally consisted of 100 soldiers.

37 *Spite on*: an expletive indicating anger or irritation.

5.4.7 *Favour . . . tongues*: a call for silence translated from the Latin, *favete linguis*.

13 S.D. *kindleth . . . gums*: i.e. sets alight the resin (in his censer).

15–16 *See . . . face*: Fortune would have been played in the earliest productions by an actor since it is just the statue's head which turns away from Sejanus.

23 *juggling*: cheating, deceptive.

27 *game*: laughing-stock, object of ridicule.

29 *Avoid*: clear away, get rid of.

31 *spicèd*: over-particular, scrupulous.

50 *unperfect*: not brought to completion.

82 *Caius*: i.e. Caligula.

5.5.23 *warn*: summon, call.

5.6.16 *to the isle*: i.e. Capri, the island to which Tiberius has retired from public life.

30–1 *'tis . . . wisdom*: i.e. I am willing to take a risk on your wise discretion.

35 *several*: separate, individual.

41 *tribunicial . . . power*: the promised honour, bestowed by emperors on their intended heirs, would make Sejanus' authority equal to that of Tiberius.

52 *quitted*: requited, repayed.

70–2 *Fill . . . hinge*: Jonson has adapted these lines from Seneca's *Thyestes* (855–77).

72 *Shake . . . hinge*: i.e. shake the earth off its axis (hinge).

76 *forkèd fire*: lightning.

5.7.15 *Harpocrates*: god of silence.

19–20 *Fates . . . thread*: the Fates were pictured as three women spinning thread; the point at which the thread was cut marked the end of one's life.

30 *He . . . will*: i.e. that person is wise who will (ironic).

5.8.3 *lictor's pace*: lictors moved quickly as they cleared the way for magistrates advancing through the streets.

14 *'say*: assay, attempt.

17 *start*: rush, hasten.

25 *slow belly*: i.e. he is sluggish or unwieldy, because overweight.

26 *here's another*: i.e. Haterius (see 5.10.140–2).

28 *Liburnian porters*: Liburnian slaves, from Illyria, were used in Rome as sedan-bearers.

30 *carriage*: burden, load.

 S.D. *Consuls*: i.e. Regulus and Trio.

5.10.10 *rector . . . isle*: i.e. ruler of Capri.

36 *calends of June*: i.e. 1 June, AD 31. This is an error, as Sejanus was condemned on 18 October.

37 *fathers*: i.e. those enrolled or elected senators.

39 *frequently present*: assembled in great numbers.

35–41 *Memmius . . . taken*: these lines are set out in the quarto in capital letters and with a full-stop between each word in the manner of a Latin inscription; the idea is presumably to create for the reader a Roman 'feel' to the speech.

47 *censure*: judgement, opinion.

73 *secure . . . necessity*: i.e. confident that it is not necessary.

77 *too sensibly*: i.e. with too sharp or acute reaction.

107 *particular*: private, personal.

117 *censure*: judge.

120 *averred*: confirmed, verified.

132 *employed*: bestowed.

142 *Your . . . tempest*: Arruntius likens the shifting movement of the senators to porpoises playing in the water, behaviour which was proverbially believed to signal the arrival of a storm.

164 *professed*: openly declared or avowed (followers of Sejanus).

169 *property*: purpose, function. This sense is not listed in *OED*, but compare the related definitions, 'means to an end, instrument' and 'distinctive characteristic of a person'.

170 *Give leave*: Sejanus indicates a desire to leave the Senate, probably beginning to make his way towards an exit; Laco immediately bars his passage.

180 *constant doom*: steadfast judgement.

189 *Typhoeus*: Macro, in a manner reminiscent of Arruntius at 4.5.12–13, compares Sejanus' upstart pride to that of the Giants from classical mythology; Typhoeus was eventually blasted into the lower world with a lightning bolt from Jupiter.

191–2 *Kick . . . nostrils*: these lines offer a guide to performance, indicating the manner in which Macro brutally assaults Sejanus in the Senate; the latter's subsequent silence and the senators' shock could be interpreted to mean that he needs to be carried off-stage.

198 *amazed*: thrown into confusion, confounded.

201 *Phlegra*: see 4.5.12–13 n.

206 *bays*: i.e. leaves of the bay laurel, woven into a wreath as an emblem of victory.

219 *Fortune's wheel*: Fortune was commonly figured as a blind woman sitting at a wheel; as the wheel turns, so changes a person's fortune. The vicissitudes of Fortune are addressed more explicitly at 249–51.

221 *popular air*: the breath of popular applause (from Latin, *popularis aura*).

229 *waiting*: attending.

241 *ravish him*: seize him, drag him off.

244 *stoops*: bows.

259 *twelve score*: i.e. 240 paces (one score = twenty paces).

270 *mankind*: human feeling, humanity.

273 *soft*: gentle, mild.

282 *Pompey's Cirque*: Pompey's Circus, or Pompey's Theatre, a large building designed for public spectacles.

284–5 *sensitive Of*: capable of feeling.

288 *odours*: perfumes, ointments.

292 *popular rage*: i.e. rage of the populace.

325 *forward*: eager, zealous.

326 *Officiously*: dutifully, perhaps with overtones of undue forwardness.

330 *staid*: modest, sober, with a pun on 'stayed with' to mean 'prevented by'.

341–2 *there . . . room*: i.e. there lacks nothing but (more) room for wrath and hatred.

348 S.D. *Nuntius*: this character-name, Latin for 'messenger', derives from the conventions of classical tragedy in which the off-stage death of the protagonist was conveyed to the audience through report.

360 *silly*: defenceless, helpless.

362 *simple*: innocent, harmless.

366 *immature*: pre-pubescent.

367 *wittily*: ingeniously.

376 *degrees*: steps.

383–4 *force . . . east*: a similar event is narrated in Seneca's *Thyestes*, the

473

horror of the crime inflicted by Atreus on his brother's children causing darkness to fall in midday.

385 *Chaos*: the most ancient of the gods; a personification of the confused abyss out of which everything was supposed to have been formed.

387 *partial dooms*: biased, unfair judgements.

399 *flexible*: easily led, impressionable.

409 *strange*: extreme, exceptionally great.

ADDITIONAL PASSAGE A

4–5 *Esmé . . . Aubigny*: Esmé Stuart (1579–1624).

The Devil is an Ass

THE PERSONS OF THE PLAY

Pug: small demon or imp.

Fitzdottrel: a dotterel is a type of bird which is easily approached and caught, hence a simpleton or fool, one easily tricked.

projector: Engine explains this profession at 1.7.10–13. The sorts of project Merecraft dreams up were in effect royal monopolies; they were prevalent in Jacobean London because they were licensed by the Crown for a fee at a time when James I was in particular need of funds.

champion: defender. As Everill makes clear at 3.3.215–23, he is the one who provides Merecraft with access to wealthy London social circles.

Engine: piece of cunning or trickery. As the broker, or middleman, Engine facilitates most of the play's deceptions.

Gilthead: any fish with gold markings on the head, with wordplay on the character's profession.

Plutarchus: as Gilthead explains at 3.1.21–5, he named his son after Plutarch, the Greek philosopher and biographer (*c.* AD 50–120).

Eitherside: the name satirizes lawyers' ability to argue either side of a case for profit.

Pitfall: trap.

THE PROLOGUE

3–4 *Yet . . . place*: acting space in the private playhouses was cramped since boxes for the audience were placed on either side of the stage; what little space there was was reduced further by the practice of gallants ('grandees') paying extra to sit on stools on the stage. Throughout this speech the Prologue complains that the gallants mar the performance by interrupting the actors and encroaching on the acting space. Fitzdottrel looks forward at 1.6.28–38 to displaying himself in his finery in this manner at the first performance of *The Devil is an Ass*.

8 *In . . . trencher*: i.e. in a space the size of a cheese platter.

tract: (small) space. This usage is ironic, since the word usually refers to a large area.

11–15 *When . . . mouth*: the player's complaint is that spectators push the actors out of the way when they are not delivering lines, thus ruining the production. The belief that threatened adders held their offspring in their mouths was commonplace.

16–18 *Would . . . pass*: the Prologue facetiously wishes for the spectators' benefit that the actors might either always face the audience head on ('stand due north'), have no backs ('no south'), or be as transparent as mica ('Muscovy glass').

22 *The . . . Edmonton*: i.e. the anonymous *Merry Devil of Edmonton*, first performed around 1602.

25 *give some*: i.e. give [the play] some [room].

26 *If . . . in 't*: a playful reworking of the title of Thomas Dekker's play, *If This Be Not a Good Play, The Devil Is In It*.

1.1.1 *Ho . . . ho!*: the folio text prints 'etc.' at the end of this line, the implication being that the actor playing Satan opens the scene with protracted roaring or diabolical laughter. This sort of entrance was a stage convention commonly associated with the traditional Vice character.

5 *puny*: insignificant, petty; perhaps also with the sense of junior.

9 *cast . . . farrow*: bear her litter prematurely.

11 *Tottenham*: a village about 5 miles north of London.

12–15 *You . . . spit*: these sorts of domestic misadventures were commonly ascribed to supernatural creatures of folktale, and hence to the devil (compare the activities attributed to Puck in Shakespeare's *A Midsummer Night's Dream*, 2.1.34–9). The belief that wrapping a cord around the churn or thrusting a hot spit into the cream would make butter come is noted by Reginald Scot in *The Discovery of Witchcraft*, and seems to have been common practice; 'tunning of ale' refers to the act of storing ale in tuns, or casks.

16–17 *Kentish . . . Hoxton*: northern suburbs of London.

19 *'gainst*: in preparation for.

26 *dull*: stupid, foolish.

34 *So*: provided that.

36 *Prove*: try.

38 *practise*: scheme, plot.

41–3 *Fraud . . . Iniquity*: throughout this scene Jonson looks back to the conventions of the popular Tudor interlude in which the Vice character, operating alongside the chief devil, was given a name such as 'Iniquity' or 'Covetousness', and was always (although not exclusively) a comic figure. The irony, as Satan makes clear at 99–102, is that such traditional vice is now taken for child's play by sophisticated Londoners.

47 *vetus Iniquitas*: old Iniquity (Latin).

44–7 *What . . . dice?*: unlike Pug and Satan, who speak in blank verse, Iniquity speaks in rhyming couplets, each line having an irregular number of syllables, but usually four or five beats; 'tumbling verse' such as this is typical of the Vice character in morality plays.

50 *by . . . nowns*: by God's wounds.

Lusty Juventus: i.e. the pleasure-seeking young protagonist in R. Wever's popular Tudor interlude of the same name (*c*.1550), who is misled by the Devil and Hypocrisy before being redeemed at the end of the play.

51–2 *In . . . belly*: i.e. the attire of the fashionable gallant, complete with French cloak, a hat projecting over the face, and an extended peascod belly doublet stuffed with bombast. Iniquity's reference to breeches 'of three fingers' might refer either to the excessive padding of the trousers or to their ornamentation with expensive guards (strips of decorative material) the width of three fingers.

56 *Paul's . . . Cheap*: i.e. from the steeple of St Paul's Cathedral to one of the fountains in Cheapside, a market street which terminated in the church-yard. Iniquity immediately betrays the extent to which he is out of touch with current London affairs, since the steeple had been destroyed by fire in 1561.

60–1 *Down . . . Kather'n's*: beginning near the cathedral and ending at the Thames, Iniquity traces a route through streets and parishes of London closely associated with thieves, pubs, and prostitutes; Smock Alley refers generally to any lane occupied by brothels, but the best known was one near Petticoat Lane.

61 *Saint Kather'n's*: i.e. the area on the north side of the Thames around St Katharine's Docks. The folio reads 'Kathernes', emphasizing the rhyme with 'patterns' in the next line.

62 *drink . . . Dutch*: perhaps a literal reference to foreign seamen, but the Dutch were renowned as heavy drinkers.

63 *Custom . . . Quay*: area near St Katharine's on the east side of London.

64 *factors*: mercantile agents, commercial merchants.

66 *Dagger . . . Woolsack*: London taverns.

69–70 *Billingsgate . . . Vintry*: i.e. start in the pubs at one of the largest ports and fishmarkets on the Thames (Billingsgate) and walk past London Bridge to the Three Cranes, a seedy tavern in Vintry Wharf.

72–3 *Strand . . . Hall*: the Strand is a street north of the Thames running between the city and Westminster; Westminster Hall is closely associated with lawcourts and lawyers.

75 *ivy . . . leather*: i.e. the money-hungry lawyers (velvet) cling as tightly to their clients (leather) as ivy to oak. The tendency of ivy to climb up oak trees is proverbial (Dent, I109.11).

80–1 *Remember . . . sixteen*: i.e. the year *The Devil is an Ass* was first performed.

85 *In . . . dagger*: the typical costume of the stage Vice; the wooden dagger, waved about ineffectually, was his traditional prop.

87 *Might . . . that*: i.e. committed the sort of sin.

93 *Cokeley*: popular contemporary jester.

94 *Vennar*: Richard Vennar, a nobleman short of cash, announced the performance of a new play at the Swan on 6 November 1602 called *England's Joy*; after collecting the admission he disappeared and the show was never performed. Satan's point is that although Iniquity may hold his own against the likes of Cokeley, he is unable to compete with Vennar.

97 *Almain-leap . . . custard*: Satan compares Iniquity to the Lord Mayor's fool, a figure of fun who traditionally jumped into a large custard at the end of a feast; an Almain-leap is a dance-step.

99 *hoods*: see note to *Poetaster*, 2.1.56–8.

104–5 *And . . . tired*: i.e. vices sent into London return to Hell exhausted.

110 *decay*: dwindle, reduce.

113 *yellow starch*: starch was regularly attacked as 'the devil's liquor' in polemical literature. Yellow starch was seen as particularly pernicious after Anne Turner, the woman who introduced the fashion to England, was sensationally tried for murder in 1615; at her execution, at which she was compelled to wear yellow ruffs, she confessed to having been possessed by the devil. When feigning possession by the devil, Fitzdottrel includes amongst his ravings references to the colour yellow which Sir Paul immediately understands as starch, 'the devil's idol' (5.8.74–5).

119 *rope of sand*: an impossible task, fit for sinners in Hell. Pug cites this torment amongst others at 5.2.1–10 as preferable to spending another hour in London.

123 *meat*: food.

126–30 *Tissue . . . nobility*: the use of extravagant and luxurious apparel beyond one's station in life was commonly cited in sermons and polemical literature as the source and symptom of all manner of immoral behaviour. Tissue is an expensive material resembling cloth of gold, roses worth eighty pounds a pair are oversized, ornamental trimmings attached to the tops of shoes, and cut-work was a type of intricate decorative sewing used on ruffs and smocks.

140 *Tyburn*: place of execution for Middlesex criminals.

142–3 *For . . . you*: a hanged criminal's clothes were the hangman's perquisite, but Satan suggests Pug might otherwise get an outfit second-hand; pawnbrokers ('our tribe') were widely criticized for dealing in stolen goods.

1.2.1–3 *Bretnor . . . Savory*: i.e. Thomas Bretnor, Edward Gresham, Simon Forman, James Franklin, Nicholas Fiske, and Abraham Savory. These men were all notorious con-artists who variously made livings at the beginning of the seventeenth century as prognosticators, astrologers, and quack-doctors. Forman is mentioned again at 2.8.33.

6–9 *crystals . . . characters*: the props and tools of necromancy with which conjurers raised demons; 'pentacles with characters' are symbols made up of three intersecting triangles inscribed with magical signs.

10–12 *I . . . picture*: Fitzdottrel might enter carrying a picture of the devil which he holds up at this point in his monologue.

15 *'Slight*: by God's light.

17 *ancient gentleman*: i.e. his gentility is of ancient date.

18 *As . . . England*: alluding to the controversial practice, begun with James I, of granting titles for money.

25 *'Sdeath*: by God's death.

31 S.D. *He . . . devil*: this marginal note may cue comic stage business (clasping of his hands, embracing of a picture of the devil) by means of which Fitzdottrel reinforces to the audience his desire to see the devil.

   An I: if I.

33 *Beelzebub*: popular name for the devil.

1.3.4 *friends*: family, kinsmen.

9 S.D. *He . . . over*: the outfit in which Pug enters, which he has stolen from Ambler (see 5.2.21–2), is the height of fashion, and Jonson satirizes his footwear by directing Fitzdottrel to wonder in excitement if Pug's shoe roses might conceal a hoof. The idea that the devil could be spotted by his cloven feet was proverbial (Tilley, D252).

33 *'Slid*: by God's eyelid.

34–5 *Derbyshire . . . Arse*: Devil's Arse is a cavern near Castleton in the Peak District.

1.4.1 *lift him*: the pun revolves around the senses of 'raise him off the ground' and 'puff him up with pride'. The wordplay on Engine's name is picked up by Wittipol in his response, and again at lines 49–51.

4 *mathematical*: precise, exact.

5 *I'll . . . piece*: i.e. I'll be answerable to you for it for half a piece of gold [11 shillings].

35 *catholic*: universal, comprehensive.

36 S.D. *'say*: assay, try.

40–1 *The . . . velvet*: cloaks were often richly decorated with embroidery and jewels, and as Engine indicates, they could be a hugely expensive fashion accessory. Plush is a silk fabric with a long nap.

50–1 *A . . . in him*: mechanisms which involve the use of a winch or pulley (playing on the pun of Engine 'lifting' Fitzdottrel).

54 *mere*: sheer, absolute.

63 *complexion*: disposition, temperament.

72 *lade*: oppressively burden—i.e. with ironic praise, but Fitzdottrel might also be referring to the cloak. Wittipol picks up the image of bearing burdens to imply in the next line that Fitzdottrel is an ass.

88 *fant'sy*: delusive imagination.

97 *defend*: prohibit, forbid.

101 *schemes*: figures of speech.

Prince Quintilian: Marcus Fabius Quintilian, Roman authority on rhetoric; Fitzdottrel's description of him as a prince is ironic.

109 S.D. *Exeunt*: Wittipol, Manly, and Engine exit the stage with Fitzdottrel and Pug, to re-enter in the next scene in Fitzdottrel's house, where the action of the rest of this act and the next takes place. The action is localized at the end of 1.6 when Mistress Fitzdottrel is sent to her room and Engine ushered in immediately after.

1.5.8–9 *Old . . . monsters*: the idea that unheard-of things come out of Africa was proverbial (Tilley A56).

11–13 *mind . . . was*: i.e. that a mind which is inwardly so coarse and vulgar should be so outwardly attractive, and laid out in the open air for everyone to see.

18 *proposed himself*: set before his mind.

21 *race . . . him*: tribe able to turn him into money for themselves.

1.6.18 *nyas*: Jonson's sidenote reads, 'A niaise is a young hawk taken crying out of the nest.'

18–21 *Which . . . at*: Fitzdottrel's point is that he is in good company since, given time enough, even prestigious families abroad give the English cause for laughter; 'seven year' proverbially suggests a long passage of time.

31 *Blackfriars Playhouse*: the indoor London theatre at which *The Devil is an Ass* was first performed.

34 *Publish*: make publicly or generally known.

40 *wusse*: variant form of 'wis', meaning 'certainly'; Jonson uses it to characterize Fitzdottrel's Norfolk dialect.

49 *in precept*: i.e. as an order or command.

56 *pragmatic*: meddling, intrusive.

57–8 *Here . . . pinnace*: a pinnace is a small light boat, used metaphorically of a woman, especially a prostitute (see the Host's description of the tailor's wife in *The New Inn* at 4.3.90). The irony underpinning Fitzdottrel's choice of metaphor is that he prostitutes his wife in order to get the cloak.

62 *they're right*: the folio reads 'th'are right', and I interpret this as a reference to the watches Fitzdottrel and Wittipol are setting. Some other editors, following the 1641 edition in thinking the elided pronoun is 'thou', emend to 'th'art right.'

63 *But . . . briefly*: a marginal note in the folio reads: 'He repeats his contract again.'

68 *yard*: a distance of three feet, with a pun on 'penis'.

73 *rush*: the stage was covered with rushes, and Fitzdottrel uses one to specify the point beyond which Wittipol is not allowed to step.

80 *glass*: mirror.

83 *court parliament*: alluding to the medieval Courts of Love, such as are enacted in *The New Inn*, 3.2.

88 *at . . . carats*: i.e. at its full value or worth.

94 *Pieces*: short spaces of time.

96 *his . . . circle*: i.e. in opposition to the circles used in necromancy to conjure the devil, referring either to his wife's arms or, more crudely, to her vagina.

97 *Lincoln's Inn*: one of the four Inns of Court (law schools), located south of Holborn. Fitzdottrel would not have travelled far to practise his conjuring, as his wife says at 2.2.53–4 that her window looks out on Lincoln's Inn.

75–99 *The . . . you*: the main thrust of this complex speech is that the cold sheets and burning candle are testimony to Fitzdottrel's neglect of his long-suffering wife.

111 S.D. *offers*: shows intention.

116 *fond*: foolish.

119 *in travail*: i.e. labouring, with a pun on 'in travel.'

125–6 *Things . . . equality*: Wittipol presents adultery as common sense through recourse to proverbial wisdom: 'Like will to like' and 'Marry your equal' (Tilley, L286, E178). He reminds Mistress Fitzdottrel at 130 of the need to enjoy her beauty while it lasts with a version of the saying, 'Beauty does fade like a flower' (Tilley, B165).

137 *Wife!*: Fitzdottrel warns his wife not to respond to Wittipol's advances; his sharp reminder might be prompted in performance by a gesture or movement on the part of Mistress Fitzdottrel.

148 S.D. *He . . . place*: the folio reads 'her place', suggesting that Manly takes up the position of Mistress Fitzdottrel while Wittipol speaks in her person. This stage direction has been emended, however, in view of the staging at 192 which indicates that it is Wittipol, not Manly, who has been standing in her place, perhaps even beside her. This makes sense of Manly's insistent protests that Wittipol must 'play fair'—that is, not break his bargain by standing closer than a yard to Mistress Fitzdottrel.

158–9 *no . . . ass*: an obscure allusion to a story attributed to Lucian (b. *c.* AD 120) called *Lucius or The Ass* in which a man is transformed back from an ass into a human by eating roses.

179–80 *change . . . ensigns*: i.e. substitute cuckold's horns for his ass's ears.

187 *mere . . . sake*: i.e. Fitzdottrel will insist on seeing the play because of its title, *The Devil is an Ass*.

216–17 *Blackfriars . . . pictures*: Blackfriars was a fashionable area of London inhabited by famous painters of the age.

219 *middling*: acting as an intermediary or go-between.

230 *motion*: bidding, prompting (i.e. that Fitzdottrel's wife forget what has taken place). Manly might also be contempuously describing as a puppet show the episode he has just witnessed.

1.7.15–17 *but . . . practise*: Engine refers to the injunction of James I to the Lord Mayor of London in 1615 to prosecute conjurors more rigorously according to the 1604 statute.

21 *courses*: personal conduct or behaviour, 'goings-on.'

29–30 *But . . . me*: this transition between the acts is unusual in that the stage is not cleared. The customary practice in indoor theatres such as Blackfriars was to allow a short break between each act, during which time music would play and the candles used to light the space would be trimmed. Here, the action is continuous from the Prologue to the end of Act 2.

2.1.3 *Via pecunia!*: Away, money! (Latin).

8–10 *Raise . . . come*: i.e. accomplish the impossible in order to gain money.

20 *Woodcock*: fool, dupe.

21 *th' Exchange*: the Royal Exchange in Cornhill was a building devoted to the distribution and exchange of currency; the area in which it was located was frequented by fashionable shoppers and thieves.

36 *undertaker*: one who takes part in a business affair, possibly also in the sense of acting as surety for the project.

38 *countenance*: credit, reputation.

46 *moiety*: half share.

53 *pan*: the hollow in which water stands.

64 *th' earldom of Pancridge*: a mock title, since Pancridge (modern-day Pancras) was a wasteland mostly occupied by thieves; the expression was proverbial (Tilley, P65).

65 S.D. *Trains . . . bag*: it is unclear who plucks out the papers during this scene. This stage direction indicates that Merecraft speaks here to Trains, but it might be dramatically effective if Fitzdottrel, getting caught up in the action, is the one subsequently to put his hand in the bag.

69 *dressing*: preparing.

71–2 *borachio . . . Spain*: large leather bag used for wine; high-quality leather (cordwain) came from Spain.

81–2 *it's . . . backside*: i.e. the profits, down to the last penny, have been calculated (cast) on the back of the paper.

83 *harrington*: brass farthing coined by John, Lord Harrington, under a patent granted him by James I in 1613.

93 *stoppling*: manner of putting a stopper, or stopple, in a bottle.

117 *England . . . dukes*: there were no dukes in England between 1572 and 1623.

129–30 *carried . . . cloud*: i.e. in a manner so as not to be perceived; the expression was proverbial (Tilley, M751).

134 *presently*: immediately, instantly.

143–4 *Keeps . . . Bermudas*: i.e. is he still living with you? The Bermudas is a slang term describing the disreputable alleys north of the Strand, near Covent Garden.

145 *Be . . . him*: i.e. do not tell him.

151 *kind*: nature.

164–5 *wafers . . . letters*: small disks made of flour, used to seal letters.

166 *vented*: spread abroad.

167 *shrewd*: vile, undesirable.

2.2.1–2 *I . . . master*: i.e. my service to Hell is not unique to me (singular), nor do I have a supreme (superlative) master!

4 *subtlety*: crafty stratagem (ironic).

10 *tract*: attraction.

48–51 *leave . . . stalking*: a dottrel is a type of bird easily caught by hunters and Mistress Fitzdottrel warns Wittipol not to assume she will live up to her namesake; her wordplay is further complicated by a pun on fowl/foul which introduces the proverbial opposition between physical beauty and moral depravity (Tilley, F29).

59 *repair*: right, remedy.

81 *spiced*: over-scrupulous.

poor gentleman: i.e. referring to Fitzdottrel, not Wittipol, and his ambitions to win a title—Pug implies that the title of cuckold is the most for which he can hope.

90 *forked top*: punning on the cuckold's horns.

122 *just complexion*: ideal constitution or temperament.

123 *truth . . . clothes*: fitted out in Ambler's new clothes, Pug suggests with false modesty that he is not well-dressed enough to attract fine ladies; a piccadill was a decorative scalloped border.

128 *jack*: fellow, lad.

Pug: his name, meaning demon, but also a term of endearment.

2.3.7 *hangings*: in the earliest performances Mistress Fitzdottrel probably would have indicated the tapestries concealing the discovery space at the back of the stage.

15 *parcel*: partly, to some extent.

33 *I'll . . . lisping*: exactly what Fitzdottrel intends by this ominous threat is never explained. At 2.5 Pug speculates that he will either be castrated or have his tongue cut out.

36–7 *And . . . enough*: one of the ways for women to flaunt their nobility was to have a coachman drive them 'bare', without a hat; Jonson mocks this pretension in *The New Inn* at 4.1.15–20.

49 *Crowland*: a town in the fens of Lincolnshire.

50 *us in Norfolk*: as Jonson's dramatis personae indicates, Fitzdottrel is of the Norfolk gentry.

2.4.6–7 *Spenser . . . Earl*: Hugh le Despenser, executed for treason in 1326, was informally known as the earl of Gloucester on the death of his brother-in-law, Gilbert.

8–11 *But . . . to*: Thomas of Woodstock was murdered, probably at the instigation of his nephew, Richard II, in 1397; Duke Humphrey was arrested on authority of Henry VI and died in custody in 1447; and Richard III (duke of Gloucester before ascending to the throne) was killed at Bosworth Field in 1485.

12 *cunning . . . chronicle*: i.e. knowledgeable in the chronicle histories, huge tomes recounting the history of Britain.

15–16 *What . . . that*: the allusion is untraced, but the whispered exchange affords opportunity for comic stage business between the two characters; 'pretends' = lay a claim to, or assert as a possession.

27–32 *Yes . . . first*: the idea that nobody could hold land in perpetuity derives from Horace (*Satires*, II. ii. 129–32); no foot = no foot [of land].

2.5.9 *seaming laces*: decorative lace used to cover a seam.

10 *And . . . 'em*: i.e. if she could show her (hidden) garters, she would soon lose them; gallants wore their lovers' garters as a trophy.

21 *speculation*: aim, purpose.

2.6 S.D. *at . . . gallery*: as Jonson's stage directions at lines 40 and 70 indicate, this scene is played behind and above the main playing area, with two windows arranged in close enough proximity to allow Wittipol to touch his lover. This upper playing space in the earliest productions may have consisted of two apertures, perhaps curtained, out of which the actors performed, or the effect of two windows may have been created along a balcony.

20 *envy*: ill-will, malice.

31–2 *'Tis . . . entire*: Pug is more concerned about the shame of being a discredit to Hell than by the possibility of injury (see 2.5.1–2).

35 *paint*: blush.

38 *perplexed*: entangled.

50 *outward . . . complexion*: i.e. external appearance.

59 *violenced*: violated.

63 *perspective*: an optical instrument such as a magnifying glass or telescope.

70 S.D. *He . . . etc.*: Jonson's fictional, as opposed to theatrical, stage direction elides the gap between the character and the body of the boy actor playing Mistress Fitzdottrel; paps = breasts.

75 *salts*: leaps.

75–6 *promontory . . . valley*: perhaps referring to her breasts and pubic area, but the precise meaning ascribed to the metaphors with which he describes individual parts of his lover's body will vary in performance according to the gestures of the actor playing Wittipol.

79 *kell*: cocoon.

107 *smutched*: sullied, dirtied.

2.7.4 *Take . . . on 't*: Fitzdottrel transfers his attention from Wittipol to his wife, perhaps pushing her behind him.

7 *proper*: excellent, admirable. The conceit throughout this passage is that of unwelcome flies (Wittipol) buzzing around and spoiling tasty food (Mistress Fitzdottrel).

14 *I . . . are*: Fitzdottrel is trying to say that he is determined to challenge

Wittipol to a fight; Wittipol reinterprets his words to mean that he is determined to be an ass.

15 *broker's . . . property*: a piece of wood on which brokers display used clothing, and stage property. Wittipol is disparaging Fitzdottrel's practice of wearing second-hand clothes.

28 s.d. *Fitzdottrel . . . down*: this stage direction indicates that the Fitzdottrels descend from the balcony to enter the main stage from the tiring-house doors.

36–7 *receive . . . pieces*: i.e. receive news from abroad as to how to dress fashionably in every point.

2.8.9 *bedfellow*: intimate.

17–18 *I . . . behalf*: i.e. she is completely out of esteem with me.

22 *make . . . postures*: bow, put one's body into artificial positions.

32 *canon*: standard of judgement or authority.

36 *quintessences*: highly refined extracts.

58 *crack*: prankster, high-spirited boy.

64 *Dick Robinson*: Robinson was a boy actor with the King's Company in 1611, and there is a good possibility that five years on Robinson played the adult role of Wittipol in the first production of *The Devil is an Ass*, a casting decision which would add layers of meaning to Wittipol's transvestite performance of the Spanish lady 'in place of' Robinson.

66 *friend's of mine*: as is made clear in 3.4, the friend is Wittipol.

69 *gossip's feast*: dinner for friends.

72 *carve*: show great courtesy.

73 *frolics*: humorous verses circulated at a feast.

92 *What birds?*: i.e. 'what happened?'; 'bir' is an obsolete verb meaning to pertain or belong to.

100 *forest*: i.e. the hunting rights in a forest.

103 *statute*: recognizance allowing the creditor to hold the debtor's lands in case of default.

104 *hedge in*: i.e. secure a debt by including it as part of a larger one with better security.

105 *Make . . . metal*: i.e. tell Gilthead Fitzdottrel is made of gold.

3.1.20 *Counters*: name of the two London debtors' prisons; 'pound' is an enclosure for animals, and figuratively refers to the prisons in which debtors were imprisoned.

28 *descent*: generation.

35 *rerum natura*: things of this world (Latin).

39 *confounds*: irreversibly mixes together; also, ruins, overthrows.

485

3.2.8 *hap*: have the good fortune to.

22 *Plutarch's Lives*: editions of the *Parallel Lives* were published in 1579, 1595, 1603, and 1607.

34–5 *plume . . . scarves*: an ostrich plume and shoulder sash were distinctive features of some military uniforms.

Cheapside . . . Cornhill: London streets near the Royal Exchange.

38 *posture book*: military drill book.

41 *Finsbury battles*: military manoeuvres conducted at Bunhill Fields. There may be a bawdy quibble on the idea of Plutarchus doing battle with his mistress.

3.3.11 *one quarter*: three months.

21 *epistles*: i.e. letters begging money. The folio prints the marginal note: 'Merecraft tells him of his faults.'

26 *Globes . . . Mermaids*: London taverns; the latter was a favourite of Jonson.

30 *Low Countries*: Netherlands.

32 *In garrison*: i.e. in a military base.

33 *Your . . . blanks*: i.e. the wife of the man who sells provisions to soldiers (sutler's wife) in the military camp (leaguer) who can be bought for the price of two small French coins (blanks).

36 *privy seals*: i.e. royal warrants demanding a loan; Merecraft uses the term ironically.

38 *Pox . . . you*: the folio prints in the margin: 'He repines.'

45 *You'll . . . day*: i.e. Will you ever stop exercising [over me] this imperial rule (empire)?

53 *Strike . . . part*: this agreement to band together against Fitzdottrel is reinforced by the folio sidenote: 'They join.'

56 S.D. *Merecraft . . . business*: this might signal some stage business, such as Merecraft collecting his bags and coat.

62 *Master . . . Dependences*: the folio adds the redundant direction: 'Merecraft describes the Office of Dependency.'

62–7 *A . . . it*: a dependence was a quarrel or affair of honour pending settlement, and 'Master' was an informal term used to describe someone proficient at duels who would advise one or the other side as to the etiquette of the process. James I set laws in place from 1614 to put down duelling, but Merecraft's idea is to regulate the practice by turning it into a monopoly overseen by Everill.

67 *book*: charter.

71 *vapours*: foolish brags, boasts.

75 *arbitrary court*: court of arbitration.

77 *distaste*: difference, quarrel.

83 *a hundred pieces*: a piece (22 shillings) was worth two shillings more than a pound.

102 *pretend to*: aspire to, aim at.

113 *concerns*: matters, is of importance.

125 *Visit . . . ground*: study the basis of the matter.

127 *proportions*: estimates, reckonings.

149 *Bermudas*: colony in the North Atlantic.

165 *St . . . tide*: this date (23 April, the feast day of St George, the patron saint of England) was traditionally the occasion of major festivities at Windsor.

170–1 *And . . . tavern*: Merecraft's military vocabulary is ironic: Pimlico was a popular destination for day outings and a place where Plutarchus could get drunk; bush = signboard of a tavern.

173 *Bristol . . . counterfeit*: British stones with the appearance of diamonds.

176 *I'll . . . mill*: counterfeit diamonds were not as hard as the real thing, and Gilthead claims these stones would endure grinding in a mill.

177 *paragon*: perfect diamond.

179 *black water*: i.e. a diamond having excellent lustre or transparency.

184 *Turnings*: chippings, shavings? Sense uncertain.

196 *just*: exact.

213 *You've . . . wisely*: alluding to Aesop's fable in which prey is divided equally between an ass, a fox, and a lion; the lion kills the ass, whereupon the fox makes division into three parts, giving the lion two.

217 *bullions*: punning on trunk-hose and lumps of gold and silver.

3.4.11 *But . . . tall*: the folio adds the marginal note: 'He excepts at his stature.'

15 *Every jot*: given that Robinson probably played Wittipol in the first production, they would be exactly the same height.

30–1 *You . . . sixpence*: i.e. you are guaranteed to share every penny of the profits.

32 *purchase*: gains, winnings.

34 *guarda-duennas*: guards in attendance on Spanish ladies; Wittipol explains the term at 4.4.77–85.

35 *provedore*: purveyor.

37 *still*: always.

40 *countenance*: patronage, support.

49 *fact and venting*: production (fact) and selling (venting).

57–8 *dealing . . . shares*: selling shares, with financial guarantees.

62 *break . . . you*: confide in you.

3.5.2 *Row*: Goldsmith's Row, mainly occupied by people of that trade.

10 *her ladyship*: i.e. the Spanish lady.

13–14 *airy . . . mouth*: i.e. glib but politic of speech.

27 *honours*: bows and curtsies.

28 *Trust . . . it*: the folio adds the redundant marginal direction: 'Gives him instructions.'

30 *French-time*: perhaps referring to the congé, a low departing bow, but the sense is uncertain.

35 *play-time*: i.e. in the mid-afternoon. Two marginal notes here read: 'He longs to see the play', 'Because it is the *Devil*.'

51–2 *You . . . office*: a marginal note beside this speech in the folio reads: 'He puts him in mind of his quarrel.'

58 *proceed—*: Fitzdottrel hesitates, not quite sure how to proceed in his dependence.

68 *assure*: render safe or secure.

77 *double*: reversible.

3.6.4 *I'll . . . fieldfare*: Merecraft puns on Pitfall's name, presenting her as a trap into which men (figured here as birds) will fall. His innuendo implies that she may have a sideline in prostitution, a suggestion Pug acts upon when she re-enters.

27 *I . . . not*: this, and Pug's next speech, could feasibly be delivered as an aside in performance. A sidenote in the folio reads: 'The devil confesseth himself cozened.'

34 *reckless*: negligent, careless.

35 *How . . . questioned*: a marginal note explains: 'Merecraft accuseth him of negligence', while the note beside Pug's response reads: 'He asketh aid.'

40 *present*: immediate.

46–7 *No . . . pride*: the sidenote reads: 'Merecraft promiseth faintly, yet comforts him.'

59–60 *And . . . perfect*: Jonson suggests the tone of Pug's speech with the marginal note: 'The devil is doubtful.'

4.1.37 *pieced*: mended, repaired.

41 *Not I, madam*: the marginal note reads: 'Merecraft denies him.'

44 *urged*: charged.

52–3 *nature . . . milk*: a proverbial expression meaning evil is innate to him (Tilley E198).

4.2.4–6 *I . . . 'em*: the fashionable complaint of the courtier; Crispinus advises Chloë to affect such boredom in *Poetaster* (2.1.119–24).

28–9 *Madam? . . . abused*: Merecraft is drawn only with difficulty to discuss the toothpicks, preferring to continue at one side his private conversation with Manly.

39 *For . . . toothpicks*: the marginal note reads: 'The project for toothpicks.'

44 *adult'rate*: impure.

53 *chawing*: chewing without swallowing.

71 *infanta*: daughter of the monarch of Spain. Wittipol, whose height has already been commented on at 3.4.11, would indeed seem like a giant when he enters dressed in high-heeled cioppinos. The implication at 3.4.12–14 was that Wittipol would wear ordinary shoes, but the women make direct reference to his elevated footwear at 4.4.72–85.

4.3.28–9 *They . . . madam*: cosmetics were in fact poisonous in this period, common ingredients including turpentine and white lead. They were strongly opposed by moralists, not for reasons of health, but on the grounds that they encouraged female vanity and pride; here and elsewhere in Jonson's plays the application of cosmetics offers evidence of a character's moral depravity (compare Livia's conversation with her physician in *Sejanus*, 2.1.60 ff.).

37–8 *I . . . too*: the marginal note reads: 'Manly begins to know [recognize] him.'

39 *Madames*: punning on brothel owners, prostitutes.

45 *servants*: lovers—in this instance, more accurately clients.

46 *reckoning*: bill.

4.4.12 *complexion*: cosmetics.

19 *Flowers of glass*: i.e. powdered glass.

17–25 *They have . . . thin-skinned*: some editors assign these lines to Wittipol, but the emendation is unnecessary since Tailbush is trying to impress the Spanish lady with her knowledge of the ingredients of cosmetics, a mastery summarily dismissed by Wittipol in his next speech.

27–8 *alvagada . . . argentata*: synonyms for ceruse, or white lead. Jonson's so-called Spanish lady moves freely between Spanish and Italian, and such inconsistencies contribute to the scene's humour since they give the impression that Wittipol is improvising his role.

30 *allum . . . pedra*: types of sulphate used, for example, to make pigments or plaster.

31 *zuccarino*: any delicate confection made out of sugar paste.

32 *soda di levante*: baking soda.

33 *benjamin di gotta*: gum benzoin, an aromatic resin used in perfumery.

34 *Grasso . . . marino*: snake fat . . . sturgeon (literally, 'little sea-pig').

35 *Oils . . . mugia*: i.e. oils of the mastic tree, gourds, and of a type of fish, perhaps mullet.

39 *Look at sixteen*: i.e. look 16.

40 *Lady Estifania's*: the identity of this woman is obscure, but the name appears in a similar context in *The Staple of News* (1.2.99).

43 *Plume*: pluck.

45 *carrnuacins*: an alternative word which appears in some copies of the folio is '*carravicins*'. Both are obscure, but the version adopted in this edition might be a variant of '*carnuccio*', meaning 'scraps of skin or hide.'

   pipitas: white scales which form on the tip of a diseased hen's tongue.

47 *gliddered*: glazed over.

50 *in decimo sexto*: i.e. 'as at sixteen', referring to youthful-looking skin and glancing back at the mention of 'sixteen' at 39; 'decimo sexto' literally describes any book in which each sheet of paper is divided into sixteen pages.

52 *oglio reale*: i.e. 'real oil.'

55 *cataputia*: spurge, a type of herb with purgative properties.

   flowers of rovistico: flowers of the privet, a bushy shrub.

56 *muta*: course; presumably a treatment lasting several days.

67–8 *clasped . . . arm*: trains were unusual in this period, and were worn only at court or on ceremonial occasions; Wittipol probably wears a trained skirt in performance and demonstrates how it could be draped over the arm.

69 *in punto*: in point, according to the precise details of fashion.

71 *pumps*: close-fitting soft shoes with thin soles. Pumps could be worn on their own, or (as Wittipol suggests) inside richly decorated cioppinos.

82 *hoop*: i.e. which gives the shape to a farthingale skirt.

85 *and . . . finger*: in performance, the actor playing Wittipol would probably extend his little finger towards the women to illustrate the point.

95 *Make love*: woo, court.

107 *What . . . sir*: the sidenote reads: 'Merecraft murmurs.'

109 *I . . . toy*: Fitzdottrel's state of mind is suggested by the sidenote: 'He is satisfied now he sees it.'

137–8 *they . . . Managers*: i.e. they manage [clandestine affairs] better.

142 *Pastillos*: meat dishes, specifically meat pies (pasties).

    Braganza: district in north-east Portugal.

143 *Coquettas*: rolls, small loaves.

    almojavanas: cheesecakes.

    mantecadas: dainty pastries ('*mantegate*').

144 *Alcoreas*: icing, sugar paste ('*alcorza*').

mustaccioli: marzipan.

145 *peladore*: depilatory.

145–6 *balls . . . itch*: i.e. pills to counter scabies.

aqua nanfa: sweet water smelling of musk and orange leaves.

146–7 *oil . . . Muja*: perfumed gloves were a popular accessory; the identity of the Marquess of Muja is unknown.

150 *piveti*: Spanish coal, an aromatic compound burned as a perfume.

160–2 *I'll . . . thread*: i.e. that woman who does not know to a hair's breadth ('within a thread') what she can get away with and still retain the reputation of honesty is not worth a pin ('rush').

163 *fame*: reputation.

168 *engaged*: obliged as if by contract (to flirt with them).

170–1 *You . . . this*: the marginal note reads: 'The devil admires him.'

185 *Against*: in anticipation of.

190 *Over smocks*: i.e. 'more than women', where smocks refers to the worst excesses attributed to women.

196 *honours*: bows.

202 *barren head*: i.e. alluding to the pretension of coachmen driving bareheaded.

204 *valley . . . waste*: i.e. his fertile valley (with a bawdy quibble on [his mistress's] vagina?) is below the barren mountain top (with a pun on waste/waist).

209 *French stick*: walking-stick.

232 *The moon . . . moon*: i.e. the position of the moon and its influence, punning on 'mooncalf', or fool. Wittipol suggests in addition finding out the dog's star sign.

233 *proneness*: (heightening) inclination (to sexual intercourse).

238 *And . . . puppy?*: the redundant speech prefix for Wittipol printed at the start of this line in the folio may suggest that a speech has been lost between 237 and 238.

241 *proficient*: learner who is making progress.

244 *All . . . abstract*: the marginal note reads: 'Fitzdottrel admires Wittipol.'

4.5.16 *livery . . . seisin*: i.e. livery of seisen, a legal term for the delivery of property into someone else's possession.

31–2 *his . . . questioned*: i.e. his monetary value, hence, ability to pay debts (valour) at the gaming table (tall board) has been challenged.

4.6.4 *friend*: with connotations of 'lover.'

41 *Madam*: the point at which Mistress Fitzdottrel leaves the stage is not marked in the folio, and she might exit here since she has no further lines. This edition has her exit with Wittipol and Manly at 4.7.73 since it seems dramatically effective for her to remain on stage with the Spanish lady throughout the discovery scene.

42 *leg . . . dottrel*: hunters would strain their legs as they stalked towards dottrels. 'Dottrel' might here represent an abbreviated form of Fitzdottrel's name.

49 *favour*: object of favour.

4.7.16 *She . . . sir*: the marginal note adds: 'He hopes to be the man.'

26 *undertake*: formally promise, pledge.

41 *falsehood . . . truth*: this variation on the proverb 'Praise by evil men is dispraise' (Tilley, P540) is highlighted with opening quotation marks in the folio.

48 *Nay . . . undertake*: the marginal note suggests Fitzdottrel's state of mind: 'Fitzdottrel is suspicious of Manly still.'

53–5 *he . . . pounces*: this metaphorical language figures Wittipol and Fitzdottrel as birds of prey; soused = beat severely, and swooped down like a hawk.

55 *ravished . . . away*: carried or dragged her away by force.

56 *to . . . ears*: i.e. to take secure hold of him.

64 *see . . . home*: i.e. see her home safely.

65 *Duke o' Shoreditch*: a mock title in use from the days of Henry VIII (compare 'earldom of Pancridge' at 2.1.64). Shoreditch was a dangerous and illicit area in north east London.

73 s.d. *baffles him*: disgraces him, treats him with insolence. In performance Wittipol might shove or otherwise assault Fitzdottrel on his way out.

85 *in case*: in a position, prepared (because he has no money).

5.1.3 *sampled you*: put you in comparison.

14 *Put . . . rack*: be at your utmost strain of words, hurry up.

18 *complexion*: physical temperament, referring to the balance of humours in the body.

27 *conduit-head*: reservoir.

29 *Lord . . . House*: a house erected for the entertainment of the mayor and aldermen of London; banqueting-houses took on a shady reputation in the early seventeenth century as the common location of clandestine assignations.

47 *Saint Giles's*: St Giles-in-the-Fields, south of Oxford Street.

48 *A . . . penance*: referring to the rugs worn by the Irish.

5.2.3 *laving*: lading, scooping.

2–8 *To . . . atoms*: proverbially futile activities.

20 *general council*: a formal assembly of ecclesiastics gathered to discuss church doctrine; here used parodically.

31 *threepenny gleek*: type of card game played by three persons.

35 *'Tom o' Bedlam'*: title shared by a few songs, and a common term for a madman, originally an inmate of Bethlehem Hospital, a London insane asylum.

40 *Sciptics*: i.e. Sceptics; those who believe that one cannot be certain of the truth of any proposition. This irregular folio spelling has been retained as a signal to the actor to mispronounce the word. The marginal note reads: 'For Sceptics.'

43 S.D. *Exit Ambler*: some editors have Pug exit here with Ambler, since he says nothing more until 5.5. However, as the folio stage direction at the beginning of 5.3 includes Pug, and in 5.5 he is fully aware of Mere-craft's plot of Fitzdottrel feigning possession, I have left Pug on stage; Ambler enters alone at the beginning of 5.5 to confront Pug with the others.

5.3.2 *As . . . fizzling*: i.e. as easy as farting silently.

4–5 *nutshell . . . fire*: the idea is to set light to the fibres of flax or hemp (tow), which would in turn set fire to a small bit of kindling (touchwood).

6–8 *Did . . . Nottingham*: i.e. John Darrel, Thomas Darling (the boy at Burton), children supposedly possessed by Edmund Hartley, and William Sommers. All of these were famous cases of people who had fraudulently pretended either to be possessed or to exorcize possession by the devil. As the marginal note explains: 'They repair their old plot.'

12 *compos mentis*: of sound mind (Latin).

28 *in potentia*: in possibility (Latin); Fitzdottrel is not yet a duke.

5.4.8 *justify*: prove, make good.

17 *Upo' . . . forks*: the marginal note reads: 'The project of forks.'

22 *signet*: seal used to authorize a document.

23 *on . . . private*: privately.

44 *in reversion*: i.e. about to succeed to a great estate.

5.5.11 *godfathers in law*: i.e. a jury of twelve men.

46 *veered*: let or paid out (a nautical image).

47 *emissaries*: people employed to rally support for a cause.

48 *Bladders*: i.e. which he can inflate with the bellows.

50–1 *A . . . day*: probably referring to John Smith of Leicester, whose feigned possession led to the execution of nine women in July 1616.

493

54 *simple coil*: complete turmoil, disturbance.

59 *you crack*: i.e. your voice breaks (continuing the musical metaphor introduced with 'ela').

5.6 S.D. *Newgate*: chief prison of London.

1 *garnish*: money extorted from a new prisoner.

12–13 *Neither . . . fact*: an obscure passage. The sense is perhaps that he does not have to wait to know (expect) what his torment will be as it is obvious from his crime (fact) of bringing the body back to Newgate.

18 *confute*: confound.

21 *session*: one of the periodic sittings of the Justices of the Peace, at which time Pug would be sentenced to hang for theft.

23 *car*: an elevated term for a cart.

29 *may be*: i.e. may well be.

39 *case*: body.

43 *proffer*: attempt, endeavour.

49 *vindicate*: revenge.

52 *no . . . devil*: i.e. no one wanting to promote or assist the devil's cause.

64 *Provincial*: head of a religious order, used here ironically.

bawd-ledger: i.e. resident ambassador of the bawds.

73 *ride*: hang in the gallows.

76–7 *The devil . . . devil*: Tudor interludes conventionally ended with the Vice riding off on the devil's shoulders; in this play, the Vice carries away the devil. 'Out-carries', a nonce verb, refers to the devil being physically carried off-stage by Iniquity, but also to the fact that Pug was bested by human vice.

5.7.1 *Justice Hall*: the name of the Sessions House in the Old Bailey.

2–3 *Faugh . . . here*: the smell of brimstone left behind by the devil was proverbial (Tilley D224); 'steam' refers to the fume given off by a substance when heated.

4 *countenance*: face.

5.8.28 *Ha . . . etc.*: this open-ended line signals maniacal laughter, and perhaps an opportunity for improvisation and comic stage business; compare 74.

33 *with a wanion*: with a vengeance.

36–7 *Oh . . . madam*: a swelling stomach was a sign of possession (cf 5.5.25 and 48), but the comedy rests on also interpreting the swelling as an erection.

40 *The . . . Coverlet*: Wittipol provides Fitzdottrel's performance with an ironic mock title.

41 *outface*: defy, impudently confront.

70–2 *What . . . delighted*: signalling that Fitzdottrel, lying on the bed, has begun miming some activity which might be interpreted as smoking tobacco.

78 *He . . . players*: Jonson's portrait of Sir Paul—opposed to alcohol, smoking, and the theatre as the devil's work—parodies the godlier sort of Protestants in Jacobean England who attacked all sorts of supposedly frivolous entertainments.

81 *figgum*: the marginal note clarifies for the reader that Sir Paul coins this word to refer to an act of sorcery or witchcraft: 'Sir Paul interprets figgum to be a juggler's game.' What exactly Fitzdottrel is doing on the bed is obscure.

99 *Out . . . circumstances*: i.e. on the basis of circumstantial evidence, what he sees in front of him.

102 *meridian*: point of highest perfection or full splendour.

104 *Justice' . . . brains*: i.e. the head and brains of a Justice; the possessive 's' has not been added after the apostrophe in order to preserve the metre of the line.

107 *purt'nance*: guts.

gilthead: a pun on the goldsmith's character name is implicit.

109 *knight . . . bowl*: although not reflected in modern pronunciation, each pair of words rhymes.

111 *Speak . . . can*: an ability to speak foreign languages was taken as one of the sure signs of possession, a belief confirmed by Sir Paul at 121; as Everill makes clear at 115, he rehearsed this part of the scene with Fitzdottrel in advance.

112–14 *Oimoi . . . muriakis*: a slightly condensed quotation from *Plutus* by Aristophanes: 'Ah me, miserable, and thrice miserable, and four times, and five times, and twelve times, and ten thousand times.' This passage, originally printed in Greek characters, has been transliterated.

116 *Quebremos . . . burlas*: 'Let's break his eye for a joke' (Spanish); Everill mistranslates 'ojo' to mean 'neck.'

118 *Di . . . parte*: 'Please, sir, if you have money, give me some' (Italian).

119–20 *Oui . . . Diabletin*: 'Yes, yes, sir, a poor devil, a poor little devil' (French).

124 *rent down*: torn down, pulled asunder.

128 *These . . . pocket*: Ambler describes the stolen belongings at 5.1.38–42.

131 *withal*: moreover, in addition.

133 *St . . . steeple*: St Sepulchre was a church on Newgate Street, opposite the prison.

134 *Ware*: a town 20 miles north of London.

142–3 *I . . . fiend*: i.e. because the devil is the father of lies. The expression is proverbial (Tilley, T566).

167 *apprehend*: understand.

The New Inn

THE DEDICATION

2 *charge*: expense.

5 *never . . . prospect*: i.e. failed to draw what they saw into a unified whole.

7–9 *To . . . play*: Jonson describes the fashionable practice at the Blackfriars playhouse of gallants sitting on the stage to display their fine clothes ('clothes of credit', with a pun on credit to mean 'unpaid for'). The same behaviour is criticized in the Prologue to *The Devil is an Ass*.

9–10 *And . . . lines*: by standing up to leave the stage (where he was seated in an 'oblique line' to the audience) in the middle of the action the gallant at once passed comment on the play and showed off his rich apparel. Fitzdottrel tells Merecraft in *The Devil is an Ass* that he does it to anger the poet and 'keep him in awe' (3.5.45); confidence = impudence.

11–12 *prejudice*: premature or hasty judgement.

12 *as*: in the same manner as.

THE ARGUMENT

3 *Sylly's . . . south*: the gentlewoman's maiden name, Sylly (or Silly), is suggestive of her character, and means helpless or deserving of sympathy.

5 *extravagant*: with the senses of both 'excessive' and 'wandering'.

11 *her . . . church*: women made a ritual appearance in church a month after giving birth, a practice known as 'churching'; ritely = with all due rites.

12 *reducing*: leading back from error.

15 *resent*: repent, regret.

24 *servants*: male suitors.

25 *Barnet*: market town 11 miles north of London.

39 *against . . . day*: i.e. on the [previous] evening, in anticipation of (against) the trip to Barnet; as = an intensive to 'on the eve'.

47 *oddly*: nobly, choicely.

48 *love . . . her*: wooed, courted.

49 *fly . . . inn*: only known by the name of Fly. A 'fly' describes one who lives

off another's hospitality; Jonson gives a fuller account of this character in the dramatis personae.

66 *presently*: immediately.

73 *court*: courtyard.

74 *Bat*: an abbreviated form of 'Bartholomew'.

broken: bankrupt.

76 *entreated*: treated, dealt with.

81 *Pinnacia Stuff*: a 'pinnace' figuratively refers to a prostitute, and 'stuff' to the material with which tailors work; her name is suggestive of her character.

82 *preoccupied in*: literally, dressed in beforehand, but with a bawdy secondary sense which turns on Stuff's practice of having sexual intercourse with his wife in his customers' clothes.

106 *portion*: dowry.

THE PERSONS OF THE PLAY

3 *Frampul*: variant form of the adjective 'frampold', meaning disagreeable or peevish; the sense of spirited or fiery (usually applied to horses) may also be implied.

8 *complete*: accomplished, consummate.

16 *affections*: inclinations.

19 *stale*: bait, decoy.

21 *beggar-woman*: i.e. the Nurse, her mother.

25 *jealous*: doubtful, mistrustful.

30 *fantastical*: capricious, impulsive.

43 *Sir . . . Tipto*: the name offers clues about his character: 'Glorious' derives from *gloriosus* (Latin) meaning vainglorious or bragging, while 'Tipto' alludes to his pretentious or haughty demeanour. The braggart soldier (*'miles gloriosus'*) was a popular stock character originating in Plautus' comedy of the same name, and the type is probably glanced at here.

46 *neglects . . . him*: i.e. he ignores the lady, as she does him.

50 *parasite . . . house*: the parasite or fly who lives off another's means was a stock character in classical comedy; visitor-general = supervisor, inspector.

51–2 *inflamer . . . reckonings*: i.e. Fly artificially inflates customers' bills.

53–4 *Pierce . . . Anon*: Part of his function was to 'pierce' barrels; the nickname derives from waiters' conventional call to customers demanding service.

55 *Jordan*: chamber-pot.

56 *tertia*: regiment or division of infantry.

58 *Peck*: measure of dry goods equal to a quarter of a bushel; horses were commonly allotted a peck of oats.

59 *in-and-in man*: i.e. someone who gambles at in-and-in, a dicing game popular in taverns.

60 *Huffle*: bluster.

65 *only . . . on*: i.e. in 4.1.

THE PROLOGUE

2 *old house*: i.e. Blackfriars Theatre.

3–4 *same . . . fat*: i.e. Jonson, who weighed nearly 300 pounds.

8 *meat*: food.

10 *secure dresser*: confident cook.

12 *loud*: emphatic, vehement.

13 *nice*: delicate, fastidious.

19 *shrewd grudging*: grievous symptom of illness.

26 *hectics . . . epidemical*: fevers which accompany consumption or other wasting diseases (hectics) are not found everywhere (epidemical). His point is that the 'disease' which makes some unable to appreciate his play will not have spread to everybody.

1.1.3 *Light Heart*: i.e. cheerful, merry spirits. Jonson puns on this title throughout the play to refer to the new inn and the host's personality.

5 *A . . . too*: the signboard outside the inn, which may have been visible to the audience and towards which the Host points, portrays a set of scales in which a feather weighs more than a heart. A second rebus (representation of a phrase through pictures) depicted on the board is explained by the Host at 14–18.

9–10 *'gainst . . . man*: i.e. against any man's temperament. In ancient and medieval physiology, 'humours' were the four chief fluids of the body, the relative proportions of which (complexion) were thought to determine a person's temperament.

15 *A . . . heart*: the sentiment is proverbial (Tilley, P655).

17 *'makes'*: companions, mates. Turtle-doves (turtles) were proverbially known for conjugal affection and constancy (Tilley, T624).

19–20 *Old . . . 'ton'*: i.e. John Islip, Abbot of Westminster (d. 1532), and Bolton (first name unknown), Prior of St Bartholomew in Smithfield, who were renowned for the rebus each made of his name (an eye with a slip of a tree, and a bird-bolt shot through a tun).

21 *grounds*: fundamental principles.

25 *Or . . . thwack*: the phrase 'to be threshed with your own flail' means to be treated as one treats others; the Host, interested in having a good time, is determined his guests will pursue pleasure as well.

27 *pounding*: impounding, confining.

29 *thorough*: through.

33 *Spanish needle*: Spanish steel was known for its excellence (cf. *Devil is an Ass*, 1.1.58); neat = clean or bright.

35–7 *As . . . hair*: i.e. as if measuring an ant's egg in relation to a silkworm's egg with a bizarre (fantastic) instrument made of thread can give you the exact (just) difference between their sizes.

39 *quaint . . . physics*: ingenious experiment of natural science.

1.2.6 *Footman's . . . end*: i.e. the stocks (glossed by the Host at the end of the line).

7 *Carrier's . . . Wain*: the allusion is untraced, but probably ironic; wain = wagon.

16 *mere . . . 'gain'*: downright libel against.

17 *commons*: rations, daily fare.

24 *magna . . . laetificat*: referring hyperbolically to what the Host perceives to be his charter of rights as landlord of an inn; 'cor laetificat' is taken from Psalm 104: 15 and translates as 'makes glad the heart' (Latin). See Lovel's amused use of similar terminology at 35.

28 *bush*: signboard of a tavern; originally a branch of ivy. The Host is speaking figuratively here, as he has already described his signboard in detail.

29 *poesy*: motto.

32 *earthy*: having the properties of the element earth; heavy, dull.

Humorous: full of humours; capricious, whimsical.

33 *airy*: i.e. of the element air—lively, cheerful—as opposed to Lovel's earthiness.

34–5 *trench Upo'*: encroach, infringe upon.

41 *shades*: sheltered, quiet spots.

1.3.1 *bird . . . night*: the precise meaning of Ferret's quibble is unclear, but either a prostitute or thief.

2 S.D. *o' the by*: aside.

5 *An*: as if.

play-boy: boy actor.

Thou—: the octavo punctuation suggests that the actor hesitates, perhaps uncertain how to respond to Ferret's ambiguous praise of Frank's Latin.

6 *pitch*: the height to which a bird of prey soars before swooping down on its prey.

8 *rubber*: towel.

quick: living.

25–6 *Subtristis ... Pulchrè*: 'You present a somewhat sorrowful appearance to my father who desires to welcome you cheerfully and so treat you.' 'Excellent'.

28–30 *Veretur ... Bellè*: 'My father fears lest that too reserved face might bring us some ill omen.' 'Prettily spoken'.

41 *institution*: custom, usage.

54–5 *vented ... outcry*: sold by public proclamation or auction; the Host criticizes the controversial practice, begun with James I, of granting titles for money.

61 *centaurs' ... Thrace*: centaurs are mythological creatures, half-human, half-horse; Thracians were known for their riding abilities.

62 *Pollux' ... fence*: i.e. Polydeuces, brother of Castor, who was famous for his skill in boxing; Lovel presents boxing and fencing as related examples of close-combat sports.

63 *Pyrrhic gestures*: war-dance of the ancient Greeks.

65 *figures ... proportions*: terms of rhetoric.

67 *Nestor ... Ulysses*: Greek heroes from Homeric legend: Nestor was renowned for his wisdom, Ulysses for his cunning.

68–9 *To ... says*: referring to the Friar as described in the Prologue to Chaucer's *Canterbury Tales*: 'Somwhat he lipsed, for his wantownesse, | To make his Englissh sweete upon his tonge' (264–5).

70–1 *Pandarus ... Cressid*: according to medieval legend, Pandarus encouraged and facilitated a sexual affair between his niece, Cressida, and her lover, Troilus, during the Trojan War.

74 *vaulting horse ... vaulting house*: a horse used for the exercise of mounting without the use of a stirrup ... a brothel.

75 *bale of dice*: set of dice, usually three.

80 *twinge*: tweak, pinch.

83 *pagery*: service as a page.

84 *tides*: times.

85 *Tyburn*: place of execution for Middlesex criminals.

87 *St ... Waterings*: place of execution for Surrey criminals. It was also a watering-place for horses, which provides the Host with a pun on Aquinas, *aqua* being Latin for water.

88 *go ... circle*: i.e. graduate with a hangman's noose (hemp circle) around his neck.

500

90–1 *come . . . cap*: occur to you, come into your mind.

94 *quick*: brisk.

100 *sons . . . hen*: a proverbial expression used to describe someone favoured by fortune (Tilley, S632).

104 *coats*: playing-cards bearing a king, queen, or jack.

106–7 *face it Out*: brazen it out.

110 *clear nostril*: the precise meaning of this expression is unclear, but presumably refers to the Host's good judgement.

117 *synonyma*: synonyms; the Graeco-Latin plural form was not unusual.

120 *tinkleth*: makes rhymes or jingles.

126 *that*: if.

128–33 *Where . . . comedy*: the image of life as theatre is a commonplace (Tilley, W882); see Lady Frampul's similar comment at 2.1.39.

133 *chuck*: chuckle.

136 *as*: as though, as if.

138 *sad*: grave, serious.

138–40 *loadstone . . . 'em*: i.e. activities used by the melancholic to pass the time: loadstone acts as a magnet, while jet will attract light objects when electrified by rubbing.

147 *Cheapside*: major market street in London.

151–2 *ploughing . . . ox*: alluding to the words of Samson to the Philistines in Judges 14: 18 after the secret of his strength has been discovered: 'If ye had not ploughed with my heifer, ye had not found out my riddle'.

1.4.13–14 *jug . . . beard*: i.e. a drinking-jug on which is painted a bearded face.

16 *this*: i.e. the Host.

17 *fant'sy*: delusive imagination.

20 *tame*: poor-spirited, servile.

1.5.2 *guests . . . game*: gamesome, merry guests.

4 *cry*: announce, proclaim.

7–8 *Old . . . ass*: i.e. Marcus Licinius Crassus, who is reported by Cicero in *De Finibus* to have laughed only once in his life; Agelastos = unsmiling (Greek).

11 *Pru*: the uncorrected octavo reads 'Cis', and as the second epilogue to the play makes clear, the character of Prudence was originally called Cicely. It is uncertain if the name was controversial because the spectators assumed that Jonson was alluding to a living person, or if the name simply sounded too much like a hiss (of a displeased audience). The

unrevised form occasionally found its way into the octavo, but these mistakes were corrected during the printing of the play.

12 *Discharge the house*: i.e. settle the bill.

30 *protested*: publicly proclaimed for non-payment of bills.

39 *canting universities*: schools in which one can learn the secret language (cant) and practice of thieves; used ironically.

43 *family*: household.

51 *bent a fant'sy*: i.e. of a capricious nature so determined and resolute.

55 *precipices*: falls, descents; alluding to the dubious social propriety of her decision to travel to an inn with her suitors.

62 *motion-man*: one who mounts a puppet-show; 'Goose' may refer specifically to a seventeenth-century showman named Gosling.

69 *lost herself*: lost her wits, became distracted.

70 *fond*: foolish.

76 *great confusion*: alluding to the confusion of languages at the Tower of Babel (Gen. 11: 9).

80 *authorized . . . riot*: sanctioned forms of debauchery.

1.6.5 *Chalk . . . rondels*: customers' tabs were chalked on the walls of inns. A 'rondel' is literally a circle; here, presumably, a symbol for a unit of money, or possibly a circle within which a customer's bill is chalked.

7–8 *To . . . window*: a proverbial expression to describe revelling (Tilley, H785).

18–19 *No . . . fist*: wearing an opal or holding the invisible seed of the fern were popularly believed to make a person invisible.

20–1 *reasons . . . ring*: i.e. reasons as complete or accomplished as the enchanted ring of Gyges which made the wearer invisible.

22 *round . . . hoop*: proverbial expression meaning 'easily' or 'quickly' (Tilley, H593). The Host's joke is contorted and obscure, and Lovel's response perhaps indicates patient tolerance rather than genuine amusement.

25 *Secretary*: one who keeps records and transacts business for another, anticipating Pru's formal encounter with Lovel as her lady's ambassador. The title also glances at Pru's knowledge of Lady Frampul's private or secret matters.

31 *in state*: i.e. made with great pomp and solemnity.

45 *suffrage*: approval, consent.

48 *envy*: begrudge, deny.

56 *nice*: reluctant, unwilling.

62 *o' . . . volley*: without consideration.

64–6 *Yet . . . others*: i.e. when women please, they will withdraw (retire) into private like anyone else and there know their true and confidential opinions (cabinet-counsel).

69 *Or . . . me*: i.e. you have taken the words right out of my mouth. Prudence's response suggests that the Host tries to kiss her at this point.

75 *Reserving*: retaining, preserving.

79 *prove*: try, attempt.

80 S.D. *Strikes . . . chest*: the Host strikes Lovel to rouse him from his reverie.

97 *Whether*: which.

98 *house*: family.

101 *impotently*: unrestrainedly.

112 *came off*: retired from the encounter.

124–6 *Arthurs . . . Pantagruels*: the heroes of popular prose romances of the period.

127 *Abortives . . . cloister*: i.e. imperfect works (abortives), specifically the Rosicrucian tracts, alleged to have come from the doctrinally unsound (fabulous) cloister of Christian Rosenkreutz.

128 *infest*: attack, trouble.

132 *fant'sy*: imagination.

129–33 *But . . . virtue*: the heroes of the Trojan War as recounted in Homer's *Iliad*: Achilles was one of the greatest Greek heroes; Agamemnon was commander-in-chief of the Greek expedition against Troy; Nestor was the oldest of the Greek commanders; Ulysses was a Greek warrior and commander renowned for his cunning and diplomacy; Tydides (or Diomedes) was a Greek warrior.

133 *Virgil*: see *Poetaster*, note to The Persons that Act.

135 *Pious*: dutiful (from Virgil's description of him as *pius Aeneas*).

religious: dutiful, conscientious.

137 *Rapt*: carried, removed.

140 *Hours*: female divinities supposed to preside over the changes of the seasons.

149 *hopeful*: promising.

154 *courting-stock . . . on*: i.e. Frances could be made the object of young, inexperienced suitors' attentions.

156 *religion*: strict fidelity, conscientiousness.

161–2 *phoenix . . . ashes*: the phoenix, a mythological bird, is renowned for its ability to rise up alive from its own ashes.

2.1.2 *with . . . biggest*: too big.

6 *Girt . . . hard*: fasten or belt yourself in tightly.

12 *still*: always, invariably.

put off: dispose of through sale.

19–20 *The . . . scissors*: the octavo punctuation at the end of Lady Frampul's speech suggests that she is cut off by Prudence, who eagerly begins imagining tortures for Stuff; cropped = to have his ears clipped.

21 *cering candle*: with a pun on 'searing candle'; tailors used cering candles to dress material.

22 *trundle*: revolve. The idea is that shorn of its ears, Stuff's head would roll freely on his pillow.

23 *cut . . . measures*: i.e. cut into tape-measures.

26–8 *Or . . . aqua-vitae*: i.e. nearly four feet of taffeta drawn through his guts in the manner of an enema and then set on fire with alcohol.

28–9 *Burning . . . him*: criminals able to read a Bible verse in Latin could claim benefit of clergy and have a death sentence commuted to branding on the hand. Jonson himself escaped execution in this manner after killing a fellow actor in a duel.

30 *Now . . . on*: i.e. got the dress on; Prudence has been struggling with the dress since the opening of the scene.

31–2 *cruel . . . strait-laced*: Lady Frampul puns on her maid's moral outlook and appearance: Prudence is neither severe nor dressed in workaday worsted (cruel/crewel), but she is morally rigorous and tightly laced into her clothing (strait-laced). This particular wordplay was commonplace.

35–6 *'Twill . . . somewhat*: it was the practice for acting companies to acquire expensive clothing for use as stage costumes second-hand from the gentry or their servants; yield thee somewhat = make you a (small) profit.

37 *illiberal . . . sordid*: i.e. ill-bred and entirely mercenary.

40 *province*: duty, office.

50 *overlaid*: punning on the senses of 'overburdened' and 'sexually laid by a man'.

54 *translated*: transformed, altered; Prudence's concern is justified, since contemporary polemicists deemed dressing above one's station a serious moral error.

57 *sentences*: sententiae, moral aphorisms.

60 *without*: outside.

2.2.14 *Frank . . . lady*: while Frank exchanges compliments with Lady Frampul, Pru takes the Host aside to discuss with him her plan to disguise his son as another (female) guest.

35 *silly*: innocent, helpless.

40 *shape*: disguise.

42 *French hood*: see note to *Poetaster*, 2.1.56–8.

56–7 *Call . . . hand*: 'Laetitia' means 'gladness' in Latin, and so the name will put them in mind of their intended mirth.

2.3.12 *figures*: rhetorical forms of expression; figures of speech.

16 *steward*: official (usually male) who controls a household's domestic arrangements.

trundling: rolling, but with the suggestion that his speech has a tendency to digress.

2.4.2 *discovery*: exploration, reconnoitring.

3 *this parasite*: i.e. Fly.

9 *property*: instrument, tool.

16–19 *I . . . remain*: in the last scene, the Host explains that Fly was a fellow traveller (5.5.127).

20 *Nothing less*: hardly.

23 *School*: i.e. Schoolmen, medieval scholastic philosophers and theologians collectively.

23–4 *Of . . . unknow*: Beaufort adapts what Jonson incorrectly believed was a disparaging comment on the learning gained at the Benedictine convent of Stratford-le-Bow in the Prologue to Chaucer's *Canterbury Tales*: 'And Frensh she spak ful faire and fetisly | After the scole of Stratford atte Bowe, | For Frensh of Paris was to hir unknowe' (124–6). William Lily wrote *A Short Introduction of Grammar* (*c*.1527) which was the standard Latin primer well into the nineteenth century.

25–7 *Only . . . rear*: describing Fly's daily activities through the use of military puns prepares the audience for the unusual manner in which Fly has ordered his so-called militia below-stairs; 'call in' means both withdraw and shout in; 'inflame' is to set alight and inflate (dishonestly); 'bill' refers to one who fights with a halberd and a customer's account; 'shot' is an armed soldier and another word for account.

29 *corporal . . . campo*: i.e. superior army officer.

32 *publish it*: bring it to public notice.

2.5 S.D. *Enter . . . Fly*: Tipto and Fly only notice the others' presence at 34, when the Host interjects into their conversation; presumably the Host and lords are standing to one side of the stage.

9 *Salamanca*: Salamanca university, founded in Spain in 1200, was one of the chief seats of learning in Europe.

12 *macte*: 'honoured' (Latin).

15 *magis aucte*: 'greater' (Latin). This is a false etymology.

17 *accession*: addition; specifically, title.

21 *side . . . meet*: i.e. run alongside each other without colliding; presumably an image of harmony.

23 *committed*: i.e. as if to prison.

26 *under-officers*: punning on subordinate, and below-stairs, officers.

31 *in ordinary*: permanent staff rather than casual labour, with a pun on 'ordinary' to mean tavern.

35–7 *Where . . . ostler*: the joke is that Fly's studying consists merely of heavy drinking and discussion with the other servants as to how best to cheat guests; the Host's wordplay revolves around 'case' to mean pair and the phrase 'case of conscience'.

40 *What . . . talks*: this gives a clue as to the costuming of the play, as the Host is presumably wearing a hat adorned with a large feather; it is mentioned again at 47.

43 *set . . . up*: i.e. as one would a top.

44 *dominus . . . Factotum*: master . . . person who does everything around the house. Conversely, the Host may be interpreted as saying that he is the 'dominus factotum', or unquestioned ruler of the inn.

45 *Host . . . maintenance*: an obscure and pretentious line befitting Tipto; 'real' means 'royal', while 'cap of maintenance' is a symbol of official dignity borne before the sovereign of England or Lord Mayor of London.

48 *in cuerpo*: without the cloak, and therefore in a state of undress. Tipto indicates at 50 that the Host is wearing doublet and hose.

51 *blank . . . half-blank*: some editors have argued that this phrase describes the Host's outfit which was simple ('blank') and the colour of his hose which were parti-coloured ('half-blank'), but the sense of the latter term is obscure and difficult to verify. When this play was first performed, hose of different colours were well over fifty years out of fashion; see 5.4.36 n.

52 *relish not*: partake not of; hence, are not appropriate to.

54 *to . . . gold-weights*: with the greatest exactitude.

62 *Savoy chain*: worn either as jewellery or as a symbol of office.

62–3 *ruff . . . cuffs*: elaborate articles of lace worn around the neck and wrists, often purchased as a set.

62–7 *The Savoy . . . Madrid*: the fashion of wearing rich foreign apparel had long been satirized in England, and Tipto's catalogue of clothing serves to characterize him as a buffoon; his 'Florentine agate' decorates a luxurious hatband.

73 *paramentos*: ornaments (Spanish).

74 *long sword*: two-handed sword with a long cutting blade.

75 *Sir . . . Hudibras*: mythical British king, and supposed founder of Canterbury, Winchester, and Shaftesbury.

506

77 *tall*: brave, valiant.

78 *Don Lewis*: Don Luis Pacheco de Narvaez studied fencing under Jeronimo de Carranza (mentioned at 87), and both were regarded as authorities on the subject in the late fifteenth and early sixteenth centuries. The joke behind the debate between Tipto and Fly as to whether Don Lewis or Euclid is the better fencer is that Euclid was a mathematician in ancient Greece, not an early modern fencer; their confusion arises from the fact that the Spanish manner of fencing was described as the Euclidian School because of the geometrical precision with which the fighters took up their stances (see Tipto's account of the Spanish style at 92–3).

82 *Go . . . Hieronimo!*: a late allusion to *The Spanish Tragedy* by Thomas Kyd, and probably introduced because Hieronimo (Jeronimo) was the name of an Italian fencing master who taught in Blackfriars around the turn of the century.

83 *played*: fenced.

83–4 *Abbot . . . bold*: the first fighter is untraced; perhaps there was a fencer in Blackfriars called Antony Abbot whose name has been inverted in Fly's speech for comic heroic effect (see Tipto's response). John Blinkinsop was a fencer of the late sixteenth century.

89 *this*: i.e. Euclid.

98 *Archimedes*: mathematician and inventor, third century BC.

99 *assure*: Tipto misunderstands the Host to use 'assure' in the sense of 'insure' rather than 'promise', and so asks at what rate the Host offers such insurance.

110 *Stevinus*: Simon Stevinus (1548–1620), mathematician and physicist, who held offices under Prince Maurice of Orange. He had nothing to do with fencing.

111–12 *thirty . . . engines*: Fly comically exaggerates the usual challenge, which would be to fight something like six bouts, each time using different weapons; engines = machines or instruments used in warfare.

116 *Scaliger*: Joseph Justus Scaliger was a classicist (1540–1609); one of his works, *Cyclometrica Elementa*, is mentioned by Tipto at 124, who gets the name wrong.

120 *Basta!*: enough (Italian).

123 *He . . . circle*: *Cyclometrica Elementa* had an appendix on the subject, hence the gallants' subsequent quips about reading only the title and index; Scaliger's work was vigorously attacked and discredited, and thus Tipto's citation of him as a mathematician is further evidence of his ignorance.

125 *indice*: the plural of index is 'indices', and this may be a rare construction of the word in the singular; 'index' could be used in its modern sense, or else to refer to the table of contents.

125   *quaere*: 'it is a question' (Latin).

128   *lightly*: commonly, often.

129   *hawk at*: attack, fly at.

138   *shadow*: spirit of the dead in Elysium.

2.6.3   *hand off*: her command indicates that Beaufort has approached or grabbed Prudence in some manner when she enters.

   8   *Speak . . . language*: i.e. play your part in the day's sports more convincingly; the Host threatens to undermine the credibility of Prudence's performance amongst the others.

10–11   *What . . . hence*: a nostalgic allusion to the forty-five year reign of Elizabeth I (1558–1603).

   18   *fair omen*: i.e. because her name means 'gladness'.

   19   *Let . . . lips*: a proverbial expression (Tilley, L326) which usually means one disagreeable thing deserves another; Beaufort puns on lettuce/Laetitia to affirm that she is beautiful (or sweet tasting) enough for him.

   28   *Vincent . . . York*: alluding to a squabble conducted in print in the early seventeenth century between two heralds, Augustine Vincent, herald of Windsor, and Ralph Brook, herald of York.

   31   *blaze a coat*: to blazon (describe heraldically) a coat of arms. There is undoubtedly a sexual pun intended here, but its sense is obscure.

   32   *single eye*: i.e. honestly and sincerely, but also literally, as the Nurse has a patch over one eye.

   36   *off . . . road*: i.e. not in the direct or obvious manner (by revealing to Tipto that Laetitia is the Host's son).

37–8   *No . . . Fly*: knowing Fly's greedy (lickerish) desire for profit, the Host warns him not to suck favour from Tipto in the manner of a fly by revealing Frank's imposture, on pain of losing his 'proboscis'—a word which refers both to a fly's sucking mouth and Fly's employment in the inn.

   38   *velvet-head*: an epithet which suggests the Host wears a velvet hat in performance.

   45   *broom*: a pun on *spártos* (Greek), meaning 'broom'.

   46   *as cuerpo*: i.e. as I might to one dressed in *cuerpo*.

   57   *spinster . . . law*: i.e. the law regards her as a spinster, and therefore she has no special rights. All unmarried women beneath the degree of a viscount's daughter were spinsters and shared an equal rank.

   66   *enginous*: i.e. 'of an engine', playing on the description of his words in the previous line as explosive devices; another possible sense is crafty, or cunning.

67–8 *He . . . it*: alluding to the image of an elephant carrying a castle on its back, common on inn-signs; the expression 'castle in the air' proverbially meant a plan or words of no real substance (Tilley, C126).

70 *Buzz!*: common exclamation of impatience, with a play on the sound made by a fly.

73 *busy*: meddlesome, prying.

80 *dresser*: sideboard or table, here used as a metonym for the kitchen.

81 *flap*: rebuke; a 'fly-flapper' was used to swat flies.

87 *Dor . . . eyes*: to 'give someone the dor' was to make them the subject of ridicule; a dor is also a type of fly or bee.

90 *thoroughfare*: i.e. Jug, the tapster, described in the dramatis personae as a 'thoroughfare of news'.

91 *relics*: forsaken or discarded people.

103 *bravery*: splendour, or more specifically, fine clothes.

116 *aloes*: the juices of this plant have a bitter taste.

118 *quintessence of either*: i.e. purest essence of each (sweetness and bitterness).

121 *distillation*: refined or concentrated essence.

132 *she-Trajan*: Marcus Ulpius Trajanus, renowned for the excellence of his rule, was Roman emperor AD 98–117.

133 *What is 't?*: here, and throughout this scene, Beaufort is too preoccupied with Frank to notice what is happening around him.

139 *Nor . . . pretences*: i.e. nor Grumbling (personified as a plaintiff) her false claims.

140 *libel*: in civil law, the document of the complainant containing his allegations and instituting a suit.

164 *latitude*: range, scope.

170 *gentle*: suitable for one of noble birth.

184 *in foro*: in open court (Latin).

191 *court o' requests*: formerly, a court of record for relief of people petitioning the king held by the Lord Privy Seal and the Masters of Requests; Beaufort continues the analogy at 195 where he describes Laetitia as a 'Mistress of Requests'.

sovereignty: supreme authority (of Prudence's court).

198 *approve*: put to the test.

221 *best . . . start*: a proverbial expression meaning that even the strongest things will sometimes bend (Tilley, B561); start = warp.

222–3 *Pru . . . sour*: a pun on 'sage', meaning both 'wise', and a type of herb known for its bitterness; sour = bitter.

229 *loose*: upshot, issue; also, the act of discharging an arrow.

233–4 *Ay . . . meant*: the Host mocks the intended sense of Lovel's line, that he is willing to sacrifice his life in the attempt to win Lady Frampul, by ironically reinterpreting 'die' to mean 'have an orgasm'.

240 *corps*: corpses.

249–51 *Sovereigns . . . conditional*: i.e. Lady Frampul has no choice in the matter; suffrage = consent, approval.

253 *regiment*: rule, government.

263 *Shelee-nien*: the nurse's full name is Shelee-nien Thomas (4.4.233). This is a bastardized form of the Gaelic 'Síle nighean Thomas', meaning Celia, daughter of Thomas.

269–72 *I . . . not*: the nurse maintains her pretence of being a herald's widow by recounting complicated family lineages. 'Serly' probably refers to the dissenting Scot-Irish chieftain Sorley Boy Macdonnell whose family was massacred by the English in 1575, but the other references are vague and difficult to trace.

3.1.1 *plot*: design, scheme.

21 *alferez*: second lieutenant or official standard-bearer (Spanish).

24 *inches*: stature. Punning on Jug's name to mean a drinking-jug, Tipto shows his affection for this member of Fly's militia by grasping him by the beard or ear (handle).

25 *don del campo*: gentleman of the field (Spanish).

28 *monosyllabe*: monosyllable, spelt after the form of the word in Greek.

29 *other horse*: Fly assures Tipto that the stables are less important to their current military arrangements than the wine cellar (30–1), punning, in addition, on 'horse' to mean 'whores'.

32 *exact*: consummate, or perhaps precise.

33–4 *Lipsius . . . Jouse*: alluding to Justus Lipsius, a celebrated and well-published sixteenth-century scholar; the grounds on which Tipto compares Fly to him are obscure.

35–6 *Old . . . now*: Tipto puns on different attributes of Ferret's name: a pioneer is a foot-soldier who digs trenches and repairs roads (in the manner of a ferret), while the verb 'to bolt' refers to the action of a ferret or fox in driving a rabbit out of its hole.

48 *lighter*: even more frivolous.

55–6 *Juno's . . . lilies*: according to Greek mythology, Hercules as a child was laid at Juno's breast while she was sleeping; when she awoke she pushed the child away and the milk that was spilled fell to earth and either created, or made white, the lilies. Pierce alludes to the myth again at 100–1.

58 S.D. *Fly . . . aside*: the exchange that follows between Fly and Peck, in which they discuss the deceits practised on horses in general, and Tipto's horse in particular, is unheard by the other characters, and is interrupted only by the sudden entry of Pierce with the wine at 93.

59 *cousin*: term of friendship; Peck and Fly are probably not related.

64 *court-dish*: hodge-podge of different scraps, or perhaps short allowance; the precise sense is uncertain.

71 *dimensum*: measured or due allowance.

73 *Keeping . . . Eve*: i.e. fasting; the day before Lady Day (Annunciation, 25 March) was observed in this manner.

77–8 *as soon . . . buttered*: i.e. the hay is so coarse or inferior (gross), a horse could only eat it buttered; the problem is that horses are unable to eat greasy hay.

81 *mystery*: punning on the senses of 'enigmatic or inexplicable thing', and 'trade or profession'.

92 *mistake*: take wrongfully or in error.

96 *Lieutenant . . . ordnance*: despite Jordan's entrance here, Fly could be speaking to any of the servants on stage; ordnance = military supplies.

103 *The . . . rose*: i.e. red wine. The legend is that Venus stepped on the thorns of a white rose and her blood dyed the flower red.

109 *Parcel Peck*: i.e. part Peck, alluding to his practice of not giving horses their full measure of food.

110 *it . . . cripples*: i.e. because they are able to spot the deceit; halting = limping. The expression was proverbial (Dent, H60).

132 *litter*: straw.

143 *double beneficed*: has two benefices, or livings. The practice was illegal but occurred nonetheless through various evasions.

144 *greasing . . . teeth*: a trick by means of which horses were prevented from eating.

146 *want*: lack.

166 *foundered*: lamed through inflammation of the foot. It is unclear why Fly insists that Peck lengthen (prolate) the word in pronunciation to three syllables.

167 *all four*: i.e. all four legs.

170 *Mass*: a shortened form of the mild expletive 'by the mass'. The word as printed in the octavo could be interpreted instead, however, as a shortened form of 'master'.

174 *Once . . . bat*: i.e. he'll never change his ways; 'bat' refers both to the shortened form of his name and to a 'bird of night', or thief.

176–7 *Genoway . . . steel*: Tipto might be alluding to the proverb, 'In Genoa there are mountains without wood, sea without fish, women without shame, and men without conscience' (Tilley, G59), implying that for Burst, as for the Genoans, bankruptcy is a prudent business strategy; Genoway = Genovese.

178 *hold*: remain faithful either to their word or principles.

181 *in-and-in*: dicing game popular in taverns.

186 *Protection*: an affected title adopted also by Pinnacia Stuff (4.2.59); vapours = brags, blusters.

190 *Politics*: Aristotle's treatise.

191 *tuftaffeta night-gear*: the point is perhaps that Huffle quietly eats his supper in a rich dressing-gown, but it seems more likely that Pierce is referring euphemistically to a prostitute.

194 *Dormit patronus*: the master sleeps (Latin).

196 *that*: such.

197 *muscadel . . . eggs*: an aphrodisiac; muscadel = strong, sweet wine.

198 *trundling cheats*: carts or coaches. 'Cheat' referred generally to anything, and was made specific through the use of a defining word; trundling = revolving.

201 *Crown*: with a pun on royal monarchy and Crown Inn.

3.2 S.D. *Musicians . . . bench*: the characters enact in this scene a formal parliament or court, reminiscent of the medieval Courts of Love. Although the musicians are brought on-stage in this edition, the music might be heard in performance from the galleries or even off-stage.

1 *set*: appoint the limits of.

5 *smell . . . without*: smell (either stink or sniff) outside the room.

11–12 *fable . . . fruit*: in classical mythology, Ladon, the dragon who guarded the Golden Apples in the garden of the Hesperides, had a hundred heads and voices; it was killed by Hercules in the course of his twelfth labour.

31 *challenge*: claim.

33 *bail*: power, jurisdiction.

37 *designed*: designated, styled.

53 *Ovid . . . Amandi*: i.e. *Ars Amatoria*, or *Art of Love*. Ovid's work was notorious for its sensuality, and by making this the book on which the lovers swear, Jonson raises (false) expectations of a discourse on sexual love.

57 *stones . . . virtue*: occult stones.

herb of grace: rue, a type of herb.

character: magical sign or emblem.

52–60 *Herbert . . . it*: the oath which the Host administers to Lovel and Lady

Frampul is a parodic reworking of the legal formula of oaths taken before entering one-to-one combat.

85 *signature*: distinctive mark.

90–3 *For . . . beloved?*: Lovel's entire argument is heavily indebted to Plato's *Symposium*, which Beaufort recalls at 97–100, in which he argues for the pre-eminence of spiritual or heavenly love (what we now describe as Platonic love) over the mere satisfaction of sexual desire.

94–5 *Have . . . freely?*: Beaufort clarifies whether he is permitted to offer his opinion on the matter under discussion (vote), and ensures that nothing he says can be held against him; writs of privilege = written notes exempting a person from a crime.

97–100 *Then . . . rejoined*: as Lovel notes at 104–5, this is the explanation of love offered by Aristophanes in the *Symposium*. His idea was that originally there were three sexes (male, female, and hermaphrodite), and each body was in effect two people joined together at the back; the gods, angered by human pride, split these creatures in two and from that time on humans have sought to reunite themselves with their lost half.

101 *Cra-mo-cree!*: i.e. 'love of my heart'.

112 *The . . . itself*: Lovel's logic is Aristotelian: the efficient cause of love is the means by which it is produced; the formal cause is the ideal essence of love; and the final cause is the end for which love is produced.

113 *larger*: at more length.

115 *corpse*: here, specifically, a living body.

114–20 *It . . . reflect*: i.e. love is a spark which is dead in one's own body (proper corps), and alive (quick) in another. One engenders love by casting in one's mind the essence or ideal form (idea) of the beloved, or conversely, by reflecting that essence back like a mirror (glass), the implication being that this is an image to which the other will be attracted. The idea derives from the commentary to the *Symposium* written by Marsilio Ficino.

125 *circular*: perfect, complete.

134 *leip*: i.e. 'leap', have sex with.

135 *lip*: kiss.

138 *Along*: at length, in full.

143–4 *I . . . Ovid*: the opposition between spiritual and physical love explored in the *Symposium* is figured in Lovel and Beaufort; sense = corporeal gratification. A poem called *Ovid's Banquet of Sense* was written by George Chapman in 1595.

155 *style*: manner of expression or discourse.

159 *frontispiece*: decorated entrance to a building.

161 *Surprised*: overcome, overwhelmed.

172 *inoculated*: engrafted.

185 *starts*: swerves.

187 *oblique*: morally perverse.

191 *philosophers' stone*: supposed to possess the capacity to turn base metals into gold, continuing the alchemical metaphor introduced two lines earlier.

195 *projection*: transmutation.

196 *parts*: assumed or feigned roles.

214 *fact*: crime.

218 *Dixi*: 'There I rest my case' (Latin); the formal method of closing a legal speech.

223–4 *Plato . . . d'Urfé*: each of these wrote on the subject of love. Heliodorus was a Greek novelist who wrote a love-story called the *Ethiopian Story of Theagenes and Charicleia*; Achilles Tatius wrote a romance about two lovers, Cleitophon and Leucippe, in the manner of Heliodorus; Sir Philip Sidney wrote his *Arcadia* and the love sonnets *Astrophil and Stella* in the sixteenth century; and Honoré d'Urfé published a pastoral romance called *Astrée* in France between 1610 and 1618.

225 *Master . . . Sentences*: a title traditionally attributed to Peter Lombard, the author of an influential theological treatise called *Sententiarum libri* published in the mid-twelfth century.

231 *irregular*: an ecclesiastical term, to mean not in conformity with the rule of the Church.

238 *Chaucer's . . . Cressid*: an ambiguous choice of texts, since this is a story of love betrayed; Lady Frampul's overblown rhetoric is perhaps at least partly ironic.

239 *vow*: consecrate, dedicate.

242 *trespassed*: wronged, violated.

234–54 *What . . . farther*: the staging of this speech is not obvious: it cannot be delivered as an aside to the audience since the other characters variously comment on the sincerity with which she speaks, and yet her closing sentence is probably not heard by her lover. Presumably either her final lines are spoken as an aside, or Lovel turns away at 218.

254 *Most . . . lady*: i.e. one who answers by not answering; Prudence continues to doubt her lady's protestations.

255 *ironic*: feigned, dissembling.

269–70 *Beware . . . lay*: a proverbial expression meaning 'don't start something you can't finish' (Tilley, D319), with a bawdy quibble on 'lay' to refer to her ability to cause an erection (the 'raised spirit') to disappear.

277 *personated*: feigned, pretended.

284 *accidental*: casual, occasional.

288 *The . . . arms*: the Host praises hyperbolically Lovel's success in the Court of Love by likening him to the classical hero Bellerophon, who stole Pegasus, the winged horse of the Muses, to defeat the monster Chimaera.

291 *bouncer*: the word is obscure, but senses of the verb include 'bluster' and 'swagger'. Presumably Pinnacia, dressed in her fine clothes and lording it over her husband, is behaving in a loud, overweening manner.

4.1.3 *As . . . chip*: a proverbial expression, here used ironically, meaning extremely dry (Tilley, C351); chip = small piece of wood.

3–4 *Good . . . jugs*: punning on 'cast' to mean a pair, and quantity of ale brewed at one time.

7 *gauge . . . capacity*: synonyms meaning capacity or measure, punning on the name Jordan to mean chamber-pot.

9 *penny-club*: a 'club' is a social gathering at a tavern, the expenses of which are paid through contributions made by each participant; here, they each contribute a penny.

15 *Highgate*: village 5 miles north of London.

18 *That . . . countess*: one of the ways women indicated their nobility was to have a coachman drive them 'bare', without a hat; Fitzdottrel promises his wife that she will enjoy this privilege once he is made Duke (see *The Devil is an Ass*, 2.3.36–7).

19 *o'er-grown duchess*: i.e. a fat duchess, referring to Pinnacia's size, but with a bawdy pun on 'overgrown', the precise sense of which is unclear, but perhaps 'pregnant'. The quibble is developed over the next two lines.

24 *rabbi*: one whose learning or authority is on par with that of a Jewish rabbi; here used to tease Jordan about his knowledge of women.

28 *man-net*: Jonson coins the word to mean 'little man'.

4.2.1 *Come . . . quart*: this scene takes place in the courtyard of the inn; in fresco = in the open air.

6 *broke-winged*: bankrupt.

9 *Hospital*: i.e. Christ's Hospital, London, a charitable institution for the maintenance and education of needy children.

10 *Inquest*: i.e. Court of Inquest, London, a court which determined debts under 40 shillings.

23 *That . . . me*: one drinker pledged another by agreeing to protect him from attack while he drank his ale.

33 *composition*: mental and physical constitution.

37 *gravedàd*: dignity, seriousness (Spanish).

44 *cuello*: ruff, or perhaps collar (from *cuello*, Spanish for 'collar').

50 *eat—*: the octavo punctuation presumably indicates that Huffle hesitates, searching for words.

52 *'Slid*: by God's eyelid.

53 *A . . . aboard*: nautical metaphors meaning 'well-dressed', and 'Let's approach her', but also carrying bawdy connotations of sexual intercourse. The verb 'to trim' was used to refer to a woman who has been sexually violated by a man.

57 *Seville*: punning on Stuff's injunction that they be 'civil'.

67 *vespertilio*: bat (Latin).

68 *gentleman . . . head*: a proverbial expression used to refer contemptuously to a social upstart (Dent, G66).

74 *Sampson*: i.e. the extant ballad of Samson, parodied in *Eastward Ho* (2.2.43–50); Samson was renowned for his valour and strength.

80 *goose*: tailor's (planing-) iron, so called because of the shape of the iron's neck. It is used as a metaphor for Stuff's tongue with which he tries to smooth out quarrels.

84 *that jacket*: i.e. one befitting his assumed role as Pinnacia's footman; see 4.3.71.

90 *see fashions*: i.e. learn people's ways (ironic).

95–7 *And . . . say 't*: Jonson is scathing about the morals of the fashionable woman; compare the similar conclusion drawn in *The Devil is an Ass* (4.4.164–9).

100 *affront*: insult, but also attack, assault.

101 *Centaurs*: mythical creatures who were half-human, half-horse. They fought their enemies, the Lapiths or Lapithae, after drinking too much at the wedding of Peirithous, a legend to which Beaufort alludes at the beginning of the next scene.

4.3.1 *Thracian*: the inhabitants of Thrace were renowned as great warriors and drinkers.

8 *knocked marrowbone*: marrow is removed by knocking the bone sharply.

17 *(As . . . somewhere)*: the enemies of Ajax are described as cowering in silence like flocks of birds when he appears before them (Sophocles, *Ajax*, 167–71), but the allusion is uncertain.

28 *bill of enquiry*: formal document directing an enquiry; more properly, 'writ of enquiry'.

30 *curious*: skilful, elaborate.

31 *As . . . fishwife*: Pinnacia's response is that of the hawker attracting customers in the fishmarket.

40 *style*: title.

45 *scruple*: doubt.

51 *say . . . on*: try . . . on.

55 *begotten*: malapropism for 'gotten', meaning obtained or won.

71–2 *Romford . . . Barnet*: each of these towns lay about 10 miles outside London, and were the common destination of day excursions.

76 *quaint*: punning on the senses of 'cunning' and 'elegantly dressed'; as a noun, the word refers to the female genitals.

species: spectacle or outward appearance (Latin).

79 *preoccupation*: i.e. occupation of the clothes before handing them over, with a bawdy pun on sexually occupying or filling his wife.

82 *credits*: punning on 'reputations' and 'unpaid bills of expenses'.

87 *censure*: condemnatory judgement.

88 *blanketed*: i.e. tossed in a blanket.

90 *Pillage . . . pinnace*: a pinnace, playing on the name 'Pinnacia', describes a small boat and a prostitute; the gallants pick up the nautical metaphor in the following lines.

97–9 *And . . . her*: women prosecuted for illicit sex were liable to the punishment of being placed in a cart and processed through the streets with one or more people banging a basin in front.

103 *nicked it*: hit the mark.

106 *type*: figure, image.

4.4.6 *lame*: imperfect, defective.

11 *curious*: elegant, elaborate.

14 *gentle*: noble, excellent.

21 *acquiesce*: rest satisfied.

32 *The . . . Love*: a book by Thomas Usk (d. 1388), published as part of *The Works of Geoffrey Chaucer* in 1532.

37–8 *It . . . danger*: Lovel's discourse on valour is a pastiche of passages borrowed from the works of Seneca; there are close parallels, in particular, with extracts from *De Ira*, *De Constantia*, and the *Epistulae*.

40 *inconsiderate*: unconsiderate, precipitate.

41 *false*: improperly, wrongly.

44 *scope*: aim, end in view.

51 *fear*: i.e. fear for.

56 *considerable*: capable of being considered. The manner in which Lovel goes on to identify the three aspects of valour is comparable to his analysis of the subject of love in terms of efficient, formal, and final cause (3.2.90–2).

68 *undertake*: enter upon an enterprise.

70 *frenzy*: madness, insanity.

83 *congregate*: assemble.

85 *Compose*: settle the debate.

86 *that*: i.e. anger.

92 *respects*: regards, takes into account.

94 *confident . . . undertaking*: presumptuous . . . bold. Lovel's adjectives are indicative of his disapproval.

110 *object*: expose.

112 *Respect*: regard, consideration.

117 *self*: personal.

132 *quiet*: peace of mind.

136 *injury*: insult, calumny.

141 *run on*: discourse on.

165 *the lie*: to 'give the lie' was to call someone a liar, often prompting a duel in which both sides attempted to preserve their honour; here Lovel argues that only worthy adversaries should be taken seriously.

179 *spice*: sort, kind.

184 *forehead*: impudence, audacity.

186 *errors*: vexations.

190 *Or . . . or*: either . . . or.

196 *Would . . . Olivares*: i.e. with overbearing (Spanish) pride; Gaspar de Guzman y Pimental, Conde-Duque de Olivares, was prime minister of Spain, 1623–43.

210 *security*: confidence, assurance.

223 *sentence*: opinion.

229 *engine*: contrivance, machine.

234 *Er . . . Chreest*: i.e. 'for the love of Christ'.

234–5 *Tower . . . doone*: i.e. 'give us a cup of whiskey'.

244 *except*: object, take exception.

248–9 *From . . . misery*: Lovel's reflections on the futility of love are voiced loudly enough for everyone on stage to hear; when the others exit with Lovel, Lady Frampul and Prudence are left with the sleeping nurse.

252 *abrupt . . . estate*: abruptly precipitous condition.

256 *prognostics*: predictions, prophesies.

268–70 *I . . . love*: i.e. I will attempt the impossible rather than remain in love; Lovel's proposed alternatives are proverbially futile (Tilley W416, W417, W451).

272 *craft of crocodiles*: Lovel assumes Lady Frampul's show of grief at the end of the hour was hypocritical, and alludes to the proverbial belief that crocodiles weep while eating their prey.

276 *baffled*: disgraced, dishonoured.

281 *leer*: sly, underhand.

297–8 *You . . . observant*: Lady Frampul, like Lovel at 1.6.115–16, assumes that the symptoms of true love are evident to anyone who cares to look; regardant = observant.

310 *doubt*: suspect.

317 *uncased*: stripped, undressed.

318 *properties*: articles of costume, stage accessories.

5.1 S.D. *[Enter] Host*: since act divisions were marked at Blackfriars with a musical interlude, the Host would not have been required immediately to re-enter the stage after his exit at the end of the previous scene.

6 *And . . . nothing*: i.e. help recover the situation; the Host is dismayed by his guests' gloom.

16 *He . . . it*: 'He had the (big) paunch of a priest'.

17 *branched*: embroidered with figures resembling flowers or foliage.
   side: long.

18 *formalities*: robes or insignia of office.

21–3 *Licence . . . about*: in place of the required marriage licence, Fly jokes that they had a 'licence of love' and lots of money; 'angels' refers to gold coins each worth 10 shillings.

30 *mine-men*: miners, humorously referring to their status as below-stairs characters.

31 *tropics*: limits, boundaries.

34 *The . . . redeemed*: the gown was supposed to have been burned (4.3.92–4).

5.2.9 *secular*: common, unlearned.

10 *claim by*: assert himself with.

11–12 *His . . . stitch*: i.e. 'he is no better even than his apprentice', but a bawdy secondary sense is available since 'needle' could also mean 'penis', and 'stitch' could be 'grudge or ground of complaint'.

14 *say*: fabric.

15–16 *With . . . miracles*: i.e. 'just by warming (chafing) the sweat (grease) left in it by Pinnacia (hind) [the dress] may work miracles'. The miracle would be that Lovel would forgive Lady Frampul and 'rise' out of bed. A bawdy interpretation is also feasible: 'with your buttocks (butt) rubbing the dress, the sweat of a bare bum (hind) may work miracles'; in this version, the miracle would be Lovel's sexual arousal (implicit in 'rise').

20 *In . . . pauperis*: a legal term designating one who is allowed, on account of poverty, to sue or defend in a court of law without paying costs (Latin).

23 *fire . . . charm*: i.e. burn the dress.

24–5 *I . . . it*: Elizabeth Shore, the mistress of King Edward IV and popular subject of moral treatises, was thought to have died in a ditch in an area of London subsequently named Shoreditch; matter = story.

29 *frampul*: this obsolete variant form of the adjective 'frampold', meaning disagreeable or peevish, has been preserved in order to make obvious the wordplay on the family name.

41 *branch it*: exalt in the highest branches? The precise sense is uncertain, but an image of pride.

55 *whe'r I am*: whether I exist.

70 *All-to-be*: completely, soundly.

5.4 S.D. *Fiddlers*: as at 3.2, the musicians might be heard in performance from off-stage.

9 *pardon o' course*: i.e. a pardon excusing ordinary procedure.

20 *expect*: wait.

29 *conceits*: fancy trifles for the table.

31 *provocative*: serving to excite appetite or lust.

34 *genial bed*: marriage bed, from the Latin, *lectus genialis*.

35 *points*: tags or laces with which garments were fastened.

36 *codpiece point*: codpieces were at least twenty years out of fashion when this play was first performed.

48 *clipped*: like a counterfeit coin, the edges of which have been fraudulently cut.

5.5.40 *inmates*: lodgers.

43–5 *There . . . truth*: English statutes prevented the taking in of poor people as lodgers, and Beaufort threatens to expose to the authorities the Host's living arrangements; the court of the Star Chamber was a powerful criminal court feared for its tyranny.

67–8 *left . . . Gaunt*: the Beaufort family was descended from the issue of John of Gaunt and his mistress, Catherine Swynford (hence 'left rib'), whom he married in 1396; the children were legitimized by Richard II a year later.

83 *Leave . . . light*: i.e. it is not difficult to ask permission. This reproof was commonly said to anyone who intruded upon another's interests (Tilley L170).

101 *she-Mandeville*: i.e. a female Mandeville. A book of travels published under the name of Sir John Mandeville was written in the middle of the fourteenth century; it had most recently been published in 1625.

102 *disquisition*: diligent search.

    S.D. *Enter . . . robes*: there is no obvious moment at which Fly should re-enter; his entrance here with the robes gives visual emphasis to the Nurse's sense of wonder at the recovery of her husband.

103 *admire*: wonder, marvel.

137 *four . . . bed*: the proverb 'More belongs to marriage than four bare legs in a bed' (Tilley, M1146) emphasizes the importance of financial security in a marriage, which Prudence is now guaranteed.

138–9 *coin Up*: fashion, shape.

    Indefinite: boundless, infinite.

148 *several*: separate.

155 *Maecenas*: influential patron of the arts portrayed in *Poetaster*; here the allusion seems to be to his frequent quarrels with his wife, Terentia.

THE EPILOGUE

  6 *numbers*: lines.

 11 *It . . . out*: Jonson had a stroke in 1628 and was confined to his room; he died in 1637.

21–2 *And . . . seen*: King Charles consequently sent him £100, a gift which Jonson acknowledges in an epigram printed in *The Underwood*.

ANOTHER EPILOGUE

  8 *Cis*: see 1.5.11 n.

 14 *province*: duty, office.

ODE TO HIMSELF

  7 *fastidious*: proud, scornful.

 13 *simple*: foolish.

 22 *Pericles*: i.e. the play by Shakespeare, printed in 1609.

 34 *quit*: absolve, acquit.

 36 *larding*: covering or lining.

 37 *comic socks*: slippers or socks (*socci*), worn by comic actors in ancient Greece.

 40 *gamesters*: actors.

    guilt: punning on 'gilt', or money.

 42 *Alcaic lute*: i.e. the lute of Alcaeus, Greek lyric poet.

 43 *Horace*: Roman satirist and lyricist, born 65 BC.

43 *Anacreon*: Greek lyric poet.

44 *Pindar*: Greek lyric poet.

60 *And . . . wain*: i.e. and raising the glory of Charles I above Charles's Wain, the group of seven stars which form the constellation called the Great Bear.

GLOSSARY

a unstressed form of 'he'

aconite type of poisonous plant

Aesculapius Roman god of medicine

affy trust, rely

after-game a second game played to improve or reverse the outcome of the first

against in preparation for

agnomination word-play in which one word alludes to another

albe albeit

Alcides Hercules

almanac-man fortune-teller, prognosticator

amelled enamelled

an if

andirons iron supports for holding wood in an open fireplace

angel gold coin worth ten shillings

antic grotesque, absurd

apozem medicinal infusion

appellant one who accuses another of a crime

apperil peril, risk

aqua-vitae term from alchemy describing unrectified alcohol; hence, in popular usage, any strong alcoholic spirit

arcana mysteries, secrets

architrabe Latinized form of 'architrave', referring to the main beam running between two columns

arras rich tapestry fabric; also 'arras cloth'

ascribe subscribe

atomi atoms

Bacchus Greek god of wine

balderdash jumbled mixture of liquors

balsamum balsam, an aromatic resin

bandog mastiff, bloodhound

bane poison; ruin, hapless fate (*Poet.* 5.2.68)

basilisk cockatrice, a mythological creature said to kill with its glance

bedlam a mad person; originally, an inmate of Bethlehem Hospital, a London lunatic asylum

bird-lime a sticky substance spread on twigs to catch birds

blanc-manger a dish made of white meats, mixed with rice, cream, and eggs; used figuratively to mean trifling

blandishment attraction, allurement

blazon record of virtues or excellences

bodge unit of measurement approximately equal to half a peck

bona-roba a showy woman, sometimes with implications of prostitution

bonny-clabber milk that has stood until it has soured

bots disease of horses and sheep caused by a parasitical worm

bottle bundle of hay or straw

bousy drunk, intoxicated

brace pair

brach female hound

brave handsome, well-dressed

bravery ostentation, splendour; more specifically, fine clothes

brawn pickled boar

breeze gadfly

bride-bowl (-cup) a spiced drink prepared for the bride and groom on their wedding night

buckram type of coarse linen or cloth

buss kiss

buttery place for storing liquor and food

caduceus wand carried by Mercury, usually represented as having two serpents twined round it

cant to speak using the jargon of thieves; also used as a noun

canter one who speaks cant (see above)

cap-à-pie from head to foot

caparison covering spread over the back of a horse or beast of burden

cargo term of contempt; the exact meaning is unclear

carline disparaging term for a woman, especially an old woman

carman carter, carrier

caroche a type of luxurious coach or carriage

cartel written challenge

castle-soap Castile soap, a hard soap made with olive oil and soda

catamite the passive partner in male homosexual intercourse

catastrophe the denouement of a play

catchpole a disparaging term for an officer who arrests for debt

cater caterer, buyer of provisions

cates choice viands, delicacies

cautelous deceitful, crafty

cavalier horse-soldier, knight

ceruse white lead, formerly used as a cosmetic

chamberlain servant in charge of the bedchambers

characterism characterization

chimera wild fancy

chink ready money, coins

choler bile, one of the four humours of early physiology thought to cause irascibility

cioppino a kind of shoe with a high cork sole

civet substance deriving from the civet cat used as a perfume

clem starve

cloak-bag bag in which to carry clothes; valise

clyster enema

coach-leaves folding blinds of a coach-window

cockatrice a legendary serpent said to kill with its glance, basilisk; prostitute, whore (*Poet.* 3.4.161)

cock-brained foolish, lacking judgement

cock-stone stone supposedly found in the gizzard of a cock and thought to be a sexual stimulant

cog cheat

cokes fool

coltsfoot a common weed, the leaves of which were used as a cure for asthma

commenter commentator

concoct digest

concomitant accompaniment

contemn despise, scorn

contentment pleasure, delight

contumely insult, abuse

cony rabbit (*NI* 2.5.69); dupe or gull

corn-ground ground used for growing grain

coronice a horizontal moulded projection which crowns a building

cothurnal pertaining to tragedy, tragic

cotquean scolding woman

cozen deceive, beguile

crambe a game in which players find rhymes for words without repeating the same rhyme twice

crisped tightly curled (said of hair)

cropshin corpion, a herring of inferior quality; used as a term of abuse

crupper buttocks

cuckold a man whose wife has sex with another man; also used as a verb

cutis skin

daw disconcert, frighten

debonair gracious, affable

denier very small sum; originally a French coin

dentifrice toothpaste, toothpowder

deprave defame, disparage

descry discover, detect

designments undertakings, designs

detrect decline, refuse

dictamen dictate, pronouncement

disjune breakfast

disposure disposal

disprized disparaged, dispraised

distich couplet

divers various, sundry

doxy prostitute, slut

draff dregs, swill given to swine

drawer one who draws liquor for customers

dropsy a morbid accumulation of fluid in any part of the body

egregious exellent, renowned

ela the highest note in the Gamut, or 'Great Scale', of Guido d'Arezzo, sung to the syllable 'la'

elenchize argue through question and answer

elysian heavenly, blissful

Elysium state or place of bliss after death; heaven

embryon embryo

emphase emphasize

engine plot, snare (*DA* 2.2.87; *Sej.* 2.2.131); ingenuity, cunning (*DA* 2.3.46, *Sej.* Arg 21); instrument, means (*Sej.* 3.3.125)

engineers plotters, layers of snares

epitasis that part of a play into which is introduced complications

equivoke double meaning, equivocation

ere before

erewhile a while before, some time ago

eryngo candied root of the plant of the same name (also called Sea Holly), considered an aphrodisiac

escudero attendant, lady's page

exampless unprecedented, unparalleled

expiscation the action of fishing out, investigation

extract extraction

fautor protector, patron (*Sej.* Chapman poem, 140); adherent, supporters (*Sej.* 2.2.127)

feoffee the person to whom a freehold estate in land is conveyed

feoffment act by which a person is invested in a freehold estate of land

fieldfare species of thrush

firebrand one who is doomed to burn in hell

firk dance

flickermouse flittermouse, bat

forswear swear falsely, commit perjury

frieze in architecture, any horizontal broad band occupied by sculpture

froward perverse, refractory

fucus cosmetics, face paint

Furies avenging goddesses sent from the lowest region of the underworld

fustian coarse cloth made of cotton and flax

gallipot small earthen glazed pot

gamester gambler

gear nonsense, 'goings-on'

gelid icy, frosty

generalty generality, general statement or notion

giglot lewd woman, slut

gimlet a boring-tool, used to pierce casks

ging gang, company

girt gird, bind

girth belt placed around the body of a horse to secure the saddle

glanders contagious disease in horses characterized by swelling under the jaw

glebe soil, regarded as the source of food

gloze flattering speech

godwit a marsh bird, popular for the table

Goody goodwife

grammaticaster inferior grammarian

grandee person of high rank or eminence

grant-parole respite(?). This is the only usage cited in *OED*

gratulate congratulate, offer congratulations; reward (*Poet.* 4.7.13)

grazier one who grazes or feeds cattle for market

gripe seize, grasp

grot grotto, cave

grudging sensation of resentment, envy; symptom of approaching illness

guerdon reward, recompense

gulch glutton or drunkard

gull dupe, fool (noun); to dupe or fool (verb)

gust taste

harpy monster supposed to have a woman's face and body, and a bird's wings and claws; used also to describe a rapacious person who preys on others

hecatombs great public sacrifices amongst ancient Romans

Helicon mountain in central Greece sacred to the Muses

heliotrope a plant, the flowers of which turn to follow the sun

hellebore name given to certain plants having medicinal and poisonous qualities, used particularly as a cure for mental disease

hobby-horse toy consisting of a stick with a horse's head on one end, which children pretend to ride

hogshead cask of liquor containing sixty-three old wine-gallons

horn-book children's primer covered with translucent horn in which was printed, amongst other things, the alphabet

horse-leech variety of large leech; used figuratively to refer to a rapacious person

hum strong ale

humorous subject to humour or mood, capricious

humours in ancient and medieval physiology, the four chief fluids of the body, the relative proportions of which were thought to determine a person's temperament; a particular (unpleasant) disposition having no apparent reason or justification (*Poet.* 4.7.8)

hybrid of mixed descent

Hydra in Greek mythology, a monstrous snake whose heads grew back as quickly as they were cut off

ibides rare plural form of ibis, a bird related to the stork and heron

importune troublesome

incubus evil spirit supposed to come to people in their sleep, especially seeking sexual intercourse with women

indifferently impartially, without bias

ingle catamite, male prostitute (noun); cajole, wheedle (verb)

ingrate(ful) ungrateful (*DA* 1.6.174, *Sej.* 5.10.161); displeasing, disagreeable (*NI* 4.4.264)

instauration restoration, renewal

interested implicated, involved

intergatories interrogatories

iwis truly, assuredly

jade ill-tempered horse; disparaging term for a woman

Jew's trump Jew's harp

jointure an estate limited to the wife to take effect upon the death of the husband

julep syrupy medicinal drink

king-at-arms chief herald

lapwing type of bird well-known for luring predators away from its nest

larum alarum, call to arms

lawn type of fine linen

lazar poor or diseased person, especially a leper

lees dregs

lick-foot the action of licking the feet, servility

limn portray

list wish, choose

lording gentleman

lotium stale urine applied by barbers to clients' hair

louting bowing, cringing

man-of-war soldier, warrior

mastic gum which exudes from the bark of some trees; formerly used in medicine

mastiff large, powerful dog

mead alcohol made by fermenting a mixture of honey and water

mechanic craftsperson

meed reward

Mercury Roman messenger god

mien carriage, bearing

migniard dainty, caressing

minceative mincing, affected

Minerva Roman goddess of wisdom and handicrafts

moonling simpleton, idiot

motley said of a fool's outfit; hence, foolish

mulct punish by fine (verb); fine (noun)

multiplying glass magnifying glass

mummia thick medicinal liquid

muster-roll list of officers and men

musty peevish, sullen

myriads countless numbers

nard aromatic ointment made from a plant of the same name

neal temper, harden through baking

necessited necessitated

neophyte novice, one who is new to a subject

noble gold coin valued at 6s 8d
nupson simpleton
obarni scalded mead
obsequiously obediently, dutifully
ore-tenus word of mouth (Latin)
ort scrap left over from a meal
ostler stableman, groom
out-term mere exterior, outward figure
ouzel blackbird or merle
Pallas goddess of wisdom
pap breast
paronomasy paronomasia, word-play or pun
pash break, dash
patten high-heeled shoe, cioppino
peccant unhealthy, corrupt
peremptory over-confident
periwig wig
perspicil microscope
petard small explosive device used to blow in a door or breach a wall
petasus low-crowned, broad-brimmed hat, frequently represented as worn by the Greek god Mercury
philtre love-potion, love-charm
Phoebus sun-god and patron god of prophecy, medicine, poetry, and music, commonly associated with the symbols of the lyre and bow; also known as Apollo
pilcher a term of abuse, the origins of which are uncertain
pinnace a small, light boat; also used figuratively of a woman, especially of a prostitute
plaining complaining
pleurisy a disease characterized by pain in the chest and side
plover type of bird
politic politician
polt-foot club-footed
pomatum pomade, ointment
post post-rider, messenger
postern back door
prentice apprentice
problematize propound problems
provocado challengee (Spanish)
provocador challenger (Spanish)
puck-fist disparaging term for a braggart or niggard

pump close fitting soft shoe with a thin sole
punk prostitute, strumpet
purslane a herb used in salads
quack-salver fraudulent doctor, charlatan
quartermaster army officer responsible for setting up camp and seeing to the provisions
quotidian ordinary, everyday
ratsbane rat poison
rebus an enigmatical representation of a name, word, or phrase by figures or pictures which suggest the syllables of which it is made up
receipt recipe
reck care
rectress female ruler, governor
recure recovery, cure
relict survivor
renown make famous, celebrate
reremouse bat
restauration restoration of something to its proper condition
Rhadamanthys one of the three judges in the lower world, renowned for his wisdom
ribibe derogatory term for an old woman
riot debauchery, wasteful living
rive tear
roister swaggering, noisy reveller
rook gull, dupe
rosmarine rosemary
rout rabble, common herd of people
rubber towel
rusher one who strews rushes on the floor
sack white wine from Spain
sad(ness) serious(ness)
saraband slow and stately Spanish dance; Jonson describes it as 'bawdy' in *The Staple of News*
saturnine born under the planet Saturn, gloomy
scape escape
scarab beetle, thought to breed in and feed upon dung, hence used figuratively of people
scroyle scoundrel, wretch

scurril scurrilous

sellary male prostitute

serenissimous most serene

shot-clog unwelcome companion who is tolerated because he pays the bill for the rest

shrive obsolete form of sheriff

siege excrement, faeces

skeldering begging, especially by passing oneself off as a disbanded soldier

skill matter, make a difference (verb)

skink serve drink

spavin a horse malady characterized by a tumour in the leg

spermaceti substance deriving from the sperm whale used in medicines

spintry male prostitute

spital charitable foundation for the housing of either poor or diseased persons

spleen an abdominal organ regarded as the seat both of melancholy and mirth

spruntly smartly, trimly

spurn kick

staff stanza, verse

staggers referring generally to any disease which causes animals to stagger

standard suit

statuminate support

still always, continually

stooter a Dutch coin

strappado a form of torture in which the victim's hands are tied behind the back and attached to a pulley; the victim is then hoisted from the ground and dropped half-way

succuba whore; originally a demon in female form supposed to have sex with men in their sleep

suit outfit

supersedeas a legal term, referring to a writ commanding the stay of legal proceedings

supposititious fraudulently substituted, spurious

switch-seller literally, a beggar who sells switches, or twigs, for use as riding whips

syllogize argue by syllogisms

table-book pocket notebook or memorandum-book

tapster one who draws liquor for customers

tenents tenets

tentiginous lecherous

thorough through

throstle thrush

tincture dye used as a cosmetic

tother other

toy trifle (*DA* 2.1.67; *Sej.* 2.4.64); trick, joke (*DA* 3.3.222; *NI* 2.1.68); trifling piece of writing (*NI* 1.6.104)

travail labour (used as both noun and verb)

treaty behaviour, usage

trump deceive, cheat

trundle roll

tuftaffeta taffeta with a pile or nap arranged in tufts

underwork seek to undermine or overthrow

usher male attendant on a person of rank

vellute velvet

venerable highly respected, esteemed

Venus goddess of love

Vertumnus god of the changing year

vervain verbena; a plant formerly thought to have medicinal properties

visor mask

vively distinctly, vividly

volary large bird-cage, aviary

Vulcan god of fire and metal-working

wapentake a subdivision of certain English shires, corresponding to the 'hundred' of other counties

weal welfare, well-being

welkin sky

whipstock term of contempt for someone who drives horses

widgeon type of wild duck

woad blue dye

woodness madness, insanity

wormseed any of a variety of drugs used to expel worms

wreak vengeance, revenge
wrest to twist or pervert meaning
wresting misinterpretation or distortion
  of meaning
yard yardstick, or a distance of three

feet; often used with a pun on
  'penis'
yond yonder, that over there
zany professional jester or buffoon,
  specifically, a clown's assistant

The Oxford World's Classics Website

www.worldsclassics.co.uk

- Information about new titles
- Explore the full range of Oxford World's Classics
- Links to other literary sites and the main OUP webpage
- Imaginative competitions, with bookish prizes
- Peruse *Compass*, the Oxford World's Classics magazine
- Articles by editors
- Extracts from Introductions
- A forum for discussion and feedback on the series
- Special information for teachers and lecturers

www.worldsclassics.co.uk

American Literature

British and Irish Literature

Children's Literature

Classics and Ancient Literature

Colonial Literature

Eastern Literature

European Literature

History

Medieval Literature

Oxford English Drama

Poetry

Philosophy

Politics

Religion

The Oxford Shakespeare

A complete list of Oxford Paperbacks, including Oxford World's Classics, OPUS, Past Masters, Oxford Authors, Oxford Shakespeare, Oxford Drama, and Oxford Paperback Reference, is available in the UK from the Academic Division Publicity Department, Oxford University Press, Great Clarendon Street, Oxford OX2 6DP.

In the USA, complete lists are available from the Paperbacks Marketing Manager, Oxford University Press, 198 Madison Avenue, New York, NY 10016.

Oxford Paperbacks are available from all good bookshops. In case of difficulty, customers in the UK can order direct from Oxford University Press Bookshop, Freepost, 116 High Street, Oxford OX1 4BR, enclosing full payment. Please add 10 per cent of published price for postage and packing.